Adult Development and Aging

Second Edition

Bert Hayslip, Jr.
University of North Texas

Paul E. Panek
The Ohio State University at Newark

HarperCollins*CollegePublishers*

To our wives, Gail and Christine,
and our children, Stephen, Patrick, Rachel and Rebecca

Acquisitions Editor: Anne Harvey
Developmental Editor: Carol Einhorn
Project Coordination and Text Design: Benjamin Production Services
Cover Design: Kay Petronio
Cover Photo: Copyright © David Brownell/The Image Bank
Photo Researcher: Karen Koblik
Production/Manufacturing: Michael Weinstein/Paula Keller
Compositor: Compset, Inc.
Printer and Binder: R.R. Donnelley & Sons Company
Cover Printer: The Lehigh Press, Inc.

Library of Congress Cataloging-in-Publication Data

Hayslip, Bert.
Adult development and aging / Bert Hayslip, Jr. and Paul E. Panek. —2nd ed.
p. cm.
Includes bibliographical references (p.) and index.
ISBN 0-06-500244-X
1. Adulthood. 2. Aging—Psychological aspects. I. Panek, Paul E. II. Title.
BF724.5.H39 1993
155.6—dc20 92-31643
CIP

95 9 8 7 6 5 4 3

BRIEF CONTENTS

DETAILED CONTENTS

CHAPTER 4

Sensory and Perceptual Processes 114

CHAPTER 5

Cognition: Learning and Memory 155

CHAPTER 6

Cognition: Intelligence 189

CHAPTER 8

Personality and Adaptation 290

CHAPTER 9

Work, Retirement, and Leisure 336

CHAPTER 10

Mental Health and Psychopathology 391

PREFACE

The field of adult development and aging is a relatively new one not only in psychology, but also in other behavioral sciences, such as education and sociology. When we wrote the first edition of *Adult Development and Aging,* we were responding to our own need for a text that could be used in courses taught in various social science departments to students with diverse academic backgrounds. Thus, we set out to present human development in holistic terms.

In order to understand the developing individual's behavior, one must recognize that he or she is affected by many interacting factors of a biological, interpersonal, psychological, and cultural-environmental nature. Given the complexity of human development, it is important to realize that the processes of aging do not occur in a vacuum. Rather, we see the developing person as embedded within the environment, acting upon that environment as well as being acted upon by it. No matter what field of study students were coming from or moving toward, we wanted them to come away from a course on adult development and aging with this sense of integration.

NEW STUDENT ORIENTATION

We originally wrote a text defined by scholarship and a broad research base, and we were gratified to receive positive feedback on these aspects of the text. However, we also feel that the everyday relevance of the knowledge generated by this research is equally central. In this second edition, we have strived to create a text that is truly student-oriented and student-accessible. Consequently, we have placed additional emphasis on the applied aspects of adult development and aging so that students can appreciate both the usefulness of basic research in these areas and the relevance of this material to their own lives and the lives of those they know.

ORGANIZATION

The text is organized topically rather than chronologically, since many of the topics are equally relevant to both older adults and younger adults. Aging is best thought of as an ongoing process, not easily segmented into discrete stages that are mutually exclusive. Yet some aspects of young adulthood, middle age, or late adulthood are unique and need to be understood in the context of biological change and/or psychosocial factors distinct to each life period. For these reasons, our discussion of issues relevant to adults and aged persons varies both within and between chapters.

We believe that organizing the material topically also helps students understand adulthood in a more integrated manner, making it more likely that topics in different chapters will be seen as interrelated rather than as independent. The chapters are also arranged so as to first lay the groundwork for the students' thinking about adult development and its research methods, and then to deal with basic psychobiological processes (i.e., biology of aging, sensation/perception), followed by topics that are distinctly psychological (i.e., learning/memory, intelligence, and personality). The later chapters are predominantly psychosocial and/or clinical in their orientation (i.e., work/retirement, mental health/psychopathology, intervention/treatment, and death/dying). This chapter organization reinforces the text's dual emphasis on basic and applied research.

We have condensed the second edition from 14 chapters to 12 so that the material fits together more logically. For example, Chapter 4 now covers both sensation and perception, and Chapter 7 now includes information on relationships in adulthood as well as on socialization. Likewise, the section on industrial gerontology is now in Chapter 9 (Work, Retirement, and Leisure), and that on sexuality is covered in both Chapter 3 (Biology of Aging and Longevity) and Chapter 7 (Interpersonal Relationships and Socialization). Other major organizational changes that we feel will enhance the book's readability and coverage include moving the discussion of myths and stereotypes of aging to the introductory chapter, so that students can evaluate their own attitudes and knowledge about the aging process as they begin learning about younger and older people. In addition, the chapter on Research Methods follows Chapter 1 to lay the methodological groundwork for all that is to follow.

COVERAGE AND PRESENTATION

We have also made a number of changes in coverage and presentation in this second edition. For example, references have been updated to include the newest studies on a variety of topics; nearly a third of the references cited are 1987 or later. Moreover, there is a greater balance between theory and application that is reflected in how material is presented in each chapter.

Because the field of adult development and aging is a dynamic, changing one, high-interest topics that are current and relevant to the lives of both younger and older adults are discussed, such as custodial grandparenting and elder abuse (Chapter 7), women's career development (Chapter 9), stress and coping (Chapter 8), intellectual and memory training with older adults (Chapters 5 and 6), drug use and abuse in older adults (Chapter 10), family caregiving (Chapters 7 and 10), the psychological effects of physical aging (Chapter 3), and psychotherapy with dying persons (Chapter 12). In addition, we have expanded our coverage of dementia in Chapter 10 and everyday memory and learning in Chapter 5, as well as discussing more fully the developmental aspects of grief and bereavement in Chapter 12, which is now the concluding chapter in the text. In addition, students can now evaluate their own likely life expectancy using information in the Appendix.

Perhaps the most important change in presentation is the overhaul of the writing style. For example, sentences are now shorter and less complex, and concepts are now explained in simpler language. In addition, references have been streamlined and moved to the end of each sentence to aid in comprehension. We have field tested these new changes with students in the classroom and have received enthusiastic support. We hope that you will feel the same about this way of presenting the material. Additionally, more numerous applied examples appear throughout to help students understand basic concepts in a way that will seem more "real-life" oriented.

PEDAGOGY

Each chapter of *Adult Development and Aging* begins with a chapter outline to give students a preview of the covered topics and to structure and guide their learning. Throughout the chapter, key terms appear in boldface type at their first usage, to call students' attention to their significance. Following each chapter, a summary and a list of key terms and concepts cue the student once again to the most important issues discussed. New review questions test student comprehension of the chapter material.

New "Adults Speak" Inserts

Another new feature we are quite excited about are the new inserts with the heading "Adults Speak" in nearly every chapter. In these quotes and excerpts, people of various ages describe in their own words how they are facing a number of aging-related issues. We think these inserts will make the text material come to life for students—and maybe some of them will even strike a chord of familiarity!

Other boxed inserts throughout the text highlight high-interest topics and applications, such as hospice care, divorce, euthanasia, marriage and parenting, Elderhostel, hearing loss, sexuality in later life, training older workers, therapy with people suffering from dementia, the Baby Boom generation, and centenarians.

A complete glossary at the end of the text assists the students in defining terms used throughout the text. A separate Instructor's Manual containing test items and a variety of classroom activities is also available. We believe that these features will not only make students' learning easier and more effective, but also make this learning more personally meaningful to them.

ACKNOWLEDGMENTS

We would like to gratefully acknowledge the efforts of the following reviewers whose critiques of the second edition manuscript at various points in its development were most valuable:

Harriet Amester, University of Texas, Arlington
William Bailey, Eastern Illinois University
Clifton Barber, Colorado State University
Paul Bell, Colorado State University
Andrew Coyne, University of Medicine & Dentistry of New Jersey
Darlene DeMarie Dreblow, Muskingum College
Jeffrey Elias, Texas Tech University
Sandra Fiske, Onandaga Community College
Joseph Fitzgerald, Wayne State University
Karen Hooker, Syracuse University
Ruth Lyell, San Jose State University
Robert Stowe, Central Connecticut State University
Mark Ziegler, York University

We would also especially like to thank our student reviewers, Martha Hipskind and Eddie Strickel, who kept us on track as we endeavored to orient the book toward students. Anne Harvey and especially Carol Einhorn at HarperCollins were extremely supportive and helpful. Their experience and insight were essential to the completion of the second edition. Finally, thanks are extended to Pat Parham for her patience and expertise in the typing of the manuscript.

We hope you like what we've done with this second edition of our text.

Bert Hayslip, Jr.
Paul E. Panek

CHAPTER 1

Adult Development and Aging

An Introduction

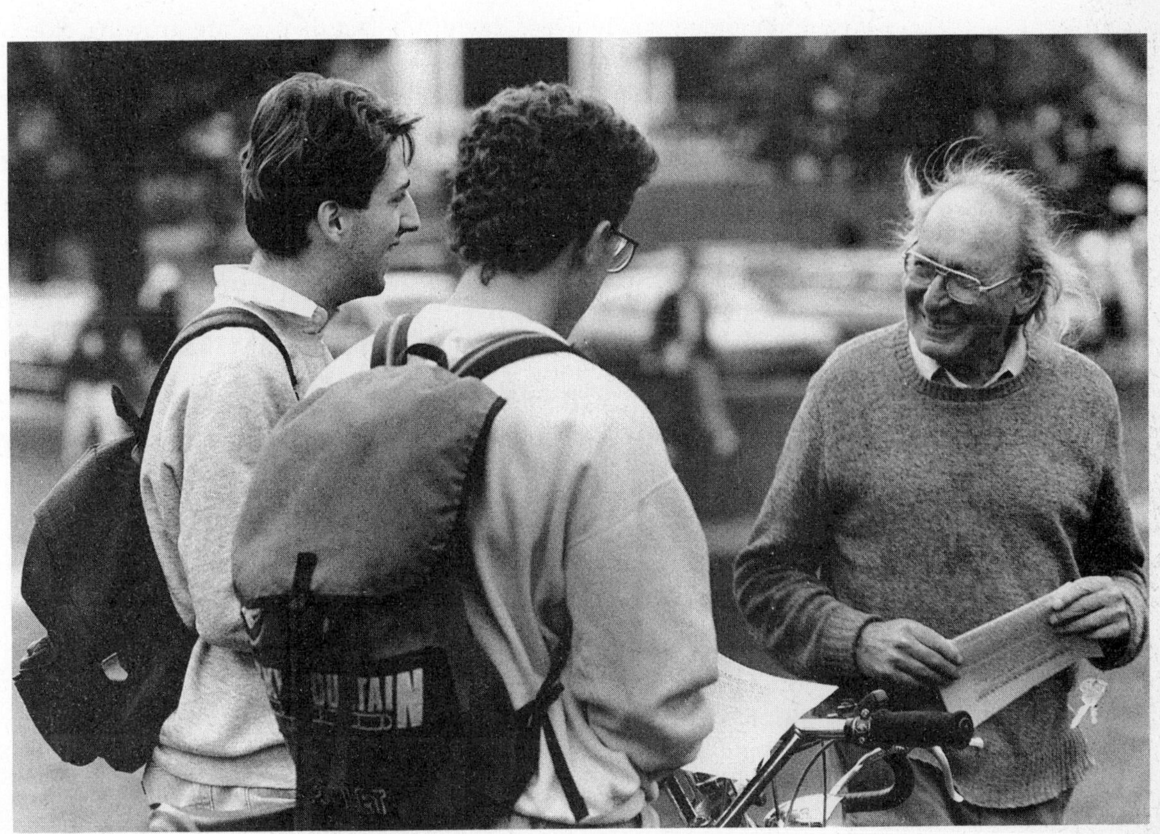

C H A P T E R   O U T L I N E

PREVIEW

We are reminded nearly every day of the fact that we are growing older. Yet the process of aging is, for many of us, a mysterious one, born out of our biases and lack of information. While we all carry around a vague picture of what our adult years will look like, we rarely take the trouble to ever find out whether that picture is an accurate one. Paradoxically, we seem to cling to definite ideas or opinions about how we or others "should" age. Some of us dread getting older, while others look forward to it. Still others have mixed emotions. In any event, our feelings color our own experiences as well as our relationships with others who are younger or older than we.

Consider for a moment the following list of individuals and phrases:

George Burns	the older person driving in front of you
Rose Kennedy	the older woman you saw crossing the street
Barbara Bush	the older person you saw in your doctor's office
Jane Fonda	the older person in a nursing home
Cheryl Tiegs	menopause
Julia Roberts	your grandmother
Christie Brinkley	over the hill
Tom Cruise	dirty old man
a retired professor	Michael Jordan
senile old goat	Arsenio Hall
your grandfather	middle-age spread
little old ladies	Madonna

How did you react as you read over this list? Do you think the individuals are aging normally, or are they exceptions? Some of the names or phrases on this list probably evoked some very positive feelings in you. Others perhaps made you feel more negative. Were you comforted or disturbed in reading this list?

It is probably safe to say that your reaction to many of the names or phrases reflects your own long-standing bias about how one "should" develop and age. Should you "age gracefully," or will aging drag you along "kicking and screaming"?

Learning about adult development and aging is important and valuable for many reasons. It can lead us to new insights about our own lives, as well as deepen our relationships with our children, parents, or grandparents. It can help us set realistic and attainable goals for ourselves in the future. If, in our professional lives, we deal with adults and older persons, separating myth from fact can enable us to be more effective and empathic in how we do our jobs. For a variety of reasons, then, being able to describe and explain what happens in our lives as we grow older can be very useful to us.

It might be helpful to think about the years that lie ahead of you as a journey of sorts that we all must travel. For some of us, the journey may be a difficult one, while for others it may be a pleasant trip. As with any journey, there are many roads, and some are bumpier than others. Which road will you take?

While we cannot predict with certainty which of the many paths your journey will take, we can provide some road signs to guide you. That is, while we cannot say what *will* happen, we can help you understand what *might* happen in the years ahead. We hope that by learning about adult development and aging, you will be able to avoid taking a wrong turn that would make your journey more difficult or more painful than it needs to be.

This text examines the process of adult development and aging. We will explore and discuss the effects of a variety of biological, physiological, psychological, sociological, and cultural factors on development during the adult years. In order to accomplish this somewhat complex task, we have organized the text topically rather than chronologically. This was done because we feel each topic is relevant to each phase of the **life cycle,** e.g., young adulthood, middle age, or old age. Moreover, chronological age, as we will see, is not a good predictor of behavior in adulthood. However, the significance of each of these topics, or factors, on behavior and development sometimes differs for adults at different points in their lives. Therefore, our discussion of issues and factors relevant to young adults and aged persons often varies within and between chapters.

The process of human development and aging is a continuous and dynamic one, not easily separated into discrete or independent stages. Consequently, factors that affect people during adulthood should be viewed as interrelated rather than as independent. For example, in Chapter 3 we will discuss the role of biological and physiological factors in the process of aging. At that time, we must be sure to keep in mind that these biological/physiological processes, often expressed in terms of observable physical changes (e.g., our hair turning gray), will also have potential psychological and social effects on us. Graying hair, for instance, may lead us to feel mildly depressed or cause us to avoid interactions with others in social situations. Thus, the process of human development and aging is best understood and studied in a holistic manner.

In this chapter we have several goals. We will first provide you with the foundation of information, concepts, and issues that you will need to appreciate and understand the complex process of adult development and aging. We will address such concepts as age and issues related to age.

We will also introduce some of the major myths about older people and the process of aging. (See Box 1.1.) One of our major concerns is to provide you with the information necessary to challenge and dispel these myths. We will also discuss attitudes toward aging in the United States as well as from a sociocultural perspective. Last, we will provide you with a theoretical framework or perspective within which to understand the processes of adult development and aging.

It is important to note that, for the most part, our discussion of adult development and aging will focus on what can be considered normal aging as opposed to pathological aging. **Normal aging** involves changes—biological, sociological, or psychological—that are inevitable and occur as the natural result of maturation or the passage of time (Drachman, 1980). These changes affect all of us as we age. They should be distinguished from **pathological aging** processes, that is, changes that result from pathology or disease. They are *not* part of the normal aging process. For example, as one ages, manifestations of underlying pathological changes, such as gray hair or hardening/calcification of one's bones and nails, are part of the normal aging process. They are not the result of pathology or disease. On the other

BOX 1.1

HOW MUCH DO YOU KNOW ABOUT AGING?

What are some of the myths regarding aging and the aging process? Take a few minutes and answer each of the following questions either True or False:

1. As people grow older, they become more alike.
2. If people live long enough, they become senile.
3. Old age is generally a time of serenity.
4. Older people tend to show little interest in sex.
5. Older adults tend to be inflexible.
6. Most older people lack creativity and are unproductive.
7. Older people have great difficulty in learning new skills.
8. When people grow old, they generally become "cranky."
9. Most older people are lonely and isolated.
10. As people become older, they are likely to become more religious.

Source: Palmore, E. (1977). Facts on aging: A short quiz. *Gerontologist, 17,* 315–320.

hand, heart attacks, cataracts, and deficits in concentration due to brain dysfunction are examples of pathological or disease processes. They are not part of the normal aging process.

WHO ARE ADULTS? WHO ARE THE AGED?

The issues we must first address are determining whom we consider adults, whom we consider aged, and determining what criteria to use in assigning these labels to particular individuals. The key factor in both issues is age. However, age is not a simple concept and has many meanings.

Types of Age

After reading this section, when someone asks you your age you will be able to answer him or her with, "Which of my ages are you talking about?" There are many types of age, and the following are the types most widely discussed concerning adulthood and aging.

CHRONOLOGICAL AGE

When one thinks of the concept of age, perhaps the first thing that comes to mind is **chronological age,** which simply refers to the numbers of years that have passed since birth. Although chronological age is widely used by people to classify themselves or others as young, old, and so forth, professionals in the field of adulthood and aging have expressed great dissatisfaction with the use of chronological age as an indicator of change or as a research variable (Hagestad & Neugarten, 1985; Wohlwill, 1970b). When we assume someone's age causes that person to behave in a certain manner, we are ascribing to age the status of an **independent variable.** But if age is truly an independent variable, we would have to be able to independently assign individuals to a given age group when investigating the effect of age on behavior or performance. Obviously this is not possible; one cannot arbitrarily designate a 20-year-old as one of a 40-year-old group of individuals. Thus, chronological age should be regarded as a nonpsychological **dependent variable** (Birren & Cunningham, 1985; Wohlwill, 1970a, 1970b). In other words, age-related changes in behavior or appearance are themselves *dependent on,* say, some underlying biological process. We will have more to say about independent and dependent variables in our next chapter dealing with research methods.

In both everyday and laboratory situations, we are often interested in those characteristics of individuals, such as personality traits or performance on a task, that make them different from, or similar to, one another. We often explain such differences in terms of age. In truth, while age cannot itself cause individuals to change, experiences or events that are **age-related,** or associated with age, may help explain why they change. Therefore, it is better to view age as an index of change, just as inches are an index of a person's height, rather than a cause of change. Although the use of chronological age may help us organize our knowledge about people and their behavior, it does not allow us to explain the how and the why of that behavior. For example, using chronological age to index differences in political attitudes toward government spending between 20-year-olds and 60-year-olds may be useful for discussion and comparative purposes. However, this common classification of individuals on the basis of chronological age does not explain how such attitudes came about or why individuals of varying ages maintain or give up these attitudes. Moreover, not all 20-year-olds or 60-year-olds share similar attitudes. In many cases, an individual's life situation, rather than age, influences what he or she is doing or feeling. For example, being laid off from your job may better explain why you are pro–government subsidies for unemployed workers than being 30, 50, or 65 years old. Likewise, as an employed worker with a family to raise, you might oppose such programs because they would increase your taxes. Many individuals, be they 20, 45, or 60 years of age, would be opposed to such a tax increase. A woman can have her first baby at age 17 or at age 45. A man might be newly married at age 25 or age 65. One might retire and begin a new career at age 40 or at age 70.

However, our society and others have found it difficult to move away from the use of chronological age to explain or predict behavioral change. One reason is that chronological age is often linked, by law, to the accessibility and nonaccessibility of specific goods, services, and benefits. For example, at age 16 you can get a driver's license, at 18 you can vote, at 21 you can purchase alcohol, and at 65 you can retire. Using chronological age in this manner has been called the legal definition of age. That is, age is defined in terms of government laws and mandates. Though the legal definition lacks scientific precision, it does mandate a specific standard for making decisions about people that affects everyone equally.

BIRREN'S THREE TYPES OF AGE

Birren (1964) suggests that in order to discuss the age of a person in a meaningful way, we must consider three types or indices of age. These are: **biological age, psychological age,** and **social age.** Each of these types of age is thought to be independent. That is, a person's biological age does not necessarily affect his or her psychological and social ages, and vice versa. In reality, however, for most individuals they are somewhat related.

There are two aspects to biological age. First, it can be considered to be the relative age or condition of the individual's organ and body systems. For example, does the 80-year-old individual's bodily processes, such as the cardiovascular system or nervous system, in fact function like those of an 80-year-old? It is quite possible for an 80-year-old who has remained physically active through exercise and running to have a cardiovascular system characteristic of someone much younger. On the other hand, a 30-year-old who has lived a very sedentary life-style (a couch potato!) and engaged in poor dietary and health practices (e.g., a diet high in cholesterol, cigarette smoking) may have the cardiovascular system characteristic of someone much older.

The other aspect of biological age is an individual's present position relative to potential life span, that is, how many years the organism could theoretically or potentially live. This varies from species to species. Flies have a potential life span of days, dogs 15 to 20 years, and humans 100+ years. Therefore, a given chronological age has different meanings for different species. An age of 15 years is of course meaningless applied to a fly, to a dog implies the later stages of its life cycle, and represents adolescence for a human. Also, being eight years old but affected with progeria, a disease where one cannot expect to live much beyond 15 or 20, makes that person biologically older than an eight-year-old whose likely life span is 70+ years. Thus, chronological age carries a very different meaning from species to species. It is important to note, however, that while biological age should not be viewed as synonymous with chronological age, for most humans they are usually quite similar.

> Age is a question of mind over matter. If you don't mind, it doesn't matter.
>
> *Satchel Paige*

Psychological age refers to the adaptive capacities of an individual, such as one's coping ability, problem-solving skill, or intelligence. These are usually inferred from the person's behavior in everyday situations or on the basis of interview or test data. While our psychological age may be related to both chronological and biological age, it cannot be fully described by their combination. For example, although an individual may be chron-

Remaining physically active can influence our biological age. We feel younger than our age.

ADULTS SPEAK

THE PRIVATE WORLD OF AN OLDER PERSON

Often, what we think getting older is like is not at all what those who actually experience it report. Malcolm Cowley, age 80, tells it this way:

The new octogenarian feels as strong as ever when he is sitting back in a comfortable chair. He ruminates, he dreams, he remembers. He doesn't want to be disturbed by others. It seems to him that old age is only a costume assumed for those others; the true, the essential self is ageless. In a moment he will rise and go for a ramble in the woods, taking a gun along, or a fishing rod, if it is spring. Then he creaks to his feet, bending forward to keep his balance, and realizes that he will do nothing of the sort. The body and its surroundings have their messages for him, or only one message: "You are old." Here are some of the occasions on which he receives the message:

- when it becomes an achievement to do thoughtfully, step by step, what he once did instinctively
- when his bones ache
- when there are more and more little bottles in the medicine cabinet, with instructions for taking four times a day
- when he fumbles and drops his toothbrush (butterfingers)
- when his face has bumps and wrinkles, so that he cuts himself while shaving (blood on the towel)
- when year by year his feet seem farther from his hands
- when he can't stand on one leg and has trouble pulling on his pants
- when he hesitates on the landing before walking down a flight of stairs
- when he spends more time looking for things misplaced than he spends using them after he (or more often his wife) has found them
- when he falls asleep in the afternoon
- when it becomes harder to bear in mind two things at once
- when a pretty girl passes him in the street and he doesn't turn his head
- when he forgets names, even of people he saw last month ("Now I'm beginning to forget nouns," the poet Conrad Aiken said at 80)
- when he listens hard to jokes and catches everything but the snapper
- when he decides not to drive at night anymore
- when everything takes longer to do—bathing, shaving, getting dressed or undressed—but when time passes quickly, as if he were gathering speed while coasting downhill. The year from 79 to 80 is like a week when he was a boy.

Those are some of the intimate messages. "Put cotton in your ears and pebbles in your shoes," said a gerontologist, a member of that new profession dedicated to alleviating all maladies of old people except the passage of years. "Pull on rubber gloves. Smear Vaseline all over your glasses, and there you have it: instant aging." Not quite. His formula omits the messages from the social world, which are louder, in most cases, than those from within. We start by growing old in other people's eyes, then slowly we come to share their judgment.

I remember a morning many years ago when I was backing out of the parking lot near the railroad station in Brewster, New York. There was a near collison. The driver of the other car jumped and started to abuse me; he had his fists ready. Then he looked hard at me and said, "Why, you're an old man." He got back into his car, slammed the door, and drove away, while I stood there fuming. "I'm only 65," I thought. "He wasn't driving carefully." I can still take care of myself in a car, or in a fight, for that matter.

Continued

continued

My hair was whiter—it may have been in 1974—when a young woman rose and offered me her seat in a Madison Avenue bus. That message was kind and also devastating. "Can't I even stand up?" I thought as I thanked her and declined the seat. But the same thing happened twice the following year, and the second time I gratefully accepted the offer, though with a sense of having diminished myself. "People are right about me," I thought while wondering why all those kind gestures were made by women. Do men now regard themselves as the weaker sex, not called upon to show consideration? All the same it was a relief to sit down and relax.

Source: Cowley, M. (1982). *The view from 80*. New York: Penguin. pp. 3–6.

ologically 90 years of age and bedridden with severe arthritis, that person may still be quite alert. He or she may be very conversational, keep abreast of current local and world events, and have sound reasoning skills. Therefore, this individual's ability levels could easily be similar to those of someone in his or her twenties.

Social age refers to the habits, behaviors, and activities of an individual relative to the expectations of society. These behaviors and activities to which our actions are compared are often called **developmental tasks.**

Basically, developmental tasks are expectancies, in terms of the acquisition and onset of specific skills, behaviors, and activities. Developmental tasks often vary as a function of culture, race, ethnicity, sex, and age. These developmental tasks provide individuals with a system of **age norms** or **age-appropriate behaviors** and activities. An example is telling one of your friends, whom you view as acting like a child, to "act your age." Society tends to reinforce individuals for acting in an age-appropriate manner and to implicitly punish individuals for violating these norms.

Social age is somewhat related to chronological, biological, and psychological age but is not completely defined by them. For instance, someone who is chronologically 80 years of age may share similar attitudes, habits, clothing preferences, and leisure activities typical of someone in his or her thirties.

An interesting way to define age is to ask individuals what they think their **personal age** is. In other words, how old do they "feel"? Barnes-Farrell and Piotrowski (1989) asked just this question of over 800 men and women aged 18 to 65. In general, people reported feeling younger than they really were more often than they reported feeling older than their actual age. However, the proportion of people reporting feeling younger *increased* with increased age, while the opposite was true for younger people. Moreover, the magnitude of the discrepancy also increased with increased age.

Montepare and Lachman (1989) surveyed nearly 200 men and women aged 14 to 83 years and found again that the older one was, the younger one perceived himself or herself to be. This was more true for women than for men. These authors also found that for younger persons, younger age identity was associated with greater fear of aging and less life satisfaction. These findings reinforce the everyday experiences of many of us who sometimes say, "I feel older today than I really am." Perhaps the best estimate of how old we are is how old we *think* we are!

FUNCTIONAL AGE

The concept of **functional age** has increased in both popularity and usage. While there are many views or definitions of functional age, they all have in common the assumption that one's functional age is an index of one's level of capacities. Capacities can range from performance on a particular job to the condition of various organ systems in the body. For example, although a person has a chronological age of 40, the condition of his or her cardiovascular system may be similar to that of a 30-year-old. In addition, this person may be just as productive on the job as someone who is 25 years of age. Functionally, this person is 25 to 30 years of age, not 40.

This example highlights the two most widely discussed views of functional age. The first type closely parallels Birren's (1964) views of biological age and is illustrated by the work of Fozard, Nuttal, and Waugh (1972). These researchers obtained and analyzed a large number of varied measures on a series of factors (biological, psychological, and social) from 600 healthy men, ranging in age from 20 to 80 years. They were able to derive six preliminary components of functional age: blood serum and urine; auditory functioning; anthropometric descriptions (observable physical characteristics, for example, grip strength); verbal, perceptual, and motor abilities; personality; and sociological assessments. Simply put,

Exercising one's mind is an important aspect of psychological age.

an individual's performance on, or measure of, each of these components could be used as an index of his or her functional age. For instance, an individual who is chronologically 65 but able to discriminate tones, or who has the hand speed of someone 40 years of age, would have a functional age of 40.

The second view of functional age is illustrated by the work of Dirken (1972) and McFarland (1973), where functional age reflects one's standing on a composite index of several measures of job performance and work capacities. The primary goal of this approach is to find a replacement for chronological age as a criterion for hiring, job rotation, and retirement. This perspective implies that it is possible for a worker who is 60 years of age to perform as adequately on the job as a person who is 20 years of age.

At present, both views of functional age are limited in that they still are in part defined by chronological age. We will examine the implications of functional age regarding the assessment of work performance in greater detail in our discussion of industrial gerontology (see Chapter 9).

AGE: CONCLUDING COMMENTS

As we have seen, there are many types of age. Each of these types has unique implications for us as we age. You have probably observed that we use the terms *aging* and *development* interchangeably. This is due to the fact that they are identical processes; from the minute we are born we are aging. Therefore, when we refer to the aging person or aging process we are not specifically referring to older adults but to changes across the entire course of adult development and aging. All of us, regardless of our age, are aging.

Just as difficult as defining the age of a person is deciding what ages (usually chronological) define periods of life, such as adolescence, young adulthood, middle age, and later adulthood. Further, as we have seen that there are different types of age, the term *age* can also have different **subjective** meanings to individuals at different points in the life cycle. A 6-year-old may view his 15-year-old sibling as an adult, or maybe even aged! Fifteen-year-olds may consider themselves adults, while most parents view them as children. Most 30-year-olds consider themselves adults, yet a 20-year old may view a 30-year-old as middle-aged, or even old. Likewise, many 60-year-olds may see themselves as middle-aged and reserve the term *old* for someone who is 75 or 80, and address a 30-year-old as a "youngster." Therefore, terms such as *young* and *old* are *relative* terms and often depend on one's perspective. In a poll of nearly 1000 adults of varying ages, their chronological estimate of "old" suggested that for 18- to 22-year-olds, 65 was considered old, while for 65-year-olds, 72 was considered old (*USA Weekend*, 1987).

At this point, you might ask yourself and discuss with others at what chronological age you feel one is an adult. By what criteria did you reach this decision? How do we know when someone is an adult, or no longer an adult, and is therefore now an older adult? (See Box 1.2.)

BOX 1.2

PERCEPTIONS OF MATURITY AND AGING

Most people, when asked, will say that one is an adult when he or she is "mature." What do people really mean when they say someone is mature? Likewise, we all probably have views about our own personal aging. What sorts of positive and negative things happen to people as they get older? Carol Ryff (1989) asked 171 middle-aged and older adults these questions and got some rather surprising and interesting answers. As you look over these adults' responses (summarized in the bar graphs below), notice that in many ways people's views about these issues varied with age. Think about how you would respond if you were asked the same questions. Do you consider yourself mature? What sorts of changes in yourself do you imagine taking place as you get older?

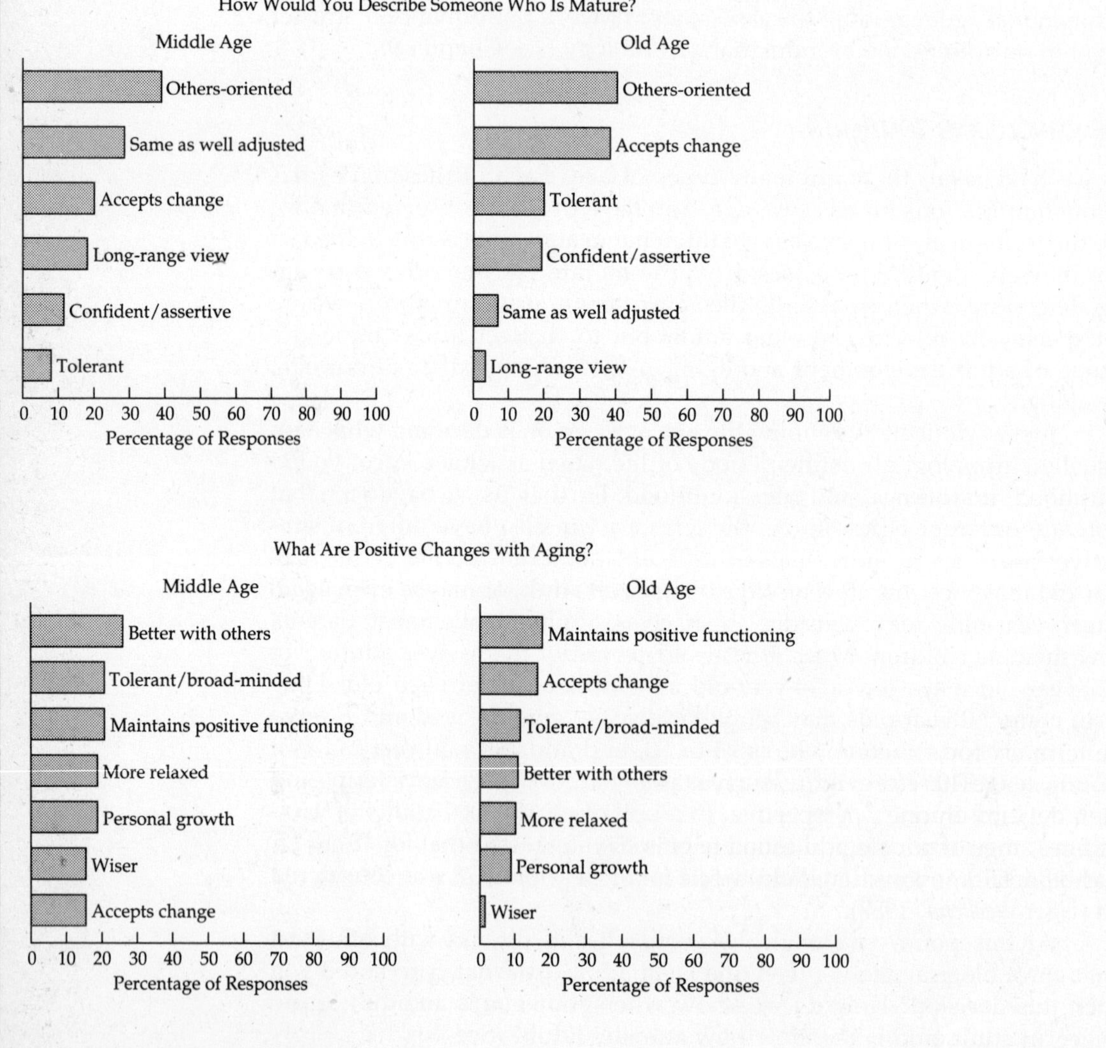

Box 1.2 *continued*

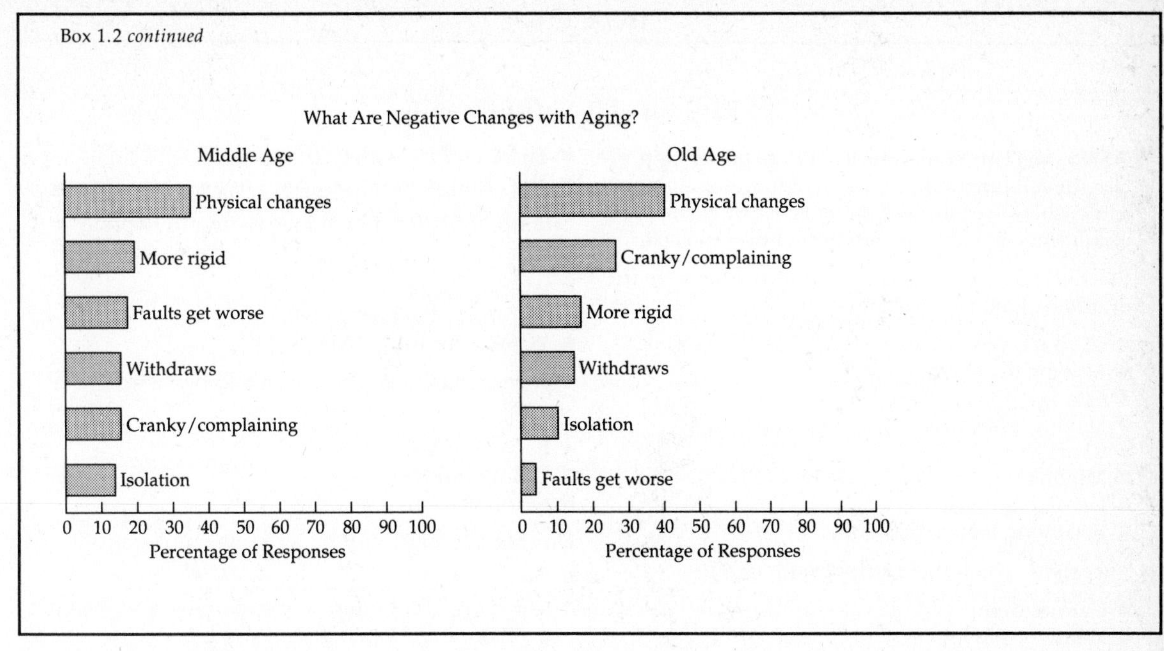

Periods of the Life Cycle

Experts in the area of adulthood and aging not only fail to agree on the value of characterizing adulthood in terms of stages, but they also have differing opinions on how to label or characterize stages or life periods along the life cycle. In addition, they debate which criteria should be used to classify individuals into these periods, such as what chronological age limits define each stage. Indeed, there have been various schemes proposed to define the stages or periods of adulthood. Since these designations are often arbitrary, they should not be considered absolute or distinct (Lerner, 1986). Their primary value is simply to help us organize and describe information about persons across the life cycle.

As individuals proceed along the life course, entrance to and exit from these purported stages is gradual. According to Levinson (1986), early adulthood theoretically ends at about age 45, and middle adulthood begins at age 40. The five-year span (ages 40 to 45) thus serves as a midlife transition during which the stage of early adulthood draws to a close and the stage of middle adulthood begins. Similarly, between the stages of middle adulthood and late adulthood is a five-year span (ages 60 to 65), for the transition to later life.

In this text, we will structure our discussion and presentation using the classification system of Levinson (1986): early adulthood (17–45 years), middle adulthood (40–65 years), and late adulthood (60+ years). Further, we will separate the stage of late adulthood, as suggested by Neugarten (1976), into young-old age (65–75) and old-old age (75+).

BOX 1.3

TYPES OF TRANSITIONS

Transitions are sometimes overlooked as important developmental events in adulthood. Nancy Schlossberg has studied many types of transitions in adulthood. Here are some examples of each.

Elected: Some are social milestones; others are individual choices

- Graduating from school
- Moving away from home
- Changing jobs
- Having a baby
- Retiring
- Moving
- Divorcing
- Becoming a grandparent

Surprises: When the unexpected happens

- Car accident
- Winning the lottery
- Death of a child
- Plant closing
- Getting a raise

Nonevents: When the expected doesn't happen

- Infertility
- The promotion that doesn't occur
- The book that is never published
- The fatal illness that disappears
- The child who never leaves home

Life on hold: The transition waiting to happen

- The long engagement
- Waiting to die
- Hoping to become pregnant
- Waiting for Mr. or Ms. Right

Sleeper transitions: You don't know when they started

- Becoming fat or thin
- Falling in love
- Becoming bored at work

Double whammies: It never rains but it pours

- Retiring and losing a spouse
- Marrying, becoming a stepparent, and being promoted to a first supervisory job
- Having a baby, developing a serious illness, getting a new job
- Caring for ill children and parents at the same time

Source: Schlossberg, N. (1989). *Overwhelmed: Coping with life's ups and downs.* Lexington, MA: Lexington Books. pp. 28–29.

Given the general dissatisfaction with the use of chronological age in explaining development, many theorists prefer to classify individuals into stages of the life span on the basis of developmental tasks. Examples of various theorists' conceptions of developmental tasks or critical issues for specific stages of the life cycle are presented in Table 1.1. While developmental tasks are often seen in normative terms, they vary as a function of factors such as cultural change, socioeconomic level, ethnicity, race, gender, marital status, educational level, and occupation. Thus, issues defining these developmental tasks and norms for behavior are always relative, never absolute. They vary from culture to culture and as a function of individual life circumstances (Riegel, 1977a, 1977b). Indeed, a developmental task may need to be redefined and reconfronted several times during one's life. Consequently, we may never finish dealing with certain developmental tasks (Oerter, 1986). Consider how many times in your life you have had to redefine "who you are." Yet questions regarding one's identity are supposedly most characteristic of adolescence.

TABLE 1.1

EXAMPLES OF DEVELOPMENTAL TASKS/CRITICAL ISSUES ENCOUNTERED BY INDIVIDUALS DURING ADULT LIFE AS PROPOSED BY VARIOUS THEORISTS

Birth	Life Span		To Death
	Chronological Age in Years		
15 20	25 30 35 40	45 50 55 60	65 70 75 80+
	Stages of Life		
?	Young Adulthood ?	Middle Adulthood ?	Late Adulthood ?
Theorists:			
Erikson (1963)	Intimacy vs. isolation	Generativity vs. stagnation	Ego integrity vs. despair
Gould (1972, 1975)	Independence from parents Career development Starting a family Questioning of self	Attempting to attain life's goal Settling down General mellowing	
Havighurst (1972)	Courtship and marriage Adjustment to marriage Beginning a family (parenthood) Child rearing Family responsibilities Career development Social relationships Civic responsibility	Helping children Adult social and civic responsibility Satisfactory occupational performance Development of leisure activities Accepting and adjusting to physiological changes Adjustment to aging parents	Adjusting to declining physical strength and health Adjusting to retirement and reduced income Adjusting to death of spouse Anticipating one's own death
Sheehy (1976)	Independence from parents Further identity formation Career and family involvement Adult responsibility	Mid-life transition or crisis Reestablishing or renewing self-concept	

AN AGING SOCIETY

Our society is rapidly becoming more attuned to the unique problems of aging, given the demographic changes in the United States during the last two decades. During this period, infant death rates have declined, and birth and death rates have stabilized. In addition, life expectancy has increased from 70 years in 1970 to 75 years in 1990 (Statistical Abstract of the United States, 1990). Improved health care, better nutrition, increased personal health care practices, and other factors have all played a role in these demographic changes. The changes indicate that in the future more people will be surviving into their seventies and eighties. Thus, demands on caregiving and services such as health care will be greater than before for current and future cohorts of younger persons.

Recent estimates indicate that in 1990 approximately 12 percent of the population in the United States were aged 65 or older (U.S. Bureau of the Census Statistical Abstract of the United States, 1990). In fact, the percentage of older persons has risen steadily over the past 20 years and is projected to exceed 20 percent by the year 2000. Figure 1.1 clearly indicates that the relative balance of younger versus older persons in our society will shift even more dramatically in the future. While the numbers of persons aged 44 or younger have already or are projected to decline, those over 45 will become more numerous. In 1990 the median age in the United States was 32.2 years.

Due to these demographic shifts, the United States, as well as other industrialized nations, is becoming what is called an aging society. That is, the percentage of "older" individuals is becoming larger than the percentage of "younger" individuals. Thus, concerns that affect all adults, especially older adults, will most likely assume more importance in the future and have an increasing biological, psychological, economic, and political impact on many aspects of our lives (see Chapter 3).

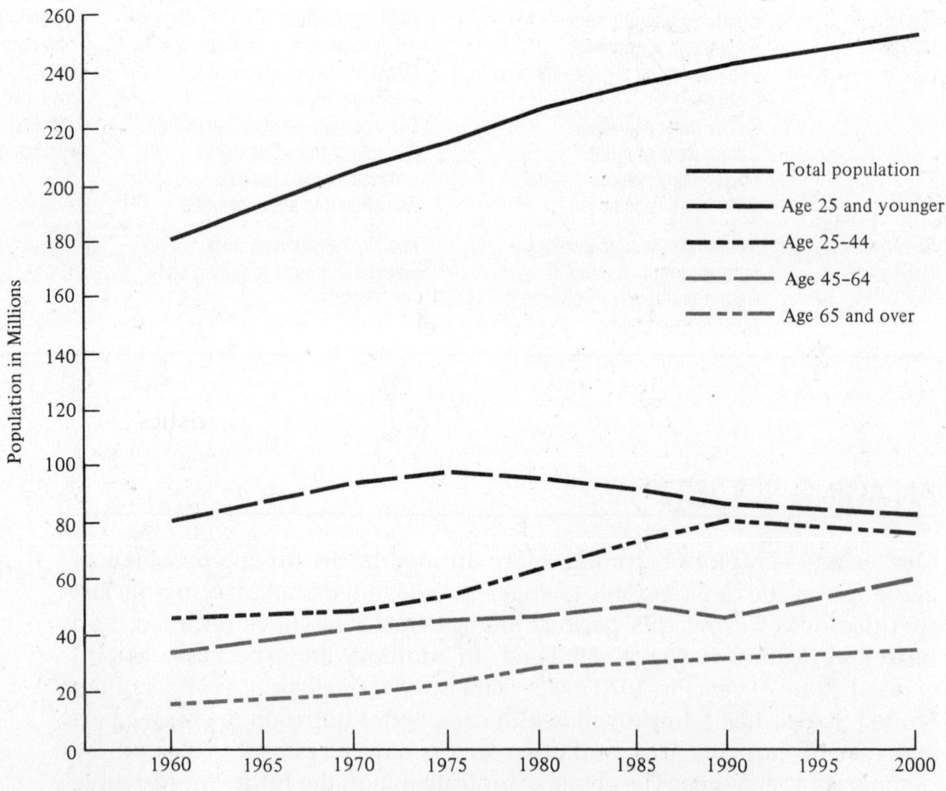

Figure 1.1 U.S. population by age: 1960–2000. *Source:* Adapted from U.S. Bureau of the Census, *Statistical Abstract of the United States: 1986* (106th ed.), Washington, DC, 1985.

Myths of Aging and Attitudes Toward Aging

Despite these demographic changes in the composition of the United States population, views about later adulthood and the aging process continue to be clouded by much misinformation. This misinformation can potentially lead an individual to subscribe to some of the common myths regarding aging and the aging process. These myths can affect in turn our attitudes toward the aging process and toward older persons.

Despite the acquisition of new knowledge and research findings, many myths, usually negative in nature, still persist today regarding the aging process. Some of these myths or beliefs can be traced as far back in history as biblical times, the Romans, and the writings of Shakespeare (Covey, 1989). For example, in an essay entitled *de Senectute* ("About Old Age"), written by Cicero, a lawyer and essayist living at the time of Julius Caesar, the major character addresses four charges against Old Age. According to Cicero, Old Age (1) prohibits great accomplishments; (2) weakens the body; (3) withholds enjoyment of life; and (4) stands near death. Interestingly, these four assumptions define the core of a number of current myths regarding old age.

So prevalent are these myths that many elderly come to believe such myths themselves (Kausler, 1991), which often makes adjustment more difficult than necessary (Bennett & Eckman, 1973). In fact, Thorson, Whatley, and Hancock (1974) found older people often hold the most negative views of old age.

Because most of us have little preparation for the experience of dealing with being old in our society (Rosow, 1985), we often avoid or make jokes about older persons. In contrast, many Eastern cultures, such as those of Japan and China, treat elderly persons with an attitude of reverence and respect (Butler, Lewis, & Sunderman, 1991; Palmore, 1975). Often our misperceptions are based on a lack of experience and knowledge. **Stereotypes,** frequently due to lack of contact or selective exposure, help people to minimize ambiguity and bolster self-esteem (Brubaker & Powers, 1976).

Many of the false beliefs surrounding elderly persons are simply not supported by statistics regarding the demographic characteristics of the aged. For example, not all old persons live in institutions—only a small minority do so (see Butler, Lewis, & Sunderland, 1991; American Association of Retired Persons, 1990). Most older persons (over 65 years old) do not live alone; only 30 percent live alone or with nonrelatives (American Association of Retired Persons, 1990). Not all old people are sick. In fact, while many do suffer from chronic diseases, these illnesses are not necessarily incapacitating. Consequently, many older persons lead worthwhile, happy, satisfying lives, despite a greater probability of experiencing chronic illness than the young (Butler, Lewis, & Sunderland, 1991). Not all older people are senile either. Senility, as Zarit (1980) points out, is a legal-medical term, often misapplied and considered untreatable. However, even when cumulative brain dysfunction has produced an organic condition that is irreversible, there can be overlays of depression, anxiety, and psychosomatic disorders that are in fact responsive to medical and psychotherapeutic interventions (Butler et al., 1991; Zarit, 1980).

In addition to the illusion of senility, several other myths of aging lack substance. An example is the tranquility myth, which sees old age as a period of serenity where people enjoy their past accomplishments. Given society's devaluation of many aged, a greater need for medical care combined with decreasing earning power to meet such costs, inadequate public transportation, losses in status, age discrimination, and interpersonal loss (death of spouse and friends), it is ludicrous to view the older person as tranquil or serene.

Clayton (1975) suggests that most older people in today's society are more likely to have a feeling of despair than tranquility (Erikson, 1959)—regret over their lives, unhappiness, and a feeling of time running out. While a sense of integrity—feelings of adequacy, self-satisfaction, and wholeness—is possible, Clayton nevertheless feels that older persons may have incompletely resolved or compromised their way through previous psychosocial crises. This, according to Clayton, leads to feelings of despair rather than ego integrity in later adulthood.

Another pervasive myth exists about aged persons: unproductivity. The notion of unproductivity falsely suggests that older people are no longer able to produce on the job or do not wish to remain active and creative. Many elderly do in fact remain employed (almost 3 million, 30 percent of the aged) and continue to work beyond retirement age when their health permits it (see Chapter 9). In fact, health may improve after retirement, permitting the older person to pursue work-substitute, leisure, or work-related interests (Butler et al., 1991).

Related to the myth of unproductivity is the stereotype of the older adult as incapable of learning. As we shall see in Chapter 5, this is anything but the case. In fact, a number of factors that are independent of chronological age (e.g., level of education, health status, culturally relevant social changes, and differential life experiences) are better predictors of learning and memory skills. Although a loss in learning ability with age may be realistic for some individuals, those who study older people have found that in many cases such declines have been overestimated. We will restate and expand on each of these points in many chapters throughout this text.

Another common misperception of the elderly is that of resistance to change, or rigidity. However, rigidity may be a function of long-established personality traits or socioeconomic pressures rather than anything inherent in the aging process (see Chapter 4). Moreover, rigidity may be adaptive for some persons, helping them structure their lives and making events more predictable.

Other myths persist: that of the sexually disinterested and incapable aged persons. Ludeman (1981) dispels this stereotype in noting that older people do retain both interest in and ability for sexual relations (see Chapter 3).

In general, then, the assumption of the so-called universal **irreversible decrement model** in capability with increased age has been questioned. A viewpoint termed the **decrement with compensation model,** which accepts losses in function that can be compensated for by using intervention strategies (e.g., prosthetics), has instead surfaced. Compensatory aids may be either physical (e.g., hearing aids) or psychological (e.g., adopting more efficient means of approaching tasks to be learned) (Schaie & Gribbin, 1975; Woodruff & Walsh, 1975).

Note that older people usually do not make the same generalizations about themselves that younger people often do. Indeed, there is evidence suggesting that the manner in which the elderly are perceived by others and their perceptions of themselves are frequently at odds. While a few studies indicate that the aged hold relatively low self-opinions (see Chapter 8), many studies report discrepancies between the perceptions of older people and those of the young, with elderly persons reporting more positive feelings about themselves than those attributed to them by younger persons.

In this light, it is interesting that Weisz (1983) and Langer (1982) suggest older persons underestimate their skills by (1) simply being labeled old (connoting inferiority), (2) being denied the opportunity to engage in tasks formerly engaged in now being performed by someone else (as in the case of retirees), and (3) allowing others to help them (implying that they cannot help themselves). Recall the experience of the older man who was offered a seat by a younger woman presented earlier in this chapter.

Indeed, when provided with no other information than an individual's age, younger people are more likely to attribute the poor performance of a 65-year-old (versus someone younger) to a lack of ability or task difficulty (Gekoski & Knox, 1983). Lachman and McArthur (1986) found that in general, older people's lack of ability was more likely to be attributed to poor performance in social, physical, or cognitive situations, while for good performance, luck or ease of the task was thought to be important. When older people's attributions (explanations) for such performance were examined, however, it was found that they were more likely to take credit for good performance and deny responsibility for poor performance, suggesting that they may have used such explanations to cope with feelings of inferiority or expected poor performance.

The most convincing data regarding the disparity between older people's perceptions of aging and those of younger people have been reported by the National Council on Aging through a Harris public opinion survey (1975) entitled "The Myth and Reality of Aging in America." This study involved polling over 4000 people of all ages to ascertain their perceptions of aging. Significant discrepancies between general public opinion of the elderly (over 65) and those who were actually 65 and over were found on such variables as brightness and alertness, being physically and sexually active, being open-minded and adaptable, and being very good at getting things done.

Significantly greater proportions of the general public than the aged felt that people over 65 spent "a lot of time" doing things such as just sitting and thinking, sleeping, "just doing nothing," and watching television. Unhappily, those over 65 saw themselves as less physically and sexually active than did those under 65, indicating that to some extent they had internalized some of the myths of aging discussed above. As Binstock (1983) suggests, it may be more fruitful to focus on relationships between younger and older people, rather than on older people per se, thus reinforcing the interconnectedness between younger and older people.

Exchange theory has been adapted to help explain negative attitudes toward aging (Kahana & Midlarsky, 1982). According to exchange theory, individuals attempt to maximize rewards and reduce costs in interpersonal relationships. All relationships are viewed on a debits-and-credits basis. Since older adults may have few credits, such as money, material possessions, and physical attractiveness, and a large number of debits, such as poor health, they are not valued by others. It is this lack of relative value that contributes to the negative images of aging.

ARE OUR IMAGES OF AGING ALWAYS NEGATIVE?

Based on all of this information it appears as though aging is viewed quite negatively in the United States. Is this really true?

Although the above discussion strongly suggests that most people hold negative attitudes toward aging, the evidence is not completely supportive of this (Austin, 1985; Lutsky, 1980). Not only do some studies not support negative attitudes toward the aged, but the belief that Americans hold negative attitudes toward the aged may itself be a myth unsupported by research (Schonfield, 1982). It may be that formerly negative biases have simply been replaced with equally inaccurate positive and negative stereotypes—for instance, that most elderly are well off, older people are a drain on our financial resources, or older people are politically self-interested—based on generalizations about them. These generalizations ignore subcultural and individual variations (Binstock, 1983).

As mentioned earlier, we often assume that older people, because they respond to society's negative view of them in certain ways, also subscribe to these same myths. We subsequently assume that they have poor views of themselves. However, this self-definition resulting in a negative view of oneself has been challenged by Brubaker and Powers (1976). They propose an alternative approach emphasizing both positive and negative aspects of the stereotype of oldness. Which aspect of this stereotype is incorporated into the older person's self-definition is a function of (1) whether the person subjectively defines himself or herself as old, (2) objective indicators of old age, and (3) previous self-concept. The refreshing advantage of this approach is that it does not predict that all elders will necessarily adopt a negative stereotype of old age. In fact, Brubaker and Powers point out that the signs of aging in our society (e.g., retirement) are not always viewed as negative by the old or the young.

Recent evidence for variability in the stereotypes held by younger persons has been provided by Schmidt and Boland (1986) and Hummert (1990). Hummert's study is unique because it investigates stereotypes of older *and* younger adults held by young persons (see Box 1.4). Schmidt and Boland (1986) found that the term *older adult* serves as a superordinate

BOX 1.4

MULTIPLE STEREOTYPES OF YOUNGER AND OLDER ADULTS

Hummert (1990) asked college students to sort a list of 84 traits to investigate their perceptions of both their age peers and of elderly people. For each target age group, multiple stereotypes of young and older adults were obtained, with those for young people being more complex. This study documents the fact that we carry around more than one general stereotype of both our age peers and non–age peers. In general, people felt more positive about some stereotypes than others. That is, some stereotypes were negatively viewed (e.g., severely impaired, shrew, underclass, redneck), while other stereotypes were more positively viewed (e.g., John Wayne conservative, perfect grandparent, mature young professional, activist, athlete/extrovert).

Source: Hummert (1990).

category (including gray hair, wrinkles, false teeth, retirement, and poor eyesight) within which different stereotypes that are both positive (e.g., John Wayne conservative, perfect grandparent, and sage) and negative (bag lady, recluse, vulnerable, shrew, severely impaired) exist. Simply put, different older persons evoke different reactions. Institutionalized, ethnic, and dependent aged are most likely to hold and be the object of negative attitudes toward older persons (Schmidt & Boland, 1986). On the other hand, independent, highly educated, and high-occupation elderly are the objects of at least ambivalent, if not positive, stereotypes of aging. In sum, this study demonstrated that college students had both positive and negative stereotypes of the elderly (Hummert, 1990).

The above studies suggest that it may not be just aged persons who are the victims of stereotypes. Young adults are *also* stereotyped by their age peers (Hummert, 1990). However, there is a conspicuous absence of research dealing with stereotypes about middle age. As we will discuss in Chapters 3 and 8, middle age can be a pivotal time of life, yet information about how individuals view middle age is, comparatively speaking, lacking.

Even if our stereotypes apply only to certain older persons, they suggest that we are denying that we too are aging and will someday become elderly. It may be a way of handling what we fear most: losing our youthfulness, good health, or a circle of friends, or facing the inevitability of our deaths and ultimately accepting responsibility for our own lives. To the extent that stereotypes and myths of aging are adopted by both the young and the old, the experience of aging becomes a self-fulfilling prophecy for the young.

Fischer (1977) has traced the attitudes toward older adults in America from colonial to modern times. During the colonial period in America, there were very few older adults. It was estimated that about 2 percent of the population was over 60 years of age at that time. Since achieving old age was so rare, due to a lack of medical care and sanitation, the presence of many diseases, and the hazards of frontier life, reaching old age was taken as a sign of being one of the "elect." During this period, then, America exhibited the **cult of the aged.** It was acceptable and positive to be old. In fact, fashions were designed to highlight old age, as illustrated by the popularity of white-haired wigs.

After the American Revolution, the status of the elderly began to deteriorate, for a number of reasons. First, society became more mobile. There was westward expansion, the result being fewer large families and individuals moving away from the family unit to seek independence and their own destinies. Second, there was industrialization. Individuals no longer had to base their economic future on the family land, property, or business; they could work in someone's mill and earn their own money independently of the rest of the family. Finally, society began to value functional roles, activity, and productivity rather than wisdom and experience. Since younger individuals had greater physical stamina and could work harder and longer than older adults, the young came to have a greater value than the old, according to society. America thus adopted the **cult of the young.**

It may be, however, that the cult of the young has peaked, and we are now moving toward the **cult of the adult.** In other words, one can be over 30 and still enjoy life! This change may be because between 1980 and 1990 the fastest-growing age group in the United States has been the *baby boom* generation—individuals now between 35 and 49 years of age who were born between 1946 and 1964 (Robey, 1984). Media programming, commercials, advertisements, and industries are beginning to take note of this fact. For example, companies such as the Ford Motor Company have established "mature advisory" boards to address "adult" consumers and their needs.

A CAUTION REGARDING ATTITUDES TOWARD AGING

The current answer to whether or not there are negative attitudes toward older adults depends quite heavily on the situation or source of the material. In fact, the study of attitudes toward older adults is quite enigmatic because of its contradictory and voluminous nature.

Perhaps a resolution of the paradox can be based on the difference between what individuals do and what they say. That is, in situations where individuals are asked to openly state negative attitudes toward older adults (as in a questionnaire), they either see through the situation or do not want to appear prejudiced toward older adults and therefore do not exhibit any bias. However, these same individuals may directly or indirectly react negatively toward older adults in terms of their actual behavior. Support for this assumption has been found by Panek (1984).

When negative attitudes toward older adults do exist, they are often based on a combination of factors such as misinformation, myths, and presentations by the media, as well as the result of other factors. For example, Kite and Johnson (1988), in a meta-analysis of the literature, found support for Lutsky's (1980) conclusion that age, in and of itself, appears to be less important in determining attitudes toward older adults than other types of information (e.g., one's personality, whether a specific or general older person is being considered). Sanders and Pittman (1987) found perceived knowledge of the elderly affected attitudes, in that "known" aged were viewed more positively than "other" aged.

CHANGING ATTITUDES TOWARD OLDER PERSONS

What can we do to change the view the young have of the old, and of the experience of being old itself? Many have found that the young come to see the aged in a more positive light and report less generational conflict with increased exposure to older persons, both in general and within the context of the family unit (Nardi, 1973; Weinberger & Millham, 1975). In this light, one study found that less than one-fourth of their sample of 3- to 11-year-old children knew any older persons outside the family (Seefeldt et al., 1977). Even for those children who had more contact, it was limited to no more than two visits per year. Kimmell (1988) suggests that ageism may be reduced by emphasizing diversity among older people.

Institutional intervention may also help matters, such as (1) by training teachers in life-span development to effect a shift in attitudes early in life, (2) age integration of classes and training in life-span development at the elementary, high school, and undergraduate levels, (3) by designing courses around interest groups instead of age groups, and (4) by encouraging the development of affective experiences and motivation (e.g., through small-group discussion) as well as cognitive skills in the classroom (Birren & Woodruff, 1973). Perhaps such efforts are paying off; Dial (1988) found that television portrayals of older adults have been improving.

We have stated that individuals age in unique ways. Yet older people who are from different cultural backgrounds are more different still.

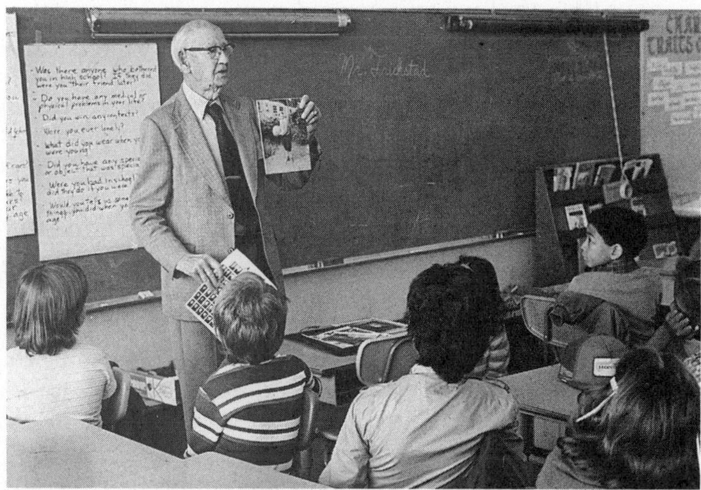

Having direct experience with older people is important to the development of realistic yet positive attitudes toward aging.

American society is a collection of different individuals who also vary in terms of race, ethnicity, and cultural background. By the year 2050, a fifth of all aged persons are projected to be nonwhite (Myers, 1985).

Keith (1985), in a discussion of the social position of the old, stresses the importance of ethnicity. Each ethnic group has its own history of traditions that affect behaviors and values. Older persons "manipulate" these traditions in a way that not only helps them cope with societal change via their relationships with younger generations but also guarantees continued status and prestige within the family. In Boston, for example, traditional kinship patterns determine who cares for the aged person (e.g., the child who lives nearest the aged person) among Irish and Chinese persons (Ikels, 1982).

CORE IDEAS IN ADULT DEVELOPMENT AND AGING

The Concepts of Differences and Changes in Adult Development and Aging

In this chapter, we have used the terms *differences* and *changes* when referring to the process of aging. These terms have specific meanings when used in the study of adult development and aging, and it is important that they be clarified. These terms are: **individual differences, intraindividual differences,** and **intraindividual changes.**

INDIVIDUAL DIFFERENCES

Difference *between* individuals in any ability, trait, or characteristic is called an individual difference. If your hair color is black and your spouse's hair is brown, that is an individual difference in hair color. Suppose you and your roommate are of the same age and gender, come from the same socioeconomic background, and are enrolled in the same course. On the first test in the course, you receive a grade of A and your roommate receives a D. This difference in test performance is an individual difference between you and your roommate. However, knowing there is a difference in performance does not explain what caused the difference. Perhaps one of you is brighter; perhaps you prepared more carefully. We would, of course, be interested in explaining this difference in class performance.

The concept of individual differences is important since the aging process proceeds at different rates for different people. Some individuals begin to lose their hair during their late twenties and have white hair by their mid-forties. Others do not lose any hair, or their hair does not turn white until their late sixties. Therefore, when we discuss various topics throughout the text, such as psychomotor ability, intelligence, and so forth, you should realize that there will be great individual differences in performance levels among individuals at any given point in the life cycle. In other words, people are different from one another even at similar ages. Consequently, not all individuals of a given chronological age will share

In many respects, people remain much the same as they age, while in other respects, they exhibit great change.

the same attitudes or evidence similar abilities of performance levels. And in fact, it is not uncommon for individual differences to become greater with increasing age (Krauss, 1980; Nelson & Daneffer, 1992). That is, greater variability in performance is observed in individuals as they age. Simply put, older persons are more different from one another than are younger persons. This is illustrated in Box 1.5.

INTRAINDIVIDUAL DIFFERENCES

Intraindividual differences refer to differences among traits, behaviors, abilities, or performance levels *within* a specific individual at any point in time (Baltes et al. 1986; Hoyer, 1974). An example would be the differences among your grades for the various courses you are taking this term. For instance, you may be receiving an A in this course, a B in Mathematics, and a C in English Composition.

INTRAINDIVIDUAL CHANGES

Intraindividual changes refer to changes *within* an individual over time on any behavior, ability, or performance skill. How your intelligence changes as a function of time or the aging process would be an example of an intraindividual change. The identification and explanation of intraindividual changes are the primary goals of research and theory in the field of adult development and aging. As intraindividual changes become more dramatic, differences between persons also widen (Baltes et al., 1986).

Overall, it will be important to keep in mind that there will be differences both within and between individuals at all points in adulthood.

BOX 1.5

INDIVIDUAL DIFFERENCES AND AGE

What do we mean by individual differences becoming greater with increased age?

Below is a list of test scores for 30 students enrolled in a college course. Let us suppose 10 of these students are young adults, 10 are middle-aged, and 10 are older adults. From examining these data, a number of points about development can be illustrated. While the average test score appears to lessen with increasing age, *variability* between persons—individual differences—becomes larger with increasing age. In view of this fact, focusing on average scores may not be desirable.

The apparent decrement in performance with age obscures the fact that older people's scores are more different from one another than are those of the younger groups. Thus, on an individual basis some older people outscore many of the younger ones.

This variability can be observed by looking at the standard deviation and range of scores for each of the age groups. This variability increases across levels of age. The standard deviation and range are two statistics that are used to describe the variability of scores. The larger the standard deviation and range, the greater the variability of scores.

Test Scores

	Young Adult Individual	Middle-aged Individual	Older Individual
	80	100	57
	95	65	100
	100	78	57
	100	99	89
	85	87	100
	99	95	94
	95	92	83
	93	81	72
	84	76	78
	96	87	91
Average score	92.7	86.0	82.1
Standard deviation	6.81	10.56	15.13
Range	80–100	65–100	57–100
N	10	10	10

Causes of Change in Adulthood and Aging

The processes of development and aging are universal characteristics of all living organisms and thus entail and imply change. As previously indicated, the primary focus of research and theory in adulthood and aging is to identify and explain change within the organism, i.e., intraindividual change. To the extent that these changes are associated with chronological age, they are termed *age-related changes.* That is, they are assumed to be the direct result of the aging process. However, changes in behavior, traits, abilities, and so forth can also be attributed to factors other than age in the sense of maturation or biology. In fact, Baltes et al. (1980) suggest that, to adequately understand changes in the context of adulthood and aging, one must consider three types of influences. These are (1) **age normative,** (2) **history normative,** and (3) **nonnormative influences** and are illustrated in Figure 1.2.

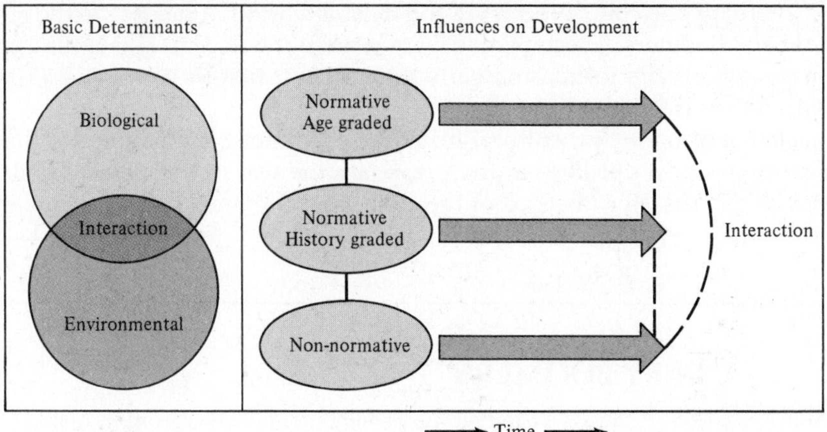

Figure 1.2 Influences that regulate life-span development. *Source:* P. B. Baltes, H. W. Reese, & L. P. Lipsitt. (1980). Reproduced, with permission, from the *Annual Review of Psychology,* Volume 31, © 1980 by Annual Reviews, Inc.

Age-normative influences are factors that are general to the process of development and are highly related to chronological age. Though the timing in terms of onset may vary for different subgroups of people, these influences generally affect persons of a specific age in a particular manner. Age-normative influences can be the result of biological-physiological processes, such as the onset of puberty or menopause. However, they can also be social-environmental, such as mandating a specific age for marriage, childbirth, or retirement, or simply expecting people to "act their age."

History-normative influences are factors or events that occur at a specific point in time (day, month, or year) and theoretically affect everyone in that society or culture. These events can have either a short-term or long-term effect upon individuals, and may also have different effects on individuals as a function of age. For instance, if a war were to be declared, the most pronounced effect of this would be on individuals who because of their age would be called upon to fight in the war—young adults. However, this does not mean that the spouse, children, and family members of the individual called to fight in the war will remain unaffected.

History-normative factors also include influences that are particular to a given cohort or generation, and can have a significant and long-lasting effect on the behavior, attitudes, and values of members of that cohort. In general, a cohort is any group of people sharing a common set of experiences. An age cohort would commonly include persons born at a particular historical time period or era. For example, the cohort of individuals who were children during the Great Depression of the 1930s, and were therefore born in the early twentieth century, is comparatively very frugal economically and very independent, having lived through severe economic hardships. McIlroy (1984) calls these prevailing attitudes, values, and beliefs shared by members of society at a particular time **cultural ethics.**

Perhaps the cohort receiving the most attention at present is the so-called Baby Boomers. These people were born in the mid- to late 1940s and are now in their late forties and early fifties. They are our next generation of older persons (see Box 1.6).

Some of the major cultural-historical events of the past decade that will perhaps affect our lives in the future are the war in the Persian Gulf, the *Challenger* disaster, the end of the Cold War, the breakup of the Soviet

BOX 1.6

BABY BOOMERS

The Baby Boom generation refers to the very large group of individuals born between 1946 and 1964—almost 80 million people. The Baby Boom was created by delays in marriage and childbearing due to World War II and the prosperity that followed. We sometimes separate this generation into the Early Boomers, born before the early 1950s, and the Late Boomers, born thereafter.

Consider that in 20 to 25 years, the ratio of older to middle-aged persons will be 253 to 100, according to census figures. If this doesn't make you aware of the tremendous shift in our population base due to the Baby Boom generation, consider that in the year 2021 Bob Dylan and Paul Simon will be 80, Linda Ronstadt will be 75, Stevie Wonder will be 71, and Michael Jackson will be 63. All of these well-known people are either early or late Baby Boomers.

In response to the sheer numbers of people growing up in the late 1940s and early 1950s, our society has changed in many ways. For example, thousands of new elementary schools were built in the 1950s to accommodate the young Baby Boomers. Colleges and universities also expanded rapidly to meet the demands of this new generation.

The Baby Boom generation was bound together by a number of significant cultural changes. For example, they were the first generation to be free of many potentially fatal childhood diseases, such as diphtheria, polio, smallpox, and whooping cough. Boomers grew up with television—Mickey Mouse, Superman, Roy Rogers, Howdy Doody, and American Bandstand, plus Barbie and Ken, I Like Ike, Elvis, and the Twist. Later on, Woodstock, Kent State, Gloria Steinem, Vietnam, the Beach Boys, the Beatles, Bob Dylan, the Pill, a concern for women's rights and for the environment, and the drug culture of the 1960s and 1970s separated the Baby Boomers from their "materialistic, traditional, middle-of-the-road" parents. Boomers spawned the development of the record industry, amusement parks, the convertible, and fast foods, notably McDonald's.

This "bulge" in our population is now middle-aged. They are confronting the realities of raising children and caring for aging parents, as well as dealing with the physical realities of aging themselves—crow's feet, double chins, and pot bellies. In general, Baby Boomers are more highly educated, are married, have children later in life, start work later, and are more likely to have two incomes than their predecessors.

Because of their sheer numbers, peer-group identity became important and was a major factor in pitting this generation against its elders over America's involvement in Vietnam in the early 1970s. While the parents of the Baby Boomers laid the groundwork for the massive societal changes many Baby Boomers grew up with, the generation following the Baby Boomers may not be as societally driven or as economically lucky. Rising inflation and increased unemployment, coupled with rising costs of housing, education, and health care, may make the next generation's life very different.

Gerber et al. (1989) forecast that in the next 30 years, due to the aging of the Baby Boom generation, (1) more women, many of whom are financially independent and who will outnumber men by almost 2 to 1, will head up families, (2) early retirement will be a thing of the past, as more people change jobs later in life, (3) age coalitions will replace age wars, (4) cancer will become a chronic illness and doctors will lose much of their power as patients become more responsible in treating themselves, and (5) as the numbers of elderly increase, senior citizen discounts will end, and a new "elderculture" will emerge, reflecting the rebellious and independent spirit of the 1960s youth culture. As America's age structure changes, our society is almost certain to change greatly.

Union, the reunification of Germany, and the increasing number of deaths from AIDS. Each of these events, or their combination, may help to define a distinct cohort of individuals who share similar attitudes and experiences. These experiences are historically unique and differ from those shared by persons born earlier or later, historically speaking. Thus, we might speak of the Depression Era cohort, or the Baby Boomer cohort (see Table 1.2).

Nonnormative influences are factors that are not related to age or history but still affect specific individuals during the life span. In a sense, these factors cannot be attributed to the normal process of development or to the impact of environmental, cultural-social events. Having an accident, becoming seriously ill, winning the lottery, or being fired are all examples of nonnormative events.

Each of these influences is considered ongoing and interactive in terms of its effect across the life span (Figure 1.2). Moreover, each of these factors exhibits different levels of influence on the individual at different

TABLE 1.2

HISTORICAL VALUES BY COHORT

	1900–1929	**1930–1959**	**1960–1969**	**1970–1991**
Communications	Face-to-face, newspaper, radio, phonograph	Movies, telephone, radio, newspaper, hi fi	Television, movies, radio, newspaper, stereos, cassette tapes	Computer, fax, videos, TV, movies, VCRs, newspaper, cassette tapes, stereos, radio
Marker events	World War I, Great Depression	Great Depression, World War II, H-bomb, postwar boom	Social upheavals, deaths of JFK, RFK, and King, Vietnam, the Pill	Nixon, hostages, Carter, Reagan, deficit, ongoing global crises, Persian Gulf war
Culture	Good guys, bad guys, pro-American	Nationalistic, work-oriented, values, conservative, naive	More leisure, travel, human potential, sex, drugs, divorce	Environmental disasters, more rich, more poor, fewer middle-class, recession
Heroes	Sergeant York, Woodrow Wilson	FDR, John Wayne	Neil Armstrong, Martin Luther King, JFK	Mother Teresa, Mikhail Gorbachev, celebrities
Mood	Idealistic, optimistic	Optimistic, realistic	From optimism to pessimism	Cynicism, overwhelmed
Worst disease	Tuberculosis	Polio	Herpes	AIDS
Generation labels	Flappers, new wealthy	Survivers, Boomers	Activists, New Age	Yuppies, punks, dinks, busters
Favorite music and dance	Charleston, tango	Jazz, big bands, fox trot, Bing Crosby, Kate Smith	Beatles, rock, Twist, disco, Paul Simon, Elton John, Judy Collins	Madonna, Prince, the Jacksons, heavy metal, rap music

Source: Hudson, F. (1991). *The adult years: Mastering the art of self-renewal.* San Francisco: Jossey-Bass. p. 188.

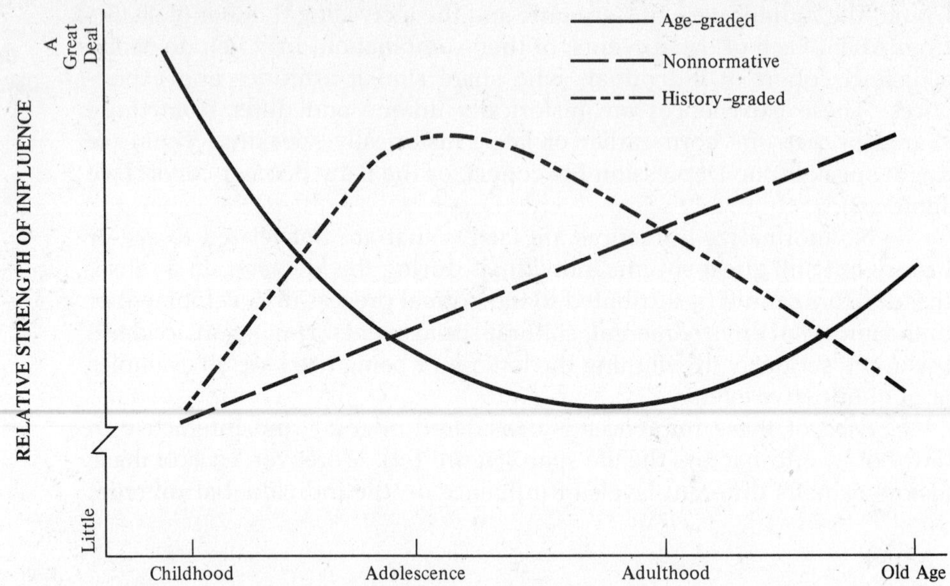

Figure 1.3 Prototypical profile of life-span influences. *Source:* P. B. Baltes, H. W. Reese, & L. P. Lipsitt. (1980). Reproduced, with permission, from the *Annual Review of Psychology,* Volume 31, © 1980 by Annual Reviews, Inc.

points in the life cycle. For instance, age-normative influences are often considered to be the result of maturation and are under genetic control. Therefore, they have the most pronounced effect during childhood and old age. History-normative influences are most pronounced among adolescents and young adults, and nonnormative events increase in significance with increasing age (Danish, 1981) (see Figure 1.3).

A Model of Development: The Life-Span Developmental Approach

A method of organizing ideas and theories about human development is called a model of development. The specific model to which one subscribes guides one's research and determines what behaviors are studied, as well as what explanations are used in interpretation of changes or differences in these behaviors along the life cycle. From our point of view, the **life-span approach** (Baltes, 1987; Baltes et al. 1986), which incorporates the work of Riegel (1975, 1976) on the dialectics of development, provides an excellent overall perspective on human development.

According to Riegel's **dialectical theory,** internal factors such as genetically preprogrammed instinctual behaviors, traits, and the like, and external factors such as aspects of the environment or culture, continuously influence and in turn are influenced by each other. That is, internal forces interact with external forces. Both affect the course of development, and both are constantly changing and being changed by the other. Consequently, there is an interdependence between internal and external factors throughout the course of development.

The life-span, dialectical approach views the process of development as complex, affected and being affected by many mediating or moderating factors, and the developing person is best understood in the context of these factors. These include inner-biological factors (health or illness), the physical or cultural aspects of the environment (outer-physical and cultural-sociological factors), and individual-psychological influences. Therefore, change during the course of development is inevitable.

The course of our development may vary in terms of the extent to which these factors are working together, or "in synchrony," or at cross-purposes with one another, or "out of sync." To put it another way, we all go through "smooth" and "rough" periods in our lives, where we are more or less in sync with others and with physical or social changes in our everyday lives. For example, one may wish to marry but not find a suitable mate; illness may interfere with one's career plans; or one may be forced to retire due to poor health or company policy. For people who are adapting well to these changes, there is more **synchrony.** For people who cannot cope with these changes, more **asynchrony** is created; that is, a bad situation becomes even worse.

During the course of development a "crisis" may result, stemming from asynchrony, for example, the often-referred-to **mid-life crisis** (Golan, 1986; Jacques, 1965). Although crises may be disruptive, dialectically speaking, they are considered normal, and perhaps even healthy, because they give individuals the opportunity to make choices and to change their lives. Whether one perceives a crisis as positive or negative, however, often depends on the individual's personal perspective and ability to cope and adapt to change.

As Neugarten (1973, 1977) notes, for some individuals a crisis may result when they consider themselves "off-time" with reference to a **social clock.** Examples of off-timeness include delaying having children until your late thirties or early forties, going to your high school reunion and observing that many of your friends have climbed higher up the career ladder than you, or retiring at age 40. Given the importance we have placed on individual differences in development, being off-time could be seen as normal. In fact, some individuals purposely plan their lives so that they are always off-time!

The life-span developmental model views development as **multidimensional,** in that there are many different dimensions or aspects of development. For example, intelligence and sensory function are very distinct aspects of development. Also, that development is **multidirectional** suggests that change can take on many forms or directions. Some forms of change are age-irrelevant; that is, they do not vary with age. For example, certain aspects of intelligence or personality do not vary by age (see Chapters 6 and 8). Others, however, are specific to certain periods of the life cycle and are therefore age-related. The process of development is **pluralistic**, in that it can take many forms, of which increments and decrements

BOX 1.7

LINEAR AND CYCLICAL VIEWS OF ADULTHOOD

Frederic Hudson's views about adulthood embrace many of the principles of life-span development. He contrasts a linear view of adult development with a cyclical one.

	Linear	**Cyclical**
The World	The world is more stable than chaotic. Order is separate from chaos, and chaos can be cordoned off by order. Social institutions sustain stability so individuals can succeed and prosper.	The world is more chaotic than stable. Order is a temporary holding pattern within chaotic experience, and chaos cannot be avoided or cordoned off. Institutions and individuals seek to monitor change together so that acceptable levels of the quality of life can be experienced by as many people as possible.
Society	Development in personal life, family, systems, work, and society is serial. Each serial point (marriage, having children, career, and so on) is something that we do in order to move on to some goal or result. The larger society governs and guides individual and family plans.	Development is continuous reprioritization and renewal of the same issues—identity, achievement, intimacy, play, search for meaning, and social compassion. These issues provoke life tasks that we do over and over again in different ways throughout the adult years.
Personal Life	Life fits into a social master plan with defined roles, timing of events, and constraints. Personal life is a series of goals and objectives requiring long-term commitment, personal discipline, and postponed gratification. The goal of life is to attain, acquire, and obtain results—a progressive conquest that holds the promise of success and happiness. Adult life is a long period of stability in which personal strengths, intimacy bonds, career development, and responsibility work toward personal fulfillment and social progress. Transitions are not viewed positively.	Life is modular, flexible, interactive, chaotic, and resilient. Personal life is lived among many conflicting plans and social forces, requiring the abilities to tolerate ambiguity and adapt to new situations. Life is flow, an adventure into the unknown that holds the promise of continuous learning through the highs and lows of life. Adult life is a process that moves from periods of stability to periods of instability and transition to new periods of stability, and so on. Adults need to know how to build life structure and how to manage life transitions.
Family	The family is a traditional, nuclear one, with the wife as the primary caretaker of the home, being responsible for friendships, social life, child rearing, and schooling matters.	The family is an extended one, with an intimate couple sharing the caretaking of the home, including the maintenance of friendships, social life, child rearing, and schooling matters with continual negotiation of these issues.

Continued

Box 1.7 *continued*

Careers	The husband has a full-time career at all times. The wife is the full-time homemaker and parent and possibly has a part-time job or career.	Both the wife and the husband have careers or job options throughout the adult years, with economic interdependence.
Education	Education is youth oriented, to prepare for the grown-up years.	Education is a lifelong process for reeducation, renewal, and redirection.

Source: Hudson, F. (1991). *The adult years: Mastering the art of self-renewal.* San Francisco: Jossey Bass. pp. 46–47.

in specific behaviors are of but one type. Furthermore, many different types of abilities and behaviors have different courses of development in terms of onset, direction, duration, and termination. In other words, development is both multidimensional and multidirectional (Baltes et al., 1986).

In conclusion, given the complexity of human development, the life-span developmental approach seems to be an appropriate model for viewing this process. This model stresses the dialectic, dynamic nature of development. Moreover, the life-span developmental approach highlights the interrelationship between individuals of particular cohorts and their environments across the life span.

Person-Environment Interaction

In order to better understand both the importance of individual differences in development and the life-span developmental model's emphasis on the relationship of the person to his or her environment, we will discuss **person-environment interaction.** This discussion will also help illustrate how changes associated with the aging process have many implications for our everyday interaction with our environment.

All aspects of behavior and performance can be seen as a result of the interaction or transaction between the individual and the environment (Pervin, 1968). The environment can be a classroom, a workplace, a neighborhood, or even an entire culture. A match, or "best fit," in terms of abilities, skills, and performance levels of the individual to the environment expresses itself via high performance, satisfaction, and little stress in the system (the individual), while a mismatch leads to poor performance and stress (Jahoda, 1961).

In order to perform successfully and adapt, individuals must match their ability levels to the demands of their environments. This is of great importance in understanding how people cope with change. Lawton and Nahemow (1973), for example, view the aging process in terms of continued adaptation to both the demands and pressures from the external environment. In addition, it is continual adaptation to the internal changes in physical and cognitive functioning that takes place during all adult lives.

Lawton and Nahemow (1973) suggest that the individual's "internal representation" of the external world mediates this person-environment interaction. By the term *internal representation* we mean how a person conceives or views the environment. We can understand person-environment interaction more easily if we separate it into its many components. To this end, Lawton and Nahemow present what they call the transactional model, which has five components: (1) degree of individual competence, (2) environmental press, (3) adaptive behavior, (4) affective responses, and (5) adaptation level. To help you understand this model, consider the example of an adult who is employed at a demanding job, such as a word processor in a busy office.

DEGREE OF INDIVIDUAL COMPETENCE

Briefly, degree of individual competence is the diverse collection of abilities that individuals possess. These include sensory processes, intelligence, learning abilities, and perceptual-motor speed. Each skill is unique and varies over time between minimum and maximum limits that are specific to each person. In other words, each of us has particular strengths and weaknesses, these skills are different from one another, and our level of each skill is different from those of our peers. If, for example, you are not adept at word processing or cannot cope with deadlines, we might say that your individual competence at your job is impaired. Your lack of skill will eventually create problems for you at work and perhaps at home.

ENVIRONMENTAL PRESS

Environmental press is defined as those demands from the environment impinging upon and affecting the individual. Examples include other individuals, the demands of a task, driving a car on a freeway, taking a test, and taking part in an activity. If your boss is very demanding or you have a tight schedule, the press of these demands will likely influence your work performance, your stress level, and your relationships with your coworkers.

ADAPTIVE BEHAVIOR

According to Lawton and Nahemow, adaptive behavior is the outer manifestation of individual competence and one result of the individual-environment transaction. Adaptive behavior is often observable as performance on a task, such as a test grade, golf score, or number of years driving without an accident. If you work after hours or during your lunch hour, or use a stress reduction technique such as relaxation, we would say that you are adapting to the demands of your job in light of your skills and abilities.

AFFECTIVE RESPONSES

Affective responses are the inner (unobservable) aspects of the individual-environmental transaction, including the individual's evaluation and emotional reaction to the environment. Affective responses also include our subjective self-evaluation and assessment of performance on a task. If we feel we performed poorly, we may feel distressed and consequently change our self-view. For example, if you are critical of your performance or feel you have let your boss down, you may respond by becoming angry or depressed.

ADAPTATION LEVEL

Adaptation level can be considered the point where the individual is functioning at a comfortable level relative to external demands. Stimuli of a given strength are perceived as neither strong nor weak (Helson, 1964; Lawton & Nahemow, 1973). If the demands on us deviate to a certain extent from our adaptation level, or comfort zone, we will respond positively, up to a limited point. Beyond this comfort zone, positive affect decreases and becomes negative as the demands push us past our adaptation level (Lawton & Nahemow, 1973). (See Figure 1.4.) For example, if you normally word-process six pages per hour, seven or eight might be a challenge. However, being asked to do, say, ten pages per hour would cause you to make more mistakes. You might become irritable, or tire more easily. You have exceeded your personal comfort zone or level of adaptation.

You might also think of adaptation level as the level at which you feel comfortable in responding to demands from the environment. For example, the loudness level at which you normally listen to your stereo is your adaptation level. If the volume is either too low or too high, you may feel uncomfortable. Note that your own adaptation level may be different from that of your roommate or your parents.

The transactional model of Lawton and Nahemow (1973) has a number of implications for how individuals cope with their everyday environments in adulthood. For instance, Barrett (1976) has presented an approach to job design—the congruence model—which suggests that there is an optimal match or congruence among one's abilities, preferred aspects of a job, and the complexity of the job. When this match is achieved, we can use our skills to their best advantage. Our productivity and satisfaction with our work increase, and we may anticipate staying on the job for quite some time. When individuals say they like their jobs, they may be expressing this congruence between their skills and the demands of their work.

One of the major tasks in designing living environments and transportation facilities is to try to match the needs and skills of the older person. In everyday life, individuals often say that their home or work environment "fits" them. For these people, there is a good match between their skills, tastes, and so on and the environments in which they live.

In conclusion, regardless of our age, in order to deal effectively and competently with our environment, we must find tasks that match our

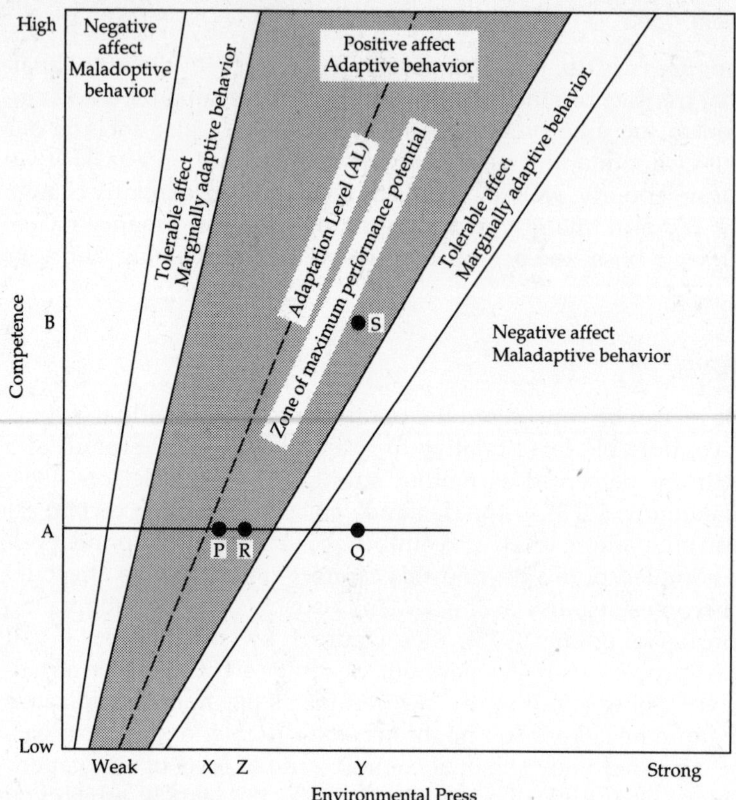

Figure 1.4 Behavioral and emotional outcomes of person-environment transactions. *Source:* Lawton & Nahemow. (1973).

ability levels. If the demands on us exceed our abilities, stress and poor performance may result. Of course, there are some people whose skills exceed the demands made on them. They might feel that their jobs are too easy, or that they are not being challenged. Simply put, they may be bored! Ironically, they might also not be performing up to par. In either case, we might define our performance under these circumstances as indicative of our functional age.

Adult Development in Context

Many times thus far we have referred to the developing individual in the context of biological, psychosocial, and cultural-environmental changes or influences. What exactly do we mean by this? Figure 1.5 illustrates adult development in the context of historical change and a variety of more narrowly defined factors that influence behavior. We hope that this working model will help you to understand adult development more completely.

To the extent that there is something systematic and age-related about our behavior, the **age continuum** serves as our individual time line, which begins at birth and ends with death. We emphasize an age contin-

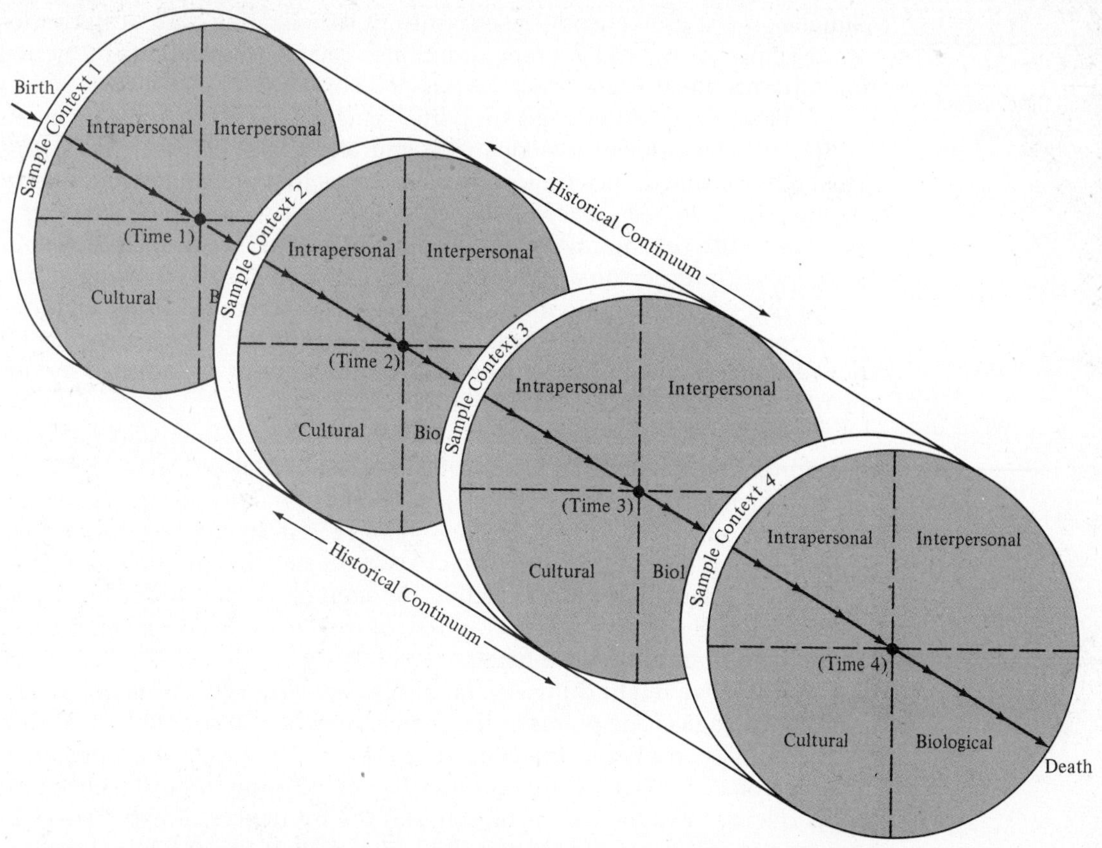

Figure 1.5 Adult development in context. Development occurs at both individual and historical levels, which interact with one another. Moreover, dimensions within individuals are in constant change, affecting how the individual reacts to the historical context and life events. To understand adequately individual development, many samples of the individual's behavior in context must be studied.

uum because, as Riegel's dialectics suggest, change in human development is the rule rather than the exception. To not change or to fail to cope seriously interferes with our development. This age continuum also serves as a focus or basis for the interaction of what might be termed various sectors, arenas, or dimensions of influence. The intrapersonal dimension deals with our feelings, goals, abilities, or attitudes, in short, how we internally represent—at present, in the past, and with respect to the future—our experiences. Learning, memory, intelligence, personality, and sensation/perception are all quite relevant to the intrapersonal dimension of development.

The interpersonal dimension reflects our relationships with others in a number of contexts or situations—as workers, parents, children, or spouses.

The biological dimension most directly relates to topics such as health and illness, death, and longevity and sexuality, while the cultural dimension not only encompasses issues of socialization, and attitudes toward aging, work, and retirement but also relates to questions of mental and physical health care.

Because we do not age "in parts," each of the above dimensions or sectors of development overlaps with and affects the others. It is for this reason that dashed lines indicating boundaries that are somewhat fluid or fluctuating have been placed between the sectors in Figure 1.5. For example, our health (biological dimension) both is affected by and affects (1) our awareness (interpersonal dimension) of the importance of eating a balanced diet or exercising (cultural dimension), (2) our prevailing attitudes (intrapersonal dimension) toward and access to health care, as well as (3) our relationships with others who provide this care or are affected by our own ill health (interpersonal dimension).

Figure 1.5 also suggests that each of these dimensions is itself changing, consistent with historical time (Neugarten & Datan, 1973), or along a historical time continuum. Each point in history serves as a larger context for our development. Besides changes in individuals, we must also consider changes in our culture that vary with the ebb and flow of historical changes and that help to define the context of development. These cultural changes affect us at each phase of the life cycle. We label this historical continuum *contextual time.*

While we might draw several samples of a person's behavior at various chronological age points in time, each must be considered a small slice of the individual's life in the context of (1) the influence of intrapersonal, interpersonal, biological, and cultural factors; (2) how that person represents relevant experiences at present; (3) the influences of experiences in the individual's past; and (4) those experiences that the individual can anticipate in the future. Therefore, numerous samples of behavior (e.g., sample context 1, sample context 2) could—and should—be taken to more fully understand this changing individual. Moreover, each sample of an individual's behavior in context is influenced by how each of the sectors is itself changing as a function of the passage of contextual time along the historical continuum. Hence, historical contexts change along a dimension of contextual time, as do individuals, who simultaneously change along an individual life time (Neugarten, 1973). As discussed above, individual life time is defined by the age continuum that begins with birth and ends with death.

We can also use the transactional model of Lawton and Nahemow to understand the relationship between the developing individual and this changing, multidimensional context. Hence, one's competence and adaptive behavior (intrapersonal, biological) and environmental press (interpersonal, cultural) all interact to produce affective and behavioral responses that should, if development is to proceed, allow for and result from the individual's adaptive coping with various aspects of the environment.

As you read about the various sectors of adult development and aging, which we have arranged topically, try not only to think in terms of their relationship to one another and their influence on development, but also to envision how these sectors have themselves changed over the last decade.

Understanding adult development in this way will help you realize that while the topics we present appear to be separate issues, dimensions of change are necessarily interwoven with one another and interwoven as well with changes in our culture. These influences both change individuals and are being changed by them. Remember that your own development and aging can be understood best in relative terms, that is, relative to how each of the sectors or dimensions in your own life is interacting across the life cycle and relative to changes in each sector across contextual time.

SUMMARY

There are a number of problems associated with classifying individuals into specific stages of development in terms of chronological age, as well as with the meaning of such age periods. Overemphasis on age as a predictor of behavior, in combination with selective exposure to individuals varying in age, can lead to unrealistically positive and negative ideas and expectations, termed *stereotypes,* of the aging process and older persons. Equally important is separating normal and pathological aging. There are *individual differences* among people in adulthood, as well as *intraindividual changes* within individuals across time in adult development. As a general rule, differences between people increase with increasing age.

Although many definitions of age exist, it is thought by many researchers and theorists that the functional age concept provides the future direction for defining and discussing the effects of the aging process. At the present time, while all theories of development are somewhat limited, the life-span developmental theory appears the most adequate relative to our present state of knowledge. According to this view, developmental change is both *multidimensional* and *multidirectional* and explained by *age-normative, history-normative,* and *nonnormative* influences.

The concept of *person-environment interaction* suggests that for successful performance or *adaptation,* an individual must have ability levels matched to the demands of the environment. This *transaction model* assumes that a match in terms of abilities, skills, and performance levels of the individual to the environment expresses itself in high performance, satisfaction, and little stress, while a mismatch leads to poor performance and more stress. These assumptions have numerous implications for the design of environments conducive to the optimization of functioning in adulthood.

A contextual model for understanding adult development was presented that incorporates *intrapersonal, interpersonal, cultural,* and *biological* factors. Each set of influences interacts to account for individual developmental change along an *age continuum* of *individual time.* These influences and their interactions are being changed as a function of the larger historical context in which they are embedded. They change along a *historical continuum* as a function of *contextual time.* Adult development and aging are therefore best understood in *relative* terms, emphasizing a changing individual in a changing environment.

Attitudes toward the aging process and the aged in the United States vary when examined from an historical perspective. Currently, many suggest that society values traits associated with young adults, such as strength, good looks, and vitality, although this seems to be changing.

It is generally assumed that older adults are at present viewed negatively in the United States, as expressed in *ageism, myths,* and *stereotypes,* but research evidence does not consistently document negative attitudes toward aging.

Variations in aging exist on both an *individual* level and on a *culture-specific* level.

KEY TERMS AND CONCEPTS

Life cycle
Chronological age
Independent variable
Dependent variable
Biological age
Psychological age
Social age
Developmental tasks
Environmental press
Age norms
Age-appropriate behaviors
Functional age
Personal/subjective age
Intraindividual differences
Individual competence
Age-normative influences
History-normative influences
Baby Boomers
Interdependence
Adult development in context
Asynchrony
Myths of aging
Age cohort
Cultural ethics
Life-span developmental approach
Dialectical theory
Social clock
Multidimensional development
Multidirectional development
Person-environment interaction
Decrement with compensation model
Irreversible decrement model
Exchange theory
Individual differences
Intraindividual changes
Age-related changes
Pluralistic
Nonnormative influences
Normal aging
Pathological aging
Synchrony
Stereotypes

REVIEW QUESTIONS

1. What are the myths and stereotypes about development and aging? How did they develop? What are their negative effects?
2. Why is it difficult to classify individuals into specific periods of life on the basis of chronological age?
3. What are developmental tasks? What role do they play in development during the life cycle?
4. Why is it important to consider individual differences in adulthood?
5. What is the life-span developmental model of human development?
6. What are the three major influences on developmental change?
7. What is person-environment interaction?
8. What are Birren's three types of age?
9. Are attitudes toward aging negative in the United States today? Have these attitudes changed?
10. What do we mean by adult development in context?
11. What is dialectics? Why is it important in understanding adult development?

C H A P T E R 2

Research Methods in Adult Development and Aging

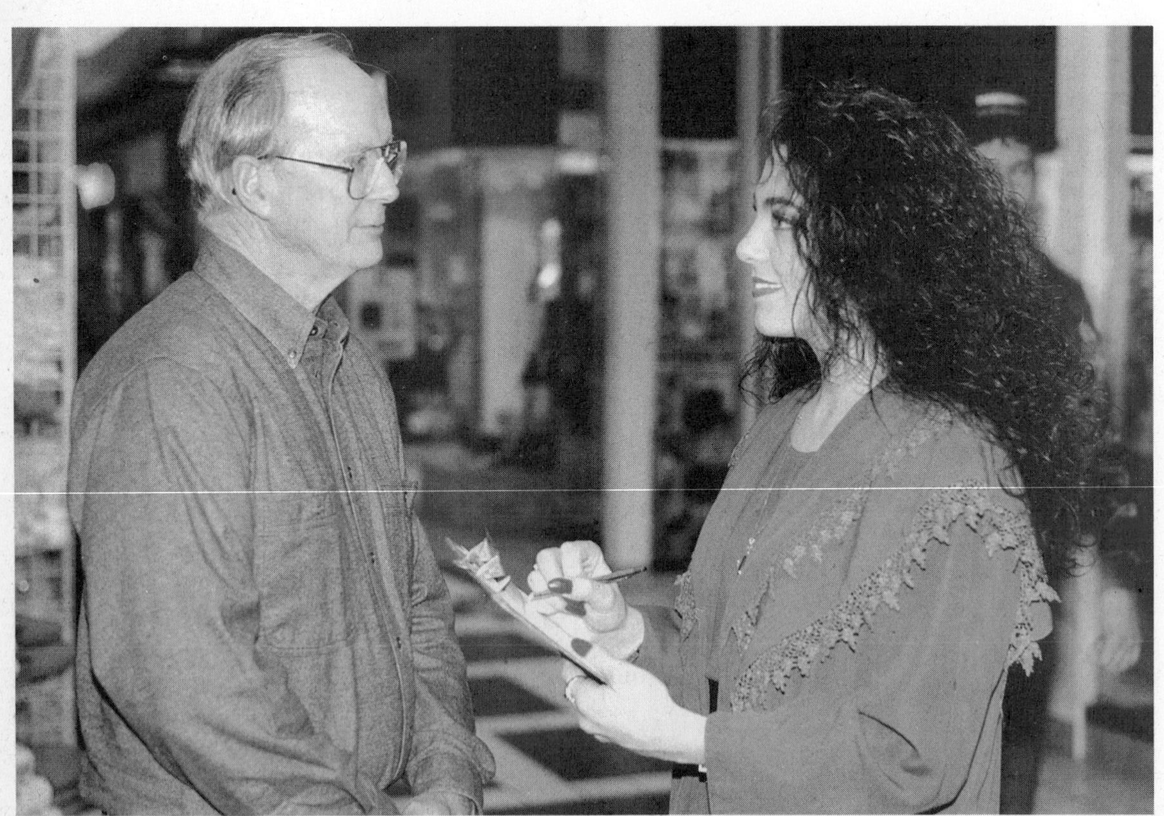

C H A P T E R   O U T L I N E

INTRODUCTION

This chapter deals with how we know what we know about adults. As we have all experienced in everyday life, how we go about gathering the facts about any issue, be it buying a new car or evaluating our health, often determines the conclusions we reach. If we do not do our research carefully, we may lose money or assume we are well when we are not.

On a daily basis, we use some form of the research methods we will discuss in this chapter. For example, we often assume that because two events are related in some way, one event must have caused the other to happen. If we notice that someone seems anxious or "down," and we also know that this person is enrolled in a number of demanding classes, we might assume that the individual's emotional state is "caused" by his or her difficult class load. In fact, the individual may not be feeling well, may have had a fight with a spouse, or may be tired from work. All of these have little to do with the difficulty of classes but may indeed better explain someone's mood on a given day.

Similarly, in class we listen to individuals express their opinions about any number of issues. If one student is young and the other is old, we might conclude that each feels the way he or she does because of age.

Moreover, if we reflect on changes in our own lives over the last ten years, we often assume that it is because we are older that we have changed.

In many ways, then, we are all "amateur researchers" who go about explaining our own and others' behavior using some implicit strategy for gathering our facts. If we are not systematic, thorough, and precise in our data gathering, however, we can easily misjudge others or reach a conclusion that has nothing to do with the way they really are. Understanding ourselves and others thus can become very difficult and frustrating.

Virtually all the facts presented in this text were gathered using some research strategy. Being able to understand the methods by which the facts of adult development are gathered will put you in a more favorable position to evaluate their relevance and validity to you personally. Moreover, the more understanding you can gain regarding the methods by which the facts about adulthood are gathered, the more useful those facts will be to you in dealing with adults of all ages.

In this chapter we will explore a variety of approaches to gathering the facts about adulthood and aging. Our goal will be to present important information regarding research methods so that you can be an informed consumer of results presented in studies of adulthood and aging. Before we talk about methods of gathering the facts about adults, we must discuss the distinctions between **nondevelopmental** and **developmental research,** and that between **experimental** and **correlational research.**

DEVELOPMENTAL VERSUS NONDEVELOPMENTAL RESEARCH

Nondevelopmental Research

Nondevelopmental research examines relationships between factors or variables that might apply to all adults, regardless of age. Such research is often, but not always, conducted with the intention of establishing a causal relationship between one factor or set of factors and another factor or set of factors. For example, we might be interested in whether there is a relationship between similarity of spouses (e.g., interests, abilities, or backgrounds) and marital satisfaction. That is, are persons who see themselves as similar to one another more happily married than those who see themselves as different? We could be interested in the role that similarity (versus other factors) plays in determining a married couple's satisfaction with their relationship. An investigator might feel that such knowledge is important for many reasons. For example, if one knows that similarity between spouses is not the most important factor in determining happy marriages, one could better provide counseling to prospective newlyweds or people experiencing marital difficulties.

Developmental Research

Developmental research, on the other hand, seeks to determine if any relationship exists between chronological age or, more accurately, the biological and maturational processes that account for aging, and some other factor of interest. The developmental researcher might define a marital problem differently. That is, among newlywed couples who are similar to one another versus those who are not, who is more happily married 10 or 15 years later? When compared with couples who have been married for many years, is similarity an essential ingredient in the relationship of newlyweds?

In other words, the developmentalist is interested in exploring the contribution that couple similarity plays in the "aging" of a relationship. The nondevelopmentalist is more concerned with the relative importance of similarity in determining marital happiness among couples regardless of length of marriage. While the couples who participate in a research project may be young or old, we would consider their ages to be irrelevant or extraneous to the problem the nondevelopmental investigator is examining. However, quite often nondevelopmental research is done as a basis for work that may be developmental in nature. For example, we might first want to know whether similarity contributes to marital satisfaction at all. Then we could investigate how powerful similarity is as a determinant of happiness in long-lived marriages. In many cases, of course, both developmental and nondevelopmental research complement each other.

EXPERIMENTAL VERSUS CORRELATIONAL RESEARCH

Another basic distinction we need to draw at this point is that between experimental, or manipulative, and correlational, or descriptive, research.

Experimental Approaches to Research

The focus of experimental research is to establish causal relationships between a factor or factors that is (are) manipulated by the researcher, which are termed independent variable(s) (IV) (McGuigan, 1983; Rosenthal & Rosnow, 1984) and another factor, called the dependent variable. This independent variable derives its name from the fact that individuals can be independently assigned to conditions (e.g., treatments or training programs) hypothesized by the researcher to be causally related to some result that he or she is seeking to produce (e.g., enhanced skills or more positive attitudes). The intended result, or dependent variable (DV), is so termed because it is dependent on the effects of the treatment. Examples of dependent variables are test scores, observations of behavior, ratings of performance, interview data, or questionnaire responses.

For example, if we wish to determine whether the type of instruction older students receive affects their attitudes toward learning, we might **randomly assign** students, as they register, to one section that is instructor-taught, or to another section that is television-taught. If extraneous factors, such as differences among our older students in motivation, previous education, intelligence, personality factors, socioeconomic status, or marital status, are thought also to influence attitudes toward learning, assigning students randomly might distribute these effects equally across class sections. In this case, type of instruction functions as our independent variable, and changes after instruction in attitudes toward learning represent our dependent variable.

In order to compare these two classes validly, we must further ensure that they are as comparable as possible in any other aspects that could also conceivably affect the students' attitudes toward their class experience. Such aspects might include the size of the class, content of the material to be learned, seating arrangement, number of class meetings, length of classes, time of day, and sex or age of instructor. We must also ensure that all participants are treated equally during the course of their classroom experience. For example, they should be tested on course content at equal points in the semester, and experience adequate lighting and temperature conditions throughout the class.

Ultimately, the conclusion should be reached that only the manipulation of the independent variable accounts for the differences between our groups' attitudes toward learning. If we are not able to equate our groups in every way except for the type of instruction received, or we are unaware of the influence of some extraneous variable on our results, the effects of the treatment (the IV) would be potentially **confounded** with, or inseparable from, the effects of the other factors we would ideally like to control for. That is, our results would be unclear in terms of cause; we would not know if the result is due to our treatment, to other extraneous variables, or to a combination of the two.

In most cases of experimental research, there is first a specified hypothesis, in this case perhaps that instructor-led classes will produce more positive attitudes. We would then label those people receiving the manipulation or treatment to be members of the **experimental group,** while those not receiving the treatment of interest, in our case, the TV-instruction class, would be labeled the **control** or **comparison group.**

Correlational Approaches to Research

Correlation coefficients describe a relationship or an association between at least two factors. A correlation coefficient has two aspects, a number ranging from 0 to 1.00, which indicates the strength of the relationship, and a sign, plus or minus, which indicates the direction of the relation. Therefore, a correlation coefficient can range from −1.00, perfect negative correlation, through 0 (zero), to +1.00, perfect positive correlation.

Regardless of the sign, the larger the number, the stronger the relationship between the two variables. With regard to sign, a positive (+) correlation indicates that both variables are associated in the same manner (direction), while a negative (−) correlation indicates that both variables are associated in an opposite manner.

Consider the following examples to illustrate these points. If a researcher were to investigate the relationship between typing speed and number of years of experience as a typist, the correlation that one would most likely observe would be positive and quite high. That is, with more experience, one's speed at typing would increase rather predictably. However, if the researcher were to investigate the relationship between years as a typist and the number of typing errors per page, the observed correlation would most likely be negative and quite high. In other words, with more years of experience, people tend to make fewer errors. The variables of years of experience and measures of typing skill are indeed related.

Correlational research seeks to establish whether or not a factor co-varies or correlates with another factor. That is, are changes in one factor accompanied by systematic changes in another? To the extent that this is true, any variables of interest, such as personality traits, assertiveness, intelligence, or age, are said to be correlated (see Figure 2.1). While **correlation** is a necessary condition for **causation**—two factors must at least be correlated in order to be causal—it is not a sufficient one in itself. Thus, correlational research allows the conclusion that two variables are associated, but not that one variable has a causal effect on the other. In other words, correlational research allows us to describe a relationship, but it cannot explain that relationship.

For example, while more assertiveness may be accompanied by greater intelligence, that is, they are positively correlated, it does not follow that greater intelligence causes one to act more assertively or vice versa. It may be that intelligent people recognize that assertive behavior is sometimes adaptive and sometimes not. In this case, intelligence would play a causal role. On the other hand, characteristics of assertive individuals, such as good interpersonal skills or the ability to analyze situations, may account for their higher intelligence. However, both intelligence and assertiveness might also be correlated because they both stem from a common third factor. For example, one's parents might foster curiosity and encourage lots of questions about the world and the people in it.

Let us say that we have found that age and intelligence are positively correlated. Is this relationship a causal one? Intelligent individuals may live longer because they are more knowledgeable about avoiding stressful situations. It could also be that intelligence and age would appear to be causally related because those who were less intelligent have since died. They may have been careless, which led to a fatal accident. Intelligent people may live longer because they are more adaptive (intelligence is causal) or the accumulation of experience and knowledge associated with age may cause individuals to behave more intelligently (age-related factors are causal). A third variable in explaining the age-intelligence relationship might be level of education. Highly educated persons not only live longer but tend to experience less intellectual decline (Jarvik, Blum, & Varma, 1972: Jarvik & Falek, 1963). They may also seek further education to keep themselves mentally stimulated and involved. In sum, some individuals live longer than others and are more or less intelligent or assertive, for a number of reasons. While any two factors might be correlated, as seen in the above situations, one should be *very* cautious about assuming that correlation equals causation.

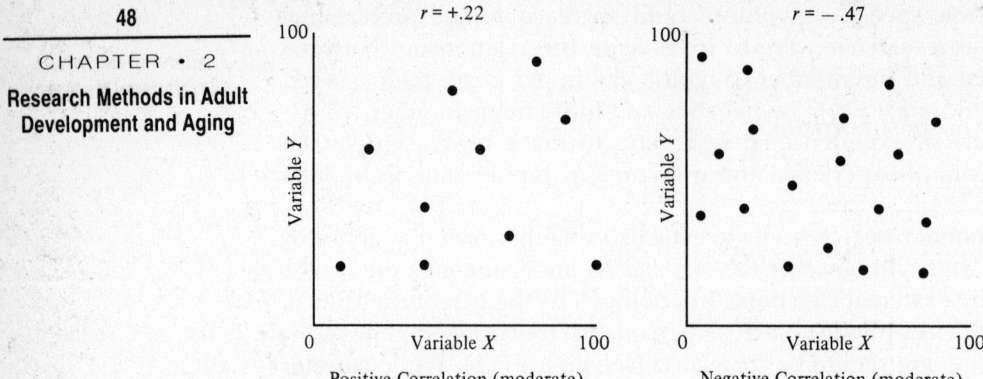

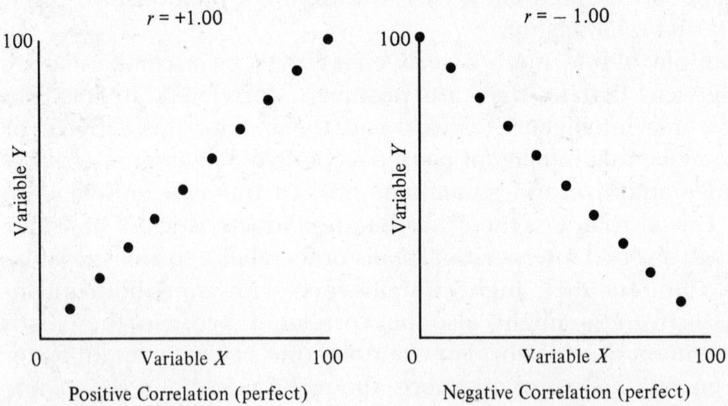

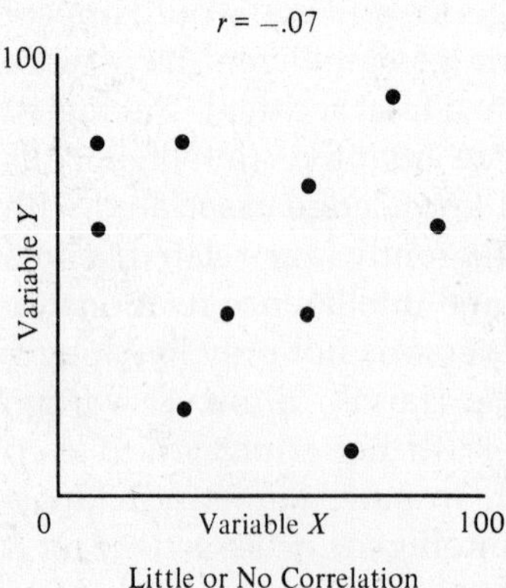

Figure 2.1 The nature of correlation: examples of varying degrees of correlation between variables.

Applications of Experimental and Correlational Research

Let us make several important points regarding experimental and correlational research.

First, whether an experimental or correlational research approach is taken is often dictated by the nature of the problem that an investigator is researching. Studies of naturally occurring phenomena (e.g., aging, retirement, marriage, parenthood, or death) deal with issues whose effects must be inferred. In other words, while we cannot directly observe such effects, we can conclude via the weight of the evidence that they are present.

Second, when participants are selected according to the criterion of whether they have experienced a given event or not, such research is by definition correlational. The problem to be studied can only be found in a naturalistic, real-world context where behavior is observed in its natural surroundings. People cannot be randomly assigned to a retired versus a nonretired group, just as an experimenter cannot arbitrarily say, "For the purposes of this research, you will be sixty years old and you will be twenty years old." A correlational-naturalistic approach to some research topics is then, by definition, necessary since the variable of interest is not manipulatable by the researcher (Birren & Renner, 1977; Wohlwill, 1970a). For example, if we were interested in studying the effects on morale of being relocated from one's home to a nursing home, randomly assigning participants to groups would be not only unfeasible but also unethical. How could one person be denied nursing-home care and another receive such care? Who would decide? Who would be responsible for any negative effects on those denied such care? On this basis, it is somewhat unfair and, in fact, inaccurate to conclude that experimental research is "better" than correlational research.

Third, experimental research can, however, if carried out carefully, lead to relatively unambiguous conclusions regarding a causal relationship between independent and dependent variables. If our independent variable (IV) is powerful enough, and we have not confounded its effects with other factors, we are more likely to reveal that the manipulation of the IV leads to a systematic impact on the dependent variable (DV). If we can draw such a conclusion, our experimental study is more likely to be **internally valid**; that is, the obtained differences in our dependent variable are solely due to the experimental manipulation or treatment.

Fourth, unfortunately, while experimental methods permit more control over extraneous factors, they sometimes lack **external validity.** If a study is externally valid, its findings are **generalizable.** This means that the findings can be generalized to other samples of people or to other measures of either our independent or dependent variables. It is precisely because the conditions under which experimental data are collected are often well specified that such research is often narrow in scope. That is, it often cannot be generalized to other sets of treatments and measures of their effects, samples of participants, or experimenters. In other words, research results are limited to a specific set of conditions and therefore lack external validity.

Fifth, it is also possible for a phenomenon being studied to itself change as a function of our studying it! In the real world, events rarely are caused by a single underlying factor or independent variable, and there are always extraneous influences that confound the study of a problem we are attempting to view in isolation. It is for this reason that correlational research must be viewed as descriptive, with the hope that future work might tease out a causal relation between two factors that are interrelated. To the extent that research reflects problems people actually confront in everyday life outside the laboratory, it is said to have **ecological validity** (Hultsch & Hickey, 1978; Schaie, 1978; Scheidt, 1980; Weisz, 1978). Because the real world often fails to mirror the laboratory, there is a great deal of merit in studying adults naturalistically.

Sixth, if our findings are valid only for a given sample of participants, or for a particular intervention, then they are going to be of limited use to both the basic researcher, as a stimulus for further work, and the practitioner, as a potential solution to an everyday problem. To the extent that our findings are reproducible, however, we can be more confident of their meaningfulness.

Note that the concerns regarding research discussed above apply equally to both experimental and correlational research, which can be either nondevelopmental or developmental in scope.

It is also important to understand that if one selects participants according to their chronological age, the study must in the strictest sense be considered correlational, because we cannot randomly assign participants to levels of age. We cannot arbitrarily designate some persons to be older or younger than they really are. Therefore, we must always correlate age and the variable we are interested in studying.

Frequently, as is the case of developmental or nondevelopmental research, experimental and correlational approaches can be combined to improve our understanding of a phenomenon. For example, we may discover under everyday conditions that being fatigued seems to correlate with the tendency for some adults to perform poorly at a task. Subsequently, in a controlled situation, we may confirm this relationship by manipulating fatigue (making a task shorter or longer) and observing its effects on performance.

It is because both internal and external validity are important that the researcher must be especially careful and precise in

1. formulating a problem and a hypothesis,
2. defining the population from which a sample of participants will be selected,
3. assigning participants to clearly defined conditions or treatment groups, if appropriate,
4. selecting and measuring the dependent variables,
5. collecting data,
6. analyzing and reporting the results of this data collection,
7. drawing conclusions based on the analysis of these data regarding the extent to which the hypothesis is supported, and

8. making inferences based on the study of the phenomenon one is interested in studying.

All of these requirements are characteristics of the **scientific method** (McGuigan, 1983; Rosenthal & Rosnow, 1984).

RESEARCH CHOICES

Once researchers have defined a problem to study, many decisions must be made that ultimately affect the internal and external validity of their findings. First, they must determine what population of individuals their findings will apply to. For example, if one wants to study older rural women who are not highly educated, it makes little sense to interview urban, highly educated older women. Should individuals or groups be studied? How many persons should be involved? How should they be recruited? What if everyone asked fails to agree to help with a project? Or, once they have agreed to participate, can one prevent them from nonrandomly abandoning the project in midstream? All of these questions and problems must be confronted and worked through.

Once researchers have defined the population of interest and selected a sample of sufficient size that is representative of this population, numerous other choices must be made. How is the information to be collected? Research in adulthood is quite variable in this respect. Some individuals prefer to interview participants over the phone or face to face, while others use formal tests or questionnaires to gather information. In some cases, information is best gathered individually, while in others, testing people in groups might be appropriate. Choices must be made about what questions to ask, how many questions to ask, and how to best ask them so that they accurately reflect what we want to know.

Sinnott et al. (1983) have discussed a number of basic problems and principles to which all researchers in adult development and aging should adhere.

1. *The research participant must be protected.* Here, questions of risk to the participant and confidentiality of findings are paramount. We will discuss ethics in research again later in this chapter. For the present, however, suffice it to say that the welfare of those who have agreed to help with a project should be first priority.
2. *The research user must be involved.* Those who are to use research findings should help in the design of the research. For example, questions that are meaningful and interesting to the participant should be explored if at all possible. In most situations, the needs of the study participants, practitioners, and researchers need not conflict.
3. *The research should balance integrity and responsiveness.* The process of research is a give-and-take affair between those who sponsor or fund research, those who will ultimately be the consumers of research findings, and those who actually conduct the research.

Practical and logistical considerations in terms of time and money must be recognized without compromising the integrity of the research project. Yet, a study's purpose as well as its findings should be understood by sponsors, participants, and colleagues.

4. *Have a clear purpose.* Research can sometimes be quite time-consuming. For this reason, a great deal of effort must be made to assure individuals that they can indeed gain something from participating. While these benefits may be monetary, they can also be in the form of increased knowledge, greater insight, or enhanced skills. The purpose and benefits of the research should be explained to people in terms they can understand so that it is clear that there are no hidden agendas.
5. *The research should be useful.* It should answer a clearly stated question, and findings should be disseminated to participants in a form that accurately represents what was found, in understandable terms. Research should enable us to better understand development in adulthood, with the ultimate goal of improving the quality of life for adults of all ages.

We now turn to specific types of research strategies that are particular to developmental research—cross-sectional, longitudinal, and time-lag designs.

DEVELOPMENTAL RESEARCH METHODS: CROSS-SECTIONAL, LONGITUDINAL, AND TIME-LAG DESIGNS

As noted above in making the distinction between developmental and nondevelopmental research, the developmentalist is primarily interested in the relationship between chronological age and some factor or factors. For the purposes of this discussion, the assessment of age effects in developmental research is likely to be the central interest of the developmental investigator.

Traditionally, the measurement of age effects on behavior has been accomplished via the use of **cross-sectional** or **longitudinal designs** (see Achenbach, 1978; Baltes, Reese, & Nesselroade, 1988; Botwinick, 1984; Friedrich, 1972; and Schaie, 1977). As with experimental and correlational research, each approach to measuring developmental change has its own unique purposes, advantages, and drawbacks. Each suffers from certain problems associated with both internal validity and external validity.

It is best to consider both cross-sectional and longitudinal designs as descriptive. That is, the data they yield may or may not indicate that chronological age causally relates to whatever we are studying, such as intelligence or reaction time. With each design, we can derive a so-called **age function,** or a picture of how age and our variable of interest are related. This age function may or may not suggest that what we are interested in studying varies with chronological age. Because cross-sectional or longitudinal studies can at best describe whether intelligence or reaction time varies with chronological age, *why* either varies is quite another matter. With these points in mind, let us discuss these basic developmental designs.

Cross-sectional Designs

A cross-sectional research design compares individuals who vary in age on one or more dependent variables at one point in time. For example, 20-year-olds, 40-year-olds, and 60-year-olds all might be tested in 1985. In a cross-sectional study, people are purposefully selected to form a cross section of the age continuum. Obviously, we could select participants so that they would vary along some other factor, such as socioeconomic class, sex, or race. The samples of individuals comprising each age range are said to be gathered independently of one another; that is, 20-year-olds are sampled independently of 40-year-olds.

The cross-sectional design measures **average interindividual age differences** on our dependent variables of interest. Given reasonably large samples that are representative of the overall population, the obtained level of performance on each dependent variable for each age group is often viewed as an age norm, or an average for that age. We use the terms *age norm* or *average* because the average level of performance is typical for an individual in each age group. Researchers interested in determining the average level of performance on any dependent variable in adulthood use a cross-sectional research design. It is perhaps the most widely used research design employed in life span research.

PROBLEMS WITH CROSS-SECTIONAL DESIGNS

In conducting cross-sectional research, the researcher must assume that the samples are relatively **homogeneous.** That is, all the people in the age groups are assumed to be similar on all other important variables that could affect the results, such as health condition, socioeconomic level, or education level. If this assumption cannot reasonably be met, it would be unwise to compare the samples on the basis of age. Even if it were reasonable to assume that age was responsible for differences in the variables of interest, with a cross-sectional design, this fact would be difficult to establish. Since age correlates with other factors that also affect our variables of interest, our cross-sectional comparison will also be hampered. These other factors, such as socioeconomic status, health, and level of education, therefore make it difficult to describe our samples accurately.

Whether the samples are similar with respect to all factors except age affects the basis upon which comparisons can be made. For example, is age or education responsible for the differences in the factor of interest? Because we cannot assign participants to levels of age, it is quite possible that these other factors would be confounded with age. That is, they are intercorrelated and thus inseparable. In an experimental sense, had random assignment to ages been possible, we might assume that the effects

Despite similar ages, older adults are very different from one another in many ways.

of these other confounding variables would be equally distributed across groups.

In younger samples, the individuals are more similar to one another, and we call such a sample homogeneous. Older samples are likely to be more **heterogeneous,** which makes overall comparisons difficult (Bornstein & Smircina, 1982; Krauss, 1980; Maddox & Douglass, 1974). This is because individual differences between individuals within age groups increase with age, as discussed in Chapter 1. For this reason alone, cross-sectional comparisons of persons varying widely in age are limited in their value to the developmental researcher.

Working with age-homogeneous groups that are heterogeneous on other factors *not* correlated with age, we might assume that the results of our cross-sectional study would yield valid conclusions regarding average interindividual age differences in the dependent variable, the factor dependent on presumed variation in the age of the samples. The term *average* is used to indicate that each individual's score within each group can validly be represented as an average, assuming relatively homogeneous groups.

Cross-sectional designs, however, reflect conditions at only one specific point in time. Thus, if the primary object of our interest is intraindividual age change, it cannot be assessed with a cross-sectional research design, as participants have not changed. Ideally, we want to know something about the process of aging that is maturational, biological, or age-graded in nature. Because cross-sectional participants are different individuals who are measured only once, they cannot provide us with information about age changes that may be maturational.

The cross-sectional researcher who is unaware of the age difference/age change issue when examining the difference between 20-year-olds and

40-year-olds is assuming that if the test were repeated on the same subjects 20 years later, the 20-year-olds would then resemble the 40-year-olds in the original cross-sectional study. But because each person in a cross-sectional study is measured only once, whether the 20-year-olds would later resemble the 40-year-olds cannot be determined.

In a practical sense, cross-sectional research can be quite useful, however. It is relatively inexpensive and efficient because a great deal of data can be gathered at one time. We can also establish normative trends, that is, judgments about an individual's standing relative to his or her age peers, using cross-sectional methods.

From a developmental standpoint, the internal validity of the cross-sectional study is especially difficult to establish. There are several rival explanations for the effects of age (maturation) on the dependent variable. That is, if we wish to infer that age is related to sample differences in the dependent variable, we may have difficulty in doing so. Work by Baltes (1968) and Schaie (1967, 1970, 1973) suggests that the following are potentially confounded with chronological age in a cross-sectional design: **cohort effects, selective sampling, selective survival,** and **terminal change.**

Cohort Effects While problems in the definition and interpretation of cohort effects have been raised (Rosow, 1978), cohort is usually defined in terms of year of birth or a range of years. Individuals from a particular cohort or generation share a common set of experiences that separate them from others preceding or following them in historical time (see Chapter 1). Thus, people who have experienced such events as the Great Depression or World War II (i.e., people born between 1920 and 1940) would differ in their world view from those who have seen astronauts land on the moon or benefited from the polio vaccine (i.e., those born between 1940 and

People who are members of a birth cohort may grow up with unique experiences particular to their year of birth.

1970). Each cohort grows up with different attitudes, experiences, skills, and values. Cohorts can also be defined in terms of specific psychosocial events such as marriage, parenthood, or retirement, on the theory that those who have married, had children, been divorced, or retired would each share a common set of experiences (Botwinick, 1984).

Baltes (1968) illustrates the potential age-cohort confound in cross-sectional findings for intelligence, where different cohorts are tested at different points in their individual life spans. Figure 2.2 illustrates that intellectual growth clearly accompanies the aging process on a within-cohort basis, assuming that cohorts begin with differing levels of knowledge. As seen in the figure, the cross-sectional comparison yields a curve that *appears* to present a picture of decline with age, however. Awareness of the substantial cohort effects in intelligence and other domains, such as personality or attitudes, bears out the misleading age effects that cross-sectional research may portray, leading to faulty conclusions about intraindividual change across the adult life span.

Selective Sampling In cross-sectional studies, age may also be confounded with selective, or nonrandom, sampling, where those who are the most able, most available, most highly educated, or in the best health tend to volunteer, producing *positively biased* samples (Baltes et al., 1988; Friedrich, 1972; Salthouse, 1982). That is, the sample presents a falsely positive picture of age differences. This sampling bias may cause one to underestimate

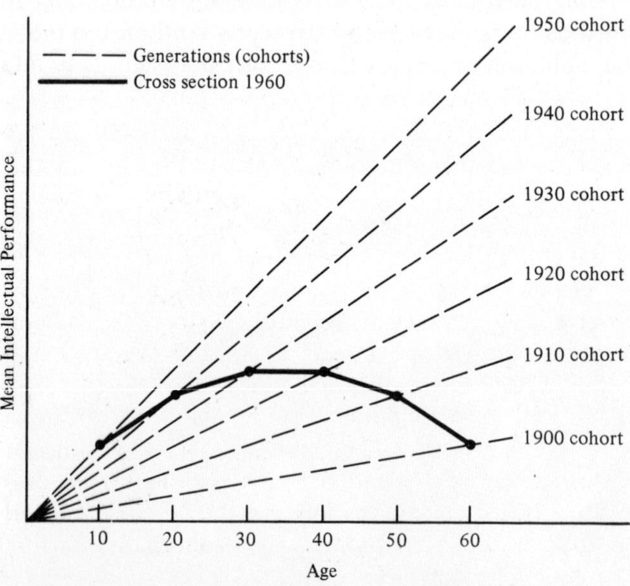

Figure 2.2 Age-cohort simulation: illustration of age-cohort confounds in cross-sectional research and cohort differences in intellectual functioning. *Source:* P. B. Baltes. (1968). Cross-sectional and longitudinal sequences in the study of age and generation effects. *Human Development, 11,* 152. Reprinted by permission of S. Karger AG, Basel.

reliable age effects. Even if one randomly selects potential participants, they cannot be forced to participate on a random basis. Thus, in many cases, what appears to be an aging effect may really be a sampling effect based on volunteer samples that are not representative of the pool of potential participants. Even in studies where surveys or telephone interviews are the method of choice, some people obviously choose not to return questionnaires or answer questions over the phone. Such people are most likely different from their counterparts who choose to participate in a study.

Selective Survival Age affects may also be confounded with selective survival, which refers to the tendency for those who live longer to differ from those with less longevity (see Chapter 3). The survival effect may also cause cross-sectional studies to underestimate age effects, especially where age-related declines actually exist. Those who are initially in better health, more highly educated, married, or employed in low-stress occupations may all live longer and consequently no longer be representative of their original cohort, that is, those who died earlier (see Baltes, 1968; Baltes et al., 1988; Riegel, Riegel, & Meyer, 1967). Because these samples represent the "cream of the crop," they are biased in a positive direction. For this reason they are termed positively biased samples.

Terminal Change Terminal change may also be confounded with age effects in cross-sectional studies (Kleemeier, 1962; Reigel & Reigel, 1972; Siegler, 1975). Terminal change refers to the fact that with increased closeness to death, individuals show declines in their functioning. For example, either their standing relative to others may be lower, or they may decline to a greater extent than others (Botwinick, West, & Storandt, 1978). Depending on how many participants are in this "terminal phase," terminal change will either depress or elevate group means in older samples, leading to faulty conclusions about the relationship of the dependent variable to chronological age (see also Chapter 3 on terminal drop).

In a cross-sectional study, the four factors listed above are all potentially confounded with chronological age differences. Because they are inseparable, the researcher cannot draw clear, unambiguous conclusions regarding the basis for the apparent age effects a cross-sectional design portrays. These confounds affect not only the internal validity of cross-sectional research but also its external validity. That is, we cannot know to what extent these age or cohort effects can be generalized to other times of measurement. Remember that a cross-sectional study is time-of-measurement specific. If there are alternative explanations for the effects of age on our data (e.g., cohort effects), results subject to these alternative factors may not be replicable.

Unfortunately, the cross-sectional researcher is never able to answer questions about confounding without replicating his or her study at a different historical point in time. And even assuming similar age groups are studied a second time, the new cross-sectional study would necessarily involve different cohorts (see Figure 2.3).

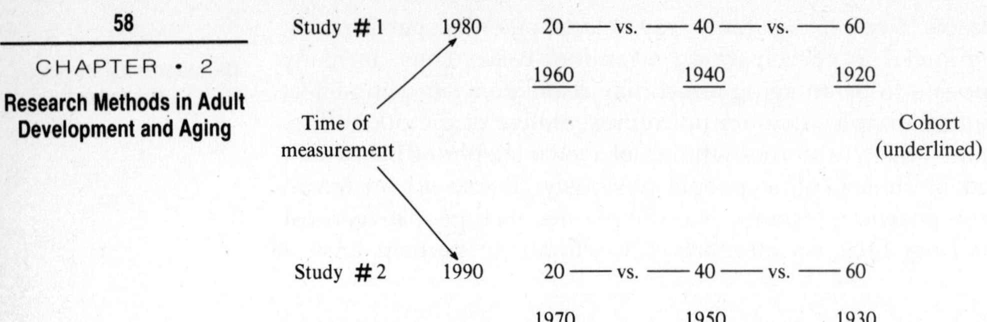

Figure 2.3 Replication of a cross-sectional study at another time of measurement.

Longitudinal Designs

Longitudinal research designs measure **average intraindividual age** changes; that is, change within an individual averaged across people on a dependent variable over time (Baltes, 1968; Baltes et al., 1988). Longitudinal studies are restricted to a particular cohort, and each person is assessed more than once. Longitudinal studies utilize dependent sampling, where data for participants at the second (repeated) sampling are dependent on those data gathered at the first testing. For example, individuals, all born in 1900, are first tested at age 20 in 1920, again at age 40 in 1940, and again at age 60 in 1960. Because different individuals may age at differing rates, the longitudinal researcher is primarily interested in exploring the basis for the resulting interindividual differences that can exist at any point in time. The researcher is not interested in between-group variability, as in the cross-sectional design, but in within-group, or cohort, variability. If we are interested in studying the cohort as a whole, our longitudinal study might permit us to estimate average intraindividual variability with age. Consequently, the longitudinal study allows us to study aging on both a group and individual level, by examining differential rates of change for a factor or factors between persons within a given cohort.

Differential changes across time in a given factor or changes in patterns of relationships among factors such as health and ability at age 20 versus age 40 within persons can also be studied longitudinally (Baltes, 1968). Because individuals are interviewed repeatedly, they obviously have the opportunity to undergo change that is perhaps in some manner related to the aging process.

PROBLEMS WITH LONGITUDINAL DESIGNS

Despite its potential for assessing developmental change, the longitudinal method is considerably more expensive than cross-sectional research, since it involves multiple observations of each person. The investigator may also face practical difficulties in the storage of data, record keeping, or changing characteristics of the measuring instruments, that is, reliability or validity.

If for some reason there is a change in researchers, this becomes a source of error in itself, especially when investigators collect their own data.

Time of Measurement The major internal validity problem for the longitudinal researcher is the potential confounding of age changes by **time of measurement.** A time-of-measurement effect is one that affects all persons, regardless of age or cohort (Schaie, 1965, 1970). For example, in general, people interviewed in 1950 might be more anxious or score more highly on a scale of intelligence than those interviewed in 1960.

While cohort effects have an impact that is relatively long term and specific to individuals born in a given year who share a common set of experiences, time-of-measurement effects are of relatively short duration and generalize across people regardless of age. For example, a researcher might ask whether longitudinal changes in personality are determined by maturational (aging) processes or whether they reflect specific events. The specific research question might be, "Do the changes in personality between ages 20 and 40 reflect the maturation of individuals born in 1900, or do those changes reflect a historical shift from post–World War I optimism to pre–World War II anxiety?" Given the potential confounding of age and time of measurement, the longitudinal researcher cannot draw clear-cut conclusions regarding the role that maturational change plays in determining age changes in, for example, political views, personality structure, or intelligence.

Note that if one is studying any aspect of development that is culturally influenced, such as the impact of economic changes, however, time measurement–specific events can influence individuals in very different ways. For example, an economic depression may affect older workers differently from younger workers, and established businesspeople differently from those just starting out (see Elder, 1979).

While selective sampling, selective survival, and terminal change can be confounded with age in *both* cross-sectional and longitudinal research, **selective dropout, practice effects,** and **regression to the mean** are internal validity problems unique to longitudinal design.

Selective Dropout Selective dropout or attrition refers to the tendency for participants to nonrandomly withdraw from a study for a variety of reasons, such as lack of interest, poor performance, lack of time, illness, or other unavailability. If the reasons for such dropout are correlated with age effects in the dependent variable, then selective dropout is said to be confounded with aging effects in the longitudinal data. Siegler and Botwinick (1979), for example, found that with repeated testings over a 20-year span of time, the less able subjects tended to drop out, yielding data falsely suggesting little age-related decline in intelligence.

Practice Effects Practice effects mean that with successive exposure to the same test materials, people score higher (Baltes, 1968; Botwinick, 1984; Cerella & Lowe, 1984). Practice effects are associated with increased test sophistication, item familiarity, or lessened anxiety. Practice can also confound age changes measured longitudinally, and in most cases, practice effects lead to more favorable estimates of age changes. Practice effects can be dealt with by creating several alternative forms of the same measure, one of which is administered to each person on each occasion.

Practice effects can be studied by comparing the scores of a sample of people who have been tested once with those who have been tested repeatedly (Labouvie et al., 1974; Schaie et al., 1974; Schaie et al., 1973). If differences do occur, the data from repeated measurements can be adjusted for the difference in performance solely due to practice (Labouvie et al., 1974).

By utilizing "fresh participants" who are not "test-wise," independent sampling may help to deal more completely with practice and attrition issues inherent in longitudinal research. There is some controversy regarding whether longitudinal samples gathered independently do in fact differ from traditional longitudinally gathered samples, however, so the data adjustment discussed above may not be necessary (see Botwinick, 1977, 1984; Schaie & Hertzog, 1983; Schaie et al., 1973).

Regression to the Mean This concept is a potential confound in longitudinal studies, especially where participants are selected along the extremes of some continuum, such as high versus low intelligence or conservative versus liberal, or where selective sampling or selective survival effects have produced biased samples (Baltes et al., 1972; Campbell & Stanley, 1963; Nesselroade et al., 1980). Those at the extremes are said to be more likely to "regress" statistically toward a less extreme position at the second measurement relative to the first one, as illustrated in Figure 2.4. For instance, those who initially score very high on whatever factor is being studied subsequently tend to score lower. In a sense, their scores cannot go much higher because they are so high already—there is no "room" for them to improve further. Alternatively, those who have initially scored the lowest

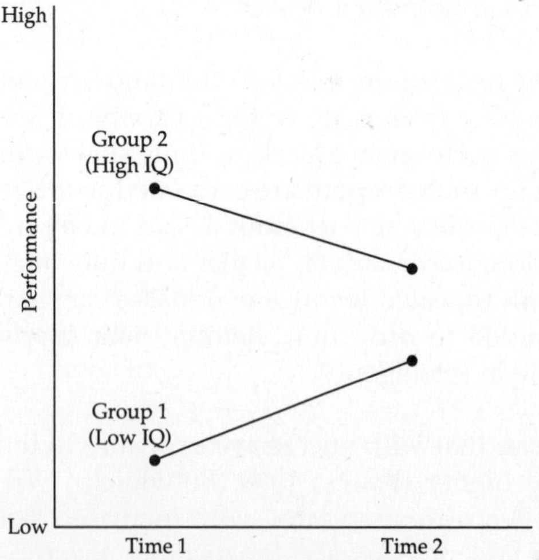

Figure 2.4 Regression to the mean.

Longitudinal Study #1	Occasion 1 (1920) →	Occasion 2 (1940) →	Occasion 3 (1960)
Cohort 1900	Age 20	Age 40	Age 60
Longitudinal Study #2	Occasion 1 (1960) →	Occasion 2 (1980) →	Occasion 3 (2000)
Cohort 1940	Age 20	Age 40	Age 60

Figure 2.5 Replication of a longitudinal study with a different cohort.

appear to improve relative to where they begin. They could not score much more poorly, thus their improvement is simply the only direction in which they can change.

Regression to the mean may mask genuine aging trends, or it may make change appear to occur when none has really come about. In either case, those at the extremes simply regress to a less extreme value at the second time of measurement relative to the first.

As with the cross-sectional design, these internal validity concerns also affect the external validity, or generalizability, of longitudinal study. If these confounding factors are substantial in their impact, it is less likely that longitudinal findings will generalize to other cohorts.

Replicating a longitudinal study with a different cohort would require a new data collection effort at a different historical point in time. If the culture has changed in any significant way, it is unlikely that results from the two longitudinal studies would agree (see Figure 2.5). Because the longitudinal study is cohort specific, the researcher cannot determine whether results will generalize to other cohorts or not. Despite these problems, longitudinal studies remain very valuable due to their ability to measure average intraindividual age change.

Time-lag Designs

In contrast to cross-section and longitudinal designs, whose focus is the assessment of age-related differences and changes, the purpose of the **time-lag design** is to assess some aspect of cultural change (Baltes, 1968; Baltes et al., 1988; Friedrich, 1972; Schaie, 1965, 1970). Chronological age effects are not the focus of the time-lag design, and the researcher may be acting on either a hunch or the results of previous research suggesting age to be a relatively unimportant influence on the dependent variable.

Time-lag studies are a valuable source of information to the extent that cultural changes, and not age-related factors, are responsible for such things as political attitudes, behaviors in various roles, or feelings about social issues. Time-lag studies therefore complement both cross-sectional and longitudinal methods.

Time-lag designs may involve two or more separate data collection efforts, or they may be accomplished archivally, utilizing existing data such as high school records or voting patterns. Time-lag research, which is lagged or delayed across historical time, equates at least two samples in terms of age, for example, 20-year-olds in 1960 (1940 cohort) versus 20-year-olds in 1980 (1960 cohort) (see Figure 2.6). Thus, a time-lag design may enable one to know whether being a young adult is a similar experience for those born in 1940 and those born in 1960. If we find the two independent samples to be similar in some way, we can infer that the aging process or, in this case, the *lack* of an aging process, *may* be responsible for the lack of a difference (recall our samples are of equivalent ages). Thus, our findings could imply that age was causally related to our variable of interest as it failed to vary when we studied two groups of people who were of similar ages. If, however, the results suggest that our samples are different, then we would have to infer that the difference is due to either differences between the samples in times of measurement (1960 versus 1980), or cohort membership (1940 versus 1960 cohort), but we could not determine which. Because we cannot separate the effects of the two, the internal validity of the time-lag study suffers. In other words, cohort membership and time of measurement can be confounding factors in a time-lag study.

From the point of view of external validity, the time-lag study is restricted to a given sample of ages for all of our participants (e.g., 20- or 40-year-olds) and a given set of cohorts and times of measurement. What would happen if we were to compare two samples of 40-year-olds, or replicate a study at different times of measurement utilizing individuals of a similar age? To the extent that all individuals were differentially affected

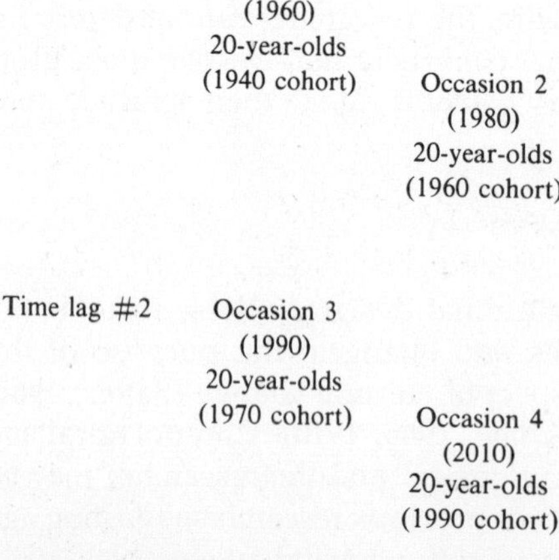

Figure 2.6 Replication of a time-lag design utilizing different cohorts measured at different times of measurement.

by what was happening in 1960 versus 1980, we could not expect the results of a time-lag study to be replicated with individuals from different cohorts assessed at different historical points in time (see again Figure 2.6).

Time-lag samples are, of course, also subject to the effects of selective sampling, selective survival, and terminal change, making identification of an age effect in a time-lag study especially meaningful. Thus, if despite these confounds a time-lagged comparison suggests that cultural changes are relatively small, it would allow us to infer that the age of participants may be important to the results. This would be an important conclusion, given the internal validity problems discussed above concerning the cross-sectional and longitudinal methods.

Summary of Cross-sectional, Longitudinal, and Time-lag Designs

Based on our discussion of the three designs, we can now reach several conclusions regarding the ability of each to measure developmental changes and differences (see Baltes, 1968; Schaie, 1965):

1. Cross-sectional, longitudinal, and time-lag designs serve very specific purposes, and can provide valuable starting points for further research. Yet, they each have some drawbacks that should be recognized so that they can be used to their best advantage.
2. Cross-sectional, longitudinal, and time-lag designs cannot provide unambiguous conclusions regarding age effects or cultural effects, respectively, due to the numerous potential confounding influences affecting each design's internal and external validity.
3. Even if these conclusions were not true, we would still be making descriptive, not causal, statements, because we cannot randomly assign individuals to age group, cohort, or time of measurement.
4. Without controls for the effects of numerous potential confounding factors, these designs cannot provide accurate estimates of intraindividual age change or sociocultural change.
5. In focusing on a single variable (e.g., age), neither cross-sectional nor longitudinal designs are able to describe adequately the possible interaction between factors, for example, age and cohort, age and time of measurement, or time of measurement and cohort (Baltes, 1968; Friedrich, 1972; Schaie, 1965).

Table 2.1 summarizes each of these basic designs from both an internal and external validity point of view.

SEQUENTIAL DESIGNS

Schaie's Trifactorial Approach

In an attempt to address these internal and external validity concerns, Schaie (1965, 1970) proposed a more complicated set of research designs, each derived from the three basic designs discussed above. Collectively,

TABLE 2.1

BASIC DEVELOPMENTAL DESIGNS

	Cross-sectional	**Longitudinal**	**Time-lag**
Type of change/ difference measured	Average interindividual differences	Intraindividual change or average intraindividual change	Cultural change
Uncontrolled factors (internal validity)	*1. Generation differences confounded with age differences 2. Selective survival 3. Selective sampling 4. Terminal change	*1. Time of measurement confounded with age changes 2. Practice effects 3. Selective dropout 4. Selective survival 5. Selective sampling 6. Terminal change 7. Regression effects	Time of measurement confounded with generation difference (age held constant)
Uncontrolled factors (external validity)	Generation generalizability (are differences between ages stable at times of measure?)	Generalizability at other generations (may be generation specific)	Generalizable at different times of measurement or different generations?

*Major internal validity problem

Age ——→ Maturation effects

Cohort ——→ Generation (genetic cohort specific) effects

Time of measurement ——→ Environmental treatment effects

Source: Adapted from D. Friedrich. (1972). *A primer for developmental methodology.* Burgess Publishing Co., pp. 35–38 and from P. B. Baltes (1968). Cross sectional and longitudinal sequences in the study of age and generation effects, *Human Development, 11,* 145–171.

these designs are termed *sequential designs.* They involve sequences of cross-sectional, longitudinal, or time-lag designs. We term Schaie's approach a **trifactorial** one, where three factors—age, cohort, and time of measurement—are the dimensions of interest. These dimensions are not independent of one another, since participants cannot be independently assigned to levels or treatment groups. According to Schaie, these three factors can both describe and explain developmental change.

While Schaie's trifactorial model specifies three sequential designs, each involves replications of the basic cross-sectional, longitudinal, or time-lag designs. For our purposes, however, we will discuss the sequential design most applicable to the study of adults. Before we do so, let us restate that chronological age may not be the only explanation for developmental changes that people experience. Thus, results from cross-sectional studies, often presenting a picture of decline, and longitudinal studies, often portraying stability or growth, frequently do not yield similar findings (see Baltes, 1968; Baltes et al., 1988; Schaie, 1965, 1970). Therefore, more complex designs are necessary to understand fully the course of developmental change.

Cohort Sequential Designs

When studying adults and the aging process, we are interested in what it is about the aging process that helps to explain why people change over time. In Chapter 1, we presented a contextual model of adult development. This model strongly suggests that historical changes can contribute to our understanding of the aging process. For this reason, the developmental researcher is often interested in whether different cohorts age in the same manner. Whether different generations age similarly is a question that can be answered by utilizing the **cohort sequential** method.

Cohort sequential studies replicate a longitudinal study utilizing a different cohort the second time. In this case time of measurement is considered irrelevant. Cohort sequential studies allow us to independently estimate age changes and cohort effects. It is illustrated in Figure 2.7. The cohort sequential design is a more comprehensive case of the longitudinal method, wherein two longitudinal studies covering the same age range are conducted.

In general, the cohort sequential design rests on a distinct set of assumptions about which component is irrelevant or confounded, and this is based on the investigator's knowledge or empirical research. The cohort sequential design tries to deal with internal validity problems by assuming one of three possible confounding factors—time of measurement—to be irrelevant, therefore allowing for unbiased estimates of the remaining two—age and cohort.

External validity problems are dealt with in the cohort sequential method by replicating a longitudinal design, thereby allowing for the generalizability of findings to other cohorts. Note in Figure 2.7 that the cohort sequential design must involve a minimum of one replication—at least two data collection efforts—of the basic longitudinal design from which it is derived. Given the effort required, it is unlikely that one would naively conduct a cohort sequential study simply based on a hunch. In most cases, previous research dictates one's choice of designs. Despite the importance of cohort effects in adulthood and aging research, it does not necessarily follow that they will be more important than age effects in all instances (Kausler, 1991).

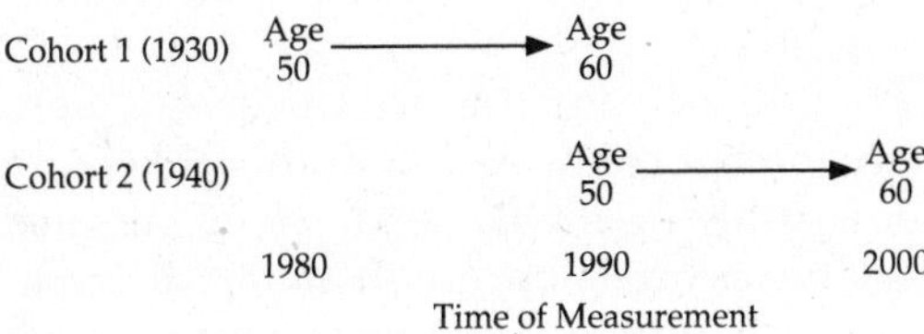

Figure 2.7 Cohort sequential design.

Which Designs Are Used Most Often?

Hoyer, Raskind, and Abrahams (1984) reviewed aging research and noted a continuing problem in accurately describing samples and the methods by which they were recruited. While the cross-sectional method continues to be the most popular, it seems to ignore the importance of cohort effects, according to Hoyer et al. (1984). Longitudinal studies, while more frequently used than before, nevertheless were found to be still comparatively rare. Arenberg (1982) has cautioned those who conduct research in aging to be especially careful, when carrying out sequential designs, to fairly assess age effects apart from cohort and/or time of measurement effects (Botwinick & Siegler, 1980). The researcher should be especially sensitive to sample biases created by selective attrition and selective survival effects (Arenberg, 1982).

These cautions suggest that despite the sophistication of our methods for gathering data about adults, we still need to be careful to design studies that are well executed to help us separate myth from fact regarding adulthood.

ETHICS AND RESEARCH IN ADULTHOOD

As mentioned earlier, the rights of those people from whom we gather our data should be given the highest priority, especially when our methods might induce anxiety or otherwise put participants at risk for physical or psychological harm. These concerns apply to research subjects of any age but are especially relevant when children or elderly people are being studied (American Psychological Association, 1982; Lawton, 1980a; Strain & Chappell, 1982; Yordi et al., 1982).

Minimizing unnecessary risks can be accomplished by obtaining **informed consent** from all participants. Informed consent implies that participants, prior to the project's start, fully understand the purpose of the research and their involvement in it, in terms they can understand. All questions about the research should be answered, and all who participate must understand that in no way will they be asked to give up anything (e.g., information or services) they normally receive from the organization conducting the research. Should they consider withdrawing from the project, it is critical for participants to understand that such withdrawal will in no way penalize them, particularly if the research is done in a "captive-audience" setting such as a nursing home.

All data collected must be confidential, and thus a participant's identity should not be shared with anyone not connected with the project. In many cases, when the researcher is studying highly sensitive or personal aspects of behavior, confidentiality is a central concern to the participant. Thus researchers need to be especially sensitive to the importance of confidentiality by avoiding even casual references to individual participants in their work.

The researcher also has a special ethical obligation to protect the welfare of those who may not be competent to judge whether they should become involved in a project and are thus unable to give informed consent. Examples of such people would be adults who are suffering from a cognitive disorder such as a stroke or Alzheimer's disease (see Chapter 10). Moreover, where a treatment is offered to an experimental group of participants, those in the control or comparison group should also be able to benefit from such treatment or intervention after the study is completed. Finally, feedback regarding the project should be provided, so as to lessen a participant's concerns about poor performance or misconceptions about the overall purpose of the research.

Despite the emphasis on the "how" of conducting research in this chapter, the design of a study is never as important as the need for it to be carried out with openness and honesty regarding the ethics of its purposes and methods. Elaborate designs answering important questions do not take priority over the welfare of research participants.

SUMMARY

Regardless of our purpose in doing so, how we gather our facts has an important bearing on what those facts are. In understanding research methods, distinctions between *developmental* (where age is of interest) and *nondevelopmental* approaches are important. Likewise, *correlational* (where correlations between variables are of importance) and *experimental* (where *causal* inferences between *independent* and *dependent variables* can be made) have different purposes. While correlational and experimental research studies are frequently conducted with different purposes in mind, they are often coordinated in a larger, more organized effort.

While *chronological* age is often assumed to cause developmental change, it cannot be manipulated and is therefore more accurately seen in terms of being *dependent on* other underlying sets of processes.

Cross-sectional studies measure *average interindividual age differences,* whereas *longitudinal studies* measure *average intraindividual age changes. Time-lag* studies assess *cultural change.* All these designs should be considered *descriptive,* since participants cannot be randomly assigned to levels of age, cohort, or time of measurement. Each of these designs has its own set of *internal* and *external validity* problems, which have been in part addressed by the development of sequential methodology.

The *cohort sequential* is an extension, or replication, of the longitudinal method. By assuming time of measurement, a *confounding factor* affecting the internal validity of the longitudinal design, to be irrelevant, cohort sequential designs address internal validity problems. External validity is dealt with by replication of the longitudinal method.

Regardless of how sophisticated we become in research design, our *ethical* obligation to those who participate in our studies must never be overlooked, particularly as it bears on obtaining *informed consent* from those who may not be competent to give such consent. In addition, we should carefully preserve the confidentiality of information we gather from each participant and protect volunteers from undue physical or psychological harm.

KEY TERMS AND CONCEPTS

- Developmental versus nondevelopmental research
- Experimental versus correlational research
- Correlation versus causation
- Random assignment
- Generalizability
- Independent versus dependent variables
- Experimental versus control group
- Internal validity
- External validity
- Ecological validity
- Cross-sectional research design
- Practice effects
- Selective dropout
- Regression to the mean
- Cohort sequential
- Positively biased sample
- Longitudinal research design
- Time-lag research design
- Homogeneous versus heterogeneous samples
- Confounding
- Interindividual age differences
- Intraindividual age changes
- Age functions
- Independent versus dependent samples
- Cohort/generation effects
- Time of measurement effects
- Selective sampling
- Selective survival
- Terminal change
- Informed consent
- Confidentiality

REVIEW QUESTIONS

1. Why is it important to study research methods? Is there a relationship between how we gather our facts and what these facts are?
2. What is the distinction between developmental and nondevelopmental research?
3. What similarities and differences exist between experimental and correlational approaches to research? What are the advantages and disadvantages of each?
4. What is internal validity? What is external validity? Why is this distinction important?
5. What are the purposes, advantages, and disadvantages of cross-sectional, longitudinal, and time-lag designs?
6. How does Schaie's cohort sequential method propose to solve the problems of one of the other basic designs discussed in this chapter?
7. What are the major ethical concerns to keep in mind when conducting developmental and nondevelopmental research?

CHAPTER 3

Biology of Aging and Longevity

C H A P T E R   O U T L I N E

INTRODUCTION

For many of us, what defines development and aging are the changes we experience in our physical or biological functioning. Some of these may be mild in nature, such as aches and pains or stiffness, or they may be severe and life threatening, as in heart disease, cancer, or stroke. However, though we often associate such changes with aging, many people are fascinated by the thought of living a long time or, for that matter, remaining ever young.

We learned in Chapter 1 that physical or biological factors are but one set of antecedents that contribute to either normal or pathological aging. Nevertheless, they color the reality of growing older for many people. Knowledge about the biological processes of aging can help us understand that there are important relationships between those changes and our feelings and cognitive abilities. It can also aid us in separating the facts of aging from the myths.

For example, many people fail to distinguish between physical changes that are determined by the biological processes of aging, and those that are due to inactivity, poor eating habits, or disease. The former are termed *primary aging* changes, while the latter are termed *secondary aging* changes.

As individual life-style or susceptibility to chronic illness changes with increased age, many of the physical changes that people experience are secondary to primary aging. That is, they are not caused by primary aging. Being overweight, becoming "winded" when going up stairs, or having wrinkles are each consequences of factors secondary to the basic processes of aging. And while secondary aging changes may affect some people, primary aging changes are experienced by everyone.

Aging-related physical changes are important in themselves, as they impact our self-esteem and behavior. Moreover, such changes also influence decisions made about us by others, which may have important consequences for our relationships with others, for our work, or in the classroom.

In our culture, judgments about an individual's attractiveness, personality characteristics, or competence are often linked to age-specific criteria. Consequently, knowing what physical changes actually occur as one gets older can indeed be valuable in many ways. At the least, it may help many adults change their life-styles so that they can avoid needless debilitating physical declines, adding to both the quantity and quality of their lives. We all must learn to adjust and cope with physical change, which can greatly affect our mobility, our relationships with others, and our self-esteem.

It is with these thoughts in mind that we discuss the interrelated topics of the biological processes of aging, that is, aging at the most basic, cellular level, and longevity, the outcome of these underlying cellular changes. We will emphasize their impact on various body systems as well as their psychosocial effects. For instance, changes in physical appearance, such as wrinkles or gray hair, may lead to loss of self-esteem for those individuals who highly value physical appearance. Depending on how we interpret these changes, we may accept them and move on with our lives. However, we might also color our hair or have plastic surgery to try to convince ourselves that we are not growing older after all!

THE PHYSIOLOGY OF AGING

Beginning in early adulthood, there are a number of internal biological and physiological changes taking place. These changes eventually show up as external physical changes. During young adulthood, most biological and physical functions are at their peak, or most efficient level. For example, by the middle to late twenties, most of the physical growth and development of muscles, internal organs, and body systems have reached a plateau. In fact, most individuals in their twenties and thirties view themselves as being at their peak regarding health, life-style, sex life, and physical condition. This belief is supported by research (Sinclair, 1969; Timiras, 1972; Zoller, 1987). However, biological and physiological changes are indeed taking place during young adulthood, but these changes are internal and are therefore not generally experienced or observed directly by the individual. Thus, they have little impact on our behavior. For this reason, biologically and physiologically speaking, young adulthood gives the illusion of being a stable period.

For most people, it is when they reach their forties and fifties that they take note of these changes. Also during middle and late adulthood, physical changes begin to affect us functionally. That is, they influence our behavior and adaptation to the everyday environment.

Musculoskeletal System

The muscular system begins to change noticeably during middle adulthood in a number of ways. Changes in overall muscle strength begin to occur at approximately age 35 (Zoller, 1987). However, the degree of loss differs widely among various muscle groups. Large-muscle groups are affected more than small-muscle groups. Men age differently than do women, and the rate of muscular aging is also influenced by one's level of physical activity. Activity level affects losses in both muscle mass and strength. Declines are greater for fast-twitch muscles, which are involved in rapid movement where strength is important, than for slow-twitch muscles, which allow us to maintain or adjust posture as well as sustain endurance during physical exertion (Whitbourne, 1985). For example, although a younger runner may have more speed in a 100-yard dash, an older runner may have more endurance and nevertheless be able to run for long distances at a slower pace.

Despite physical changes with aging, older people may still retain flexibility and endurance.

At age 45, muscle strength is approximately 90 percent of the level at age 25; 75 percent at age 65; and 55 percent at age 85 (*Newsweek*, 1990). Muscle mass reaches its peak by the early twenties and begins to decline in the thirties (Roseman, 1990). Furthermore, muscle tone changes, and there is a redistribution of fat and subcutaneous tissue with aging (Whitbourne, 1985). However, if one exercises regularly, age-related muscle atrophy can be minimized.

On average, all of the skeleton within the body has been transformed to bone by age 18, at which time we achieve our maximum height (Roseman, 1990). Thereafter, due to increased loss of calcium, increased porosity, and erosion, the bones start to become more brittle, and the articulating surfaces begin to deteriorate. After reaching its peak, bone mass for both men and women then begins to drop by about 1 percent a year (*Time*, 1988). These changes have numerous effects on the aging individual. Brittle bones are the major cause of fractures, especially the hip, which cripple many elderly persons. These processes also contribute to arthritis (Wantz & Gay, 1981). Furthermore, due to the settling of bones within the spinal column, changes in body curvature, and shrinkage of the intervertebral disks and vertebrae, individuals may shrink one to two inches in height over the life span, usually beginning during their fifties (Garn, 1975).

Perhaps the most serious problem associated with aging and bone density is **osteoporosis.** Osteoporosis is a disease characterized by progressive decline in bone density (Rowe & Kahn, 1987). It contributes to over 1 million bone fractures a year, according to the National Osteoporosis Foundation. Although osteoporosis affects both males and females, it is most common among elderly women. With osteoporosis, bone mass actually deteriorates, posture declines, and it is much easier to fracture the spine, hips, and other stressed parts of the skeleton (American Association of Retired Persons, 1986). The disease progresses slowly, often with no pain or visible symptoms, making it difficult to detect. With proper nutrition, specifically a diet with calcium supplements, and regular exercise, the chances of developing osteoporosis can be reduced.

Cardiovascular System

The cardiovascular system also undergoes systematic changes with age. At approximately age 25, heart rate is at its peak efficiency and the average cholesterol level is 198. By age 45, heart rate is at 94 percent of peak efficiency and the average cholesterol level is 221. By age 65, heart rate is at 87 percent of peak efficiency and the average cholesterol level is 224. At age 85, the heart rate is at 81 percent efficiency and the average cholesterol level is 206 (*Newsweek*, 1990).

The distinction between normal (primary) and pathological (secondary) aging was discussed in Chapter 1. It is important to understand that many of the debilitating effects of cardiovascular changes are the result of disease, not a consequence of normal aging. In fact, coronary disease accelerates the effect of aging on the functioning of the heart, particularly for people over the age of 60 (Lakatta, 1990). During middle adulthood, the frequency of heart disease, cardiovascular failure, and hypertension begins to increase. Heart disease, specifically coronary artery disease, is the number 1 cause of death in men over 40. When blood flow is restricted to the heart muscle due to sudden occlusion of a coronary artery, damage to the heart muscle occurs, resulting in an often-fatal myocardial infarction—a heart attack.

Other parts of the body are also targets of blood vessel disease, including the brain, which is subject to cerebrovascular disease, or stroke. Stroke occurs when blood is cut off to a region of the brain due to weakened or blocked cerebral arteries or a rupture with bleeding (hemorrhage) into surrounding tissues. Loss of blood may result in permanent damage to the brain cells and related cognitive or physical disability, or death. Stroke affects one-and-a-half times as many men as women, and survivors are often left with permanent disabilities, requiring constant care by family members or professionals.

In the absence of disease, however, the heart functions smoothly and even adapts to the normal changes of age. For those who are free from coronary disease and who are moderately active, age declines in cardiac output, heart rate, blood pressure, and stroke volume (the amount of blood pumped per contraction) and aerobic capacity are less dramatic than for those with disease (Lakatta, 1990). Changes that do occur in the heart with age are thought to help maintain normal function. Such changes include thickening of the left ventricle, which sends oxygenated blood to the body. Also, the heart compensates for a slower heart rate during exercise by increasing the amount of blood pumped per heartbeat.

Overall, although the structures within the cardiovascular system show signs of change and degeneration with age, these disorders are highly dependent on both genetic and environmental factors such as smoking, stress, diet, and exercise (Elias & Streeten, 1980; Wantz & Gay, 1981; Whitbourne, 1985). Indeed, people can reduce their risk of stroke and cardiovascular disease by making changes in their diets, life-styles, and levels of physical activity. In fact, exercise training seems to lessen age-related declines in cardiovascular performance, as it is measured under stressful testing conditions such as a treadmill test. It is under such conditions that coronary disease is most likely to be detected (Lakatta, 1990).

There are also age-related changes in the blood, which relate to immune system function. The immune system starts to decline at around age 30 (Miller, 1990). For instance, white blood cells, which fight off viruses and bacteria, lose their effectiveness with age. Therefore, the weakening of the immune system makes it harder to fight off illnesses. After age 65, hemoglobin and red blood cell count also decrease (Zoller, 1987).

Respiratory System

The aging process has some effect on the respiratory system (Zoller, 1987). The maximum breathing, or vital, capacity of the lungs decreases progressively between 20 and 60 years of age. The lungs lose, on average, 30 percent to 59 percent of their maximum breathing capacity between the ages of 30 and 80 (*Time,* 1988). This decrease in breathing capacity is due to a loss of elasticity in the joints of the rib cage and the lung tissue itself, as well as weakened muscles that support the lungs.

The primary harmful effects on the lungs, however, are caused by environmental factors. These include smoking and the inhalation of noxious agents such as asbestos, which have been linked to disorders of the respiratory system such as lung cancer, asthma, emphysema, and pneumonia. Of course, people who quit smoking and begin a regular exercise program can regain some respiratory function or vital capacity (Whitbourne, 1985). Likewise, feeling winded or fatigued after climbing stairs or brisk walking can be lessened with regular exercise.

Digestive System

Although the digestive system may work less efficiently with aging, the changes that occur are usually minor. Such changes may include slower action of the muscles that move food through the system, reduced acid production, and impaired ability to absorb nutrients. Metabolism begins to slow at around age 25. For each decade thereafter, the number of calories required to maintain one's weight drops by at least 2 percent. Since muscle mass also shrinks gradually, people generally accumulate fat around the middle of their torsos, and there is an increase in body fat with age (*Time,* 1988). Because of these changes, it is important to pay attention to the quality and types of food one eats. A diet of whole grain breads and cereals, fruit, vegetables, poultry and fish, meats, and dairy products, in that order, is recommended. A balanced diet can lessen such problems as constipation, diarrhea, intestinal gas, or nausea, leading to feelings of physical well-being and sounder sleeping (Whitbourne, 1985).

The most serious disorders associated with the digestive system and age are colon cancer and diabetes. Next to lung cancer, colon cancer claims more lives than any other form of the disease (National Cancer Institute, 1991). The incidence of colon cancer is highest among white men. When detected early, however, this type of cancer can be arrested with surgery. Diabetes is a metabolic disorder that can cause a number of debilitating symptoms, including blindness, damage to various organs of the body, and in some cases, death. The frequency of this disease increases with age (Whitbourne, 1985). The effects of both diseases can be lessened with proper nutrition, a healthier life-style, and prompt medical care and treatment.

Finally, the loss of teeth and periodontal disease become more common in middle and old age, which decreases the individual's ability to chew foods adequately (Zoller, 1987). These dental problems can contribute to poor nutrition and dietary habits. Also, there is some decline in the secretion of gastric juices and in the metabolism of proteins and fats (Whitbourne, 1985). When the digestive system does not work as efficiently as it once did, it is not uncommon for individuals to begin to noticeably gain weight, even when they are careful about diet and exercise.

Skin and Hair

Often, it is the external and observable changes to our body, such as wrinkles on the skin and thinning and graying hair, that remind us that we are aging. As any of us who watch TV knows, there is no shortage of products available that claim to slow down the aging process by reconditioning the skin or thickening or coloring the hair. Hair transplants, especially for men, are becoming more popular.

The majority of changes to the skin with normal aging are cosmetic in nature and the result of internal biological or physiological processes, such as a decrease in the flexibility of collagen fibers, which inhibits the skin's ability to conform to moving limbs. With age, areas that are darkly colored ("age spots") become more numerous, and the skin begins to lose elasticity and wrinkles appear, though exposure to the sun plays a significant role in this process (Roseman, 1990). The loss of small blood vessels and subcutaneous fat with age also contributes to dry, wrinkled skin. Furthermore, after many years, the forces of gravity and aging tend to produce flabby skin. In general, blood vessels and bones become more visible, particularly in the arms and in the face, as the subcutaneous fat layer is reduced. Other changes include a yellowing of the nails and hair loss (Zoller, 1987). In addition to a decrease in pigment in the hair, loss of hair is common after age 30 in men and after menopause in women. Table 3.1 summarizes age-related changes in bodily systems with age.

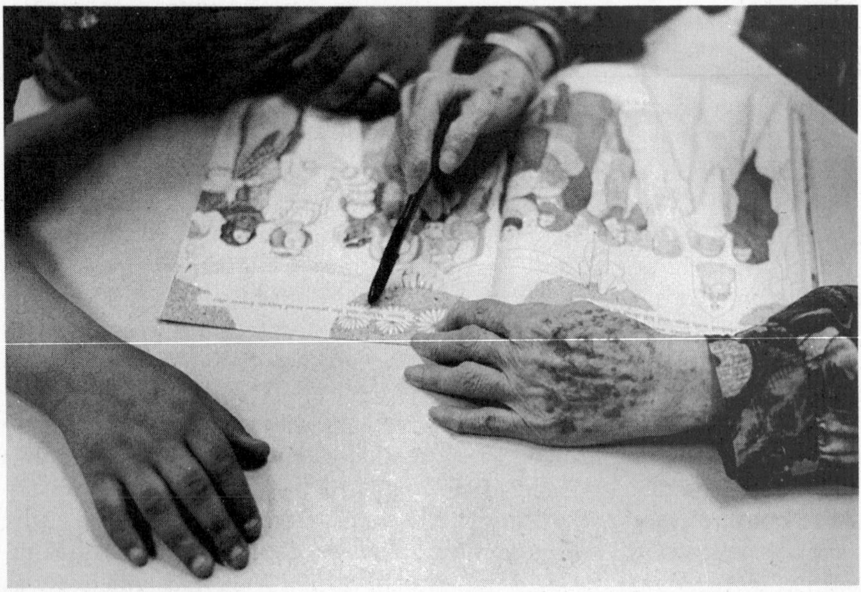

One common physical manifestation of the aging process is the accumulation of lipofuscin, which appears as liver spots on the skin.

TABLE 3.1

AGE-RELATED CHANGES IN PHYSIQUE AND PHYSIOLOGICAL SYSTEMS

The Human System	Description of System Changes
Skin	Increase in wrinkles and dark pigment with frequency, intensity, and duration of sun exposure related to rate; skin is less pliable, thinner, drier
Body weight	Muscle cell density increases until about 40, followed by shrinkage due to fiber loss and disuse. Muscle tone, strength, flexibility, and speed decline, but contingent on activity level. Fat tissue increases with age. Weight gain until 50s, usually followed by loss later
Body height	Shrinkage of 1″ in males, 2″ in females due to posture, thinning disks, and water loss. Reduction of bone mass due to loss of calcium. The ability to repair bone is maintained, but more slowly. Osteoporosis can occur with age, most common in postmenopausal women. Hormone treatment and calcium supplements recommended
Hair	Follicles shift from vellus hair (fine) to terminal (coarse) or the reverse; ear hair becomes terminal for older men; scalp hair can shift to vellus. Reduction of scalp hair for men and women, other types of hair loss (e.g., leg, armpit, pubic) contingent on hormones. Hair-color loss related to protein shifts. Some data suggest stress related to graying and hair loss; malfunctioning thyroid can also be cause
Nails	Rate of growth slows; rigidity; splits; dull yellow-gray or -green appearance with age
Respiratory	Decrease in chest wall muscle and pulmonary tissue compliance (tissue tends not to relax after inspiration, chest wall expanded) due to alveoli and bronchioles increasing in size. 10–50% decrease in oxygen content of blood, especially when stressed, but no increase in blood carbon dioxide level in the blood, as in pulmonary emphysema, asthma. Decrease in lung elasticity and vital capacity; reduced transportation of oxygen to organs and muscles. All changes mediated by activity level
Muscular	Decrease in strength and endurance; increase in time to relax/contract or be restimulated. Stamina declines related to activity level
Cardiovascular	Decrease in maximum heart rate, cardiac output, stroke volume; increase in blood pressure; lower system efficiency. These changes hasten the onset of fatigue; altered positively by activity level
Kidneys	30% of nephron functioning lost by age 85; reduced renal mass; 50% decrease in renal blood flow and glomerulus filtration rate between ages 20 and 90

Central Nervous System

Without a functional central nervous system, it would be impossible to do most of the things we do on an everyday basis. Our ability to think, reason, and act in response to incoming stimulation from the environment depends on the integrity of our central nervous system, that is, the brain and spinal cord. Changes in the structure and function of the central nervous system help to explain a variety of the behavioral and performance changes that occur with age.

The principal changes in the central nervous system occur in the brain. In most cases, our information about such changes comes from studies of animals and from postmortem studies of individuals who have given permission for such analyses.

Whitbourne (1985) emphasizes the difficulty in getting accurate information about age-related changes in brain tissue. Autopsies may not be done quickly enough, and death itself may cause changes in the brain. Moreover, when people die, they are probably not "normal"; that is, either disease or injury may alter the structure and function of the brain. In addition, there may be important species differences that limit the validity of certain information about brain function gleaned from animal research. At present, we cannot routinely study aging changes in an individual's brain function while the person is alive, although newer computerized brain techniques can be used in vivo (Carlson, 1986). Thus, our studies are limited largely to cross-sectional comparisons of autopsied brains from individuals of varying ages.

GROSS CEREBRAL CHANGES

The aging of the central nervous system occurs at different rates for different people, and different regions of the brain change differentially. Generally, the number of cells in the central nervous system decreases, and the overall size of the brain decreases with age (Scheibel, 1992; Sinclair, 1969). The central nervous system reaches its peak in terms of functioning neurons by age 30 (Howath & Davis, 1990; Vogel, 1977).

Between the ages of 20 and 90, the brain loses from 5 to 10 percent of its weight. The extent of this loss varies with the individual's health and with the region of the brain studied (Whitbourne, 1985). Brain volume also declines with age, especially after age 50, by approximately 15 to 20 percent. As the volume of brain tissue shrinks, the brain's appearance also changes. The gyri—swellings—of the brain become smaller, and the fissures or sulci—valleys between the gyri—widen (Scheibel, 1992). Again, such changes vary with health status. With age, too, the volume of the ventricular fluid increases, compressing adjacent tissue and leading to increased ventricular size, due as well to the loss of brain cells (Bondareff, 1980). By age 80, there is a 7 percent reduction in overall cerebral hemisphere mass (Zoller, 1987).

NEURONAL CHANGES

The central structural feature of the aging brain is the loss of neurons, or nerve cells, which receive and transmit information. The brain is very complex and contains more than 20 billion neurons and even more—120 billion—glial cells, nonneuronal brain cells that serve a nutritional and supportive function (Carlson, 1986; Thompson, 1975). The interconnections between these neurons are nearly infinite. While some neurons degenerate and die, others do not. When a neuron dies, all its connections—the small spaces between neurons referred to as *synapses,* and there are thousands per cell—with other neurons die as well. Synapses, which also help integrate information from various parts of the nervous system, occur on the cell body and the dendrite of the neuron. These parts of the brain cell are the sites of the neuronal electrical and chemical activity characteristic of brain function. With age, cell bodies change in appearance and accumulate the yellowish pigment called *lipofuscin,* which interferes with neuronal function. In addition, the fluid surrounding the nucleus of the cell body develops spaces called *vacuoles* (see Figure 3.1).

Extending from each cell body are dendrites, whose function is to receive incoming information from other neurons. While they are normally intricately intertwined, with age this organization becomes simplified, and eventually the cellular dendrites disappear altogether, meaning that less information is received by each neuron (Whitbourne, 1985). Consequently, less information can be transmitted via the axon to other neurons, muscles, and glands. Also with age, **neurofibrillary tangles** are more likely to develop, which means nerve fibers in the cell body and dendrites increase in number and become interwoven, pushing the nucleus aside and interfering with cell functioning (Adams, 1980; Bondareff, 1980). These neural tangles are found in normal brains but are especially prevalent in the brains of people with certain forms of **dementia** (see Chapter 10).

Neuronal structures may also degenerate due to a reduction in cerebral circulation. This can result either from normal age-related changes in cardiac output or from heart disease. Often heart disease creates a pro-

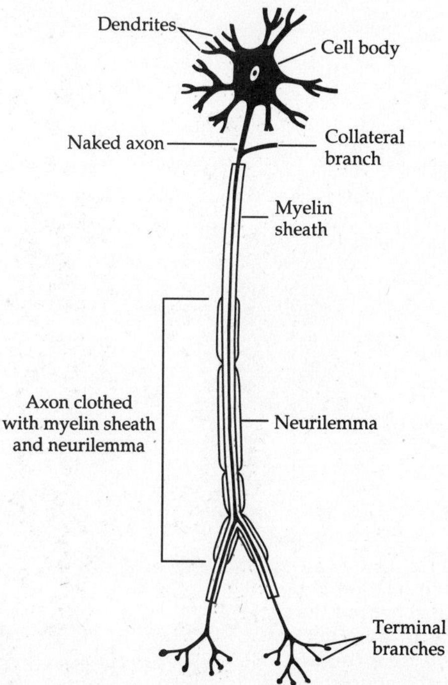

Figure 3.1 A neuron. *Source:* Rockstein & Sussman. (1979).

gressive narrowing (**atherosclerosis**) and hardening (**arteriosclerosis**) of arterial walls. At worst, blood flow is shut off altogether by infarcts of varying sizes or by stroke. All of these pathological changes damage or kill neurons, but there are many who believe that regular aerobic activity such as running, swimming, or tennis can slow down this degenerative cardiovascular process (Whitbourne, 1985). Bondareff (1980) suggests that changes in the volume and composition of the fluid surrounding the neurons may also contribute to neuronal loss.

With age, and especially in certain forms of dementia, **senile plaques** are more likely to form. Senile plaques are abnormally hard clusters of damaged or dying neurons, present in specific areas of the brain, which interfere with neuronal function. As neurons die, certain types of glial cells also increase in size. With age, glial cells may also perform less adequately their function of providing nutrients to brain cells.

Thus, we can observe a number of structural changes in the brain with age. Such changes may be caused by a so-called critical loss of a certain number of neurons especially important to the storage and reception of information (Whitbourne, 1985).

The cortex is the part of the brain mediating the most complex behaviors and is organized into hemispheres that function somewhat independently of one another. The left hemisphere controls speech, language and verbal activity, and mathematical and symbolic skills, while the right hemisphere primarily controls spatial and complex perceptual abilities

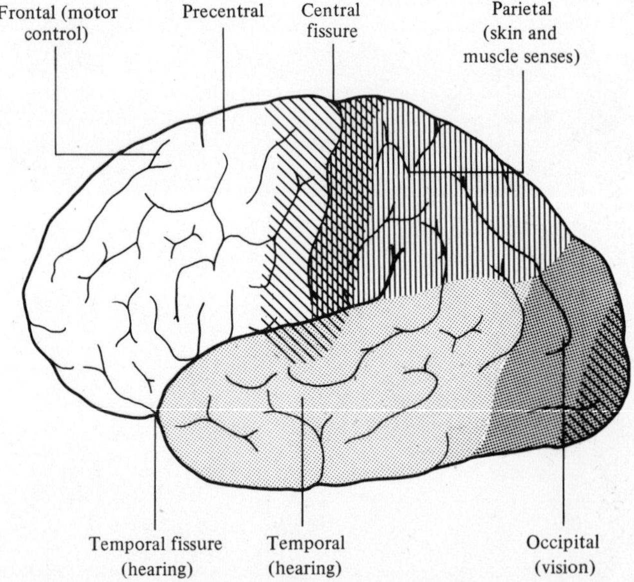

Figure 3.2 Major subdivisions of the brain in relation to fissures (sulci). All remaining parts (noncrosshatched) of the parietal, preoccipital, temporal, and frontal areas that are not sensory or motor in nature are termed *association* areas (higher mental process). *Source:* R. F. Thompson. (1975). *Introduction to physiological psychology.* New York: Harper & Row. Reprinted by permission.

(Carlson, 1986; Thompson, 1975). Right-hemisphere functioning appears to decline at a greater rate with age than does left-hemisphere function (Klisz, 1978).

In addition to the above structural changes, the concentration of neurotransmitter substances, which make synaptic transmission possible, appears to decline with age (Adams, 1980; Whitbourne, 1985). Thus, synaptic transmission and coordination are impaired.

Various functional areas of the cortex controlling sensory experience lose neurons, particularly the occipital (visual), parietal (skin and muscle senses), and parts of the temporal (hearing) and frontal (motor control) lobes (see Figure 3.2). In the various areas of the associative cortex that control higher cognitive functions, such as long-term memory, abstract reasoning, and symbolization, as well as coordinate the sensorimotor areas, the loss is less severe (Thompson, 1975; Whitbourne, 1985).

With appropriate stimulation or experience, however, neuronal connections may be regenerated, or neuronal loss may be lessened. We call this potential *plasticity.* It is the redundancy of neurons in the cortex, resulting in more frequent activity by fewer cells or more constant activity by healthy cells, that makes such plasticity possible (Whitbourne, 1985). (See Figure 3.3.) Transmitter substances in these areas remain relatively

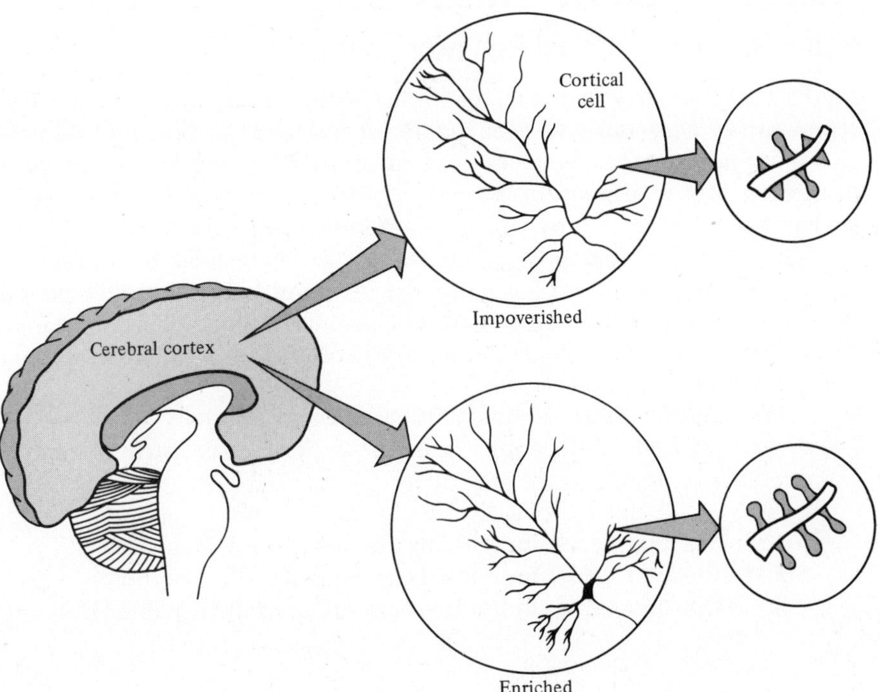

Figure 3.3 Brain plasticity as a function of environmental enrichment. Cells from cerebral cortex of rats put in an enriched environment show more numerous branching of dendrites that stretch out to other brain cells and more fully developed dendritic spines, which receive chemical messages from the other cells. *Source: New York Times.* (1985, July 30). Copyright © 1985 by The New York Times Company. Reprinted by permission.

constant, and thus wisdom, abstract reasoning, judgment, foresight, and long-term memory may be relatively unaffected by aging (Bondareff, 1980, 1985).

In addition to neuronal loss in the cerebral cortex, evidence for such degeneration is found in certain areas of the brain stem, which connects the cortex with the spinal cord. Neurotransmitter deficits in certain areas of the brain stem seem to be linked to disturbances in sleep patterns, short-term memory deficits, and overarousal (Adams, 1980; Thompson, 1975; Whitbourne, 1985). Changes in fine motor coordination, large-muscle control, and both visual and auditory function, however, seem to be linked to age-related changes in the various cortical areas (discussed above).

Overall, deficits in brain function vary both within—by cortical or subcortical area—and between persons. It is important to realize that age changes in brain structure and function are highly subject to, and confounded by, disease. While these alterations in brain structure and function do occur, many older persons can compensate for behavioral deficits in memory, fine motor coordination, or learning new information by relying on their experience, planning, and organizational skills to maintain effective functioning on an everyday basis.

SEXUAL BEHAVIOR IN ADULTHOOD

Myths Regarding Sexual Behavior and Aging

Myths are beliefs that lack a factual basis. Myths about sex and aging persist in part because our data base is sketchy and because most middle-aged and older adults today were not reared in a time when there was open discussion of sexual matters. Moreover, the interpretation of findings is subject to contamination by young and middle-aged values. For example, one might conclude that older adults would lose self-esteem by finding out their level of sexual activity is less frequent than that of younger people (Thomas, 1982). In discussing sexual behavior in adulthood, it is important to realize that it is both a biological and psychosocial issue; sexuality is as emotional in nature as it is physical.

We reinforce many myths about aging and sexuality when we tell jokes about sex and older people, or use such phrases as "dirty old man." Common myths are:

1. In the later years, individuals are not sexually desirable
2. In the later years, individuals are not sexually desirous
3. In the later years, individuals are not sexually capable (Hotvedt, 1983)

While there is ample support for the fact that both older and younger persons *believe* the above statements to be true, there is little or no factual basis for any of them (O'Donohue, 1987). It is because they are false beliefs, not supported by fact, that they are termed myths.

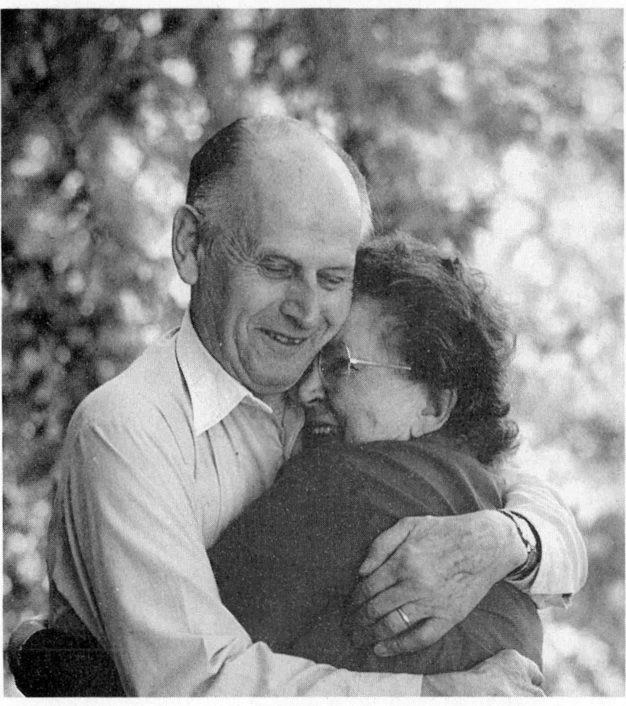

Intimacy and togetherness are an essential aspect of sexuality at any age.

As with other myths of aging, maintaining such beliefs may reflect cohort-specific biases, experiences, and lack of information about sexuality particular to middle-aged and older cohorts, who did not grow up with effective contraception or sex education. For some younger people, holding these beliefs may make them feel more secure about their own sexuality. For older ones, these myths may mirror their ignorance of the facts about sex and aging, or reflect a lack of viable role models. For example, how often are older people portrayed on TV and in the media as sexually attractive, sexually interested, or sexually capable? Many myths regarding sexual behavior during old age are held even by the old themselves (Salamon & Charytan, 1984).

It is quite normal for older adults to engage in sexual behavior until their eighties and nineties, contrary to the belief that the elderly do not, should not, or cannot do so. Cameron (1970) examined beliefs about sexuality in the young (18–25 years), middle-aged (40–55 years), and old (65–79 years). In all age groups, even the oldest, the old were seen as below average on the following dimensions: desire for sexual behavior, skill in performing, capacity for sexual behavior, frequency of attempts at sexual behavior, social opportunities for sexual behavior, and frequency of sexual activity. Findings such as these indicate there is a discrepancy between the physical capacity of older adults to engage in sexual behavior and their own attitudes as well as those of others.

Life-span Trends in Sexual Behavior

In adulthood, it is important to distinguish between sexual interest and sexual activity. Sexual interest is primarily a psychological experience and pertains to an individual's desire to engage in sexual behavior. Sexual activity refers to actually carrying out sexual behavior. Life-span trends for each are illustrated in Figure 3.4, which is based on a collection of experimental studies and reports (Comfort, 1980; Pfeiffer, Verwoerdt, & Wange, 1968; Masters & Johnson, 1981; O'Donohue, 1987). Remember that the data reported in the figure should be seen as generalizations only, since there are individual differences within all age groups in terms of both sexual interest and sexual activity.

ADULTS SPEAK

SEX AFTER SIXTY

Contrary to the popular notion that sexual interest and prowess disappear in aging adults, research shows that many members of the over-60 set continue to lead active sex lives. Here are some excerpts from personal observations offered in group discussions that were conducted in a retirement community after the participants saw a film on sexuality and aging.

A 68-year-old married man: I have to admit that I used to think that older people didn't have sexual relations. I never really thought about it in personal terms, though, so when I got to my sixties and found my needs were still there, I wasn't all that surprised.

A 72-year-old woman: I think that the thing that surprises people is that we even think about sex, but why shouldn't we? If sex is still fun, and doesn't cost anything, and you've got a person you love to be with, it's no sin.

A 76-year-old widow: I say that you're as young as you think you are. If you think you're over the hill, you will be in a hurry. If you leave all the fun to younger people, you'll just sit in a rocking chair feeling old.

An 81-year-old man: To me, it's like knowing how to ride a bicycle. Once you learn, you never really forget. Even though my friends don't talk much about sex except to make jokes, I still think about sex and even have dreams about it. And a couple of years ago, when I was having trouble with my prostate, my doctor was certainly surprised when I told him I still have sex twice a week.

A 71-year-old widow: I think it's perfectly all right to stop having sex whenever you want to. When my husband was still alive, we continued to love one another long after we stopped having sex.

A 70-year-old married woman: You have to admit that sex isn't exactly the same when you get older. I enjoy myself, and I know my husband does, but the passionate responses simmered down years ago, and sometimes I think we respond more out of memory than excitement.

A 69-year-old widower: One thing that nobody ever talks about is the pressure you get from women if you're an eligible man who is reasonably healthy and secure. They flirt, they hint, they make outright propositions—and I don't always like it, although I must admit that sometimes I do. But it's embarrassing to find that you've got a willing partner and you're not capable.

Source: Masters, Masters, & Kolodny. (1992).

Figure 3.4 illustrates a number of important facts. First, in adulthood there is a discrepancy between interest in sexual behavior and actual sexual activity; interest and desire are always higher than activity. Second, there are gender differences in both age of peak sexual interest and age trends in sexual interest. Specifically, for males, sexual interest peaks in early adulthood (roughly ages 17–25) and then gradually declines with age. For females, the peak in interest is not reached until approximately the thirties and then declines more gradually. We will discuss the reasons for this decline later in this chapter. Third, during adulthood the activity level of males and females is almost identical. This is because individuals usually engage in sexual activity only with their spouses or a limited number of partners.

Longitudinal investigations of sexual interest and activity find that sexual interest remains fairly constant throughout most of life and does not begin to decline until after age 75 (Pfeiffer et al., 1968; Schover, 1986). In terms of activity, Comfort (1980) reported that 47 percent of all individuals between 60 and 71 years of age, and 15 percent of individuals over age 78, engaged in regular and frequent intercourse. On the other hand, some studies have found that sexual activity begins to decline in the sixties (Ludeman, 1981).

As age increases, the discrepancy between interest and activity widens for women (see again Figure 3.4). In fact, male interest and female activity seem to be parallel. Although older unmarried women report little or no sexual activity, about 25 percent still express interest (Wantz & Gay, 1981).

For males, there are a number of causal factors involved in the decline of sexual activity. These include monotony and boredom, preoccupation with career or other activities, mental or physical fatigue, poor physical health, and fear of failure (Masters et al., 1992). It is, however,

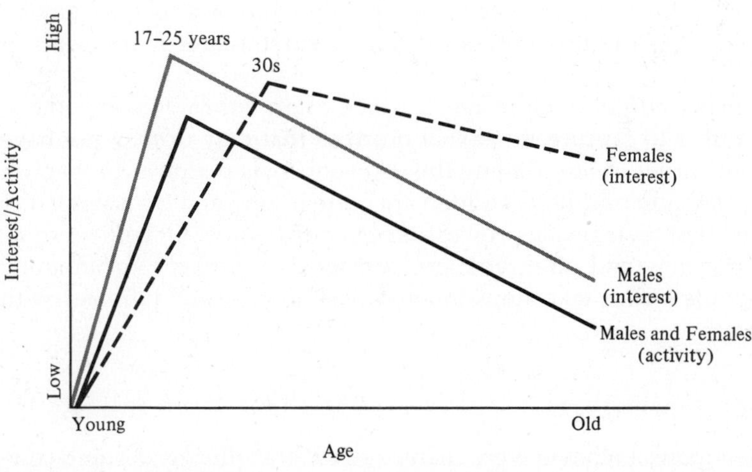

Figure 3.4 Suspected life-span trends in sexual interest and activity for males and females.

difficult to determine which is the most significant reason for reductions in sexual activity. For some older men, difficulty in maintaining an erection can reflect lowered expectations of themselves as vital older persons. For others, declining health or hormonal changes are the major difficulty. While there is little risk of heart attack during intercourse, strokes, hypertension, arthritis, diabetes, or the side effects of medications can also interfere with sexual activity (O'Donohue, 1987). Interestingly, Masters et al. (1992) maintain that if forms of sexual activity such as oral sex, masturbation, and touching and caressing are recognized, the frequency of sexual behavior in later life is much more common than is often believed. For example, many adults of both sexes over the age of 60 masturbate (Bretschneider & McCoy, 1988). For many older couples, where intercourse is difficult due to disability or heart difficulties, simply touching one another and embracing are highly sexual in nature.

Sexuality in young adulthood is characterized by the desire to become sexually experienced and knowledgeable, perhaps as a prelude to marriage (Masters et al., 1992). Masters et al. (1992) identify several patterns of sexual behavior in young adults: *experimenters,* who value proficiency and variety in sexual behavior; *seekers,* who see sex as a way of searching for the ideal marriage partner; and *traditionalists,* who reserve intercourse for serious relationships. It is clear that young adults have become more sexually active over the last few decades, in part due to the popularity of cohabitation (Bumpass & Sweet, 1989). However, heightened activity is tempered by a growing discontent with casual sex and of course the fear of contracting AIDS (Masters et al., 1992).

After people get married, the frequency of intercourse generally declines, in part because of the demands of work and parenthood and because sex is balanced with the other rewards of a marital relationship (Greenblatt, 1983; Masters et al., 1992). If a couple divorces, sexuality is redefined and characterized by sexual freedom but hampered by dating and courting skills that have become rusty. In some cases, uncertainty about sexual attractiveness reappears, and individuals may be embarrassed about revealing themselves to another person after many years of marriage.

For many adults, middle age is a time of growth, while for others, it may be a time to capture the sexual prowess that may or may not have been present earlier in life. Calling this a sexual crisis period is probably a misnomer, as many middle-aged men are quite happy and do not need to be reassured that their sexual prowess is not on the wane. Of course, some do seek out a new and often younger partner as a cure for an unhappy marriage, while others take steps to reestablish new sexual intimacy with their spouses.

MENOPAUSE

In 1963, menopausal women were characterized as acquiring "a vapid cow-like feeling called a 'negative state.' It is a strange endogenous misery. . . . The world appears as though through a grey veil, and they live as docile, harmless creatures missing most of life's values" (Wilson, 1963, p. 12).

It is perhaps the lack of distinction among sexual interest, attitudes, and behavior that predisposes many to assume that menopause implies less sexuality. **Menopause** refers to the cessation of menstruation (fertility), accompanied by decreased estrogen production, atrophy of the breasts and genital tissues, and shrinking of the uterus. While symptoms such as hot flashes or night sweats are experienced by most women, expectations about growing older and level of investment in the mothering role are more important to the negative psychological impact of menopause on women (Newman, 1982). Women whose identity does not rest solely on bearing and mothering children may be more likely to get involved in new tasks, such as returning to school or community work, and feel less negatively about menopause.

While many women feel relieved when they actually stop menstruating, beforehand they often view menopause negatively. For example, several studies have found that before menopause, as many as 70 to 80 percent of women believe that both depression and atypical behavior should accompany menopause (*APA Monitor*, 1991). For women who have a variety of interests, however, symptoms such as hot flashes often go unnoticed. But women who were previously depressed or angry not only reported more menopausal symptoms but also seemed to be more negatively affected by them (*APA Monitor*, 1991). Thus, it indeed appears that the impact of menopause on women depends on their expectations of menopause or their personalities.

The negative perceptions of menopause and the generally negative sexual connotation given to oldness contributes to the myths about sexuality in later adulthood that were discussed above. These attitudes seem to apply to women in particular (Laws, 1980).

General Factors Related to Sexual Behavior

If there are so many myths about sexuality in adulthood, then exactly what is true? In this section we will discuss **extrinsic factors** and **intrinsic factors** that affect sexual behavior for both males and females (Broderick, 1982; Masters et al., 1992).

EXTRINSIC FACTORS

One factor that affects an individual's sexual behavior is his or her personal attitude toward sex. Some individuals enjoy engaging in sexual activity more than others, have more liberal views than others, and so forth. Second, the beliefs and attitudes of our ethnic, cultural, and/or social group affect our sexual behavior. For example, individuals from middle and upper socioeconomic classes tend to have a more open or liberal attitude toward sex (Crooks & Bauer, 1980). A third factor is educational level; individuals with more education are generally more sophisticated and liberal regarding sexual behavior. Fourth, being married affects sexual activity. That is, married individuals are more likely to engage in sexual activity because of the availability of a partner. Another factor related to sexual behavior is the quality of the marital or interpersonal relationship. The closer and warmer the relationship, the greater the potential for sexual activity. Personal religious beliefs also affect sexual behavior. Often, religious beliefs set standards and expectations regarding sexual behavior, for example, that only engaging in sexual behavior to have children is permissible. Despite the many influences on sexual behavior, individuals tend to maintain a particular pattern of sexual activity throughout the life cycle in terms of frequency. The frequency of such activity varies among individuals, however, based on a number of factors.

INTRINSIC FACTORS

There are a number of specific biological-physiological changes in body structures and organ systems that are part of normal aging which relate to sexual behavior (Ludeman, 1981; O'Donohue, 1987). These changes have a more significant effect upon one's interest and desire to have, rather than one's ability to engage in, sexual behavior. We will discuss the changes for males and females separately.

Males Based on interviews and laboratory observation of men ranging in age from 50 to 90 years, Masters and Johnson (1966, 1970) found a number of biological-physiological changes with age. Some of these include: the time required for erection increased with advancing age; the penis did not get as hard or extend its maximum length; the amount of pre-ejaculatory fluid decreased; although ejaculatory control increased, the force of ejaculation and volume of seminal fluids decreased; orgasm was briefer; and the refractory period increased with age. Kolodny, Masters, and Johnson (1979) report that the level of testosterone (sex hormone in men) decreases in older males. Since low testosterone levels are usually associated with a loss of sexual desire and erectile dysfunction, it is likely that this hormonal decline leads to a decrease in sexual activity (Schover, 1986). These changes may affect both sexual interest and activity.

Females Masters and Johnson (1966, 1970) also studied women ranging in age from 40 to 80 years, finding a number of biological-physiological changes that could affect sexual behavior with aging. For example, the production of vaginal lubricant becomes slower, the vaginal barrel constricts in size, and vaginal walls become thinner. These changes were found to result in pain during intercourse. Finally, orgasm is of shorter duration. The primary hormonal change associated with aging is related to menopause, a decrease in estrogen and progesterone produced by the ovaries (Schover, 1986). However, even though hormonal changes accompany menopause, only a minority of women reported a loss of sexual desire. Lack of a male partner seems to be the primary cause of decreased sexual activity in older women.

It is important to realize that there is no evidence that any of these changes, in themselves, affect an older person's ability to engage in normal sexual activity. Thus, it is not physical condition itself that reduces activity but rather beliefs about physical condition, such as anxieties about a heart ailment or enlarged prostate. Fear and misinformation can be just as harmful as can hormonal changes.

Note, too, that the age-related sexual decline found in the studies to date may really be due to a cohort effect, that is, a product of the era in which the subjects grew up (George & Weiler, 1981; O'Donohue, 1987). George and Weiler (1981) interviewed married men and women between the ages of 46 and 71 years of age at two-year intervals over a period of six years. The most common pattern for an individual man or woman over the six-year period was stability of sexual interest and activity (58%). Only 20 percent decreased sexual activity with their partner. The oldest participants (65+ years) were most likely to report a sexual decline.

Overall, the frequency of sexual activity and desire in later life corresponds directly to the importance one places on sexuality earlier in life (George & Weiler, 1981; Biambra & Martin, 1977; Martin, 1981). Perhaps the most accurate statement regarding sexual activity during old age was made by Masters and Johnson (1981), who stated that older men and women must "use it or lose it."

SEXUAL DYSFUNCTION

Sexual difficulties and impairments in normal functioning are termed *sexual dysfunction*. It is estimated that at least half of all married couples at some time may be affected by some form of sexual dysfunction (McCary & McCary, 1982). Most sexual dysfunctions are due to psychosocial factors, such as fear of failure, guilt, and low self-esteem (Hyde, 1982; Kaplan, 1974, 1975; Masters & Johnson, 1992). Some examples of sexual dysfunction are presented in Table 3.2. When couples experience sexual dysfunction, psychological interventions can be very helpful, regardless of age (Broderick, 1982; O'Donohue, 1987; Zarit, 1980), although research in this area is seriously lacking.

In fact, there is still the need to accumulate additional reliable data regarding sexual behavior that is both normal and dysfunctional at all points along the life span. Very little is known about the incidence and types of sexual dysfunction in elderly persons, for example (Schover, 1986). This may in part be due to emphasis on genital sex rather than the whole sexual relationship. Butler et al. (1991) point out that sex can also be a means of expressing emotions and loyalty toward another, reaffirming personal identity and self-esteem, as well as affirming physical vitality and feelings of aliveness. As many of us know but often fail to communicate to others, sexual contact and sexuality are quite distinct. Sexuality embodies trust, admiration, safety, security, warmth, affection, and romance, while sexual contact can and does occur in the absence of sexuality.

Information about sexual behavior and sexuality is needed by counselors, nurses, physicians, social workers, and other mental health professionals in order to deal more effectively with individuals who are experiencing sexual problems both inside and outside the context of marriage. Salamon and Charytan (1984), O'Donohue (1987), and Masters et al. (1992)

TABLE 3.2

EXAMPLES OF SEXUAL DYSFUNCTIONS IN MALES AND FEMALES

Dysfunction	Definition	Estimated Prevalence
Males		
Erectile dysfunction	When intercourse is unsuccessful 25% of the time or more, due to an inability to have or to maintain an erection	50%
Premature ejaculation	Absence of voluntary control of ejaculation	50%
Retarded ejaculation	Inability to ejaculate into the woman's vagina, though the person may be able to ejaculate through other means of stimulation (e.g., masturbation)	unknown
Females		
Orgasmic dysfunction	Inability to have an orgasm	10–20%
Vaginismus	Severe involuntary contractions of the muscles surrounding the vaginal entrance that make intercourse too painful	unknown, but thought to be rare

Source: Hyde (1982); Kaplan (1974, 1975); Masters & Johnson (1970); Masters, Johnson, & Kolodny (1992).

discuss programs designed to deal with medical, emotional, and social problems related to sexuality in the aged.

PSYCHOLOGICAL EFFECTS OF BIOLOGICAL AND PHYSIOLOGICAL CHANGES

The physical and biological changes with aging discussed so far do not occur in isolation. It is not hard to imagine the potential effects that biological and physiological change and resultant observable physical changes might have on actors, models, television news authors, athletes, laborers, carpenters, or plumbers. These individuals' self-concept, identity, or occupational security may hinge on their physical appearance or physical capability. But the psychological impact of changes in skin texture, hair color, hair density, as well as overall appearance can be quite debilitating for many people.

Individuals are identified quite easily by others on the basis of their physical characteristics (Schmidt & Boland, 1986). Thus, being labeled or perceived as old by others on the basis of one's appearance is probably quite common and contributes to our own as well as others' evaluations of us as physically attractive or not. Moreover, not looking young anymore may cause some people to feel inferior to others. Looking old can also be an occupational disadvantage, particularly for women, whose appearance is often unfairly used as a barometer of their skills and worth as employees. Professional models, actors and actresses, corporate managers, media personnel, salespeople, and flight attendants may all be discriminated against on the basis of age changes in their physical appearance.

For men, too, the mere appearance of frailty may make it difficult to get promoted or retain a job. Wrinkled or sagging skin, graying hair, or even being overweight can be a disadvantage. Given the emphasis we place on our appearance, it is no wonder we are obsessed with appearing forever young by resorting to creams and lotions, hair colors, exercise, diets, and plastic surgery to retain "that youthful look." Beauty may only be skin deep, but many adults seem to behave otherwise!

In light of these physical changes, middle age can be a difficult time of transition, change, confrontation, and crisis (Sarason, 1977). It can be

ADULTS SPEAK

OVER THE HILL?

Over 3500 *USA Today* readers aged 35 to 43 were asked to say what bothered them most about aging as well as what they missed about youth. In many cases, their responses suggested that they do not distinguish between aging and disease or life-style. Moreover, they often failed to realize that many of the physical and psychological changes they experienced could be totally avoided, or at least minimized, by exercise, diet, or decrease in stress level. Here is a summary of the *USA Today* findings:

"What bothers you most about aging?" For *men*, tiring quickly (31%), bad back (19%), poor memory (12%), sags and wrinkles (6%), and diminished sex drive (5%) were the most troubling. For *women*, sags and wrinkles (28%), tiring quickly (26%), poor memory (15%), bad back (11%), and diminished sex drive (4%) were the most distressing.

"Which body part has aged the most?" For all respondents, the waist (35%), face (20%), back (19%), knees (14%), and feet (13%).

"What do you miss most about youth?" Can't stay up late (64%), can't play sports without getting stiff (18%), can't drink as much (10%), and can't touch toes (8%). Before 40, people complained most often of weight gain. After 40, they were most distressed by failing eyesight.

This increased awareness of bodily changes, and acceptance of them, is illustrated by several comments:

A 35-year-old man said, "Everyone else reaches for a beer after the ball game. I reach for Ben-Gay."

A 43-year-old woman said, "I'm beginning to feel as if aspirin is one of the four basic food groups."

A 41-year-old man stated, "My favorite exercise is a nice, brisk sit."

To what extent do these opinions mirror reality? How are they influenced by myths and stereotypes of growing older?

It need not be all bad. For example, an over-40 woman proclaimed, "Sure there are some things I'd like to change, but I ain't bad for 42. I'd love to show how good this age can be!"

Many take such changes in stride and can even make light of the physical realities of middle age. As one 42-year-old woman quipped, "Recently, I found myself shopping for support shoes and a sexy teddy on the same day. Reality versus illusion."

Source: USA Weekend (December 29–31, 1989). *The ache age.* pp. 4–5.

viewed as a time of confrontation between the realities of one's present life and the myths and dreams of one's youth. The greater this discrepancy, the greater the potential for stress and crisis. While this self-examination is usually associated with middle age, it can occur at any point in the life cycle (Romaniuk & Romaniuk, 1981).

Seeing ourselves, our peers, and our parents aging physically and eventually dying, as well as watching our children growing up and entering adulthood, often results in the first realization that we are in the middle of the life cycle. Individuals at this point in the life cycle are often called members of the **sandwich generation.** That is, they are caught in the middle between meeting the demands and needs of their children and the demands and needs of their aging parents. For some people, such demands, on top of the growing discomfort with their own aging, can be overwhelming. These stresses may contribute to alcohol or drug abuse, family violence, impaired social and work performance, or depression. Others, however, are quite able to cope with care-giving demands and the physical realities of growing older. We will have more to say about family care-giving later on, when we discuss intergenerational relationships (Chapter 7) and dementia (Chapter 10).

EXPLANATIONS FOR THE AGING PROCESS

Given the complexity of the human aging process, there is currently no one single theory that adequately explains why it happens. Some explanations are best considered hypotheses in the attempt to explain the nor-

ADULTS SPEAK

ON REACHING 40

A few middle-aged people probably do experience a mid-life crisis, and react by becoming anxious or depressed. They may have made sudden, unwise, or irrevocable changes in their lives (Colarusso & Nemiroff, 1981). However, many people see middle age simply as a time to reevaluate the direction of their lives. They often set new goals for themselves, realizing that they no longer have unlimited time to get things done.

As one 43-year-old woman says, "I think being 40 caused me to kind of stop and take stock. . . . I wondered if I wanted to be a professional organist all my life." She has since returned to school to pursue a degree in counseling.

Her most sobering realization at turning 40 was that "I'm not going to have time to do everything. . . . Like I always had the idea of going to medical school. That's not going to be a possibility now. . . . It's kind of a splash of cold water when you realize that some of the things you thought you would be doing just aren't going to happen."

Her advice to young people? "Shake loose, and look at all the possibilities."

mal aging process. The fundamental assumption of all biological and physiological theories, however, is that the life span of any organism—how long a member of a species will live on average—is ultimately determined by an inherited genetic program (Hayflick, 1988). Otherwise, there is no shortage of ideas about why we age.

Biological Theories

Biological theories of aging are usually divided into two major categories: (1) genetic, which concentrate on genetic structure, formation, and processes, and (2) nongenetic, which focus on changes that occur at the cellular and tissue level (Finch & Hayflick, 1977; Hayflick, 1988; Shock, 1977). We will highlight one or two specific approaches for each major category to give examples of the most common assumptions about aging.

GENERAL GENETIC THEORIES

The basic assumption of genetic theory is that there is some genetic program that sets the average upper limit of the life span for all species. While all cells reproduce a specific number of times and then die, this upper limit differs from species to species. For example, while the mayfly has an average life span of only one day, the dog's life span is 12 years, the horse's life span is 25 years, and the human's life span is 70+ years (Comfort, 1964; Shock, 1977). In addition, in humans, individuals who have long-lived parents and grandparents live, on average, longer than those who do not. Moreover, identical twins' life spans are more similar than those of fraternal twins. This explanation makes common sense and is supported by the literature (Hayflick, 1988; Shock, 1977).

Hayflick's Aging Clock Hayflick and his associates (1965, 1977) have demonstrated that normal human cells survive and reproduce in a culture medium for a certain period but eventually enter a state of degeneration and then die. This is termed the aging clock. More specifically, human cells reproduce themselves almost 50 times (± 10 times), then they die. On the basis of normal rates of metabolism, Hayflick has estimated that the maximum potential human life span is thus no more than 110 to 120 years. If Hayflick is correct, and even if all pathological causes of death were eliminated, a human would eventually die anyway, merely as a result of the expiration of the programmed life span of the cells.

NONGENETIC THEORIES

All nongenetic cellular theories of aging assume that with the passage of time change takes place in molecules and structural elements of cells that impair their effectiveness to function after these cells have been formed.

Wear and Tear This theory is based on the assumption that living organisms behave like machines. That is, when things get very old, they wear out.

BOX 3.1

CENTENARIANS

People who live to be at least 100 years of age are termed *centenarians*. In 1980, there were approximately 15,000 people 100 or older; by 1985, this number had increased to 25,000. By the year 2000, estimates are that 100,000 people will be alive who are centenarians. This suggests that the oldest-old are the fastest growing segment of our population. Indeed, the probability of reaching age 100 has increased immensely over the last century. According to census figures, the odds of living 100 years in 1920 was 400 to 1; by 1980, the odds had increased to 87 to 1.

Based on ongoing research at the University of Kentucky Medical Center, a key to living to this advanced age is keeping busy. However, the choices people make to do so are highly individual ones. Several centenarians offered other bits of advice:

"If you get to thinking too much about your age, you're going to die."

"If somebody gives you a cussing, pray for that person. That releases both you and him."

"I read a newspaper every day. Don't go to bed ignorant."

"Eat blackeye peas and cornbread, and don't eat between meals."

Most centenarians are women, but centenarian men seem to be in somewhat better relative health. Most do not smoke, drink, or eat red meat, and few are overweight. Relative to what one might expect, they have lost fewer neurons, have better memories, and have the more effective immune systems. Many have been raised on farms, and because of this their lives have a sense of orderliness about them. Centenarians seem to be relatively religious and to have a well-developed sense of humor. While heredity seems to play a role in determining long life, people who survive to 100 are very strong-willed. They persist in overcoming life's obstacles despite poor health and poverty, which are common among centenarians. Many do not have health or life insurance, having underestimated how long they would live.

Perhaps the most important factor in living to 100 is the ability to be oneself and maintain individuality throughout life. In spite of their great age, centenarians remain future-oriented. As one researcher put it, "These 100-year-olds are not sitting around waiting to die; they're really alive." Of one 102-year-old man, who was writing his autobiography and had gotten up to age 30, the researcher stated, "He has every intention of finishing it."

However, this process may or may not be predictable (Hayflick, 1988), and although this theory appears to be good common sense and is easy to understand, the machine analogy is not adequate. Unlike machines, which cannot repair themselves, living organisms have developed many mechanisms that permit self-repair, such as new skin tissue replacing old tissue.

Accumulation Theories Cellular aging has also been attributed to the accumulation of deleterious (toxic) substances in the aging organism (Shock, 1977). The metabolic waste theory suggests that aging occurs as metabolic waste products, which are considered injurious, gradually accumulate in the cells of the body. One such waste product is lipofuscin (age pigment), which begins to accumulate in various organ systems with advancing age. It is assumed that the deposit and accumulation of lipofuscin results from age-related changes in the body's ability to metabolize or effectively process certain nutrients. Therefore, metabolic waste accumulation appears to be more of a symptom of aging than a cause.

The collagen theory is based on the established relationships between changes in the body's fibrous proteins, collagen and elastin, and aging (Shock, 1977; Whitbourne, 1985). Basically, collagen and elastin fibers are quite abundant within the body. In fact, they are the two most common proteins in all connective tissues. These fibrous proteins are found in muscles, joints, and bones. With increased age, these fibrous proteins become thicker, less elastic, and less soluble (Whitbourne, 1985). They tend to mass and replace existing tissues. Age-related changes in collagen and elastin fibers are associated with various external signs of growing older, such as wrinkling of the skin (exacerbated by exposure to sunlight), sagging muscles, and slower healing of cuts and wounds. Although this theory is plausible, it must still be considered only a tentative explanation for aging while waiting for further experimental verification.

The nongenetic theories discussed above appear to explain internal and external changes that are associated with the aging process, such as liver spots, but do not adequately explain the cause of the aging process itself.

Other nongenetic theories are (1) the deprivation theory, which assumes aging is due to deprivation of essential nutrients and/or oxygen required by the cells of the body; (2) the free radical theory, which suggests that cell death, and consequent aging, are results of the damaging effects of the formation of free radicals, unstable atoms, in the cell; and (3) the cross-linkage theory, which postulates aging as the result of the formation of cross-linkages between the protein molecules that form the intercellular material in the body.

Physiological Theories

Physiological theories attempt to explain the aging process and life span of organisms on the basis of either (1) a breakdown in the performance of a single organ system, or (2) impairments in physiological control mechanisms. Generally, physiological theories of aging have focused attention on a single organ system in order to explain all the effects of aging and are therefore often referred to as single-organ-system theories (Shock, 1977).

SINGLE ORGAN SYSTEMS

Failures in a number of specific organ systems have been proposed as the cause of aging. For example, since failure of the heart and blood vessels represents a primary cause of death among the aged, failure of the cardiovascular system has often been regarded as a primary cause of aging. Another theory assumes aging can be attributed to the slowing of metabolic processes at the cellular level. Since the rate of cellular metabolism is regulated by the thyroid gland, aging is thought to be due to the inability of the thyroid gland to supply adequate amounts of hormones. It has also been suggested that since the pituitary gland plays a central role in the control of the adrenal and thyroid glands, aging could be caused by a failure of the pituitary gland to carry out its functions properly.

TABLE 3.3

THEORIES OF BIOLOGICAL AGING

Genetic Theories	Nongenetic Theories	Physiological
Genetic program	Wear and tear	Cardiovascular system
Hayflick's aging clock	Accumulation of toxins	Thyroid gland
	Metabolic waste (lipofuscin)	Pituitary gland
	Collagen	Breakdown of immune system
	Deprivation of nutriments	Autoimmune (self-destruction of normal cells)
	Free radical theory	
	Cross-linkage of proteins	

See N. W. Shock (1977). Biological theories of aging. In J. E. Birren and K. W. Schaie (Eds.), *Handbook of the psychology of aging*. New York: Van Nostrand Reinhold. pp. 103–115.

PHYSIOLOGICAL CONTROL MECHANISMS

The human immune system protects not only against microorganisms that invade the body but also against atypical or mutant cells that may form in the body. The immune system carries out this protective function by generating antibodies that form special cells to engulf and digest foreign cells and substances. The aging process has a marked impact on the functioning of the immune system. Production of antibodies reaches a peak during adolescence and then declines thereafter. This decline is so dramatic that in some species senescent (old) animals retain only one-tenth of the immune capability of younger ones (Shock, 1977). This approach is referred to as the immunological theory of the aging process. Variations on this theme involve loss in ability by the immune system to recognize slight deviations in molecular structure and cellular characteristics. Therefore, mutated cells, which earlier in life would have been destroyed by the immune system, are no longer recognized as such and are permitted to grow and develop, to the detriment of the organism.

Finally, the autoimmune theory of aging (Blumenthal & Birns, 1964) suggests that aging results from the development of antibodies that destroy even the normal cells in the body. That is, the autoimmune antibodies come to function in a self-destructive manner. This theory further posits that various organ systems may begin to reject their own tissues.

The variety of biological theories on the aging process are summarized in Table 3.3.

LONGEVITY/LIFE EXPECTANCY

As discussed above, theories of aging explain the aging process at the biological, or molecular, level. One necessary but unfortunate outcome of living is that when physiological changes are disruptive enough to interfere

While numerous factors contribute to life expectancy, the quality of our lives is especially important in influencing how long we live.

with vital functions, we die. How long we have lived when we die, or how much of our potential life span we achieve, is called **longevity.**

Closely related to longevity is **life expectancy.** Life expectancy refers to how much of the maximum life span for a particular species an individual organism may anticipate attaining, or the average length of life for a member of that species. Currently, humans usually have a life expectancy—longevity—of 70 to 80 years, though they have the potential to live 110 to 130 years—the maximum life span. For purposes of our discussion, we will use the term *life expectancy.*

Human life expectancy has exhibited a phenomenal change from the time of the ancient Greeks to the present. Life expectancy at birth in ancient Greece was 18 years (500 B.C.), 25 years in ancient Rome (A.D. 100), and 35 years in thirteenth-century England. It is estimated that the median age in the American colonies just prior to the Revolutionary War was 20.

From 1775 to 1900 in the United States, the increase in life expectancy was from about 15 years to 35 years. This increase in life expectancy can be attributed to factors such as improved housing, sanitation, and the development and use of antiseptics. Since 1900, life expectancy has increased due to the passage of public health laws, better sanitation and hygiene, immunization for childhood diseases, improved medical care and medical practice, and better nutrition (Strehler, 1975).

The most significant increases in life expectancy in the United States occurred between 1900 and 1940; increases have been relatively minor since then. For white males, during the 50-year period from 1900 to 1950, predicted life expectancy at birth increased by approximately 20 years (46.6

to 66.5 years). But for the 28-year period from 1950 to 1978, predicted life expectancy at birth increased only about 4 years (66.5 to 70.2 years). This is due to the fact that the major causes of death are diseases that have no known cure at the present time.

Data from government sources (U.S. Senate Special Committee on Aging, 1987–1988) indicate the leading cause of death for middle-aged and older adults to be chronic disease. The likelihood of having a chronic illness increases with age, and it is not uncommon for people in their eighties and nineties to have more than one chronic illness, particularly those in nursing homes. The major causes of death for both genders in the United States are cardiovascular diseases and malignancies—cancer. These diseases account for three-fourths of all the deaths of older adults. While younger people do die of such disorders, death from these causes is comparatively rare. Accidents and violent death kill most young adults.

Factors Related to Life Expectancy

INTRINSIC/PRIMARY FACTORS

Intrinsic or **primary factors** are generally considered fixed, since they are inherited or otherwise related to universal biological and physiological processes (Timiras, 1972, 1988). The major intrinsic factors related to life expectancy appear to be genetic inheritance and health. Although these factors have been demonstrated to be related to life expectancy, they cannot be considered causal. Their impact varies with other, secondary influences on life expectancy such as life-style or stress. In addition, because our information is based on studies of lower animals, there may be a problem in generalizing to humans. Finally, there are vast individual differences in these factors, since humans do not develop in a vacuum and the factors themselves do not function in isolation.

Heredity There is an association between the life spans of individuals and those of their immediate ancestors (Birren & Renner, 1977; Timiras, 1972). Simply put, long-lived parents tend to have long-lived children. This relationship, although significant, is quite complex. In general, however, how long you live in relation to your parents' life span will depend on the interaction of the other intrinsic/primary and extrinsic/secondary factors such as diet and exercise. As noted above, a genetic program sets certain limits for the potential life span; this limit varies by species (Shock, 1977). However, for individuals, the expression of this basic genetic program can be altered by many internal and environmental factors. One might say that heredity "deals the cards," but we "play the hand."

The major familial characteristics that affect life expectancy in humans are gender, ethnicity, and health.

Gender In the United States and in most nations of the world, females today live longer than males by a margin of 7 to 8 years (Timiras, 1972; Wantz & Gay, 1981). However, this difference in life expectancy for males and females has increased since 1900. For males and females born in 1900, females outlived males by approximately 2 years; for males and females born in 1960, females are expected to outlive males by 6.5 years; and for those born in 1975, women are expected to outlive men by approximately 8 years. Females may have a genetic program for a longer life, or they may be the stronger and healthier members of the species and therefore live longer. Their greater life expectancy also may be the result of other primary or secondary factors.

The fact that females live longer than males of the same cohort has a significant impact on interpersonal relationships during late adulthood. Because the majority of women marry men who are older than themselves, the chance of their outliving their husbands by 10 or 15 years is quite high. Women would do well to acquire the skills necessary for independent living, such as paying bills, simple home maintenance, and driving a car, since it is quite likely they will need these "independent living survival skills" after the deaths of their spouses. Likewise, women should begin economic planning, such as by saving for retirement or building a credit history, since it is likely they will have to support themselves after the deaths of their husbands.

Ethnicity Whites generally tend to live longer than members of minority groups (Timiras, 1972, 1978; Ward, 1984). However, experts in the field of population statistics report what they call the **crossover effect** (Schwartz & Peterson, 1979), which refers to the fact that black females will have a longer life expectancy than white males born in the same year.

Health It is not surprising that the better your health and the better your access to health care, the longer you are likely to live (Siegler & Costa, 1985). However, many individuals overlook the fact that a number of the major diseases and causes of death—for example, heart disease and diabetes—can occur at any point in adulthood. This is where a familial pattern of incidence can come into play, as in the case of an aged father and his middle-aged son both having heart disease. A number of diseases, several forms of mental retardation, Tay-Sachs disease, and sickle-cell anemia all have either a familial or racial genetic pattern and contribute to shortened life span.

Exclusive of accidents, both acute and chronic illnesses commonly cut our lives short. Older adults tend to have not only more chronic diseases than the young, as noted above, but also have about twice as many hospital stays as do young adults. Also, their stays last almost twice as long (Hickey, 1980). Additionally, many older people suffer from multiple ailments (Siegler, 1989). However, the majority of older adults report themselves as being in good or excellent health. The major difference between subgroups of aging people in health status appears to be between whites and nonwhites: more whites report good to excellent health than do nonwhites, and fewer whites report fair to poor health than do nonwhites. Perhaps this difference can be attributed to the greater availability of medical care and services to whites earlier in their lives.

Certain chronic illnesses tend to vary by gender. Older women have higher rates of arthritis, diabetes, high blood pressure, and vision impairments than do men. Men have higher rates of asthma, chronic bronchitis, hernias, ulcers, and hearing impairments.

While self-perception of health and actual health status are not identical, self-assessments of health by older adults are usually quite accurate (LaRue et al., 1979; Siegler & Costa, 1985). In some cases, however, the perception of one's health as good may serve as a defense against the anxiety about growing older, becoming dependent, or being institutionalized. Moreover, persons with significant cognitive impairment may not be capable of judging their health status, be it good or bad. On balance, most adults seem to do a reasonable job of assessing their overall health. Yet, these assessments should not substitute for a thorough physical exam!

Individuals of both sexes over age 60 tend to perceive their own health in a significantly more positive manner than do younger age groups (Cockerham et al., 1983). This may be due to successful adjustment to the medical or physical conditions common to elderly persons, such as arthritis and high blood pressure.

In general, physicians tend to give low priority to the medical needs of older adults, for two reasons. First, they assume that being sick is a necessary part of being old, and second, many elderly believe that the symptoms of illness they experience are normal and inevitable results of aging and therefore do not seek help. For example, Harris and Cole (1980) report a study conducted by the University of Illinois of 900 older adults who were homebound. It was found that many of the individuals were too ill even to walk to the door and had gone for months without seeking medical aid. They thought that because they were old they were supposed to be sick. Also, physicians tended to write off many symptoms as normal in the elderly. Often, highly treatable, acute illnesses such as heart attacks, viral infections, and even appendicitis went undiagnosed!

Another explanation for why physicians give low priority to the needs of elderly people rests with their medical training, which primarily emphasizes acute illness. Since older adults are more likely to suffer from chronic illness, often with no known cure, the situation is frustrating and depressing to many physicians. Until recently, geriatric medicine has received little, if any, attention in U.S. medical schools, a situation that creates a void in the physician's knowledge about caring for and treating older adults. Recent attention to geriatric medicine, however (Rowe & Minoker, 1985), reflects an emerging sensitivity to the unique health care needs of older adults.

As medical care and technology improve in a society, life expectancy increases. For example, medical science has developed vaccines to prevent diseases that used to kill people during childhood or early adulthood, such as whooping cough and polio. As medical care and knowledge progress, and cures and treatments are discovered for diseases such as cancer, life expectancy is likely increase further (Davis, 1985).

Fries and Crapo (1981) have developed the *rectangular survival curve,* which predicts relative stability in life expectancy until approximately 85,

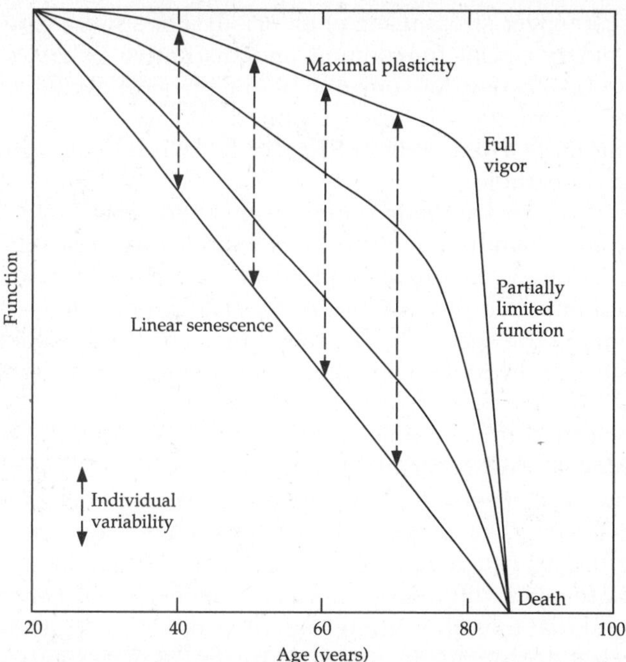

Figure 3.5 The individual rectangular curves for vigor, representing a lifetime of vigor followed by terminal collapse. *Source:* Fries & Crapo. (1981).

after which survival declines precipitously (see Figure 3.5). This means they predict that while more people will live longer, they will also be sicker. In view of this trend, Callahan (1987) has argued that because of the high cost of medical care, elderly people with chronic illnesses should be sacrificed so that available resources can be used to care for the young. This issue obviously creates an ethical dilemma for physicians caring for older patients and has a major impact on patient-doctor relations as well as relationships between younger and older people in our society. Can we put a price on the worth of a person's life based on age alone? Can quality of life be exchanged for its quantity? Interestingly, physicians often underestimate the quality of life in older persons with chronic illnesses such as diabetes, cancer, or arthritis, when compared with the older persons' own reports (Pearlman & Uhlmann, 1988).

When an older person is ill with a chronic disorder, or requires hospitalization, intergenerational conflict between the older parent and adult children may result (Hall, 1989). This conflict may result from the disruption of activities and life-style of the adult child. That is, the adult child may suddenly be called on to provide care and assistance for a chronically ill parent. In many cases, the health of the adult care-giver suffers.

Correlates of stress and burden for adult children appear to be the older person's functional and mental impairment, disruptive behaviors, sharing a household with the care receiver, and the gender of care-giver (Miller, 1989). Female care-givers, spouses, and those sharing housing report higher levels of care-giver stress (Gatz et al., 1990). For spouse care-givers, problems in elders' social functioning and disruptive behavior, rather than the demands of caring for someone with a physical disability, are primary correlates of care-giver burden (Deimling & Bass, 1986). We will discuss care-giving more extensively in Chapter 10, which deals with mental health and psychopathology.

Health is also related to economic status. In this light, many older adults have difficulty in obtaining adequate health care, illustrating the relationship between economic conditions and health. Moreover, Gerson et al. (1987) have found impaired physical health to relate strongly to lessened mental health among the aged. That is, they found that when older people could not engage in everyday activities, their mental health was impaired as well.

Since health is related to a number of behaviors and activities, as well as personality, intelligence, and mental health status (Siegler & Costa, 1985), it is important for researchers and practitioners to take a more active interest in the health disorders of adults. As medical science makes new discoveries regarding disease, such as cures for cancer and heart disease as well as organ replacements, life expectancy may again go up. Davis (1985) has already found that mortality among elderly people has dropped substantially over the last decade due to improved treatment of cardiovascular disease alone.

Although the factors discussed above have been reported to be related to life expectancy in humans, they are not causally related, nor is the relationship among them a simple one; thus, in reality they do not function independently. That is, they interact in a complex manner. For these reasons, it is impossible to predict exactly how long you will live. However, a rough guide to charting your life expectancy can be found in the Appendix to this text.

EXTRINSIC/SECONDARY FACTORS

Extrinsic or **secondary factors** modify the limits projected for life expectancy by intrinsic factors. They are not inherited, but are instead the result of environmental, social, and psychological conditions or events. Usually, individuals do not have any control over the primary factors but can exercise control over the secondary factors to some extent. Moreover, the effects of these extrinsic/secondary factors can be positive or negative; that is, they can enhance or detract from life expectancy.

The major extrinsic/secondary factors influencing life are nutrition and diet, climate or physical environment, exercise and activity, stress avoidance, interpersonal relationships, work and work satisfaction, education and economic status, cognitive/intellectual factors, and personality (Elias et al., 1990; Siegler & Costa, 1985; Timiras, 1988). In some cases, they interact with intrinsic factors. For example, diet and exercise both affect and are influenced by health. Moreover, many extrinsic factors interact with, and in some cases are dependent on, each other. For example, highly educated individuals often have the economic resources available for good nutrition, high-quality medical care, and work satisfaction.

Nutrition and Diet Most of us now know that avoiding obesity and eating a diet low in animal fats is beneficial to our health (Wantz & Gay, 1981). Although dietary restrictions that lead to low blood-cholesterol levels may not be directly related to longevity, they are directly related to high blood pressure and cardiovascular disease, which in turn may shorten life.

But nutritional factors are related to more than just life expectancy, especially in older adults. Chronic nutritional deficiencies in older adults (and in young adults as well) can lead to vitamin deficiencies, which in turn may have negative effects upon various organs and organ systems in the body (Eisdorfer & Cohen, 1978). These deficiencies can eventually lead to disorders that produce dementia, which is often reversible but often misdiagnosed (see Chapter 10). Individuals with a dementia-like condition sometimes manifest rapid and sudden cognitive dysfunction, high levels of anxiety, and even delusions and hallucinations (Eisdorfer & Cohen, 1978).

The distinction between dementia and nutritional deficiencies is particularly relevant for individuals who work with older adults living in the community. When one visits older adults, especially those that live alone, one should attempt to assess their dietary intake. That is, are they eating at all, eating junk food, or eating a balanced diet?

Individuals of all ages who live alone often do not eat nutritionally balanced meals, but instead eat meals that are expedient and quick. One major reason for this is that the process of eating is a social event in most cultures, including ours. Consequently, eating alone may lead to feelings of isolation and loneliness. Thus, rather than cook a big meal or go out to get a balanced one when we are alone, we may find it easier not to eat at all or to eat something quickly.

Diet is significantly affected by economics at all age levels, since it may be difficult to eat nutritious meals if one does not have the money to purchase good food. This problem is particularly relevant for older adults, who often have a number of economic difficulties (Chen, 1985). For this reason, many communities and agencies sponsor programs for elderly people to provide meals that are free or at greatly reduced cost based on the person's ability to pay. These projects serve two important purposes: they provide elderly people with nutritious meals, and they provide opportunities for social interaction.

Climate and Physical Environment Each species has specific requirements in terms of temperature and climate in order to sustain life. For instance, tropical birds cannot live for a prolonged time in a cold climate. Other factors, however, such as exposure to chemicals, noise levels, and pollution, can also affect life expectancy, directly or indirectly. For example, if you work on a job in which you are repeatedly exposed to dangerous chemicals or live in a city with a high pollution level, these factors have the potential of either contributing to disease or otherwise reducing your life expectancy.

Quality of Housing The most obvious aspect of the physical environment for older adults is housing. In fact, housing and the immediate surroundings influence well-being and the quality of life significantly for the elderly, for whom the home is the center of virtually all activities (Lawton, 1985). Due to poor health or lack of physical mobility, older adults spend an increasingly larger proportion of time at home. Housing plays an important role in their lives (Lawton, 1985). For example, Qassis and Hayden (1990) found that elderly people living in either their own homes or retirement homes reported greater well-being than their matched counterparts in nursing homes.

About seven out of every ten community-living older adults own their own homes (Chen, 1985; Lawton, 1985). Since the homes were usually obtained when their owners were young, they are generally older, located in older neighborhoods, and more likely to need repairs. The remainder of community-living older adults (30%) live in rental properties. Many older adults who rent live in older apartment buildings, located in run-down areas of a city, where rents and services are low and crime rates are high.

Exercise and Activity Regular physical exercise throughout life is thought to have many positive physical and psychological effects for both men and

1991
1951
Creators Syndicate, Inc.
©1991 Leigh Rubini
". . . Therefore, after a 40-year case study, it is my contention that couch potatoes actually begin to develop early in life as tater tots."

Creators Syndicate Inc. © 1991 Leigh Rubini.

women (Blumenthal et al., 1989; Buskirk, 1985; Whitbourne, 1985). These include improved cardiovascular and respiratory-system functioning and better muscle tone. In terms of psychological functioning, it is assumed that the better your body feels physically, the better your psychological feeling of well-being. For this reason, running is often prescribed as a treatment for depression. A general relationship between regular, long-term exercise or physical activity and life expectancy is also well documented (Emery & Blumenthal, 1990; Whitbourne, 1985), although consistent empirical data are lacking. For example, Lee and Markides (1990), in a longitudinal study of older Mexican Americans and Anglos, found that activity was not a significant predictor of mortality when factors such as age, gender, education, marital status, ethnicity, and self-rated health were controlled for.

It is likely, however, that a program of physical exercise, in combination with a clearly designed diet regimen, will contribute to less weight gain, lower blood pressure, and lower cholesterol levels. People who follow such a program lower their risk of heart attacks and strokes. Overall, it would appear that exercising at least half an hour three times a week is an important aid to controlling weight, keeping bones strong, building muscle strength, conditioning the heart and lungs, and relieving stress.

Education and Economic Status In general, the higher one's educational level and economic status, the longer one is likely to live (Bengtson et al., 1977; Chen, 1985; Pfeiffer, 1970; Rose, 1964).

As one would expect, being highly educated and earning a comfortable salary usually implies work satisfaction and good medical care (Shanas & Maddox, 1985). People who earn more and who are highly educated generally also eat a nutritious diet and live in a safe physical environment. Thus, although educational level and economic status are not causal factors in life expectancy, they are directly related to many other secondary factors that affect life expectancy.

We sometimes believe that many older adults are wealthy and live a life of affluence. This is far from the truth. Although there are some affluent older adults and the economic position of older adults has improved in recent years (Chen, 1985; *Wall Street Journal*, 1983), many are still poor or just getting by. In fact, some older adults are in such a disadvantaged economic position that they constitute a major social problem for our society today.

Interestingly, elderly people tend to disapprove of receiving financial assistance from adult children (Hamon & Blieszner, 1990), yet elderly people living alone—both men and women—have the lowest incomes.

Poverty also varies among subgroups of older adults. Approximately 10 percent of elderly whites were considered poor in 1988, while 32 percent of elderly blacks and 22 percent of elderly Hispanics were considered poor during this same year (U.S. Bureau of the Census, 1990).

Older adults often face economic hardships during periods of high inflation, since they live primarily on fixed incomes. This is especially true for those who worked at lower-level occupations their entire lives, earning minimal wages (Wilson, 1984). Since Society Security and pension benefits are closely tied to earnings, these people then receive low benefit payments. Some individuals who earned just enough to get by when they were working experience poverty for the first time in retirement (Wilson, 1984).

Work and Work Satisfaction There is a clear relationship between working conditions and work satisfaction and life expectancy (Palmore, 1969; Rose, 1964). For instance, working in hazardous conditions, such as being exposed to pollution or dangerous chemicals, potentially shortens one's life span. Also, individuals who have high work satisfaction tend to have higher self-esteem and a more positive outlook on life than those who are dissatisfied with their work. The type of work performed is also highly related to socioeconomic level and other secondary factors related to life expectancy. We will have more to say on the relationship between aging and work-related issues in Chapter 9.

Interpersonal Relationships Valued interpersonal relationships, such as those with friends and a spouse, exert a positive influence on many psychological factors like self-esteem and life satisfaction (Kahn & Antonucci, 1980), as well as on life expectancy (Bengston et al., 1977; Wantz & Gay, 1981). The presence of valued others makes us feel worthwhile and reduces feelings of isolation, loneliness, and depression. That is, they provide necessary and beneficial psychological and social support for us. Such relations are more critical to us as we get older due to the deaths of friends, relatives, and spouses. And since having animals as pets has also been shown to facilitate psychological well-being in people (Lawton et al., 1984; Levinson, 1972), they too can provide many positive effects for both older and younger individuals (Cusack & Smith, 1984).

Personality and Stress Avoidance An individual's personality type, particularly how he or she reacts to stress, is related to life expectancy (Siegler & Costa, 1985). For instance, Friedman and Rosenman (1974) investigated the relationship between personality type and incidence of coronary disease among men. Their research suggested there are two personality types, **Type A** and **Type B,** and found a significant relationship between so-called Type A behaviors and coronary heart disease. Basically, Type A individuals can be viewed as having a stressful personality type, since they tend to respond to most situations with stress. People with Type A traits are hard driving, highly competitive, impatient, always rushing, and striving to accomplish more than is reasonably possible. Type B individuals, on the other hand, are more low-key and relaxed.

Both day-to-day stress and major stress events are a normal part of life. Stress may be found on the job, at home, on the highway, and in personal life. There are differences in the perception of stress as well as individual reactions to it. However, as we age, the more we are likely to encounter those situations generally perceived as very stressful. For older people, these include the death of a spouse, retirement, a change in health, and the death of close friends (Holmes & Rahe, 1972).

In addition to the influence of the major life stressors, daily life events play an important role in influencing both physical and mental health in adulthood. Such daily events have been termed **hassles,** or negative small events, and **uplifts,** or positive small events (Zautra et al., 1986). While everyday stressors are often overlooked as sources of distress, these seemingly minor events can have a major impact on both physical and mental health in adulthood (Zautra et al., 1988). Examples of hassles are losing a wallet or purse, not having a phone call returned, being late for work, arguing with the boss, or having a car break down. Examples of uplifts might be getting a good grade on an exam, receiving a refund, being praised or complimented by one's spouse, or successfully solving a problem at work (Zautra et al., 1986). Of course, our emotional state can either help or hinder such situations. For example, if we are tired, angry, or depressed anyway, mild daily hassles can seem worse, and we may fail to derive any satisfaction from a small uplift.

The study of stress and adaptation to it is significant for older adults since the frequency and intensity of stressful life events often increase at a time of life when economic, physical, social, and psychological resources and abilities are generally decreasing. Examples of common adaptations required of older people are new life-styles required by retirement, learning to cope with widowhood, and the many changes in daily living that accompany relocation to a new home or nursing home (Kahana & Kahana, 1983). Moreover, many middle-aged and older adults find themselves in a care-giving role with either a physically or cognitively impaired spouse, parent, or in-law. When the care-giving involves parents, note that it is likely to be delegated to the wife, regardless of whose parents are involved (Bumagin & Hirn, 1982).

Of particular relevance to this discussion of stress is the work of Selye, who found that stress and our reaction to it are related to both medical conditions and life expectancy (Eisdorfer & Wilkie, 1979a; Siegler, 1989; Siegler & Costa, 1985). More specifically, the prolonged and repeated exposure to stressful situations and events may contribute to a number of psychological and medical/physical problems, such as ulcers during middle age and heart disease in old age (Selye, 1976).

Selye sees such effects in terms of a theory of stress referred to as the **general adaptation syndrome.** This theory postulates three stages the body goes through in reacting to stressful situations.

Stage 1, the alarm reaction, is characterized by a general mobilization of the body's physical and psychological resources in order to deal with the perceived stressful situation, that is, to attack the source of stress, defend oneself, or retreat from the stress.

If the stressful situation continues or new ones develop, the second stage, called the stage of resistance, begins. During this phase, all physical and psychological systems continue to function at a high level of strain in order to cope. This reaction to prolonged stress can lead to physiological and/or psychological problems, including high blood pressure and depression. Furthermore, if the system becomes depleted and the stress remains, individuals may begin to take drugs or medications to cope with the situation, on which they may then become dependent.

According to Selye, if the stress continues even longer, the individual's bodily systems move into the third and final stage, the stage of exhaustion. During this stage, bodily systems become so fatigued they can no longer cope with the stress. This may lead to feelings of resignation, mental and physical breakdown, and even death. Moreover, with increasing age, it takes longer to return to prestress levels of functioning (Siegler, 1989).

Selye's ideas suggest that as we develop, we repeatedly encounter stress, which may eventually weaken our psychological and biological system—our resistance and adaptive capacities. We normally think of such high-stress events (Holmes & Rahe, 1967) as the death of close friends or a spouse, retirement, and being a victim of crime (Eisdorfer & Wilkie, 1979a, 1979b) as being typical of adulthood. However, it will come as no surprise to readers of this text that work, school, and raising children are also stressful! Regardless of age, any of these events potentially may have a more pronounced effect if an individual's ability to cope is already weakened.

If we experience a decline in our capacities with age or inactivity, previously nonstressful events and tasks, such as climbing stairs, can become stress producing. Thus, it is important to develop appropriate coping mechanisms early in life, because stressful situations obviously do not disappear as we get older.

COGNITIVE/INTELLECTUAL FACTORS

Numerous investigations have linked cognitive/intellectual factors with life expectancy. Individuals with better or higher cognitive/intellectual abilities tend to live longer, and this is often referred to as the **wisdom factor** (Birren & Renner, 1977). More specifically, Fozard et al. (1972) demonstrated that an individual's performance on a number of verbal, perceptual, and motor tasks, as well as measures of blood serum, urine, and personality, were all related positively to life expectancy.

Other research has attempted to link life expectancy and survival to sudden and dramatic declines in cognitive/intellectual performance from a few days (Kleemeier, 1962; Lieberman, 1965) to a number of years prior to death (Jarvik & Blum, 1971; Jarvik & Falek, 1963; Riegel & Riegel, 1972). For example, Kleemeier (1962) administered an intelligence test on four occasions, at 2- to 3½-year intervals during a 12-year period, to 13 older adult males. Not surprisingly, Kleemeier observed that the performance of all participants decreased over the 12-year period, but that there were substantial individual differences in the magnitude of this decline. Furthermore, following the last retest it was observed that the decline in test scores was faster and greater in magnitude for those who died than those who survived. This decline was labeled **terminal drop.** In other words, impend-

TABLE 3.4

INTRINSIC AND EXTRINSIC INFLUENCES ON LIFE EXPECTANCY

Intrinsic	Extrinsic
heredity	nutrition and diet
ethnicity	climate and physical environment
gender	exercise and activity
health	stress and personality
ethnicity	work and work satisfaction
gender	education
socioeconomic status	socioeconomic status
	interpersonal relationships
	cognitive/intellectual factors (wisdom factor, terminal drop)

ing death was often preceded by a terminal drop in cognitive/intellectual functioning. Numerous other investigators have since then examined the ability of specific measures of intellectual or memory functioning to predict terminal decline and terminal drop, with some success (Botwinick et al., 1978; Hayslip et al., 1989; Palmore & Cleveland, 1976; Siegler et al., 1982). Despite substantial evidence at this point, the phenomenon needs to be viewed cautiously due to a number of methodological problems in the research (Siegler, 1975). For instance, the poor physical health of the individuals who died may have been responsible for their decrease in test performance, rather than cognitive factors.

Self-reflection regarding how each of us stands on all the factors discussed above may lead to positive and happy feelings for some, and to negative and pessimistic feelings for others. However, it is never too late to improve the quality of our lives, for example, by watching our diets or beginning exercise programs. Table 3.4 summarizes the intrinsic and extrinsic influences on life expectancy we have discussed.

Developmental Health Psychology

Developmental health psychologists study the relationship among aging, health and illness, and behavior. These professionals are interested in the distinction between normal aging and disease, as well as the impact of health behaviors and age on various diseases common among middle-aged and older adults, such as coronary heart disease, hypertension, and Alzheimer's disease (Siegler, 1989).

It is important to realize that the relationship between behavior and health is a two-way street. Of course, health affects our behavior in many ways. However, many behaviors we engage in also affect our health. If we can understand and modify our health behaviors, we can potentially increase the number of healthy, functional years to our lives. Unfortunately, we may also be able to increase the number of disabled, dysfunctional years in our lives (Brody et al., 1987). Either way, this most certainly has real implications for family care-givers as well as health care professionals.

Developmental health psychology recognizes that aging and illness are indeed distinct. Moreover, health and illness are not opposite sides of the same coin, since individuals perceive and interpret symptoms in unique ways (Siegler, 1989). Of particular interest here is the study of health behaviors and their impact on health.

Age, sex, and family history are often used to assess biological risk of various diseases. However, there are behaviors and other characteristics

TABLE 3.5

RISK FACTORS AND PREVENTIVE BEHAVIORS FOR ILLNESS IN ADULTHOOD

Risk Factor	Symptom/Disease
Smoking	Bone loss/osteoporosis Coronary heart disease (CHD) Myocardial infarction/sudden death In elderly: death Cancer of lung, mouth, larynx, bladder Emphysema
Alcohol	Cancer of stomach, breast Falls
Obesity	Hypertension, diabetes mellitus
High lipids	CHD
High fat/Low fiber	Cancer of colon, rectum, breast, prostate
Hypertension	CHD
Diabetes	CHD
Type A behavior	CHD
Hostility	CHD
Job strain	CHD
Sexual behavior	AIDS, cervical cancer
Preventive Behavior	**Effect on Symptom/Disease**
Diet: Vitamin D Diet: Calcium supplement	Reduce bone loss
Exercise	Reduce bone loss Reduce heart disease mortality
Aspirin	Reduce heart disease
Fat reduction	Reduce heart disease
Social support	Reduce mortality
Internal control	Increase self-care

Source: Siegler. (1989).

that also put one at risk, and these have been identified in many cases (see Table 3.5). Once these high-risk behaviors are understood, we can then advise individuals of the most likely avenues for behavioral or environmental change to lower their risk. Examples of the preventive behaviors are also shown in the table.

Developmental health psychologists tend to be very flexible and broad in their conceptions of disease-behavior relationships. Other disciplines are integral to understanding disease and health: physiologists, geriatricians, and sociologists are all essential in the work of developmental health psychologists. Moreover, because health, illness, age, and their relationship to behavior are approached holistically, the design of everyday environments that permit control and decision-making is crucial (Elias et al., 1990; Siegler, 1989).

We have much to learn about disease and health in adulthood, over and above their biological roots. But we know that the severity of diseases and age-related biological changes, ranging from osteoporosis, to incontinence, diabetes, menopause, arthritis, and coronary heart disease, can be lessened by practicing preventive or ameliorative behaviors. We can also lessen risk by understanding and addressing individuals' belief systems about health and illness. Moreover, polypharmacy, the use of and interaction among many drugs, as well as medication adherence can be treated behaviorally. Indeed, by modifying behavior and life-style, we can add "life to years" rather than simply "years to life"!

SUMMARY

In this chapter, the biological and physiological aspects of the aging process were discussed. There are clear age-related changes in the muscular, cardiovascular, respiratory, digestive, and central nervous systems. While *neuronal loss* with age is characteristic of the brain, such losses vary within (by cortical area) and between individuals. Moreover, recent evidence suggests some *plasticity* in brain function well into later adulthood. The effects on *behavior* and *well-being* of these changes for the individual were also discussed; these seem to be most apparent in middle and later adulthood.

Life-span trends differ in both sexual interest and activity for both males and females, as does the peak of sexual interest. However, there are significant individual differences between interest and activity at all points along the life span. Specific factors that relate to decreased sexual activity for both male and females with increasing age were discussed. For females, the primary factor resulting in decreased sexual activity is lack of available male partners; for males, the factors are less clear. We still do not have an extensive and reliable data base regarding sexual behavior in adults, especially from middle age to older adulthood. This research area is still considered somewhat taboo, which contributes to our lack of definitive information.

There are numerous psychosocial implications of the changes in our bodies and bodily systems as we age. These may be interpersonal or occupational in nature. Their impact probably becomes most apparent to us in middle adulthood, although it is inaccurate to assume that mid-life is a crisis-filled period of life. Unfortunately, women may be especially affected by such changes, due to society's biases about their physical attractiveness and care-taking roles.

A number of biological and physiological theories—*genetic, nongenetic,* and *physiological*—of the aging process were presented. Due to the complexity of aging, however, no one specific theory can adequately explain all its aspects, and thus these theories remain educated guesses or speculations about the process.

The historical, current, and future trends in life expectancy in the United States and other nations were presented. Research suggests that specific intrinsic or primary and extrinsic or secondary factors are related to longevity in humans. Intrinsic factors are those generally considered fixed or determined, since they are inherited from our parents or are related to biological/physiological processes. These factors are *genetic inheritance, gender* and *race,* and *health condition.* Extrinsic factors include *nutrition* and *diet, climate* and *physical environment, exercise* and *activity,* and *personality* and *stress avoidance.*

Developmental health psychologists focus on the relationship between health behaviors and health, so that preventive behavioral or lifestyle changes can be made to enhance the quality of life for all adults.

KEY TERMS AND CONCEPTS

Osteoporosis
Neurofibrillary tangles
Dementia
Senile plaques
Extrinsic factors (sexual behavior)
Intrinsic factors (sexual behavior)
Hayflick's aging clock
Metabolic waste theory
Cross-linkage theory
Autoimmune theory
Life expectancy/longevity
Intrinsic/primary factors (life expectancy)
Crossover effect
General adaptation syndrome
Terminal drop
Stroke
Atherosclerosis
Arteriosclerosis
Plasticity
Menopause
Primary aging
Secondary aging
Rectangular survival curve
General genetic theory
Wear and tear theory
Collagen theory
Free radical theory
Hassles and uplifts
Extrinsic/secondary factors (life expectancy)
Developmental health psychology

REVIEW QUESTIONS

1. What are some of the major biological and physical changes experienced by most individuals during young adulthood? middle adulthood? late adulthood?
2. What are the implications of changes in one's biological and physical condition for individuals of varying ages?
3. What are some of the theories that attempt to explain the aging process? How are these theories classified?
4. What are some of the stresses of middle age? old age?
5. Why is it difficult to obtain accurate information regarding sexual behavior? How do these problems relate to myths about sexuality and aging?
6. What extrinsic and intrinsic factors are related to sexual interest and activity across the life cycle?
7. Why do some individuals reevaluate their lives and goals during middle age?
8. What diseases are responsible for the deaths of the majority of adults?
9. What are some of the major structural and functional changes in the brain as we age?
10. How do intrinsic and extrinsic factors affect life expectancy?
11. What is developmental health psychology?

CHAPTER 4

Sensory and Perceptual Processes

CHAPTER OUTLINE

INTRODUCTION

The focus of this chapter is on sensation and perception in adulthood. We define **sensation** as the reception of physical stimulation and the translation of this stimulation into neural impulses. **Perception** is the interpretation of sensory stimulation. For instance, imagine yourself walking across campus, and off at a distance you see an individual approaching you. When you are able to more closely examine this person's features, you realize it is one of your friends. Here we see the distinction between sensation—the reception of a shape or form by the visual system—and perception—the interpretation of this form as a friend. In real life, sensation and perception are closely intertwined. For example, the clarity with which you hear a sound (sensation) influences your interpretation (perception) of that sound (e.g., is that Dad's voice on the phone?).

Sensation and perception are important in adulthood for a number of reasons. First, our ability to cope and interact with our environment is in large part due to our ability to detect, interpret, and respond appropriately to sensory information (Kline & Scheiber, 1985). Think of the amount of contact you would have with the environment and the people in it if you were unable to hear, see, and taste. Second, there are clear relationships between numerous perceptual processes and many other behaviors and traits, such as driving, accidents, personality, and learning style (see Chapters 5 and 8). For both these reasons, it is important to know what effect changes in these processes have on our behavior and performance with increasing age.

The importance of studying age changes in sensation and perception, as well as other abilities such as memory, learning, and intelligence, discussed in other chapters, can be further underscored by embedding them in an information-processing approach to aging.

INFORMATION-PROCESSING (IP) APPROACH TO AGING

Information-processing models have become very popular in psychology, human development, and education. By viewing the individual in information-processing terms, one can easily understand both individual differences in performance and the implications of age changes in the various abilities used in interacting with the environment. Simply put, we all process what happens to us, on a daily basis.

While there are many information-processing (IP) models, they all attempt to explain human behavior and performance in machine-like terms, such as those used in discussing computers. The person, like a computer, receives certain inputs or data from the environment. Inputs are processed by various systems which in turn produce outputs, or behaviors. An example of an IP model, illustrated in Figure 4.1, is based on the work of Panek et al. (1977). This figure can help us understand the implications of age changes in sensation and perception.

The IP approach suggests that once a person has received stimulation from the environment, this stimulation (information) must pass through four distinct information-processing stages before a response in the form of observable behavior occurs. A breakdown in functioning at any of these stages can affect the relationship between stimuli (input) and responses (output).

What are the functions and processes involved in each stage of information processing? Stimuli from the environment can be viewed as all the experiences and events that repeatedly impinge on us. These include sounds, sights, sense impressions, feelings, conversations, and questions—in short, all our daily experiences. The person's first contacts with the environment come at the first stage of IP, called the *preperceptual stage* or *sensory store.* The main function of this stage is to receive and register sensory information and experience, that is, to notify the person that this store or filter has been stimulated. We commonly term the type of information processing in this stage *sensation.* Examples of sensation rele-

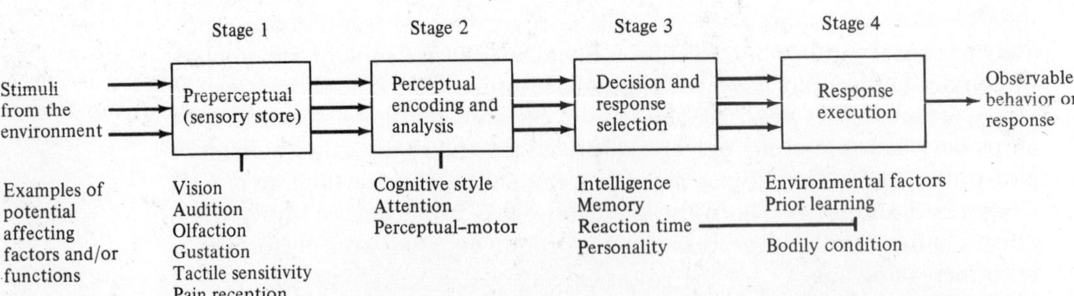

Figure 4.1 Four stages of information processing. *Source:* P. E. Panek, G. V. Barrett, H. L. Sterns, & R. A. Alexander. (1977). A review of age changes in perceptual information-processing ability with regard to driving. *Experimental Aging Research, 3,* 388. Copyright © EAR, Inc., 1988.

vant to this stage of IP are vision, audition (hearing), olfaction (smell), gustation (taste), tactile sensitivity (touch), and pain sensitivity. As you can imagine, if the receptors for these processes are not functioning well, the quantity and quality of information received from the environment will be quite limited. Furthermore, if we have limited or faulty input at this stage of IP, later stages will have less, or perhaps incorrect, information to process and work with.

The second stage of IP is labeled *perceptual encoding and analysis*. The basic functions of this stage are to encode, interpret, and classify the information received in the preperceptual stage, that is, to analyze the information received by the senses. Psychologists often label the type of processing going on at this stage *perception*. Examples of perception at this stage of IP are cognitive (perceptual) style, selective attention, and perceptual-motor reaction time.

Again, if limited or incorrect information is received in stage 1 and passed on to stage 2, the quality and quantity of the information interpreted and classified are severely impaired.

Information is then passed on to the third component of the IP system, which is termed *decision and response selection*. The primary function of this stage is to make a decision about the information received from the preceding two stages and, in turn, to decide upon the appropriate response or course of action. Many abilities, traits, and experiences of the individual come into play at this stage, such as intelligence, memory, and personality. As before, if incorrect input has reached this stage, the probability of making a correct decision and responding appropriately is reduced.

After information has been received and processed by the other stages, a specific response is executed, which is the final stage of information processing. This is usually expressed in some type of behavior or course of action: answering a question, fighting, fleeing, turning left in a car, and so forth. These behaviors can be viewed as a result of both the information processed at preceding stages and factors such as past experiences, situational factors, and physical or health condition.

By returning to our example of the person approaching us on campus, we can perhaps better understand how this information-processing model operates in everyday life. Stage 1 of our IP model, preperception, involves simply receiving sensory input about this person, that is, facial features, voice tone, height, and build.

Stage 2, perceptual encoding and analysis, permits us to label these features as perhaps belonging to someone we know. If, for example, our friend were tall, blond, and slim, and the person approaching us were tall, heavy set, and brunette, we would most likely not consider greeting this person in a friendly, outgoing manner. In this stage, by comparing our friend's features with those of the person we see, we can then interpret or label this individual as friend or stranger. Of course, if our input is poor—if we do not get a close look at the person because he or she is running or has his or her back to us, we may misinterpret this person as someone we know or don't know. It usually causes most of us a fair amount of embarrassment if we fail to greet a friend, or mistake a stranger for someone we know!

The third stage, decision and response selection, allows us to decide "friend" or "stranger," based on our perception of the person's features, and to select an appropriate response. For example, we may choose to say nothing, or make eye contact and extend a hand in the anticipation of hearing our friend's voice. The fourth stage, response execution, simply involves doing what we have chosen to do, based on the information about the person we have taken in and interpreted in one way or another.

Adopting an information-processing approach can enable us to more easily understand the implications of age changes in sensory abilities. For example, sensory loss can have a serious impact on an older person's ability to make sense of the environment, leading to maladaptive behavior or faulty decision making. People with a hearing loss may have difficulty in talking to others, since this loss affects their ability to process auditory stimuli (words). Consequently, they might well avoid others, leading to isolation and feelings of loneliness.

We can select almost any topic discussed in this text and potentially explain behavior differences between people in terms of how their information-processing systems are functioning. Our goal in this chapter is to make you aware of the changes that our sensory and perceptual processes undergo through adulthood so that you can understand the implications of these changes for everyday living.

SENSATION

When we speak of *sensation,* we are simply referring to sensory experience at the receptor level, such as the experience of pain, taste, or temperature. That is, some form of stimulation has been registered by the *sensory receptors*.

Each of the primary senses responds to particular types of stimuli and is associated with a specific type of receptor. These are listed in Table 4.1.

When researchers discuss the change in the senses from early adulthood to old age, they often make reference to the **absolute threshold.** An absolute threshold is the minimum level of stimulus energy or intensity required for one to detect the stimulation. Examples of absolute thresholds for the various senses are presented in Table 4.2. Related to absolute threshold is the **difference threshold,** which is the degree to which a stimulus such as sound or light must be louder or brighter to be perceived as such.

Most research reported in this section has utilized cross-sectional designs, and in light of the methodological problems inherent in such approaches (see Chapter 2), we urge you to be cautious about overgeneralizing the age-differences data to reflect age changes. We also want to stress that there are individual differences within and between groups of young

TABLE 4.1

CLASSIFICATION OF SENSORY SYSTEMS IN TERMS OF THE TYPES OF STIMULI TO WHICH THEY RESPOND

Stimulus	Sense	Receptors
Electromagnetic energy	Vision	Rods and cones in retina
Mechanical energy		
Sound waves	Audition	Hair cells in the basilar membrane, inner ear
Displacement of skin pressure	Skin senses	Various types in skin and tissues
Movement of joints	Kinesthetic body sense	Nerve endings in tendons, muscles, and joints
Gravity, acceleration	Vestibular body sense	Hair cells in semicircular canals of ear
Thermal	Skin senses	Various types in skin and tissues
Chemical substances		
Dissolved in saliva	Taste	Taste buds on the tongue
Molecules in air	Olfaction (smell)	Cells in upper nasal cavity

Source: R. E. Smith, I. G. Sarason, & B. R. Sarason. (1982). *Psychology: The frontiers of behavior* (2d ed.). New York: Harper & Row. p. 132.

TABLE 4.2

APPROXIMATE ABSOLUTE THRESHOLDS FOR SELECTED SENSES

Sense Modality	Absolute Threshold
Vision	Candle flame seen at 30 miles on a clear, dark night
Hearing	Tick of a watch under quiet conditions at 20 feet
Taste	1 teaspoon of sugar in 2 gallons of water
Smell	1 drop of perfume diffused into the entire volume of a large apartment
Touch	Wing of a fly or bee falling on your cheek from a distance of 1 centimeter

Source: R. E. Smith, I. G. Sarason, & B. R. Sarason. (1982). *Psychology: The frontiers of behavior* (2d ed.). New York: Harper & Row. p. 144.

and old individuals on many of the abilities and processes discussed in this chapter (Hoyer, 1974).

Sensory Processes

VISION

Of all of our sensory processes, we probably obtain the most information about our world through the visual system. Therefore, as we discuss vision, think of the impact that visual declines might have upon your ability to interpret what you see, as well as your everyday behavior. For instance, what effect would decreased vision have on your reading, driving, or interacting with others? While the extent of visual impairment does vary from person to person, it is quite likely that you will eventually experience visual impairment sufficient to require treatment or influence your daily activities (Kline & Schieber, 1985). The loss of vision is the second most feared consequence of aging, next to cancer (Verrillo & Verrillo, 1985). Current estimates suggest that there are 2 million adults over the age of 65 who are visually impaired; by the year 2000, this figure could reach 2.5 million (Nelson, 1987). In addition, visual impairment is not uncommon during middle adulthood.

Age differences in visual functioning are the result of two types of changes in the structure of the eye (Fozard et al., 1977; McFarland, 1968). The first type is related to transmissiveness—the ability of light to pass through—and accommodative—adjustment or focus. These changes begin between the ages of 35 and 45 and influence visual functions such as distance vision, sensitivity to glare, depth perception, and color sensitivity.

The second type of changes concerns the retina and usually occurs between 55 to 65 years of age (Panek et al., 1977). These affect the metabolism of the retina and influence the size of the visual field, sensitivity to low levels of light, and sensitivity to flicker.

Structural Changes in the Visual System With normal aging, a number of visual structures undergo change. In most instances, peak visual functioning occurs during late adolescence or early adulthood, is fairly constant through adulthood, and then begins to decline during one's late fifties and early sixties. These changes can influence both the quality and quantity of visual information available to the individual. In some cases, these changes, if they are severe or untreatable, can force people to change their life-styles or change jobs. Thus, the adequacy of our visual system is a topic of more than academic importance. To facilitate our discussion, an illustration of the structure of the eye is presented in Figure 4.2.

Beginning in early adulthood, many of the eye structures begin to change, causing some loss of efficiency and effectiveness in functioning (Kline & Schieber, 1985; Verrillo & Verrillo, 1985). However, decrements in our vision are often so gradual that we do not notice the changes until our fifties or sixties. And since there are individual differences in the magnitude of these changes, you may or may not experience them as rapidly as someone else.

Some of these changes are as follows: (1) the lens of the eye gets thicker and yellows, which results in less light being projected onto the retina; (2) the ciliary muscle gets weaker, which affects the focusing capability of the lens; and (3) the iris loses pigmentation, resulting in a lack of luster in eye color. These changes are considered normal aging processes.

In addition, there are a number of visual disorders associated with the structures of the eye, which can occur at any age and significantly affect vision. Some of these disorders are the result of normal aging processes, while others are caused by pathological disease processes or physical in-

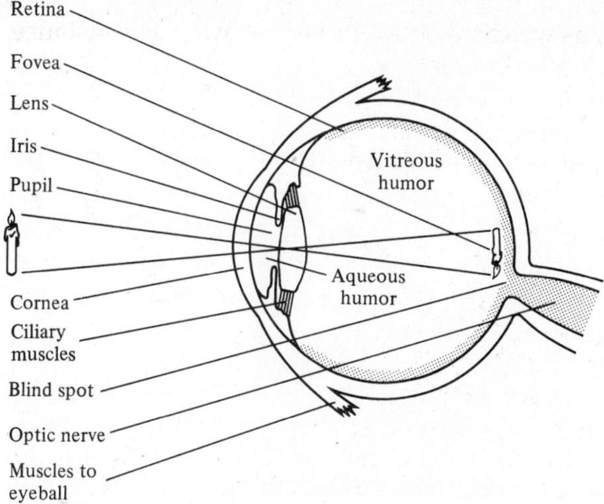

Figure 4.2 Cross section of the eye. *Source:* R. E. Smith, I. G. Sarason, & B. R. Sarason. (1982). *Psychology: The frontiers of behavior* (2d ed.). New York: Harper & Row. Reprinted by permission. p. 133.

jury. For example, diabetes is a major cause of blindness for individuals at all age levels. In addition, cataracts and glaucoma are often problems for older people, particularly if these diseases are left untreated.

CHANGES IN VISUAL ABILITIES WITH AGING

Absolute threshold for vision refers to how bright an object must be in order to be seen. Older individuals require a greater intensity of light—higher illumination—than younger individuals to detect a stimulus (McFarland, 1968; Verrillo & Verrillo, 1985). In other words, one's absolute threshold increases with age. Perhaps the most important consequence of this increase has to do with the mobility of older people when it is dark. Generally speaking, as we get older we also require higher levels of illumination to perform most visual activities, including reading. Moreover, since many older adults do not see well in the dark, they are often afraid to go anywhere at night. Driving a car, reading street signs, or recognizing the faces of family or friends may become more difficult. Thus, due to the difficulty of seeing at night, many older adults become homebound in the evening, which limits their interactions with friends and family.

Difference thresholds also increase with age, making it more difficult to distinguish between brightnesses of light (e.g., a 60-watt versus a 75-watt bulb). This inability to discriminate may result in lower levels of ambient light, which also interferes with tasks such as reading. **Accommodation** is the process whereby the eye adjusts itself in order to attain clarity. The accommodation process involves an adjustment of the ciliary muscle, which changes the refractive power of the lens by altering its focal length. The outcome of this process is the eye's ability to alternately focus near and far and to discriminate detail.

Driving is an activity that is affected by changes in our visual system.

With increasing age, there is a decrease in the ability of the eye to focus on objects at varying distances (Panek et al., 1977). The most common manifestation of this process is a decline in the eye's ability to focus on near objects. This is termed **presbyopia** and results mainly from a loss of elasticity in the lens. This is why many individuals in late middle age start to need glasses for reading, or for working with objects that are close to them. Many times, farsighted individuals must hold objects farther away from them so that they can read or see. For this reason, it is common for older people to say, "My arms have gotten shorter as I've gotten older!"

In addition, with increased age, the time required for refocusing, or changing focus from near to far, increases. One major implication of the increased time required for accommodation pertains to driving skills. While driving on a highway, drivers must constantly focus on the instrument panel (near), monitor vehicles immediately in front of them (near), then refocus on exit signs and autos in the distance (far), and then refocus on objects that are near again. Since a longer time is often required to refocus with advancing age, many older drivers may accidentally miss important signs (Panek & Reardon, 1987). They may compensate for this increased accommodation time by driving more slowly.

Visual acuity refers to the eye's ability to resolve detail and is most often equated with the accuracy of distance vision compared with that of a "hypothetical normal person." Anyone who has taken an eye examination is probably familiar with how visual acuity is measured by means of a chart, called the Snellen chart, which is a standardized series of letters, numbers, or symbols that must be read from a distance of 20 feet. The ability to read this chart is termed *static visual acuity.* Each line of the chart contains letters of a different size, which correspond to the standard distance at which the letters on that line can be distinguished by a person of normal vision. For example, if an individual with normal vision can read a designated letter on the Snellen chart at a distance of 20 feet, this is called

20/20 vision. A person who can distinguish at only 20 feet a letter that a person of normal vision can distinguish at 100 feet is said to have a visual acuity of 20/100.

Studies of visual acuity across the life span show that visual acuity tends to be relatively poor in young children, improves in young adulthood, and follows a slight decline from the mid-twenties to the fifties. Beyond this point, the rate of decline is accelerated (Colavita, 1978; Panek et al., 1977). The average acuity of individuals over age 65 is 20/70. This decrease in visual acuity can easily be simulated by putting on a pair of clear glasses that have a piece of wax paper placed over the lenses.

There are also clear age decrements in dynamic visual acuity (Long & Crambert, 1990). *Dynamic visual acuity* refers to the ability to accurately identify a moving target, such as a television message, a weather warning, or a street sign seen from a moving car. The more quickly the target is moving, the more disadvantaged older people are relative to younger ones. The deficit with age in dynamic visual acuity appears to be related to changes in the thickness of the lens and the size of the pupil. It is for this reason that providing more ambient light, or making objects larger and more distinct, seems to lessen the older person's difficulty, as does slowing down the moving object to be identified (Long & Crambert, 1990).

There are many manifestations of decreased visual acuity with advanced age, such as greater difficulty in reading, watching television, reading instructions on medicine bottles, driving, and reading a newspaper. Imagine how much less you would learn if you could read only the headings in a textbook or the headlines in a newspaper! For middle-aged and older employees, providing more ambient light to work by can be critical, especially if one is working with moving parts. Consider the implications of not being able to "read the fine print" for an older customer signing a contract, or for the senior lawyer who must determine its accuracy or legality. In driving situations, simply illuminating the road more completely can help older drivers compensate for deficits in both static and dynamic visual acuity. Although visual acuity clearly worsens with age, most people maintain fair acuity—at least 20/40—well into their eighties (Gittings & Fozard, 1986).

Color vision refers to the faculty by which colors are perceived and distinguished. The registration and detection of color is due to light-sensitive cells in the retina of the eye called *cones*. Cones are employed primarily in daylight vision and are concentrated in the center of the retina in an area called the fovea (see Figure 4.2 again).

What limited research is available on color vision suggests that with increased age, there is increased difficulty in discriminating among the blues, blue-greens, and violets—the low to middle range of the visible light spectrum—and much better successes in discriminating among the reds, oranges, and yellows, the upper middle to high range of the visible light spectrum (Kausler, 1991). Color vision deficits are more apparent when levels of illumination are low and when fine discriminations in shades of blue and green are being made, as when one wants to match a tie and a coat (Fozard, 1990). The consequences of distortions in color vision are minor compared with those of other visual functions. It can, however, be embarrassing to come to work with clothes that don't match!

Adaptation is defined as the change in the sensitivity of the eye as a function of change in illumination. There are two types of adaptation: *dark adaptation,* the improvement in sensitivity to light in a dark environment, and *light adaptation,* the increased sensitivity to light in a light environment. For example, when you enter a dark movie theater, your pupils will automatically expand in order to increase the amount of light entering your eyes. This process takes about 30 seconds. The reverse happens when you leave the theater, that is, your pupils will automatically contract to cut down the amount of light entering your eyes. This process requires a shorter time than does dark adaptation.

The time required for both of these processes increases with age (Kline & Schieber, 1985). The primary consequence of this change is that it will make you more susceptible to environmental hazards during the first few minutes of being in a differently illuminated environment. For example, coming out of a theater into bright sunlight may temporarily blind you, to the point where you stumble off the curb. If one is older, there might also be a greater tendency to experience snow blindness. In both cases, falling is a real possibility, the consequence of which can be very serious for people in their fifties, sixties, or seventies.

Relatively bright light that results in unpleasantness or discomfort and/or interferes with optimum vision is termed *glare.* Glare is produced when light rays are diffused via a change in the composition of the vitreous humor (see again Figure 4.2). The most vivid examples of this process occur during night driving when drivers shine their high beams at your car and when you are reading material printed on glossy paper.

The effects of glare on visual performance increase with age, with greater deterioration of performance from age 40 on (Burg, 1976). With regard to driving, the longer vision is affected by glare, the less information from the environment can be detected and the greater the potential for one's attention to the road to be disrupted. We have all experienced the glare created by diffusion of light from an oncoming car's headlights, but for middle-aged and older drivers, this temporary blindness can easily cause an accident.

The visual field is defined as the extent of physical space visible to an eye in a given position—the whole area you see when your head is in a fixed position. The peripheral field is the outer area of your overall visual field. The peripheral field shrinks several degrees per decade after age 45 (Kline & Schieber, 1985). For example, the overall visual field for a young adult is typically 170 degrees. By age 50, it has decreased to approximately 140 degrees (Kline & Schieber, 1985; Panek et al., 1977) and continues to decrease with advancing age. It is as though one has blinders on. The more your visual field is restricted, the more you must turn your head to see what you used to see "out of the corner of your eye," with your peripheral vision.

Are there everyday parallels to the visual changes we have discussed? In a unique study, Kosnik et al. (1988) asked over 400 adults, aged

With increased age, we become more sensitive to glare. This may interfere with many daily activities, such as shopping.

18 to 100, questions about the visual difficulties they experienced on a daily basis. Older adults reported having more difficulty processing visual stimuli quickly, and being more sensitive to glare and inadequate illumination. They had difficulty in reading small print, locating and reading signs, and reading signs on moving vehicles. Middle-aged adults, however, reported having more difficulty in adapting to bright lights and reported more eye strain. Each visual difficulty changed at varying rates. Visual slowness, seeing in a dim environment, and near vision problems increased with age most frequently, while visual search and dynamic vision difficulties increased with age more gradually. Such difficulties undoubtedly affect everyday activities such as driving, shopping, reading, sewing, and reading music.

One can readily comprehend the difficulty experienced by people who have visual problems in performing simple, routine tasks we tend to take for granted. For those whose vision has always been good, such effects may be particularly distressing—they may cook, watch TV, or listen to their favorite music less, or be more fearful in social situations due to their inability to process new facial features or remember old ones.

In extreme cases, where full or partial blindness has been caused by disease or injury, and in cases where visual changes are more gradual and age-related, adults and their families face a number of difficulties. These difficulties are likely to be greater for those whose sight has been good in the past. For example, being labeled developmentally disabled can significantly affect one's views about the ability to function independently and care for oneself. Contacts with sighted peers are often adversely affected, leading to isolation (Vernon, 1989). Needs for support services, accessible health care, and transportation increase. Having to wear bifocals, some people even feel less attractive (Whitbourne, 1985). On the other hand, one may come to understand the needs of visually impaired people more clearly. In many respects, visually impaired people are very much like those who still have their sight (*Aging & Vision News*, 1990); in fact, their ability, not their disability, becomes a focus for their interactions with others.

Because visual changes are so gradual, individuals usually do not notice them and so they may not seek professional help to correct these deficits. Tragically, some older individuals who do realize their visual abilities have declined may not seek professional help because they feel these changes are just signs of getting old; that is, they think their vision is supposed to get worse. They may also believe that because declines signal aging, these deficits cannot be corrected. And in some cases, people simply deny changes until circumstances force them to acknowledge that there is a problem—after they have an automobile accident or accidentally take an overdose of medication. However, many such changes can be corrected or prevented via routine eye examinations.

Intervention Techniques The older individual experiencing visual impairments can be helped in many ways (Shore, 1976). For example, many books and newspapers are now printed in large type, and talking books are also available. Large numbers on rooms, clocks, and elevator doors can facilitate the functioning of visually impaired older adults. Color coding of rooms, floors, and steps can be helpful. Illuminating halls and stairways well may help people avoid falls. The use of flat paints versus enamels may help to reduce glare. As obvious as it sounds, getting prescription glasses and turning up the light without creating glare can remedy things a great deal!

Perhaps the most effective strategy to deal with visual problems is preventive—educating adults about the importance of having regular eye exams, so that diseases like glaucoma can be treated before their effects are irreversible. In this way, too, prescriptions can be checked to make sure that they still match the individual's visual capacity. In light of the necessity for the individual to find a new identity as a visually impaired person, the support of his or her family is very important (Ainlay, 1981; Moore, 1984).

CHANGES IN AUDITION WITH AGING

Audition With aging, we rely on audition, or our hearing sense, to obtain information about our surroundings. Alarm clocks wake us; the phone rings. If our hearing is impaired, we may oversleep or miss an important call. If we cannot hear well, our communication with others is also disrupted. If for no other than these obvious reasons, it is important to understand that changes in auditory functioning are part of aging. Changes in ability to hear are a function of both normal aging processes and external forces such as exposure to high levels of noise.

The ability to hear decreases quite dramatically across the life span, to the point that by late adulthood, many individuals have some form of hearing disorder (Olsho et al., 1985). Age changes in hearing ability are often characterized as progressive, irreversible, and detrimental to successful adaptation and interaction in the later years (Olsho et al., 1985). In a sample of normal older adults, using standard criteria for the definition of hearing impairment, 46 percent were hearing impaired (Thomas et al., 1983).

The most common auditory disorder of older adults is **presbycusis.** Presbycusis is a progressive bilateral (meaning both ears) loss of hearing for tones of high frequency due to changes in the auditory system. Thirteen percent or more of older adults show signs of presbycusis, which suggests the need for expanding existing audiological services for the aged.

The human auditory system consists primarily of two subsystems, which interact: (1) the structural system—outer ear and inner ear, and (2) the neural pathways—auditory nuclei and fiber tracts. Figure 4.3 illustrates the structures of the auditory system.

Outer, Middle, and Inner Ear With aging, there are a number of changes in the structure of the outer, middle, and inner ear that may have implications for receiving auditory information. The pinna, a structure in the outer ear, becomes hard and inflexible, and may change in size and shape (Olsho et al., 1985). There may also be an increase in wax buildup. The functional significance of these changes, if any, has not been investigated.

The two primary structures of the middle ear are the eustachian tube and the ossicular chain. Often, people have an accumulation of fluid in the middle ear due to an obstruction in the eustachian tube. The cause of this

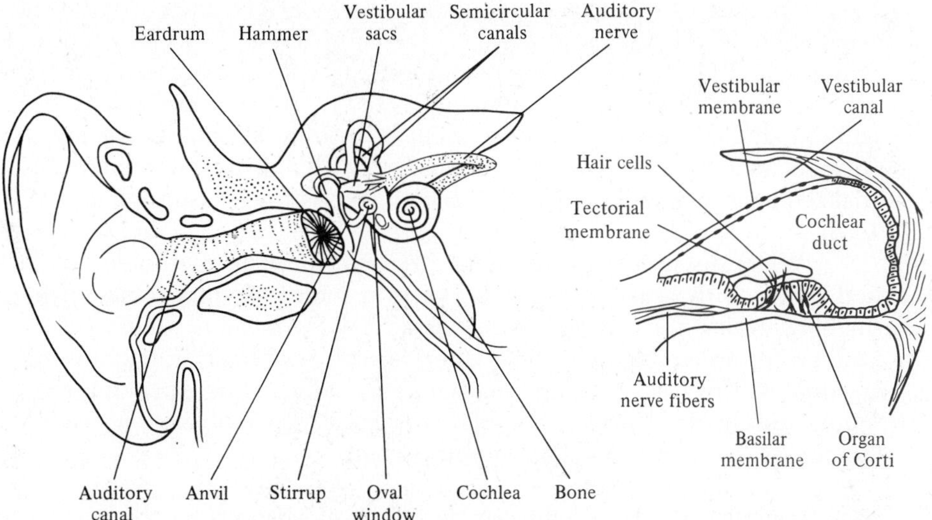

Figure 4.3 A cross section of the ear showing the structures that transmit sound waves from the auditory canal to the cochlea. There they stimulate hair cells in the organ of corti. The resulting nerve impulses reach the brain via the auditory nerve. The semicircular and vestibular sacs of the inner ear contain sense organs for equilibrium. *Source:* R. E. Smith, I. G. Sarason, & B. R. Sarason. (1982). *Psychology: The frontiers of behavior* (2d ed.). New York: Harper & Row. p. 140. Reprinted by permission.

blockage is usually a cold, and hearing difficulties will be present as long as the tube remains closed. Regarding the ossicular chain, there are arthritic changes in the middle-ear joints with aging (Whitbourne, 1985). While arthritic changes become more severe over time, they do not appear to impair sound transmission through the middle ear.

Schuknecht and Igaraski (1964) suggest there are four general types of disorder observed as a function of age in the structures of the inner ear: (1) atrophy and degeneration of hair cells in the cochlea, called *sensory presbycusis,* (2) loss of auditory neurons, called *neural presbycusis,* (3) changes in the supply of nutrients to the cochlea, called *metabolic presbycusis,* and (4) atrophic changes in the cochlear partition, called *mechanical presbycusis.*

Each of these types of disorders shows a characteristic hearing pattern. Sensory presbycusis produces a high-frequency hearing loss that does not involve the speech frequencies. Neural presbycusis affects speech discrimination without an accompanying loss in pure-tone thresholds. With metabolic presbycusis, there is a nearly uniform threshold loss for all frequencies. Finally, mechanical presbycusis produces increasing hearing loss from low to high frequencies.

Absolute Threshold There is a loss in the ability to hear higher frequencies of sound that occurs as part of the normal aging process. It has been estimated that 70 percent of all individuals over age 50 have some type of hearing loss (Anderson et al., 1969; Olsho et al., 1985). Men seem to experience hearing loss to a greater extent as they get older than do women (Whitbourne, 1985).

The rate of this loss depends on several factors, including (1) the population of individuals studied, (2) the cumulative history of exposure to noise, and (3) the population's homogeneity with respect to hereditary and environmental factors (Bergman, 1971a, 1971b). For example, cross-cultural studies indicate less decrement in hearing sensitivity for higher frequencies with normal aging in nonindustrialized cultures than in industrialized ones, due to less exposure to high levels of noise (see Baltes et al., 1988).

When discussing the absolute threshold for hearing in older adults and others with hearing disorders, keep in mind the importance of the ongoing level of noise in the environment. That is, the more noise in which your words are embedded, the greater difficulty the hearing impaired individual will have in hearing what you are saying. Thus, speaking more loudly and clearly, especially in noisy situations such as a party, or seeking a quiet area in which to talk is very important.

Pitch Discrimination The ability to detect small changes in the pitch of sounds not only is important for listeners and performers of music but is also an important factor in the perception of speech. Since presbycusis involves high-pitched tone hearing loss, pitch discrimination is poorest for those consonants that have higher frequency components in their acoustic patterns (Corso, 1977). Older adults may be unable to discriminate between phonetically similar words, and thus they may have problems in following normal conversation, especially in noisy environments. Because women's voices are more highly pitched, conversation with them in noisy situations is especially difficult. Although this difficulty in speech discrimination is well documented (Olsho et al., 1985; Whitbourne, 1985), its cause is still in question.

Hearing Loss and Exposure to Noise There is a strong relationship between excessive noise exposure and permanent hearing loss for people of all ages (Corso, 1977; Kryter, 1970). The basic question seems to be whether hearing loss due to noise exposure and age is additive or interactive. That is, is hearing loss due to constant and repeated amounts of excessive noise (additive), or is it due to the contribution of many factors, each of which contributes to eventual hearing loss (interactive)? Overall, research suggests that the effects of age and noise exposure are independent and nonadditive. This implies that hearing loss can be attributed to external noise factors alone, or to age factors alone; and that in most instances the effects of external noise are more pronounced than those of normal aging. In fact, Corso (1977) terms the damaging effects of repeated noise exposure *premature presbycusis.* For this reason, many industries require workers, such as municipal street workers and airport baggage handlers, to wear protective ear plugs. In light of this fact, you should consider the long-term consequences of listening to a car stereo or portable radio turned up to nearly full volume.

RELATIONSHIP BETWEEN SPEECH AND HEARING

As you would expect, any serious impairment of hearing will probably produce a problem in speech communication. That is, hearing disorders may lead to speech disorders, which will eventually lead to decreases in normal verbal and social interaction. For example, if people have to speak quite loudly for you to hear, they may not want to interact with you at a social gathering if they feel embarrassed by talking loudly. In turn, you may avoid conversations with others, causing you to feel less confident and more isolated. Therefore, hearing disorders can affect the social and psychological adjustment of people at any age, but this is especially so during later adulthood (Whitbourne, 1985).

Speech Comprehension In a recent review of research, Stine et al. (1989) discuss "on-line" speech processing. How we process what is said to us in a conversation is "on-line." Unlike reading, the input for what we hear is sequential; that is, the listener must attend to every word if what is said is to be accurately understood (Stine et al., 1989). Words must be recognized and a context for understanding must be constructed (Fozard, 1990). For adults with uncorrected, age-related hearing loss, the basic sound information needed for processing and understanding is distorted, resulting in faulty reception and understanding of speech. Even when speech is rapid, older adults are able to effectively select longer segments of words to compensate for the increased rate at which speech must be processed (Stine et al., 1989). This seems to enable them to compensate for a deficit, more common among older adults, in processing individual words or word elements.

For people with hearing disorders, therapeutic approaches run the continuum, from hearing aids and medical-surgical procedures, to rehabilitative therapy programs, depending on the nature and extent of the hearing disorder as well as the age of the individual (Olsho et al., 1985). Two rehabilitation programs widely used with older adults whose level of hearing impairment is not classified as severe are speech reading, or lip reading, and auditory training. Both these procedures are based on the integration of both visual and auditory information. Speech reading is a skill that enables someone to understand language by carefully observing the speaker's lips move. The technique is widely practiced by older adults as a compensatory adjustment to the effects of hearing loss. Auditory training involves the client attending to certain key sounds or words in a conversation while simultaneously watching the speaker's lips move.

Interestingly, although hearing rehabilitation procedures can be effective with older adults, they tend to be underutilized, for three reasons. First, although most older adults with speech and hearing problems believe they need professional assistance, many feel they do not have the time, money, or motivation to attend rehabilitation programs. Some older adults may not have the money to pay for aural rehabilitation if they do not even have enough money to pay for more basic necessities. Second, the staff of such programs may sometimes see older adults as being dependent and incapable of managing themselves. Thus, they alienate the individuals they hope to treat by talking down to them, as they would to young children. Finally, older adults are often targets of unscrupulous individuals who attempt to portray themselves as insurance agents, investment counselors, and health professionals. Consequently, older people often regard health professionals, and others, with distrust. However, while these are certainly major concerns in older adults' use of these services, we should be cautious about overgeneralizing to all service providers or all aged individuals.

Language and Voice Impairments There are four major classifications of speech disorders: (1) articulation, excessive repetition of phonemes, or sound substitutions; (2) stuttering; (3) voice, where the processes of phonation and resonation are altered with deviations in pitch, loudness, and vocal quality; and (4) symbolization, or aphasia, the inability to associate meaning with language symbols in a normal manner (Bergman, 1980; Obler & Albert, 1985).

These disorders are found in people of all ages and may stem from vascular insufficiency, neoplasms (tumors), trauma, stroke, or progressive degenerative illnesses. Their incidence, especially that of aphasia, however, increases with advanced age as a result of strokes and cardiovascular conditions (Obler & Albert, 1985).

Changes in the communication processes of older adults are not restricted to language and hearing impairments, but may also involve the acoustic characteristics of the voice. Specifically, the frequency range becomes smaller, vocal intensity is decreased, and voice quality is impoverished, depending on the kind and extent of organic changes that have occurred in the larynx (Benjamin, 1981, 1982).

EFFECTS OF AUDITORY CHANGES

Hearing plays an important part in our communication with others. Thus, it should not be surprising to find that decrements with advancing age cause some older adults to experience social and/or emotional disturbances (Campanelli, 1968). The magnitude of adjustment problems experienced by individuals with hearing disorders is directly related to the severity of the hearing disorder and the time of its inception—at what age it began. That is, the later hearing loss begins in life, and the greater its severity, the greater the adjustment problems individuals experience (Corso, 1977). Probable consequences in such cases are the following: (1) not being able to hear adequately leads to lower self-concept, and (2) not being able to hear adequately leads to feelings of paranoia—"Are those people talking about me?" (Eisdorfer & Stotsky, 1977; Whitbourne, 1985) (see Figure 4.4).

The hearing-impaired aged individual is often pictured as withdrawn, insecure, depressed, confused, and isolated (Thomas et al., 1983). A research study dramatizing this point is that of Eisdorfer (1960), who administered a projective personality test, the Rorschach (see Chapter 8), to 48 community-living older adults, who were divided into six groups on the basis of three visual and two auditory levels of functioning. Eisdorfer found that there were substantial differences in personality between older adults with normal hearing and those with impaired hearing. Individuals reacted to hearing loss by withdrawal and increased rigidity of personality

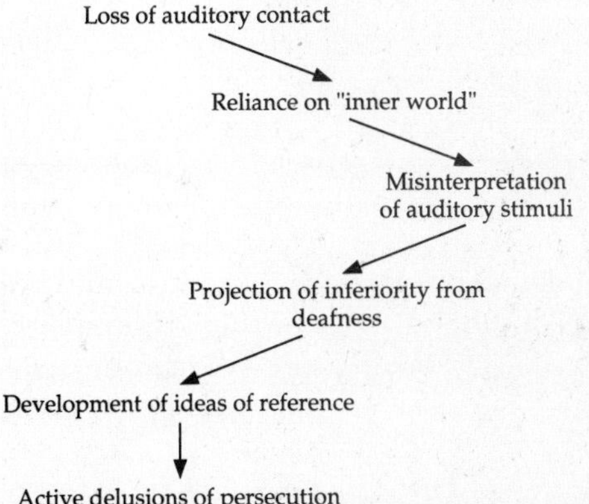

Figure 4.4 Hypothetical link between deafness and paranoid reactions. *Source:* Kermis. (1984). p. 273.

(Eisdorfer, 1960). This study suggests that the effects of hearing disability, especially with aging, are at least as dramatic as are the effects of visual impairment.

Although it makes common sense to believe that hearing deficits have severe effects on people, these effects are not clear-cut. They depend on a number of factors, such as the seriousness of the problem, its locus, age of onset, and support from others.

Thomas et al. (1983) investigated the relationship between untreated hearing deficits, emotional state, cognitive functioning, and social interaction in otherwise healthy older adults. These researchers could not find any negative effects of uncorrected hearing impairment on the person's emotional status, memory, or social interaction.

On the other hand, Granick et al. (1976) and Ohta et al. (1981) have reported a significant relationship between hearing loss and intellectual functioning in older adults, and this appears to be greater for verbal intellectual measures than for nonverbal intellectual measures. This finding has recently been confirmed using longitudinal data by Sands and Meredith (1989), who studied middle-aged and older adults. Having impaired hearing of course alters the input we use to enhance our verbal skills.

It is important to realize that the difference in results between these studies vividly illustrates many of the factors discussed in Chapter 2 on research methods. For example, the differences among these studies may be partially attributed to sampling differences, as well as to differences in the measures of intellectual functioning utilized. The contradiction highlights the need for additional research regarding the extent and effects of

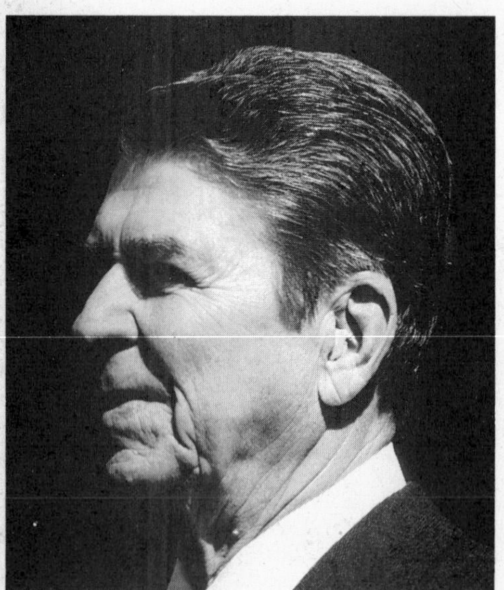

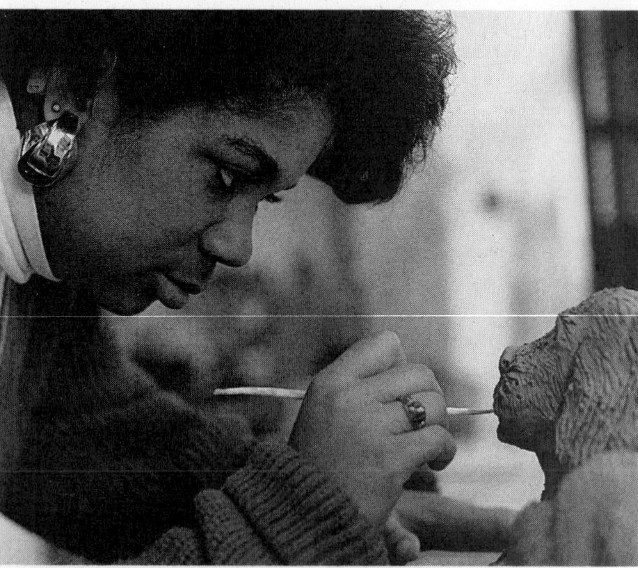

Wearing a hearing aid that is unobtrusive helps many adults cope with hearing loss, yet it does not interfere with their relationships with others.

hearing disorders on the well-being and everyday functioning of individuals in adulthood.

Patience and support from one's spouse and children are critical in both the adjustment to hearing loss and its rehabilitation (Ashley, 1985). It is important here to distinguish between a measured hearing loss, via an audiometer, and a conversational hearing loss that is obvious to the individual or others. For example, if hearing loss is progressive and mild, the individual may adapt to the problem. But some middle-aged and older adults play down their hearing loss or minimize its effects on others by concealing a hearing aid. That perceptions of hearing loss and hearing aids are negative supports education as a means of coping with such denial (Elliott, 1987) (see Box 4.1).

Intervention Techniques Many things can be done to help adults who have hearing impairments. Shore (1976) suggests numerous methods for improving the everyday communication skills of such older adults. One example is facing the individual directly and speaking slowly and distinctly; this allows the listener to lip-read. Also, facial expressions and arm and hand movements help communicate information. It may also be helpful to

BOX 4.1

DO YOU HAVE A HEARING LOSS?

The American Association of Retired Persons (1984) recommends these simple tests as indicators of mild hearing loss. Early detection and treatment are very timely!

1. *Sit down, cross your feet, and rub your shoes together.* Rubbing your shoes together makes a very soft sound, similar to a whisper. If you can't hear this you may have borderline normal hearing ability or a mild hearing loss.
2. *Listen to your watch. (No digital watches please.)* You should be able to hear your watch when it is held close to your ear. If you can't, this may indicate that you have a mild hearing loss for certain pitches.
3. *How many times this week have you said, "I wish they would stop mumbling"? (Aloud, or to yourself.)* Frequently the loudness level (intensity) of speech seems fine, but it's not as clear as it used to be.
4. *Have someone else adjust the volume on a radio or television, so that it's pleasing to that person, then listen.* Do you have to strain to hear it at all? Your response to an irritated, "Are you deaf?" is probably "No!" but you may have a hearing loss that could disrupt communication with others. Conversely, there may be some sounds that seem painfully loud.
5. *Adjust the water faucet so it drips, and listen.* You may have a mild hearing loss if you can't hear the dripping water.
6. *When you are driving with someone else in heavy traffic, roll the window down and continue your conversation.* For many of us conversation becomes more difficult when there is a noisy background. Noise interference reduces listening effectiveness.
7. *When you are talking with someone, close your eyes and see if your ears "close" too.*
8. *When you are talking on the phone, switch the phone from ear to ear to judge if conversation sounds the same.*
9. *Have you avoided restaurants, theaters, or social functions?*
10. *Has anyone complained because you have failed to answer the doorbell or the telephone?*

Source: Have you heard? *Hearing Loss and Aging.* AARP (1984, pp. 7–9).

carry a paper and pencil for communication purposes. Other suggestions involve avoiding background noise and providing clues to create a context for understanding. Because people with hearing loss are sometimes ashamed, they may make matters worse by shouting or monopolizing the conversation. They do not inform others of the importance of speaking clearly and not shouting, and do not get others' attention before speaking (American Association of Retired Persons, 1984).

TASTE AND SMELL

Interestingly, although we are exposed to numerous tastes and smells every day, we know comparatively little about what exactly happens to these abilities as we age. Results of studies regarding age differences vary as a function of the method employed to assess taste and smell, as well as the substance investigated. Therefore, many of the facts presented in this section will lack consistent research support.

Our taste (gustatory system) and smell (olfactory system) sensitivities function interactively. For example, when you have a cold and your nose is stuffed up, you are often unable to taste your food. However, for presentation purposes, we will discuss these two systems separately.

Taste Humans are able to detect four basic taste qualities: sweet, salty, bitter, and sour. Figure 4.5 illustrates a taste bud and the location of the taste buds for each taste quality on the tongue. While research has attempted to determine what happens to our ability to detect these taste qualities with age, the evidence presents a paradox. This is the apparent discrepancy between objective assessments of older adults' ability to taste in the laboratory, and their subjective reports regarding their inability to taste food in everyday situations. It may be only when sensitivity is drastically altered that the objective and subjective aspects of taste coincide. In

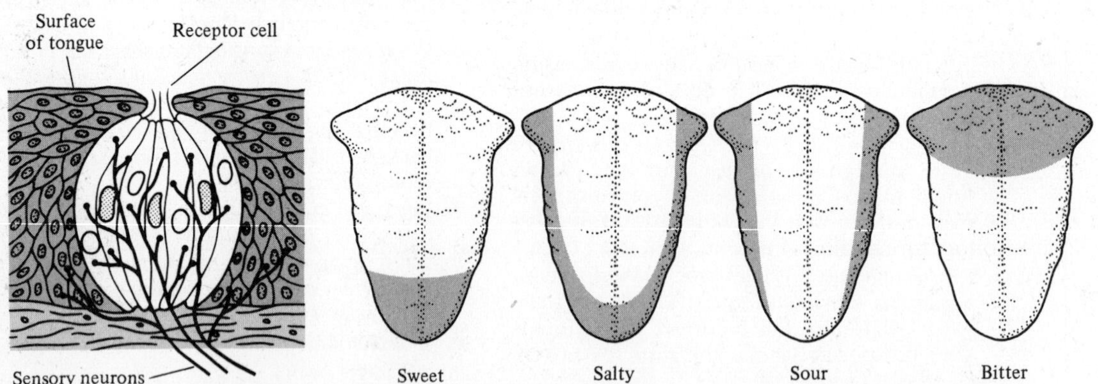

Figure 4.5 The receptors for taste are specialized cells located in taste buds in the tongue. The taste buds are grouped in different areas of the tongue according to the taste sensation to which they respond. The center of the tongue is relatively insensitive to taste qualities. *Source:* R. E. Smith, I. G. Sarason, & B. R. Sarason. (1982). *Psychology: The frontiers of behavior.* (2d ed.). New York: Harper & Row. p. 141. Reprinted by permission.

tasting food, cues regarding shape, color, odor, and of course knowledge of the food itself come into play (Bischmann & Witte, 1990).

Laboratory studies in this area have used various procedures to determine the so-called concentration threshold necessary for a participant to identify a certain taste quality. For example, what concentration level of sucrose is required to make a solution taste sweet to the individual? The keener the sensitivity, the lower the concentration threshold.

Structural Changes in the Taste System As we age, the basic structure of our taste system changes. El-Baradi and Bourne (1951) report a gradual decrease in the number of taste buds with increasing age. It appears that the taste buds become fully developed in early adolescence and remain relatively unchanged until the mid-forties, when signs of atrophy begin to appear. Harris (1952) estimated that as many as two-thirds of the papillae atrophy by old age.

Additional age changes include loss of elasticity in the mouth and lips, decrease in the flow of saliva, and fissuring of the tongue. Although these changes may appear to be important, they do not seriously affect taste sensitivity until relatively late in life, if at all. Weiffenback et al. (1990) found little evidence for oral sensory change except pressure sensitivity of the tongue. Others have found that sensitivity to the four taste qualities remains fairly constant and unimpaired until the late fifties, followed by a sharp decline in all four qualities (Engen, 1977; Whitbourne, 1985).

The discussion above implies that applied research in taste sensitivity is difficult to do. For example, older adults often report in experimental laboratory situations that they can taste and differentiate among all four qualities. Yet eating later at a restaurant, it would not be uncommon for the same people to state that the food is tasteless, does not contain enough salt, or is too salty.

Of course, severely diminished taste sensitivity could result in malnutrition (Whitbourne, 1985). However, due to the discrepancy in findings from the laboratory and in the real world, we now understand that food complaints and taste aberrations are in part the result of psychosocial influences. That is, the high incidence of food complaints among older people is based, not on sensory decrements, but on factors such as problems in personal adjustment, attitudes toward self, or feelings of abandonment. This explanation appears to make sense, since eating is such a social event in our culture. Isn't it more fun to eat with others rather than alone? Eating is often a time of social interaction, and companionship may be more important than the meal itself.

Recently, Spitzer (1988) has found that thresholds for sour, salt, and bitter increased with age, but that sweet remains constant. When institutionalized people were compared to noninstitutionalized age peers, it was found that taking prescription medication elevated sour thresholds in those who were institutionalized. Similarly, those who were on high blood pressure (hypertension) medications had higher salt-detection thresholds. Thus, medication and illness can often lead to a greater than normal decrease in taste sensitivity in older people (Schiffman, 1983; Spitzer, 1988).

Again, it is important to realize that elevated taste thresholds may not, however, mirror ability to discern the tastefulness of foods in real life (Spitzer, 1988). Instead, complaints about the ability to taste foods may indicate mild degrees of depression or side effects of medication prescribed for a health problem (Bischmann & Witte, 1990). Indeed, people who are depressed often have acute or chronic health difficulties that are being treated with medication. Those who are depressed may also complain more about their health (Bolla-Wilson & Bleecker, 1989).

Based on what we know at present, we cannot make recommendations that are of practical use for such things as diagnosing taste deficits or planning diets. Clearly, the possibility for such deficits must be recognized as a first step in designing any nutritional program for the aged. However, psychosocial influences such as isolation may undermine even the best efforts in this area.

Smell (Olfaction) Although there is a substantial amount of research on olfaction, very little of it is life-span in nature. It is also difficult to separate the effects of the interaction between olfactory and gustatory sensitivity.

Since the primary olfactory receptors are the neurons on the olfactory bulb, most research investigations have concentrated on studying the olfactory bulb and tract. Liss and Gomez (1958) found in postmortem examinations of aged individuals that changes in the olfactory bulb and tract are similar to those that occur in the central nervous system with age (see Chapter 3). That is, there is a generalized atrophy, with a moderate loss of neuronal elements. Yet, the severity of this loss was not correlated with age. In fact, these researchers reported that one individual over 100 years of age had only a mild loss of neurons. This suggests that damage to the olfactory bulb and tract are likely due to environmental factors, such as occupational odors, airborne toxic agents, and smoking, rather than age per se. If individuals who are isolated experience deficits, they may, for example, not pick up on body odors that may offend others, further contributing to their isolation (Whitbourne, 1985). There is some evidence suggesting that using olfactory abilities tends to preserve them (Engen, 1982). Clearly, however, deficits in olfactory sense can have some potentially disastrous consequences. As sensitivity to natural gas may be impaired with age (Chalke et al., 1958), gas leaks in the home would be a major safety concern, particularly for smokers.

AGE CHANGES IN TOUCH, VIBRATION, TEMPERATURE, KINESTHESIS, AND PAIN SENSITIVITY

Our sensitivities to touch, vibration, temperature, kinesthesis, and pain are collectively known as **somesthesis;** they arise from normal and intensive stimulations of the skin and viscera (Kenshalo, 1977). Age changes in somesthetic sensitivity can best be understood in terms of changes in the anatomical and physiological characteristics of the aging skin, muscles, joints, viscera, and nervous system. Age changes or differences in these senses vary as a function of the method used to assess them, and by the part of the body involved. For example, sensitivity of the feet starts to decrease at an earlier age than does that of the forearm (Kenshalo, 1977).

Touch Although we rely on our sense of touch every day, we know comparatively little about the effects of age on touch sensitivity. In addition, the absolute threshold for touch varies with the part of the body stimulated. In certain areas of the body, such as lips, tongue, and fingertips, touch receptors are more dense. If neural transmission is affected by damage to the brain, the lower part of the body may receive garbled messages, leading to less sensitivity. Touch sensitivity appears to remain relatively unchanged through about age 50 to 55, with a rise in the absolute threshold thereafter. This is usually attributed to a loss of touch receptors, but this explanation is still considered tentative (Whitbourne, 1985).

Vibratory Sensitivity For older adults, vibratory sensitivity differs by the part of the body stimulated. For example, vibratory sensitivity is better for the wrists, elbows, and shoulders than for the ankles, shins, and knees (Corso, 1971). It appears the lower extremities are more affected by age than the upper extremities. This loss may occur for several reasons: (1) inadequate blood supply to the spinal cord, which damages the nerve tracts; (2) a decline in the number of myelinated fibers in the spinal roots; (3) dietary factors, such as Vitamin B deficiency; and (4) diminished blood flow in peripheral structures of the body (Corso, 1971).

Temperature Sensitivity The *American Society of Heating, Refrigeration, and Air Conditioning for Engineers Handbook,* which sets standard conditions for comfort in heated and air-conditioned spaces, reports that the preferred temperature for people over 40 years is about 0.5 degrees higher than that desired by younger persons.

Although thermal comfort criteria may not change dramatically with advancing age, the ability of the temperature-regulating system among the elderly to cope with extreme environmental temperatures—both hot and cold—appears to be somewhat impaired. Apparently, older adults may not accurately detect how hot or cold it actually is and thus suffer physical or medical complications, such as hypothermia, heatstroke, and frostbite, more readily than younger adults. What has been found is that there is a slight rise with age in the absolute threshold for both cold and warmth (Whitbourne, 1985). But whether this is a genuine physiological change or due to psychosocial factors is not known.

Kinesthesis One of the most important and distressing problems for older adults is their susceptibility to falls and the complications—sometimes fatal—that occur as a consequence (Ochs et al., 1985). It is conceivable that decreased or failed input from the kinesthetic receptors may be a contributing factor. Despite the importance of this sensory system for everyday interaction and mobility among people of all ages, the specific sensory receptors responsible for the kinesthetic sense are still a matter of debate.

The risk for falls varies for older men and women (Campbell et al.,

1989). For men, less physical activity, stroke, bodily sway, and lower limb arthritis predict falls. For women, muscle weakness, increased psychotropic drug use, low blood pressure, and the use of medications that reduce blood pressure in the lower body make falls more likely. Reducing household hazards and a thorough diagnostic evaluation are critical in case of falls (Campbell et al., 1989).

Susceptibility to falling can be quite debilitating, in both the physical and psychological senses. The likelihood is quite high that a fall will result in a broken hip, requiring surgery, hospitalization, and rehabilitation (Cummings & Nevitt, 1989). Being unable to walk or fearful of walking can contribute to becoming isolated from others, the sense that one is no longer able to walk without help, and thus depression. For this reason, contributing factors, such as lack of knowledge about how to fall and decreasing bone strength, must be recognized and acted on in order to avoid hip fractures due to falls (Cummings & Nevitt, 1989). In some cases, vestibular disease or neural changes may be responsible for either dizziness or vertigo, the sensation that the surroundings are spinning (Whitbourne, 1985).

Discussion of the kinesthetic sense usually centers on two forms of movement, passive and active. Passive movement describes a situation where the individual is stationary but is in a vehicle or apparatus that is moving, such as an airplane. Active movement pertains to actual movement of the body or body parts, such as walking. Regarding passive movement, deterioration in perception of movement for the great toe occurs with increasing age, as well as for several joints, the knees, and the hips (Ochs et al., 1985). Concerning active movement, judgments of tension of differing degrees of muscle or tendon strain are relatively unaffected by age.

As with the other senses, individuals differ in their kinesthetic sensitivity. Although there are definite age-related changes in the vestibular system that create balance difficulties for older people, other sensory systems such as vision may help them compensate to avoid losing their balance (Kenshalo, 1979). We can facilitate the mobility of older adults by providing environmental aids such as handrails in corridors and benches for resting (Shore, 1976). Many older adults also use the backs of couches, chairs, tables, and other furniture to navigate from one area to another.

Pain Age-related changes in pain sensitivity are the most well researched of all changes in the skin senses (Harkins et al., 1986). However, reports of pain thresholds vary strikingly between individuals, and between parts of the body in the same individual. In addition, the experiences and report of pain are more than just sensory phenomena; they involve cognitive, motivational, personality, and cultural factors as well.

Research evidence suggests older people do not feel pain as intensely as do younger individuals. Schuldermann and Zubek (1962) investigated pain sensitivity in five areas of the body across the life span. Results indicated that overall pain sensitivity remains relatively constant until one's fifties, after which it shows a sharp decline. The decline after 60 years was highly significant. Decreased pain sensitivity with increased age was greater for the forehand, upper arm, and forearm than for the thigh and leg.

The decrease in pain sensitivity with increased age may be due to degenerative changes that occur in the receptors and the peripheral nervous system. These include: (1) a decrease in the number of receptor-end organs in the skin, (2) a decline in the number of myelinated fibers in the peripheral nervous system, (3) changes in the elasticity of the skin, and (4) changes in blood flow and/or other characteristics of the circulatory system. Sun exposure could also produce changes in the thickness and elasticity of the skin, which would lessen the effectiveness of a stimulus to elicit pain (Corso, 1971).

Recently, Arena et al. (1988) have successfully used relaxation therapy to treat tension headaches in elderly people. This approach may hold much potential in the treatment of other types of pain in the aged as well.

TABLE 4.3

EXAMPLES OF THE EFFECTS OF SENSORY DECLINE WITH AGE UPON INTERACTING WITH THE ENVIRONMENT

Sensory System	Structural/Anatomical Changes	Functional/Ability Changes	Possible Behavioral Implication
Gustatory	Decreased taste buds (papillae)	Inability to correctly determine taste qualities?	Loss of appetite? Distorted taste? Decreased socialization
Olfactory	Degeneration of neurons on olfactory bulb	Inability to correctly detect and determine various odors?	Loss of appetite? Distorted odors? Inability to detect the presence of potentially harmful odors?
Somesthesis (touch, vibration, temperature, kinesthesis, pain)	Decreased number of sensory receptors for each somesthetic sense	Inability to correctly detect stimulation from the environment	Exposure to potentially dangerous temperature levels Susceptibility to falls Inability to discriminate among clothing materials
Visual	Deposits forming on lens Atrophy of ciliary muscles	Decreased ability in accommodation Decreased visual activity Decreased visual field	Difficulty in reading Difficulty in mobility Difficulty in driving Difficulty in writing letters Difficulty in watching television Decreased activity
Auditory	Wax buildup Accumulation of fluid in middle ear Degeneration of hair cells in the basal coil of cochlea Loss of auditory neurons	Increased absolute threshold Difficulty in pitch discrimination Hearing loss	Inability to hear on the telephone Inability to hear during normal conversation Difficulty in hearing questions on intelligence test Difficulty in interpersonal communication

It is important to realize that pain is in many respects a very elusive sensory experience. Tolerance for, or willingness to report, pain may or may not lead a family member or physician to conclude that someone is truly in pain. Aches and pains may be a symptom of an underlying illness; or they may be an expression of depressed mood.

EFFECTS OF SENSORY DECLINE ON EVERYDAY FUNCTIONING

Now that we have discussed some major age changes in sensory processes, it should be obvious that they can have a real impact on ability to adapt to the everyday environment. But again, we must stress caution. Individual differences in such changes are substantial. Examples of how decrements in sensory abilities with increasing age can affect people are found in Table 4.3. These examples should not be considered exhaustive; you may be able to suggest others.

PERCEPTION IN ADULTHOOD

Perception

What mediates the impact of sensory changes on our behavior? This, of course, is the heart of **perception.** How one interprets and processes sensory input is a major influence on how adaptive one's behavior is. Several general types of perceptual phenomena come to mind that have implications for everyday functioning in adulthood. Taking an information-processing approach, we will briefly discuss vigilance, attentional skills, and reaction time as critical types of perceptual changes influencing how we interact with the environment.

VIGILANCE

Vigilance is the ability to maintain attention to a task for a sustained period (Panek et al., 1977). This ability is very important for driving, assembly-line work, and other activities where the individual must maintain attention for a fairly long period of time, as air-traffic controllers or computer programmers must. Thackray and Touchstone (1981) found age differences favoring young adults in performance on simulated tasks for air-traffic controllers. Older adults were less accurate at detecting targets, responded more slowly, and reported more false alarms than did young adults. Middle-aged adults were intermediate in their performance relative to the young and the old. Vigilance is usually studied via monitoring or inspection tasks, such as monitoring a pointer on a clock-like device.

Age differences in vigilance vary as a function of a number of factors, such as the nature of the task, the sensory modality studied, the length of time one is expected to be vigilant, and whether one must respond quickly or not (Griew & Davis, 1962; Survillo, 1964; Thompson et al., 1963). Of course, individuals also vary in their ability to be vigilant.

Air-traffic controllers are required to be vigilant for long periods of time. This skill appears to decline with age, although there are individual differences in vigilance throughout adulthood.

The only longitudinal investigation of age changes in vigilance is that of Quilter et al. (1983), who investigated changes 18 years later in individuals who originally participated in vigilance research by the authors. Quilter et al. (1983) reported that at about age 70 there was a noticeable reduction in vigilance performance. Moreover, there were individual differences within age groups. Results indicated that the largest performance decrement for the older adults was in an auditory task such as listening to an ongoing sound or sounds. Giambra and Quilter (1988) found that when vigilance tasks minimize memory, age effects are minimal. However, these investigators also found that when long-term vigilance is required to monitor a stimulus, detection accuracy, and speed of response all generally decline with age. Fatigue may also contribute to this decline (Belmont et al., 1989).

Kausler (1991) suggests that vigilance is most impaired in older people when a task is rapidly paced or lengthy, or when individuals must hold information in memory. On tasks of **pattern recognition**—for example, when a certain kind of blip on the screen means a small plane and another type means an airliner—older people seem to be at a greater disadvantage when the two stimuli are semantically dissimilar, or mean different things, than when they are perceptually dissimilar, or look different (Kausler, 1991).

To the extent that two bits of information—blips, patterns of speech, faces—are of varying importance, how do older persons fare? Studying the detection of audio signals that are imbedded in background noise (static), as you might encounter in tuning a radio or listening to a garbled telephone conversation, can help us understand whether performance differences are a function of sensory loss or some perceptual process (Kausler, 1991). In most cases, researchers have found older persons to make fewer mistakes but also to make fewer correct identifications than young adults in situations where the signal-to-noise ratio is nearly equal or where the signal is only slightly louder than the noise. Older people tend to be more cautious or conservative (see Kausler, 1991).

Implications for Everyday Life You may be wondering how vigilance influences your everyday life. Two excellent examples concern driving and industrial performance. While driving, a person must constantly be vigilant, looking at the center line on a road at night for long periods of time, and monitor the road in order to avoid accidents. The successful assembly-line worker must constantly monitor the line despite fatigue or monotony. Murrell and Griew (1965) believe that the experience gained over months or years of work on such a job may compensate for a decrease in performance with age. That is, the older worker, realizing his or her performance may not be as good as it used to be, compensates by being more vigilant. In this sense, an older person may be a better employee, making fewer mistakes and doing better-quality work.

It is important to realize that many of the age differences in sensation discussed earlier may be partly a function of older persons' reluctance to report seeing or hearing a stimulus until they were absolutely certain it was present. We must therefore consider individuals' "private threshold" in interpreting research dealing with, for example, the perception of pain or symptoms of illness. In short, any time someone makes a decision about either physical or environmental stimulation (Is one head of lettuce heavier than another? Is one grapefruit bigger than the other?), **response biases** may be involved. Those who market products of any type, particularly if they are targeting an older audience, should take such decision-making processes into account to be successful. As our information-processing model illustrates and these examples reinforce, the processes of sensation and perception are closely related to one another.

PERCEPTUAL/COGNITIVE STYLE

The construct of **perceptual style** has been developed to help explain individual differences in perception (Kogan, 1973; Witkin et al., 1954). One's perceptual style more or less "sets the stage" for those aspects of the environment one attends to. How attention is divided, as well as what information one chooses to process, is likely to be influenced by a general perceptual orientation to the environment.

One aspect of cognitive style is **field dependence/independence.**

People who are field-dependent make judgments that are heavily influenced by the immediate environment, while field-independent people's judgment is not.

An individual's perceptual or cognitive style is usually measured by performance on: (1) the Embedded Figures test, which requires the location of an element embedded in a geometrically complex figure; (2) the Rod-and-Frame test, which requires accurate adjustment of a luminous rod to true vertical when it is suspended within a tilted frame; or (3) the Body Adjustment test, which requires the individual to adjust his or her body to true vertical following rotation of a chamber in which the person is sitting in a non-upright position (Kausler, 1991; Kogan, 1973). Good performance on one or more of these measures indicates field independence, while poor performance indicates field dependence.

Extensive cross-sectional data suggest that there is a shift from field dependence to independence during adolescence, continuity during adulthood, and a return to field dependence during old age (Panek et al., 1978). While it may be difficult to explain, this shift toward field dependence with increased age has many implications for interaction with the environment. One consequence of this shift toward field dependence concerns driving behavior (Panek et al., 1977). Perceptual style is highly related to emergency behavior in a controlled driving simulation (Barrett & Thornton, 1978; Barrett et al., 1969) and actual accident involvement (Mihal & Barrett, 1976) in adults.

SELECTIVE ATTENTION

Selective attention is an essential aspect of perception and human information processing (Panek & Rush, 1981). Attention plays an important role in almost all areas of our daily lives, including reading this book and taking notes in class.

Although many have studied selective attention in adulthood, it is difficult to define properly (Kahneman, 1973; Panek & Rush, 1981). However, the most encompassing definition was proposed by Plude et al. (1983), who defined it as the control of information processing so that a given source of information is processed more fully than any other simultaneous sources of information. In many situations, we engage in divided attention, or the allocation of attentional resources to two simultaneous sources of stimulation. That is, although we are constantly exposed to numerous sources of information at the same time, we try to attend selectively to specific information. A good example of this process is attempting to read this text while your roommates are carrying on a conversation and listening to the stereo. We have all probably experienced how difficult that can be, especially when there's an exam the next morning.

Since the literature on attention is quite extensive, our discussion will concentrate on studies that attempt to apply their results to everyday problems. Studies of attention focus on either auditory or visual selective attention.

Auditory Selective Attention One widely used measure of auditory selective attention is a dichotic listening task. In a dichotic listening task, the individual wears headphones and is presented with simultaneous but different specific stimuli (numbers or letters) or messages in each ear, usually at a high rate of speed. The individual is required to repeat a particular stimulus or stimuli designated as the target, such as all the odd numbers. Dichotic listening is a fine example of a fast-paced situation that causes special problems for many older people since successful performance requires simultaneous attention to two alternatives.

Panek and Rush (1981) found that the ability to maintain and reorient attention decreased substantially with age. Furthermore, within all age groups, reorientation of attention was more difficult than its maintenance, or vigilance. Moreover, the difference in performance between these two components of selective attention, maintenance and reorientation, was magnified with increasing age.

Even when not distracted by irrelevant information, older people are deficient in selective attention relative to the young and middle-aged (Barr & Giambra, 1990). Yet there are individual differences; not all older adults perform poorly. As most studies in this area are cross-sectional, it is certainly possible that the age differences reported are influenced by cohort differences or due to sampling effects. However, it may be that cross-sectional research is appropriate, given the low probability of cohort effects (Kausler, 1991).

On divided-attention tasks, the performance of both young and old individuals declines as the tasks increase in difficulty. Yet, the decline is generally greater and more rapid for older adults (Wright, 1981). When the attentional demands of the task decrease, the performance of older adults improves (Madden, 1982; Lorsbach & Simpson, 1988).

Visual Selective Attention The most common measure of visual selective attention is the Stroop test (Stroop, 1935), which assesses the capacity to maintain a course of action in the face of intrusion by other stimuli. The task is composed of three cards. The *A* card consists of the words RED, BLUE, and GREEN printed in black ink each 100 times but arranged in random order. On this card the individual has to read the words aloud as quickly as possible. Card *B* consists of 100 randomly arranged rectangular color patches of red, blue, and green. The task is to correctly name the colors as quickly as possible. Card *C* presents, in random order, 100 color words—again, RED, BLUE, and GREEN—printed in a different color from one designated by the word. For example, the word BLUE might be printed in red ink. In this case, because reading is overlearned, inhibiting the response "blue" might be very difficult (Kausler, 1991).

There are marginal life-span differences in the response time for naming the ink color of color patches, or the color-naming response (Eisner, 1972). However, older adults are significantly slower than young adults when the color is inconsistent with the color word stimulus, which is now called the *Stroop effect* (Burke & Light, 1981). In general, for the Stroop effect, there is a curvilinear trend across age groups, beginning with a large effect for young adults, stability for middle-aged people, and then increasing again for older adults (Panek et al., 1984).

There are numerous explanations for why age differences occur on the Stroop test. For example, Burke & Light (1981) suggest that encoding and retrieval processes appear to be crucial (see Chapter 5). That is, older adults have extreme difficulty in encoding the cognitive-semantic information (color/word) and then retrieving the correct response because of the incongruence between the color and word. Young adults have more efficient encoding and retrieval processes and therefore perform the task faster. Support for this view was found by Panek et al. (1984). As there are wide differences in Stroop performance in older adults, however, we should be cautious in generalizing these visual attentional findings to all older people (Rush et al., 1990).

A related task that tells something about the selective attentional capacities of adults is where individuals are asked to sort cards into specific categories. For example, cards are sorted into *A*s and non-*A*s. People must search for the same letter(s) amid other letters that are irrelevant and distracting. Across practice trials, if these distractors are constant, then the task situation is termed **consistent mapping.** In consistent mapping, the target letter is always the same. If the letters to be searched for vary from session to session, as do the distractors, then the task situation is termed **varied mapping.** Older adults have considerably more difficulty in varied mapping tasks than they do in consistent mapping ones (Plude & Hoyer, 1979). As the number of distractors or targets is increased, older persons have more difficulty (Plude & Hoyer, 1981). Consistent mapping makes little demand on memory and attention, while such demands are great in varied mapping. Sorting bills, addresses, mail, or holiday cards along a single dimension, such as bills paid or not paid, versus along multiple dimensions—bills paid by check, cash, or charge versus not paid—is a real-life equivalent to the card-sort task used to study consistent versus varied mapping.

DIVIDED ATTENTION

A closely related topic to selective attention is divided attention (McDowd & Birren, 1990). As mentioned above, driving, talking with more than one person at a time, or reading the paper and listening to someone on the phone are everyday examples of divided attention. When people must attend to two simultaneous tasks, older individuals are again compromised (Kausler, 1991). Some attribute this to diminished ability to divide attention (McDowd, 1986), short-term memory impairment (Inglis & Caird, 1963), or left hemispheric dominance (Clark & Knowles, 1973). More recent explanations point to the complexity of performing two tasks at once for everyone, young and old (McDowd & Craik, 1988). It should be mentioned, however, that older people, when confronted with difficult or complex tasks, often respond anxiously (Hayslip, 1989). Anxiety can interfere with attentional resources in situations where mental effort is expected, as can depression and fatigue (Hayslip et al., 1991; Kennelly et al., 1985).

As mentioned above, an interesting application of divided attention is driving. When older people performed a simulated driving task where they were required to perform two activities simultaneously, such as steering and pushing buttons, they had problems with integrating the two activities, specifically due to difficulty in making decisions about how to move back and forth between tasks (Ponds et al., 1988). Decision-making by itself requires attention, and since attention is divided while driving anyway, decision-making problems may leave less attention to devote to scanning the traffic environment for cues and potential hazards such as traffic lights, other cars, or pedestrians. Of course, when driving fast, there is even less time to process and respond to what is going on.

VISUAL INFORMATION PROCESSING

There are many everyday situations in which we must process visual information sequentially. For example, in reading a weather report on TV, in searching for gate numbers from one's car at the airport, or in reading road signs that are flashing, we process sequences of letters. Indeed, to the extent that we are able to selectively attend to people, signs, cars, trucks, so that we are not overwhelmed, many situations in our everyday lives must be processed sequentially. The most obvious auditory parallel is listening to someone speak: words must be processed in the order that they are spoken.

In the lab, visual information processing is often investigated by procedures known as stimulus masking or stimulus enhancement. In a masking study, the individual is presented, usually for an extremely short time, a stimulus that is called the first test, or target stimulus, then a second stimulus called the masking stimulus. It is called *backward masking* when the first stimulus obscures the second (Hoyer & Plude, 1980). In an enhancement study, the second stimulus is integrated with the first; that is, both stimuli have overlapping presentation times.

According to **stimulus persistence theory,** older adults should experience the effects of the first stimulus for a longer time than younger individuals (Botwinick, 1984). That is, if the trace of the first stimulus takes longer to clear through the nervous system, then the second stimulus will, depending on its nature, either mask or enhance the first stimulus. Thus, it should take longer for older adults than younger ones to encode, retrieve, and process the stimulus information (Till, 1978). Salthouse (1980) suggests that performance decrements in these situations reflect the lower efficiency of the older person's nervous system to separate relevant and irrelevant aspects of perceptual stimuli, that is, that older people require greater time intervals and more stimulus exposure time to process perceptual cues accurately.

Results from backward-masking studies generally suggest that processing deficits of middle-aged and older adults can be reduced by (1) making visual stimuli more distinct, or (2) increasing the time interval from one visual pattern to another—slowing the rate of presentation (Kausler, 1991).

This deficit in visual information processing has more to do with the individual's ability to make decisions about the comparability of the stimuli (same or different?) than it does with a peripheral sense-organ difficulty (Kausler, 1991). In any case, with practice older people can improve their information-processing skills (Hertzog et al., 1976).

When searching for an object in the visual environment, as in traffic or in a crowded room, older people process visual information less efficiently and are more easily distracted, leading to still slower processing (Madden, 1990). If older people are not actively searching the environment for cues, then the presence of distracting information is less troublesome (Plude & Hoyer, 1986).

When visually processing information, particularly in a complex environment, such as traffic, two stages of processing occur: (1) feature extraction, where an object's unique sensory qualities are extracted, and (2) feature integration, where an object's features are then reorganized with other objects in the environment to reform a complex stimulus (Kausler, 1991). Reassembling an object's features with other, perhaps irrelevant or distracting features of the environment seems to be more difficult for older people, who may have to focus their attention to many aspects of the everyday environment. When a single feature like color or form can be extracted and reprocessed simply, however, older individuals can overcome their general inability to selectively process visual (and possibly auditory) information (Plude & Doussard-Roosevelt, 1989).

An alternative to the stimulus-persistence model has been proposed by Kline and Scheiber (1985) based on the assumption that different types of visual stimuli are processed by different neural channels in the visual system. **Sustained neural channels** detect stable high-spatial-frequency stimuli—slow-moving objects such as fine print—with little contrast and respond more slowly yet more persistently over a longer span of time. **Transient neural channels**, on the other hand, respond to low-spatial-frequency (coarse) stimuli that are moving or flickering and respond more quickly and for shorter periods of time.

Older adults, relative to younger ones, tend to process less efficiently (1) high-spatial-frequency (finely detailed) objects that are stationary versus low-spatial-frequency ones, and (2) low-spatial-frequency stimuli (coarsely detailed) that are moving (Kline & Schieber, 1985). Older people tend to experience a loss in the effectiveness of transient visual channels and rely more heavily on sustained channels, leading to greater stimulus persistence. Where information is presented sequentially, older individuals need a greater time interval between the first and second letter or number to process them accurately, consistent with their reliance on sustained channel functioning (Kausler, 1991).

Overall, research clearly indicates that with aging there is a significant decrease in the speed and efficiency of both auditory and visual processing ability, often found among people in their forties and fifties. But at present, there is no adequate single theory of age-related changes in attention (Kausler, 1991; Madden, 1984; McDowd & Birren, 1990).

Reaction Time

One of the reliable changes with increasing age is a slowdown in performance and behavior (Birren et al., 1980). From age 40 onward, accuracy appears to be emphasized at the expense of speed in performing a psychomotor task (Welford, 1977). This is often referred to as the **speed versus accuracy trade-off,** and simply means concentrating on performing correctly rather than quickly.

Studies of reaction time are concerned with the speed of the individual's response to some external or internal stimulus. The study of reaction time performance in adulthood and aging is very important due to the fact that many situations in our everyday work and life involve reacting to stimuli quickly and accurately. Common examples are driving a car, working on a machine in industry, typing, and avoiding everyday hazards such as burning oneself with hot water while cooking.

Researchers currently describe reaction-time tasks as *perceptual-motor reaction-time tasks,* since successful performance involves a great deal more than just a single motor response.

In a reaction-time task, the individual must (1) perceive that an event has occurred, (2) decide what to do about it, and (3) carry out the decided-upon action (Welford, 1977). Thus, poor performance on a perceptual-motor reaction-time task can often be attributed to one or more of these other factors rather than to just the speed of motor performance. Consequently, the previous discussion of sensation and perception should be a valuable asset to your understanding the material in this section and its everyday implications.

TYPES OF REACTION-TIME TASKS

There are three types of perceptual-motor reaction-time tasks: simple, choice, and complex. In a simple reaction-time task there is only one stimulus to be associated with only one response. An example of this type of task would be having a person seated in a chair at a table on which there is a light bulb and a key. The individual is told to press the key as soon as the light comes on. The person's reaction time is the length of time elapsed between the onset of the light and the key being pressed. With this task, we can derive two components of reaction time: (1) **decision/premotor time,** and (2) **motor time.** For instance, we could have the participant rest a finger on another key while waiting to respond to the light stimulus. The time lapsed between the onset of the light stimulus and the removal of the finger from the resting key would be considered decision time, while the time between removing the finger from the resting key to the completion of the appropriate response would be motor time or movement time.

There are consistent age differences in overall simple reaction time as well as in each of these individual components (Panek et al., 1978). However, the most noticeable age difference is in decision time. That is, it takes older adults a longer time to initiate the response than those who are younger (Clark et al., 1987).

In a study of over 5000 people aged 10 to 70 by Wilkinson and Allison (1989), the slowest response times to a simple reaction-time test were found for persons under 10 and over 60, who were also the most variable among themselves. On the other hand, the fastest times were distributed among all ages, with those in their twenties the quickest. The authors speculated that when people must wait to respond, their reaction times are most impaired. This was true for the youngest and the oldest.

In a choice reaction-time task there is only one response paired with only one stimulus, yet there is more than one stimulus-response pair. An everyday example of a choice reaction-time task is typing (Salthouse, 1984). Research investigating performance on such tasks usually indicates slowing, or increased reaction time, with increased age (Rabbitt, 1965). The magnitude of such differences increases with the number of distracting stimuli, response/stimulus complexity, and cognitive (memory, attention) demands (Welford, 1977). For example, a typewriter with few keys on it would be, for most typists, especially older ones, easier to type quickly on than one with more keys. However, older typists may compensate for greater complexity by being more efficient in their hand movements (Salthouse, 1984).

A good example of a complex reaction-time task is driving an automobile. In driving, the stimuli are infinite; responses are also diverse. For example, if you drove your car to class, you probably encountered many critical situations to which you had to react quickly and accurately to avoid an accident. Moreover, in each case you could respond in a variety of ways. For example, as you were driving down a street, a car pulled out of a driveway about 25 yards in front of you. To this one event, you had the choice of many responses: to step on the brakes, honk the horn and continue to drive, quickly turn left, or quickly turn right. As the task to which one must respond becomes more complex, reaction time increases disproportionately with age (Cerella et al., 1980).

For older people performing complex tasks, selecting an appropriate response from the many available is a major cause of slowness (Kausler, 1991). They also seem to have difficulty in preparing themselves to respond and in using cues effectively to help select an appropriate response (Gottsdanker, 1980; Stelmach et al., 1987).

EXPLANATIONS FOR SLOWNESS IN REACTION TIME

Why do people slow down as they age? **Peripheral explanations** view the loss of speed as a result of decrements in the sense organs and/or peripheral nervous system (Botwinick, 1984). **Central explanations** are now seen as the major cause of the slowdown in behavior with aging (Clark et al., 1987; Salthouse, 1985). All central explanations view the slowdown in behavior/performance with age as being due to some higher-level internal process.

Of the central explanations for behavioral slowing, the inability to maintain "set" (as in get ready, get set, go) and complexity are worth discussing further. Expectancy or set theory views the slowdown with age in responding as the result of older individuals' inability or difficulty in preparing their response to the stimulus (Birren, 1964). This explanation has received extensive support (Kausler, 1991). But perhaps older people's difficulty lies in the inability to ignore distractions or maintain attention. Moreover, although the set hypothesis makes good common sense, it is not readily applicable to many situations where stimuli are not presented in a predictable, paced manner. For example, in driving, we very rarely have time to prepare to look for a stimulus and then respond. In reality, we are most often confronted with an unexpected situation to which we must act immediately to avoid an accident.

The complexity explanation is also a most tempting hypothesis to explain slowing (Cerella et al., 1980). Complexity is defined in terms of such factors as increased cognitive demands, increased numbers of stimuli, and increased response attention. We noted above that as task complexity increases, reaction time slows down for older persons to a greater extent (Panek et al., 1978).

Other Explanations for Slowing Cautiousness has also been proposed to explain slowness in reaction time (Okun, 1976; Panek, 1982c). However, this conclusion is not definitive. That is, exactly what factors are responsible have not yet been identified.

An increase in cautious-like behavior has many applied implications. These include explaining psychomotor slowing with age, driving behavior, and industrial performance. Taylor (1972), for example, found that older business managers tended to acquire more information, took longer to reach a decision, and were less confident of the decision they eventually reached than younger managers. Accidents typically sustained by older drivers seem to be due to slowness and a tendency toward confusion, while accidents among young drivers are due to various kinds of recklessness (Welford, 1977).

Rigidity has also been offered as an explanation for slowing. For example, we may tend to hesitate rather than act, or we may adhere rigidly to a routine.

While studies of the rigidity hypothesis have not been unanimous in their conclusion that older adults are more rigid than young adults, this myth still persists. For example, many of the studies discussed earlier regarding cautiousness and aging could easily be reinterpreted as supporting the notion of rigidity. However, cautiousness can be viewed as quite adaptive, as it allows more time to make decisions. Perhaps we are quick to accept the notion of rigidity because it is consistent with the negative expectations we often have about older adults. Moreover, what passes for rigidity may simply reflect cohort-specific experiences. For example, growing up in a politically conservative time may exert a long-term influence on attitudes or risk-taking behavior that might falsely be interpreted as rigid. Thus, if rigidity as a construct does exist, we do not know if it is a personality construct or a behavioral construct.

Individuals who appear to be rigid in one situation may not be so in another. This was nicely illustrated by Ohta (1981), who investigated response-selection tendencies of older adults in two spatial problem-solving situations: (1) a hypothetical life situation, and (2) an actual problem-solving situation conducted in a real physical environment. Results indicated that in the hypothetical situation there was a marked tendency for elderly people, as opposed to young individuals, to choose to avoid an alternative course of action, no matter what the probability of success—an indication of rigidity. But in the real-life situation, there were no age differences in selection of approaches to solve the problem. That is, neither young nor old participants appeared to be rigid. These findings illustrate the complexity of investigating concepts such as rigidity and cautiousness and demonstrate that behavior in one type of situation may not be related to behavior in others.

EFFECTS OF TRAINING ON PSYCHOMOTOR PERFORMANCE

Only recently has training become popular in the study of adulthood and aging, due for the most part to the belief that decrements in performance in most human abilities associated with aging could not be improved.

Training may involve providing older people with regular physical (aerobic) activity to speed their performance. Baylor and Spiduso (1988) found that for older women regular aerobic exercise improved both premotor and motor aspects of reaction time to both simple and choice reaction-time tasks.

Clark et al. (1987) demonstrated that response selection by elderly adults, which is critical to responding quickly in complex situations, could be improved by appropriate training. Their training program for an experimental group of elderly subjects consisted of playing a video game for 2 hours per week over 7 weeks. They reasoned that practice on a video game would facilitate response selection because playing the game successfully requires speeded-response selection. Their control group of subjects received no training on the video game. Subjects performed tasks under either compatible (left light on, press left button) or incompatible (left light on, press right button) conditions. The training procedure was especially effective in facilitating reaction times under the condition of incompatibility. Experimental subjects were actually faster on incompatible trials than on compatible trials. By contrast, subjects who did not receive training were considerably slower on incompatible trials than on compatible trials. The investigators reasoned that video game–playing altered the strategy used by their elderly subjects in speeded tasks in general. That is, they became more effective in transmitting stimulus-response information into short-term memory in preparation for responding.

In studies in business and industry where speed is a necessary performance component, older workers are able to partially mask the slowdown in their behavior by taking advantage of improved skills and knowledge gained through experience (Schwab & Heneman, 1977). Plus, the effects of psychomotor slowdown with age are often avoided by job change and promotion. In other words, as individuals gain experience and seniority, they are often transferred or promoted to positions where speed is not

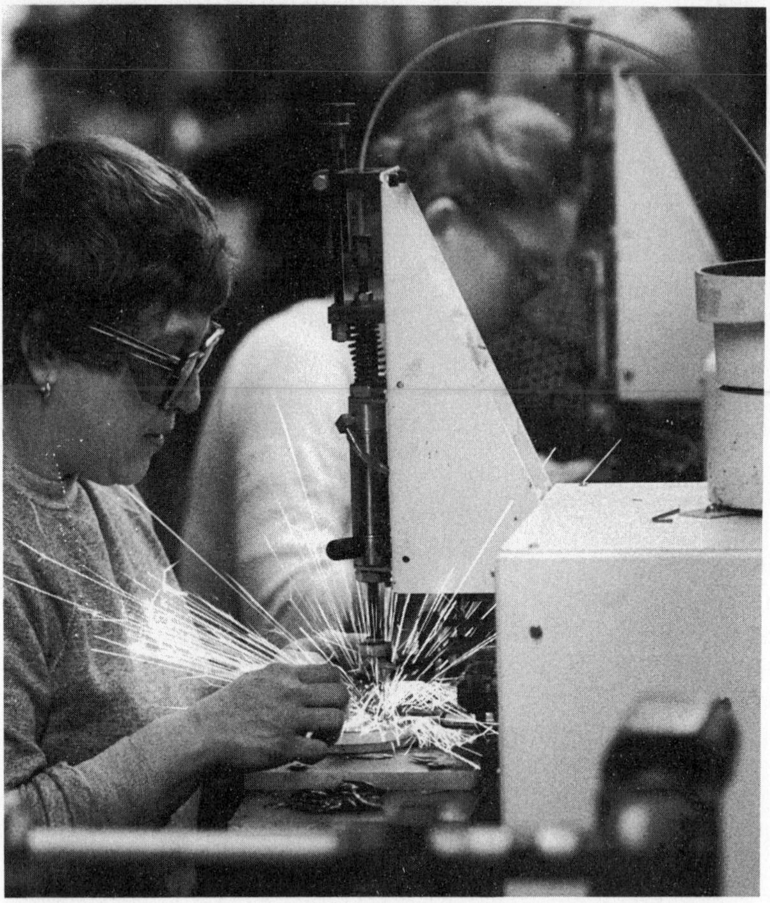

Many jobs require skilled psychomotor performance. A careful assessment of both the job and an individual's psychomotor skills is essential for both the employee and the employer.

a primary prerequisite for successful performance. Therefore, the aging worker is taken off a physical/psychomotor task prior to the time when a slowdown in responding would be a serious detriment to productivity.

Real-world parallels to the reaction-time laboratory tasks we described here are typing (Salthouse, 1984) and word processing. While younger and middle-aged adults can acquire these skills relatively quickly, the rate at which older adults learn such skills is somewhat slower (Elias et al., 1987). Of course, a general uncertainty about or lack of confidence in one's ability to learn new skills, as well as specific fears about computer technology, may also help to explain this finding.

SUMMARY

In this chapter, we discussed age differences in *sensation* and *perception*. The relationship between these processes can be understood in terms of an *information-processing model* of aging. The numerous changes with age in *vision, hearing, taste, smell,* and the *somesthetic* senses were described and their implications for our everyday functioning were discussed. Although a fairly large number of visual and auditory functions decrease with age, there are *individual differences* in the degree to which persons experience deficits in visual and auditory functioning. In contrast, definitive findings in terms of the effects of the aging processes on the other senses, such as taste, smell, and touch, are less clear.

Also in this chapter, we described a number of perceptual processes. Information about several important perceptual processes such as *cognitive style, vigilance,* and *selective attention* was presented. As a general rule, in cases where adults must divide their attention in complex situations, their performance suffers.

In cases where information is processed *sequentially,* both the speed and efficiency of such processing seems to be affected by the aging process. These age-related differences have been explained in terms of *stimulus persistence* and *transient* versus *sustained channel* theories. Research investigating perceptual processes has suggested that while these skills appear to decline with age, numerous decision-making biases such as *cautiousness* also obtain in older persons. These biases clearly affect the reporting of sensory impressions, illustrating the interrelatedness of sensation and perception. Where deficits in sensory or perceptual functioning exist, they have a number of implications for everyday functioning.

We also discussed *psychomotor performance* and concluded that one of the most noticeable changes with age is a slowdown in speed of performance. Decrements appear most reliably in *complex reaction-time* tasks. Numerous explanations have been proposed for declines in psychomotor performance, ranging from deficits in sensory receptors to task complexity. Yet, there are individual differences in psychomotor performance, and reaction time can be improved via extended practice. Researchers suspect the moderator of the slowdown to be *central,* rather than *peripheral,* in nature.

Two commonly held assumptions regarding causes of psychomotor performance of older adults are prevalent: (1) increased *cautiousness in decision making* and behavior with advancing age; and (2) increased *rigidity* of behavior with increasing age. These constructs are difficult to define and appear to be influenced by numerous factors that argue against their being intrinsically related to aging and reaction time.

KEY TERMS AND CONCEPTS

Information-processing approach to aging
Sensation
Perception
Absolute threshold
Glare sensitivity
Peripheral field
Audition
Presbycusis
Kinesthesis
Somesthesis
Sensory information-processing tasks

Presbyopia
Accommodation
Adaptation (dark, light)
Sustained and transient visual channels
Perceptual information-processing tasks
Stimulus persistence theory
Speed versus accuracy tradeoff
Perceptual-motor reaction time
Decision/premotor time
Motor time
Difference threshold
Field dependence/independence
Selective attention
Vigilance
Pattern recognition
Response bias
Divided attention
Cautiousness
Rigidity hypothesis
Peripheral explanations
Central explanations
Complexity hypothesis
Pain sensitivity

REVIEW QUESTIONS

1. What is the relationship between sensation and perception?
2. How will our behaviors and activities change as a result of changes in sensation and perception with aging?
3. What are the major structural changes in the visual system that accompany aging? How do these changes affect visual abilities?
4. How do the structures of the auditory system change with age, and what implications do these changes have for our behavior?
5. What happens to our ability to taste and smell substances as we age?
6. What are some of the changes in somesthesis?
7. Does attentional ability decrease with age? What are some of the implications of this?
8. What are the implications of changes in our ability to process information?
9. Why is it important to study psychomotor reaction time in adulthood?
10. Is there a general slowdown in behavior with advancing age? What implication could such change have for the aging individual?
11. What factors affect whether age differences are observed in reaction time?
12. How can training or practice improve the performance of older adults on perceptual-motor reaction-time tasks?
13. Do individuals become more cautious in their behavior and decision making with increasing age?
14. Do individuals become more rigid with advancing age?

CHAPTER 5

Cognition: Learning and Memory

CHAPTER OUTLINE

INTRODUCTION

Learning and memory during adulthood have been areas of great interest in the last decade (see Kausler, 1991; Labouvie-Vief & Schell, 1982; Poon, 1985; Salthouse, 1991). Moreover, understanding how adults learn has many implications for their well-being, regardless of age. Indeed, continued growth and change is one of the hallmarks of adult development, as we pointed out in Chapter 1.

Universities now face the prospect of declines in the numbers of students who are 18 to 22 years of age. Middle-aged and older adults who have been laid off or faced with early retirement, many of whom are women, may need to be retrained. Given these changes, it is imperative that we try to understand the basic processes of learning and memory as well as whether these skills vary with age.

As the demands of older employees and older students increase, educators also face the challenge of designing appropriate learning environments for those who want to upgrade their existing skills or acquire new ones (see Lumsden, 1985).

This may be especially important to many adults for their jobs and in their relationships with others. Not being able to learn new procedures at work, or being unable to remember others' names, can be embarrassing and detrimental to both personal and professional well-being. Moreover, forgetting an important doctor's appointment or when to take medication can have serious consequences for one's health. For these reasons, learning environments or training programs designed for adults should reflect their interests, strengths and weaknesses, backgrounds, and goals.

All of the topics we deal with in this text are related to our capacity to learn and remember—intelligence, personality, interpersonal relationships, parenthood, retirement, and so on. Our feelings about and the facts regarding nearly endless experiences are accumulated and processed by each of us. If we could not do this, we would never be able to learn from the childhood experiences that enable us to become better parents. Nor could we learn from our school experiences, which help us to make decisions about our careers. Once formed, our attitudes and prejudices would remain unchanged forever. Indeed, all that has happened to us throughout our adult lives would cease to have meaning if we could not learn or remember (Kausler, 1991).

LEARNING AND MEMORY DEFICITS: A CONSEQUENCE OF AGING?

Despite the potential of continued learning to enrich our development through adulthood, the major issues and concerns regarding learning and memory usually have been limited to childhood or old age, for example, at what age human beings begin to learn, or whether they cease learning at a certain age. Answers to such questions might influence practical decisions about whether to retire or whether to institutionalize an elderly relative.

While psychosocial issues such as parenthood, divorce, work, sexuality, and marriage are often linked to young adulthood or middle age, learning and memory are often considered crucial only when we discuss late adulthood. There are several problems with this reasoning. First, it segregates the study of learning and memory from the study of aging. Second, it reflects a continuing bias or myth implicitly suggesting that older adults cannot continue to grow cognitively. The idea that memory loss with aging is natural and inevitable is centuries old (see Box 5.1).

Everyone suffers from memory lapses and has difficulty in learning from experience from time to time. Yet, these difficulties rarely concern most adults until they feel that it is time for them to be experiencing such problems. It is when people reach their forties and fifties that even temporary slips of memory or difficulty in learning new ideas sensitize them

BOX 5.1

AGE DEFICITS IN LEARNING AND MEMORY—ANCIENT HISTORY?

Lowered expectations about older people's ability to learn and remember are by no means new. In fact, Aristotle (384–322 B.C.), the Greek philosopher whose empiricism greatly influenced psychology, felt that learning and memory each clearly decline with age.

In 330 B.C. he wrote:

In those who are strongly moved owing to passion, or time of life, no mnemonic impression is formed; as no impression would be formed if the movement of the seal were to impinge in running water; while in others in whom, owing to the receiving surface being frayed, as happens to old walls, or owing to the hardness of the receiving surface, the requisite impression is not implanted at all. Hence, both very young and very old persons are defective in memory; they are in a state of flux, the former because of their growth, the latter, owing to their decay.

Source: The Works of Aristotle Translated into English. (vol. 3.) Oxford University Press. In W. Dennis (Ed.). *Readings in the history of psychology.* New York: Appleton-Century-Crofts, 1948. pp. 1–9.

to the fact that "they must be getting old." To elaborate, not many of you reading this text are likely to give a second thought to forgetfulness, whether it be on an exam or in an everyday social situation (e.g., in forgetting a phone number, someone's name, or an address). Nor are you probably particularly concerned about any difficulty in mastering new course material. Instead, you might feel that the material is too difficult or that you have not studied enough. Yet, for many older adults in the classroom or in everyday life, these same difficulties are seen as signs of impending senility and are a cause for alarm, anxiety, or depression. The senility myth leads some older learners to lose self-confidence in their skills. For those who value "brain power," it may even cause loss of self-respect. Other people may then expect less of them because they are forgetful. A vicious cycle has thus been established: Further problems with learning or memory create more worry, and the worry contributes to more difficulties in concentration, thereby interfering further with learning and memory skills. Rather than read a new book, try a crossword puzzle, or attend a lecture, these adults give up. "I'm too old for that" may now be the silent message that our learner sends him- or herself. Thus, learning difficulties or memory loss with increased age can become a self-fulfilling prophecy for some people (see Figure 5.1).

Because many adults fall victim to this fallacy, it is important to separate fact from myth. Does age inevitably bring losses in learning and memory skills? Are losses reversible? Under what conditions and for what types of individuals do we observe declines in learning and memory abilities? It is with these questions in mind that we now turn to the topic of memory and learning in adulthood. Let us first briefly discuss exactly what we mean by learning and memory. After our review of memory and learning in adulthood, we will discuss factors that get in the way of efforts to learn or recall information—whether it be what you had for lunch yesterday or the name of your first pet.

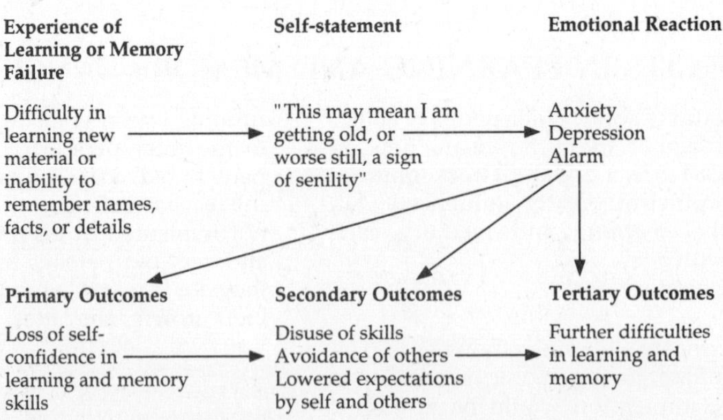

Figure 5.1 Learning and the cycle of memory loss.

How Do We Define Learning and Memory in Adulthood?

Learning is often understood in terms of the acquisition of stimulus-response (S-R) associations (Kausler, 1991). In other words, all learning is associative. The stimuli (S) evoking a response (R) may lie in your environment, as when a sound causes you to turn your head, or be produced by you yourself, as when a sensation of pain in your leg causes you to walk more slowly. In order to be effective in bringing about a response, stimuli must first evoke an internal connection, which may be a particular thought or image (e.g., the sound I heard means class is over). This internal connection mediates the observable, external response (R), such as putting one's notes away and leaving the classroom. In either case, a threshold—a certain loudness of sound or a critical level of pain in the cases above—must be reached in order for you to respond appropriately (Kausler, 1991).

While learning requires some effort or intention on the part of the learner, **memory,** while also requiring effort, is also dependent on experience but not necessarily tied to a specific situation, as is learning (Estes, 1975; Kausler, 1991).

Craik (1977) suggests that how learning and memory are defined depends on one's point of view. From an S-R associative point of view, learning involves the acquisition over time of S-R associations, while forgetting is defined as the breakdown or loss of these associations. The strength of our memory for associations is usually assessed somewhat later; thus, we use the labels short-term and long-term memory.

In contrast, an information-processing approach stresses that learning and memory are best understood in terms of the cognitive processes of registration, encoding, storage, and retrieval of material. In this case, we view learning in cognitive terms, where the adult learner is seen as an active processor of information (Schwartz & Reisberg, 1991). In other words, cognitive processes or operations that we actively perform on information to be learned and remembered are the focus of this approach. For example, we might organize or categorize information that we store for later retrieval or recall, as we often do when trying to remember groceries to buy or when learning and recalling people's names at a party.

Still another approach to learning and memory relies on the integrity of the network of cells in the brain termed neurons. Depending on how this neural network is organized, we are more or less efficient in learning and recalling information (Kausler, 1991).

Recent research has explored the ability to learn and recall a variety of specific behaviors or skills. **Instrumental learning** requires learning a sequence of responses that lead to a goal, as in maze learning. **Motor skill learning** involves either discrete (e.g., drawing a line of a specified length) or continuous (e.g., tracing a figure) responses. In either case, a precise bodily movement of some kind must be learned. Everyday examples of both instrumental and motor skill learning are quite diverse: playing golf, tying one's shoes, typing, playing the piano, maneuvering a wheelchair, learning a route from home to work, ascending stairs, and unlocking a door (Kausler, 1991). Many such behaviors are acquired early in life, and become overlearned, while others are more novel. Some are complex, others involve simple responses. It is true that age deficits have been found in both instrumental learning and motor skill learning (Kausler, 1991). However, individuals with high degrees of experience and expertise may not show these losses (Salthouse, 1991). Moreover, some skills can be recaptured rather easily even if they have not been used for some time, such as riding a bike, typing, and playing the piano.

Most research in learning and memory, however, deals with verbal material—words, pictures, symbols, and numbers—so we will focus on verbal learning and memory for the remainder of this chapter.

In research on learning in adulthood, two basic types have been studied most often: **rote learning,** where an association is acquired repetitively, and **mediated learning,** where the learner utilizes a visual or verbal mediator acquired in the past (e.g., 30 days hath September, April, June and November . . .). The mediator links the stimulus and response elements of the association, as this rhyme reminds one that February has only 28 days. The more active the rehearsal, or the more efficient the use of a mediator by the learner, the more effective learning and memory should be. And in fact, more rote learning and better mediated learning usually makes for more efficient performance in younger adults (Schmeck, 1983). However, this does not necessarily hold when explaining how older adults learn and recall information, as we shall see.

We can also distinguish between memory for general rules or basic meanings, termed **generic** or **semantic** memory, and memory for specific events, termed **episodic** memory (Craik, 1977; Kausler, 1991). Memory may also be intentional or **explicit**, or it may exist without an awareness of remembering, in which case it is termed **implicit** (Hultsch & Dixon, 1990). Explicit memory for specific events or general rules may be enhanced by learning the material either rotely or by the use of mediators, depending on a number of factors, which we will discuss below.

Measuring learning in adulthood usually involves creating a situation where such associations can be acquired, and memory is assessed somewhat later by asking the individual to recall the associations acquired during learning. Examples of learning situations or tasks that allow us to measure and understand both learning and memory are discussed briefly here. In a **paired-associates** task, pairs of words to be associated are presented together for a certain number of trials. In a **serial learning task,** a string of numbers, words, or letters is presented several times for later recall. While the tasks per se are relatively unimportant, they do provide us with examples of the individual adult learner's behaviors in highly structured learning situations.

DISTINGUISHING BETWEEN LEARNING AND MEMORY

Although we have so far treated learning and memory as separate functions, in reality they are related to one another. Because neither learning nor memory can be observed directly, they must be inferred from perfor-

TABLE 5.1

MEMORY STRUCTURES AS SEEN FROM AN INFORMATION PROCESSING POINT OF VIEW AND EVIDENCE FOR AGE DEFICITS IN EACH

Memory Structure	Major Characteristics	Age Deficit
Sensory store (iconic-visual information, echoic-auditory information)	Preattentive, very short duration of memory trace (e.g., ½ second).	yes/no
Primary memory short-term store (measured via serial recall of a span of letters, digits, or words)	Temporarily (e.g., up to a minute) stores and organizes information—information is processed in terms of its physical qualities (e.g., loudness, form, location, brightness). Limited capacity, relatively short duration. Memory trace decays unless further processed.	yes/no
Secondary memory (measured via learning/retention of lists of words)	Relatively short duration. Stores newly learned information. Involved when primary memory capacity is exceeded.	yes
Tertiary memory (long-term store)	Permanent duration, very large capacity. Highly organized episodically (regarding time and place) or semantically (regarding personal meaningfulness) recall of overlearned information.	yes/no

Source: Adapted from J. Fozard. (1980). A time for remembering. In L. Poon (Ed.), *Aging in the 1980's: Psychological Issues* (pp. 273–290). Washington, D.C.: American Psychological Association.

mance. When the ability to learn a list of words is assessed, for example, it is often only through the recall of the list that conclusions can be reached about how many words were originally learned. One obviously cannot recall information that has not been learned to begin with! As Botwinick (1978, p. 261) states, "If a man does not learn well, he has little to recall. . . . If his memory is poor, there is no sign of his having learned much." Thus, in practice, the distinction between these two processes is often difficult to make. For example, in studying for a test, you acquire information by reading, organizing, and reviewing. If your test is in two days, you must also be able to store or hold the information you learned in your memory for a time until you need to retrieve it—when you actually take your exam. Thus, we infer both learning of and memory for the test material on the basis of your test score.

MEMORY—STORES AND PROCESSES

Memory in adulthood can be understood by an emphasis on memory structures and the use of associated memory processes, as illustrated in Table 5.1. One approach to studying memory suggests that there are distinct structures or "hypothetical entities" defining memory. Typically, differences between different types of memory stores are expressed in terms of the time elapsing from exposure to recall of information. While such terms as short-term and long-term memory, as well as working memory, are often used for different types of memory stores (see Craik, 1977; Fozard, 1980), we will adopt here those used by Poon (1985): the sensory, primary, secondary, and tertiary memory stores.

Briefly, each memory store serves a different function within our multistore memory system. **Sensory memory** is preattentive or precategorical—what exists is in the form of unprocessed image. As Craik (1977) notes, the notion of capacity is somewhat difficult to apply when discussing memory. Instead, items in sensory memory are said to decay very rapidly (within 1/3 to 1 second).

Primary memory contains items that are within conscious awareness. Access to this information is limited; it decays if it is not processed further. While its capacity is small, primary memory plays an important role in the control and assimilation of information (Poon, 1985). It serves more as a temporary holding and organizing process, and less as a formal storehouse of information (Craik, 1977). When the older adult's attentional resources are divided, age deficits are more apparent (Craik, 1977).

When material to be remembered exceeds primary memory, it enters the **secondary memory** store, whose capacity is less limited (5–7 items). This is most likely what the layperson refers to as *short-term memory.* Age differences favoring young adults are commonly found in measures of secondary memory, such as immediate or delayed recall of long spans of digits or paired associates (Poon, 1985). However, more highly educated, brighter older adults may maintain relatively efficient memory systems.

Short-term memory in part encompasses both primary and secondary memory. However, **tertiary** or long-term memory, whose storehouse is in theory limitless and permanent, refers to recall of remote events or extended recall for recent events. Researchers studying remote or tertiary memory typically use questionnaires to gather their data. There is little decrement with age in tertiary memory (see discussion below).

Given the recent attention to memory processes, it is perhaps better to consider the sensory-primary-secondary-tertiary memory distinction as a continuum rather than as distinct memory stores (Craik, 1977).

Rather than rely solely on memory structures, a newer, more widely accepted approach to memory emphasizes processes that explain how material is transferred from one memory store to another (Craik, 1977; Poon, 1985). In this case, we are interested in how adults use various memory processes to deal with material that has been learned and stored for varying amounts of time in each of these memory stores. Figure 5.2 (Craik, 1977, p. 386) illustrates how each of these stores can be linked together via memory processes. These processes are referred to as *registration, encoding, storage,* and *retrieval.* They build on and interact with one another. *Registration* refers to whether material is heard or seen, that is, whether its size or loudness exceeds one's sensory threshold. In other words, if you do not hear what someone says, or you are not listening or paying attention, we

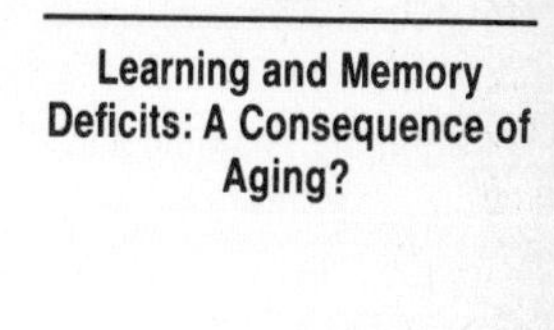

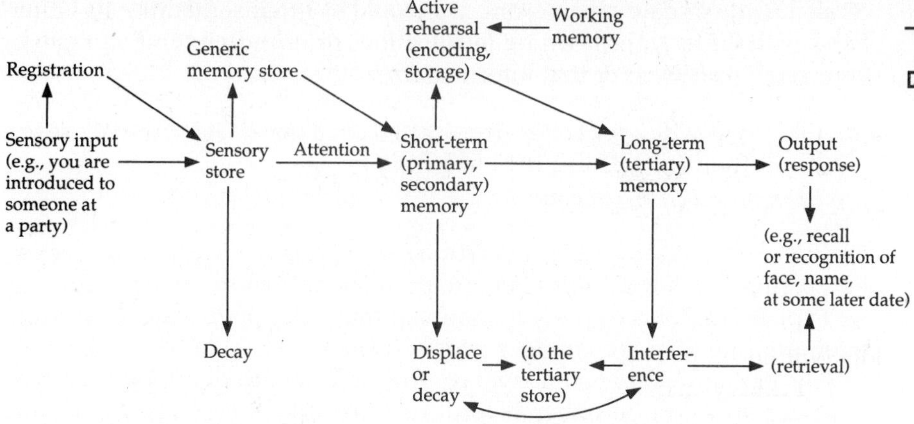

Figure 5.2 Links between memory stores via memory processes. *Source:* Modified from F. Craik. (1977). Age differences in human memory. In J.E. Birren and K.W. Schaie (Eds.), *Handbook of the psychology of aging* (p. 386). New York: Van Nostrand Reinhold; and D. Kausler, *Experimental Psychology and Human Aging* (2d Ed.) (p. 294). New York: Springer-Verlag.

might say that the words spoken do not enter your sensory store—they are not registered (see Chapter 4). Thus, whether information is registered or not is an obvious prerequisite for your processing that information in some way so that you can learn and recall it later. If, for example, an older adult suffers from sensory loss such as poor eyesight, it is unlikely that what is presented visually will be adequately registered.

Encoding refers to the process of giving meaning to incoming information after it has been registered and has entered the sensory store. Creating a visual or verbal mediator (e.g., a rhyme or an image) to help you learn and recall a list of words reflects encoding. Encoding information requires that we attend to and rehearse (actively process) information that has been registered. The ease with which material stays in the system is determined by the efficiency of the learner's encoding system.

Storage suggests that information, having been encoded in some form, is then organized in a hierarchic general-to-specific pattern, where general categories are first created, within which more specific categories are developed.

On the basis of current research, it appears that older adults often encode and store information differently than do younger adults. For example, they are less likely to organize spontaneously or use mediators, and they store information less efficiently (Kausler, 1991; Poon, 1985). A good way of expressing this relationship involves first establishing a memory trace, then maintaining or rehearsing it in storage until it can be retrieved (Kausler, 1991).

Retrieval is, quite simply, the "getting out" of information that has been registered, encoded, and stored. If you are anxious, that anxiety may make it difficult for you to retrieve what you have in storage. This explains the tip-of-the-tongue phenomenon we have all experienced. If you cannot recall a name or date on an exam, we would say that something has interfered with either your learning (acquisition, or encoding, and storage) or your recall (retrieval) of that information.

Understanding Learning and Memory

INTERFERENCE AND TRANSFER

Obviously, we do not recall everything that we have learned. Moreover, our learning for some things is more permanent than for others. How can we explain this? It is commonly assumed that older people are more interference prone than are younger people (Goulet, 1972). And, as the observations of many older people will confirm, the wealth of information they have acquired can be either helpful or hurtful to their learning of, and memory for, new or old information.

Interference is thought to occur by either **unlearning** or **competition at recall** (Hulse et al., 1980; Kausler, 1991). Unlearning occurs when a new association interferes with the maintenance of an old one. Thus, the old association loses some of its strength and may be partially or entirely forgotten. For example, learning a new address at college may actually interfere with the recall of your address at home. Competition at recall occurs when old associations, perhaps not completely unlearned, interfere with the learning of new information. For example, learning a woman's married name is often difficult if you have known her by her maiden name all your life. Interference between old and new associations is created via unlearning and competition at recall can be understood by using the examples of remembering names and adjusting to streetlights.

If, for example, Miss Jones and Mrs. Smith are similar in some way, or perceived to be so, the potential for **negative transfer**—interference—exists. Negative transfer occurs when the learning of Miss Jones's or Mrs. Smith's name is interfered with because of their similarity to one another. To use another example, playing racquetball and playing tennis involve similar movements, but playing racquetball a great deal usually detracts from one's tennis game. That is, there is negative transfer from racquetball to tennis. Learning to ride a tricycle helps in later riding a bicycle, as many of you recall from your childhood. In this case, similarity between activities or types of information creates **positive transfer.**

Educators who work with younger and older adults want to minimize conditions that make interference and thus negative transfer more likely, and capitalize on situations that allow for positive transfer from previous learning experiences. There are some recent indications that when we adjust for how much information has been initially acquired, older adults are no more interference-prone than younger adults (Kausler, 1991).

Learning, Memory, and Aging

What conclusions can be reach regarding differences among adults in learning and memory processes? What factors contribute to differences with age in learning and memory?

Current research suggests that the ability to learn and remember with age is highly dependent on a number of factors. As mentioned above, most of this research has concentrated on verbal learning performance, using either paired associates or serial learning tasks.

Compared to explicit memory, implicit memory performance is relatively stable with increased age (Hultsch & Dixon, 1990). This is true for both recall of the occurrence of specific bits of information (items) known to the learner, as well as memory for associations between unrelated items.

There are few clear age differences or age changes favoring young adults regarding sensory memory (Craik, 1977; Fozard, 1980; Kausler, 1980; Perlmutter, 1983; Poon, 1985). However, what little information that does exist argues against age effects in both **iconic** (visual) and **echoic** (auditory) sensory memory (Kausler, 1991; Poon, 1985). Furthermore, it is difficult to demonstrate that sensory memory even exists in elderly adults experiencing serious sensory or attentional deficits.

Most life-span research on learning and memory has focused on primary and secondary memory (see Table 5.1). Both primary and secondary memory may reflect our ability to recall information that is only seconds or minutes old, although tertiary memory may also be involved with newly acquired information (Craik, 1977). As a general rule, if information is not actively rehearsed, it will be forgotten. The limits of primary memory seem to be between two and four distinct bits of information, such as digits or words (Craik, 1977). In general, there seems to be a moderate age decrement in primary memory (Hultsch & Dixon, 1990; Kausler, 1991), as shown in measures of memory span derived from a digit-span task. This is where digits of varying span lengths (2–7 digits) are read to an individual, who then repeats this span in the same order. However, when digits are repeated in reverse order, age differences favoring younger people are stronger, largely due to deficits in working memory (Hultsch & Dixon, 1990; Dobbs & Rule, 1990).

Working memory is an active aspect of memory that enables us to rearrange or process information while holding it in the short-term store. When the limits of primary memory are exceeded, as they would be in repeating digits backward, secondary memory becomes active. In order to keep this information "on tap," so to speak, it must be actively rehearsed, processed, or organized in some way. Even when age deficits in primary memory occur, they generally reflect lessened capacity of the short-term store, influenced by secondary or working memory deficits (Kausler, 1991). Older adults may be slower or less efficient in searching the context of the short-term store, and they may organize information to be stored less efficiently, whether the words to be organized are related to one another or not (Kausler, 1991). Moreover, older adults rehearse to-be-remembered items less actively and search for such items less efficiently. This contributes to both primary and secondary short-term memory deficits (Kausler, 1991).

Arenberg and Robertson-Tchabo (1977) reported six-year longitudinal age deficits in secondary memory across a wide age range (30 through 80 years) in a highly selective sample of men. Such deficits appeared to be linked to a more basic problem in encoding and retrieving information

(Poon, 1985). When original rates of learning were controlled for, what were formerly believed to be storage deficits with age, due to interference, were nearly absent (Poon, 1985).

It is particularly important to understand the basis of age declines in secondary memory so that efforts to minimize such losses can be developed. It is secondary memory losses to which most of us respond with some concern. "I must be getting old because my memory is poorer than it used to be" is an often-heard remark, frequently indicating not only modest concern about such failures but also belief in their irreversibility. We will have more to say about memory interventions shortly.

With enough rehearsal, information enters the tertiary, or long-term, store, which is nearly limitless and holds information permanently. While age differences in tertiary memory do exist, they tend to favor older adults (Perlmutter & Mitchell, 1982). Deficits with age in tertiary memory would be difficult to demonstrate, however, given the confounding of the age of the individual and the age (datedness) of that which is recalled (Botwinick, 1984). That is, when we ask someone to recall an event, name, or the like from long ago, we may be assessing many things. For example, people who know more because they are older, more experienced, or educated may actually appear to show poorer long-term memory because what they have stored is more complex and extensive. This places a greater burden on their encoding, storage, and retrieval skills. Likewise, it may appear that people who have less material to search through have better memories! However, older individuals, with their greater storehouse of information, may be able to accurately recall a greater percentage of what they know. Because we cannot know exactly what they knew at the time the memory was originally encoded and stored, it is difficult to know who has the better long-term memory.

If older adults can recall more information removed from the present, it may be because they can efficiently encode and store (rehearse) information that is more personally meaningful to them. When we control for rehearsal effects by using test items that are equally salient rather than differentially personally meaningful or dated, age differences in tertiary memory are nearly absent (Botwinick, 1984; Craik, 1977; Poon, 1985). In fact, some evidence suggests that older adults actually recall more recent events than they do remote events (Kausler, 1991). Perhaps this is because the former are more meaningful and thus more actively rehearsed. Where age deficits in long-term memory do exist, they seem to be understood best in terms of the older person's problems in retrieving the old information (Botwinick, 1984; Kausler, 1991).

Finding out exactly where a person's memory problems lie can be accomplished via the use of certain experimental procedures. For example, if information is presented in a **recognition** format, as in a multiple-choice test, versus a **recall** format, as in an essay exam, deficits in recall performance only allow us to infer retrieval as the locus of the problem. Recognition tests provide learners with clear retrieval cues to guide their search for an answer. It is probably safe to say that college students benefit from being given a multiple-choice test versus an essay exam, which many people find more difficult.

If someone were to have a memory deficit in both recall and recognition situations, this would suggest not only retrieval but also encoding and storage problems. Typically, recognition formats show fewer age differences than do recall tasks (Poon, 1985). This highlights retrieval as a critical skill that is essential to both secondary and tertiary memory (Craik, 1977; Poon, 1985); both recognition and recall scores are better for pictures than for words (Kausler, 1991). When faces are the items to be recognized, however, older people's performance is poorer (Flicker et al., 1989).

As we learned in Chapter 2, cohort differences are often confounded with age differences in cross-sectional research. A study by Storandt and associates (1978) clearly suggests that older people remember more accurately items pertaining to them personally when they were young. In other words, they have better memories for "old" information, whereas younger adults have better recall of "younger" information. Thus, cohort effects in tertiary memory do seem to exist.

Perlmutter et al. (1980) asked younger and older adults to make so-called recency judgments—judgments about when something occurred historically—for events occurring in each of three time periods between 1862 and 1977. These authors found no age differences in the number of correct recency judgments. They did, however, find evidence for both encoding and retrieval deficits with age; older people remembered fewer recent events and events in their youth than did younger adults. These authors attribute educational differences between their research subjects and those of Storandt et al. (1978), and the influence of the media focusing on current events, as explanations for their age deficits. While memory for general historical facts may not be impaired, Perlmutter et al.'s results indicate that recall for more detailed, episodic, historical information is affected by cohort differences.

Here we want to briefly mention a somewhat different approach to learning and memory, emphasizing levels of processing (Craik & Lockhart, 1972; Craik, 1977). Craik separates **shallow processing,** where only an item's sensory features are stored (e.g., the image of a boat), from **deep processing,** where the item is processed and stored semantically, in terms of its meaning (what does *boat* mean?). While shallowly processed information is more susceptible to interference via a variety of factors, including anxiety and fatigue, deeply processed items are more permanent and less likely to be forgotten. It is commonly assumed (see Craik, 1977) that older adults process information less deeply than do younger ones. However, they do benefit when instructed to process test items semantically. In this case, their recall is better, although still lower than those of younger adults (Kausler, 1991). When instructed to process information shallowly, recall is equal for younger and older adults (Kausler, 1991).

CONTEXTUAL INFLUENCES ON LEARNING AND MEMORY AMONG ADULTS

In explaining everyday cognitive functioning, it is important to understand the adult learner in the context of many interacting systems, including the family system and the cultural system (Sinnott, 1989a). In addition to a learner's memory system, there are other systems that influence how learning and memory function in everyday life, such as motivational, perceptual, and sensory systems. We cannot understand the learning-memory system apart from the other intrapersonal systems with which it must interact or those real-world systems in which the individual is embedded (Sinnott, 1989a). Learning and memory in everyday life therefore must be studied and understood in relative, rather than absolute, terms, especially if we see individuals as acting on the learning environment. This view suggests that a learner's skills are simply more or less functional in solving everyday problems, rather than viewing a learner as competent or incompetent.

Whether one is a superior learner or has a good memory is relative to (1) the nature of the information to be learned, (2) the needs, abilities, and motives of the individual involved, and (3) the requirements of the situation in which one uses learning and memory skills (Cockburn & Smith, 1991; Hultsch & Dixon, 1980; Willis, 1985). For these reasons, methods of intervention we might use to help people improve learning and memory skills must be flexible. Approaches that work for some, such as organizing the material to be learned, for others will fail miserably! Either consequence—success or failure—must also be understood in light of (1) what we are asking someone to learn, (2) that person's own needs, abilities, and skills, and (3) the environment in which the person learns. Our discussion here reflects the information-processing approach introduced earlier in this chapter.

Goulet (1972) has pointed out that the learning-memory distinction is more difficult to make for older adults than for younger adults. Older people typically need more practice or familiarity with a task used to assess learning and recall. Thus, for the older adult learner, it is especially important to create an environment that maximizes learning and memory. To understand learning and memory deficits among adult learners, it would be advantageous to (1) identify the nature of the memory store involved (what kinds of information present the most difficulty?), and (2) identify what processes need to be strengthened (how was the information processed?).

Willis (1985) has advocated studying the adult learner in terms of efforts to enhance performance (see Figure 5.3). The factors Willis suggests as important in this process are:

1. The learner's characteristics: factual knowledge and existing skills (versus self-assessment or metaknowledge of abilities) and susceptibility to factors, such as anxiety and fatigue, that may interfere with the learning process
2. Activities/behaviors the individual is expected to engage in: asking more effective questions, using mediational aids, more effective rehearsal, utilizing techniques to reduce anxiety
3. Nature of the training/intervention program regarding content (use of materials that are meaningful, concrete, organizable, clearly read and understood) and process (rewarding participants for responding to all items, reducing anxiety, providing feedback, and practice with learning materials)

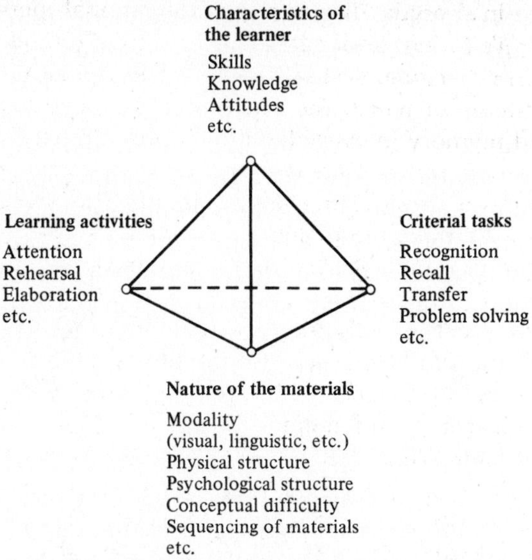

Figure 5.3 Willis's (1985) four-dimensional approach to educational intervention in adulthood: The learner in context. *Source:* Adapted from Jenkins (1979) and Smith (1980). In J. E. Birren & K. W. Schaie (Eds.), *Handbook of the psychology of aging* (2d Ed.) (p. 835). New York: Van Nostrand Reinhold. Used with permission of the publisher.

4. The specific goals/behaviors the learner is expected to acquire: whether or not the person is narrowly focused in terms of skills to be learned and whether the problems are personally meaningful to the learner

Using this fourfold approach can more fully illuminate those factors that facilitate learning and memory throughout adulthood.

PACING, LEARNING, AND MEMORY

Deficits in learning and secondary memory have been found when the material to be learned is presented at both fast and slow rates of presentation (Arenberg & Robertson-Tchabo, 1977). However, when various aspects of a task, such as the amount of time given to learn an item or to search one's memory for a correct response, are paced, age deficits in secondary memory increase. In paced tasks, the time per item or between items is restricted. A paced task would require that one learn and recall material at a fixed rate of presentation, say one item per minute, for example. Proceeding through the items at one's own speed would be learning in an unpaced situation.

Most of us get jittery when we must respond quickly in a situation, and older people are no exception. They recall the fewest correct words when they are not given sufficient time to respond. In a paired-associates task, the **inspection interval** is the time needed to register, correctly associate, and rehearse a particular stimulus-response pair (Arenberg, 1967; Canestrari, 1963; Monge & Hultsch, 1971). When the inspection interval is lengthened, the memory of older adults is somewhat less impaired. However, increasing the **anticipation interval,** which refers to the time available to search for and retrieve a correct response, seems to be more important in lessening age differences in learning and memory. In short, the inspection interval involves registration and encoding, while the inspection interval reflects storage and retrieval. In addition, allowing more time overall for a task clearly aids the adult learner, in that more time can be taken to register, encode, search for, and retrieve an appropriate response (Kinsbourne & Berryhill, 1972).

MEDIATED LEARNING

In addition to pacing, much research has also suggested that the extent to which encoding is supported or impaired may determine secondary memory deficits among adults. For example, encouraging and training adults in the use of verbal mediators (verbal associations involving the words to be learned) and visual mediators (mental pictures involving the words to be linked) seem to help matters greatly (Canestrari, 1968; Hulicka & Grossman, 1967; Rowe & Schnore, 1971).

Robertson-Tchabo et al. (1976) and Anschutz et al. (1985) had great success with the **method of loci**, where a learner was asked to imagine a walk through his or her home, picking out several stopping points during the journey. The learning and memory of words was greatly helped by instructions to associate each of the familiar loci with a word. Closely related to the method of loci is the **keyword method**, where a learner forms a word (e.g., whale) that sounds like the word to be remembered (the name Whalen) and also elicits a clear image (a whale swimming). This too was found to be helpful for both younger and older learners. Unfortunately, in the long term (by three years after training), older learners frequently abandon the method of loci even though it has been effective (Anschutz et al., 1987).

Likewise, specific instructions to organize material have been shown to enhance learning and memory (Denny, 1974; Hultsch, 1974, 1975). Hultsch (1969, 1971, 1975) has effectively used the alphabet as an aid in the organization of a list of words to be learned, for example, words beginning with *A* might be learned or recalled first, followed by words beginning with *B*, and so on. Schmidt et al. (1981) also found that specific instructions to organize items by category aided in their recall. Moreover, simply asking adults in advance to retrieve words seems to enhance later recall (Rabinowitz & Craik, 1986). This seems to be a specific form of practice that is beneficial to the adult learner.

It is especially important to create a positive environment for learning by being emotionally supportive and expressing confidence in the learner (Ross, 1968). This makes it more likely that he or she can use learning aids, termed **mnemonic devices,** such as visual or verbal mediators and organization by category. Note that the strategies you use and which might work well for you may not work so well for people who are older and who

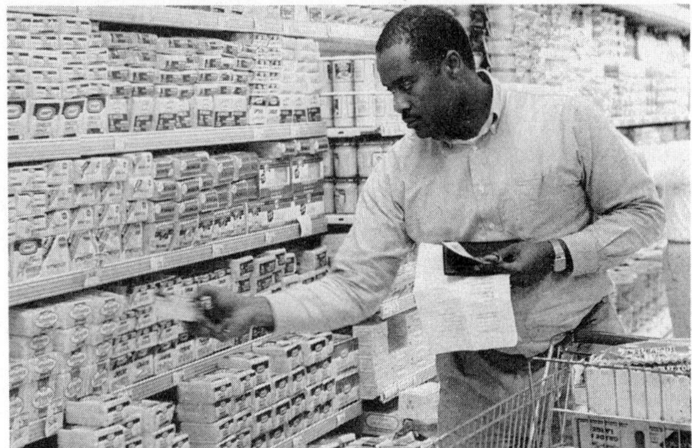

Organizing what one must learn and recall is essential to skilled performance.

can generate their own learning aids (Treat & Reese, 1976; Treat et al., 1981). In some cases, individuals may be incapable of generating their own helping mechanism. The inability to use a particular mnemonic aid is termed a basic *mediational deficiency.* Alternatively, people simply may not wish to use a mediator of their own or one you might provide for them. This is termed a *production deficiency.*

It may also be helpful to reward individuals for making any effort, even if it is wrong. Research by Leech and Witte (1971) has shown that rewarding learners, particularly older adults, for making *errors of commission* as well as correct responses improves performance. Lessening *errors of omission* makes people better able to take advantage of whatever mediational aids are provided (Botwinick, 1984).

Being supportive and rewarding any response, right or wrong, reduces the chances that individuals will become anxious or too excited (Botwinick, 1984; Eisdorfer, 1968; Furchgott & Busemeyer, 1976; Kooken & Hayslip, 1984; Wine, 1971). For example, at some time you have probably been so "psyched-up" for an exam that this extra energy or emotion actually interfered with your performance. Perhaps you did not listen carefully to instructions, or failed to read each question thoroughly. If you could manage to be relaxed yet alert, your performance would likely improve. If the test material were subject to the use of a variety of learning aids, such as mediators and organization, the effort required to deal with your anxiety could be used instead to deal with the requirements of the test!

The debilitating effects of the inappropriate use of your attention are also observed in adults, when the tasks require a great deal of cognitive effort or concentration. As mentioned in our discussion of sensation and perception (see Chapter 4), when older people must divide their attention because they are anxious, or when they are confronted with either a complex task or a simple task requiring a complex response, their attentional resources are compromised by having to devote effort to *how* their attention is used (Perlmutter, 1983; Plude & Hoyer, 1981; Hoyer & Plude, 1980).

This leaves them few resources to deal with and respond appropriately to the task itself.

A common example of such a situation would be driving at night on a strange highway. Dealing with fears about whether you are lost might cause you to miss road signs, or perhaps cause you to drive faster when you should drive slower in order to read the signs. In cases such as this, encouraging adults to process information in a more systematic manner is most helpful. For example, they should drive slower or stop, try to relax, get out the map, or get out of the car to get their bearings. In general, to the extent that a task is adversely affected by use of attentional processes (see Chapter 4), and is itself a complex task, the adult learner will have even further difficulty (Botwinick, 1984; Wright, 1981). For example, learning to program a computer and running a program are complex tasks that demand a great deal of concentration and attention. Many of you have probably had some difficulty with computers because of "computer phobia"; these fears make a hard task even harder! Once you are able to conquer your fear, however, working with computers becomes easier.

Noncognitive Influences on Learning and Memory

Earlier in this chapter, we raised the question, How can we best develop the adult's learning and memory skills? One approach is utilizing the variety of **cognitive** interventions, such as mediational aids or organization of information, discussed above. Another approach is the **noncognitive**, or ability-extraneous (Botwinick, 1967), aspects of learning and memory in adulthood (Kausler, 1990).

Hayslip and Kennelly (1985) suggest that a variety of noncognitive factors interact with the learning situation and the learner's personality and skills to create an overly negative picture of the adult's continued ability to learn with increased age. Saying that an older person's potential for learning is impaired implies a high correspondence between some outward sign of this learning (e.g., poor performance on a task) and those cognitive abilities or skills the individual is inferred to have. If other factors "cover up" or mask the expression of underlying ability, they are termed *noncognitive,* and they affect the expression of the qualities we are interested in knowing about. For example, fears about getting lost at night are noncognitive factors that actually make it more difficult for you to find your way.

A number of factors considered noncognitive have already been discussed: overarousal, willingness and ability to use learning or memory aids, not wanting to guess and be potentially wrong, anxiety about failure, sensory or attentional deficits, task pacing, and cautiousness. Most important among these is minimizing any sensory deficits that exist (see Chapter 4 on sensation), thus enhancing registration of the material to be learned or recalled. Arenberg (1976), Taub (1975), and Dixon et al. (1982) have all demonstrated that, for material that is personally meaningful and that can be reviewed, visual presentation may be most helpful. On the other hand, for more complex and less familiar material, auditory augmentation of visually presented material may be helpful, such as by presenting slides while speaking.

Other noncognitive variables affecting learning and memory are health problems such as cardiovascular disorders (see Abrahams, 1976; Hertzog et al., 1978), the perceived relevance of the learning and/or memory task (Calhoun & Gounard, 1979; Hulicka, 1967; Hultsch et al., 1975), and fatigue (Cunningham et al., 1979; Hayslip & Sterns, 1979; Hayslip et al., 1990).

Personality is a noncognitive factor that also has an important influence on learning and memory in adulthood (see Kausler, 1990). An individual's personal beliefs, values, and perceptions of whether it is even important to maintain skills can and do also influence learning and memory skills (Kausler, 1990, 1991). Believing that one has little control over events in one's life, not valuing one's intellectual skills, or undue anxiety about failure can all set the stage for poor learning and memory performance in adulthood. Believing that one is too old to learn new things, or that memory naturally diminishes with increasing age, can not only undermine the development of new skills in adulthood, but lead as well to decline of the skills one already has (Hayslip, 1989a). Thus, we should examine individuals' beliefs about the wisdom of learning new things and the inevitability of memory loss with age before undertaking efforts to develop new skills or enhance old ones. For example, an estimate of one's own memory skills and memory self-efficacy each seem to predict memory performance (Cavanaugh & Poon, 1989; Hertzog et al., 1990).

Hayslip and Kennelly (1985) point out that when the adult learner must divide attention in complex learning situations, or when *depression* is present, becoming fatigued makes the learning and/or retention of new material particularly difficult (Gribbin & Schaie, 1979; Kennelly et al., 1985; Zarit, 1980).

Depression is often associated with memory deficits among adults, particularly when the material to be remembered places demands on one's use of attentional resources (Breslau & Haug, 1983; Salzman & Shader, 1979). People who show symptoms of depression also tend to report more memory complaints (O'Hara et al., 1986). Thus, if depression is suspected, a separate evaluation is in order and treatment recommended, if necessary, prior to making any efforts at new learning (see Chapter 10).

Hayslip and Kennelly (1985) conclude that when adjustments are made, more accurate conclusions about older people's learning and memory capacity can be reached. These adjustments are listed in Box 5.2.

These recommendations and the research discussed above emphasize the potential of cognitive interventions in helping adults of all ages increase their learning and memory skills. Goulet (1972) and Poon (1985), among others, have noted the importance of the adult's learning the to-be-remembered material to the greatest extent *before* an assessment of memory is made.

Improving Learning and Memory Skills

From an intervention standpoint, we might improve an adult's learning and memory skills by altering

Developing good study habits enhances both learning and memory for adults of all ages.

1. the material (task) to be learned, by making it more meaningful or easily seen or heard;
2. the learner, by a skills-training program, altering one's expectations of success or failure and motivations for improvement, or by minimizing noncognitive factors such as anxiety or fatigue; or
3. the context in which learning occurs, by using instructions that are easily comprehended and task pacing (Willis, 1985).

Langer et al. (1979), in working with institutionalized elderly, found that by simply providing either interpersonal or practical rewards for attending to and recalling recent events in the everyday environment, real improvements in short-term memory could be achieved. Beck (1982) found that when nursing-home residents were provided with incentives for re-

BOX 5.2

FIGHTING FORGETFULNESS

Everyone experiences memory loss, and there is some normal aging decline in episodic memory, termed *age-associated memory impairment* (AAMI, Crook et al., 1986).

You don't have to accept memory loss passively. Various mnemonic techniques do work.

Reminders

Some memory-enhancing techniques involve focused mental effort. Much of the time, though, you can simply let reminders do the work for you.

- Keep a small notebook or tape player with you—even by your bed at night—to record ideas, points you want to make in conversation, and plans.
- Record appointments in a portable date book.
- Use Post-it™ notes, those removable adhesive notes that are "probably the single most important memory aid ever invented."
- Set a watch alarm or cooking timer if you forget to do things, such as turning off the stove.
- Remember to take medicine by keeping your pills near something you use routinely, such as your toothbrush. "To keep track of whether you've taken your pills," suggests Robin West, Ph.D., a memory researcher at the University of Florida, author of *Memory Fitness over Forty* (Triad Publishing), "fill out a calendar with *P*s for each time you're supposed to take them. Circle the *P* when you do."

Mental Notes

When memos and timers aren't practical, there are other ways to remember. It helps to become a creature of habit:

- Establish fixed places for things you commonly misplace—keys, hat, gloves, wallet, or important papers. Always return them to their assigned places. Designate a certain spot for anything you'll want to take with you when you go out, then put the object there as soon as you decide you'll need it. Also, Dr. West suggests that you establish standard places to put your things when you're away from home—the left side of your chair in a restaurant, or a certain spot in a friend's house.
- Decide where things belong so you'll notice when you've forgotten them. Keep your handbag or briefacse on the front seat of your car whenever you go out. If you routinely visualize it there, you'll instinctively check the front seat whenever you get in the car.
- Get in the habit of doing things at the same time each day. Feed the dog, for example, when the morning and evening news come on.
- Pay extra attention to things you want to remember. If you sometimes wonder whether you locked the door or turned off the lights, for example, focus on those actions. Say to yourself, "I'm locking the door now." To help remember that you did it today, not yesterday, note the weather or what you're wearing as you lock the door.

Focusing

Focused attention is the key to remembering names. Take the time to rehearse and repeat.

- Before you go to a meeting or party, think of who might be there and practice linking names and faces.
- Repeat names to yourself, even aloud. Don't hesitate to ask new acquaintances to repeat their names.
- At a social gathering, concentrate on learning a few new names, rather than those of everyone you meet.

Other mnemonic devices take a little more imagination:

- Organize thoughts, objects, or actions. To remember a list of things, categorize them according to similarities, importance, location, or whatever method fits. For example, if you've got several errands to run, remember them according to the route you'll be taking.
- Visualize yourself going through the steps of a new process. West suggests that, once you've deciphered the instructions on a new VCR, you should imagine yourself performing all the operations.
- Invent an acronym. For example, FILM (Fred, Irene, Louise, Mary) would help you recall the names of a relative's children. Even if you can't come up with a good word, the attempt itself may fix the names if your mind. Telephone numbers lend themselves especially well to acronyms. Even a nonsense word like *ADJUGAR* (235–8427) is useful, but with extra effort and a little luck, the same number yields more memorable results—*CELTICS*.

membering aspects of their daily lives, they not only increased their memory performance but were also rated more socially involved by the staff.

Poon (1985) suggests that intervention studies demonstrating the positive benefits of many of the above learning aids on learning and memory performance among older people reveal (1) great individual and situational differences in the benefits of mnemonic training, and (2) short-term but not long-term benefits. Older people often choose not to use such memory aids unless reminded to do so (Poon, 1985; Schaffer & Poon, 1982). Attending to the older learner's reasons for using or not using such techniques needs to be our prime focus. How can such techniques be helpful? How can I benefit from them? These are questions that must be answered up front. It is interesting to note that Cavanaugh et al. (1983) and Schaffer and Poon (1982) have found that internal learning and memory aids, such as imagery or organization, are rarely used by either younger or older adults in everyday situations. Instead, they use external techniques, such as lists, notes, and a string tied to the finger (see Poon, 1985).

Recent discussions of how to best improve learning and memory in adulthood clearly reflect a sensitivity to the variety of influences on learning and memory performance. Enhancement techniques involve (1) assessing the learning and memory demands one faces, (2) identifying helpful strategies that individuals are capable of and are willing to use in improving their skills (e.g., organization, mnemonic aids, overlearning, verbal elaboration), and (3) ensuring that such gains can be maintained and that they are generalizable (West, 1989).

Before concluding this section, let us qualify what we know about learning and memory in adulthood. Much of the research investigating age-related differences in learning and memory has been cross-sectional (Perlmutter, 1983). With a few exceptions (Arenberg & Robertson-Tchabo, 1977), this evidence must be viewed cautiously, since it simply describes the performance of individuals of varying ages who have been presented with various learning and memory tasks. These performance differences varying by age may be confounded by cohort differences in learning histories and thus do not tell us about intraindividual age changes in learning and/or memory processes (see Chapter 2). Despite these limitations, however, a great deal of research has investigated numerous factors that either lessen or magnify these age differences. At the least, what we now know about learning and memory should enable us to better understand those factors that influence cognitive change across the adult life span.

Learning and Memory in Everyday Life

What we know about learning and memory in everyday adult life has grown from interest in studying the basic processes of learning and memory in the lab. Ultimately, however, what psychologists and educators know about these basic processes is important to the layperson if it can be used to predict and improve everyday cognitive functioning. It is this challenge, to which basic research must respond, that determines its value in understanding behavior.

While the researcher continually searches for parallels in the everyday world, the practitioner looks to research findings in hopes of finding ways to solve everyday problems. This laboratory–everyday world relationship reflects the *ecological,* or external, validity of research in learning and memory, where findings obtained under well-controlled conditions, using somewhat contrived tasks, may or may not generalize to the real world.

Banaji and Crowder (1989) argue that studies purportedly examining everyday learning and memory do not ensure such generalizability. They feel it useful to distinguish between studies using methods that may or may not be ecologically valid to produce results that may or may not be generalizable. Many disagree, arguing that *both* laboratory and naturalistic research is necessary to study learning and memory (Ceci & Brofenbrenner, 1991; Conway, 1991; Tulving, 1991). As a way of resolving this issue, it may be helpful to distinguish between mechanistic explanations of memory, where underlying processes can be identified, and functional explanations, which identify the everyday uses of these processes (Bruce, 1991).

Several topics in everyday, ecologically relevant learning and memory in adulthood have generated a great deal of recent interest: (1) memory for text materials, (2) metamemory, (3) speech comprehension, (4) memory for spatial information, (5) prospective memory, and (6) memory for activities.

MEMORY FOR TEXT MATERIALS

Many who have studied adults' memory for text (e.g., sentences, prose paragraphs) reach difficult conclusions about whether younger or older people's performance is superior. While some findings suggest that age differences in the learning and memory of real-life discourse (text materials) favor the young, it may be lower levels of comprehension in the aged that account for memory deficits with meaningful material (Botwinick, 1984). This again illustrates the close relationship between learning and memory, which we discussed earlier. Such age differences are also dependent on how comprehension and memory for text materials is assessed, that is, whether the materials to be learned and recalled are visually or orally presented (Hartley et al., 1980). Thus, age differences in performance of real-life tasks is determined by those tasks' characteristics as well as the learner's skills and personal attributes.

It is important to realize that text comprehension is an active, constructive process, where the learner processes each sentence selectively, piecing it together with existing knowledge to generate a new interpretation about what the sentence means (Hultsch & Dixon, 1984). Indeed, the processing of text materials reflects a variety of logical operations the learner goes through in constructing the meaning of the text, based on a hierarchical organization of arguments linked together by verbs (Hultsch & Dixon, 1984). In the learner's mind, arguments may or may not be connected in the text, depending on their relationship to one another. Out of this organization that the learner constructs, a sentence's meaning can be understood and sentences can be linked together and summarized to glean an overall meaning of what has been read.

There are a number of factors that affect the ability to efficiently process and recall text (Hultsch & Dixon, 1984). If the learner is given instructions to process deeply (at the level of meaning) a list of words preceding the text material, recall of text is enhanced among young adults but interfered with among older people. Other influential factors include whether (1) a recall or recognition format is used, (2) recall is immediate or delayed, (3) presentation is oral or visual, and (4) recall for details or main ideas is examined.

Depending on breadth of prior knowledge, level of education, and verbal ability, older and younger adults may or may not show adequate memory performance for text material (Meyer & Rice, 1989). For those with little prior knowledge of the topic, who are poorly educated, and who have the least verbal ability, performance is poorest. Hartley (1986) found that the effectiveness of reading ability, rather than age, determined memory for text. In that age differences in the processing of more ecologically valid tasks are also dependent on a number of factors, we must ask under what circumstances age differences in memory for text exist.

One's goals and strategies, reading habits, and personality (e.g., needs for intellectual stimulation) also influence memory for text material. While reading tasks such as news articles, biographies, essays, and stories seem to demonstrate adequate ecological validity, in the real world readers are rarely required to absorb a passage with the goal of being able to recall it accurately. It is for this reason that what actual strategies adult readers use remain as questions yet to be answered (Hartley, 1989).

METAMEMORY

Metamemory refers to how much we know about what we can remember (Lachman et al., 1979). The study of metamemory is important because confidence in one's own abilities influences the amount of preparation for or effort put into dealing with everyday tasks. For example, whether one makes a grocery list before leaving for the store depends on a preestimate of memory skills. A common observation is that many adults rely heavily on calendars, datebooks or diaries to keep track of appointments because they underestimate their learning or memory skills.

The literature regarding age differences in metamemory is mixed (see Kausler, 1991). Many have found that older adults are as accurate as younger adults in predicting what they can remember, regardless of whether old or new information is being dealt with (Lachman & Lachman, 1980; Rabinowitz et al., 1982). However, Murphy et al. (1981) found that older people tend to overestimate what they can remember compared with younger adults, as did Bruce et al. (1982). Zelinski et al. (1980), on the other hand, found older adults to be more accurate in estimating their performance than were young adults.

Similarly, some researchers have found little relationship between older people's subjective estimates of their memory skills and objective performance (West et al., 1984; Sunderland et al., 1986; Zarit et al., 1981), and others have found that older people's predictions about performance and their actual performance were related (Dixon & Hultsch, 1983; Poon & Schaffer, 1982; Zelinski et al., 1990). A key to resolving these inconsistent findings lies in measuring metamemory accurately (Poon, 1985).

Table 5.2 illustrates a frequently used metamemory questionnaire (Gilewski & Zelinski, 1986). It is somewhat complex, measuring a number of aspects of an individual's metamemorial skills. In light of the complexity of metamemory, it is not surprising for studies to disagree on whether younger or older adults have superior metamemorial abilities. Results also vary depending on whether adults are asked to estimate everyday memory performance versus performance on a task in a lab (Kausler, 1991).

Despite the mixed character of these findings, this newly emerging area of research can perhaps provide a more accurate base for training pro-

TABLE 5.2

SCALES AND SAMPLE ITEMS FROM THE METAMEMORY QUESTIONNAIRE

Scale	Sample Item
1. General rating	1. How would you rate your memory in terms of the kinds of problems you have?
2. Reliance on memory	2. How often do you need to rely on your memory without the use of remembering techniques, such as making lists, when you are engaged in . . . (a) social activities?
3. Retrospective functioning	3. How is your memory compared to the way it was . . . (b) one year ago?
4. Frequency of forgetting	4. How often do these present a memory problem for you . . . (a) names?
5. Frequency of forgetting when reading	5. As you are reading a novel, how often do you have trouble remembering what you have read . . . (a) in the opening chapters once you have finished the book?
6. Remembering past events	6. How well do you remember things which occurred . . . (a) last month?
7. Seriousness	7. When you actually forget in these situations, how serious of a problem do you consider the memory failure to be . . . (a) names?
8. Mnemonics	8. How often do you use these techniques to remind yourself about things . . . (a) keep an appointment book?
9. Effort made to remember	9. How much effort do you usually have to make to remember in these situations . . . (a) names?

Source: Adapted from Gilewski and Zelinski. (1986). Table 11.7. (Copyright 1986 by the American Psychological Association. Adapted by permission.)

grams for the adult learner. Programs may be more effective if they are targeted to the particular older learner whose metamemorial skills are poor, perhaps because of poor self-esteem. If such individuals are depressed and complain a great deal about their loss of skills, they may not have used their memory and learning abilities for some time. They may also have lacked feedback about the status of their skills (Hayslip & Caraway, 1989). Reminding older adults to use memory strategies that have been learned and proven effective in the past, promoting an awareness of metamemorial skills, and clearly specifying goals are all viable strategies by which to enhance the memory performance of older people both on laboratory tasks and in everyday situations (Poon, 1985).

Improving individuals' estimates of their own abilities, by reducing anxiety or altering self-perceptions, might also be an effective way of increasing everyday memory (Hayslip, 1989b). This again suggests that noncognitive factors might influence learning and memory and indicates that we should be interested in how adults explain their learning and memory problems and in their own sense of intellectual **efficacy** (Bandura, 1977; Lachman & Jelalian, 1984; Lachman & McArthur, 1986). For example, when older people experience memory difficulties, these problems are usually attributed to lack of competence. However, when such failures are experienced by younger people, they are explained in terms of expectations that both the young and the old have about the cognitive skills of younger people.

SPEECH COMPREHENSION

Speech comprehension is a topic that is relevant to adults of all ages if they are to interact with others effectively. How we process what is said to us in a conversation is "on-line." That is, relative to what we read, the input for what we hear is sequential; the listener must attend to every word if what is said is to be accurately understood. Words must be recognized and a context for understanding must be constructed. For adults with uncorrected age-related hearing loss (presbycusis), the basic sound information requisite for processing and understanding can be distorted, resulting in faulty reception and understanding of speech (see Chapter 4). However, even when there is noise or when speech is rapid, there is little decline in the ability to construct a linguistic context essential to comprehension and later recall with increased age (Stine et al., 1989). When speech rates are increased, younger and older adults are both nevertheless able to effectively select longer segments of words to compensate for the increased rate at which such speech must be processed (Stine et al., 1989). This seems to enable a listener to compensate for a deficit in processing individual words or word elements, which is more common among older adults.

MEMORY FOR SPATIAL INFORMATION

When we search for an object that we usually put in a given place, such as keys or glasses, or when we try to get our bearings if lost in an unfamiliar place, our knowledge of and memory for spatial activities and relationships come into play (Kivasic, 1989). As with other ecological tasks such as memory for prose, the learner's skills are of importance. Available findings indicate clear age-related declines in memory for spatial locations, in both small-scale (e.g., locations of features on a map) and large-scale (e.g., knowledge of one's residence or landmarks in one's hometown) situations (Kivasic, 1989). Moreover, one's spatial abilities seem to predict knowledge of one's own neighborhood (Krauss et al., 1981). In a study involving shopping in a familiar versus an unfamiliar supermarket, younger adults' ability to execute an efficient shopping route in a new setting was not affected by familiarity with an old setting, yet older adults' performance was so affected (Kivasic, 1981). However, there was no consistent relationship between adults' spatial skills and the efficiency of their shopping behavior. While spatial skills predicted shopping behavior in the novel setting for older persons, they did so in the familiar setting for younger people. As with other ecological tasks, we have much to learn about the everyday spatial behavior of adults.

PROSPECTIVE MEMORY

One is using prospective memory skills when one intentionally commits to memory a list of things to be done in the future. Obviously, in making intelligent decisions regarding the future, in planning upcoming activities such as vacations, and even in getting through a hectic day, the memory for actions required to carry out plans or reach previously set goals is involved (Sinnott, 1989b). Research in this newly emerging area is just appearing, and that which exists often uses tasks such as remembering to mail a postcard or make a phone call at a certain time in the future because one has been told to do so. In almost every case, either no age difference or superior performance by older people over young adults has been observed (Sinnott, 1989b).

A recent study found that there were no age differences in prospective memory when performance was measured by the likelihood of remembering to press a key when the word *rake* appeared in a list of words to be recalled later (Einstein & McDaniel, 1990). In addition, short-term memory was unrelated to prospective memory skills. When both younger and older adults were permitted to formulate a memory aid such as a note or a string tied to a finger, their prospective memory performance improved (Einstein & McDaniel, 1990). Moreover, as the uniqueness of the stimulus to which they were to respond in the future increased, their performance also improved. Unfamiliar or unique cues presumably create less interference, leading to better prospective memory.

In using prospective memory, it is important to remember not only that one must do something in the future, but also the particular cue or target that should elicit this behavior. For example, knowing that you must make an important call at noon three days from today does little good if in three days you fail to remember that it is at noon when this important call must be made. While many methodological issues, including the artificial nature of the task involved, need to be addressed (Sinnott, 1986b), research on prospective memory may prove it to be a most relevant, ecologically valid process enabling adults to continue to function adaptively.

MEMORY FOR ACTIVITIES

Another type of everyday memory comes in the form of memory for personal activities, which are rehearsal-independent, that is, independent of active rehearsal, as opposed to rehearsal-dependent, which is effortful and active (Kausler, 1991). Memory for our own activities or actions is relatively unimpaired by aging, compared to effortful forms of memory where we intend to recall to-be-learned items (Hultsch & Dixon, 1990; Kausler, 1991). In this respect, it is similar to implicit memory, which is also stable across age groups.

Education and the Adult Learner

Peterson (1985) and Courtney (1989) see education as a very powerful means by which to normalize the roles older people play in our society, as well as an activity that can preserve a sense of personal dignity to facilitate personal growth and actualization (Beder, 1989; Sterns & Mitchell, 1979). Their approach to continued education is self-expressive, rather than instrumental—leading to a clearly defined goal (Hiemstra, 1976). Research examining the impact of formal educational interventions on adult learners is comparatively rare (Davenport, 1986; Deshler & Hagan, 1991; Peterson

Learning is a lifelong endeavor.

& Eden, 1981). However, it should be clear that older people are quite capable of acquiring new cognitive skills in a variety of ways.

Hiemstra (1985) and Pearce (1991) have discussed the importance of self-directed learning—learning that is self-initiated and tied to one's personal experiences—as an important factor in the education of adults. Such learning should have positive effects on adults' involvement in learning, self-esteem, responsibility for self-improvement, and self-fulfillment.

Indeed, among adult learners, a major goal for continued learning is personal growth (Pearce, 1991). This predisposition toward learning for either meaning (internal) reasons or achievement (external) reasons has been termed **learning style.** That is, for some adults learning is self-expressive, while for others it is instrumental, or leads to a goal.

Davenport (1986) suggests that the personal and educational benefits of Elderhostel (see Box 5.3) for older participants varies with sex and learning style but not age. Kaye et al. (1985) found factors such as age, sex, previous teaching experience, and level of formal education, as well as both race and ethnicity to all play a role in determining older people's ac-

ADULTS SPEAK

STILL GOING STRONG AT 94

Grace Jordan is 94. She has been slowed recently by fading vision, but she had no trouble climbing the steep slope leading to her pier which juts into the clear water of the lower Corrotoman River.

"Joy in the heart, pleasure in the mind, a body free of pain," she says. "If you have that, you can be happy all day.

But one has to begin with an enthusiastic embrace of life.

"He who wakes at dawn with enthusiasm may expect satisfaction at sunset," Jordan explains.

"Youth is enthusiastic and old age likes to sit. It's crazy to do nothing. There's no enthusiasm in nursing homes. They're just sitting around. Life is over. They're just waiting for the end.

"Have something to look forward to," she says. "Before I go to sleep at night, I plan what I want to do the next day."

Her lifelong love of learning was the reason she took the Dale Carnegie course in Effective Speaking and Human Relations. "I might get something to think about," she says.

As it turned out, "she gave her 34 classmates something to think about," says instructor Buck Stahl.

"A deep respect grew from all classmates for her," Stahl says. "When she got up [to speak], you could hear a needle drop. People didn't even squirm in their seats. She was an inspiration to all of us."

In addition to intellectual exercise, Jordan is an avid believer in keeping the body active.

Loading a cassette into her tape player, she placed a 5-foot-long wooden rod over her shoulders and started waltzing, slowly pulling the rod down her back. The exercise "keeps the chin out of the navel," she says.

Her husband died in 1979 and she has no children, but Jordan says she doesn't get lonely.

"I would if it wasn't for the fact I've learned how to accept what is. I'm interested in life and learning and getting ahead."

Source: Adapted from B. Baskevill, "Getting old isn't the same as aging." Associated Press.

BOX 5.3

ELDERHOSTEL: CONTINUED OPPORTUNITIES FOR GROWTH IN LATE ADULTHOOD

Using the youth hostels in Europe as a model, *Elderhostel* provides older persons with both intellectual stimulation and physical challenges. Developed by Martin Knowlton in 1975, *Elderhostel* began with five institutions of higher education offering programs to 200 *Elderhostelers.* The growth of the program has since been quite dramatic; in 1983, over 700 schools in the United States and Canada and 67,000 elderly learners participated in *Elderhostel.* Moreover, *Elderhostel* programs are offered in Great Britain, Denmark, Finland, Norway, Sweden, France, Germany, and Holland. They are based "in the belief that retirement does not mean withdrawal, that one's later years are an opportunity to enjoy new challenges" (*Elderhostel* brochure, 1984).

Elderhostel offers a wide variety of liberal arts and science courses at low cost that "explore various aspects of human experience." Students usually enroll for one or two weeks' duration for one to three courses and participate in a variety of extracurricular activities at each campus. There are no exams and no required homework assignments, though instructors often make suggestions for outside reading. Each course assumes no previous knowledge of the subject, so that elders regardless of background can enroll. Participants, living in college dorms and eating with other students, often travel from campus to campus or combine *Elderhostel* with family visits or vacations.

The following is a smattering of the offerings to *Elderhostel* students. *Elderhostel's* aim is to provide those interested in continued learning with high quality education that is rich in content, personally relevant, and fun!

Meet the Southwest
Historical approach to ranching, mining, railroads, and lumbering through on-site visits supplemented by lectures, slides, and optional Narrow Gauge Rail trip. Relive the years that the Southwest was "tamed."

Bites, Bytes, the Computer, and You
An introduction to the development and use of microcomputers in the home, classroom and industry. Hands-on experience with word processing, spread sheet, and database software packages. Located in a new computer facility.

Backstage at the Theatre
Class includes involvement with a summer theatre production, including a backstage visit during rehearsals, meeting the actors, learning about sets, costumes, etc., as well as attendance at a performance.

Holistic Health Workshop
Introduction to the holistic health concept, including wellness, prevention, and self-responsibility. Intervention for stress-management with relaxation techniques, nutritional support, as well as identification of health and lifestyle behaviors.

Drawing—From the Inside Out
How many times have you said, "I can't draw a straight line!"? Using a step-by-step approach, you will learn how to look at an image and coordinate the use of eyes and hands to interpret your unique vision as a permanent creation.

Comedy, Wit and Humor
Psychology of humor and wit in contemporary America. What makes us laugh? Why? What humor reveals about ourselves, others. Its various forms of expression—political, social, economic—are examined through anecdotes, stand-up comics, etc.

Source: Elderhostel Catalog, Summer 1988, Vol. 19, No. 2.

quisition of leadership skills in an older adult-teacher training program. However, while these skills were retained on a short-term basis, participants did not always maintain their original level six months later.

By taking into account all of the factors discussed above, we can not only encourage adult learners in their pursuit of educational goals but also reinforce the perception that one's mind can still work quite well! Willis

(1985) notes a study by Flanagan and Russ-Eft (1976), which found that among project TALENT volunteers, those in their mid-thirties were least satisfied with their status regarding use of their minds "through learning, attending school, improving your understanding, or acquiring additional knowledge." These individuals had been followed up 15 years after they originally participated in the project as high school students. Given the generally negative views about change in abilities with age held by some people, these individuals might be prone to even more negative expectations of their own intellectual lives as they age. Altering expectations about continued learning throughout adulthood could provide an important influence on adults of all ages.

Predictions about adult learners suggest that they will be more diverse and more highly educated in the future (Engle, 1990). Education will not only help individuals to maintain their survival skills, but also meet the needs of those who wish to be retrained for new careers (Long, 1990). For these reasons, interventions based on individual differences in abilities, interests, and educational and personal goals are critical to enhancing learning skills. Wanting to learn new skills may be influenced by changes in one's career plans, or may simply reflect a desire to acquire new knowledge for its own sake (see Daniel et al., 1977; Hiemstra, 1985; Romaniuk & Romaniuk, 1982).

Reflecting this broader perspective toward lifelong learning and education, Willis (1985) has suggested five possible goals that the adult learner might achieve, through either formal education or more informal (noncredit, self-directed) activities. These goals are

1. Aiding the individual in understanding the changes in body and behavior that reflect basic biological processes of aging;
2. Helping the adult learner to understand and cope with technological/cultural change (e.g., becoming computer literate);
3. Making possible the development of skills to help overcome the obsolescence created by rapid cultural change;
4. Helping in the pursuit of second, or third, careers; and
5. Facilitating the formation of skills that are personally relevant, rather than occupationally relevant, after retirement; gaining information to find satisfying leisure activities or volunteer roles.

Thus, education can serve many ends for different adult learners at different points in their lives. But it is important that such efforts begin early in adulthood (Ansello & Hayslip, 1979; Willis, 1985). This makes it more likely that individuals will see their learning and memory skills positively. Positive views about one's learning skills reflect what existing skills might be used for and also influence the individual's efforts in developing new skills (Sterns & Hayslip, 1990).

Many adults see no reason to develop their cognitive skills, because they see these efforts as being doomed to failure based on their expectations of decreased ability with increasing age and the youth-oriented "production mentality" (Ansello & Hayslip, 1979). The production-mentality mind-set suggests that skills, interests, and abilities must lead to the attainment of a well-defined goal, such as a college diploma, new or better job, or preparation for a future life role.

A shift toward the production mentality was dramatically illustrated in a recent poll of college-age students taken by *Newsweek,* which showed that greater numbers of students are attending college solely to get better jobs or make more money. This orientation toward learning (i.e., that learning must lead to a better job) may prevent many adults from pursuing formal education. They may be denied access to such opportunities and the educational process (Ansello & Hayslip, 1979). It may also simply hinder the desire for new learning.

We want to encourage the adult learner to continue to be "alive" mentally and to continue to develop his or her learning and memory skills. To do so, we must not only focus on the means by which to achieve this, but also change our own attitudes about the adult's ability to learn. In this regard, too, we should distinguish instrumental (goal-oriented) interventions from expressive (non-goal-oriented, individually centered) ones in order to meet each learner's needs (Danish, 1980; Hiemstra, 1976). In short, the ends as well as the means for enhancing cognitive abilities in young adulthood and old age need to be given equal consideration.

Quite suddenly and without warning, Herb fell victim to the old adage, "If you don't use it, you lose it."

Robertson-Tchabo (1980, p. 516) has suggested that "the answer to the question, 'Why should old dogs learn new tricks?' is the same as that for younger dogs—because they want and need to learn new behaviors." The question of how best to enhance the potential for continued cognitive growth in adulthood, which we raised at the beginning of this chapter, needs to be accompanied by the question, To what end are these newly acquired skills to be put? If at all possible, these goals should be relevant to the adult's abilities, personality, interests, and life goals.

SUMMARY

In this chapter we discussed *learning* and *memory*, which are both inferred processes. They are inferred because we cannot observe them directly. Furthermore, they are of great importance and have many implications regarding how all of us develop and learn during the adult phase of the life cycle. We pointed out that learning and memory are separate but interrelated processes, since one cannot remember what has not yet been learned. Learning in its most basic sense involves the making of stimulus-response (S-R) associations. Memory loss, or forgetting, refers to the *breakdown* of these associations. *Unlearning* and *competition* at recall are forms of *interference* that cause this breakdown.

Research in learning and memory during all phases of the adult life cycle has focused on the distinction between *rote learning* and *mediated learning*. In addition, we can separate *structural* (sensory, primary, secondary, and tertiary memory stores) and *process* (registration, encoding, storage, and retrieval) approaches to memory. Deficits with aging occur at the *encoding* and *retrieval* stages of memory processing and in the *secondary* memory stores. Findings for *primary* and *tertiary* memory in some cases are unclear. Memory and learning deficits, where they exist, can be lessened in learners of all ages via a number of different types of interventions, such as *organization* or the *method of loci*. Learning and memory performance can also be improved by a number of *noncognitive* interventions, such as reducing anxiety about failure and treating depression.

Recently, attention has been directed to the study of learning and memory in *ecologically valid contexts*. The context in which learning occurs has been recognized as an important factor in the design and implementation of adult education and life-long learning programs. Such programs serve a number of diverse needs for the adult learner. We must place equal emphasis on the *ends* and the *means* by which to improve the cognitive skills of individuals during adulthood.

KEY TERMS AND CONCEPTS

Learning
Memory
Acquisition
Negative/positive transfer
Paired-associates task
Serial learning task

Retrieval
Deep versus shallow processing
Recognition versus recall tasks
Inspection versus anticipation intervals
Memory for text
Secondary memory
Tertiary memory
Registration
Encoding
Storage
Generic or semantic memory
Episodic memory
Interference
Stimulus-response (S-R) associations
Cognitive/noncognitive influences
Rote versus mediated learning
Explicit versus implicit memory
Ecologically valid learning
Unlearning
Task pacing
Self-efficacy
Mnemonic devices
Sensory memory
Primary memory
Metamemory
Method of loci
Motor skill learning
Instrumental learning

REVIEW QUESTIONS

1. Why is the study of learning and memory in adulthood important?
2. In what ways are learning and memory similar? How are they different from one another?
3. Define interference. What is its relationship to memory?
4. Why is the context in which learning and memory occur important in adulthood?
5. What is the difference between rote and mediated learning?
6. What is the difference between a structural approach and a process-oriented approach to understanding memory?
7. What is a levels-of-processing approach to memory? How does it help us to understand memory and aging?
8. What is the distinction between cognitive and noncognitive influences on learning and memory in adulthood? What are some examples of noncognitive factors affecting performance?
9. What is task pacing? How does it affect learning and memory in younger versus older adults?
10. What is ecologically valid learning? What are some examples of ecologically valid learning tasks that have been used with older adults?

CHAPTER 6

Cognition: Intelligence

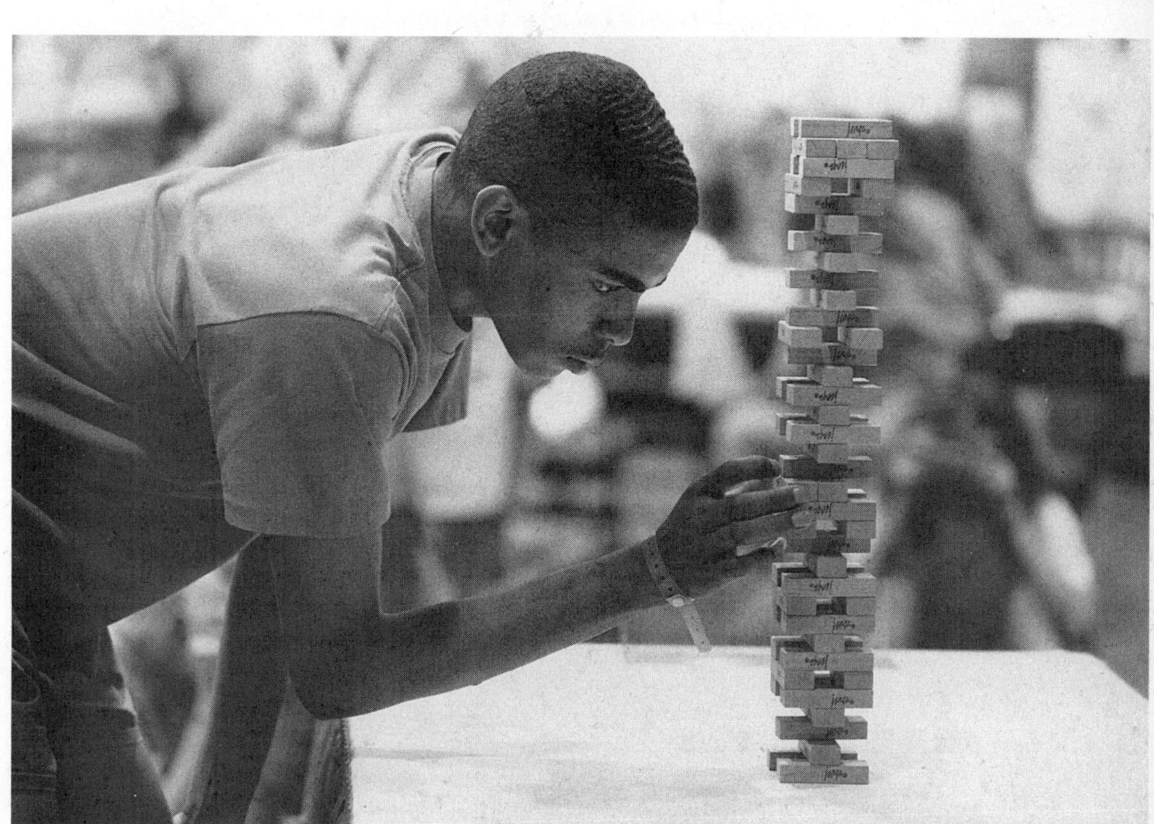

CHAPTER OUTLINE

INTELLIGENCE: ITS RELEVANCE TO OUR DAILY LIVES

People make many important decisions about our lives and others' based on an estimate of how intelligent we are. Entering school, being hired for or promoted to a new job, being forced to retire, and being institutionalized are all in some measure influenced by our own or others' judgments about our intellectual skills.

In everyday life, we often use the concept of intelligence to aid us in assessing our own or another's behavior and underlying competence (see Box 6.1). Consequently, our ideas about whether intelligence declines with age affect not only estimates of our skills at present, but also decisions we make about our goals and plans for the future. Thus, the answer to the often-heard question, "What do you want to do when you graduate?" for many of us involves an evaluation of our general ability, or perhaps an evaluation of our ability in a specific area of expertise (Should I go on to medical school?). Identifying someone as "bright" or "dull" can therefore have important emotional and vocational consequences for that individual.

Intelligence is a value-laden term, one we are quick to fall back on in explaining behavior but nevertheless have difficulty in defining. It means different things to different individuals, depending on (1) their

HOW DO ADULTS VIEW INTELLIGENCE?

We all have our own ideas about what intelligence is. We use particular behaviors to make inferences about our own and others' intellectual ability. What behaviors are these?

Fitzgerald and Mellor (1988) looked at adults' so-called implicit theories about intelligence (Sternberg et al., 1981). In other words, what behaviors do adults usually associate with intelligence? Approximately 100 adults between the ages of 18 and 79 years, when asked about a variety of specific behaviors, were able to separate "unintelligent" behaviors from intelligent ones, as follows:

Unintelligent Behavior	*Intelligent Behavior*
Has a narrow perspective on problems	Is on time for appointments
Refuses to accept the ideas of others	Displays varied interests
Does not communicate effectively	Aware of new problems arising out of solutions to old problems
Does not consider range of options	Identifies connections among ideas
Cannot articulate goals of action	Reasons logically and well
Lacks interest in solving problems	Reads widely
Does not understand other people	Makes fair judgments
Lacks respect for others	Listens well
Does not adapt quickly and well to new situations	Is sensitive to other people's needs and desires
	Able to cope with everyday environment

In a second study, Fitzgerald and Mellor studied whether these conceptions of intelligent behaviors could be meaningfully organized. Again, sampling adults, who represented a somewhat more narrow age range, they concluded that perceptions could be grouped into three highly related clusters of behaviors. Examples of each are:

Cluster 1: Practical Problem-solving Items

Reasons quickly and well

Identifies connections among ideas

Is able to apply knowledge to problems at hand

Sees individual elements in their overall context

Thinks before speaking and doing

Makes good decisions

Aware of new problems arising out of solutions to old problems

Cluster 2: Verbal Learning and Culture Items

Speaks clearly and articulately

Appreciates the arts

Displays good vocabulary

Is verbally fluent

Converses well

Reads with comprehension

Reads widely

Cluster 3: Social Competence and Character

Is sensitive to other people's needs and desires

Able to cope with the everyday environment

Emotions are appropriate to the situation

Displays common sense

Accepts others for what they are

Admits mistakes

Remains calm under pressure

In general, people were more able to clearly separate intelligent from unintelligent behavior than they were able to organize intelligent behaviors into distinct groups. Perhaps we use the more general judgments about intelligent and unintelligent behaviors to evaluate our competence on an everyday basis. In any case, people are "smart" or "dumb" to us, based on our observation of their behavior.

background and training, and (2) the everyday behaviors they are attempting to understand or predict. For many reasons, then, intelligence is a concept that demands clear definition over the entire life span.

This chapter discusses the concept of intelligence and its development over the adult life span. How and why intelligence grows and changes with age has been the subject of much research and debate among professionals in the fields of developmental aging psychology and education over the last 30 years (see Jensen, 1969; Matarazzo, 1972).

We will organize our discussion of intelligence and its development during adulthood around (1) major ideas and approaches to intelligence and their relevance to adult development and aging, and (2) whether intelligence actually declines with increasing age.

Defining Intelligence: A Brief History

Historically, definitions of intelligence have evolved from being very philosophical in nature to being more empirical and objective. This shift tends to be associated with Binet's (1905) development of the concept of **mental age.** Mental age refers to an individual's performance on a variety of intellectual tasks relative to that of other people of the same age (Matarazzo, 1972). While it was first used to study simple intellectual capacity, the popularity of the **intelligence quotient** for this purpose soon waned. The primary reason for this was that the method of determining IQ—mental age divided by chronological age—did not allow children of different ages to be compared. For example, a child of six and a child of ten with the same mental age, say eight, would not be equally intelligent for their ages. In fact, the six-year-old would be considered bright and the ten-year-old would be considered dull using this method of computing IQ. Moreover, age changes in mental age might be more rapid at some points in development than at others, also making it difficult to compare children using the mental age approach. Furthermore, adults could achieve a top mental age of only 16. Thus, a 50-year-old would have an IQ of only 33 using this method (see Rebok, 1987).

These problems led to a shift away from a concept of IQ based on mental age to one calculating IQ based on deviation from the mean. That is, each person's IQ was expressed in terms of the extent to which it differed or deviated from an average of 100 for people of a given age range. **Deviation IQ** therefore allows us to compare individuals, regardless of age, in common terms, that is, to what extent someone's IQ is above or below 100. In order to compare people of different ages, however, an **age credit** was given to the older persons to allow comparison of the standardized scores, using data collected from people 20 to 34 years old. Likewise, an **age debit** was used to compute the IQs of individuals who were younger (Botwinick, 1973). Based on a presumed decline of IQ with age, the resulting scores were then set equal to an average IQ of 100 using this method of correction (see Figure 6.1). Here we see that bias against individuals' to maintain and/or increase their intelligence as they age has literally been "built into" the method of calculating IQs, which are derived

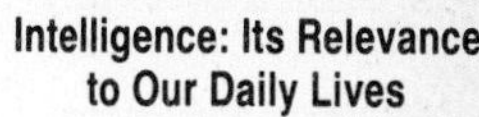

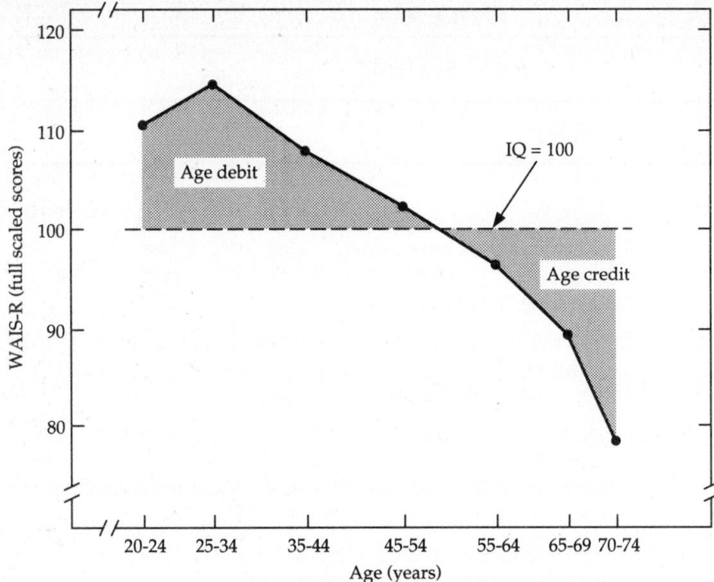

Figure 6.1 WAIS-R full-scaled scores as a function of age. Data were obtained from Table 20 of the WAIS-R Manual (Wechsler, 1981, pp. 97–109) by culling sum of scaled scores of IQs of 100. *Source:* Botwinick. (1973).

from the Wechsler Adult Intelligence Scale (WAIS) (see Table 6.1). Note that the WAIS is perhaps the most commonly used test of intelligence among psychologists and educators today.

It is important to realize that an IQ of 100 indicates average intelligence and is an arbitrary decision or value judgment; the figure could just as easily be 150, or 60. Whether these numbers necessarily indicate anything about an individual's innate ability is certainly arguable. Moreover, the particular items that appear on any intelligence test are quite arbitrary—a function of the test constructor's own beliefs about what exactly intelligence is.

For example, traditional IQ tests, which rely on middle-class words, values, and experience, might unfairly penalize people who are not highly educated, or individuals of various racial and ethnic groups (see Rebok, 1987). While there is some controversy over whether IQ tests are unfair to minorities (Barrett & Depinet, 1991), most educators agree that traditional standardized IQ tests do a poor job of measuring intelligence in people who are from lower socioeconomic-class backgrounds, due to the combined effects of poverty, ill health, malnutrition, impoverished living environments, and lack of education (Rebok, 1987). If test items were geared to the experiences of such people, scores would most likely paint a different picture. Thus, an individual's IQ is somewhat arbitrary since it is influenced by a number of factors.

You might more easily understand this point if you think about your grade-point average. For any number of reasons, that number is also some-

TABLE 6.1

WAIS-R SUBTESTS

Scale	Sample Items
Verbal tests	
General information	1. How many wings does a bird have? 2. How many nickels make a dime? 3. What is steam made of? 4. Who wrote "Tom Sawyer"?
General comprehension	1. What should you do if you see someone forget his book when he leaves a restaurant? 2. Why is copper often used in electrical wires?
Arithmetic	1. Sam had three pieces of candy and Joe gave him four more. How many pieces of candy did Sam have altogether? 2. Three women divide eighteen golf balls equally among themselves. How many golf balls did each person receive?
Similarities	1. In what way are a lion and a tiger alike? 2. In what way are a circle and a triangle alike?
Vocabulary	This test consists simply of asking, "What is a ______________?" or "What does ______________ mean?" The words cover a wide range of difficulty.
Performance tests	
In addition to verbal tasks of the kinds illustrated above, there are a number of performance tasks involving the use of blocks, cut-out figures, paper and pencil puzzles, etc.	

Source: Adapted from Wechsler Adult Intelligence Scale—Revised.

what arbitrary; it depends on the particular courses you have taken, your energy level, state of health, whether you were motivated to do well during a particular semester, your family or work responsibilities, and whether the course load itself was a heavy one. Someone with an undergraduate GPA of 3.8 who has few responsibilities, whose academic load is light, and whose course work is composed of beginning-level offerings might not be seen as doing as well as someone whose GPA is 3.0 but who works full-time, who is raising a family, and whose course load is a comparatively heavy one composed of upper-level courses. In this case, who is the better student?

Using this same analogy, we could also ask whether grades give us reliable information about who will ultimately be the most successful in real life, or who will even be the better graduate student. For example, scoring high on certain scales of the WAIS-R, such as Vocabulary, Comprehension, or Information (see Table 6.1), may reflect one's formal educational background or simply be a function of an avid interest in reading and acquiring diverse facts. Being intelligent, in this sense, may predict success in fields such as Library Science or English but do little to explain why an individual might have difficulty in following directions or reassembling a lawn mower engine!

We use our intellectual skills in many ways, and intelligence is often relative to the everyday demands on us.

We need to take into account a number of diverse factors in both defining and measuring intelligence in adults, whether the person tested is 25 or 75 years old. For example, the individual's health, work or living environment, family background, interests, motives, personality, and skills in other areas such as memory all influence performance on any test of intelligence. We will have more to say later about these factors as influences on whether intelligence declines in adulthood.

It is also important to point out that one should rely on intelligence-test data sensibly and without bias for both practical and basic research use. In this sense, how individuals *use* their intelligence can reveal a great deal about their personalities and relationships with others at school and at work. Ultimately, what we are seeking to predict is intelligent behavior, which we believe reflects an underlying set of abilities or skills that intelligence tests measure.

If we are aware of the many influences on performance, however, intelligence tests can indeed help us measure what skills individuals actually have in order to help them adapt to everyday life. Because intelligence tests are closely related to academic abilities and school achievement, they may be able to predict academic difficulties, later occupational involvement, or vocational success (Anastasi, 1988; Barrett & Depinet,

1991). In any case, they are currently used in primary and secondary schools, industry, the civil service, the armed forces, mental hospitals, and private clinics for a variety of purposes, including personnel selection and evaluation, diagnosis, treatment, and vocational counseling, with much success.

Only when we thoroughly understand what intelligence is—and is not—as well as why it changes with age, are we in a position to help individuals use their abilities to the fullest. Let us review some major ideas about intelligence to introduce some order to the confusion about just what the concept means.

ADULTS SPEAK

VIEWS ABOUT INTELLECTUAL GROWTH AND CHANGE

Some of us have fairly negative expectations about our intelligence and learning ability as we grow older and hold similar views about older people themselves. Yet, not all adults share this rather pessimistic view, and still others are somewhat ambivalent. Bits and pieces of each perspective are expressed in the statements of the adults we interviewed about learning and intelligence.

Keeping current and constantly working to learn new skills are very important to many adults, as is having a healthy, positive attitude about one's ability to do so. There is much truth to the notions "what you see is what you get" and "use it or lose it" when it comes to the aging of our cognitive skills.

A 29-year-old man said: "I believe older people can be taught new ideas. I do not believe they are as capable of learning as someone who is younger. I feel this is so because they do not like to learn new things. They would rather stick with what has worked in the past. However, I do respect older people for their wisdom about life. Older people obtain lots of information from experience. . . . I also believe intelligence increases with age if it is worked at."

A 44-year-old woman had this to say: "An old person is without hope. An old person has a "wearing-out" attitude written on his face because society looks and judges old people this way. Most people think of gray hair, wrinkles, stooped posture, lack of metabolic functioning, and hopelessness when old age is mentioned. Wrong! Age is in the mind; the body follows faster or slower because of the mind-set. . . . If the older person is willing to learn, behavior modification is possible. I am certain that a person's willingness to survive motivates activity. The personal characteristics of the individual, regardless of age, will regulate the rate and volume of learning new things. . . . Intelligence is a capability. If you don't use, you lose it. It is that simple. Barring disease, age has no impact on intelligence. Now wisdom, that's a whole different ballgame!"

A 70-year-old woman said, with a tone of resentment: "One should keep changing and not get in a rut. I believe the learning process continues across the life span, providing one wants to learn. At the moment, I am in a rut! . . . Intelligence does not increase. Its manifestations change, but it does not decrease either. . . . A person becomes old around the age of sixty. Other characteristics would be slowing down, and gray hair."

PSYCHOMETRIC APPROACH TO INTELLIGENCE

Historically, ideas about intelligence have been heavily influenced by research derived from the **psychometric tradition.** The psychometric approach to intelligence focuses on the assessment of an individual's testable intelligence via the use of distinct scales. This approach assumes that scores obtained from these scales reflect real qualities or abilities that exist within the person. What has emerged from this tradition is a concern for how intelligence is organized structurally. That is, is there one general ability under which all types of performance can be organized, or is intelligence more complex, say, 2 factors, or 7, or 100?

From a very practical point of view, the answer to this question will influence one's ideas about the development of intelligence or its assessment. For example, how many different measures must one choose in order to assess an individual's intellect adequately? Should similar scales be used to assess individuals of varying ages and backgrounds?

For instance, for a group of high school students we might require only one scale, measuring general ability, to adequately assess intelligence for the purpose of predicting college performance. On the other hand, for a sample of adults, for the purpose of predicting performance in a complex job situation, we might require measures of five different abilities. For this reason, it would not be appropriate to compare the scores obtained from the two groups. Not only are different types of abilities being measured—general versus specific skills—but what we are trying to predict (school success versus job performance) is also very different.

For our purposes, how intelligence is organized also deserves consideration because of its implications for the development of intelligence in adulthood. If intelligence is composed of more than one general ability, it challenges the wisdom of comparing individuals of different ages in terms of some overall index of intelligence (IQ). If, as in the example above, we were trying to predict different types of intellectual performance, we might not want to use the same ability measures for both cases.

Howard Gardner (1983) has proposed a theory of multiple intelligences that is decidedly practical. It specifies many domains of intelligence that seem to relate to the everyday world and/or to occupational success. These domains include linguistic, musical, bodily-kinesthetic, and logical-mathematical intelligences (see Gardner, 1983, for a thorough discussion). It remains to be seen whether this view will come to be accepted as a viable approach to intelligence, particularly as it relates to knowledge of adult development and aging.

Most psychometric concepts of intelligence rely on a statistical technique known as **factor analysis.** Factor analysis provides an empirical guide to how many underlying factors explain relationships among a number of scales measuring various abilities and skills. For example, if we were to administer 20 ability measures to each of 200 individuals, factor analysis would enable us to identify any common ability or set of abilities accounting for performance in this battery of 20 scales. Depending on what specific

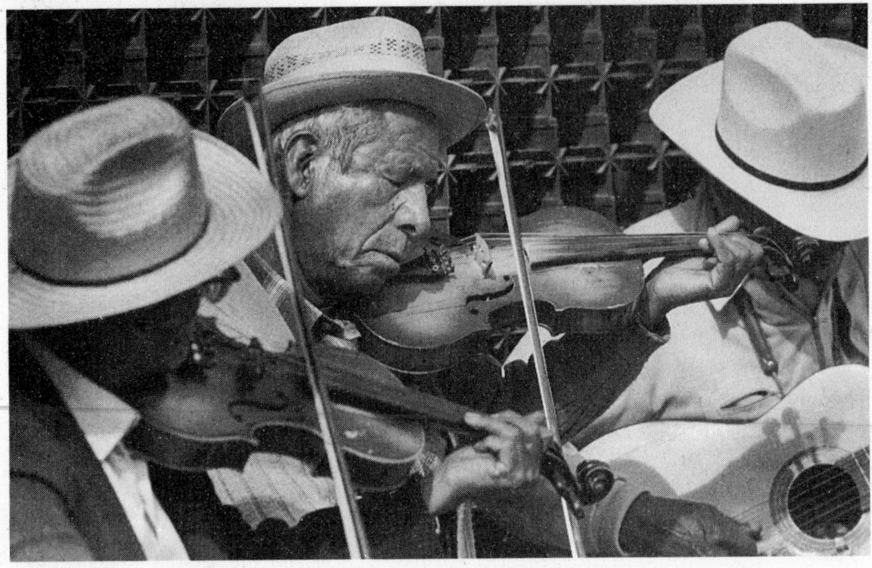

Many intellectual abilities are domain-specific (e.g., musical ability). Often, with continued use, one's intellectual skills can be maintained well into adulthood.

scales are used, how they are administered, and the nature of our sample (whether it is a very diverse one), one or more common factors could be derived by factor analysis.

Factor analysis, however, cannot provide us with a guide as to what scales to select in the first place. We would have to develop guidelines for this separately, based on a particular theory or our experience in everyday life. In addition, the factors identified by factor analysis are merely statistical abstractions. When we label factors, for example, as "verbal" or "performance," we are making value judgments based on the nature of the scales comprising that factor.

Thus, depending on a number of variables, including our choice of scales, method of administration, or the nature of the people comprising our sample, we can arrive at somewhat different conclusions about whether intelligence is explained by a single factor or by many factors. As a result, there are probably many equally plausible answers regarding the structure of abilities in adulthood.

We now turn to two theories that historically have been closely identified with adult developmental research in intellectual functioning. These theories are Thurstone's primary mental abilities approach, and the Horn-Cattell theory of crystallized and fluid abilities. Both are highly psychometric in nature.

Thurstone's Primary Mental Abilities Theory

Many researchers have considered general intellectual ability to be most important (see Rebok, 1987). However, Thurstone's ideas emphasize the opposite. Thurstone's theory of **primary mental abilities** (PMA) specifies several factors: spatial ability, perceptual speed, numerical ability, verbal relations, words, memory, and induction (see Figure 6.2). These abilities are correlated with one another to a certain degree. Thus, an estimate of someone's general intelligence could be obtained by measuring performance on the sales for each PMA factor.

Primary mental abilities have served as the framework within which Schaie has conducted perhaps the most extensive studies of adult intellectual development to date, which we will discuss more later in this chapter (Schaie, 1979).

Crystallized and Fluid Abilities

While Cattell presented his ideas about the existence of crystallized (Gc) and fluid (Gf) abilities in the early 1940s, it was not until 1965 that Cattell's doctoral student John Horn more or less popularized the theory, based on his research with a group of adults whose ages ranged from the twenties to the sixties. In contrast to previous ideas about the structure of intelligence, the distinction between Gc and Gf abilities is especially suited to adult development in that both intelligences are defined in such a way that predictions about developmental change are possible.

Crystallized and **fluid abilities** are formally defined as the "processing of perceiving relationships, educing correlates, maintaining span of immediate awareness in reasoning, abstracting, concept formation, and problem solving" (Horn, 1978, p. 220). Gf can be measured using unspeeded as well as speeded tasks involving figures, symbols, or words (see Figure 6.3). What is perhaps most distinctive about fluid ability is that it can be measured by tasks in which relatively little advantage comes from intensive or extended education and acculturation (Horn, 1978). Crystallized ability, however, reflects "relatively advanced education and acculturization either in the fundaments (contents) of the problem or in the operations that must be performed on the fundaments" (Horn, 1978, pp. 221–222). In other words, crystallized skills come about as a function of more organized, systematic, acculturated learning.

As the term suggests, Gf is fluid, or fluctuates with the demands made on us in novel situations. On the other hand, Gc crystallizes, or takes on a definite form or character with experience, making our early learned skills the basis for those acquired later on in life. In cases where a problem or situation demands that we manufacture a novel response to it, Gf will come into play, whereas when previously learned skills are required, Gc will be called on. Horn (1970, 1978) suggests, however, that this distinction is in some cases not as clear-cut as it would appear, since some tasks could require the exercise of either general ability.

Gf, then, is largely situational in character, whereas Gc is a function of the accumulation of formal and informal experience and skill over time. Different sets of underlying causal factors determine each skill. For example, decreased neurophysiological functioning with age influences changes in Gf, while cumulative intensive acculturation and education influences

A. **Verbal Meaning (V)**

This is the ability to understand ideas expressed in words. It is used in activities where information is obtained by reading or listening to words. The task requires verbal recognition via a multiple-choice format. In the following example the subject must select that alternative which is the best analog of the capitalized stimulus word:

BIG A. ILL B. LARGE C. DOWN D. SOUR

The test contains 50 items in increasing order of difficulty with a time limit of 4 min.

B. Space (S)

Measured here is the ability to think about objects in two or three dimensions. It may be described as the ability to imagine how an object of figure would look when it is rotated, to visualize objects in two or three dimensions, and to see the relations of an arrangement of objects in space. The more recent technical definition of this ability is *spatial orientation.* Space is measured by 20 test items, with a time limit of 5 min. In the example given below every lettered figure that is the same as the stimulus figure, even though it is rotated, is to be marked. Figures that are mirror images of the first figure are not to be marked.

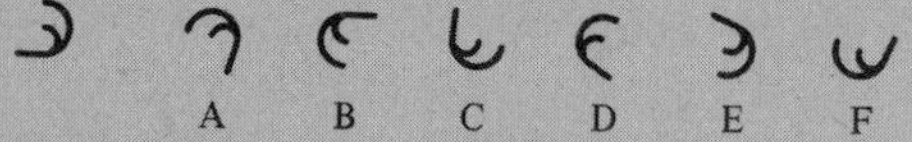

C. Reasoning (R)

The ability, which in current factor taxonomies is often more specifically identified as *inductive reasoning,* involves the solution of logical problems—to foresee and plan. The Thurstones (1949) propose that persons with good reasoning ability can solve problems, foresee consequences, analyze a situation on the basis of past experience, and make and carry out plans according to recognized facts. Reasoning is measured by such items as the following:

a b x c d x e f x g h x h i j k x y

The letters in the row form a series based on a rule. The problem is to discover the rule and mark the letter which should come next in the series. In this case the rule is that the normal alphabetic progression is interrupted with an x after every second letter. The solutions therefore would be the letter i. There are 30 test items with a time limit of 6 min.

D. Number (N)

This is the ability to work with figures and to handle simple quantitative problems rapidly and accurately. It is measured by test with items of the following kind:

17
84
29
140 R W

The sum of each column of figures is given. However, some of the solutions given are right and others are wrong. Sixty test items are given with a time limit of 6 min.

E. Word Fluency (W)

This ability is concerned with verbal recall involved in writing and talking easily. It differs from verbal meaning further in that it concerns the speed and ease with which words are used, rather than the degree of understanding of verbal concepts. The measurement task requires the subject to write as many words as possible beginning with the letter S during a 5-min. period.

Figure 6.2 Thurstone's Primary Mental Ability (PMA). *Source:* Reprinted by permission of the publisher from *SRA Primary Mental Abilities, Ages 11–17, Form AM* by L. L. Thurstone & T. G. Thurstone. Chicago, IL: Science Research Associates, Inc. Copyright 1948 by Science Research Associates, Inc.

Induction (Letter Series)

In these questions, write the letter that comes next in a series of letters.

Example:

A B C D E F G ____NA

The next letter in this series is H. Try another example.

Example:

A B B C C C D D D D E E E E ____NA

This time the next letter is E. You can see that A occurs once, B twice, C three times, D four times, and so E should occur five times. But there are only four E's listed. Therefore, the next letter in the series should be E.

Here are some examples with the right answer given. Study these examples to make sure you understand this kind of question.

Example:

G F E D C B A Z __Y__ NA

In this series the alphabet is written backwards. When the series comes to A, it goes to the end of the alphabet to the letter Z, and continues on backwards, so Y is next in the series.

Example:

R S R T R U R V R __W__ NA

Here the letters in the series S T U V are separated by an R. The last letter to appear is one of these R's, so the next letter is W.

Figural Relations (Matrices)

Find the picture on the right that should be in the empty square on the left. Write the letter that corresponds with the correct answer in the space to the far right next to the problem number.

Example:

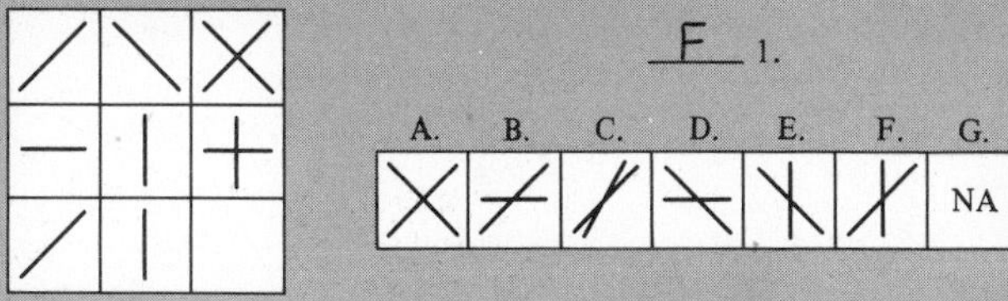

The correct answer –F.–has been written in the answer space. Make sure you understand why this is the correct answer. Here is another example for you to try:

Example:

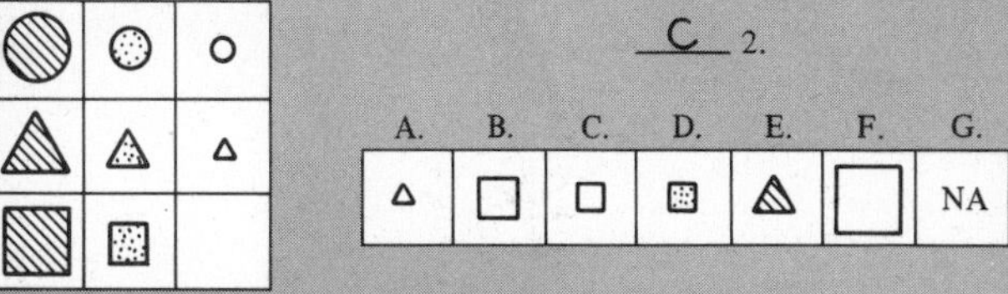

Figure 6.3 Measures of Gf-typical induction and figural relations items. *Source:* Adapted from J. Horn (1975). Gf-Gc Sampler. University of Denver Mimeo. Reprinted by permission of the author.

Gc. Gf is thought to increase and then decline over the life span, whereas Gc should generally increase or remain stable over the adult years (Horn & Cattell, 1966, 1967; Horn, 1970, 1978).

The distinction between fluid and crystallized intelligence (Horn, 1978, 1982) reinforces the complex picture of intelligence and aging painted thus far. In this case, the curves of stability and growth for Gc and decline for Gf suggest intelligence to be both multidirectional and multidimensional in nature. In this case, too, it would be inappropriate to compare older and younger adults in terms of IQ, since the scales measuring IQ are partially crystallized and partially fluid in nature.

You can see in Figure 6.4 that the two abilities exhibit a different path of development, and also vary greatly from a global index of intelligence, or general IQ (Horn, 1970). Global tests fail to separate crystallized and fluid intelligences.

Horn (1982) points out that apparently simple distinctions such as learned/unlearned and verbal/performance are in fact complex and are not equivalent to the Gc-Gf distinction. He underscores the unique nature of Gf and Gc in terms of the kinds of learning experiences that underlie each. Gc is determined by purposeful, acculturational learning provided by societal institutions, such as the home environment, the school, and by implication, the work environment. Gf is, on the other hand, determined by idiosyncratic, largely self-determined casual learning influences. Horn also maintains that Gc and Gf are each, to a certain extent, a function of neurological factors, such as the number of active brain cells or the effects of stroke damage. However, the evidence for the differential relationship be-

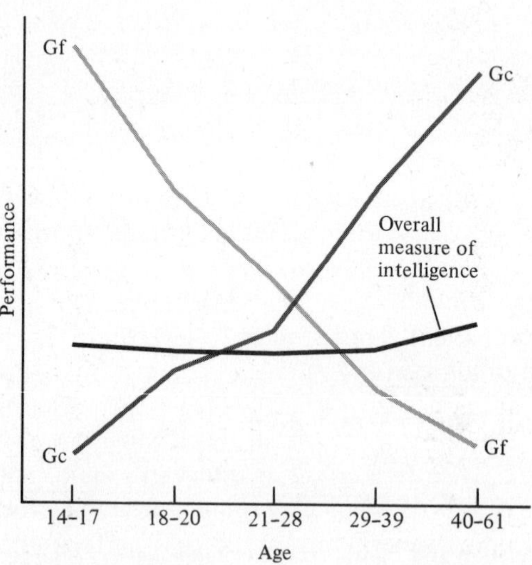

Figure 6.4 Age curves for Gc and Gf versus overall intelligence. *Source:* J. Horn. (1970). Organization of data on life-span development of human abilities. In L. Goulet and P. Baltes (Eds.), *Life-span developmental psychology: Research and theory* (p. 463). New York: Academic Press. Reprinted by permission of the author.

tween neurological damage and Gf versus Gc is indirect and somewhat sketchy (see Horn, 1982, 1985).

Physiological influences are but one set of causal factors that Horn sees as critical to the development and maintenance of intelligence in adulthood. Other influences are selective learning, family size and composition, values of parents or peers, one's own attitude toward aging, or whether one is labeled by others as disadvantaged or old. Consequently, in adulthood, a number of factors contribute to the growth and/or decline of Gc and Gf abilities, both within and between individuals. Some of these are traceable to earlier experiences, and some are in the present environment.

Gc is best assessed via measures of vocabulary skill, general information, and remote associations. An example of a remote-association question is, With what word can plain, Tarzan, and Dick be associated? The answer is Jane—as in plain Jane, Tarzan and Jane, and Dick and Jane. Gf is best measured via figural relations (matrices) tasks and induction (letter series) tasks (see again Figure 6.3).

It is also possible to choose measures that tap both kinds of intelligence. For example, verbal analogies where the content or meaning of the words is emphasized (e.g., edema is to medicine as homicide is to law) assesses Gc and to a lesser extent Gf. In the opposite case, which emphasizes a relationship between words whose meaning is well known (e.g., happy is to sad as dark is to light), Gf might be more important.

In recent years, Horn has expanded the notion of Gf and Gc to include other components. To accomplish this, Gf and Gc have been interrelated with other measures of personality traits such as carefulness, sensory/perceptual-motor slowing, short-term memory, and attention to more fully explain those processes that contribute to intellectual functioning. As a result, we can more completely explain *why* Gf and Gc exhibit differential paths of growth and decline over the life span (Horn, 1982, 1985). This approach is hierarchical; that is, the general factors are organized by level, from sensory, the most basic, to thinking, the most general.

Considerable variation can be observed both within and across individuals in Gf and Gc functioning. Some individuals may make more effort to sharpen their skills than do others (Horn, 1978). Moreover, some people are more prone to fatigue, anxiety, or attentional lapses than are others (Horn, 1978; Kennelly et al., 1985). These factors may either raise or lower the Gf or Gc performance of a given individual.

Because Gf performance is particularly variable, there has been considerable debate regarding losses with age in fluid ability and whether these losses in Gf are reversible by training or other interventions (Baltes & Schaie, 1976; Baltes & Willis, 1982; Donaldson, 1981; Horn & Donaldson, 1976). We will have more to say about improving intellectual performance shortly.

Whether the Thurstone or the Horn-Cattell approach is more valid is arguable, and most likely depends on what one is seeking to predict—vocational success? school achievement? everyday intelligent behavior? competence in later life?

We want to caution you about comparing theories of intelligence such as the PMA or Gf/Gc approaches. Because they rest on different assumptions and use different scales and methods for data collection, and because of sampling differences, studies based on different theories are difficult to compare (Reese & Overton, 1970). However, the evidence overwhelmingly indicates that general intelligence is *not* adequate to explain performance on the many tests and scales investigators have devised to assess intelligence. Intelligence is complex, and thus it should not surprise us if different aspects of intelligence change in different ways, and for different reasons in different people, as they age (see Chapter 1).

A practical implication of the fact that there are multiple intelligences is that no one need see him- or herself as more or less intelligent than others in an overall sense. Rather, it is more accurate to say that some individuals are brighter than others with regard to certain classes of abilities. For example, the highly educated older individual may have excellent verbal skills or command a wealth of information but do poorly in visualizing relationships between objects in space, a critical skill in assembling or disassembling an engine. Moreover, this person may still have difficulty in understanding and recalling directions despite being highly educated.

Thus, we see that the very complexity of intelligence supports the notion that we can all develop skills in some areas to perhaps compensate for deficiencies in other areas. One can frequently observe this among older adults who make an effort to maintain and even improve their vocabulary skills, while shying away from tasks or situations in which they cannot use past experience to their advantage. Such situations are often seen as too difficult, personally irrelevant, or simply requiring of too much effort (Hayslip, 1989). Thus, some adults develop skills that are already intact, while neglecting those they do not see as critical or necessary to everyday life experience (Hayslip, 1988).

INFORMATION-PROCESSING APPROACH TO INTELLIGENCE

A newer approach, termed the **information-processing perspective,** has enabled researchers to understand intelligence differently (Resnick, 1976; Sternberg, 1985; Sternberg & Detterman, 1979). An information-processing approach to intelligence stresses the person as an active processor of the information contained in a problem or in the real world. Individuals develop logical operations and strategies by which to understand and analyze information presented to them. For the most part, the intelligence and aging literature has been dominated by the psychometric approach, mainly due to the ease with which numerous batteries of scales can be administered relatively quickly to large numbers of people varying in age. Nevertheless, it is important to understand the general thrust of this newly emerging area of intelligence research.

By more clearly specifying the "representations, processes, and strategies" (Sternberg, 1985) individuals use in solving questions that measure intelligence, we can better understand and thus facilitate intellectual development among adults of all ages. Research in this area is very diverse, focusing on the various specific tasks or types of items most commonly found in intelligence tests, for example, spatial relations, analogies, and block design (Carroll, 1979; Keating, 1982; Sternberg, 1979).

Proponents of this approach to intelligence argue that while factor analysis has demonstrated that intelligence is complex, a more promising approach is to focus on so-called component processes that are themselves functions of the interaction between task influences and person influences. Examples of component processes are encoding, storage, retrieval, rule formation, and pattern analysis. It is principally through the study of this complex interaction between the person and the task that intelligence can best be understood, according to the information-processing theorists. Typically, this is accomplished through a task analysis, whereby performance on an intelligence test item is broken down into more basic units, or processes, that can be studied thoroughly.

Information-processing researchers have distinguished between *bottom-up* and *top-down* approaches to accomplishing this goal (Keating, 1982). Briefly, a bottom-up approach studies intelligence in terms of the basic qualities of individuals, seeing them as information-processing systems, without reference to intelligence per se. For example, a person's perceptual or memory skills might be crucial to understanding how people process information in an intelligence test. In a sense, intelligence as such no longer exists if we can understand it in terms of more basic processes (see Chapters 4 and 5).

A top-down approach, on the other hand, assumes that an intelligence test item is itself a complex task and breaks down this task into the basic skills essential to its solution. Thus, in this approach, the task's characteristics are important, not the skills of the person solving the task.

For example, performance on a measure of fluid intelligence can be broken down into the two basic components of content and process (Pel-

Complex tasks often require the use of our information-processing abilities. These skills are closely tied to fluid intelligence.

legrino & Glaser, 1979). This top-down approach to intelligence has been used with much success as a basis for enhancing performance on measures of Gf among the aged. For example, in such training, A, BB, CCC, _____, can be solved by simply adding one more of the next letter in the series, a simple arithmetic operation one can use to solve such a letter-series task, which measures Gf. In this case, the content is straightforward (letters); however, the process of solving a letter series item is critical.

In a sense, the top-down approach represents a kind of "marriage" between the psychometric and information-processing approaches. While factor analysis has defined fluid ability as an important dimension of intellectual development that varies across age, the identification of the basic processes critical to the solution of tasks measuring Gf has been accomplished by the componential researcher.

Crucial to the information-processing approach is the selection of tasks, such as reading and arithmetic analogies, that relate to the everyday world (Keating, 1982). Ideally, then, by using an information-processing approach to intelligence, we may discover and foster the component skills that individuals of all ages use on an everyday basis. This approach to intelligence, particularly if combined with the psychometric view, may be very fruitful in many ways and ultimately shape the intelligence tests of the future.

PSYCHOMETRIC INTELLIGENCE IN ADULTHOOD

We have so far discussed how intelligence has been defined, under the assumption that understanding the concept can lead to better understanding of its development in adulthood. On the basis of this discussion, we concluded that the idea of intelligence as a single underlying ability can probably be rejected. In contrast to, yet complementing, a psychometric approach to intelligence, the information-processing approach tries to understand how intelligence is exercised, through the study of underlying processes, which individuals utilize to demonstrate competence in situations requiring intelligent behavior. We now turn to a central topic of this chapter: whether intelligence declines with age.

Early cross-sectional studies (Doppelt & Wallace, 1955) found that overall WAIS performance peaked between ages 20 and 34, then declined slowly with age until about 60, with more severe declines afterward. However, longitudinal studies typically have displayed an increase in overall WAIS performance with age (Schaie & Labouvie-Vief, 1974).

A number of other studies using the WAIS have found the so-called "classic aging pattern" in intelligence (Botwinick, 1977, 1978). This refers to a decline in performance scores but relative stability in verbal scores (see Figure 6.5). However, we can more profitably understand intellectual aging by focusing on more specific abilities. Schaie's work using primary mental abilities and Horn's research using the crystallized-fluid abilities distinction are two outstanding examples of these focuses.

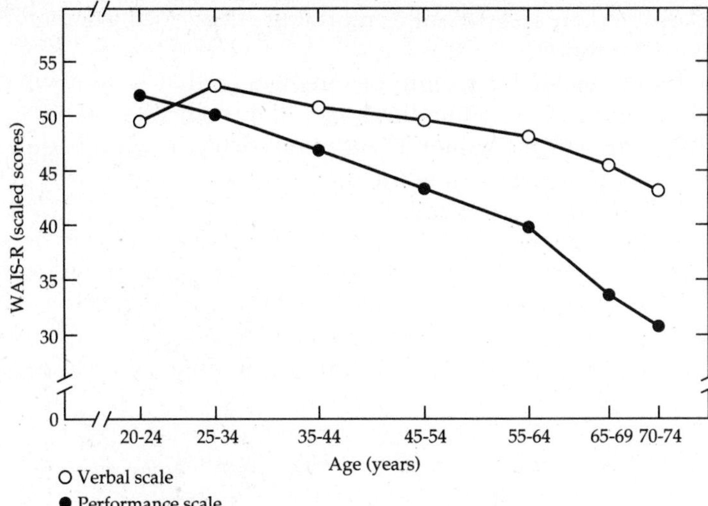

Figure 6.5 WAIS-R Verbal and Performance scores as a function of age. Data were obtained from Table 20 of the WAIS-R Manual (Wechsler, 1981, pp. 97–109) by culling sum of scaled scores of IQs of 100. (The Verbal scaled scores were multiplied by 5/6 to develop a common base with the Performance scaled scores.)

Schaie's PMA Research

As noted above, developmental research on intelligence has, to this point, been dominated by the psychometric tradition. Schaie's work on intelligence and aging best exemplifies the work done in this area.

In a comprehensive account of his research program, Schaie (1979) described a series of cross-sectional and longitudinal studies that began in 1956. Initially, he carried out a cross-sectional comparison of over 500 adults, ranging in age from 20 to 70 years and spanning seven different cohorts. In 1963, a new cross-sectional sample was drawn. In addition, a seven-year longitudinal follow-up of the subjects tested in 1956 was begun, using a battery of scales based on Thurstone's Primary Mental Abilities theory of intelligence. In 1970, a new random sampling of subjects was taken, and follow-ups of subjects originally interviewed in 1956 and 1963 were conducted. Also in 1970, new random samples from those originally tested in 1956 and 1963 were drawn. In 1977, this process was essentially repeated, so that Schaie now had independent samples from each of seven cohorts at 1956, 1963, 1970, and 1977, and longitudinal follow-ups (dependent samples) involving people of seven age ranges who had been originally interviewed at each of the four measurement points (Schaie & Hertzog, 1983).

By amassing data collected in this fashion, Schaie was able to examine the relative impact of age, cohort membership, and time of measurement on different aspects of intelligence in adulthood using a combination of cross-sectional and longitudinal analyses (see Chapter 2). These analyses also permitted an assessment of mortality effects (see Chapter 2) on intelligence in adulthood.

Schaie's results yielded a picture of intelligence that is somewhat complex and consistent with the multidimensional, multidirectional nature of development discussed in Chapter 1. Although Schaie's work is quite comprehensive, we will focus on only the most relevant findings bearing on the question of intelligence and age.

Data from the first cross-sectional study, conducted in 1956, suggested that different types of abilities demonstrated diverse age-related peaks of functioning (see Figure 6.6). Schaie found PMA reasoning to peak earliest, and space, verbal fluency, word fluency, and number abilities to peak later. Moreover, younger people had strengths in different areas than did those who were older.

The 1963 data found evidence for a time-of-measurement effect; those tested in 1963 were superior to those tested in 1956 at comparable ages. Moreover, longitudinal (1956–1963) findings suggested that age-related changes in intelligence were minimal until subjects reached their sixties.

Recall from Chapter 2 that sequential analyses can pit longitudinal time-of-measurement changes against age-cohort differences. Schaie's sequential data suggested that cohort differences were more important than chronological age in explaining the sectional or longitudinal age effects found for many abilities. These sequential analyses, however, also implied that, in early adulthood and very late adulthood, age effects on abilities within cohorts might also be substantial.

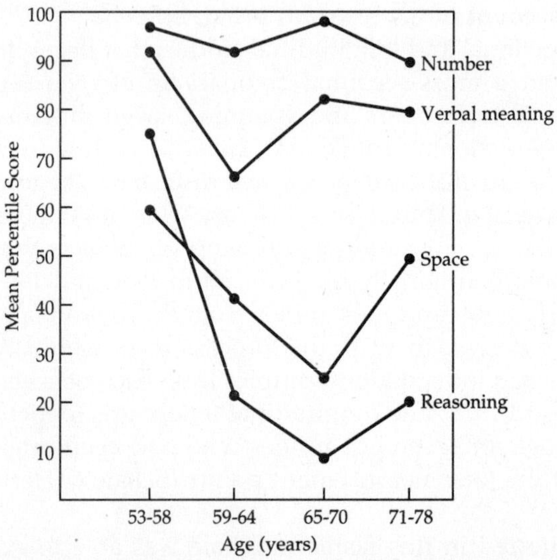

Figure 6.6 Age differences in scores on the factor components of the Primary Mental Abilities (PMA) Test. (Adapted from Schaie, Rosenthal, & Perlman, 1953, Figure 2. Copyright © 1953 by the Gerontological Society of America. Adapted by permission.)

Additional analyses of these data suggested positive cohort effects, that is, more favorable performance in successively younger cohorts, for verbal meaning, space, and reasoning. For number abilities, cohort effects were minimal, while for word fluency, cohort effects were slightly negative—younger cohorts scored more poorly (see Figure 6.7).

The 1970 follow-up analyses clearly suggested what Schaie's earlier data had pointed to: what had initially appeared as a decrement associated with age was attributable to cohort differences. Furthermore, the extent to which age decrements were found varied with both (1) the type of ability examined and (2) cohort membership (see Schaie, 1990).

Cross-sectional and longitudinal replications of seven-year follow-up analyses (1956 vs. 1963; and 1963 vs. 1970) to a large extent yielded similar findings. Clearly, the extent of age decrement in abilities varied with cohort membership. Moreover, for most abilities, a decline was apparent only relatively late in life, at age 67.

The third cross-sectional study in 1970 yielded substantial time-of-measurement effects, with advantages to those tested in 1970 for all PMA factors except word fluency. When the data were rearranged by cohort (see Schaie, 1979), dramatic cohort-specific patterns, again varying by PMA ability, emerged. Cohort sequential analyses (in 1970 and 1977), which allowed Schaie to measure age changes over seven-year intervals from 25 to 81 years and cohort differences for cohorts 1889 to 1938, again clearly indicated that cohort membership was more important in explaining these data than was age per se (Schaie & Hertzog, 1983). Schaie and Hertzog (1983) also found clear declines in most PMA factors after age 60, with

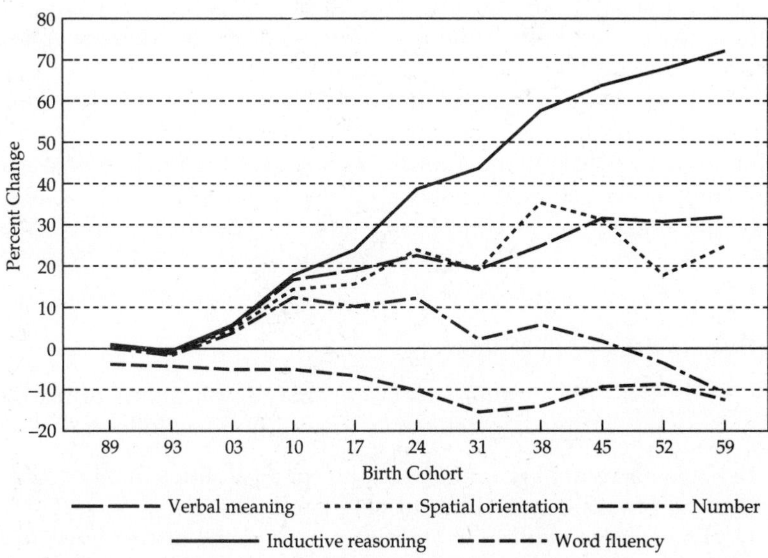

Figure 6.7 Cumulative cohort differences from 1889 base cohort for the mental abilities. *Source:* Schaie (1990). Cohort differences in mental abilities. *Late life potential* (p. 48). Gerontological Society of America.

minimal evidence for decline somewhat earlier. Schaie (1990) also reported that men and women score differently in some aspects of PMA performance. Across cohorts, women outscore men in reasoning and number, while for later cohorts only, men are generally superior in word fluency.

Schaie's analyses have also indicated that, in general, dropouts tended to initially score more poorly than those who did not drop out (Baltes et al., 1971; Schaie et al., 1973). Thus, longitudinal findings (varying by cohort) suggesting minimal declines with age may have been presenting an unduly positive picture of intellectual change with age.

WHAT CAN WE LEARN FROM SCHAIE'S RESEARCH?

What is perhaps most important to learn from Schaie's 21-year study of adult intelligence is that the notion of irreversible, biologically based decline in abilities with age is clearly unfounded. For the most part, it is the interaction of the sociocultural environment and aging that reduces or intensifies age decrements in intelligence. Simply put, different cohorts age intellectually in unique ways. And since the interaction between historical content and aging seems to vary with cohort membership, a complex picture of intelligence and aging emerges. Thus, according to Schaie, there is no such thing as universal, true decline (Baltes & Schaie, 1976).

Schaie's data indicate that declines in ability are largely restricted to those 70 or over. More importantly, they paint an optimistic picture for educators and for the young, middle-aged, and elderly individuals who believe that declines in their mental abilities are inevitable or beyond remediation.

Schaie (1983) also recommends caution regarding the everyday significance of a "statistically significant" drop in performance. For example, does recalling two fewer digits, solving arithmetic problems three seconds more slowly, or defining five fewer vocabulary items correctly imply that abilities in these areas have declined to the point where they will interfere with an individual's daily life? Perhaps not, especially if the individual uses "helpers" such as calendars and calculators, lists of things to be done or remembered, notes, or dictionaries and library resources. These aids can enable the individual to compensate for any losses in ability (see Chapter 5).

SUMMARY OF SCHAIE'S PMA RESEARCH

Schaie (1979, pp. 104–105) summarizes the primary implications of his research regarding the decline of intelligence in adulthood as follows:

1. Reliable decrements cannot be found for all abilities in all people. Decline is not likely at all until very late in life.
2. Decline is most evident in abilities where speed of response and the peripheral nervous system (external to the brain and spinal cord, involving the sensory organs or muscles) are involved.
3. Declines are evident in most abilities for individuals of any age

who have severe cardiovascular disease and those in their fifties and sixties who live in deprived environments (see Hertzog et al., 1978).

4. Data on intelligence and aging obtained from independent samples overestimate loss of abilities where losses in fact occur since these subjects do not have the benefit of practice. Repeated-measurement samples data accurately estimate age changes for those in better health and in more stimulating environments, while underestimating loss for those in worse health and/or living in impoverished situations.
5. Cohort effects account for more of the variance in intelligence with age than do ontogenetic (age-related), biologically based factors, with age effects assuming more importance only late in life.
6. Individual differences in what skills decline, as well as the extent of such decline, are substantial. Many older people, dependent on their health, their educational background, whether they are isolated from others, and whether they have maintained skills developed earlier, sustain and even improve their skills, while others decline much earlier in life.

While Schaie's research program has provided us with the most extensive knowledge base about intelligence and age, it is by no means the only program devoted to this task. A great deal of equally valuable information has been collected by others.

PIAGETIAN ABILITIES AND AGING

In contrast to psychometric intelligence, it is only recently that Piaget's notions of intellectual development have been applied to adult development and aging (Hooper et al., 1984). Piaget and Inhelder (1969) have suggested that intellectual development progresses through a series of discrete, biologically based stages from infancy through adolescence. According to Piaget's theory, what distinguishes later childhood and early adolescence (ages seven and up) from infancy and early child childhood is **operational thought.** Operational thought is characterized by the ability to use symbols (words) to solve problems and perform various mental activities. It is in contrast to **preoperational thought,** which requires the child to physically act out things in solving problems (Piaget & Inhelder, 1969).

Children at the preoperational stage are influenced by what their senses tell them. For example, after comparing two rows of equal numbers of blocks, one of which is longer than the other, they will say that the longer row has more blocks, even if the extra length is caused by spaces between the blocks. Older children, however, whose thinking is operational, realize that regardless of how the blocks appear, the two rows have an equal number of blocks. They can manipulate or transform the space between the blocks mentally to make a judgment; they have the ability to conserve on number. Their thinking is less egocentric, in that they can make judgments and solve problems more independently of what their senses tell them. While children in the so-called concrete operational stage can solve problems logically, as in the above example, operational thinking, characteristic of adolescents, is more abstract. Such individuals can reason logically and solve hypothetical problems—those that they have not necessarily had direct experience with.

Under the assumption that older people regress to an earlier level of development, many early researchers in this area investigated performance on Piagetian tasks of intelligence among aged people. Specifically, the hypothesis was that older people regress from formal operations back to a concrete operational or, in some cases, to a preoperational level of thinking. Whether such regression occurs at all is difficult to ascertain since nearly all the studies to date have been cross-sectional in nature (see Papalia & Bielby, 1974). Moreover, if regression in fact accompanies the aging process, whether it occurs for the same reasons that are responsible for cognitive growth in childhood and adolescence, such as biological change, is dubious.

Nevertheless, these studies clearly reveal age differences in Piagetian task performance. Older individuals are less able to successfully solve tasks requiring the transformation of number of objects or dealing with changes in the weight or volume of different objects. As in the above example, older adults fail to conserve on number; the number of blocks in each row is thought to vary with the length of the row. Their thinking is more egocentric because they draw conclusions on the basis of what their senses tell them, rather than their understanding of concepts and relationships—that four blocks are still four blocks regardless of how they are arranged.

Hornblum and Overton (1976), however, suggest that older people may see Piagetian tasks such as arrangements of blocks as childish or irrelevant to them personally. Moreover, Kausler (1991) notes that deficits in Piagetian task performance are rarely found in healthy, educated elderly people, and that errors on these tasks are also common among younger individuals. Thus, rather than interpret these findings as evidence for a qualitative shift in intellectual functioning with age, or regression, we might see them as quantitative in nature (see Blackburn & Papalia, 1992). That is, older people might solve these tasks more slowly, or simply make more errors; but they are indeed capable of solving them.

Postformal Operations in Adulthood

Rybash and associates (1986) have suggested that Piaget's formal operational stage of cognitive development is of limited use to the adult developmental theorist and researcher. According to these authors, formal operational thinking is characterized by a rational, logical, deductive approach to problem-solving and understanding the world. Formal operational thinkers must therefore ignore the context in which a problem is embedded. Formal operational thinking may also overemphasize abstract thinking, and the importance of emotion in making everyday decisions of a social or interpersonal nature must be recognized in order to understand adults' formal operational skills (Rybash et al., 1986).

Everyday problems may be ambiguous and ill-defined. Rybash et al. (1986, p. 32) note that "real-life problems, in contrast to formal operations problems, are 'open' to the extent that there are no clear boundaries of a problem and the context within which it occurs." As an example, they provide the problem confronting a woman who is deciding whether to have a child. **Postformal** operational thinkers would not see this decision as a purely abstract, logical one. Instead, it is influenced by a number of factors, for example, the woman's self-concept, demands on her time by her career, her socioeconomic status, her relationship with her husband, and whether she has his support to have a child, whether she has other children, and her health. How she defines the problem, as well as its solution, depends on the particular factors that both influence and are influenced by her decision to have or not to have a child. In other words, postformal operational thought is dialectical in nature (see Chapter 1). Postformal operational thinking is better understood as problem-finding, or discovering a new question to be answered, rather than problem-solving, or logical thinking that leads to a well-defined answer.

Postformal reasoning is relative; that is, knowledge is temporary rather than absolute. For example, we often solve a problem only to realize that there are new things to learn and new questions to ask about it. We enter the working world with a specified set of skills we think will enable us to be successful, only to find that our success brings new challenges and problems. Our working world is different from what it once was because of our success.

Many adult developmental researchers have explored age differences in the extent to which older versus younger adults engage in formal or postformal thinking. Labouvie-Vief et al. (1983), for example, presented to children and adults of varying ages the story of a woman who threatened to leave her husband if he came home drunk again. Each person was asked what the woman might do if this indeed were to happen. With increased age, respondents were *more* likely to give answers that failed to ignore different situations (contexts). For example, whether the woman could support herself, or whether the couple had children, might influence her decision to leave him should he come home drunk again.

Cohen (1979) presented college students and older adults with a short passage involving a grandfather and a mother engaged in different activities, such as cooking in the kitchen and reading in the living room. There is traffic outside, which is closer to the front of the house, where the living room is situated. Each person was asked who would be most disturbed by the traffic. College students invariably said "the grandfather," a product of logical deductive (formal) thought. Older adults, on the other hand, were more likely to offer interpretations based on other possibilities (see Labouvie-Vief, 1985). For example, the grandfather may be deaf, the traffic may not be constant, or the grandfather might move to a different part of the house to read.

It is possible to infer some breakdown in the logical thinking processes of the older adults from these data. However, as Labouvie-Vief

(1985, p. 525), notes, "Is it not possible that the adults in this study perceived different logical reasons from the ones of interest to the experimenter rather than none at all?" In contrast to thinking that is regressive, Labouvie-Vief (1985) argues for an important qualitative difference in the thinking processes of older adults that is characteristic of the *problem-finding* stage (Arlin, 1984) of postformal operational cognitive development.

On this basis, however, Rybash et al. (1986) suggest that postformal thought represents a different style of thinking, rather than a new stage of cognitive growth. Adults may also think in different ways about how to solve problems because these problems are emotionally salient (Blanchard-Fields, 1986).

While research in postformal operations in adults is comparatively sparse, it represents a new, exciting approach to intelligence in adulthood that has emerged as an alternative to the psychometric and information-processing approaches. Such research may lead to a merging of these positions, increasing the ecological validity of our work in intellectual aging by allowing us to more fully understand the thinking processes adults use to cope with everyday problems.

DOES INTELLIGENCE DECLINE WITH AGE?

What shall we make of the data we have presented relating to declines in intelligence with increased age? A simple answer to the question of whether one theory is correct, or whether one is even better than another, is nearly impossible. In fact, debates between Schaie and Horn have raged over the validity of Schaie's analyses, focusing specifically on the issue of whether decline in intelligence is a myth (see Baltes & Schaie, 1976; Schaie & Baltes, 1977). In addition, while some might argue with Schaie's choice of Thurstone's PMA framework (see Schaie, 1979), the wealth of data he has gathered has proven invaluable in getting "the big picture" about intelligence and age.

On the other hand, the Horn-Cattell notions of Gf and Gc are by definition developmental and, since they incorporate other processes, a great deal more complex than the PMA approach. However, they lack the broad empirical base of Schaie's approach. For example, nearly all of Horn's research to date either has been cross-sectional or has focused on descriptions of single samples of age-homogeneous subjects. Nevertheless, at the risk of oversimplifying the issue, there are some similarities between Schaie's findings of developmental (age-related) change in PMA performance as well as cohort-specific effects on PMA factors, and Horn's findings regarding changes in Gf-Gc performance with age.

Factors Affecting Intelligence in Adulthood

We have already suggested that cohort effects may modify the aging of intelligence. Yet, there are a number of other influences on declines in intelligence with age.

For example, sensory deficits in hearing and vision may put many adults at a disadvantage (Sands & Meredith, 1989). Thus, items assessing intelligence in adults must take into account those who are sensorially impaired (Botwinick, 1984). Similarly, people who are in poor physical and mental health tend to perform more poorly on measures of fluid ability (Perlmutter & Nyquish, 1990).

Hertzog et al. (1978) found that people suffering from hypertension perform more poorly over time. However, if they are treated for hypertension, declines in intelligence are minimal (Schultz et al., 1986, 1989).

Another factor found to influence intelligence in adulthood is education. On the average, those who are more highly educated tend to age less, intellectually speaking. This seems to be more true for crystallized skills than for fluid skills, which are less dependent on formal education. On an individual basis, however, findings are somewhat mixed. Some people who are initially more able actually appear to decline more rapidly because they have more to lose, while those who are less able appear to gain somewhat (Alder et al., 1990). However, other researchers have found that those who are initially more able decline less (Birren & Morrison, 1961; Eisdorfer & Wilkie, 1973). It certainly seems that one's standing relative to others does in some way influence the rate at which certain aspects of intelligence (e.g., vocabulary) change with age.

Another influence on intelligence is speed, but the waters are muddied here as well. It could be that emphasis on speed unfairly penalizes those adults who respond slowly in timed tests; or slower performance could result from lessened ability to process information quickly (Hertzog, 1989; Kausler, 1991; Schaie, 1990). There may be some truth to both points of view.

There may also be a relationship between personality factors and intellectual performance, but the reasons for this relationship remain unclear. It may be that persons who have adaptive personalities age better intellectually; or intelligence may permit more flexibility in adulthood. In one study, the relationship between personality and Gf and Gc was examined (Hayslip, 1988). The results suggested some personality-related reasons for higher functioning in the two ability areas. For example, people who were more anxious about their intellectual skills had higher Gc scores. Higher functioning individuals may utilize defense mechanisms that serve to "insulate the older individual from feelings of self-worthlessness and failure and/or a loss of control over external forces via the development of intellectual skills" (Hayslip, 1988, p. 79).

Depression could also have harmful effects on intellectual performance. Depression is frequently accompanied by impaired attention, concentration, and overall levels of energy (see Chapter 10). Hayslip et al. (1990) studied the effects of depression on several measures, which included Gc, Gf, verbal-auditory short-term memory, and visual-spatial short-term memory, using individuals classified as either depressed or nondepressed. In the study, individuals completed a pretest, engaged in either effortful/fatiguing tasks or noneffortful/nonfatiguing tasks, and then completed a posttest of all intellectual and memory measures. These authors found that while depression and task effortfulness did not affect Gf and Gc directly, they did influence short-term memory performance. And active short-term memory that requires our effort and attention is a skill that seems to be involved in fluid ability performance (Cunningham & Tomer, 1991; Hayslip & Kennelly, 1982; Stankov, 1988).

To further separate the relationships between personality factors and cognitive abilities, Lachman et al. (1982) developed a personality inventory that specifically addressed intellectual aging issues. One study (Lachman & Leff, 1989) examined the relationship among Gf, Gc, and perceived control of intellectual functioning in elderly people. The authors reported that control beliefs did not predict changes in intellectual functioning. However, changes in intellectual-control beliefs were predicted by fluid intelligence. Thus, they concluded that "intellectual performance influences changes in beliefs, and not the converse" (p. 729). This study is unique because it examined changes in intellectual ability and control beliefs over a five-year period. While it may be difficult to understand the many factors that may have contributed to the intellectual changes during the five-year period, the authors suggest that the increased impact of negative stereotypes about older adults' cognitive abilities may be important. However, another possibility is that perceived changes in ability over the years may not be accurate.

Schooler (1987) has emphasized the possible impact of the complexity of our everyday environment on cognitive performance. Complexity is dependent on the numbers of stimuli, decisions, and contingencies associated with the environment as well as the amount of structure in the environment. Individuals in optimally complex environments who are reinforced for "using their heads" may develop higher cognitive skills that generalize to other situations and may be better in problem-solving.

Schooler (1987) suggests that one complex environment during adulthood that may be beneficial is a cognitively challenging work situation (see Box 6.2). Many factors may affect the choice of level of complexity of one's environment, however. These might include health issues, economic factors, self-image, and personality characteristics.

One personality construct that may be especially relevant to intelligence in adulthood is **self-efficacy.** Self-efficacy refers to a belief in one's ability to perform a task successfully. Bandura (1977) proposed that self-efficacy is crucial to behavioral change. For example, we often avoid taking the courses we feel would be the most difficult for us. By the time we actually take them, they appear doubly hard! Thus, level of self-efficacy not only affects the type of tasks an individual will attempt, but also his or her level of mastery and persistence in completing the task (Bandura, 1982).

Older adults may be susceptible to decreased self-efficacy because of negative cultural stereotypes, belief in the physiological effects of aging, and negative comparisons of current abilities with earlier ones (Bandura, 1981). Thus, the negative evaluative self-statements individuals make adversely affect their choice of actions in a downward spiraling manner, leading to lower self-expectations and perhaps depression (Brockner, 1983;

BOX 6.2

INTELLIGENCE AND WORK

Since work takes up a great deal of our time and energy as adults, it should not be surprising that work's potential to enhance or impede our intelligence has been debated. Likewise, the ability of intelligence tests to predict occupational success has been widely discussed.

Rebok and associates (1986) asked over 200 mid-level managers a variety of questions regarding how they processed information at work. The questions focused on two aspects of processing style: the use of delegation ("I delegate responsibilities to others whenever possible") and time-management strategies ("I keep a daily log or list of tasks to be done," "I try to schedule my most important activities during 'peak' energy times"). Delegation suggests that people give up control over all aspects of their work, while time management is more self-control-oriented. Questions were also asked regarding perceived competence ("In general, I feel competent about the way I perform the work duties expected of me") and perceived mental decline ("My mental activity or sharpness is declining").

Respondents who saw themselves as less competent reported more cognitive decline and utilized time-management strategies less often. Those who felt they had declined the most also used time management less frequently and delegated responsibility less often. These findings were equally true for both younger and older managers, and for those who dealt primarily with people, ideas, or things.

These authors speculate that managers who have a strong sense of personal efficacy will persist in controlling the work environment and will see themselves as more effective in controlling their own behavior.

Indeed, the competence and experience of older managers may help them compensate for self-perceived declines in memory, intelligence, or health, since more experienced and more self-efficacious managers used delegation more often.

Another aspect of work that can positively influence intelligence is complexity. Higher work-environment complexity seems to stimulate intellectual growth at any age (Kohn & Schooler, 1983; Schooler, 1984). Being able to deal with the glut of information that accompanies such environments, particularly among managers who must make many decisions and have multiple responsibilities at work, *is* associated with perceived self-efficacy and positive views about one's intellectual skills with advancing age.

Does intelligence predict occupational success? It seems to do so quite well, according to Barrett and Depinet (1991). Moreover, it does a better job in predicting driving safety or success in a service occupation such as police work than do specific competencies such as actual driving behavior, or patience on the job, contrary to what McClelland (1973) has claimed.

It therefore seems, according to Barrett and Depinet, that intelligence is a valuable quality that one must have information about to select workers who may later be successful on the job. This is in direct contrast to the many assertions that intelligence cannot predict real-life outcomes such as career success.

Intelligence thus seems to both predict and be a consequence of competence at work. Our work environments can indeed help us to maintain our intellectual skills as we age, and being able to function well at work promotes positive views of our own intellectual prowess.

Bandura, 1981). For example, simply thinking, "I'm too old to learn," sets the stage for failure. Individuals with positive self-efficacy expectations perceive difficult tasks as challenges, and see failures as related to effort, and, thus, under their control. They have an emotional resilience to difficulties (Bandura, 1989). Bandura (1989) says of such people, "They are active cognitive processors of information and remain highly efficient in their analytic thinking in complex decision situations" (p. 731).

It thus appears that in addition to age and cohort, a number of factors influence intelligence in adulthood. As some people are affected by some factors and not others, intellectual aging is best seen as an individual phenomenon. That is, individuals should be understood in terms of their own personalities, life histories, health, and education, as well as the nature of the everyday environments they live in. Of course, these everyday living environments may or may not encourage intellectual curiosity and continued growth.

Explaining the Data: Schaie's Stage Theory

On the basis of his research, Schaie (1977–1978, 1979) has advanced a **stage theory** of adult intellectual development that he claims is environmentally grounded. In contrast, theories such as Piaget's see intellectual development in childhood and adolescence as biologically based. As shown in Figure 6.8, intellectual development in childhood and adolescence is best seen in terms of acquisition, as skills and abilities are being acquired. During young adulthood, in the stage of achieving, these skills are directed to the creative application to and solution of real-life problems. If these skills are used in this fashion, growth will continue. In middle age, next follows the responsible stage, where such skills are applied to the management of "increasingly complex environmental demands" (p. 109) varying with individual and historical change. Such demands may stem from career choice and advancement or the balancing of multiple roles such as parent, worker, and spouse. Simultaneously, many middle-aged individuals are establishing an orientation toward future goals, including retirement planning and planning for the children's futures, and may be coping as well with technological changes in their jobs they were not originally trained for, such as new computer languages and systems. Coinciding with the responsible stage, Schaie suggests an executive stage, which more specifically targets the use of skills to deal with "systems transcending the nuclear family or self-confined job responsibility" (p. 109). The executive stage applies more

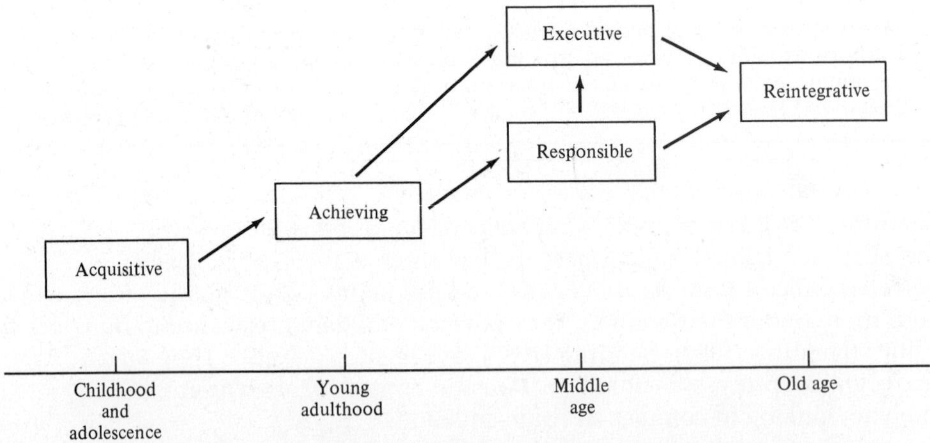

Figure 6.8 Schaie's stage theory of intelligence. *Source:* K. W. Schaie. (1977–1978). Toward a stage theory of adult cognitive development. *International Journal of Aging and Human Development, 8,* 133. Copyright © 1977 Baywood Publishing Co., Inc.

to individuals of higher educational and occupational status, who often make higher level decisions affecting others. The last stage, termed *reintegrative,* is a highly personal, pragmatic one that in many respects bears little resemblance to the previous stages. In the earlier stages, issues such as job-related achievement, occupational responsibilities, and actively raising one's family were important. In the reintegrative stage, intellect may instead be applied to the solution of more ecologically relevant intellectual tasks (Schaie, 1978; Scheidt & Schaie, 1978). Such skills require "the organism to restrict attention to those aspects of the environment which continue to be meaningful and adaptive, while ignoring those formal aspects which have lost interest and relevance" (Schaie, 1979, pp. 109–110). As Schaie and Geiwitz (1982) have observed, this last stage is characterized by

BOX 6.3

CREATIVITY AND AGING

Consider the following views about creativity:

> If you haven't cut your name on the door of fame by the time you've reached 40, you might just as well put up your jackknife. (Oliver Wendell Holmes, poet)
>
> A person who has not made his contribution in science before the age of 30 will never do so. (Albert Einstein, physicist)
>
> Age is, of course, a fever chill that every physicist must fear. He's better off dead than living still when once he's past his thirtieth year. (Paul Dirac, physicist)
>
> When age is in, wit is out. (William Shakespeare, poet and playwright)

Do you think that these statements are true? We can cite many examples to the contrary. Benjamin Franklin, Galileo, Tennyson, Grandma Moses, Michelangelo, Leonardo da Vinci, Alexander Graham Bell, and Eubie Blake all produced significant and important creative work well into later life.

Defining and measuring creativity precisely can be very elusive, however. Creativity has been defined as (1) a process such as problem-solving or reasoning, (2) something that one produces, such as a painting or a poem, (3) a characteristic of the individual, such as the ability to use objects in unique ways, or (4) an act of persuasion, as when one impresses another with his or her creativity; and akin to a distinct type of leadership (Simonton, 1990a).

Using the last definition, Simonton has evaluated the literature on creative products deemed classics, masterpieces, or breakthroughs in research. The empirical data appear to paint a picture wherein, with increased age, less creative potential and output is offset by a gain in wisdom (Simonton, 1990a, 1990b). Specifically, we find that as one's career ages, creative productivity apparently rises and reaches its peak in one's late thirties and early forties, or the second and third decades of one's career, then declines thereafter (Simonton, 1990a). Of course, there are generally more creative people who are in their thirties and forties than there are those who are in their seventies and eighties, a reflection of sheer longevity. Moreover, as one ages, the number of people with whom one must compete in order to be deemed creative increases, making it less likely that even highly creative works will be acknowledged as such.

In addition, different research disciplines have different criteria by which to label someone's work as creative. In some, a single book or scientific paper may suffice, while in others, a sustained record of productivity is necessary. In Dennis's (1966) and Cole's (1979) studies of over 15 disciplines, productivity at age 60 ranged from 9 to 90 percent of what it was at 40. Thus, there is a great deal of individual and disciplinary variation in creativity. Declines may be influenced by illness, personal problems, stressful working conditions, or personal characteristics such as enthusiasm, flexibility, conformity, or intelligence (Dennis, 1966; Kogan, 1973; Lehman, 1953; Simonton, 1990a).

How do you define creativity? What do you predict for yourself in later life?

intellectual integrity, which implies a reintegration of all that has been acquired and experienced up to that point in life.

This point of view emphasizing stages of intellect contrasts with those ideas about intelligence that stress its study at a processes level or define it solely in terms of tasks that are specific to certain areas, for example, tasks that are achievement-oriented or educational in nature.

Intelligence and Everyday Life

Schaie's ideas about late adulthood—the reintegration stage of intellectual development—are indeed intriguing. It remains to be seen, however, whether the approaches to intelligence and its assessment that psychologists and educators have devoted nearly 70 years of effort to can further our understanding of the "intelligence of everyday life."

In 1957, Demming and Pressey developed tests "with content and tasks more natural or 'indigenous' to adult life" (p. 144) because of the inadequacy of then-current tests to measure adult abilities. They developed items for their tests from several sources: newspapers and popular reading material, records of daily activities, and questions directed to individuals. They found that people scored progressively lower on traditional tests of intelligence across the life span but that the reverse pattern was evidenced on their "indigenous" tests.

Cornelius and Caspi (1987) constructed a test of everyday problem-solving in adulthood. Their test contained six content domains sampling experience in (1) being an economic consumer, (2) handling technical information, (3) home management, (4) managing interpersonal family conflicts, (5) managing problems with friends, and (6) handling co-worker conflicts. They compared scores on the everyday problem-solving test, verbal ability tests (Gc), and an abstract problem-solving test (Gf) that were administered to people ranging in age from 20 to 78.

While they found a significant correlation between scores on all tests, these relationships indicated that all three tests measured distinct aspects of intelligence. In examining age differences, they found that scores on everyday problem-solving and verbal ability increased with age, while abstract problem-solving declined with age. Educational background was positively correlated with verbal ability, moderately correlated with abstract problem-solving, and unrelated to everyday problem-solving. Thus, they concluded that both verbal ability and everyday problem-solving may be fostered by acculturation but gained through other means—one through formal education and the other outside the educational setting.

An important step in everyday-intelligence research has been provided by Scheidt and Schaie (1978). These researchers developed a system for classifying situations that reflect everyday-intelligent behaviors. They did this by simply having older adults list those situations they felt were critical to their intellectual competence. This represents a first step in the process of understanding intelligence in everyday life, and it may prove valuable in future research with older people. The results could be used by architects, for example, who might design environments for the specific purpose of improving the various aspects of older adults' intellectual functioning believed to be related to everyday skills they actually need for survival and continued growth.

Measuring everyday intelligence has proven to be anything but easy, and there are very diverse opinions about this new area of research (Cornelius, 1990; Hayslip, 1989; Kausler, 1991; Schaie, 1990; Willis, 1991). Some aspects of intelligence are **implicit**, that is, they reflect people's own beliefs about intellectual functioning, while others are **explicit**—they reflect researchers' efforts to measure intelligence using specific tests (Sternberg et al., 1981).

Research on everyday intelligence has used both approaches. When people are asked to assess their own intellectual skills, the ratings do not always correspond to their tested intelligence, or to measures of everyday problem-solving (Cornelius, 1990). When asked to describe intelligence, practical intelligence and social competence emerge as distinct from problem-solving and verbal intelligence or knowledge (Cornelius, 1990). Thus, everyday ability and testable ability seem to be different from one another to a degree. Perhaps actually observing individuals behaving intelligently in the real world will be necessary to understand everyday intelligence.

Willis and Schaie (1986) and Hayslip and Maloy (1991) have found that, among older adults, measures of fluid intelligence and, to a lesser extent, crystallized ability correlated highly with performance on a variety

Reading maps may be an aspect of our everyday intelligence.

of everyday tasks such as reading maps, understanding labels, filling out forms, and understanding charts and schedules. Cornelius et al. (1983), however, found that, among older adults, indicators of Gf and Gc were positively related to a general measure of coping and negatively related to a general measure of defensiveness. Moreover, these relationships were less strong when situational measures of coping were used.

These studies provide a starting point for understanding those abilities common to a variety of everyday intellectual situations—specifically, their adaptive value—and thus can help us to design training programs more precisely in order to enhance adults' use of these basic everyday skills.

Optimizing Intelligence in Adulthood

On the assumption that declines in intelligence with age are not irreversible and that intellectual functioning in old age is characterized by a great deal of **plasticity**, many investigators have developed training programs to help older adults enhance their intellectual skills. One such project is termed ADEPT, the Adult Development and Enrichment Project (Baltes & Willis, 1982). The originators focused on skills required to solve items measuring fluid intelligence (Gf). By comparing elderly people who received such training with those who received no training and those who simply practiced without benefit of training, they concluded that older adults can in fact enhance their intellectual skills. They based their conclusions about the efficacy of their training program on evidence they gathered suggesting (1) a hierarchical pattern of transfer and (2) maintenance of training effects over time. This hierarchical pattern of transfer suggests that tests measuring fluid ability (near-transfer tasks) should be affected by training to the greatest extent, and those measuring crystallized ability (far-transfer tasks) should be least affected. For those who had simply been allowed to practice with items measuring Gf, no hierarchical pattern of transfer to Gf versus Gc was found. Moreover, the magnitude of training effects was greater for training-program participants than for those in the control group, where only practice but no training was provided. These effects were maintained one month after training and to a somewhat lesser extent after six months.

Similarly, the training data collected by Schaie and Willis (1986) using Primary Mental Abilities has demonstrated that training can apparently reverse 14-year declines in PMA performance. For people who participated in several subsequent training programs over a seven-year interval, intellectual performance still exceeded their original levels.

These results as well as similar training data collected by Schaie and Willis (Willis, 1991; Willis & Schaie, 1988; Willis & Nesselroade, 1990) have provided the main thrust for cognitive/intellectual training in adults.

Despite the breadth of these data, other recent studies have demonstrated that improvements in fluid-ability performance can be achieved by other means as well. For example, Hayslip (1989) found that providing older individuals with anxiety-reduction techniques, such as using success self-statements instead of failure self-statements (Meichenbaum, 1989), and relaxation techniques were both almost as effective as direct, specific, rule-based training and superior to no training at all (see Figure 6.9). Practice seemed to help everyone, regardless of whether they received training.

Another means of enhancing intellectual performance is to allow older people to generate their own intellectual problem-solving strategies, rather than providing such strategies formally to them (Baltes et al., 1989; Blackburn et al., 1988). This research suggests that even in the absence of explicit instruction and feedback, older adults can perform adequately.

Research to date therefore indicates there are a number of ways to ensure that older individuals' intellectual skills do not deteriorate. However, the breadth of these training effects, whether people respond equally to each type of intervention, and whether a combination of the above approaches works best remain questions as yet unanswered (Hayslip, 1989b). These findings also vividly demonstrate that aging need not be characterized by loss and decline, and that if given the opportunity, older adults can indeed continue to grow intellectually. Such a view should give both the old and the young the message that being "over the hill" intellectually

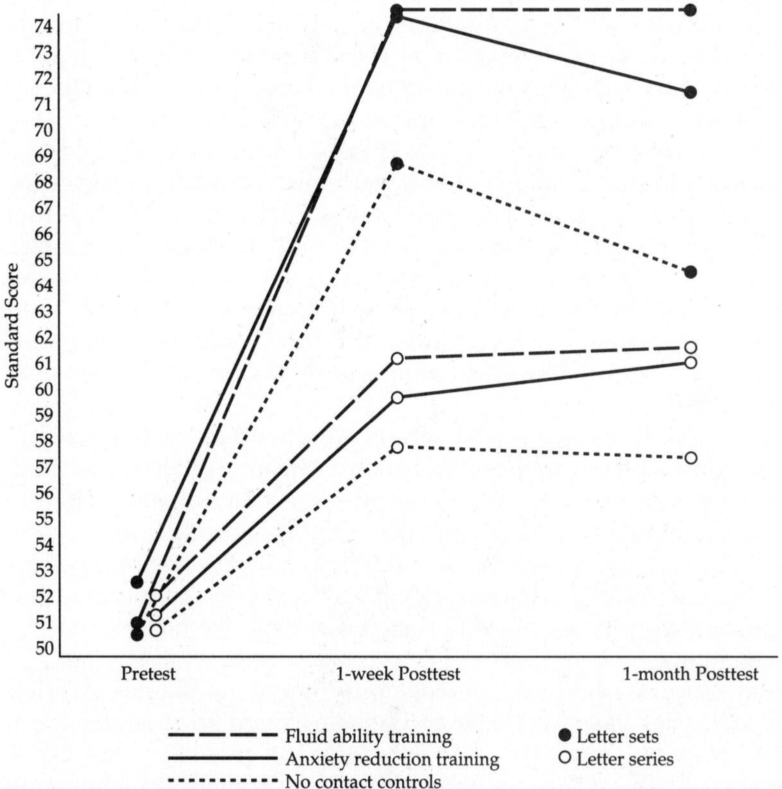

Figure 6.9 Improving fluid-ability performance using anxiety-reduction techniques.
Source: Adapted from Hayslip. (1989).

is clearly without basis in fact. To perpetuate this myth of intellectual decline does both the young and the old a terrible disservice. Older adults can use a number of strategies to help them compensate for declines in intellectual skills brought on by disease or disuse of skills that were once functional. Older people thus demonstrate **intellectual plasticity**.

NEWER IDEAS ABOUT INTELLIGENCE AND AGING

Baltes: Mechanics and Pragmatics

Baltes et al. (1984) and Baltes (1987) have proposed a theory of life-span intellectual development that does not rely on the notion of stages. Baltes et al. (1984) instead suggest a **dual-process** concept of intellectual development, emphasizing a distinction between the **mechanics** of intelligence, which are the basic cognitive skills such as speeded performance, or Gf; and the **pragmatics** of intelligence, which reflect more organized systems of knowledge, such as social intelligence, and wisdom, or Gc. The mechanics of intelligence are more structural and involve basic skills such as logic, information processing, and problem-solving. The pragmatic aspects of intelligence are more applied or adaptive and thus reflect intelligent behavior in a specific context or situation (see Box 6.4). What characterizes infancy, childhood, and adolescence is the development of mechanics, while "intellectual pragmatics appear to be the centerpiece of intelligence during adulthood and old age" (Baltes et al., 1984, p. 64).

Baltes et al. (1984) suggest that mechanics form the basis for pragmatics during adulthood, and that the mechanics of intelligence can be trained or improved if necessary. According to Baltes et al. (1984), future research should involve "testing the limits" of older people's pragmatic/mechanistic aspects of intelligence. Thus, intervention research with older people might improve the mechanics of intelligence and therefore indirectly affect its pragmatics. Even under the best conditions, however, younger people will outperform older ones in mechanics while the opposite is true for pragmatics.

Baltes et al. (1984) see intelligence in adulthood as enabling the individual to cope with a variety of age-graded, history-graded, and nonnormative events (see Chapter 1). Intelligence thus helps all individuals to *selectively optimize* their continued growth, or to compensate for biological/social losses by narrowing their frame of reference. That is, they apply their pragmatic abilities only to problems that affect them personally. All of this is accomplished within the context of each individual's life history and current life situation.

Intelligence in adulthood, then, helps different individuals in different ways to master life's problems and age successfully. It is consistent with each person's interests, interpersonal and financial resources, educational background, health, and current environment. In contrast to Schaie's approach emphasizing stages, Baltes et al. (1984) advocate a more functional or adaptive approach to intelligence in adulthood.

BOX 6.4

WISDOM AND AGING

One important aspect of the pragmatics of intelligence is the role that wisdom plays in helping older adults to continue to flourish and grow throughout life. Paul Baltes and Jacqui Smith have explained what wisdom is and how to measure it in adults. Wisdom emphasizes expert knowledge in life pragmatics and can be defined very precisely, according to Baltes et al. (1990):

Theoretical Definition

Expert knowledge in the domains of fundamental life pragmatics (life planning, life management, life review).

Functional consequence: Exceptional insight into human development and life matters, exceptionally good judgment, advice, and commentary about difficult life problems.

Family of Five Criteria

1. Rich factual knowledge about life matters.
2. Rich procedural knowledge about life problems.
3. Life-span contextualism: Knowledge about the contexts of life and their temporal (developmental) relationships.
4. Relativism: Knowledge about differences in values and priorities.
5. Uncertainty: Knowledge about the relative indeterminacy and unpredictability of life and ways to manage.

Using verbal protocols, where individuals reflect on how they would go about dealing with real-life problems pertinent to both young and old adults, Baltes and Smith discovered that middle-aged and older adults indicated a greater awareness of uncertainty and seemed better able to deal with problems specific to their age. For example:

Subjects are asked to "think aloud" about the following:

Life-planning Joyce, a widow aged 60 years, recently completed a degree in business management and opened her own business. Although she has been looking forward to this new challenge, she has just heard that her son has been left with two small children to care for. Joyce is considering the following options: She could plan to give up her business and move to live with her son, or she could plan to arrange for financial assistance for her son to cover child-care costs. What should Joyce do and consider in planning for her future? What extra information would you like to have available?

Life review Martha, an elderly woman, had once decided to have a family and not to have a career. Her children left home some years ago. One day Martha meets a woman friend she has not seen for a long time. The friend had decided to have a career and no family. She retired some years ago. This meeting causes Martha to think back over her life. What might her life review look like? Which aspects of her life might she remember? How might she explain her life? How might she evaluate her life retrospectively?

Note. Tasks vary in type of problem (e.g., normative vs. nonnormative), age, and gender of target character. Furthermore, prompting questions are given at the completion of the spontaneous protocol.

This exciting work suggests that wisdom, although often seen as characteristic of old age, evolves and is continually transformed throughout adulthood.

Denny: Exercised and Unexercised Abilities

The dual-process approach of Baltes can be compared to Denny's (1982) distinction between *unexercised* ability and *optimally exercised* ability, which is improved via use or training. In contrast to Baltes, Denny maintains that both unexercised and optimally exercised abilities will decline with age over the course of adulthood. Furthermore, due to biological and environmental factors such as poor health or isolation from others, the differences between the levels of unexercised and optimally exercised abilities will be least for a given person during childhood and old age than they are during adolescence and adulthood. It is important to see that Denny's distinction is a quantitative one (unexercised vs. optimally exercised abilities), while Baltes's is a qualitative one (mechanics vs. pragmatics of intelligence). Unexercised abilities can decrease in frequency, and then with practice become exercised ones, while mechanics and pragmatics are essentially different from one another.

Sternberg: Triarchic Theory of Intelligence

Sternberg has developed a triarchic theory of intelligence that is in many respects similar to the distinction between the pragmatics and mechanics of intelligence made by Baltes. He is very explicit in rejecting IQ as a meaningful way of measuring intelligence. Sternberg's approach understands intelligence in terms of the following three domains:

1. The internal world of the individual, that is, the mental processes that underlie intelligent behavior (componential);
2. Experience, or the degree of novelty or lack thereof involved in the application of information-processing skills (experiential); and
3. The external world of the individual, where the individual uses the above mental processes to adapt to the environment (contextual) (Sternberg, 1985, 1988, 1991) (see Box 6.5).

All of the above domains of intelligence work together.

Three aspects of intellectual functioning underlie our adaptative behavior, according to Sternberg. The first is the mental mechanisms listed above, which are referred to as **metacomponents** of intelligence, or executive processes, and plan what one is going to do, monitor while one is

BOX 6.5

EXAMPLES OF STERNBERG'S TRIARCHIC THEORY

Componential—Critical, Analytical, Intelligence
Alice had high test scores and was a whiz at test-taking and analytical thinking. Her type of intelligence exemplifies the componential subtheory, which explains the mental components involved in analytical thinking.

Experiential—Having Good Ideas, Being Creative
Barbara didn't have the best test scores, but she was a superbly creative thinker who could combine disparate experiences in insightful ways. She is an example of the experiental subtheory. She is able to see old problems in new ways, or see how what she already knows applies to this new problem.

Contextual—Adaptive
Celia was street-smart. She learned how to play the game and how to manipulate her environment. Her test scores weren't tops, but she could come out on top in almost any context. She is Sternberg's example of contextual intelligence. She is practical in a real-world sort of way.

Source: Trotter, R. J. (1986). Three heads are better than one. *Psychology Today*, 56–62.

doing it, and evaluate it after it is done. Thus, a problem must be recognized, a solution must be developed and executed, and the success or failure of the solution must be evaluated. Second, and more specific to the task, are **performance components**, which are the actual mental operations people use to solve specific problems (e.g., encoding, making inferences, making comparisons). The third dimension of intelligence is the **knowledge-acquisition components**, which help us gain new knowledge. For example, separating new from old, and relevant from irrelevant information in solving a problem, and being able to form new knowledge by combining specific bits of information into a new "whole," are aspects of knowledge acquisition.

For example, surgeons and lawyers must learn to recognize what is important and be able to put things together to form a theory about a legal case or make a diagnosis. Metacomponents help them select a strategy or plan to operate on or try a case, performance components actually enable them to analyze the "nuts and bolts" of the specific task at hand, and knowledge-acquisition components help them learn from their experience so that they can use their knowledge in new situations.

Berg and Sternberg (1985) found younger adults to be superior to older ones in most metacomponents of intelligence as well as performance components. Older adults have more difficulty in defining problems to be solved, in managing their attention to solve problems, and in monitoring solutions effectively. These skills may improve with practice, however. Making inferences and combining and comparing information are also impaired in older people. It may be that the knowledge-acquisition components that are based on experience do not decline with age, especially if they are critical in helping people to cope with new situations (Cunningham & Tomer, 1991).

Sternberg argues that each of the above aspects of intelligence helps us to cope with both new and old information and enables us to use our experiences to adapt to our everyday environment. In some cases, though, we may need to change that environment, or even select a new one. Consider the person who must learn a new job, or adapt a job to fit his or her new skills or needs. If either of these approaches fails, a new job must be found that is different from the old job. In any case, each aspect of intelligence is involved when we deal with words, numbers, or figures, as in knowing that a stop sign looks different from a caution sign.

Sternberg's ideas encompass the "hardware" of intelligence (e.g., information processing), the higher-order planning and evaluating aspects of intelligence that enable us to set goals and make decisions; and the "software" of intelligence, the practical, behavioral aspects of coping with our everyday world, using our experience when necessary.

Using Intelligence Findings Intelligently with Adults

We assume that whatever index or score we obtain from an individual accurately reflects the quality or qualities we term intelligence, but does it? In interpreting any test finding, or more generally data on intelligence and age, we need to be aware that other factors contribute to measured performance on our test(s). What Botwinick (1970a) and Furry and Baltes (1973) have termed **noncognitive** or **ability-extraneous factors** can cover up or cloud accurate assessment of an individual's skills, creating a falsely negative picture of intellectual deficits, with sometimes disastrous consequences for the individual.

Interestingly, Lachman and Jelalian (1984), using tests of Gc and Gf, have found both older and younger adults to attribute good performance to their own ability but poor performance to task difficulty. In other words, successes were internalized and failures were externalized.

The older person takes credit for personal strengths and attributes weakness to the difficulty of the task, rather than to lessened ability. Much of this tendency to externalize failure may be due to the relative difficulty or unfamiliarity of many tasks put to older people, especially Gf tasks. Despite the fact that others may attribute their success to luck and their failure to a lack of ability, older people are nevertheless accurate in estimating their own strengths and weaknesses, consistent with the attributions they made for good or poor performance. Perhaps this "style of attribution" can be traced to a lifetime of self-assessment—one comes to know over time what one is good at. It can also be that this attributional style is an ego defensive response to the message from others that one necessarily becomes less able with age (Hayslip, 1988).

Regardless of theory, we must take into account the effects of such factors as the clarity of the test materials, whether the individual understands the nature of the task, whether the individual is fatigued or anxious, whether the task demands a speeded response, and perhaps most importantly, the individual's overall attitude toward the testing. Is the testing important or meaningful to the individual? What does the individual think—or fear—will become of the data? How will the individual react to success or failure?

While recent research has placed less emphasis on the importance of noncognitive factors such as response speed (the use of time limits) per se or fatigue, than was the case earlier, in practice, it is wise to assume that these factors influence performance to a certain extent in adults of all ages. Such factors might particularly influence those who lack formal education, who have poorer self-images, who are in poorer health, or who lack confidence in their existing skills. Perhaps these people are also the most failure-prone and therefore less likely to take credit for successes they do experience during testing. Consequently, establishing rapport, clearly explaining the purpose of the testing as well as what is to be done with the data obtained, and conducting the testing at a pace the individual sets are very important. It is also imperative to clearly explain the instructions preceding a task, rereading them if necessary, and perhaps include practice items to reduce the individual's fears about failure (Hayslip, 1989; Labouvie-Vief & Gonda, 1976; Kooken & Hayslip, 1984). Using a setting that is quiet and adequately lighted, and rewarding the individual for attempting to solve every item, can also be very helpful (Birkhill & Schaie,

1975). Rewarding individuals for responding more quickly (Denny, 1982; Hoyer et al., 1973) and using cohort-appropriate materials (Popkin et al., 1983) can also ensure that performance reflects the individual's underlying ability.

In interpreting the evidence we have discussed regarding intelligence and age, factors such as cohort differences, education, and individual differences in level of education make it difficult to assign a causal role to the aging process (Botwinick, 1977; Schaie, 1983). Moreover, such factors as selective survival (see Chapter 2) and the lack of recent use of one's skills all complicate matters regarding whether or not intelligence declines with age. Considering these factors, we certainly might question whether low test scores necessarily imply lessened ability, even among younger adults.

Existing norms may not be useful, given the tremendous variability among adults and cohort differences in the level of performance for many abilities. An individual's intelligence test scores are thus better utilized ipsatively—on a within-person basis, by creating a profile of high and low abilities—to examine that person's strengths and weaknesses relative to one another. Rather than complicate matters by comparing one person to someone else, using test scores ipsatively can enable us to understand an individual more completely. Where inferences about intelligence are being made, getting accurate data and using those data wisely are equally important to young adults and older adults.

SUMMARY

Regardless of age, our own or others' assessments of how intelligent we are is likely to be important to us. While intelligence can be defined in numerous ways, one's definition hinges on personal bias about the concept and the behaviors one is attempting to predict or understand via use of the term.

Based on early biases about whether IQ continues to increase with age, a mental age–based concept of intelligence was developed, then abandoned in favor of one where individuals can be compared to others their own age. While this remains the most popular method of measuring intelligence today, it reflects a bias against older adults in the IQs so derived.

The *psychometric* approach treats intelligence as a *structural* concept, composed of various well-defined abilities that relate to one another in various ways. These abilities can be identified by a technique known as *factor analysis*. A number of theories about how intelligence is structured have been proposed. The Cattell and Horn two-factor theory of *crystallized* and *fluid* intelligences and the Thurstone *Primary Mental Abilities* (PMA) approach have most influenced research on intelligence in adulthood. The *information-processing* approach to intelligence specifies the underlying processes individuals use when they behave intelligently. Extensions of Piagetian formal operations to *postformal operations* have opened up new avenues for research as well.

Intelligence both does and does not decline with increased age, depending on how one chooses to define and measure it. Research by Schaie and by Horn has confirmed the complex nature of intelligence in adulthood. Its growth and development depend on both the influence of the immediate environment (*time of measurement*) and cultural differences between *cohorts* of individuals born at different points in historical time.

Recent attempts to explain intellectual development emphasize the *pragmatics* versus the *mechanics* of intelligence, *exercised* versus *unexercised* abilities, a *stage*-theory approach to intelligence, and Sternberg's *triarchic theory,* which sees intelligence as both an information-processing ability and an adaptive characteristic.

In light of research on intelligence and age, it is important to distinguish between *cognitive* (ability-sensitive) and *noncognitive* (ability-extraneous) influences on intelligence. Noncognitive influences often cover up what might otherwise be adequate intellectual functioning, particularly among elderly people. When allowances for these influences are made, one can more accurately assess an individual's true abilities.

Recently, the application of intelligence to everyday life has received some attention, highlighting the distinction between *implicit* and *explicit* approaches to intelligence. Also, a great deal of work has demonstrated that adults can improve their intellectual performance by a number of means. In addition to *direct instruction* in intelligence test item strategies, *self-instruction,* training in *anxiety reduction* and *relaxation techniques,* as well as *practice* seem to be effective in this regard.

KEY TERMS AND CONCEPTS

Intelligence
IQ
Mental age
Deviation IQ
Age credit
Age debit
Factor analysis
Crystallized ability
Intellectual plasticity
Information processing
Primary mental abilities
Wechsler Adult Intelligence Scale (WAIS)
Triarchic theory of intelligence
Noncognitive influences
Psychometric tradition
Fluid ability
Postformal thinking
Schaie's stage theory of adult intelligence
Mechanics versus pragmatics of intelligence
Exercised versus unexercised abilities
Implicit versus explicit theories of intelligence
Everyday intelligence
Metacomponents
Knowledge acquisition components
Performance components

REVIEW QUESTIONS

1. What is intelligence, and why is an understanding of intelligence important to everyday life?
2. What are the major approaches to understanding and measuring intelligence?
3. What approaches to intelligence are most useful in understanding its development in adulthood?
4. Does intelligence decline as we age?
5. What factors influence intelligence in adulthood?
6. How can intelligence be optimized in adulthood? By what means can this be accomplished?

C H A P T E R 7

Interpersonal Relationships and Socialization

CHAPTER OUTLINE

INTRODUCTION

John Donne, the seventeenth-century English poet, wrote:

> No man is an island, entire of itself; every man is a piece of the continent, a part of the main. . . . Any man's death diminishes me because I am involved in mankind, and therefore never send to know for whom the bell tolls; it tolls for thee.
>
> *Meditation 17*

Everyone is connected in some way with everyone else.

As humans, we are all born of parents, and many of us grow up with brothers or sisters. These bonds often form the basis for our friendships at school and at work, and perhaps later on in our lives, for a relationship with a husband or wife. Indeed, it is the rare adult whose ties to parents, siblings, a spouse, children, or a close friend or two are not in some way intimately bound with who that person is—his or her likes, dislikes, interests, and values. Even our basic personalities are shaped by and influence our relationships with others.

While we might often argue with or even cut ourselves off from these special people, our ties to them run deep and exert a powerful influence on us throughout our adult lives. Our lives would indeed be very lonely without loved ones with whom we can share our innermost feelings, successes, achievements, disappointments, and failures.

In this chapter we will discuss these very important **interpersonal relationships** in adulthood, as well as the process of **socialization** through which we acquire the roles that enable us to maintain these relationships. Of course, relationships with others play a vital role in affecting the quality of our lives in adulthood. For example, our relationships with others are critical to our satisfaction with life, our self-concepts, and our physical health (Cobb, 1976).

People with whom we share a relationship also play an important role in socializing us. Our parents and grandparents, for example, may guide us in helping to make important life decisions, in shaping our values, and in setting personal or professional goals. These relationships are played out within those roles that parents and grandparents also play as spouses, workers, citizens, caregivers, and friends. Thus, interpersonal relationships and socialization are closely related to one another.

In order to adequately understand socialization from a life-span perspective, we will discuss a number of diverse but related topics, such as roles, role transition, gender stereotyping, families, parenting, and grandparenting. As we shall see, each of these plays an important part in the socialization process, and therefore affects our relationships with others. How we view our roles as men or women, as husbands or wives, and as parents or children exerts a substantial influence on whether we get along with the opposite sex, on the quality of our marriage, and on our ties with our own parents and children.

THE PROCESS OF SOCIALIZATION

Socialization is the process by which we acquire the roles appropriate to our age, gender, social class, or ethnicity (Neugarten & Datan, 1973). Through socialization we gain the skills, values, and behaviors to function in the roles we currently occupy or will occupy in the future. It is important to realize that socialization is a dynamic process that occurs throughout the life span. As we are constantly undergoing socialization or anticipating socialization (Albrecht & Gift, 1975), with time, these expectations are eventually internalized.

Important to our discussion of socialization is the term *roles*. Roles are the behaviors, traits, and characteristics expected by others of individuals who occupy a specific social position in society (Hagestad & Neugarten, 1985; Rosow, 1985; Sears et al., 1986). Individuals are assumed by others to know what is expected of them in their roles, and in turn, these roles are influenced by society's norms, values, and attitudes. As society changes, the roles ascribed to people change (Rosow, 1985). Socialization can be viewed as a four-step process: (1) learning the content of roles, (2) rehearsing roles, (3) receiving feedback from others about one's performance, and (4) adjustment and full acceptance of a new role (Steinmetz et al., 1990).

Theories of socialization vary in terms of the means by which societal representatives perform their function of shaping us in certain ways. On the one hand, *social learning theory* emphasizes environmental and interpersonal influences as socializing agents. Other social learning theorists, however, attribute this process to characteristics lying within the person (Emmerich, 1973). Theories such as Kohlberg's, specifying levels of *moral development*, stress the importance of one's cognitive level as a shaper of how individuals define themselves and how they respond to social situations (Kohlberg, 1973). *Psychodynamic* (Freudian) and *trait* approaches emphasize enduring qualities such as the ego and superego, and traits such as sociability as structures that permit persons to respond to cultural-societal influences.

A perspective on socialization that combines both external and internal (inside the person) influences is **symbolic interactionism** (Thomas & Thomas, 1937). This approach stresses socialization as a learning process that develops out of our interactions with others. Through such interactions, information about ourselves is communicated to us symbolically, through the meanings that are attached to what others say or gesture about our looks, behaviors, or attitudes. When others reinforce, or reward, us for behaving in ways they feel are appropriate based on our age, sex, looks, ethnicity, race, or socioeconomic status, our role has therefore been defined for us given our position in society relative to others (Steinmetz et al., 1990). Of course, as our roles change through adulthood, this process may occur over and over. Since adults often play many roles simultaneously, for example, parent, spouse, worker, citizen, friend, and child, the process of being socialized into these roles becomes quite complex. In some cases, role expectations may conflict, as when one must take time away from the fathering role to fulfill the requirements of the role as worker or breadwinner, as a man may have to work late and therefore sacrifice time at home with his wife or children.

Perhaps the most in-depth attempt to describe the socialization process throughout the life span has been proposed by Brim (1966). Although socialization is a life-long process, Brim suggests that the process of adult socialization is distinctly different from that of childhood. According to Brim, the major factor contributing to socialization is the individual learning the "role of other." That is, the person learns to anticipate another individual's response to his or her behavior, and reflecting on this behavior then judges it either good or bad.

During adulthood, people who socialize us are concerned with our learning occupationally specific role behaviors, such as supervisor or coworker (Brim, 1966). We may look to our age peers or to those who are

Parents are important socializing agents and may serve as role models for us. In so doing, their own roles as parents may also change.

older for guidance in fulfilling role responsibilities as parents, spouses, or citizens.

Lerner and Spanier (1978) and Zeits and Prince (1982) argue for a bilateral, bidirectional view of socialization between children and parents (and perhaps grandparents as well). Each member of this dyad represents a host of personal and historical-cultural influences that have a dynamic effect on other individuals and the family as a whole. Children, for example, may influence not only their parents' tastes in music, TV, or clothes, but also political opinions and values. Parents and grandparents, of course, are important socializers of their children regarding sexuality, values, peer relationships, aggressive and/or moral behavior, career orientation, and self-concept. This bidirectional, dynamic process continues through life (Hess & Waring, 1978). In adulthood, for example, socialization continues to involve choices, values clarification, and role expectations revolving around parenthood, marriage, and retirement.

Late adulthood is often considered a "roleless" period of life (Rosow, 1985). Very few roles with status, with the exception of senior citizen, retiree, and grandparent, are available to older adults in our society (Rosow, 1985). Since roles contribute substantially to identity and self-esteem

(Sears et al., 1986), the unavailability of viable roles can have negative effects on the picture one has of oneself. We may feel that we no longer "count," or that others no longer value our opinions or ideas simply because we are old.

Role Types in Adulthood

To understand socialization during adulthood and aging, we must discuss specific roles in greater depth.

As adults, we are expected to acquire and perform behaviors associated with many roles simultaneously, for example, those of teacher, parent, husband, and male. Later on in this chapter, we will examine in more detail two significant types of roles usually associated with adulthood. These pertain to the family and gender.

In adulthood, many roles are age-graded (Atchley, 1975; Rosow, 1985). Exercising the right to vote, obtaining a driver's license, getting married, and purchasing alcoholic beverages are some of the privileges associated with reaching a specific chronological age in our culture. Age serves as a normative criterion with regard to both role entry and exit, as well as influencing the types of socialization agents (parents, grandparents) with whom we have contact (Nardi, 1973).

Rosow (1985) separates roles in terms of their characteristics, each type of role assuming a varying degree of importance across the life span. Each can assume positive or negative status. **Institutional role types** assume a given status, with accompanying well-defined roles, such as social class, sex, race, or age. **Tenuous role types** apply to people in definite social positions (status) who do not have well-defined functions or roles, such as aged people, younger divorced women, or the unemployed. **Informal role types** have no institutional status but have definite roles attached to them, for example, the family scapegoat, heroes, and blackmailers. **Nonrole types** have neither status nor definite roles.

Each of these role types varies in importance over the life span. Among older adults compared to younger people, institutional role types decrease in relative importance, while tenuous role types increase in relative importance. This generally negative trend has important implications for the socialization of, and attitudes toward, older people. With increased age, important, well-defined roles are lost and replaced with less well-defined ones. This contributes to the perception of late adulthood as a roleless period of life.

Role Transition and Role Change

As we move along the life span, we are constantly shifting roles (George, 1990). Role shifts may occur in two ways: through **role transition,** such as from mother to grandmother, or through **role change,** such as from student to professor. While role transition is simply the process of evolving from one form of a specific role to another form of that same role, role change involves the complete shift from one type of role to a different one. For this reason, the shift from father to grandfather is substantially less difficult than from husband to widower.

If older adults are to maintain positive feelings about themselves, new social roles must be adopted to replace those that are lost (George, 1990). This is accomplished by becoming involved in new activities that can provide new roles. For example, one might shift from the role of mother to grandmother, or from bank president to president of the senior adult volunteers' organization.

INTERPERSONAL RELATIONSHIPS IN ADULTHOOD

The Convoy

Kahn and Antonucci (1980) have used the term *convoy* to describe the interpersonal support system we all utilize to help us cope with change. Much as a convoy of destroyers accompanied supply ships through hostile waters in World War II, an interpersonal convoy serves as a psychological buffer to help support us in times of stress. That is, when we are faced with changes in our lives brought on by marriage, divorce, parenthood, illness, retirement, job loss, and death, the convoy is important to us, and especially so when changes are unforeseen or unwanted. The function of the convoy in adulthood is similar to that of the infant's attachment to its parents or primary caretakers. In adulthood, however, this convoy differs from person to person and changes as our life circumstances change, providing us with different types and levels of support at different times and in different situations. For example, as we get older, we often seek support from friends and spouse rather than from parents. We might also rely on our children for support after the death of a husband or wife.

Adults with well-defined convoys of support can generally cope with changes more effectively than those without (Lerner & Ryff, 1978). As Figure 7.1 illustrates, a typical convoy includes supportive relationships with others that are intimate and stable, as well as those that are more role-bound, instrumental, and changing (Kahn & Antonucci, 1980). Our convoy includes friendships, professional or work relationships, and close family members, that is, parents, grandparents, children, and spouse. Aspects of this convoy change over time; we break and remake relationships with others who define our convoy over the course of our lives. But it is the more stable types of relationships defining the convoy (e.g., friendships, close family, and spouse) that we will discuss in this chapter.

The first year of life is critical to the process of attachment that is the foundation of an individual's basic sense of trust in others (Bowlby, 1969). Trust is thought to develop from individuals' experiences with their primary caretakers—mother, father, grandparent, or other relatives. These early experiences serve as the foundation on which other relationships are built (Brim & Ryff, 1978; Erikson, 1963). If these first relationships are de-

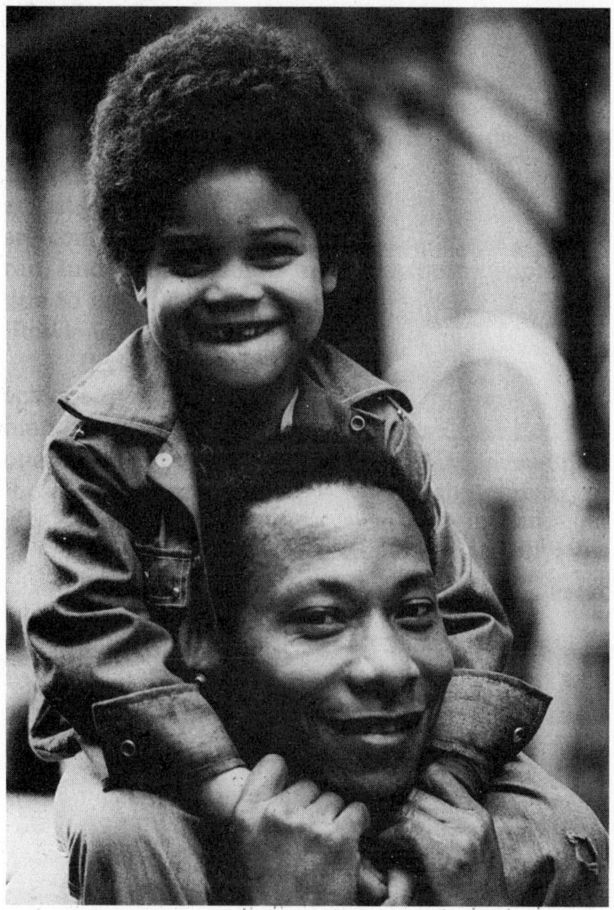

The family is an important component of our personal convoy of support in adulthood.

structive, we may have difficulty in forming and maintaining interpersonal relationships throughout life. Our convoy becomes ill-defined and unstable; it may not fulfill its supportive function well.

Hartup (1988) believes two types of attachment relationships, vertical and horizontal, are necessary for normal development. **Vertical attachments** are the first to form and refer to people who have greater knowledge and social power than the child, such as parents. They provide children with protection and security, meeting their basic needs. It is within this context that our basic social skills develop.

Horizontal attachments begin to emerge about the third year of life. They are relationships with other individuals who have the same amount of social power as themselves, that is, child-child relationships. These relationships are characterized by reciprocity and egalitarian expectations. They provide the framework in which children elaborate and enhance their basic social skills. Within these relationships, the complexities of coopera-

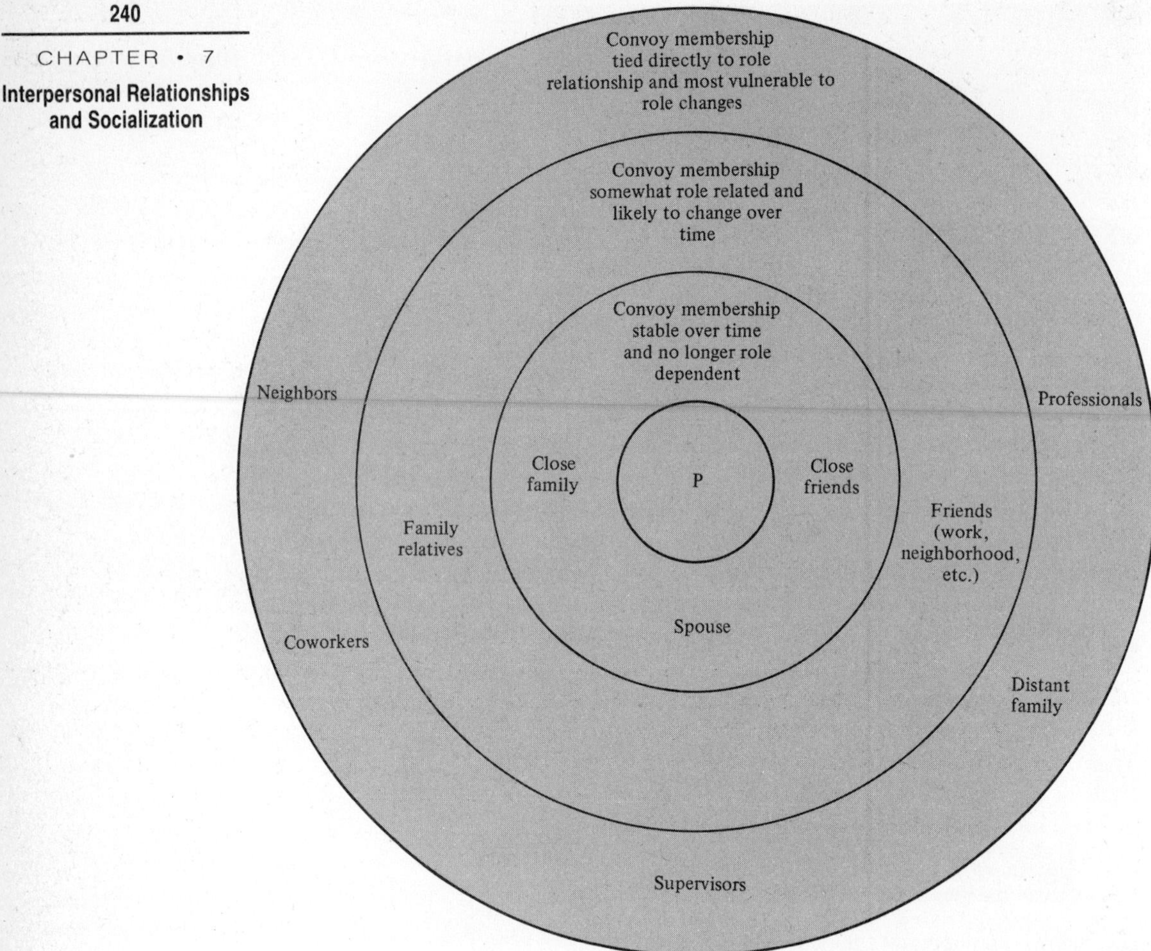

Figure 7.1 A hypothetical convoy. *Source:* R. Kahn & T. Antonucci. (1980). Convoys over the life course: attachment, roles, and social suppport. In P. B. Baltes and O. G. Brim, Jr. (Eds.), *Life-span development and behavior* (vol. 3, p. 273). Orlando, FL: Academic Press. Reprinted by permission of Academic Press and Robert L. Kahn.

tion and competition are mastered, and intimacy in social relations is first achieved.

Both vertical and horizontal attachments are carried over into adulthood. For example, learning to relate to one's boss or teacher is an extension of vertical attachments, while relationships with co-workers, fellow students, and one's spouse are extensions of earlier horizontal attachments.

Many types of relationships define our convoy of support, some stable, some not. We will discuss those relationships that can provide us with love and support, and help us throughout adulthood.

Friendships

In adulthood, friends can be important sources of support and affection. They can give our lives meaning and help us get perspective on things. Friendship is thought to contribute to a person's psychological well-being by providing supportive exchanges between the individuals who express mutual liking (Carlson & Vaughn, 1990). These supportive exchanges may include sharing intimacies as well as giving and receiving assistance and emotional support (Rook, 1987). To understand this, reflect on a friendship that is important to you. What were you doing when you first met the person? What changes in your life have you been able to share with him or her over the years? If you were hurt or experienced a tragedy in your life such as the death of someone you loved, would you want that person to be with you?

Wheeler et al. (1983) and Williams and Solano (1983) have found that, among college students, feelings of loneliness are primarily determined by whether people thought they had both intimate and meaningful friendships with others. Larson et al. (1986) found that, among retired adults, friendships were an even greater source of satisfaction than were family members.

Many factors contribute to the selection of our friends, including characteristics such as honesty, understanding, kindness, and sympathy, as well as perceived similarity and proximity (Freedman et al., 1981). Self-disclosure is an important component in the formation and maintenance of friendship (Jourard, 1961). The relative importance of each of these factors will vary as a function of the type of friendship and the age of the individuals involved.

Stevens-Long (1984) suggests that friendships among adults are defined in terms of *mutuality,* that is, mutual self-disclosure, mutual commitment, and mutual expectations of the relationship. Friendships can therefore have an important socializing influence on us (Dickens & Perlman, 1981), as well as help to strengthen our personal convoy.

While proximity and similarity may be important components of friendship among the young, Cohen and Rajkowski (1982) did not find similarity in age or gender to be an important factor in elderly persons' definitions of friendship. Subjective importance principally separated friends from nonfriends in this study. In addition, long-term emotional ties with individuals who did not live close by most often defined friends for these individuals. These close relationships can help stabilize our convoy of support throughout our lives.

Studying friendships reveals that numerous factors may affect friendship patterns (Usui, 1984). These include age, gender, race, marital status, ethnicity, religion, occupation, and educational level. Aizenberg and Treas (1985) note that the death of one's spouse often changes friendship patterns developed during marriage, though Lopata (1973) suggests that age peers can fulfill an important supportive role in adjusting to widowhood.

Researchers suggest there are two major categories or types of friendships. These are interest-related friendships and deep friendships.

INTEREST-RELATED VERSUS DEEP FRIENDSHIPS

Interest-related friendships are based on some similar life-style or interests between the individuals, such as sports, pets, or hobbies (Bensman & Lilienfeld, 1979). **Deep friendships** are those in which there is an intimacy between the individuals going beyond interests, that is, based on a feeling of personal closeness to another individual.

Once deep friendships are formed, they tend to be permanent and are usually broken only by death. People tend to have only one or two deep friends throughout life.

There appear to be gender differences in friendship patterns. Women tend to cultivate more deep friendships. Men tend to have a greater number of friendships overall, but they are less close than women's. In fact, for older males, intimacy with friends appears to have little influence on psychological well-being (Keith et al., 1984).

The importance of distinguishing between deep and interest-related friendships was highlighted by Roberto and Scott (1986), who studied the importance of equity in older people's satisfaction with friendship. Equity in a relationship refers to the perception that the costs of giving something to the friendship are at least equal to the rewards. These researchers found that older people who felt they were part of an inequitable relationship were less satisfied with that friendship. Where these relationships involved best friends, however, satisfaction was high regardless of their equity. Men were involved in more equitable friendships than were women and were more intimate and self-disclosing. Women had fewer but more diverse friendships, reported being more intensely involved, and were more concerned about equity. This study suggests that intimacy needs may be defined and fulfilled in different ways for older men and women. While this component of the personal convoy may differ greatly by sex, there are many positive effects of a confiding relationship on the quality of life for both older men and women (Connidis & Davies, 1990).

We know comparatively very little about opposite-sex friendships, but males are more likely to report having opposite-sex friendships than are females (Usui, 1984).

Sibling Relationships

One type of interpersonal connection that has generated much recent interest is sibling relationships. Most adults and elderly people have siblings, although the number of surviving siblings obviously decreases with age (Hays, 1984). It appears that earlier interaction patterns developed among siblings tend to be maintained into adulthood and old age. That is, siblings who had a close relationship during childhood also tend to be close during adulthood; close friends also link one to the past (Mosatche et al., 1983).

Regardless of age, sister-sister pairs are closer than either brother-brother or mixed-sex pairs (Adams, 1968). Although proximity to one's brothers or sisters is important and siblings tend to maintain some form of regular contact throughout their adult years, this contact is not extensive (Cicirelli, 1985).

As with deep friendships, siblings can provide considerable interpersonal support for individuals in times of crisis (Matthews et al., 1990; Rosenthal, 1985). They can act as trusted confidants (Cicirelli, 1989; Kendig et al., 1980). In fact, older people who have close relationships with a sibling (especially, a sister) feel less depressed than those who report conflict with or indifference about a sibling (Cicirelli, 1989). Cicirelli (1980) suggests that sibling rivalry, thought to dissipate with age, may continue to occur in some situations, such as inheritance, but not in others, such as illness. In general, however, feelings of closeness increase with age, and conflict between siblings dissipates (Cicirelli, 1985).

Intergenerational Relationships

Intergenerational relationships are interactions between individuals of different cohorts or generations (Troll & Bengtson, 1982). Intergenerational relationships can occur within the context of the larger family or kinship network including aunts, uncles, and cousins, but typically involve grandparents, parents, and children. Of these, parent-child relationships tend to be the strongest (Troll & Bengtson, 1982). Helping patterns that occur among child, parent, and grandparent within a family are referred to as *lineage-generational* in nature (Dunham & Bengtson, 1986).

Demographic shifts have tended to make us more aware of the importance of intergenerational relationships. For example, Watkins et al. (1987) suggest that increased longevity makes four-generation—and even five-generation—families more likely, while declines in birthrate are simultaneously decreasing the number of people in each generation. On average, most adult women will spend more years with parents over 65 than with children under 18. Moreover, since couples seem to be delaying both marriage and childbirth, defining lines between generations will become sharper (Cantor, 1991). All of these factors increase the likelihood of greater chronological-age differences between grandchildren and grandparents and therefore highlight intergenerational relationships as important socializing influences in adulthood (see Box 7.1). It is important to realize, however, that this interaction is likely to be different when grandchildren are little and grandparents are in good health than when grandchildren are adolescents and grandparents are frail (Troll & Bengtson, 1982).

Intergenerational contacts can serve many functions for each person. Among other things, older members transmit political and religious information about expected gender roles and sexual behaviors, as well as about family values work and achievement. Family solidarity is a source of support and identity for many adults (Bengtson et al., 1990). Older people are both recipients and donors of help, and, in general, emotional ties are

BOX 7.1

THE CHANGING FAMILY: WHO ARE THE CARE-GIVERS?

Numerous sociodemographic changes have forced the family, as we have known it, to change. No longer is there a typical American family, where parents and children live together under one roof, as TV images of the Nelson family ("Ozzie and Harriet") and the Seavers ("Growing Pains") suggest. Diversity of family forms has replaced this somewhat idealistic view of the family. Consider such shows as "The Golden Girls," "Who's the Boss?" "Webster," "The Jeffersons," "The Odd Couple" or "The Simpsons." Each is a family in its own way.

The new diversity pertains to both the structure and the quality of relationships among family members. This diversity has clear and definite implications for the care-giving and social support families used to provide to their young and old. Thus, the convoy of the future may look and function very differently than it does today!

What are these demographic changes, and how will they affect families?

Greater longevity

Increased likelihood of chronic illness

Families are more verticalized, leading to the "beanpole" family—more intergenerational connections and fewer within-generational relationships

Increases in proportion of older versus young people

Slowing of birth rate

Children are fewer in number and spaced more closely

Greater incidence of teenage parents, divorce, cohabitation, childless marriages, remarriage

Women outlive men

Dual-career families more common

Multigenerational families are now the norm; four- and five-generation families not uncommon

Kin networks have more older family members than younger ones

Average married couple now has more parents than children

Fewer siblings, potentially greater care-giving responsibility on each sibling, fewer aunts and uncles to depend on

More time in the role of adult child with older parent than in the role of parent with a dependent child

Increasingly greater care-giving burden and responsibility, especially for women and both younger and middle-aged people

Unique parental and/or care-giving relationships, e.g., single parents, stepfamilies, same-sex parents

Generational differences widen

Increased age at which one becomes a care-giver

In light of these changes, you might ask yourself, "If my parent or grandparent were to become ill and require constant attention and care, whose responsibility would it be to provide this care? Would this responsibility be shared? Would it be easy or difficult to be a care provider? How would care-giving affect my family as a whole? How would it impact my relationship with my husband or wife? my children? my work relationships? my friendships? my work performance? my leisure time?"

strong between parents and children (Rossi & Rossi, 1990). When there are differences, parents usually report being closer to their children than their children are willing to acknowledge (Bond & Harvey, 1988).

There are many individual and cultural differences in intergenerational relationships, since family values and patterns clearly vary as a function of ethnicity (Sussman, 1985) and race (Schneider & Smith, 1973). Troll and Bengtson (1982) note more similarity between parents and children in political and religious views than in other areas. Friends may mediate transmission of certain values (e.g., drug use) from one generation to the next.

KINSHIP NETWORKS

Within the family kinship network, individuals usually give assistance to and interact and visit with the older members of the family (Troll & Bengtson, 1982).

Especially for the oldest-old (those over 85), children are an important link to grandchildren, great-grandchildren, and other relatives as sources of support; in their absence, help may be difficult to come by (Johnson & Troll, 1992). This forces people to find other sources of support, as from friends, neighbors, or social service agencies. On the other hand, Bankoff (1983) notes the positive supportive role that older parents can play in helping a daughter adjust to widowhood.

However, family support has its limits. Ingersoll-Dayton and Antonucci (1988) found that while most exchanges between older adults and their children were viewed as reciprocal, mutual exchanges of help were weaker for family than for friends. Thus, it appears that the quality of help, not its quantity, is crucial in this regard (McCullock, 1990).

Relationships between family members of different generations tend to be better when the individuals do not live in the same household and everyone feels independent and autonomous (Sussman, 1985). Children and adults enjoy visiting with their older relatives and vice versa, but they prefer to do it on a voluntary and mutual basis. While adult women are quite willing to adjust family schedules and help with the costs of health care to help an elderly parent, they are generally not willing to adjust work schedules or share households (Brody et al., 1984). For both children and parents, receiving emotional support or help in money management is more acceptable than is receiving supplemental income.

FILIAL RESPONSIBILITY

When children are just beginning their lives as adults, help of a psychological and economic nature flows from the parents to the children (Adams, 1968). This changes, however, when children are middle-aged and parents are elderly. Here, **filial responsibility** comes into play (Brody, 1979). Filial responsibility is the perceived obligation regarding the various types of services and social support that children should provide for their older parents (Hanson et al., 1983).

A recent study by Horne and associates (1990) found that college students believed it likely they would care for one or both of their parents, and that they viewed such care with anxiety. These researchers also found that women exhibited more anxiety than men regarding the provision of such care. Finley et al. (1988) found that filial responsibility in caring for an aging parent varied by gender of the child, maternal/paternal kinship status of the parent, how far away the parent lived from the child, and how much role conflict children felt about care-giving, particularly for an in-law or parent.

In some cases, there are disagreements between parents and children regarding filial responsibility, particularly with regard to living with a parent, adjusting one's work schedule, or offering financial aid (Harmon & Blieszner, 1990). Moreover, providing more help does not necessarily increase the elder's morale (McCulloch, 1990). Filial responsibility continues to serve as an ideal in many Asian cultures, where it is based on the values of respect, responsibility, family harmony, and sacrifice (Sung, 1990).

In filial responsibility, *ideally* there are "no strings attached." Help is offered freely by children, and parents feel they can count on them without being a burden to them. It is termed **filial maturity** when we see our parents as real people who need our help (Blenkner, 1965).

The obligations adult children feel toward the care and support of their aged parents can be very revealing. Sussman (1985) suggests that *intimate* support, or that based on love, commitment, and caring, is more enduring and satisfying than is *instrumental* aid, which is obligatory or born out of guilt or criticism. These two types of support highlight the difference between filial maturity and filial responsibility as a basis for intergenerational exchanges.

EXTENDED FAMILIES

In many cases, race and ethnicity have a very powerful influence on intergenerational relations, that is, there are ethnic or racial norms regarding familial obligations or expectations. In groups that are typically defined as **extended family** groups, there is greater importance placed on filial responsibility than in groups that are not viewed as extended family (Hanson et al., 1983). Extended families represent a significant proportion of families in the black community (Wilson, 1989). The black extended family serves as a mechanism for meeting the physical, emotional, and economic needs of individuals at all age levels (Sussman, 1985). There is a strong sense of familial obligation that underlies this family support network (Wilson, 1989).

Contrary to the expectation that older minority individuals might be most disadvantaged in terms of support, research has shown that frequency of supportive contact with family and friends is no less among Mexican American and black aged than among white elderly (Dowd &

The extended family often plays an important role in shaping intergenerational relationships.

Bengtson, 1978). There is some disagreement about this, however (Maldonado, 1975). Markides (1983) suggests that Mexican American and black families tend to provide more contact and support in the care of aged family members than do white families. Such support may help aged people maintain an independent life-style to avoid nursing home care, but increased contact with one's family may not always be positive for all family members. Also, within the extended black family network, elderly persons are usually the donors of services rather than receivers (Wilson, 1989).

In view of the diversity among older minority individuals, one must be especially cautious about overgeneralizing about kinship networks among ethnic and racial groups. Each subcultural group responds differently to available social services, holds different values regarding their relationships with whites, and interacts differently with service providers who might aid the family in caring for an elderly member.

Hanson et al. (1983) found that, for all age groups and races, filial responsibility was not considered very important. Contrary to expectation, whites had a higher belief in the importance of filial responsibility during adulthood and middle age than did blacks. In old age, however, the differences between the races were smaller. Thus, the quality and quantity of intergenerational relationships depends on a family's particular economic or physical situation rather than general factors such as ethnicity or race.

Even among families that are financially well-off, some may be more helpful in certain situations than in others. Older people typically turn to their adult children or another close relative in the case of serious illness or death (Shanas, 1962). Middle-aged parents who are dealing with the stresses of raising adolescents may find it necessary to provide support or take primary responsibility for an aging parent as well (Aisenberg & Treas, 1985). In such cases, pathological *role reversal* may occur: parent-child conflicts may reemerge, and the parent, lacking decision-making power as an older person, may assume a passive-dependent role. While this may take place in some families, its importance has probably been overstated (Aisenberg & Treas, 1985). Pathological role reversal may emerge only when past conflicts have not been resolved and when the adult child feels that pressure or obligation is the primary reason for caring for a frail parent. In such cases, the elder may be physically or emotionally abused.

Adding to the stressfulness of some care-giving situations are the physical, psychological, and financial pressures of caring for an ill parent. Such pressures affect both adult parents and their children. In intimate care-giving situations, fears about becoming dependent can be talked through and settled. In Chapter 10 we will discuss more extensively the unique difficulties adult care-givers face in caring for an elderly parent with Alzheimer's disease.

Why Individuals Are Attracted to Each Other

Before we discuss marriage, it is important to examine what brings individuals together to begin with. This phenomenon is widely studied by social psychologists and sociologists and is often generically referred to as interpersonal attraction. Our goal is to highlight the factors that appear to be related to eventual selection of a partner.

A number of factors tend to facilitate attraction and interpersonal relationships, some of which may result in marriage. These factors are familiarity and propinquity, satisfaction of personal needs, similarity, predictability, reinforcement, and parental models.

FAMILIARITY AND PROPINQUITY

In order for people to meet and become familiar with each other, they must have some form of regular contact or association (Zajonc, 1968). Through regular contacts such as being in a class together, individuals have more opportunities to develop and nurture interpersonal relationships.

PERSONAL NEEDS

We are attracted to individuals who satisfy our needs and desires, such as those for love and emotional support. Social psychologists have found that physical attractiveness also plays an important part in the choice of friends and potential mates, though this effect appears stronger for males than for females (Sigall & Landy, 1973). Individuals with needs for strong emotional support tend to be attracted to individuals who will meet these needs; and individuals who seek wealth are attracted to those with great financial resources.

An alternative view suggests that individuals are attracted to those who complement their needs. This is referred to as **complementarity,** and simply means that opposites attract. Although this view appears to make good common sense, research has not generally supported it (Bentler & Newcomb, 1978).

SIMILARITY AND PREDICTABILITY

We tend to be attracted to individuals who are similar to us in terms of socioeconomic level, race, religious beliefs, and education level. For example, Hill and Stull (1981) found that women and, to a lesser extent, men preferred roommates who possessed similar values. Furthermore, being similar to other individuals allows us to predict how they will react to specific events and situations. In fact, Bramel (1969) found that predictable people are liked, while unpredictable people are usually disliked.

REINFORCEMENT

People tend to be attracted to those who reinforce and support their own opinions, values, and ideas, or share similar interests. Such individuals provide mutual support for one another. According to this exchange-theory point of view (Murstein, 1982), the rewards and costs of relationships are likely to balance out; and each person is likely to perceive the relationship as an equitable one.

PARENTAL MODELS

We may be attracted to individuals who possess the traits of our opposite-sex parent. Thus, males are attracted to females who possess the traits of their mothers; and females are attracted to males who have the traits of their fathers (Murstein, 1982).

Although these factors help explain how individuals are initially attracted to each other, they do not explain the individual's choice of a particular marriage partner from a group of potential mates who may qualify on a number of these factors. Moreover, the actual selection of a marriage partner is highly subjective and based on the many personal and individual preferences we often refer to as love.

FILTER THEORY

Udry (1974) developed **filter theory** to describe how many of the factors discussed above are used to select a potential mate. This theory suggests that in selecting a mate, people use a hierarchical set of "filters." Simply put, the person who passes through all of these filters is the person you will marry. These filters, in order of importance, are (1) propinquity, (2) attractiveness in looks, build, and age, (3) similarity of social backgrounds, which also implies similar values and goals, (4) consensus or similar attitudes about specific topics such as abortion, sex, women's roles, and money, (5) complementarity, and (6) readiness. The readiness filter excludes people who are "off time," maritally speaking. Thus, people who want to marry earlier or later than usual are likely to have a difficult time finding someone who meets this last criterion.

STAGE THEORY

Murstein (1982) proposes a **stage theory** of mate selection, where couples go through a series of stages during which they come to know one another well enough to make a decision regarding the other's marriageability. The first stage of this process is the *stimulus stage,* where observable characteristics such as physical attractiveness or knowledge of occupation dominate. If both people's stimulus attributes are equal, the couple moves on to the *values comparison stage,* where evaluations of mutual interests, attitudes, personal beliefs, and needs are made via gathering of verbal information. If such evaluations are positive, the courtship reaches the *role stage,* where the couple make clear their feelings about each other. Expectations of the relationship, individual self-concepts, and perceptions of the other person are confirmed. Evaluation of one's own and the other's ability to function in the role of married person is made in this last stage. As couples progress through these stages of courtship, the importance of the stimulus and value-comparison dimensions lessen relative to marital-role expectations.

MARRIAGE

Marriage is still quite popular; nine out of ten people eventually do marry (Glick, 1977). Statistics reflect two trends regarding marriage in the United States at the current time. First, there has been a noticeable shift in the age of first marriages of males and females during the past 40 years. For females, the median age at the time of first marriage was 20.3 years in 1950, 21.8 years in 1978, and 23.8 years in 1989. In other words, starting in the middle of this century, the median age for first marriage has gradually increased. The same general trend is observed for males. In 1950, the median age of first marriage for males was 22.8 years, 24.2 years in 1978, and 26.2 years in 1989 (U.S. Bureau of the Census, 1991). These data also suggest that males generally tend to be older than females at the time of their first marriage. Furthermore, as age increases, men stand a better chance than do women of being married; most older women are widowed (Bengtson et al., 1990).

How do we form our ideas about marriage? Certainly the culture has an influence, through popular writings, movies, and the media; so do the experiences of our own parents. We may be socialized to believe that those who are happy personally are the most satisfied maritally, that people whose parents were happily married are also likely to be so, that those who are overinvolved in their work are necessarily less happily married, or that to be happily married, one must be sexually fulfilled via one's partner.

Some of these notions, such as the idea that coming from a home where the marital relationship is sound contributes to marital satisfaction, seem to be true (Doherty & Jackson, 1982). As we will see, however, being happily married is dependent on a number of factors, and it is difficult to say in an absolute sense what characterizes all satisfying marriages.

At this point, you might ask yourself some questions: Which of the above factors in mate selection is most important? Which are least important? What does being happily married mean to me? to my parents? to my grandparents?

Why Marry?

Marital relationships, of course, are a central part of our support convoy. Perhaps during our high school years we begin to define those qualities and characteristics that an ideal marriage partner should have. For some, this special person never seems to appear. For others, it is only after a "false start" or two that they come to know what it is that truly makes them happy in a marital relationship.

People get married for a variety of reasons. For many of us, it is a response to the **social clock** (Neugarten, 1973), in that we learn, implicitly or explicitly, that one *should* get married within a particular age range, such as 20 and 30. Going much beyond this range may evoke criticism, or, at the very least, a stream of questions from peers or relatives. One's own anxiety about "marriage-ability" is also likely to increase after 30, although the growing tendency is for couples to marry somewhat later now (Aizenberg & Treas, 1985).

People also marry for security, or to compensate for perceived social and/or personal inadequacies. They may wish to get away from their parents, to enhance their position in business, or to settle down. Still others put off marriage until they have reached a certain valued goal or attained some stability in their lives. This might mean delaying marriage until graduation, discharge from the service, landing that "first job," or one's income reaches a certain level. Of course, many do marry for love, but it is often difficult to separate the "chicken from the egg." Looking back on one's decision to marry after the fact makes it difficult to know for sure what led to what. Did you marry because you were in love, or did love grow out of your relationship?

Developmentally, we can see that the choice to marry can grow out of what Erikson (1963) terms a person's *intimacy needs.* Newman and Newman (1987) define intimacy as "the ability to experience an open, supportive, tender relationship with another person, without fear of losing one's identity in the process of growing close. . . . Intimacy implies the ability for mutual empathy and mutual regulation of needs." It is this ability to share oneself with another that is perhaps the central component in the establishment of intimacy. If you are uncertain that part of you will not be lost in the process, or feel that making compromises with another, which is ultimately necessary in any relationship, will require you to give up

ADULTS SPEAK

MARRIAGE

People marry for many reasons, some of them wise and others not so wise. Among those who marry, there may be a relationship between why one marries and the later success of that relationship. Consider the diversity of the following views:

Heather (age 21): "I want to get married in the future. I want to be sure that I really love the person and that the person really loves me. I don't want to make a mistake, but if I do, I won't stay married. I'll get a divorce as soon as I realize that I've made a mistake.

"I've had a couple of casual intimate experiences, but I'm not so quick to do that now because of AIDS."

Joan (age 30): "I guess I got married for all the wrong reasons. At the time it was the thing to do. 'Here are all my friends getting married, what am I gonna do? I'm a senior in college, that's pretty old. I better start thinking about marriage. I don't know what else I can do. I can teach but that's not enough.

"The person I married was a very popular man and I was a very insecure person, *very* insecure; and I thought, well, golly, I'm going with this person and everybody likes *him,* so maybe if I marry him, everybody will like *me*! The man I married, I didn't feel he really listened, but I did feel security. That, and not knowing what I'd do when I graduated—that's why I got married."

Ann (70 years old): "Arthur and I met at a USO dance. While we were dancing, we discovered that we had grown up near each other in New Jersey and that we had even attended the same high school. I really believe it was love at first sight. We met on the fifteenth of December and married on the twenty-fifth.

"I was 22 and Arthur was 25 when we married. We shared 30 years together. He died of a heart attack in 1973.

"I have positive feelings about marriage. We had such a good one, he was a good friend and confidant, we worked and played together and it was good. When we fought, it was over little petty things."

A 45-year-old woman says: "I think that marriage is a wonderful thing. I say that even though my first marriage did not work out. I think that my first marriage did not work because the people who were involved felt quite a bit of pressure. I mean my ex-husband and I loved each other very much. However, there were other circumstances that created some pressure for us both.

"For example, I do not think that my mother liked my first husband very much. Sometimes I wonder if our parents got along much at all. I mean, his parents and my parents were from such different backgrounds and had different interests.

"However, with my second husband, things were quite different. There was not that much pressure from our parents. We came from much more similiar backgrounds and our parents got along well together."

A 53-year-old woman had very definite views on why she married: "I married my childhood sweetheart. I felt that I would always get married. I wanted that to be my life-style. It was also what everyone did. At 18, with limited exposure to the world, I don't think I was very farsighted about what I expected from a marriage. I was just in love. I think you always use your parents as role models. There are always certain things you see in your parents' relationships that you like and dislike. You promise yourself that you will do it differently or the same. Whichever the case may be. Today it is a mix. At times I feel like it is active and passive, but in retrospect and with a more mature perspective, it is give and take. There are certain areas where I give more and he gives more in some areas. It all evens out."

something crucial to your well-being, you will not get married at all, delay marriage, or experience a great deal of conflict within marriage.

Above all, perhaps, marriage presupposes a sense of knowing who one is, and happy (but not necessarily long-lived) marriages are characterized by willingness and ability to compromise, be flexible, and accept failure and inadequacy in oneself as well as someone else. Successful marriages are also characterized by a sense of *mutuality*, or being able to satisfy your own needs, in part, through meeting someone else's.

It is difficult to describe the precise function of the love that is characteristic of marriage. While love may bring individuals together, it can also develop out of a commitment to one another. It is important to remember there are many definitions of love, but in this discussion we are referring to romantic love, which consists of a number of components. For example, Kelly (1983) assumes romantic love has four components: caring, needing, trust, and tolerance for another's faults.

Research suggests that the meaning of love and the factors related to why people love each other vary with age. Reedy et al. (1982) investigated the relative importance of six factors or components of love—emotional security, respect, communication, help and play behaviors, sexual intimacy, and loyalty—for young, middle-aged, and older adults. This study demonstrated two important facts regarding the components of love across the life span.

First, the rank order (position) of these six components was identical for each age group. This ranking, from highest to lowest, was as follows: emotional security, respect, communication, help and play behaviors, sexual intimacy, and loyalty.

Second, although individuals ranked these factors identically, the amount of importance attached to each factor was different for different age groups. Thus, emotional security was the most important component for all age groups but increased in importance during old age. Respect, the second-most important factor, decreased with increasing age. Communication decreased in importance with increased age, while help and play behaviors remained fairly constant. The importance of sexual intimacy, which ranked fifth for all age groups, was highest during middle age and decreased substantially during old age. Finally, although loyalty was ranked the lowest for all age groups, its rated importance increased with age.

TYPES OF MARRIAGES

Just as it is difficult to specify exactly why people choose to marry, it is also not easy to contrive a definition of marriage that is all-encompassing. What type of relationship you consider marriage to be depends on your personal views, religious orientation, sexual preference, and value system. There are several types of relationships between individuals that might be considered marriages. These types are traditional, companionship, colleague, open, group, and homosexual relationships.

BOX 7.2

STERNBERG'S THREE-FACTOR THEORY OF LOVE

Robert J. Sternberg has developed a three-factor theory of love, illustrated in the form of a triangle. The three components of love, according to this theory, are intimacy, passion, and decision/commitment (Sternberg, 1988a, 1988b).

The *intimacy* component includes giving and receiving emotional support to and from the loved one, as well as other behaviors that foster a feeling of warmth in a loving relationship.

The *passion* component includes both sexual passion and other needs that elicit a passionate response, such as self-esteem or affiliation with others.

The *decision/commitment* component of love has two parts. The short-term part is the decision that a person loves someone. The long-term part is the person's degree of commitment to maintaining that love.

Comparing the involvement of each partner in a love relationship can be done by seeing how closely the two people's love triangles fit each other.

As each person's needs may change over time, it is important to be flexible. Sternberg notes:

> Perhaps the most important use of the triangle theory is to help people recognize that relationships are, almost inevitably, dynamic. "Living happily ever after" need not be a myth, but if it is to be a reality, the happiness must be based upon different configurations of mutual feelings at various times in a relationship. Couples who expect their passion to last forever, or their intimacy to remain unchallenged, are in for disappointment. The theory suggests that we must constantly work at understanding, building, and rebuilding our love relationships. Relationships are constructions, and they decay over time if they are not maintained and improved. We cannot expect a relationship simply to take care of itself, any more than we can expect that of a building. Rather, we must take responsibility for making our relationships the best they can be.

According to Sternberg, each dimension of love will change in a particular way if the relationship is to succeed.

Commitment increases gradually at first and then grows more rapidly as a relationship develops. It eventually levels off if the relationship becomes long-term, or falls back to zero if the relationship fails.

Intimacy grows steadily at first and then tends to level off. It may be hidden, or latent, in some successful relationships, but if it disappears completely the relationship is likely to fail.

Passion has a positive force that is quick to develop and a negative force that takes hold more slowly and lasts longer, accounting for the heartache that remains when love has gone. The negative force eventually returns to zero.

Source: Trotter. (1986). The three faces of love. *Psychology Today* (September), p. 50.

The **traditional marriage** is a relationship between a male husband and female wife, and the husband is considered the head of the family. He supports the family and is the major decision maker, while the wife's role is well-defined and usually limited to child care and household matters (Duberman, 1974). While traditional marriages still exist, their relative frequency is decreasing, for a number of reasons. One of these is the increase in the number of women working outside of the home. The current rate of maternal employment for two-parent families is 71 percent; and the dual-wage family is the modal family style in the United States (Hoffman, 1989).

In a **companionship marriage,** there is no differentiation made between male and female roles (Duberman, 1974). Each partner can take on the rights, obligations, and duties of the other. Companionship marriages are common among individuals who are highly educated. In **colleague marriages**, the partners recognize role and responsibility differences (Duberman, 1974). Each partner assumes responsibility and authority for specific duties and tasks within the family, and these are generally stable. This type of marital relationship takes into account individual differences in abilities, interests, and preferences, and is popular among highly educated, middle-class and upper-middle-class couples. The **open marriage** is based on a legally sanctioned union between husband and wife. Partners in an open marriage feel that it is perfectly acceptable for each to have intimate and/or sexual relations with other partners. A **group marriage** is one in which a number of couples are legally married in a traditional manner (a husband to a wife), but these individuals share living arrangements, duties, responsibilities, and sexual partners. As with open marriages, it is difficult to obtain an accurate picture of the frequency and popularity of this type of relationship due to society's views about it, but such arrangements were more common in communal situations in the 1960s and early 1970s.

Gay relationships involve a personal commitment by gay or lesbian individuals to each other to live together as married partners, although their relationships may not be legally sanctioned. Partners share or take individual responsibility for specific roles and duties within the relationship. Until recently, there was comparatively little data regarding gay or lesbian relationships (see Corby & Solnick, 1980). However, as societal attitudes toward gay individuals have changed, more information has become available, particularly relating to older gay life-styles. For some people, fear of AIDS (acquired immune deficiency syndrome) influences the durability of such relationships among homosexual men, although it is clear that heterosexuals also acquire AIDS.

Corby and Solnick (1980) suggested that we know more about the impact of aging on the individual who is predominantly homosexual than about the frequency of homosexual behavior per se among older people. Aging was perceived to be particularly difficult for older male homosexuals, who may be labeled old as early as age 30, leading to the stereotype of all older gays as lonely and isolated. Corby and Solnick (1980) also suggested that older gays may actually be insulated from the stresses of aging, having learned much earlier in life to cope with loneliness because of their homosexuality.

Wall and Kaltreider (1977) interviewed 100 females ranging in age from 19 to 75 years, and found that about one-third of the sample reported they had seriously considered bisexuality and felt it was an acceptable alternative for others. Approximately one-quarter reported incidental homosexual feelings. Although this study utilized a very select sample of respondents (gynecological outpatients), it does suggest that individuals can be accepting of alternative sexual life-styles. It also underscores heterosexuality and homosexuality as a continuum, not a dichotomy (Masters et al., 1992). It remains to be seen what impact AIDS will have on such attitudes, although it is clear that AIDS has already affected sexual behavior.

Homosexuals grow old, as do heterosexuals, and current estimates are that there are between 3 and 4 million gays and lesbians over the age of 65 (Friend, 1990). How do older gay men and women fare? While older gays have been portrayed as lonely, bitter, and isolated (see above), many same-sex partnerships are quite enduring and satisfying (Butler et al., 1991). Despite ageism and discrimination, older gay men may be more independent and experience less redefinition of roles than their heterosexual counterparts (Kimmel, 1978; Kimmel et al., 1984).

As with older people in general, older gays may require support from others to deal with ill health, bereavement, or retirement. Fortunately, services geared specifically toward such needs of gay people are available in most major cities. While acceptance of homosexuality may be gaining strength, gay men and women still face ridicule and rejection from others, as well as discrimination in getting both medical treatment and health insurance (Masters et al., 1992).

In a recent series of studies, we have learned a great deal about how gays and lesbians adjust to aging. Adelman (1990) found that men who were more satisfied with being gay adjusted better to growing old. They expressed higher life satisfaction, had more self-esteem, and reported few psychosomatic problems. They also had less involvement with other gays, reflecting their experience of not having grown up in a culture that accepted their sexual preference. Bennett and Thompson (1990) found that homosexual men may, in some cases, experience "accelerated aging," that is, they are considered old at an earlier age than their heterosexual counterparts. However, they still maintained an interest in sexual relationships and retained their sexual ability (Pope & Schulz, 1990). Although we know less about older lesbians, they may maintain high self-esteem because of carefully developed and nurtured support from other older lesbians (Dorrell, 1990).

Despite this progress, and a much more accurate and positive picture of older gays and lesbians, we have much to learn about homosexual relationships in middle age and later life. Longitudinal studies are needed, with larger, more representative samples of old gay men and women, but they still may be reluctant to volunteer due to the stigma they feel is attached to their homosexuality (Cruikshank, 1990). In particular, we need more reliable information about gay and lesbian couples who have grown old together, gay widows, single older gays, and married bisexual gay men and women (Lee, 1990). Therapeutic and social services, especially for those facing illness or death, need to be developed (Lee, 1990). Fortunately, progress is being made in our knowledge. If anything, the AIDS epidemic ideally should heighten our sensitivity to the unique difficulties gay men and lesbians face in later life.

In sum, if we know comparatively little about older gay men (Bengtson et al., 1990), our knowledge about older lesbians is virtually absent.

Marital Satisfaction in Adulthood

Most of us believe that happily married couples are in love. But what does it mean to be happily married? There is a great deal of confusion about how marital satisfaction is best defined. For some, the extent to which a partner carries out expected duties—meets the other partner's expectations regarding child care and being steadily employed—would define a good marriage. For others, sharing common interests or activities suffices. For still others, mutuality may be uppermost in their definition of being happily married. Perhaps the most realistic solution to this problem is to see people as "compartmentalizing" aspects of their marital relationship, some of which are satisfactory, some of which are not.

What do we know about marital happiness in adulthood? There appears to be a curvilinear relationship between marital satisfaction and stage in the life cycle, with marital satisfaction peaking before children are born and after they leave home (Lupri & Frideres, 1981; Rollins & Cannon, 1974) (see below). Also, males are more satisfied than females with marriage (Rhyne, 1981).

In a series of studies, Glenn and McLanahan (1981, 1982) categorized couples by educational level, religion, race, gender, employment status, and age, and found that child rearing had a negative impact on marital enjoyment for all subgroups. Furthermore, in an older sample (age 50+) whose children were grown and not living at home, there were no general positive effects on marital happiness of having had children.

Perhaps the most extensive study of marital satisfaction throughout the life cycle was conducted by Rhyne (1981). Based on a sample of 2200 Canadian couples, Rhyne investigated quality of marital satisfaction in terms of factors such as friendship and sexual fulfillment, love, interest, and help at home. The presence of children, age of the eldest child, and number of children at home were criteria used to determine the stage in the family life cycle (Hill, 1965).

People's evaluations of overall marital quality were lower during the child-rearing stages of the family life cycle and highest when all the children had left home. Men generally evaluated their marriages higher than did women, except for the preparental, preschool years. Women were more variable in their ratings in all stages than were men. It is important to recognize that couples raising children may not necessarily be unhappy; they simply are less happy than after children have left home. It is possible that many people define their marriages as happy *because* they have children. For these individuals, being married and being a parent are highly interrelated.

Marital satisfaction may change further in later adulthood. For example, Gilford (1984) investigated two dimensions of marital satisfaction, positive interaction (desirable aspects of relating to one another) and negative sentiment (negative feelings about the relationship), among three age groups of older married couples, 55 to 62 years of age, 63 to 69 years of age, and 70 to 90 years of age. Gilford found that higher levels of positive interaction were found for the middle group of older adults, while they were lowest for the youngest group. The lowest negative-sentiment scores were found in the middle group and the highest in the oldest age group.

Gilford suggests these results may be due to what can be called a honeymoon stage stemming from recent retirement. That is, individuals in this group are still in good health, have more leisure time, and now do the things they have always wanted to do. For older persons, commitment to spouse and to marriage as an institution, in addition to a spouse's personal characteristics, contribute to marital stability (Lauer & Lauer, 1985).

Early views about marital development stressed its regularity—a sequence of progressive stages along the life cycle, each with its own developmental task. Featherman (1983) and Riley (1983), however, have argued that this simplistic view of the family life cycle may no longer be useful. They suggest that, just as chronological age has proved to be an inadequate means of predicting individual development, age-graded events such as the birth of one's first child, empty nest, or retirement are not sufficient to understand the course of family development. These newer ideas about the family make it more difficult to say who is happily married and who is not.

An approach has emerged that sees the family as a dynamic, changing system, composed of individuals who are themselves changing (Featherman, 1983; Weeks & Wright, 1985). As families change because of rising divorce rates, to be replaced by stepfamilies, singles, or widow(er)s, the static, predictable concept or idea of the family life cycle will change as well. Families, like individuals, are constantly evolving. Thus, many feel that more dynamic, reciprocal approaches, where family members both influence and are influenced by the others, make more sense (Featherman, 1983; Lerner & Spanier, 1978; Parke, 1988).

Understanding the family in terms of developing parent-child and husband-wife relationships has been further clarified by newer ideas about the family life cycle (Carter & McGoldrick, 1988). One concept of the family is quite dynamic, despite its apparent stagelike character. Individual family members' life changes affect and are affected by the age-graded developmental tasks families often face. The family quite obviously changes over time, and in order to retain its identity and supportive, socializing function, it must be flexible enough to absorb the entry, exit, and reentry of its members into the family system without interfering with individual development (Goldenberg & Goldenberg, 1991). Table 7.1 illustrates the family life-cycle approach, within which the roles of parents, children, and grandparents can be understood as either adaptive and fulfilling or maladaptive and destructive, in terms of both the family system and individual members.

The family as an institution has obviously changed over the past several decades, and the concept of the intact nuclear family has given way to a diversity of family forms (see Box 7.1). For this reason, a modified family life-cycle approach describing family development has been proposed. It is presented in Table 7.2, and it applies to divorce and the reconstitution of a new family afterward.

We must recognize that a family life-cycle approach, even a modified one, has its limitations; it is descriptive, not explanatory. It fails to take into account individual differences in the timing of life events such as marriage, parenthood, or retirement, and it ignores important periods of transition between stages (Goldenberg & Goldenberg, 1991).

TABLE 7.1

LIFE-CYCLE STAGES FOR INTACT MIDDLE-CLASS AMERICAN FAMILIES

Family Life Cycle Stage	Emotional Process of Transition: Key Principles	Second-Order Changes in Family Status Required to Proceed Developmentally
1. Leaving home: Single young adults	Accepting emotional and financial responsibility for self	a. Differentiation of self in relation to family of origin b. Development of intimate peer relationships c. Establishment of self re work and financial independence
2. The joining of families through marriage: The new couple	Commitment to new system	a. Formation of marital system b. Realignment of relationships with extended families and friends to include spouse
3. Families with young children	Accepting new members into the system	a. Adjusting marital system to make space for child(ren) b. Joining in child-rearing, financial, and household tasks c. Realignment of relationships with extended family to include parenting and grandparent roles
4. Families with adolescents	Increasing flexibility of family boundaries to include children's independence and grandparents' frailties	a. Shifting of parent-child relationships to permit adolescent to move in and out of system b. Refocus on midlife marital and career issues c. Beginning shift toward joint caring for older generation
5. Launching children and moving on	Accepting a multitude of exits from and entries into the family system	a. Renegotiation of marital system as a dyad b. Development of adult-to-adult relationships between grown children and their parents c. Realignment of relationships to include in-laws and grandchildren d. Dealing with disabilities and death of parents (grandparents)
6. Families in later life	Accepting the shifting of generational roles	a. Maintaining own and/or couple functioning and interests in face of physiological decline; exploration of new familial and social role options b. Support for a more central role of middle generation c. Making room in the system for the wisdom and experience of the elderly, supporting the older generation without overfunctioning for them d. Dealing with loss of spouse, siblings, and other peers, and preparation for own death; life review and integration

Source: Carter & McGoldrick. (1988). p. 15.

TABLE 7.2

DISLOCATIONS IN THE FAMILY LIFE CYCLE REQUIRING ADDITIONAL STEPS TO RESTABILIZE AND PROCEED DEVELOPMENTALLY

Phase	Emotional Process of Transition Prerequisite Attitude	Developmental Issues
Divorce		
1. The decision to divorce	Acceptance of inability to resolve marital tensions sufficiently to continue relationship	Acceptance of one's own part in the failure of the marriage
2. Planning the breakup of the system	Supporting viable arrangements for all parts of the system	a. Working cooperatively on problems of custody, visitation, and finances b. Dealing with extended family about the divorce
3. Separation	a. Willingness to continue cooperative coparental relationship and joint financial support of children b. Work on resolution of attachment to spouse	a. Mourning loss of intact family b. Restructuring marital and parent-child relationships and finances; adaptation to living apart c. Realignment of relationships with extended family; staying connected with spouse's extended family
4. The divorce	More work on emotional divorce: Overcoming hurt, anger, guilt, etc.	a. Mourning loss of intact family; giving up fantasies of reunion b. Retrieval of hopes, dreams, expectations from the marriage c. Staying connected with extended families
Postdivorce family		
Custodial single parent	Willingness to maintain financial responsibilities, continue parental contact with ex-spouse, and support contact of children with ex-spouse and his or her family	a. Making flexible visitation arrangements with ex-spouse and his or her family b. Rebuilding own financial resources c. Rebuilding own social network
Noncustodial single parent	Willingness to maintain parental contact with ex-spouse and support custodial parent's relationship with children	a. Finding ways to continue effective parenting relationship with children b. Maintaining financial responsibilities to ex-spouse and children c. Rebuilding own social network

Source: Carter & McGoldrick. (1988). p. 22.

Despite these limitations, taking a newer systems-oriented perspective on family development makes it easier to see that each family is unique. Given the changing, dynamic nature of marriages, it is not surprising that satisfaction with a marital relationship varies with age. We will have more to say about family systems in our discussion of family therapy in Chapter 11.

Despite the difficulties of measuring marital happiness across the life span, a number of factors do appear to contribute to a good marital relationship (Stinnett et al., 1984). Good marital relationships reflect mutual respect for one another, commitment and responsibility for meeting each other's needs, and concern for one another's happiness and welfare. Persons who are happily married report strong emotional support and understanding from one another; each feels that his or her good and bad qualities are accepted by the other spouse. (See Box 7.3.)

What characterizes happy marriages and satisfying relationships with others is a feeling of intimacy—mutual trust, respect, commitment, closeness, and openness. Shyness, aggressiveness, self-centeredness, selfishness, lack of empathy, and unrealistic expectations all interfere with the development of intimacy (Masters et al., 1992).

BOX 7.3

HAPPY AFTER ALL THESE YEARS!

Couples married for over 15 years were questioned regarding what qualities keep their relationships going and growing. Here is what they said:

What Keeps a Marriage Going?

Here are the top reasons over 350 respondents gave, listed in order of frequency

Men	Women
My spouse is my best friend	My spouse is my best friend
I like my spouse as a person	I like my spouse as a person
Marriage is a long-term commitment	Marriage is a long-term commitment
Marriage is sacred	Marriage is sacred
We agree on aims and goals	We agree on aims and goals
My spouse has grown more interesting	My spouse has grown more interesting
I want the relationship to succeed	I want the relationship to succeed
An enduring marriage is important to social stability	We laugh together
We laugh together	We agree on a philosophy of life
I am proud of my spouse's achievements	We agree on how and how often to show affection
We agree on a philosophy of life	An enduring marriage is important to social stability
We agree about our sex life	We have a stimulating exchange of ideas
We agree on how and how often to show affection	We discuss things calmly
I confide in my spouse	We agree about our sex life
We share outside hobbies and interests	I am proud of my spouse's achievements

Source: Lauer, J. & Lauer, R. (1985). Marriages made to last. *Psychology Today* (June), pp. 26–28.

Communication, which can be both verbal and nonverbal, is an essential ingredient to marriage and, for that matter, to all intimate relationships. Despite the fact that we often think we know how to communicate effectively, many of us do not. Communication, of course, is a two-way street; we are both communicators and listeners. Table 7.3 provides some suggestions for improving communications skills. Remember, communication, trust, and sharing are vital ingredients in any relationship that people find mutually satisfying and rewarding.

TABLE 7.3

DEVELOPING EFFECTIVE COMMUNICATION AND LISTENING SKILLS IN RELATIONSHIPS

1. Think through what you want to say and how you'll say it, particularly if it's an important or emotionally charged message.
2. Let your partner know what your priorities are; try not to crowd in so many requests and instructions that it's difficult to grasp your key points.
3. Be concise. Long-winded discussions are more likely to confuse than clarify. On the other hand, being concise doesn't mean being simplistic or superficial. Don't leave out important information about your feelings or desires in order to be brief.
4. Don't talk *at* your partner. Give him or her a chance to respond and interact.
5. Try not to begin communications by criticizing or blaming your partner. Starting on a negative note puts your partner on the defensive and makes objective listening difficult.
6. Don't be afraid to put what you need to say in a letter if you're having trouble saying it face to face. Writing it down shows that you cared enough to take the time to say it carefully.
7. Ask for feedback from your partner to be sure you've been understood and to get his or her reactions.

1. *Effective listening requires your undivided attention.* Trying to listen while you're doing something else, like watching TV or reading, tells your partner that you don't think that what he or she has to say is very important.
2. *Effective listening is an active rather than passive process.* The best listeners show the speaker that they are involved in the communication process even though they are temporarily silent. This can be done by eye contact, nodding your head, or asking an occasional question to clarify a point without disrupting your partner's message.
3. *Effective listeners are patient in their listening style.* The patient listener realizes that a bit of encouragement early in a conversation can set the stage for a more meaningful dialogue later on. At the same time, patient listeners refrain from the temptation to barge in with their own comments before the other person has completed his or her message.
4. *Effective listeners avoid putting undue emphasis on one word or phrase in a message and wait for the message to be completed before they react to it.* This is particularly true in sexual matters, where many key words (such as "orgasm" or "satisfaction") can trigger an emotional response.
5. *Effective listeners pay attention to what the speaker is actually saying instead of approaching conversations with preconceived notions of what might be said.*
6. *Effective listeners are attuned to their partners even when there's been no request for a discussion.* Sometimes the most important communications occur in odd, offhand moments rather than in planned, formal dialogues.
7. *You don't have to agree in order to listen—in fact, it can be useful to disagree.* The point of being a good listener is to understand what the speaker is saying; this doesn't mean that you have to endorse the message.

Source: Masters et al. (1992). pp. 322–326.

Violence Within the Family

At the other end of the spectrum from happily married couples are marriages that are termed *conflict-habituated* (Stevens-Long, 1984). These relationships are characterized by open fighting of a verbal and/or physical nature. Within such a context, child abuse is common. Often, very young and helpless children are the victims. Abused children learn that they are not worthy of love by another, and they lose trust in their ability to receive love as well as to give it. Often, they grow up to become abusing parents, and they place inordinate demands on their children to provide the emotional closeness they themselves lacked as children. While early research suggested that the majority of abusing parents were poor, came from large families, felt negatively about themselves, and had more difficulty in dealing with the demands of child rearing (Cater & Easton, 1980), we now know abuse also occurs in families that are financially well-off and highly educated.

Children are not the only victims of physical and psychological abuse. Adults and the elderly can also be targets. In general, women more often than men are the objects of spouse abuse (Wetzel & Ross, 1983). Battered women are often overpowered by their husbands, who in many cases are the primary earners in the family (Rosewater, 1985). Battered women tend to be submissive, have low self-esteem, sometimes accept traditional female roles, and feel that they have few basic rights as human beings. Such women are frequently prone to deny the serious nature of their situations and paradoxically cling to the relationship, often out of fear, isolation from others, or guilt. Batterers, usually men, are often insecure, violent people who have learned that physical and psychological abuse are forms of control. They often drink excessively and tend to come from violent families (Hotaling & Sugarman, 1986).

Older people are not immune to physical and psychological abuse, known as **elder abuse.** Although interest in this type of family violence is high, our knowledge about the extent of the problem, and more importantly, about why older people are abused, is comparatively limited (Reinberg & Hayslip, 1991). In many instances, the abuse is cyclical: some elderly people abused their children and, as a consequence, may be more tolerant of the treatment they receive from them as adults (Hickey & Douglass, 1981). Physical or psychological abuse may also result from stress and frustration stemming from the daily demands on an adult child's physical, psychological, and financial resources in caring for an aging parent. Feeling guilty about not caring for a parent and a history of violence in one's past are also critical factors in the abuse of the elderly, who are often both physically and psychologically vulnerable (Costa, 1984; Reinberg & Hayslip, 1991).

Any evidence of neglect or deliberate physical or psychological abuse should be followed up with referral to a social worker or other professional who can pursue matters further. Counseling is, of course, an option for many families in which abuse occurs.

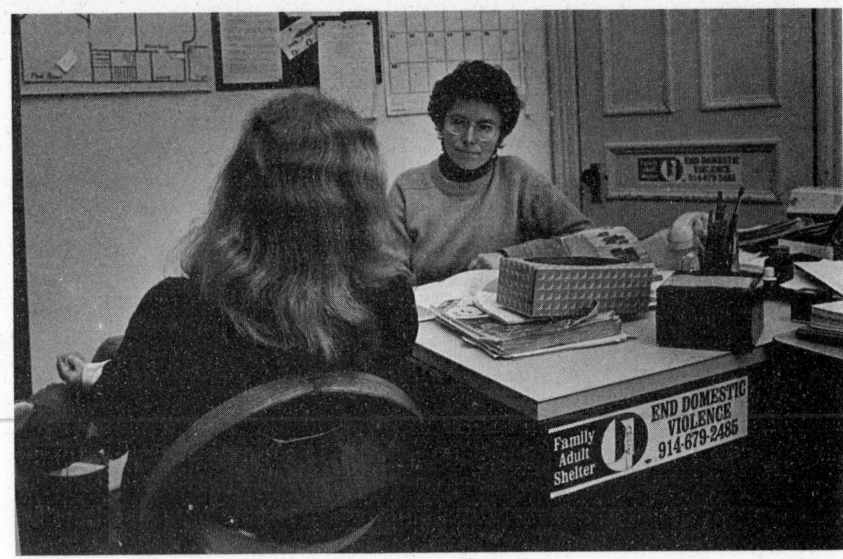

Timely intervention and counseling are essential to dealing with abuse within the family.

Violence in marital or other close relationships usually contributes to its dissolution; husbands and wives, for example, may divorce.

DIVORCE

Just as people make the decision to marry for a number of reasons, they also choose not to divorce due to a variety of factors that have little to do with the breakdown of mutuality. They may continue to stay married "for the sake of the children," for economic or business reasons, or because divorce would evoke social disapproval from friends or relatives (Kelly, 1982). Emotionally speaking, however, the couple might have divorced at some point much earlier, when each person determined that the costs of maintaining the relationship had become greater than the benefits.

During the past 20 years, the divorce rate has risen substantially, and it is estimated that nearly 50 percent of all current first marriages will end in divorce (U.S. Bureau of the Census, 1991). From 25 to 40 percent of divorced people will remarry, with divorce rates for second marriages 25 percent higher than for first marriages (U.S. Bureau of the Census, 1991). The increase in divorce may be linked to many factors, such as the belief that divorce is a reasonable alternative to an unhappy marriage, the Women's Movement, the removal of the social stigma attached to divorce, and legislation making divorce easier. There is, however, some recent evidence that the divorce rate has either declined very slightly or flattened out over the last decade (U.S. Bureau of the Census, 1991). This may be due to the odds of remarriage for women being lower than for men, the odds of the second marriage breaking up declining, or the loss in income women usually face after divorce.

In some cases, divorce may come as a complete surprise, leaving one of the partners with a deep sense of failure and rejection (Kelly, 1982). In other cases, extended absences due to job responsibilities can split up couples in spite of their genuine affection for one another.

Divorce is a painful, disruptive experience for the entire family and often leads to more life changes. For example, in a longitudinal study of the impact of divorce, people who had divorced, compared to others experiencing normative life changes (parenthood, retirement, or empty nests), reported both more positive and more negative life events. The older the individual, the more negative life events were reported (Chiriboga et al., 1991). Interestingly, three and a half years after separating, women 40 years and older and men in their forties were happiest of all; men in their fifties and older fared the worst. Many people reported that they had begun to "return to normal," relative to what they had experienced shortly after divorces.

Wallerstein (1989) found that the effects of divorce were quite pervasive and could last as long as ten years. She found, for example, that (1) in only one of seven cases studied did children describe both parents as being happily remarried; (2) ten years after splitting up, one-third of the women in the study and one-quarter of the men felt that life had been unfair, disappointing and lonely; and (3) five years after their parents' breakup, more than one-third of the children studied were doing markedly worse than they had been before the divorce.

Divorce creates a new set of difficulties for people (Bloom et al., 1983). Divorces are expensive and often lead to many life-style changes. One may need to find a new place to live, learn to manage on a day-to-day basis, arrange for child care, make new friends, find a new job, establish credit, and so on. This may be especially difficult for women who have never worked outside the home, as well as for middle-aged and older women. At the same time, the individual must deal with feelings of guilt, sorrow, and anger over the perceived failure of a primary relationship (Kelly, 1982). Often, people who have custody of the children believe they must serve as "both parents." Arrangements for custody, alimony, and visiting rights must often be made, creating additional difficulties to overcome (Warshak & Santrock, 1983). There literally may not be time to see others socially or become intimately involved with another person. Furthermore, children may object to increased demands on them to assist with chores or other activities, or to the intrusion of a new mother or father into their lives. Such families are often termed *blended families.* We will elaborate on stepparent-stepchild relationships in our section on remarriage.

In light of the unforeseen problems many divorced people face, it is not surprising that they might later question whether getting divorced was a wise choice. Many, overwhelmed by these pressures and lacking help and support from others, become depressed, suffer physical or work difficulties, or have difficulty in forming new relationships with others, fur-

BOX 7.4

COPING WITH DIVORCE

Dr. Susan Sturdivant, a divorce counselor, offers the following advice to those going through a divorce:

Being divorced means more than just no longer being married; divorced people, used to functioning socially as part of a couple, have to get used to thinking and living as a "single" again. To ease the process of separation:

Maintain your friendships during divorce. . .

- Don't wait for friends to call you. Call them first to ease their fears of saying the wrong thing or not knowing what to say.
- Build a wide support network. Don't place all the burden on one or two good friends—they may feel overwhelmed by your needs.
- Resist the temptation to ask friends about your ex's activities—it may make them feel like spies, and they'll start avoiding you.
- Don't force friends to take sides by insisting that anyone who doesn't completely support your anger at your spouse is "against you."
- Discuss with your spouse how each of you will continue friendships you made as a couple.
- Don't criticize your former spouse to your friends; it may alienate them altogether.

Be kind to yourself. It's normal to be a little crazy during a divorce! Be patient with yourself as you go through the emotional highs and lows. Just as it took time to form your marriage, it will also take time to develop your single identity. The longer the marriage, the longer the recovery time.

Consider formalizing your divorce. Some British courts ask divorcing couples to say to each other: "Goodbye—thank you for the good times in our marriage. I wish you all the best. Our relationship will continue as mother and father of our children, but not as husband and wife. Good luck."

Find a good therapist to help you figure out what went wrong in the marriage so you don't repeat destructive patterns. As George Santayana observed, *those who do not understand the past are doomed to repeat it.*

Take advantage of singles' groups in your community. *Parents Without Partners* (7910 Woodmont Ave., Washington, D.C.) has branches nationwide, as does MOMMA, an organization for single mothers (P.O. Box 567, Venice, CA 90291).

Regarding your children:

- **Explain the divorce simply and honestly** in words the child can understand. Don't try to hide or deny marital problems; the explanations children create for such tension are usually far worse than the actual facts.
- **Avoid placing blame** for the divorce. Disparaging the other parent only confuses children, who still love both of you. Make sure the children know *they are not to blame.* Don't assume they'll know this without being told.
- **Make it clear that you aren't "divorcing" your children** along with your spouse. Reassure them that both parents love and care for them even though you won't all be living together. Don't ask children to decide which parent to live with. It's a no-win situation for them, since they can only please one parent by rejecting the other.
- When you feel guilty about the effects of the divorce on your child, remember that **unhappy homes cause emotional problems** and delinquent behavior as often as divorce. The pain of divorce is a crisis that lessens with time; the tension of unhappy parents is constant.
- **Avoid unnecessary changes.** If possible, keep children in the same neighborhood and school during the period immediately after the divorce.

Source: Divorce. *Update on Human Behavior, 8* (2). (1988). Human Services Inc. Dallas, TX.

ther isolating them from support they need. Women report more anxiety and conflict prior to separation, while men experience more "practical" problems during the year following divorce (Hetherington et al., 1982). While many divorced individuals do report feelings of enhanced self-esteem and ultimately remarry, the immediate aftereffects of divorce are very stressful for both individuals, children, family, and friends. Bloom et al. (1983) note, however, that support from others in the workplace can lessen the stressfulness of the divorce and its aftermath.

Single-Parent Families

The percentage of single-parent families has been increasing during the past few decades. Clingempeel and Reppucci (1982) reported that approximately 40 percent of families in 1982 were headed by one parent. Of these families, 85 percent were headed by females and only 15 percent by males, since the courts traditionally favor mothers where physical custody of children is concerned (Meredith, 1985).

According to Norton and Glick (1986), there are four types of one-parent families, mostly headed by women. The first type is the household maintained by a parent with at least one child under 18 years and no spouse present. Generally, the younger the children, the more likely they are to be living with the mother, while older boys are more likely to be living with the father. The second type of one-parent family consists of a household with one parent but no children under 18 years of age. However, sons and daughters over 18 live in the household. The third type is called a *related subfamily* (Norton & Glick, 1986). A related subfamily lives in a house maintained by a relative. An example of this type would be a young mother and her children living in the home of the mother's parent. Approximately 22 percent of one-parent families are of this type, and 90 percent are mother-child situations. Statistically, one-parent families of this type are most likely to be young never-married mothers, and more likely to be black than white. The fourth type is called a *unrelated subfamily* (Norton & Glick, 1986). An unrelated subfamily lives in a house maintained or shared with someone to whom the subfamily is not related. An example is two divorced men or women and their children living with a friend and his or her children.

The majority of research has focused on maternal one-parent families maintaining their own households with children under 18 in the household. Interest regarding one-parent families headed by fathers is growing, however. In 1990, there were 2.9 million single fathers and 10 million single mothers raising children in the United States (U.S. Bureau of the Census, 1991). Fathers who head one-parent families tend to be older, more highly educated, raising children who are older, and usually better off economically than such families headed by mothers (Luepnitz, 1982; Risman, 1986). It is clear that fathers can be quite successful and effective in child rearing (Ambert, 1982). For example, in one study, single fathers reported deeper relationships with their children than before the separation (Smith & Smith, 1981).

Divorce in Later Life

It is interesting to note that there are increasing numbers of middle-aged and older adults divorcing (Hayghe, 1984; Uhlenberg et al., 1990). Divorce at any age has numerous economic, social, emotional, and psychological effects on individuals. For mid-life and older women, however, the transition from married to single life can be particularly difficult. They often find they are unprepared for lives as divorced single people (AARP, 1987). Women of all ages emerge from divorce with a decrease in their standard of living due to less income. This is especially difficult for mid-life and older women, who may have little, if any, work experience outside the home, which limits their employment options. They may lose their rights to their husband's pension, Social Security, life insurance benefits, and health care coverage. There is also severe stress associated with loss of support caused by the loss of friendship networks, which are usually couple-oriented. There is a decrease in self-esteem stemming from these factors; and as women get older their opportunities to remarry diminish (AARP, 1987).

While we still do not know why the divorce rate among older adults is increasing, it may be partially due to couples remaining together for the sake of the children. When the children in these cases finally leave home, there is no longer any reason for the couple to stay together (Glenn & Supancic, 1984). Especially if the husband and wife now see more of each other because they have retired, they may become aware of how unhappy they are with their relationship and consequently divorce.

While we need to gather further information regarding the causes and effects of divorce after young adulthood, preliminary work suggests that divorce's effects can extend well into the adult life span (Chase-Lansdale & Hetherington, 1990).

Remarriage

Most divorced individuals remarry, usually within three years of the divorce (Furstenberg, 1982). However, the rate of divorce for such persons is also high. Because 75 percent of divorced mothers and 80 percent of divorced fathers remarry, many children are exposed to a series of marital transitions and household reorganizations. Therefore, divorce and remarriage should not be viewed as single events, but as part of a series of transitions modifying the lives and development of children (Hetherington et al., 1989).

The majority of remarried individuals of both sexes tend to view their second marriage as being somewhat better than their first on a number of dimensions (Furstenburg, 1982). Remarriages that involve children nevertheless often present difficulties (Hetherington et al., 1982). And although individuals often describe their second marriages as happier than their first, statistics indicate that the divorce rate for remarried individuals is somewhat higher than for first marriages (Glenn & Weaver, 1978). The group of remarrieds who have the most difficult adjustment problems are those in which both husband and wife have children from previous marriages living in the household (Kampara, 1980).

Since a majority of divorced individuals remarry, a large number of children experience a relationship with a parent who is not biologically related. The period of adjustment to remarriage appears to be longer than that for divorce, especially for older children. As is the case with divorce, there is great diversity in children's responses to their parents' remarriage.

A particular problem seems to be that:

> There are no rules for stepchildren and stepparents to follow. . . . They don't know how they're supposed to act toward each other—whether, for example, the stepparent is supposed to spank the stepchild. . . . Just as losing a parent can be stressful, so can gaining a parent be stressful (Cherlin, 1990).

The majority of studies of stepfamilies have compared children living in stepfamilies to nuclear families and/or single-parent families on global measures of psychosocial adjustment or cognitive functioning. Generally, these studies have found negligible differences in psychological outcomes for children living in stepfamilies and nuclear families (Clingempeel & Segal, 1986). The three factors that have been consistently found to affect a child's response to remarriage are age, temperament/personality, and gender.

Older children usually adapt better over the long term to remarriage. Like younger children, however, older children and adolescents experience pain and anger when their parents divorce (Allison & Furstenberg, 1989). But they may be better able to assign responsibility for the divorce, resolve loyalty conflicts, and adapt to a new family.

Children who are temperamental and less adaptable to change are more likely to be the target of criticism, anger, or anxiety on the part of a parent and stepparent, and they are less able to cope with the situation. The negative effects of divorce, life in a single-parent family, and remarriage are more pervasive for girls than for boys (Hetherington et al., 1985; Vuchinich et al., 1991).

Cohabitation

Before discussing singles, we discuss cohabitation, a life-style that fits somewhere between being married and being single. Cohabitation is either a precursor to or substitute for marriage (Crooks & Bauer, 1980). Numerous factors account for the increase in couples living together in recent years. One possibility is younger cohorts' tendency to question traditional mores and values as well as the availability of more effective methods of birth control. Among older adults, cohabitation is also increasing in popularity. For this group, the primary purposes of cohabitation are companionship/emotional support and economic purposes or necessity, such as sharing the costs of everyday living.

Overall, marriage, cohabitation, and other types of companionable relationships are an important area of study in adulthood and aging be-they have been found to be related to life expectancy as well as psychological well-being (Wantz & Gay, 1981). Of course, they also help to define the convoy and thus serve the important function of emotional and psychological support in dealing with the stresses of life (Doherty & Jackson, 1982).

Singles

Singles are those individuals who have never been married, are widowed, or are divorced. Of those individuals currently viewed as single in the United States, approximately 58 percent have never been married, 27 percent are widowed, and 15 percent are divorced. Single adults are considered the heads of about one household in four (U.S. Bureau of the Census, 1991).

THE NEVER-MARRIED

Individuals who never marry remain unmarried for a variety of reasons: personal choice, professional/occupational demands, caring for aging parents or other family members, and so forth. Older never-married individuals, however, may be better adjusted than widows of the same age, never having had to cope with the death of a spouse. This may also be due to the fact they have experienced living alone, being independent, and doing things for themselves for a longer time (Bengtson et al., 1990). Furthermore, they do not experience the dramatic changes in life-style that can occur as the result of losing a spouse, and they have developed friendship networks independently of another person.

For married adults, family relations center around the family of procreation—parent, child, and grandchild. For singles, relationships involve the family of orientation—parents, siblings, aunts, and uncles. However, as the health of aging single people declines, their support convoys seem to function less well than do those of their married peers (Bengtson et al., 1990).

Approximately 80 percent of all individuals over age 65 live alone, often due to the death of a spouse, and living alone may contribute to medical and physiological difficulties, such as susceptibility to falls, malnutrition, and loneliness (Ward, 1984).

Widowhood

One of the most catastrophic events people experience is the death of a spouse (Holmes & Rahe, 1967). While most of us associate widowhood with old age, the death of a spouse can occur at any time during the life cycle.

During later adulthood, the largest group of single adults are those who are widowed. Statistics indicate that by age 65, three in five women will be widows; by age 75, four out of five will be widows (U.S. Bureau of the Census, 1991). Men do not usually become widowers until after age 85; widowhood is considerably less common for men.

The death of a spouse and a person's subsequent widowhood are experiences that are typically perceived as stressful and disruptive to daily life (Gentry & Shulman, 1988). One's ideas about the sanctity of marriage and the quality of one's marriage are also factors that determine how one adjusts to widowhood (Carey, 1980). Emotional reactions to widowhood are complex and can include denial, anger, relief, and guilt. Widowhood can, under some conditions, predispose people to serious illness or death, due to isolation from others, loneliness, or preexisting health difficulties (Rowland, 1977).

Persons who are widowed are vulnerable in many ways and need active support, not only immediately after the death but also for many months afterward. In most cases, the grief that accompanies the death of one's spouse is very personal and intense (see Chapter 12). Resolution of these feelings may require a great deal of time and support; and for some, it is never resolved.

Becoming a widow or widower seems to cause many different types of problems. Thompson and associates (1983) investigated multiple indices of self-perceived physical health for 212 older widows and widowers, ranging in age from 55 to 83 years, two months following the loss of their spouse and compared them to a control group. Results indicated that widows and widowers reported significantly more recently developed or worsened illnesses, greater use of medications, and poorer general health ratings. These differences were independent of sex and socioeconomic level.

For widows and widowers, who may be vulnerable in many ways, dealing with loss is much easier when others can provide support and help.

GENDER DIFFERENCES IN WIDOWHOOD

There is a fairly high predominance of widows compared to widowers in old age, for two primary reasons. First, there is a difference in life expectancy between males and females in favor of females (see Chapter 3). Second, as is the social custom in most cultures, men tend to marry women younger than themselves. For current cohorts, females tend to manifest greater stress at losing a spouse in old age than do males, due to the loss of status, friendship networks, and financial support that usually derive from the husband (Gallagher et al., 1983). Since more women are now entering the work force, it will be interesting to see if men in future cohorts exhibit increased stress on losing a spouse because of the loss of financial support and other benefits derived from the wife's occupation and income.

While widowhood later in life is quite stressful, conjugal bereavement in young adults also leaves men and women emotionally scarred (Allen & Hayslip, 1990). A unique aspect of widowhood in young adulthood is that the death of one's spouse is typically unanticipated, whether accidental or due to illness.

Being widowed is so common, especially during late middle age and old age, that society has ascribed a variety of roles to widows (Lopata, 1975). However, what roles women play seem to depend on their former relationships with their husbands. For some women, the role of a widow is to work to keep the family together and keep the husband's memory alive; they are not supposed to be interested in other men. For women whose lives have evolved more independently of their husbands' all along, role changes are less drastic than others', though these women are of course still lonely and grieve for their husbands. When initial support is withdrawn soon after a husband's death, many women experience difficulty in adjustment, as clear role expectations do not exist (Lopata, 1975).

It is important to recognize that women adjust to the loss of their husbands in idiosyncratic ways, depending on age at widowhood, health, socioeconomic class, race, and ethnicity (Bengtson et al., 1990; Pelham & Clark, 1987). Comparatively speaking, we still know very little regarding widowers (Marshall, 1980), except that, in many ways, widows and widowers are as much alike as they are different regarding adjustment (Mathews, 1987).

REMARRIAGE AMONG WIDOWS AND WIDOWERS

Remarriage after widowhood is less likely to occur than following divorce. The tendency to remarry following the death of a spouse is highly related to the age and gender of the widowed individual (Ward, 1984). With increasing age, the tendency to remarry following the death of a spouse decreases, although remarrying can be an effective coping mechanism for dealing with the problems and concerns of widowhood (Gentry & Shulman, 1988).

Widowers are more likely than widows to remarry, especially with advancing age. For instance, although less than 20 percent of males over

ADULTS SPEAK

REMARRIAGE AFTER WIDOWHOOD: HAROLD AND NANCY

Harold is 67 years old, and has been a university professor for over 30 years. He retired two years ago, and now teaches part-time. He is outgoing and friendly, is in good health, and takes care of himself. He was married to Chris, whom he met in college, for 43 years. Together, they raised two sons and a daughter, all of whom are happy, well-adjusted adults. Harold is the proud grandfather of two boys.

For the last seven years of their marriage, Chris suffered from Parkinson's disease, which eventually left her nearly helpless and bedridden. Harold cared for his wife until the day she died in October of 1989. Chris's death hit Harold very hard. Despite the loving support of his family, he took long drives by himself and often ate out alone.

Nancy is 68 years old and has three children and four grandchildren. She divorced her husband 18 years ago and did not look forward to getting married again. In fact, she enjoyed being single. She is a fun-loving, kind person who has a wonderful sense of humor and quite obviously enjoys other people.

Harold and Nancy have known one another since high school, and in fact were sweethearts during their high school days together. Harold played on the football team and had lots of girlfriends, while Nancy did well in school, and was very attractive and popular. Because they grew up together, they had many friends in common, and saw each other at the yearly high school reunion. They were good friends despite the fact they went their separate ways after high school. Nancy and Chris also knew one another well.

One year after Chris died, Nancy and Harold met at the annual high school reunion. They were "dancing to Sinatra," having a good time, and fell in love. Harold insists that Nancy locked the seat belt in her car so that she could kiss him, but Nancy denies this. Several months later, they got married. They had a small wedding with their immediate families there to offer love, support, and good wishes.

Nancy describes Harold as fun-loving, with a wonderful sense of humor. She feels quite lucky to have him, and says, "We could do nothing and have a good time." She thought about marriage carefully, not wanting to be disappointed and hoping that their relationship would not be changed by getting married. "I was afraid things would change, as they might for other people who don't know one another so well."

Harold, too, was somewhat concerned about marriage: "I was afraid my children would not approve."

Having known one another for over 50 years has proven to be a big advantage, as has having finished raising their children. Nancy says, "We just have fun, and he's the same all the time. He'll start a conversation at 2 A.M. and keep you in stitches. We don't have the problems some young people have, such as paying for a house and a car, raising children, and worrying about money."

Harold and Nancy both feel very strongly about how happy they are and expect to be. "We can both be ourselves, and we don't feel censored or judged at all. You know, it's so good it's scary. We just don't have to work at it, yet we both have our individual interests." (Harold enjoys woodworking and playing golf, and Nancy enjoys playing bridge.)

It is clear that marrying Harold late in life has been wonderful for Nancy, who spent many years single. "It's been lots better than I ever dreamed it could be. He could make any woman happy."

For Harold, marrying Nancy meant an end to days of feeling very lonely and somewhat lost without Chris. "I just never thought my life would turn out this way."

age 65 remarry, less than 5 percent of females over age 55 remarry. There are numerous reasons and explanations for this. First, given gender differences in life expectancy, there are simply fewer available males with advancing age. Also, females tend to be in better health than males with advancing age; thus widows may not want to risk losing another spouse to a health-related problem. In contrast, males are usually unprepared or inexperienced in the skills required to live alone, such as cooking, cleaning, and grocery shopping (Marshall, 1980). When individuals do marry following the death of a spouse, especially after age 50, they tend to marry someone they have known for a long time and to do so for companionship and affection (Bengtson et al., 1990). We will have more to say about widowhood in Chapter 12.

ROLES IN ADULTHOOD

Gender Roles

As mentioned earlier in this chapter, people who occupy specific roles help to define our convoy. For this reason, we will discuss major roles adults play and their relationship to the support people can provide to another.

One of the most significant roles we acquire during the life span is our **gender role.** Gender role affects our role within the family and may often affect our choice of occupations (see Chapter 9).

Gender roles can be defined as those behavior patterns that are considered appropriate and specific to each gender. They are formed or acquired early in life and maintained until death. Because the expected traits and behaviors associated with males and females are highly related to factors such as culture, ethnic group, socioeconomic level, and occupation, our discussion of gender roles will be in general terms.

There are a number of explanations about how gender roles are formed. They may be acquired by a child through identifying with the same-sex parent or model and thus adopting that person's traits, attitudes, and behaviors (Hall & Lindzey, 1985; Sears et al., 1986). These acquired traits and behaviors are subsequently reinforced by society as a whole, institutions, and other individuals—"You're just like your father!" Through continued reinforcement, these behaviors and traits become further internalized, eventually becoming part of the individual's identity and self-concept (Kohlberg, 1966).

Interpersonally, beliefs about roles and behaviors particular to each gender are termed gender stereotypes (Sears et al., 1986). People's views about men's and women's roles can interfere with other relationships as well as marriages in adulthood. These issues pull many marriages apart. For example, women may feel frustrated that their roles as wife and mother are limiting while men's roles are diverse. Women may also feel that being a housewife can be boring and come to feel less important than working counterparts. Even if both spouses work, women still do most of the household chores, and may face discrimination at work as well. In this case, as a married woman, her role may be unclear. For example, how assertive should she be in public, particularly if her behavior may impact her husband's work situation? What would her life be like should she divorce or should her husband die? Could she raise her children alone? Could she support herself? Should she remarry? What are her chances of remarrying or being employed as she gets older?

Work-Related Roles Within the Family

Families are generally the primary socializers of individuals at all stages of the life span (Emmerich, 1973). Expectations about roles within the family do change with age, however, and individuals may play several family roles at once, such as father, son, and brother (Nock, 1982). Given the importance we place on parenting, it is not surprising to attribute a great deal of importance to the caring and socializing roles fathers, mothers, and children play (Biller, 1982; Field & Widmeyer, 1982).

The primary functions of families of all types, in all cultures and societies, are to provide care and socialization for the young and serve as a network of support and identity for individuals within the family or clan unit. As noted above, families are changing. Old ideas have been outstripped by the diversity characterizing families today. Keep this in mind as you read about roles within the family.

DUAL-CAREER RELATIONSHIPS

U.S. Bureau of the Census data indicate that in 1970 approximately 40 percent of families were of the nuclear type, where both parents and children live under the same roof. This percentage decreased to approximately 31 percent in 1980, and to 27 percent in 1990. This is not surprising, given our previous discussion of divorce and single parents. One characteristic of nuclear families that has been changing is family size. It is gradually decreasing; that is, couples are having fewer children (see Box 7.1).

The second major change in families has been the number of parents who are employed outside the home. According to Hoffman (1989), the dual-wage family is now the modal family style in the United States; the current proportion of two-parent families with dual-wage earners is 71 percent. More women are pursuing careers and obtaining higher education. This is due to recent economic pressures, the influence of the Women's Movement, and the need to develop self-identity (Davidson & Cooper, 1986). With childlessness becoming increasingly common, we have seen the emergence of dual-career families without children, or DINKs (Dual Income, No Kids).

EFFECTS OF MATERNAL EMPLOYMENT

Hoffman (1989) has conducted a comprehensive review of the literature regarding the effects of the mother's employment in the two-parent family.

When a mother enters the work force, there are effects on all members of the family unit.

Effects on the Mother One major effect of employment on the mother is an increase in morale, self-esteem, and self-concept. That is, being employed enhances a woman's life by providing her with stimulation and opportunities for interaction and socialization, as well as an escape from the routines of housework and child care. Mothers working often results in changes in marital relationships, divisions of labor within the family, and the quality of interaction between parents and children. Obviously, employment results in additional income for the mother as well as the rest of the family unit, thus affecting the life-style of all members of the family. However, the dual roles of worker and mother can be stressful (Hoffman, 1989). Many, if not most, working mothers are uncertain whether they can be good mothers when they are away all day, and are equally uncertain that they can put enough energy into their work.

Effects on the Father The effects of maternal employment on the father are quite complex and influenced by a number of factors, such as social class, attitudes toward gender roles, and the extent to which he and the children participate in household tasks and child care. Fathers with very traditional attitudes toward gender roles have more difficulties and fears about their wives' employment, since these men are no longer the only breadwinners in the family. They may believe certain household duties are "women's work" (Hoffman, 1989). For blue-collar families, as the mother's employment status increases, the fathers' morale declines, but in upper middle-class families, a wife's employment tends to increase her husband's morale (Hoffman, 1989).

The major effects of maternal employment on the father seem to depend on how labor is divided; he has to take on additional household duties and child care. Quite obviously, taking on household tasks and duties is likely to interfere with his own activities, such as playing golf or spending nonwork time with friends. Such changes may or may not affect the father negatively. In any case, compromises need to be made.

Effects on the Children While generalizations regarding the impact of maternal employment of children are difficult, the one finding that has been reported most consistently is that children of employed mothers have less restricted views of sex roles (Hoffman, 1989). That is, they have less stereotyped views of males and females. However, a child's age determines what effects maternal employment may have on him or her. For example, infants and very young children most likely spend extended periods of time in day care or with a babysitter, and for some children, this may interfere with their relationship with their mothers (Clarke-Stewart, 1989). Additionally, older children are more likely to have to take on additional household tasks that were routinely performed by the mother or father.

Families in which both the husband and wife are employed in full-time jobs outside the home are referred to as *dual-career couples* (see Box 7.5). A study that illustrates the potential for stress within dual-career couples is that of Rawlins et al. (1985). They found that women reported more stress about parenting and family-career conflict, while men were more concerned about their wives earning more money. Women were found to be more accommodating than men, by being willing to change locations, compromising domestic standards, and prioritizing responsibilities. Given the increasing number of dual-career couples and the potential for stress and conflict in these relationships, they are likely to continue as the focus of considerable research in the future.

While many women work solely for economic reasons, there are many psychological difficulties as well as advantages dual-career couples face. Marcus and Hayslip (1987) found that, even among higher socioeconomic women who worked part-time to enhance self-image and sense of personal achievement, a substantial amount of *role strain* (having less than enough time to fulfill the roles of wife, mother, and worker) and *role overload* (having multiple demands from both family and career) was present. Supportiveness on the part of a husband was in this case no less important than for women who worked full-time. Women who were either highly committed to parenting and not highly committed to a career or vice versa

BOX 7.5

DUAL-CAREER RELATIONSHIPS—DO THEY WORK?

Dual-career relationships offer many psychological and economic advantages, yet they tend to be quite stressful and demanding for most couples. Both men's and women's roles, as well as their identities, often undergo substantial changes.

Factors Influencing How Couples Combine Work and Family Roles

Personal Factors

Personality (e.g., how important is it for a person to have an intimate relationship, to be emotionally close with children, to be number 1 in her or his field?)

Attitudes and values (e.g., what are a person's beliefs about who should rear a child, who should be breadwinners?)

Interests and abilities (e.g., how committed are persons to their work, how satisfying is it to them, how successful are they at what they do?)

Relationship Factors

Sources of power in the relationship (e.g., who decides on major purchases, who has the final say?)

Tasks that need to be done to maintain the family (e.g., who does the grocery shopping, who pays the bills?)

Environmental Factors

The work situation (e.g., how flexible are the hours, can one work at home if a child is sick?)

Employer's views (e.g., if a parent leaves at 5 to pick up a child, will he or she be viewed as not ambitious enough?)

Societal norms and attitudes (e.g., is quality child care readily available, do employers offer paid paternity leave?)

Support systems (e.g., are there friends or relatives to help out with parenting; are colleagues supportive?)

Source: Adapted from Gilbert. (1987). *What makes dual-career marriages tick?* Austin, TX: Hogg Foundation, p. 10.

experienced the greatest degree of difficulty, compared to those who were either very committed or not committed at all to their dual-career lifestyles. Interestingly, while voluntary childlessness is now more common despite the pressure many feel to have children, not being able to conceive (being infertile) can be a source of stress to many young dual-career couples (Matthews & Matthews, 1986). We will have more to say about dual careers in Chapter 9.

Specific Roles Within the Family

For each individual within the family, there are specific roles and expected behaviors. When individuals have a mutual understanding regarding what these roles are, the family can perform its socializing and care-giving functions more effectively (Goldenberg & Goldenberg, 1991). All families, however they are specifically constituted, establish rules and communicate and negotiate differences between members to help them define themselves and cope with change (Goldenberg & Goldenberg, 1991).

Family roles, however, do not exist in a vacuum and are not static. They change in response to society and to family dynamics. For example, during early adulthood, the father may fulfill the role of provider (Biller, 1982). At the same time, the mother may provide care and nurturance for other members of the family (Field & Widmayer, 1982). As we noted above, these role responsibilities often change in dual-career relationships. As these individuals enter middle age, they may now start to plan for their children's futures by not only assisting in their educational planning and careers, but also providing maintenance, support, and care for older and younger members of the family. Finally, in later adulthood, the parents may continue to assist in the care and maintenance of younger members of the family unit (Nock, 1982).

In the next section we will discuss one of the major roles within the family, that of parent. Although parenthood and the roles associated with it are crucial for child development, and while society has definite expectations of parental behavior, individuals often become parents without any formal training in how to parent. In a sense, you learn how to parent on the job!

PARENTHOOD

As noted above, parents are an important part of the convoy for many, and parents serve as important socializing agents with regard to roles within the family, as well as roles that are age- and gender-related.

Parenting: Joys and Ordeals What does it mean to be a parent? Who affects whom—does the parent primarily affect the child, or does the child have an impact on the parent? In truth, there is a mutuality in parenting; it must be understood in terms of a bond between parent and child. That is, being a parent is likely to mean different things to parent and child, depending on a variety of factors: (1) where a child is developmentally and what is

A D U L T S   S P E A K

ON PARENTHOOD: IT ALL DEPENDS ON YOUR POINT OF VIEW

Heather (age 21): "I'm not ready for motherhood. You don't have a life after you have kids. I have a friend with a baby, she always has trouble finding sitters. I babysat for her once, the kid didn't like me and it cried the whole night. I was so glad when she came to get it. It's harder to have a career when you have kids; I mean you need to work less hours and then you have to mess with doctors' appointments and stuff like that. I think it will be a long time, if ever, before I have a baby."

Jean (age 30): "I tried to be a good mother but I always had to be at work and I couldn't afford daycare so they spent a lot of time alone. My two sons really gave me a hard time; they wouldn't do their school work and they had lots of behavior problems at school.

"My daughter did good school work and behaved well there, but she and I fought terribly. The kids didn't get to spend time with their real dad; he remarried and had a new family. I didn't pick very good role models for them either. We don't visit much; they call or come by to see if I'll babysit. Most of the time I do, it's like a second chance. I love them and I'm proud of them."

Ann (70 years old): "I feel like I was a good mother. I loved them and I showed it to them by hugging and kissing them and by listening to anything they wanted to tell me. I was strict. We had rules and if they broke them I punished them. I didn't push it off on their daddy. They were good boys; even during the sixties when our friends' children were taking drugs, our kids didn't. They wore long hair and trashy clothes, and peace symbols the priest said were actually satanic symbols. We were concerned but tolerant. I'm very proud of them."

A 21-year-old woman says: "Do I want to be a parent? It all depends on my life situation and whether I feel it would be fair to bring a child into the world at that time.

"Are there certain things I would like to wait for? Yes, economic stability, parental stability, marriage stability. I feel the world right now has so many problems, it would be really unfair to bring a child into the world unless you feel you can give a very stable, realistic environment. Not protective, but where you can teach that child how to live in the world he is going to be brought into.

"What values are important to instill in my children? Honesty, not being judgmental or hypocritical, being able to have a basic understanding about the realism of life and not the quantitative things that society tries to bring upon you, be your own person and have your own opinion about things."

An 80-year-old woman states: "Is there anything I wish I had done differently with my children? I regret that I wasn't more affectionate and expressive. I don't think they were slighted. My sisters and I are still that way. My parents were not affectionate. I didn't know how to be. The last few years in my life there have been more hugs and kisses than ever. I ask my kids sometimes if I was a mean old witch. They assure me that I wasn't. . . . What values did I want to instill in them? Along the same lines as my parents did. Honesty, strive to be your best. If I was in trouble in school, I was in trouble at home. The same goes for my children. These were definitely achieved."

A 25-year-old man wrote: "Becoming a parent is not a gradual thing. Instead, it is instantaneous and a little otherworldly, like waking up one morning to a new gravity and having to learn to drink coffee without spilling it on the ceiling.

"A good deal of anxiety generally precedes it. But one finds that he or she adjusts to parenthood quickly—so quickly, in fact, it is difficult to realize one has adjusted to anything at all. Parents learn to walk, talk, breathe, and think in a world of whole new universals. But because they learn to do it so swiftly, new parents often don't realize anything has changed until long after it has already happened. By that time, spilling coffee on the ceiling is as natural as spilling it on the floor."

important to him or her; (2) whether a child is male or female; and (3) when the child is born, in terms of what is most likely going on in the lives of the parents at that point (e.g., whether they are working) (Parke, 1988). Thus, parenting needs to be seen from the point of view of both the child and the adult (Lerner & Spanier, 1978). Parent-child relationship influences are not unidirectional, from parent to child, but bidirectional, each affecting the other.

Most of us have our own ideas about what parents do, and what is expected of us as fathers or mothers, long before we marry and have children of our own. Regarding parental roles, then, we all go through a process of **anticipatory socialization** (Ahammer, 1973). We learn these roles early in childhood by observing our own parents, and they are reinforced by others. One can continue to fulfill the parental role for an adult child who asks for advice or support (emotional or financial) long after that person has left home, married, and established a family of his or her own (Alpert & Richardson, 1980).

Why Couples Have Children Couples decide to have children for a variety of reasons. They may do so in the belief that their own relationship will be further strengthened, or may simply be responding to what others such as parents, peers, or in-laws expect of them ("When are you going to have children?"). They may see a child as a way of mending a not-so-satisfying marital relationship or as an extension of themselves that will live on beyond their own deaths. Sometimes parenthood is couched in socioeconomic terms, as a tax deduction, or a child may be perceived as someone to care for his or her parents when they are old. If people put off having children, it is also for a variety of reasons (aside from an inability to conceive), such as not being able to afford them and conflicts over children versus career.

Alpert and Richardson (1980) have stated that "people in this society have little idea of what is entailed when they make the decision to be a parent" (p. 444). And once the child is born, he or she cannot be "sent back": by virtue of having a child, you are a parent, and he or she is your child. Moreover, our culture does not endorse, nor have experts agreed on, an ideal way of raising a child. How a child is disciplined, whether parents are open regarding to family discussions and responsibilities, and whether they are affectionate toward and interested in their children as individuals—all have a bearing on a child's development. These factors obviously also affect adults' perceptions of themselves as good or poor parents (Sarafino & Armstrong, 1986).

There is, however, no guarantee that decisions regarding the raising of our children will be the "right" ones. Feeling as if we are to blame for our children's failures and disappointments has created much unhappiness for many a parent. This fear of failure may cause many couples to put off having children, based on the experiences of peers or their experiences with their own parents. They may also be anxious about raising a child in a society where violence, drug abuse, discrimination, or AIDS are realities.

Children can meet many of our basic needs to love and be loved. Erikson (1963) expressed this in terms of **generativity**—for our purposes here, being the caretaker and protector of someone we have created, as well as guiding and supporting that person throughout life. The intimacy we seek with someone else within the context of marriage can also find expression in having children. The love we feel toward a spouse is, by extension, given without reservation, with "no strings attached," to our children. Being needed by someone who is fragile, vulnerable, and dependent on us can be very rewarding.

Despite the many advantages of parenting, there is ample reason to believe that most couples experience having a child as a "crisis" of sorts, regardless of their preparation. And women, irrespective of their attitude toward childbearing and their own body image, tend to see pregnancy as an anxiety-filled period in their lives (Liefer, 1977). However, women who see pregnancy as a chance for personal growth, "rather than a symbol of security or status," seem to report more positive feelings (Stevens-Long, 1984).

As for their effects on men, having children may represent the first intrusion into their relationships with their wives or, alternatively, be viewed as extensions of their relationships. They may reevaluate their relationships with their fathers (as can women with their mothers) and experience bouts of anxiety or depression both as a pregnancy progresses and after the birth itself (Biller, 1982).

PARENTS AND CHILDREN

The early and middle years of parenting, from infancy to adolescence, are often characterized by a great deal of strain, brought on by the intense, constant demands of children on parents, and financial/occupational stress. Alpert and Richardson (1980) point out that regardless of their individual preferences, men and women are forced into traditional sex-typed roles by the presence of children. While parents may initially see children in terms of personal growth, or have children out of choice, the limitations children place on them account for reports of lower marital happiness during the years children are at home (Lewis & Spanier, 1979). Children change the family configuration and force parents to redefine their lifestyles. They make new friends, spend their time doing different things such as homework, attending school-related functions and outings, and have less time with each other.

Parenting adolescents is sometimes seen as a power struggle between child and parent over a number of issues—values, sexuality, discipline, and performance in school. These differences between parents and children are not quite as great as is generally believed (Bengtson & Troll, 1978). Yet, it is clear that parents may fulfill the function of interpreting and representing the world to their children, and the adolescent may in turn serve as a representative of the culture, thereby influencing his parents in such areas as politics, religion, sex roles, personal tastes in dress, and work-achievement orientation. Thus, the generation gap may not be so great as we previously believed.

Parents of adolescents are often the children of aging parents; they are popularly referred to as the **sandwich generation**. They face the dual responsibility of caring for their children and their own parents. They may be in the process of coming to terms with their own aging as well as the aging and eventual death of their parents. Moreover, the so-called post-parental years, when children have left home and are on their own, is in many respects a misnomer. Even when children are no longer living at home, they may continue to visit regularly and ask for support or advice on a variety of matters (e.g., child care, marital problems, financial planning, and job changes), many of which pertain to the parental roles they continue to see their parents as playing. Many middle-aged parents, however, having given up the parent role, resent playing it involuntarily when the divorce of an adult child requires that they care for grandchildren.

THE EMPTY NEST

Some parents become depressed when children leave home, because it signals the end to their parental role as such. Most, however, do not react this way to the empty nest. In fact, they may welcome this time as an

ADULTS SPEAK

THE SANDWICH GENERATION

Caring for children and an aging or ill parent can be quite stressful and draining, leaving one with the feeling that all that has been sacrificed—security, peace of mind, and even health—is done so with little or no appreciation from others. A recent study found that 31 percent of women will be care-givers to both children and parents, a process that can continue for as long as 20 years in each case (*Akron Beacon Journal,* 1991). Imagine spending 40 years of your life caring for someone else, even if that someone is a person you love dearly.

One woman, who left her job to care for her father after having an anxiety attack at work, said,

> I felt I was never giving [my father] enough time, never giving my job enough time, and felt like I couldn't do anything right. I just could not work and every time I was away from work, I was feeling guilty.

Another woman quit her job and left her husband to care for her ailing 91-year-old mother, who lived 900 miles away:

> Mother's in the process of dying. It could take an hour, could take a year, could take 10 years. It's like sitting on a stick of TNT with the fuse lit. You never know when it will go off.

Another man who, with his wife, was caring for two young children and an ill mother said, with regard to his child's requests to stay with him at home:

> He's a very understanding kid. He doesn't hold grudges . . . and his judgment is that my mother makes too many demands. That's the cost of being in "the sandwich." You try to balance, but sometimes you can't. . . . Where do the loyalties lie? They have to lie with the future and not with the past. It's not triage; we've been able to do both. Look at the metaphor. Sandwich generation. What's in the middle? Chopped meat.

opportunity to renew their relationship, pursue new interests, travel, or simply relax, knowing they have raised and "launched" their children successfully (Nock, 1982). What seems to be crucial is whether a person has principally defined him- or herself in terms of the role of mother or father. If this is so, when the children leave a parent is left with nothing to "hang onto."

On an individual basis as well, there are many advantages to the empty nest. For a woman, this period may bring a particular sense of relief if the burden of child care fell upon her. She is also less likely to need to worry about becoming pregnant. As one woman put it, "We've had kids for so many years, we're thinking how wonderful it's going to be. We'll have a lot more free time, and we'll be able to talk to each other without scheduling an appointment. Plus, by then we'll probably have grandchildren."

For a man, the financial pressures brought on by children are lessened considerably; he may be free to explore new interests, or even a second career, with little economic risk to his family.

There is a considerable amount of parent-child interaction (visiting, communication, helping) during this time, which may be mutually satisfying. Thus, it is certainly inaccurate to characterize older parents as ill and dependent on their adult children (Bengtson et al., 1990). In fact, most want to live close to, but not with, their adult children. Most can expect good health well into their seventies. As discussed above, the most satisfying parent-child relationships are nonobligatory, where children are seen as dependable, and help is given and received with love and concern.

The primary role transition relating to parenthood during middle adulthood is from parent to grandparent. Grandparents, too, can serve as important socializing agents. In the next section, we will discuss grandparenting in the United States.

GRANDPARENTING

Being a grandparent is often considered by society to be a developmental task of middle or late adulthood. For many, having a grandchild may be considered a symbol or marker of middle age or getting old. Individuals who are overly concerned with being considered young may react with anxiety when others know they are "old enough" to be grandparents.

Interestingly, although most of us have experienced a relationship of some sort with our grandparents, literature on grandparenting is not extensive. It does suggest, however, that there are many styles or types of grandparenting, and that these are affected by a number of individual, environmental, and socioeconomic factors. Grandparenting is a **tenuous role,** having no clear criteria for what constitutes appropriate behavior (Rosow, 1985). It is for this reason that grandparenting is largely an individual experience. Whether one finds grandparenting satisfying depends on numerous factors, such as race, gender, the life stage of the grandchild, and the age and health of the grandparent (Kivett, 1985; Thomas, 1986; Wilson, 1986). Positive yet voluntary relationships with grandchildren and a close relationship with that adult child also contribute to how grandparents perceive their role (Johnson, 1988; Shore & Hayslip, 1992).

Because life expectancy has increased, the chances of becoming a grandparent have also increased. What does being a grandparent mean? Is it satisfying?

The once-popular image of the grandparent as a kindly, elderly person in a rocking chair is often inaccurate. Grandparents are more likely to be men and women who are much younger, employed, and even have adult children still at home! This same individual may also be caring for a mother or father who is quite old.

While the frequency of contact between grandparents and their grandchildren is fairly regular (often daily), it is rare for grandparents, children, and grandchildren to live under the same roof (Troll et al., 1979). It is important to note that grandparenting styles and contact with grandchildren are affected by forces such as age, gender, divorce, and family separation (Strom & Strom, 1987).

Meanings of Grandparenthood What do grandparents value about their role? Obviously, one does not become a grandparent by choice! Nor is being a valued grandparent automatic. Whether grandparenting is satisfying seems to be dependent principally on the relationship with one's adult children (Cherlin & Furstenberg, 1986). If that relationship is positive and lacks conflict, the grandparent role is likely to be more fulfilling to all involved. Conflicts often pertain to three issues—responsibility for raising the grandchildren, relations with adult children, and feelings about being a grandparent (Thomas, 1990).

Grandparenthood means different things to different people. How one perceives this role most likely influences one's style of grandparenting. Meaning is also affected by the quality of one's relationship with the grandchildren. Thomas and King (1990) found that both white and minority young adult grandchildren believed their grandparents were good role models and good sources of advice and support. Indeed, it is common to find that grandparents and grandchildren both gave and received tangible and emotional support to one another (Bengtson et al., 1990). This type of mutually satisfying, reciprocal relationship strengthens one's convoy of support.

Wood and Robertson (1976) classified grandparents into four types, based on the perceived meaning of grandparenthood:

1. *Apportional*—deriving satisfaction from one's own personal experiences and social norms (providing a role)
2. *Remote*—not deriving any meaning from either personal experience or social expectations
3. *Symbolic*—seeing grandparenthood as rewarding in terms of social norms, and
4. *Individualized*—finding satisfaction primarily through one's personal experience

In general, apportioned and individualized grandparents spent more time with their grandchildren. These people were also older and had more grandchildren. Wood and Robertson found, however, that having grandchildren did not substitute for having friends of one's own age.

Robertson (1977) found that the largest percentage of grandmothers surveyed described themselves as being the remote-figure style. Most grandmothers enjoyed the role because it made them feel younger, and they felt they were assisting in carrying on the family line. They got satisfaction from providing things for the grandchildren that they could not provide for their own children. Moreover, they achieved satisfaction and enjoyment from helping their grandchildren achieve more than their parents or grandparents were able to achieve.

Most recently, Kivnick (1985) has defined five dimensions of grandparental meaning: centrality, valued elder, immortality through clan, reinvolvement with personal past, and indulgence. While these multiple dimensions have been most useful in understanding grandparenting, they may not be independent of one another (Miller & Cavanaugh, 1990).

Styles of Grandparenting Perhaps the first detailed analysis of grandparenting styles in the United States has been the work of Neugarten and Weinstein (1964), who suggested there are five distinctive types: (1) *formal,* (2) *fun-seeker,* (3) *surrogate-parent,* (4) *reservoir of family wisdom,* and (5) *distant figure.*

The formal style includes grandparents who are highly interested in their grandchildren. Although these grandparents often care for their grandchildren, they should not be viewed as primary or surrogate caretakers. However, they often have authority and control over the children in the absence of the parents. The fun-seeker style includes individuals who are involved in playful, free relationships with their grandchildren and do not exert any control or authority over them. Grandparents exercising this style look on being with their grandchildren as a leisure activity. Surrogate-parent style grandparents are often the primary caretakers of the children. This style is quite common today, due to the increasing number of single-parent families and families where both parents work outside the home. For many grandparents, caring for a grandchild after an adult child has divorced is a full-time job. Such grandparents are termed *custodial grandparents* (Shore & Hayslip, 1992). Reservoir-of-family-wisdom-style grandparents provide special skills, resources, and knowledge to younger members of the family. This style is comparatively rare and usually associated with the grandfather. The distant-figure style was relatively rare when Neugarten and Weinstein proposed their styles in 1964, but due to society's increasing mobility, as well as more older adults moving to the Sun Belt, it is becoming more common. In this style, contacts are infrequent—usually on holidays—and grandparents are perceived as benevolent, yet remote physically.

More recently, Cherlin and Furstenberg (1986) have developed new categories of grandparental styles. These are *companionate, remote,* and *in-*

BOX 7.6

CUSTODIAL GRANDPARENTS

For many reasons, but principally due to physical abuse of the grandchildren or the divorce of an adult child, many grandparents have had to assume full-time custodial responsibility for their grandchildren, even though in some cases they do not have legal custody. Obviously, they love their grandchildren and want to raise them as best they can.

Shore and Hayslip (1992) studied 200 custodial and traditional grandparents and found that the disadvantages of reassuming the parental role in one's forties, fifties, and sixties outweighed the advantages. Custodial grandparents tended to be younger, were more likely to be the mother's parents, tended to have poorer health and fewer social and economic resources, were less highly educated, and were more likely to be raising boys.

Custodial grandparents reported a number of common difficulties:

1. Less satisfaction with grandparenting
2. Less meaningful grandparenting
3. Impaired or strained relationships with their grandchildren
4. Isolation from friends because of their parental responsibilities
5. Overloaded and confused about their roles as parents *and* grandparents
6. Likely to be caring for children who had behavioral or school difficulties, for which these grandparents were *less* likely to seek help

A 59-year-old grandmother expressed her ambivalence about her new role in this way: "You feel this hostility. You feel this frustration. You lose your identity—what are you going to do with these kids? And then, when they look up at you, you say, 'God, just let me get through another day because they really need me.'"

These findings underscore the problems custodial grandparents face, as well as suggest the need for psychosocial services to support them in this new role. They also reinforce grandparental relationships with grandchildren as *voluntary,* yet with a sense of responsibility toward their welfare (Johnson, 1988; Thomas, 1989).

volved. Companionate grandparents are described as affectionate but somewhat passive. They do not play an active role in caring for and disciplining the grandchildren. Remote grandparents, similar to the distant-figure style, are geographically distant but not necessarily emotionally distant. The involved grandparent appears to be similar to the formal and surrogate-parent styles, in that he or she enforces discipline and family rules (Tomlin & Passman, 1991).

Gender Differences in Grandparenting There are often gender differences in attitudes toward grandparenting. Kahana and Kahana (1970) found that maternal grandmothers and paternal grandfathers tended to display closeness and warmth toward their grandchildren. In contrast, maternal grandfathers and paternal grandmothers appeared to manifest the most negative attitudes toward their grandchildren. Thomas (1986) found grandmothers to be more satisfied with their role than grandfathers. This was perhaps due to their relative familiarity with intimate family relationships, having been principally responsible for raising their own children. Men who expressed satisfaction were older, had active relationships with their young grandchildren, and were happy with their involvement in the tasks of child rearing. Thomas (1986) and Kivett (1985) suggest that exposure to such grandfathers may have an impact on grandchildren's tendency to define themselves androgynously (see also Kivnick, 1985).

Information on grandparent-grandchildren contact is important, since most of our contact with and attitudes toward older adults are partly influenced by our interactions with grandparents or other elderly relatives. For example, Kennedy (1990) reported that college students' perceptions of grandparent and grandchild roles were generally positive, indicating affection and respect for grandparents. Black students saw the grandparent role as a more active one in the family than did white students, reflecting racial and cultural differences in perceptions of the extended family network (Bengtson et al., 1990).

On the basis of what we know, which is largely limited to grandmothers, grandparenthood can indeed be satisfying to those who value the role, who have the opportunity to interact with grandchildren, and whose relationships with their adult children are positive. As Troll (1980) has noted, the real value of grandparenthood for many middle-aged and elderly adults is that it reinforces the sense of family. Wilcoxon (1987) terms such people *significant grandparents.* That is, these grandparents derive a great deal of satisfaction in knowing that the "family theme" is being carried on by their grandchildren, even if their contacts with their adult children and their children's children are minimal. There is a preference for fulfilling voluntary, nonparental relationships with grandchildren among grandparents (Shore & Hayslip, 1992).

Grandparents can both influence and be influenced by their grandchildren. Thus, as with parenthood, we see the bidirectional nature of socialization. An older family member can communicate values, instruct, make history "real," and support grandchildren regarding issues related to work and education. In Hagestad's (1978) research, satisfying grandparent-grandchild relations were also characterized by decisions to avoid discussing certain topics—notably sexuality, religion, and politics—to minimize conflict and enrich the relationship. Simply being older does not guarantee that one will derive a great deal of personal satisfaction from having grandchildren. As with many things in life, the grandparent role must be actively shaped if it is to have meaning for both grandchild and grandparent.

Grandparents and Divorce Recently many grandparents who were earlier recruited to assume the child-rearing roles of their adult children have been thrust into the arena of divorce (Matthews & Sprey, 1984). In some cases, they are not permitted to visit the grandchildren they used to take care of, and legal counsel may be required to guarantee their visitation rights, over the objections of their adult child (Thompson et al., 1989). In times of family crisis, however, their visitation rights are often ambiguous or unenforceable, cutting them off from the important emotional nourishment of ongoing warm relationships with grandchildren (Wilson & DeShane, 1982). When adult parents remarry, stepgrandparenting often creates more problems than satisfaction. Because grandparents have no biological ties to their "new" grandchildren, their role in a reconstituted family is often ambiguous and stressful, which complicates the difficulties blended families already face (Novatney, 1990).

SUMMARY

A major topic discussed in this chapter was *interpersonal relationships*. A variety of relationships, such as *sibling relationships*, *friendships*, *intergenerational ties*, and *marital bonds*, help to define the *convoy*, an emotional support system that contributes to feelings of well-being in adulthood. Distinctions were made between *interest-related* and *deep* friendships, which seem to vary with both age and gender.

Although most individuals eventually marry, they obviously get married for a variety of reasons. In many respects, *similarity* and *complementarity* seem to determine why individuals are attracted to each other. Alternatively, we might view marital attraction in terms of *filter theory* and as a series of *stages* through which a couple learns more about one another along several dimensions. While marital satisfaction seems to vary with the presence of children, the *family life cycle* approach to family development has been criticized in favor of one emphasizing the *dynamics of family interactions*.

We also discussed the process of *socialization*, with specific reference to crucial roles based on gender and those related to the familial or occupational status that have important implications for life-span development. Socialization is a *dynamic*, lifelong process that is *bidirectional*. Furthermore, throughout the life cycle individuals are constantly acquiring and changing roles via the process of *role transition* and *role change*. People are socialized along a number of dimensions, with *gender* and *age* being two of the most important. Roles within the family, such as *parent* and *grandparent*, are also important socializing forces. While parents and children influence one another, the joys and ordeals of parenting vary in part with age-related demands of children. People obviously have children for a variety of reasons, which are social, economic, and psychological in nature. Like socialization, parenting is a dynamic process of interacting with one's children and redefining one's role which often continues well into one's sixties or seventies.

Grandparenting is not limited to older adults and is characterized by very diverse *styles*. Grandparenting means different things to each person, and satisfaction with grandparenting varies with one's *style* and *gender*.

KEY TERMS AND CONCEPTS

Interpersonal relationships
Interest-related friendships
Deep friendships
Kinship network
Spouse abuse
Single parents
Stepparent-stepchild relationships
Socialization

Filial responsibility
Filial maturity
Extended family
Social clock
Traditional marriage
Group marriage
Gay and lesbian relationships
Convoy
Attachment
Vertical attachments
Horizontal attachments
Filter theory of mate selection
Stage theory of mate selection
Complementarity
Similarity
Types of widows
Elder abuse
Institutional role types
Tenuous role types
Informal role types
Nonrole types
Role transition
Role change
Gender roles
Androgyny
Traditional nuclear family
Dual-career couple
Effects of maternal employment
Empty nest
Effects of parenthood
Styles of grandparenting
Meanings of grandparenting
Custodial grandparents

REVIEW QUESTIONS

1. What is a convoy? What functions does it serve?
2. What are interest-related and deep friendships? How do they differ by gender?
3. What is filial responsibility? How is it different from filial maturity?
4. What is the family life cycle? What are its advantages and disadvantages?
5. Why are individuals attracted to one another? What theories have attempted to explain attraction?
6. Do individuals' ratings of marital satisfaction change over the course of the life cycle? If so, what factors influence this change?
7. What is elder abuse? Why does it occur?
8. What are some of the major factors related to divorce? What effects does divorce have on the individual?
9. What are some of the special problems single parents and stepparents face?
10. What is socialization, and why is it viewed as a life-long process?
11. What are roles, and how are they developed at different stages of the life cycle?
12. What are some of the major advantages and disadvantages of parenthood?
13. Do dual-career relationships work? Why?
14. What are some major types of grandparenting styles common today? What is it about grandparenting that is meaningful and fulfilling?

CHAPTER 8

Personality and Adaptation

C H A P T E R   O U T L I N E

DEFINING PERSONALITY IN ADULTHOOD

Most of us have spent some time talking to our parents about what we were like when we were young. We might also talk with a friend about our experiences together as we browse through our high school yearbook. After we have had children, it is not uncommon to talk to them about how we have changed as we have gotten older—or perhaps how we have not changed.

This chapter deals with personality in adulthood, especially personality stability and change in the adult years. Some people see stability as a cause for pride, while others value the ability to change and be flexible. Personality has a major impact on our health, survival, and intellectual functioning (Field, 1991; Gold & Arbuckle, 1990: Hayslip, 1988; Schaie & Willis, 1991). For these reasons alone, it is an important dimension of adult development to understand.

Answering the question of whether our personalities change with age would seem to be easy. However, a major difficulty seems to be that no one agrees on exactly what is meant by "personality." In light of these disagreements, it should not be surprising to find that the answer to whether we change with age can be both yes and no depending on how we define personality.

What do we mean by differing views about personality? An approach to personality emphasizing variations in our behavior across situations is in direct contrast to one emphasizing consistency in our behavior determined by underlying qualities. According to the first perspective, our behavior can vary from day to day and from situation to situation. We see given situations as requiring certain behaviors and not requiring others. Thus, an individual can be quiet when necessary, as in class while a professor is lecturing, and quite social when a situation calls for it, as at a party. According to this view, if our behavior (personality) is stable across time, it is only because the situations involved have not changed (Moss & Sussman, 1980).

The other approach assumes that there exists an underlying set of qualities, or **traits,** that give meaning to an individual's behavior in most situations. This underlying constancy accounts for stability in personality across time (Costa & McCrae, 1980). Who is more correct—the individual who assumes an underlying set of qualities and characteristics, or the individual who emphasizes the situation?

Rather than think solely in terms of these extreme views, we can better approach personality as a continuum, where those who emphasize internal processes and constructs (e.g., ego, id, and superego), or qualities (traits) are at one end, and those who emphasize observable behaviors individuals display in response to the immediate environment are located at the other end.

Between the extremes of this continuum lies the **cognitive theory** of personality, which emphasizes the perception of oneself (Ryff, 1984; Thomae, 1980). According to the cognitive view, whether personality change occurs depends on whether the individual perceives or recognizes this change.

Closely related to the cognitive view of personality is the **social learning** perspective stressing external, observable responses to either internal or external sets of factors (Bandura, 1977; Mischel, 1981). According to this view, individuals construct a set of internal standards to govern their own behavior in the absence of external guides. Through the observation of valued, competent models, whose behaviors are internalized, personality development takes place.

The social-learning view stresses the interaction between an individual's expectations or constructs about how the world works and the environment (Kelly, 1955). People select aspects of the environment to relate to in accordance with their strengths and weaknesses. Individuals who maintain a stable personality are better able to cope with experiences that do not agree with these established constructs. Those whose personalities are not consistent or are negative are not as effective in coping with their environment (Atchley, 1982).

Personality and Development

While the many approaches to personality are difficult to compare, Maddi (1990) has attempted to reconcile them by emphasizing the commonalities among people rather than the differences. This broader approach makes possible the study of all aspects of behavior—those that generalize across individuals and those that do not. Maddi distinguishes between the pervasive, inherent "characteristics or tendencies" that give individuals direction, that is, their personalities, and behaviors, which are learned and vary with the situation. The internal forces that give people direction are referred to as the **core** of personality. Behaviors that vary with the situation are termed the **periphery** of personality. Maddi's definition of personality reflects this dual emphasis on universal qualities and situation-specific behaviors in order to understand what personality is and how it changes over time.

The core statement provides the framework within which core characteristics interact with the external environment to produce peripheral aspects of the individual. Most important for our purposes here is that the link between the core and the periphery is accomplished via development.

Maddi suggests that there is an ideal set of developmental influences that express core tendency and peripheral characteristics. Of course, there are also less-than-ideal developmental experiences, producing less adequate personality types and more detailed peripheral characteristics (traits).

Regardless of approach, we assume that it is personality that makes someone's behavior consistent or lawful. That is, each approach to personality is governed by sets of assumptions or laws that make behavior understandable and predictable. Moreover, most personality theorists are concerned with the whole individual as he or she copes with the environment.

As we will soon see, each theory of personality is limited because of the way the theorist has defined it. No approach can be all things to all people. Because each point of view begins with different assumptions about what personality is, what is to be studied, and how it is to be studied, you should resist the temptation to say that approach *A* is better than approach *B*. Rather, you should see differing approaches as either more or less useful in studying personality in adulthood (Hall & Lindzey, 1985). Ultimately, you should make your own choice about whether to agree with a given approach; and you may pick and choose from several to define personality for yourself.

STABILITY AND CHANGE IN ADULT PERSONALITY: MAJOR THEORETICAL VIEWPOINTS

Thinking about personality in terms of stability versus change with age has a number of important implications. One is that it may be necessary to think of adult personality as distinct from that in childhood. Also, we may need to reconsider how to implement interventions designed to help adults of all ages solve their problems.

As we have all observed in our daily lives, we seem to change in some readily observable ways as we age—in our tastes and interests, for example. Yet, in many fundamental ways we are the same people we were when we were young—we may be outgoing, dependent, or self-confident. Many of us have compared ourselves to others at special times in our lives—at high school graduation, when we marry, when we first become parents, or when we retire. In so doing, we realize that everyone's life does not turn out the same. This is because different people adjust to these events in distinct ways.

For example, high school graduation opens up new possibilities for some of us, and we move ahead with our lives feeling enthusiastic and optimistic about the future. We may go away to college or begin our careers. For others, graduating brings an end to a happy period in their lives. Now, they must make decisions about an uncertain future. Some individuals react by feeling overwhelmed. They never become autonomous adults and thus the future is closed off to them. They may remain at home simply to be close to their parents or have difficulty in making new friends. They see many of their high school friends leaving home, and they feel left behind. Yet, they seem powerless to do anything to change. Rather than feeling excited about the future, they seem threatened by it.

Neugarten (1977) suggests that two questions come to mind when examining the relationship between age and personality: Does aging affect personality—do people change with increased age? And does personality affect aging—does one's personality influence adaptation to the aging process? These two questions will guide our discussion of personality in adulthood in this chapter. A commonsense approach to both questions suggests an answer of a qualified Yes to each. People do change in some ways as they age, and different types of people cope with aging in unique ways.

The answers to each question are a function of (1) one's definition of stability and change, (2) one's theoretical biases, (3) the particular design utilized to gather facts about personality, (4) the level of personality one studies, and (5) how one assesses personality. Depending on these factors, personality can be at once stable and changing in adulthood. This should confirm your own self-assessment. In some ways, you are much like you were years ago. In other ways, however, you have changed.

Definitions of Stability and Change

While stability and change seem to be straightforward enough, they are really somewhat complex concepts. How we define them in part dictates whether we see personality as changing or stable in adulthood. Several types of stability have been identified (Caspi & Bem, 1990) (see Figure 8.1):

1. *Absolute stability*—constancy in the quantity (level) of a personality attribute or behavior over time. Typically, we examine absolute stability in longitudinal comparisons of group averages over time. For example, are people, on the average, more or less outgoing as they get older?
2. *Differential stability*—consistency of individual differences in a sample of people over time. A person is differentially stable if that individual's *relative* standing compared to others remains the same over time. For example, while you and a friend may each have become more self-confident over the last year, you are more self-confident than your friend both this year and last year.
3. *Ipsative stability*—consistency across time in a particular individual for a given personality attribute or behavior. For example, you might be equally self-confident or equally anxious relative to how self-confident or anxious you were a year ago.
4. *Coherence*—consistency over time of underlying personality styles or patterns despite changes in observable behaviors. For exam-

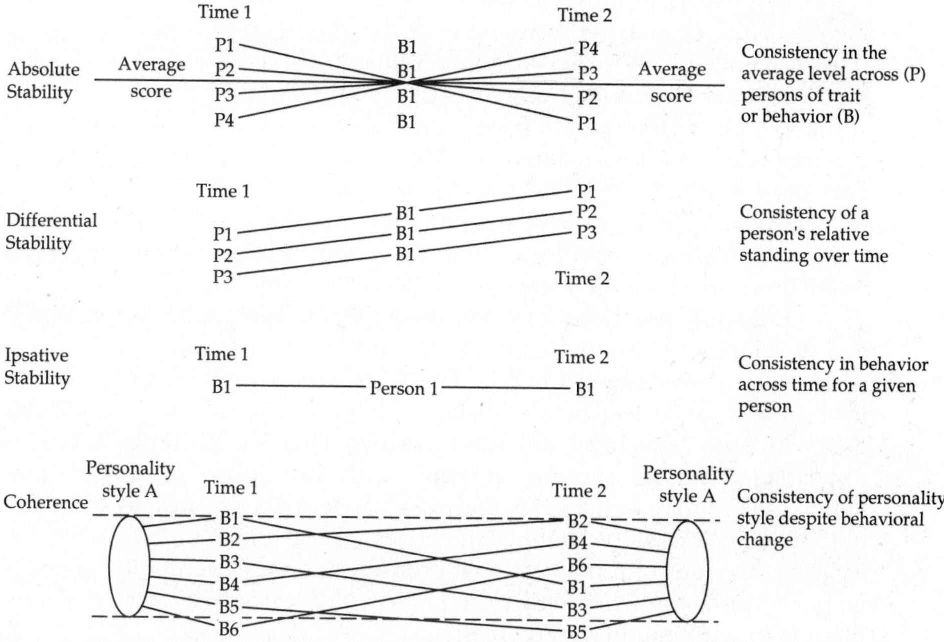

Figure 8.1 Types of personality stability.

ple, Caspi et al. (1989) found that men who were highly dependent on others as children were, as young adults, calm, warm, sympathetic, and needy of reassurance. As middle-aged adults, they were happily married and able to be nurturant. Although they were dependent on others as children, they were able to transform this into a mature, nurturant style that served them well in later intimate relationships. Thus, there is consistency in how these men affected others in spite of changes in their overt behaviors.

In this chapter, most studies deal with absolute stability, differential stability, and coherence.

STAGE THEORIES OF ADULT PERSONALITY CHANGE

Just as definitions of personality differ, so do the theories about how personality develops through the life span. How one conceptualizes personality affects conclusions about personality stability or change in adulthood.

Erikson's Psychosocial Approach

Erikson (1959, 1963, 1982) sees personality development—specifically ego development—in terms of eight **psychosocial crises.** Erikson feels that each psychosocial crisis can be resolved either positively or negatively. The ego is that aspect of the personality that must mediate the instinctual demands of the id and the restrictions of the superego to cope with reality (Hall & Lindzey, 1985). According to Valliant (1977), as one ages, the ego becomes more mature and more clearly differentiated from the id and the superego, permitting one to cope with the demands of the outside world in a more decisive, rational manner. More specifically, as one ages, the ego uses more sophisticated, effective defense mechanisms (e.g., sublimation or intellectualization) to deal with anxiety brought on by loss of control over one's instincts (residing in the id) or that related to the superego's restrictions on pleasurable experiences that are immoral.

Erikson's psychosocial crisis theory is an age-graded approach to ego development closely aligned with developmental tasks particular to various life periods (see Chapter 1). While Freud preferred to speak of fixation at a given psychosexual stage, Erikson suggests that individuals deal with each crisis in a cumulative manner. That is, difficulties in resolving earlier crises can seriously interfere with, but do not completely prevent, resolving later crises. Furthermore, each crisis, regardless of its resolution, comes to help redefine later crises. These crises are *epigenetic;* that is, they arise out of a maturational ground plan and eventually come together to form the whole individual. We will discuss those especially applicable to adulthood (see Figure 8.2).

Individuals vary in terms of their timing of each crisis, and, as noted above, crises are never "left behind." Thus, the *trust-mistrust* crisis, which

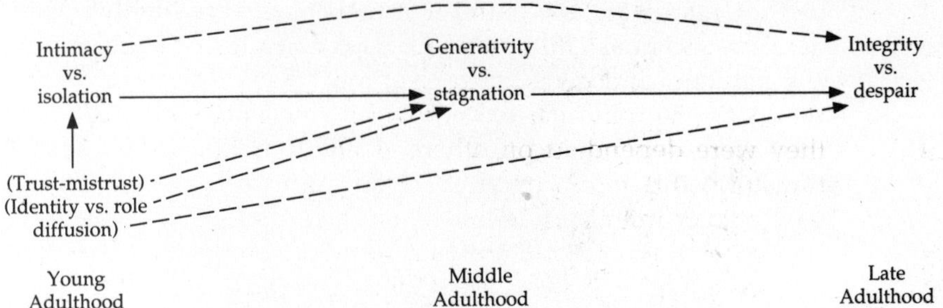

Figure 8.2 Erikson's psychosocial crises of adulthood.

is especially relevant to being cared for in a timely way and is the characteristic crisis of infancy, may reemerge in adulthood. It is at this time in our lives when we often make decisions about educational or career goals. Moreover, values regarding our ideals and relationships with the opposite sex are being crystallized. Each of these requires the ability to project oneself into the future. To be able to come to grips with these issues requires trust in one's own skills and abilities, and more importantly, a sense of trust in time itself. In other words, one must have faith that goals can be realized, whether this means being successful in one's work or becoming a parent and raising children. Clearly, while adults are not dependent on one another as infants are on their mothers, issues regarding trust in time reemerge later on in our lives, according to Erikson.

The crisis central to young adulthood, **intimacy versus isolation**, is about the ability of the individual to merge with another person to form a relationship built on mutual trust and love. If resolved successfully, the young adult develops the sense of interdependence that characterizes this relationship. But the ability to enter into a relationship that is mutual, reciprocal, or intimate is a function of the individual's previous efforts in establishing a stable sense of ego identity, versus identity confusion, in adolescence. If one's identity is formed poorly or not at all, the crisis of intimacy will be perceived as threatening. An inability to commit oneself to another person, or in a sense merge one's identity with that of someone else, is termed isolation.

Characteristic of middle age is the crisis of *generativity versus stagnation*. Here, individuals are redefining their lives in terms of "time left to live" versus "time since birth." To be generative literally means *to generate*—to produce things or people that symbolize one's continued existence after death. The reality of death implores individuals to accept their own mortality and to make preparations for future generations.

Generativity may be expressed by being productive in one's work (e.g., writing or teaching), creativity (e.g., finding a novel solution to a problem, painting an original picture), or most directly, by having children, caring for them, and raising them to become adults (Erikson, 1959, 1963). Thus, in selecting a career, in deciding to marry as well as whom to marry, and in one's relationships with children, choices made earlier in life

Mutually enjoyable relationships between husband and wife are characteristic of what Erikson calls intimacy, and having children is an expression of the need to feel generative.

predispose one toward generativity in adulthood (see Erikson, 1963). Obviously, a change in identity will accompany this process as well. Intimacy will likewise be redefined to include relationships with one's children and perhaps a few trusted friends. In contrast, stagnation implies a withdrawal into oneself. Those who are stagnated may become self-indulgent, bitter, and isolated from others. They may not feel needed; that which they have to give is not worth giving.

The **integrity versus despair** crisis characterizes old age. Integrity implies a sense of completeness, of having come full circle. Persons who have integrity are able, through the process of introspection (looking inward and examining what one finds), to integrate a lifetime full of successes and failures to reach a point where they have a "sense of the life cycle." Despairing individuals fear death as a premature end to a life—good or bad—that they are unable to take personal responsibility for. The person who has a sense of integrity accepts death as the inevitable end of having lived.

As Erikson (1963, pp. 268–269) notes,

> Only in him who in some way has taken care of things and people and has adapted himself to the triumphs and disappointments adherent to being the originator of others or the generator of products and ideas—only in him may gradually ripen the fruit of these seven stages. I know no better word for it than ego integrity. . . . Each individual, to become a mature adult, must develop to a sufficient degree all of the ego qualities, so that a wise Indian, a true gentleman, and a mature peasant share and recognize in one another the final stage of integrity.

In paralleling the trust of infancy and integrity, Erikson (1963, p. 269) writes, "And it seems possible to paraphrase the relation of adult integrity and infantile trust by saying the healthy children will not fear life if their elders have integrity enough not to fear death."

Despite the popular influence of Erikson's work in adult development, it has not gone uncriticized. Ego integrity, like the other concepts defining psychosocial crises, is difficult to define (Neugarten, 1977). However, attempts to measure the concepts of intimacy, generativity, integrity, and wisdom have been made, with some success (Clayton & Birren, 1980; Walaskay, Whitbourne & Nehrke, 1983/84). Moreover, Clayton (1975) argues, rather than accept complete resolution of crises as the norm, it is more realistic to see individuals as "compromising" their way through previous crises. This does not, however, permit them to reach Erikson's last stage, as Erikson defined it. Peck (1968) felt that Erikson's stages, particularly the last two, were entirely too global and really reflected new solutions to previous crises. He felt that too much emphasis was placed on adjustment during the first 20 years of life, to the detriment of the adult years.

Levinson's Life Structure

Another stage approach to personality development is that of Levinson (1978, 1986). Levinson (1978) conducted an intensive study of 40 men aged 35 to 45 to investigate the process by which they created a **life structure.** This is defined as a coherent relationship between one's own goals and the various life arenas of career, family, marriage, and social roles. The life structure is "the basic pattern or design of a person's life at a given time" (Levinson, 1978). On the basis of detailed interviews and psychological test data, Levinson found that the life structure evolves through a sequence of distinct periods. Moreover, this changing life structure shapes and is shaped by decisions each individual makes at varying times in adulthood.

Life structure is three-dimensional. It includes, first, the individual's sociocultural world—the multitude of social contexts such as occupational structure, social class, ethnicity, and family. The life structure also encompasses the individual's self, to the extent that certain aspects of this self are expressed or inhibited. This includes one's wishes, conflicts, anxieties and ways of fulfilling or controlling them, skills and abilities, and feelings. Last, the life structure is defined by the manner in which the individual participates in the external world.

Thus, life structure refers to how a man defines and uses the variety of roles he wishes or is required to play in the world—husband, father, citizen, lover, worker, boss, or friend. Levinson clearly says that his concept of life structure is not equivalent to ego development and/or occupational developmental stages, but instead refers to the more general, diverse framework in which each of the three dimensions listed above changes as they relate to one another.

Before discussing Levinson in more detail, we should point out several limitations of his work. Because his subjects were aged 35 to 45, information they provided about the years other than this age range was retrospective (young adulthood) and prospective (later adulthood). Levinson (1978) admits that his initial interest was to study what he intuitively thought to be a crucial period in adult development, ages 40 to 50. You should also realize that his sample was small, involved subjects who were economically well-off, and was limited to men. For these reasons, his ideas are somewhat limited in their usefulness as a general statement about adult development.

The **Early Adult Transition** (approximate ages 17–22) links adolescence and early adulthood (see Figure 8.3). During this period, the individual reevaluates the preadult world and his role in it. Relationships with people and institutions, such as parents, siblings, extended-family members, friends, and teachers, are either terminated or altered. The man's adolescent (preadult) life structure is left behind, and an initial step in the adult world is made—a kind of "testing the waters." He becomes less psychologically dependent on parental support and authority, and more autonomous and independent. Levinson notes, however, that this process is never fully complete.

Entering the Adult World (ages 22–28) functions to allow the individual to create a provisional life structure providing a link to adult society. The young man first enters the *novice* phase, where important decisions are shaped about what may later become more permanent fixtures of his life structure. Examples are occupational choice, marriage and family, peer relationships, values, and life-style. In this novice phase, the individual must leave alternatives for himself and, thus, not prematurely commit himself to a given course. At the same time, he must create a stable life structure and make some decisions indicating that he is behaving responsibly.

Many of these decisions are made within the context of one's **Dream**. Levinson defines the Dream as "a vague sense of the self-in-adult-world" (p. 91). It may be occupational or parental in nature, such as being president of one's own company, being a loving father, or being good at one's trade. The novice's task is to more precisely define this Dream and then realistically live it out. He must overcome setbacks and disappointments and learn, as well, to accept and profit from his successes so that the "thread" of his Dream is not lost in the process of moving up the ladder or revising his life structure.

The **Age-Thirty Transition** (ages 28–33) "provides an opportunity to work on the flaws and limitations of the first life structure, and to create the basis for a more satisfactory structure with which to complete the era of young adulthood" (Levinson, 1978, p. 58). Levinson found this transition to be a traumatic one for most men, in that the changes made at this point are ill advised—out of step with the individual's wishes or abilities—or based on a poorly formed initial life structure. Levinson found only a minority of men who viewed this transition as a smooth one.

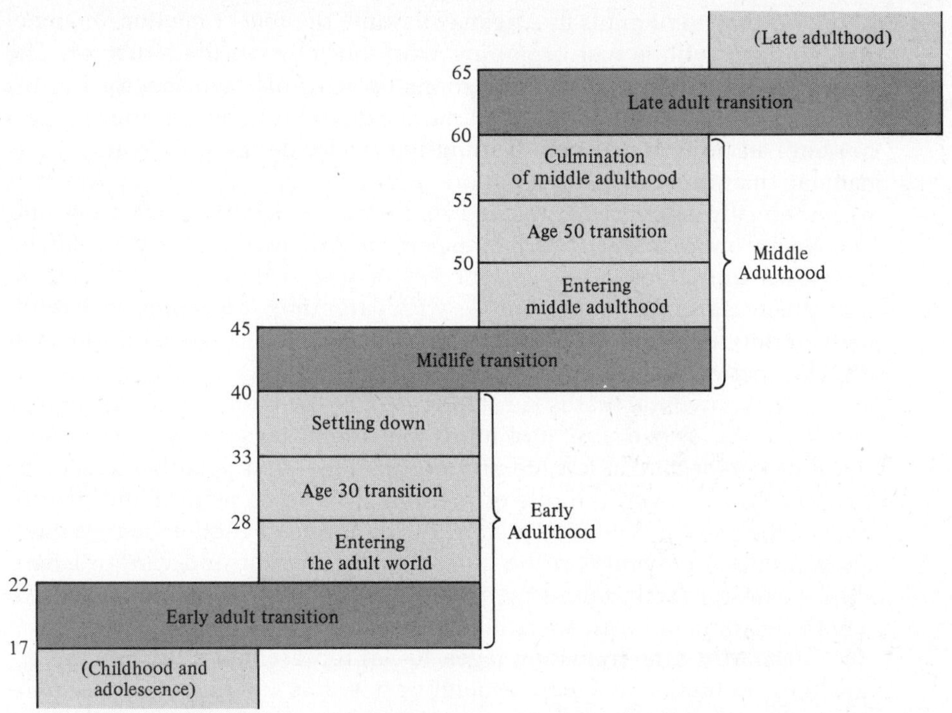

Figure 8.3 Levinson's changes in the life structure. *Source:* D. Levinson. (1978). *The seasons of a man's life* (p. 57). New York: Knopf. Reprinted by permission of Alfred A. Knopf, Inc. and by permission of the author.

The Age-Thirty Transition represents a shift away from tentative choices regarding family and career to those that are more permanent, possibly almost irreversible. It leads to the **Settling-Down** period, where the man reinvests himself in those aspects of his life structure that were somewhat tentative earlier. These aspects are the "nuts and bolts" of a framework that allows him to "establish a niche" for himself and to succeed at whatever is most important, where his progress can be monitored by himself as well as others (authority figures). He begins to map out a path for success in his work and/or his roles as husband and father.

This Settling-Down period shows a strong sense of commitment to a personal, familial, and occupational future that implies, "I am a responsible adult now," rather than, "I'm just beginning to find out what is important to me and what my opinions are," which is characteristic of the first life structure. At the end of this period (ages 36–40), the individual is **Becoming One's Own Man** (BOOM), and begins to ascend the occupational ladder to become a respected authority.

At this point in his life, he may assume the role of **mentor** for someone younger who is just beginning work on his own life structure. The man may have terminated his relationship with his own mentor by this point. Mentors can fulfill a formal, more external role, where they serve a guiding, teaching function in helping the novice define his Dream. Alternatively, mentors can also fill a more informal, internal advisory role that is emotionally supportive, much like that of a parent. Some men and women are more adept at certain aspects of the mentor role than others; their own unfulfilled needs for success or insecurity can cause them to manipulate those they supervise. As with parenting, the young adult (willingly or not) will leave his mentor when he reaches his own Settling-Down (BOOM) period and becomes someone else's mentor.

We know little that is substantive about the mentor role. It can be a very enriching experience, and much like parenting, can help one gain a sense of perspective about life and occupational and personal goals (see Chapter 7). However, the role of mentor can also be painful and disruptive—if the mentor is manipulated by his underling. Whether being a mentor is fulfilling depends on the quality of the mentor-underling relationship. Levinson rarely found men over 40 who still maintained an active mentor relationship with someone their senior.

The **Mid-Life Transition** (ages 40–45) represents a shift from an acquisition orientation to a more evaluative one. It is a period of soul-searching, questioning, and assessment regarding the extent to which all that has been accomplished in the life structure to date has any real meaning. It is similar to a mid-life crisis, as discussed earlier in this text. For some, it is a rather gradual, relatively painless change; for others, it is full of uncertainties and has an either/or quality to it. Either one starts anew or perceives that he has failed in some way to define what is important to him. Levinson notes that, either way, several years may be needed "to form a new path or to modify an old one" (p. 60).

After resolving issues regarding whether his commitments to people and things are really satisfying to him, Levinson finds the man next **Entering Middle Adulthood**. Here, he must again make choices regarding a new life structure. In some cases, these choices are defined by so-called marker events—divorce, illness, a shift in occupations, or the death of someone close. In other cases, changes are less obvious but nonetheless significant—subtle shifts in enthusiasm for his work or changes in the quality of his marriage. As before, the resulting life structure varies on the basis of its ability to truly satisfy the individual. The life structure is intrinsically happy or fulfilling only to the extent that it is connected to his self. The quality of this newly revised life structure more or less sets the tone for the remainder of the fourth decade of life.

Levinson tentatively proposes an **Age-Fifty Transition** (ages 50–55), which basically represents an opportunity to further solidify and/or change the life structure established during middle adulthood. For some, it may be experienced as the Mid-Life Transition, if they did little to alter their life structure earlier or were not very successful in doing so. It is important to note that, for Levinson (1978, p. 62), "it is not possible to get through middle adulthood without having at least a moderate crisis in either the Mid-Life Transition or the Age-Fifty Transition."

The period from 55 to 60 is seen as a relatively stable one, analogous to Settling Down, where the life structure is solidified. It is followed by a **Late-Adult Transition** (ages 60–65), which terminates middle adulthood and prepares one for older adulthood. Of course, since Levinson did not interview men in their fifties and sixties, his view on later middle age and old age are highly speculative, culture-bound, and obviously influenced by his own biases. Although Levinson tended to emphasize general changes in the life structure, these changes are nevertheless experienced in unique ways by specific individuals (Levinson, 1978).

DOES LEVINSON'S WORK APPLY TO WOMEN?

Although Levinson studied men, there is some indication that his concept of the life structure, and its accompanying personality changes, may also apply to women. Roberts and Newton (1987) found that women experienced changes in their life structure at times similar to men's, but that they worked on these tasks differently and achieved different outcomes.

Two cross-sectional studies of women's development from ages 30 to 45 generally support the viability of Levinson's work (Reinke et al., 1985; Harris et al., 1986). Ages 27 to 30 seemed to bring the most dramatic changes in women's lives. In the initial phase, beginning at age 26 to 30, personal disruption was a major theme. Women reported seeking some unknown change and often sought professional help. The second phase began between the ages of 28 and 31, and had as its major thrust a focus on the self and self-development. Women felt less oriented toward others, set personal goals, and often experienced separation and divorce at this time. The third period, starting between ages 30 and 35, reflected a new sense of well-being. The questioning and soul-searching of the two previous periods ceased, and women felt more self-confidence and greater satisfaction with their lives (see Reinke et al., 1985).

Rather than the Age-Forty crisis found for men, this study suggests an Age-Thirty crisis for women. Perhaps this is due to an awareness of their "biological clock," and thus an urgency in beginning a family; or increased autonomy due to greater career opportunities (see Wrightsman, 1988).

A separate cross-sectional study of women aged 45 to 60 found them to experience increased satisfaction with life and marriage and greater "mellowing, patience, assertiveness, and expressivity" (Harris et al., 1986, p. 415). Changes at this time, such as launching children from home and grandparenthood, are in contrast to those experienced earlier in life, which appeared to be more personal in nature. This study, too, did not find the upheaval at age 40 that Levinson found for men. It may be that the differences in the timing of men's and women's personality development is due to the greater diversity of women's lives (Wrightsman, 1988).

Gould's Transformations

Gould's ideas, like Erikson's, are stagelike in character. Gould feels that there is a shift in time perspective across the adult life cycle, from the infinity of time that seems available to us when we leave high school, to a more limited sense of time that leads to winning the Prize, which is similar to Levinson's Dream. This prize is also freedom from restrictions by those who have formed us—our parents. Gould feels that the sense of time becomes more restricted in one's late twenties, when he or she begins to realize that there is not enough time to test out all the choices that have opened up. Beginning with the late thirties and early forties, time becomes precious as we become more aware of our own mortality and begin to question whether our Prize was worth it—or if the Prize even exists!

In order to travel this bumpy road to its end, we must free ourselves of the **Illusion of Absolute Safety.** This process involves **transformations** whereby we give up the security of the past to form our own ideas, which is a troublesome task according to Gould. Note that while Levinson feels that one begins adulthood with no life structure, Gould feels that the structure (illusion) we have created for ourselves must be given up in order for growth to occur.

For Gould, adult development consists of alterations in or challenges to this Illusion of Absolute Safety. So, through leaving home to go to college or work; making decisions about work, family, or marriage; and experiencing early successes in, and conflicts among, these dimensions, people in their late thirties begin to rid themselves of the Illusion of Absolute Safety. It is at this point that we begin to confront the ultimate loss of power of our parents that comes with advancing age. Especially if our parents are very ill or have died, we also come face to face with our own eventual deaths, and our time orientation shifts to the more limited future that lies before us. We question where we are going and decide that wherever we should go, we'd better get on with it before time runs out.

By about age 50, we are forced to see our lives in terms of "I own myself," with its own sense of potential for success and failure, rather than "I am theirs" (parents'). Ultimately, we give up trying to control the world and thus no longer experience feelings of safety stemming from this sense of ultimate control. After 50, Gould says, one may come to accept what one is—good or bad, successful or not—growing out of or giving up childhood illusions of control.

Of course, Gould's ideas are perhaps the most obvious extension of Freud's psychoanalytic theory, which is not a very fruitful one for the study of adult personality development (Havighurst, 1973). It is childhood-centered, with growth or maturity more or less boiling down to a complete resolution of the separation anxiety we feel in childhood when we are first forced to stand on our own psychologically. It is in direct contrast to the view of adulthood espoused by the life-span developmental theorists (see Chapter 1), who see changes in adulthood as influenced by many factors. For them, those rooted in childhood are but one set of influences.

Gould's ideas are in many respects similar to those of Levinson and Erikson, in breaking down the adult life span into different sets of issues or tasks that are age-related. Both Gould and Levinson deal with changes in how people deal with culturally relevant shifts in the self (e.g., career, marriage, and family) brought about by and causing changes in the life structure (Levinson) and by transformations in the Illusion of Absolute Safety (Gould). Erikson and Levinson advocate positions suggesting *qualitative* changes in adult personality. By contrast, Gould's position supports a stability of personality stemming from transformations in the self that are all extensions of childhood separation anxiety.

DEVELOPMENTAL STAGES IN PERSONALITY—DESCRIPTIVE OR PRESCRIPTIVE?

One should always keep in mind that any approach to personality development emphasizing developmental stages is more properly viewed as a descriptive framework rather than a prescriptive one (see Birren & Renner, 1977; Lerner, 1986).

The desire to predict the crises of adult life, presumably so that one can prepare for them, perhaps accounts for the popularity of Gail Sheehy's (1977) book, *Passages*. In fact, depending on one's definition of crisis, one could easily argue that crises are, by definition, not predictable. They are instead individual-specific and therefore nonnormative (see Chapter 1). On the other hand, one may feel that any adjustment to life constitutes a crisis of sorts, because demands on adaptive skills or changes in identity may be required (Atchley, 1982; Eisdorfer & Wilkie, 1979; Lowenthal & Chiriboga, 1973).

Layton and Siegler (1978) suggest that crises may or may not accompany the aging process because individuals seek to maintain a *consistent* sense of physical, occupational, familial, and interpersonal identities. Challenges to our sense of mastery or **self-efficacy** are brought about by so-called marker events, such as birthdays, occupational changes, marriages, births of children, divorces, retirement, or even having one's picture taken (Bandura, 1977). Such events cause us to compare ourselves at present with ourselves in the past. We then can project into the future some ideal we have set for ourselves. Depending on the nature of the event and the adaptiveness of our efforts to cope with that event, a crisis may be experienced. For example, while some people shrug off routine physical exams, this alerts others to the possibility that in the future something *may* go wrong with their bodies, even if they pass with flying colors! They turn a harmless comment about their weight into a compulsive diet or exercise regimen. Instead of alleviating their fears, the physical magnifies them.

Likewise, normative life events, such as parenthood or marriage in one's twenties, may be expected or even prepared for via anticipatory socialization to the roles of parent or spouse (see Chapter 7). Yet, some individuals obviously cope with the changes these roles bring about more positively than do others.

Whether psychosocial crises or developmental tasks are prescriptive and/or inherently stressful is a function of a complex set of internal processes and external events. Personality change may or may not accompany experiences that some, but not all, people have as they age. How individuals cope with such changes seems to be most important.

References to developmental stages are really attempts to explain the behaviors of individuals, at a given point in their lives, that are exhibited most of the time—their modal behaviors (Lerner, 1986). As noted in Chapter 1, there may be great differences between individuals who are at a given stage of development. Also, people may display behavior that is characteristic of more than one stage. Thus, the transition from one stage to another is a gradual process, not an all-or-none affair.

Taken too literally, stages become "shoulds" rather than "maybe's." One should keep in mind that they are intended to be normative; that is, they are intended to apply to most individuals at given points in their lives. However, there are substantial differences among individuals regarding when such crises or stages are experienced, and how they are experienced. We suggest that stages are best seen as "hurdles" to be overcome or as one in a series of many choice points or decisions to be made throughout adulthood. Consequently, they may or may not meaningfully apply to you.

Although stage-theory approaches have provided a viable descriptive framework for understanding adult personality development, they need to be evaluated in terms of their potential for understanding intraindividual change or stability. This potential is limited by (1) individual differences in the timing and meaning of each stage, (2) the impact of the culture on the response to a given psychosocial crisis or developmental task, and (3) the interaction between individuals and their environments that affect and are affected by their efforts to cope with changes such as marriage, family, or career.

Riegel's Dialectics of Adjustment to Developmental Stages

Resolving a crisis can be seen as a hurdle to be overcome, and between each two hurdles one might feel that all is well. Klaus Riegel (1975, 1976) suggests that the *process* of resolving crises is really most crucial. In fact, Riegel suggests that the periods of stability coming between these crises are the exception rather than the rule. Although Riegel would not necessarily be considered a personality theorist, his ideas about coping with change can help us put the developmental stage theories of personality in focus.

For Riegel, the cultural-historical context in which we live influences whether a crisis is experienced at all (Riegel, 1977). That is, if society is in synch with individual life events, no crisis will occur. For example, while childbirth at age 20 normally would not be seen as a crisis, it could be considered as such, depending on the culture's prohibitions about birth control, day care, abortion, equal job opportunities, or single parenthood.

In such a case, having a child could present a major problem for a young woman. Similarly, depending on a man's or woman's options in retirement (e.g., access to part-time work or viable volunteer roles), leaving the work force may or may not precipitate an identity crisis.

Riegel uses the term **dialectical operations,** an extension of Piagetian formal operations, to define the individual's continual efforts at coping with life events, such as parenthood at age 40 or early retirement. Dialectical operations involve the cognitive ability to recognize and work through contradiction and crisis (Riegel, 1973).

In a dialectical sense, we must assume that at least one of the consequences of the individual's efforts to cope with his or her environment is that the environment will also change. For example, in disciplining our children, our relationships with them will change. This change will have repercussions for the individual, who is embedded in the continuous person-environment dialectic. In some cases, this change works against the individual—if we feel less close to our children, and they rebel against us—while in others, it works to his or her benefit—we feel loved and appreciated by our children. In the former case, the individual-environment dialectic becomes even more out of synch, and a crisis might be precipitated. We can, therefore, distinguish between the processes or efforts individuals bring to bear in coping with change, and the consequences or outcomes of these efforts (Danish, 1981). A dialectical approach to personality development emphasizes continual change.

COGNITIVE PERSONALITY THEORY

As noted at this chapter's beginning, distinct from a trait approach to personality is a cognitive approach. In this approach, one's perception of the environment or one's experiences is critical. We have all told others or heard, "It's all in your head." Yet, there is some truth to the idea that "what you see is what you get" in life. Those who consistently look on the bright side of things tend to be happier, well-adjusted people who can overcome adversity. Recently, Seligman (1991) has captured this outlook in his study of optimists, whose viewpoint on life he defines as positive yet realistic.

Thomae's Cognitive Theory

From a cognitive point of view, personality is one of many factors that mediate one's response to life events or role changes such as parenting, job skill obsolescence during middle age, the empty nest, institutionalization, widowhood, poor health, or impending death (Thomae, 1980). Essentially, how we think about or interpret what happens to us is the focus of the cognitive approach to personality.

Thomae (1980) refuses to provide a list of adaptive personality traits or personality types, due to the complexity of the cognitive or process approach to personality. In other words, certain traits or personality types may or may not be adaptive in a certain situation for a given individual at

BOX 8.1

IS WHAT YOU SEE WHAT YOU GET?

Cognitive views about personality emphasize the individual's perception of change, which may or may not parallel objectively measured change. Ryff (1989) asked middle-aged and older adults questions about the extent to which they had changed over the past 20 years. Her results showed that both groups were aware of both change and stability in aspects of their personalities, their lives in general, and their relationships with others.

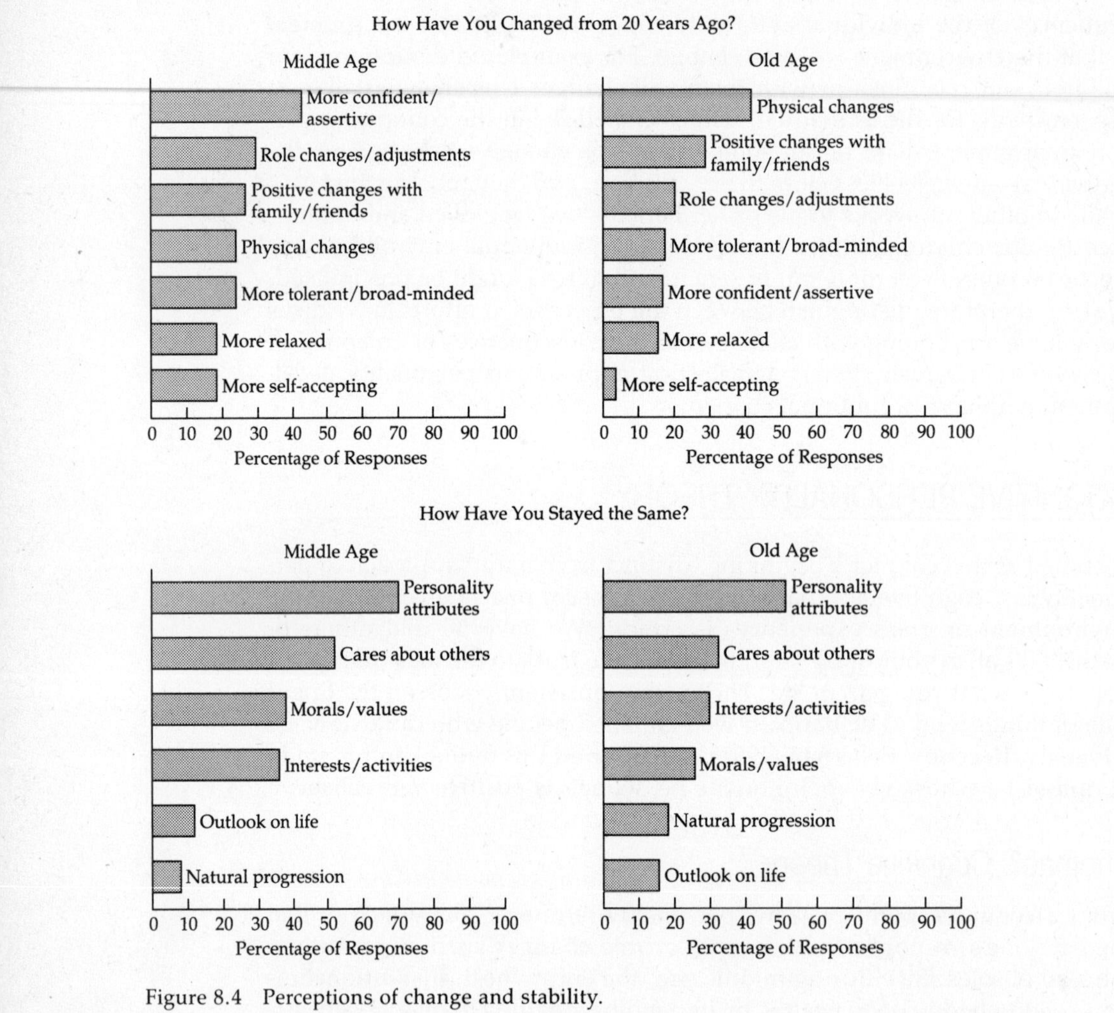

Figure 8.4 Perceptions of change and stability.

a particular point in his or her life. Thomae (1980) suggests that patterns of successful aging are best understood in terms of a complex interaction of a number of subsystems. These subsystems may be heredity, change in health or income, changes in intellectual functioning, or a shift in values or adaptive skills.

This view about personality is consistent with Riegel's dialectics, because the ongoing relationship between the individual and a changing culture is emphasized. It is crucial to understanding how people change over time. Many of the changes to which we must adapt are programmed into our lives and are a consequence of constraints on our behavior, which may have positive or negative effects for us. Personality processes play an important role in helping us adapt to such changes. They can help by either assisting us in evaluating degree of threat or change or modifying our response to the situation or task to be coped with (Hultsch & Plemons, 1979; Lieberman, 1975; Thomae, 1980). Accurately appraising a situation can also enable us to better utilize our resources, whether financial, physical, psychological, or interpersonal, to deal with change. It is variation in these personality processes that accounts for why some individuals deal with numerous normative and nonnormative events better than others (Brim & Ryff, 1981). Thus, how we appraise what happens to us seems to be very important.

STRESS AND COPING IN ADULTHOOD

When individuals are confronted with a life change, they engage in a series of cognitive appraisals that lead to behaviors that may or may not be successful in helping them adapt. **Primary appraisals** allow people to evaluate an event in terms of its being positive, neutral, or stressful and negative (Lazarus & Folkman, 1984). **Secondary appraisal** allows the individual to decide what options are available to cope with the event, if a chosen course of action is possible, and if the behaviors chosen will produce positive or negative outcomes. **Tertiary appraisal** or **reappraisal** allows one to incorporate new information into the equation. At this point, for example, the individual might evaluate whether the course of action taken was effective in either a short-term or long-term sense; in other words, "Did things actually work out as I planned? Are there outcomes I did not anticipate?" (see Figure 8.5).

Secondary appraisal is similar to what Bandura (1977, 1986) terms *efficacy expectations* and *outcome expectations*. That is, when individuals encounter a stressful situation, they ask themselves "What are the chances of adapting to this?" (efficacy expectations) and "What is the likelihood that my behavior will lead to the outcome I desire?" (outcome expectations).

Consider an individual who is offered a promotion. Assuming that being promoted is evaluated as positive (primary appraisal), one must next decide if he or she has the skills to actually do the job or can get along with new co-workers (secondary appraisal). Assuming positive efficacy expectations, the person must then evaluate whether the promotion will lead to desirable outcomes, such as higher pay or better hours or working conditions (secondary appraisal). The worker may turn down the promotion because (1) he or she lacks confidence in his or her job skills, or (2) while more money would be earned, longer hours or a more hazardous working environment would also be likely.

Let us suppose that our worker actually accepts this promotion. Tertiary appraisal of the new position may be necessary because time with one's family needs to be sacrificed, or little contact is possible with former co-workers or friends in order to do the new job well. Reappraisal might also be necessary because the individual cannot cope with the unanticipated side effects of earning more money (the extra is spent foolishly) or of having more responsibility (failing to ask for advice from others, feeling overwhelmed or isolated from others). Because the individual's efforts at coping with job demands are not effective (e.g., not budgeting time efficiently, staying up too late, not discussing the demands of the new position with a spouse), a reappraisal of the wisdom of being promoted becomes necessary. At this point, the individual might choose to be reassigned to the old job because the costs of accepting the promotion outweigh its benefits.

Hultsch and Plemons (1979) and Lieberman (1975) emphasize that personality factors such as self-concept, self-efficacy, or the tendency to deny threat influence whether people evaluate a situation or event as threatening, and whether that event is seen as personally meaningful (Lazarus & Delongis, 1983).

Our emphasis on stress and coping processes also highlights the individual's beliefs about personal control over events or personal commitments to a set of values and ideals as influences on how people assess and respond to change over the life span (Lazarus & Delongis, 1983). Lazarus and Delongis (1983), for example, suggest that with increased age, individuals may withdraw energy (disengage) from commitments they have made earlier in their lives because of poor health (if they can no longer work, which has been very important to them) or nonreward (if they are passed over for promotion, demoted, or forcibly retired, even though their work

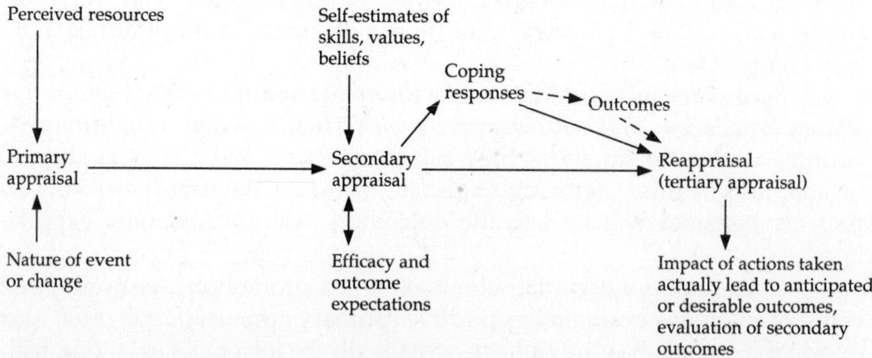

Figure 8.5 Process approach to personality: Adaptation to change. Adapted from Lazarus & Folkman. (1984).

may be of high quality). In these situations, disengagement is adaptive: it allows the individual to cope with stress. Such control beliefs are central to what Seligman (1975) has termed **learned helplessness.** Helpless individuals do not see a causal relationship between their behaviors and important events or consequences in their lives. Perhaps these people have a history of being exposed to events over which they have little control.

Seligman's model of helplessness has been reformulated by Abramson et al. (1978) to include the individual's tendency to attribute (interpret) patterns of behavior and consequences in particular ways. For example, individuals who are most easily made helpless may attribute failure (nonreward) to internal, stable causes, such as their own lack of ability, and success to external, unstable ones, like luck. We will have more to say about learned helplessness later in this chapter.

Cutrone, Russell, and Rose (1986) have found that, while reliable, nurturant social support by others predicted physical health over a six-month period, such support in concert with the extent of stressful life events experienced by older people predicted more positive mental health.

These results underscore the complexity in understanding adaptation to aging via the cognitive or process approach to personality. In contrast, the trait approach stresses the generalizability of traits across situations and persons.

Whitbourne's Identity Style

A relatively new approach to personality that is cognitive is Whitbourne's, which emphasizes the concept of **identity style** (Whitbourne, 1986, 1987). An individual's identity style is his or her manner of representing and responding to life experiences. This identity style is the accumulated self-representations of experiences that date back to childhood. As individuals interact with others in the environment, they begin to separate the self-as-agent (the "I," or subjective self) from the self-as-object (the "me," or objective self). In other words, the self exists both privately and as seen by others.

How do experiences with others influence these selves? It is through the particular identity style of the individual that experiences are processed to contribute to our selves. These identity styles can be **assimilative, accommodative,** or **balanced.** Assimilation and accommodation are Piagetian concepts (see Chapter 6). In identity assimilation, new experiences are fit into the existing identity of the individual, while in identity accommodation, identity is changed to fit a new experience.

As individuals have new experiences or interactions with others, they attempt to fit these into how they see themselves along the dimensions that are important to them. For example, if it is important to be a loving parent, experiences with one's children will be processed in a way that reinforces the perception of oneself as a loving father or mother (Whitbourne, 1987). In other words, these new experiences are assimilated into one's existing identity. Likewise, if being productive is an important aspect of the self, then retiring will be processed in a way that complements one's view of him- or herself as productive. Retirement might, therefore, be seen as an opportunity to pursue a new career or become involved in meaningful volunteer work.

Experiences for which one's identity must be changed or accommodated so that the individual can cope with them are those that are discrepant from the individual's views about self. And in some cases, assimilation is not even possible. For example, if divorce separates someone from his or her children, or someone is forcibly retired, these experiences cause them to redefine themselves. The self is accommodated or changed to fit the new events in one's life.

Successful development or adaptation occurs when there is a balance between identity assimilation and identity accommodation. This changes both the subjective ("I") and objective ("me") self. That is, there is a give-and-take to our experiences and interactions with others, and it is out of these interactions that we are changed. Using the example above, when one must discipline a child, this experience might be assimilated into one's identity as a loving parent, via "I am disciplining my child because I love him." But this same experience may require that one's identity as a loving parent be accommodated to fit the negative experience of being violent, the child's crying, or hurt and guilt at having to discipline the child. Thus, one's identity may shift—"I love my child, but maybe I am not the perfect parent. Perhaps I should seek advice from my spouse."

Whitbourne (1987) feels that it is clearly more adaptive to accommodate one's identity rather than try to assimilate an experience that is discrepant with one's self-view. For example, feeling that one is a loving parent and then abusing a child are too different to assimilate into a valued aspect of the self as a nurturant, reasonable, understanding parent. Likewise, adjusting to chronic illness or forced retirement may require accommodation. In a study of 94 adults aged 24 to 61, Whitbourne found several forms of both identity assimilation and identity accommodation. Some were more adaptive than others (see Table 8.1).

The *balanced* identity style is a stable one, neither overly assimilative or accommodative. Persons with balanced styles are relatively consistent, yet flexible enough to deal with experiences that contradict their self-views. They are autonomous and secure in the knowledge that new points of view and new experiences can be understood and learned from, without losing themselves in the process. Assimilative persons, by contrast, have a controlling style and need to win most arguments, while accommodative individuals give in without considering any alternatives because they lack confidence in their ideas or they need to please others.

As aging involves adaptation to physical change and new roles, it is not surprising that people with each identity style cope with stress and change differently. Neither is it surprising that each style has its advantages and disadvantages (see Table 8.1). While some people react emotionally in coping with stress, others adopt a more cognitive coping style (Lazarus et al., 1985; Roth & Cohen, 1986). Each style might be adaptive in

TABLE 8.1

BENEFITS AND COSTS OF IDENTITY STYLES FOR PSYCHOLOGICAL ADAPTATION TO THE AGING PROCESS

Identity Style	Benefits	Costs	Manifestations
Assimilative	Optimism toward present situation	Use of projection as defensive strategy, leading to social isolation	Unwillingness to change one's identity
	Self-perception of good health	Depletion of psychological energy required to maintain denial of age changes	Attributing negative identity characteristics to others rather than oneself
	Positive evaluation of life accomplishments	Alienation from "real," i.e., aging, self	
Accommodative	Secure basis of self-definition in identity of "aging person"	Overreaction to physical symptoms of aging and disease that blocks effective remediation	Unwillingness to recognize that a negative identity attribute exists
Balanced	High motivation to take advantage of preventive as well as therapeutic health practices, favorable adjustment to aging integrating	Frustration and a sense of helplessness in the face of age changes and events beyond one's personal control, direct confrontation with loss and mortality	Accepting into one's identity positive or negative identity attributes, considering a neutral identity attribute
	Favorable adjustment to aging that integrates age changes into a consistent sense of self	Direct confrontation of issues related to loss and mortality	

Adapted from Whitbourne. (1987).

some situations but not in others. For example, defensiveness, withdrawal, denial, or acting out, which are all assimilative coping styles, may be helpful in an emergency. In contrast, seeking advice and information or problem-solving—each a more balanced style—are more advantageous when making an important purchase such as a car or house.

Whitbourne's approach is a cognitive one because it emphasizes the developing individual's interpretation of events and experiences as a core element in the use of a particular identity style, which can lead to either stability or change in self-concept. As we all age, we are constantly in the process of shaping, fine-tuning, or maintaining views of ourselves, which allows us to adapt to new experiences. In this respect, Whitbourne's views are much like Riegel's, because they enable us to understand how people cope with changes in their lives. Because Whitbourne suggests that people with distinct identity styles cope with aging in distinct ways, her views also apply to the second question we asked earlier, "Do people with different personalities adjust to getting older in unique ways?"

TRAIT APPROACHES TO PERSONALITY AND AGING

Trait theory (Allport, 1961; Cattell, 1950; Guilford, 1959) has provided a most promising framework for recent personality research in adulthood and aging. Traits are inferred mental structures that motivate and guide an individual's behavior across a variety of situations or across time (Hall & Lindzey, 1985). Traits are enduring dispositions particular to individuals that structure or give meaning to their behavior. Using a trait approach, different individuals can be located along a continuum, in that people can be described as possessing a certain degree of one trait. Thus, traits are bipolar in nature; that is, they have negative and positive poles. For example:

Aggressive ________________ Passive
Dominant ________________ Submissive

Alternatively, people might be understood in terms of the degree to which they possess a trait, that is, from very dominant to not dominant at all. Lerner (1976) suggests that by using traits, or clusters of traits, that form more general personality factors or types, one can understand whether through development, people can be differentiated along a number of bipolar trait dimensions. Some people, for example, as they age become more aggressive than do others. This sorting-out process is very similar to Maddi's ideas about personality, where the core and periphery are linked through the process of development.

This approach is often heralded as more objective for studying personality in adulthood than those relying on clinical interviews or projective methods (see Costa & McCrae, 1980; Costa et al., 1983; McCrae & Costa, 1990). However, it is an after-the-fact approach (Lerner, 1976). That is, while it may provide us with a wealth of information describing individual differences in traits at a given point in time, or in changes in the levels of traits across age, it cannot provide us with an a priori answer to how people "get to be the way they are" (Lerner, 1976; Riegel, 1977). We still must ask questions such as, "Are personality changes across time qualitative or quantitative?" "Does aggression mean that same thing in young adulthood as in late adulthood?" "Are such changes learned or innately determined?" The trait approach has also been criticized as essentially ignoring the whole person, focusing instead on the characteristics (traits) themselves (Caspi & Bem, 1990).

Despite these shortcomings, using the trait approach, researchers have demonstrated both absolute and differential stability with age for most traits. Notable exceptions are the traits of general activity, masculinity, thoughtfulness, friendliness, and tolerance for others, all of which decrease with age. Douglas & Arenberg (1978) obtained these findings using the Guilford-Zimmerman Temperament Study (GZTS), a personality inventory yielding scores on each of ten different traits. The GZTS was administered twice by these researchers to over 900 men, aged 18 to 98, over a six- to ten-year period in the Baltimore Longitudinal Studies.

Similar evidence for absolute stability, using a measure of personality assessing 16 diverse traits, has also been found in sequential studies by Schaie and Parham (1976), Costa and McCrae (1978) and Siegler et al. (1979) (see Kogan, 1990; McCrae & Costa, 1990, for reviews).

Some age differences in terms of specific traits are found, partly due to sample differences in the age range of those tested and disparities in the time interval from initial testing to second testing (Botwinick, 1984). One might expect more age effects when the time interval separating testings is greater and when the sample is homogeneous (Botwinick, 1984; Neugarten, 1977).

Others have also found evidence for cohort effects in some personality traits (e.g., superego strength, restraint, social adjustment), as well as some indication of time-of-measurement effects (e.g., thoughtfulness, tolerance of others, friendliness) (Douglas & Arenberg, 1978; Schaie & Parham, 1976; Schaie & Willis, 1991; Woodruff & Birren, 1972). Schaie and Willis (1991) have also found cohort effects for self-reported measures of behavioral and attitudinal flexibility as well as social responsibility. But there was great absolute stability within cohorts.

Collectively, these studies also found that individuals tend to maintain their standing relative to others—differential stability—in levels of a trait over time.

Why do individuals tend to be stable over time? Part of the reason may be genetic (Lachman, 1989). For example, Pederson et al. (1988) and Pomin et al. (1988) studied 99 pairs of identical twins reared together versus those reared apart and found that there was a genetic influence on neuroticism and extraversion. Bergman et al. (1988), however, found that both environment and heredity interact in complex ways to influence personality in adulthood, depending on the strength of genotypic influences. While individuals with different personalities may react to the environment by changing it, one's preexisting characteristics (e.g., emotionality) are often accentuated when faced with novel or unstructured life changes (Caspi & Bem, 1990).

We are just beginning to learn about the complexities of change and stability in psychological traits in adulthood. Some people do change more than others, and life circumstances also change (Bem & Caspi, 1990). This exciting and complex aspect of the relationship between personality and aging will require a great deal more research before we understand it completely. We must incorporate the whole person as well as both genetic and environmental influences into our efforts.

Costa and McCrae's Five-Factor Approach

Perhaps the most impressive evidence for stability comes from a series of investigations emphasizing psychological traits (Costa et al., 1983; McCrae, 1991; McCrae & Costa, 1990). Costa et al. (1983) found stability in what they term the Neuroticism-Extroversion-Openness to Experience (NEO) trait model of personality. Somewhat later, two other factors, Agreeableness and Conscientiousness, were added to form the *five-factor model* of personality (Costa & McCrae, 1989).

In a series of studies, Costa and McCrae have clearly defined these basic personality factors (see Table 8.2). For example, neurotics are high in anxiety, depression, self-consciousness, vulnerability, impulsiveness, and hostility. They tend to be preoccupied with both physical and mental health and have more marital and sexual difficulties than other types. They also have more financial troubles, are unhappy, and lack self-esteem. They consequently express less life satisfaction (Costa et al., 1991).

On the other hand, extraverts are high in attachment, assertiveness, gregariousness, activity, excitement-seeking, and positive emotions. They are happier, less anxious and depressed, and express more life satisfaction than do those high in neuroticism. Introverts, though low in these qualities, are not pathological.

Persons high in openness to experience have high scores on ideas, feelings, fantasy, esthetics, actions, and values. They seem to have more eventful lives, full of positive events such as beginning a new line of work. They also express more positive emotions. However, those high in openness to experience also experience more negative life events, such as quitting or being demoted, being involved in a lawsuit, or becoming separated or divorced. It could be that being more open enables one to better prepare

TABLE 8.2

THE FIVE-FACTOR MODEL OF PERSONALITY

Neuroticism	*Agreeableness*
Calm—Worrying	Ruthless—Soft-hearted
Even-tempered—Temperamental	Suspicious—Trusting
Self-satisfied—Self-pitying	Stingy—Generous
Comfortable—Self-conscious	Antagonistic—Acquiescent
Unemotional—Emotional	Critical—Lenient
Hardy—Vulnerable	Irritable—Good-natured
Extraversion	*Conscientiousness*
Reserved—Affectionate	Negligent—Conscientious
Loner—Joiner	Lazy—Hardworking
Quiet—Talkative	Disorganized—Well organized
Passive—Active	Late—Punctual
Sober—Fun-loving	Aimless—Ambitious
Unfeeling—Passionate	Quitting—Persevering
Openness to Experience	
Down-to-earth—Imaginative	
Uncreative—Creative	
Conventional—Original	
Prefers routine—Prefers variety	
Uncurious—Curious	
Conservative—Liberal	

Adapted from Costa & McCrae. (1986c).

for or cope with change; or that experiencing such changes and coping with them successfully could cause one to become more open (Costa & McCrae, 1980a). While occupational choice was unrelated to neuroticism, extraverts tended to be social workers, lawyers, administrators, or advertising executives, while introverts preferred architecture, carpentry, or physics as professions.

Agreeable individuals are trusting, cooperative, and sympathetic, while conscientious persons are competent, feel a sense of duty, and are both planful and self-disciplined; they are especially good problem-solvers (Costa et al., 1991).

Costa and associates (1986), in a carefully designed large-scale cross-sectional study, found substantial evidence for absolute stability in personality using their NEO model of personality. Agreeableness and conscientiousness are also stable over time (McCrae, 1991; McCrae & Costa, 1990). In addition, they found a lack of evidence for the impact of a mid-life crisis on traits (Costa & McCrae, 1984), which was consistent with previous large-scale trait research by the same authors (McCrae & Costa, 1980a). McCrae and Costa (1987) have validated their results against peer and spouse ratings of measures of the same traits. Also, Costa and McCrae (1980b) found neuroticism and extraversion to predict negative and positive emotions ten years later.

Costa and McCrae (1980a) also found that the structure of personality itself remains basically the same across age, regardless of time-of-measurement and/or cohort effects. This means that the cluster of traits defining the five-factor model of personality is itself stable over time. Thus, individuals can be meaningfully compared in terms of changes in the level of each factor, and we can then assume we are measuring more or less of the same factor—a great advantage in understanding people in the same terms over time (Costa & McCrae, 1980a). Recall our discussion of Maddi's system of understanding personality, which attempted to spell out this aspect of personality in terms of core characteristics. Longitudinal stability for most traits across age in adulthood seems to be the rule.

Recently, Field and Millsap (1991) studied 51 women and 21 men from the Berkeley Study at age 69, in 1969, and 83, in 1983. They used a five-factor approach similar to that of Costa and McCrae. They found that satisfaction—absence of neuroticism—showed the greatest absolute and differential stability. Moreover, with the exception of the trait they termed energetic, all aspects of personality—extraversion, agreeableness, and intellect—showed high differential stability over 14 years. In terms of absolute stability, satisfaction and agreeableness were highest, while energetic, intellect, and extraversion showed declines. For both intellect and satisfaction, differences between men and women found in 1969 disappeared in 1983. For the oldest-old (those over 85), declines relative to the old (74–84) were found for intellect and energetic, but the oldest-old were more agreeable.

These findings, for the most part, confirm the picture of stability in traits we painted earlier and extend it to very late in life, where absolute stability is less often observed. It is very important to understand, however, that, while socialization and peer pressure may foster stability, life events such as divorce, serious illness or death of a child or spouse can change people forever (Field, 1991).

STATE ASPECTS OF PERSONALITY

In contrast to traits, which are assumed to behave somewhat predictably over time, recent interest has emerged in what are termed *state-dependent aspects* of personality. State aspects of personality fluctuate from day to day or week to week, due to hormonal or social factors (Nesselroade, 1988). Recall that our discussion of stability versus change in personality referred to years, not weeks or days. However, variations in our personalities (ipsative stability) do indeed occur over days or weeks, and affect our relationships with parents, children, care providers, and/or spouses. Fatigue, anxiety, feelings of control, mood states (feeling good or bad), and hostility are aspects of our personalities that show short-term fluctuations over days or weeks (Nesselroade, 1988). Because these changes influence and are often influenced by the everyday context, they are termed *contextual* (Kogan, 1990).

A broader dimension of the contextual aspect of personality is change in the historical context of events to which individuals are exposed and with which they must cope. In general, we know little about the process by which historical changes exert influence on personality development (Bem & Caspi, 1990). An exception, however, is research by Elder and Caspi, to whose work we now turn.

ELDER'S STUDIES OF THE GREAT DEPRESSION

The work of Elder (1979) is perhaps the best example of the influence of cohort-historical influences on personality. Elder compared two cohorts: children of the Oakland Growth sample (1920–1921 cohorts) and those of the Berkeley Guidance sample (1928–1929 cohorts) in their respective adolescent years during the Great Depression of the 1930s and again 30 years later. Elder found that (1) the impact of the Depression was specific to and more pervasive in the Berkeley cohorts, (2) males were more severely affected than were females, due to their being deprived of a father figure at this time in their lives (such fathers were out looking for work, or had to work two jobs), and (3) in Berkeley families who were experiencing marital difficulties prior to the Depression, their impact on personality (e.g., submissiveness, self-inadequacy) was far more negative.

Elder concluded that the earlier the Great Depression occurred in the lives of the boys, the more negative was its impact. Interestingly, the effects of the Depression on girls were the opposite. Daughter-mother relationships were strengthened. When families had experienced preexisting marital difficulties, these effects on boys and girls were less strong. Thirty years later, especially for the father-deprived boys in the Berkeley sample, psychological health was better. This appeared to be due, in part, to experience in the military in World War II, or Korea, which caused them to marry later (they were more mature), and allowed them to go to college through the G.I. Bill. They were also, in some cases, able to escape jobs that were unsatisfying and family situations that were emotionally aversive, giving them more self-confidence, stability, and a realistic set of goals to pursue. These all led to greater work success later on. While the deprived Berkeley males were rated somewhat less healthy relative to others, these differences were small 30 years later. What enabled these individuals to cope with the negative effects of the Depression, father absence, and marital discord? They seemed to have developed the cognitive skills of *positive comparisons* (Things are not so bad, compared to the Depression) and *selective ignoring* (looking for the good aspects of the Depression) (Elder, 1979).

Caspi and Elder (1986) studied the 1900 cohort of the Berkeley Guidance sample at age 30 forty years later and found that having more adaptive skills—being good problem-solvers or being healthier emotionally—predicted life satisfaction, depending on social class. While having higher intellectual and social skills was crucial for middle-class women, being emotionally healthy was most important for working-class women. For working-class women, living through the Depression lowered life satisfaction, while it enhanced life satisfaction for middle-class women.

Caspi and Elder suggest that women from lower socioeconomic classes were socialized in such a way as to interfere with their learning coping skills to deal with stress. On the other hand, many middle-class women, not having had to deal with stressful experiences before the Depression, were ill-prepared to deal with the potentially negative impact of growing old.

This study better enables us to understand not only cohort effects in personality, but also the role of personality as a mediator of an individual's response to a cohort-specific life event, as well as its effects on one's adaptation to aging. Elder (1986) has found a similar cohort difference regarding the influence of World War II on men, depending on when they entered military service and their socioeconomic level.

A last example of the influence of social change on personality is a study by Stewart and Healy (1989). These authors found that the impact of changing women's roles on women themselves were influenced by when such changes were experienced in the life cycle and by cohort membership. For example, older cohorts of women, whose traditional identities were already formed, were less affected by the Women's Movement than were younger ones. In contrast, younger cohorts of women, whose identities were still being formed, felt more pressure to combine work and family. For the earlier born cohorts, parental models were most influential.

Table 8.3 summarizes each theory of personality discussed and its position on the question of personality stability and change.

TABLE 8.3

THEORETICAL VIEWS ON PERSONALITY STABILITY OR CHANGE IN ADULTHOOD

Theorist	Core Ideas	Position on Stability or Change
Erikson	Psychosocial crises	Change
Levinson	Life structure	Change
Gould	Transformations, illusion of absolute safety	Stability
Riegel	Dialectics	Change
Whitbourne	Identity style	Stability and change
Thomae, Ryff	Cognitions about self	Stability and change
Maddi	Core, periphery	Stability and change
Elder and Caspi	Cohort, historical events	Stability and change

PERSONALITY AND ITS EFFECTS ON AGING

Activity and Disengagement

We can conclude from the discussion so far that one's theoretical orientation in part determines whether personality in adulthood is stable. While approaches such as Whitbourne's help us to understand how people cope, there has emerged a distinct body of literature dealing with the second basic question of this chapter, What is the impact of personality on aging? At this point, we might modify this to, How might one best adjust to the aging process? As we will see, different types of people tend to utilize different styles of adaptation to the aging process.

The issue of coping with change can best be understood in light of the difference between **activity theory** (Havighurst & Albrecht, 1953; Maddox, 1964) and **disengagement theory** (Cummings & Henry, 1961; Cummings, 1963).

Activity theory suggests a positive relationship between activity—involvement in social roles, interpersonal relationships, solitary activities, and formal commitments—and life satisfaction or morale (Adams, 1969; Lawton, 1975; Havighurst et al., 1969; Lemon et al., 1972; Maddox, 1965). The older person maintains, or substitutes for when necessary, as through death or retirement, those activities and relationships carried over from earlier times.

Disengagement theory suggests the opposite. Not only is decreased involvement beneficial, but the process of disengagement is a mutual one. That is, society and the individual withdraw from one another, with benefits to both. The individual gains because unwanted commitments can be given up, and the individual can disengage from others and become more self-absorbed. Society gains because younger, more productive individuals can replace those who are older. Cummings (1975) has since modified and

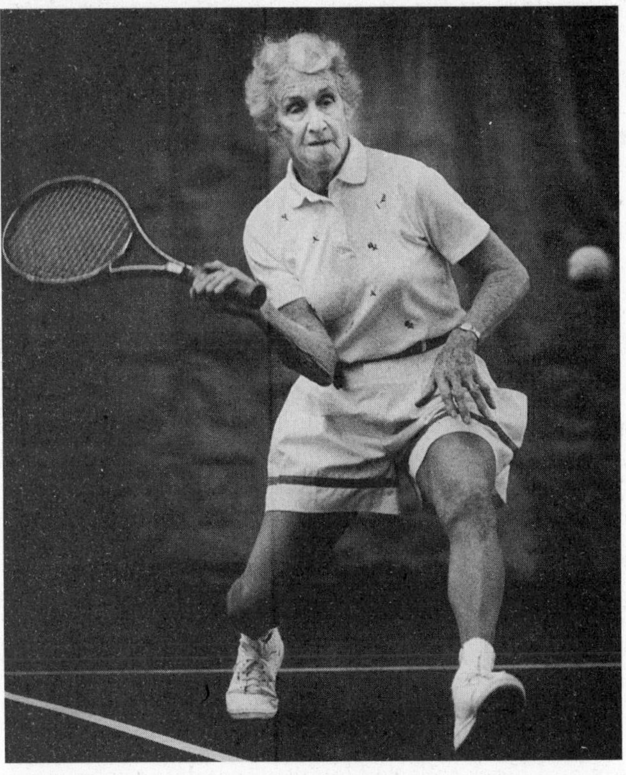

Activity theory suggests that older adults who remain both mentally and physically active cope more adequately with the aging process.

clarified the concept of disengagement somewhat, claiming that it does not necessarily imply passivity, loneliness, or isolation from others, nor was the theory ever intended to predict morale or life satisfaction.

In reality, both approaches involve value judgments about how to age optimally (Havighurst et al., 1963). Each might refer to a legitimate process by which some individuals come to terms with the many changes that accompany aging. Viewed in this way, they can be seen as options that may or may not be exercised by the older person.

It is also important to distinguish between psychological disengagement or decreasing emotional investment in the outside world, and social disengagement or decreasing formal commitments to social roles and activities. Note that disengagement may be involuntary, via relocation or poor health, or voluntary, as in avoidance of a stressful situation. High levels of activity that are involuntary, such as having to work for economic reasons or despite poor health, can be very maladaptive. A great deal of controversy and subsequent research has been generated by these two theories (see Botwinick, 1984; Neugarten, 1973, 1977; Thomae, 1980).

Consistent with the cognitive approach to personality, a number of factors have been found to mediate the relationship between the aging process, activity, and life satisfaction. For example, health status, the presence of a confidant, expected or desired levels of activity, and socioeconomic status all influence life satisfaction (Larson, 1978; Maddox & Eisdorfer, 1962; Maddox, 1965). Those who are in better health, who can share intimacies with someone else, who are more highly educated and are better off financially can maintain higher levels of activity that is fulfilling to them (Maddox, 1965). In fact, Neugarten (1977) points out that to the extent that individuals differ on these factors, evidence for personality change may not show up. For example, homogeneous cross-sectional and longitudinal samples are more likely to demonstrate age-related change in adaptation because there is less confounding of age and other causal factors (see Chapter 2).

Atchley (1989) maintains that people make deliberate choices to preserve their pasts. In so doing, they create continuity in their lives, in terms of both their feelings about themselves and how they deal with others every day. Continuity is therefore adaptive. Thus, some people are better at adapting to the process of getting older than are others. Several major studies have investigated this process of adaptation.

PERSONALITY TYPES AND ADJUSTMENT TO AGING

Berkeley-Oakland Longitudinal Studies

In the early 1970s, Haan and Block collected longitudinal data dealing with personality and adjustment among people living in the Oakland and Berkeley, California, areas (Block, 1971; Haan, 1972). To measure personality, these investigations used Q-sort methodology (Block, 1962). Briefly, in a Q-sort, individuals sort statements along a continuum of "least like me" to "most like me." This method allows researchers to gain a picture of people's self-perceptions of qualities or characteristics in terms of their relative applicability.

Livson (1973) identified two types of stability. **Genotypic continuity** refers to a pattern of stability where individuals with certain clusters of traits change in different but predictable ways. On the other hand, **phenotypic persistence** refers to stability in specific traits over time. While many longitudinal studies show phenotypic persistence, the Berkeley-Oakland studies suggest that genotypic continuity also exists (N. Livson, 1973; F. Livson, 1981; Livson & Peskin, 1981; Peskin & Livson, 1981). For example, traits such as responsibility predicted psychological health for men at age 40, but they did not at age 30, and almost the opposite pattern was observed for women.

Livson (1981) separated women into traditional and independent types. While traditionals seemed to maintain satisfaction with life and with close relationships over a ten-year period, ages 40 to 50, independents moved from a less satisfied pattern to a more satisfied one over the same period. Livson suggested that when children leave home, independents are able to fulfill their needs for achievement. Patterns for men were similar, in that men who improved in their adaptation to life became close to and more intimate with others (Livson, 1981). On the other hand, men who conformed to the controlled, rational, realistic, cultural-bound (macho) image of men were more stable in their happiness.

Strong evidence for genotypic continuity also comes from a 40-year follow-up of men and women—surviving original parents—in the Berkeley studies conducted by Mussen et al. (1982). For women, a "buoyant, responsive attitude toward life," and for men, "emotional and physical health" at age 30 predicted high life satisfaction at age 70. Interestingly, for men, their wives' emotional stability at age 30 was an even stronger predictor of life satisfaction at age 70.

More recently, Haan et al. (1986) followed up on a selected subsample of subjects from the Berkeley-Oakland longitudinal studies. Using objectively defined aspects of these individuals' Q-sorts (self-descriptions), they compared early to late childhood (ages 5–10) to early to late adulthood (50 years later). The dimensions of personality they focused on were (1) self-confident/victimized, (2) assertive/submissive, (3) cognitive commitment (achievement-oriented and innovative), (4) outgoing/aloof, (5) dependability, and (6) warm/hostile. The authors saw the dimensions of cognitive commitment, dependability, and outgoing/aloof as more developmental; that is, they showed continuous evolution over time. However, the characteristics of self-confident/victimized, warm/hostile, and assertive/submissive were experiential or situational in nature.

These investigators thus found evidence for both consistent, orderly development in the comparative short term, and complex, highly unstable, non-age-related change in personality. This apparent contradiction can be resolved by understanding personality in terms of both enduring qualities that change with age in a predictable way, varying in their level, and characteristics that vary with the situation and the individual. Reviewing our initial discussion of personality, especially Maddi's ideas of core and periphery, might be helpful to understand this apparent contradiction.

In general, personality change in the Haan et al. (1986) study suggested childhood as a period of systematic development and stability, whereas personality changes in adulthood were more dynamic and experiential in nature. Thus, personality changes were equally likely in adulthood, contrary to the emphasis on change in childhood espoused by the psychoanalytic tradition. Sex differences in experiences and situational differences requiring problem-solving skills, outgoingness, and dependability outweighed consistent, predictable life-span trends in personality change (Haan et al., 1986).

Based on the longitudinal studies discussed above, we can conclude that perhaps the most important mediator of styles of adaptation to aging is **personality type** (Filsinger & Sauer, 1978; Havighurst et al., 1963; Maas & Kuypers, 1975; Neugarten, 1977). This view suggests that individuals form distinct, characteristic styles of coping that are maintained across time. However, some styles of adapting produce higher levels of life satisfaction or morale than others (Adams, 1969; Havighurst et al., 1969; Lawton, 1975).

These personality types cover the continuum from activity to disengagement, though they are somewhat different for men and women (Guttman, 1975, 1977; Maas & Kuypers, 1975; Neugarten et al., 1964; Reichard et al., 1962).

Kansas City Studies

Another classical example of genotypic continuity comes from what have become known as the Kansas City studies.

The Kansas City studies were a series of cross-sectional age comparisons of 700 individuals aged 40 to 70 and six-year longitudinal studies of 300 individuals aged 50 to 90 conducted by Neugarten and her colleagues. These investigators used measures of personality tapping the inner world of the individual. These measures to studying personality are termed **projective techniques,** because individuals project their own wishes and needs on a neutral stimulus, such as an ambiguous picture, an inkblot, or an incomplete sentence.

In addition to information about the inner world of the individuals, data were gathered on their judgments about the extent of involvement in a variety of daily activities and performance in various roles such as worker, parent, or spouse. Ratings of life satisfaction were also taken.

From these data, the investigators were able to ascertain how ego-involved people were in their roles, as well as their feelings about current levels of role activity.

The Kansas City data yielded four clusters of personality types, broken down into eight specific patterns of adaptation, each varying from high, to medium or low on a continuum of role activity and yielding varying levels of life satisfaction (Neugarten & Hagestad, 1976; Neugarten et al., 1968). These personality types and their respective subtypes were as follows:

I. Integrated—well-functioning, complex people who are psychologically intact and competent—high in life satisfaction
   A. Reorganizers—maintaining high levels of activity, their lives have been successfully reorganized after retirement
   B. Focused—showing moderate levels of activity, but their involvement is selective
   C. Disengaged—well-integrated, life-satisfied individuals who are not active—their disengagement is voluntary and preferred

II. Armored or Defensive—very achievement-oriented, hard-driving individuals who experience anxiety about aging that must be controlled by defenses—they maintain control over, rather than being open to, their own desires and inner needs—moderately life-satisfied.
   A. Holding On—aging is seen as a threat; these individuals hold onto their past—their high levels of activity defend them against their fears of growing old

  - B. Constricted—these people defend against aging by withdrawing from others and become preoccupied with losses and deficits—this constriction permits them to maintain a sameness in their lives to ward off the inevitable losses of aging

- III. Passive-Dependent—less highly life-satisfied, for whom a source of happiness in life is letting others care for and make decisions about them
  - A. Succorance-Seeking—very dependent on others, may be both moderately active and life-satisfied, but physical and emotional needs are met by leaning on someone else
  - B. Apathetic—markedly passive, not very active, medium life satisfaction—most likely always passive and apathetic, and aging simply reinforces this pattern of meeting needs
- IV. Unintegrated—physically and emotionally incapacitated, low levels of life satisfaction
  - A. Disorganized—grossly psychologically dysfunctional, not active, but maintaining themselves in the community

While these types differed somewhat for males and females (see Neugarten, 1968), they do suggest that individuals develop consistent patterns of dealing with biological changes and/or shifts in role-related responsibilities brought about by age-graded, nonnormative, and history-graded events (see Chapter 1). The study of personality style measures personality at the level of **socioadaptational processes**.

On an **intrapsychic** level, Neugarten and her colleagues found that aged individuals utilized less energy in dealing with the outer world and more energy investing in one's own "impulse life." Thus, substantial change toward a more inner-directed orientation, termed **interiority,** seemed to occur with increasing age (Neugarten, 1977).

Not all studies find this pattern of interiority, however. For example, Fox (1979), using the Rorschach Inkblot Test, did not find an age-related pattern of increased interiority across a 12-year period, based on sequential analysis (see Chapter 2).

However, the Duke University longitudinal study found that, with time, individuals, regardless of age or cohort, tended to be more effective in overt, behavioral mastery of their environment (Siegler, 1980). These investigators also used the Rorschach test. Hayslip and Panek (1991), however, relying on projective data gathered from two samples of elderly people over a ten-year interval, found no cohort or time-of-measurement differences in personality functioning. This finding reinforces Neugarten's age-related interpretation of the personality changes she termed interiority.

Maas and Kuypers's Longitudinal Research

Maas and Kuypers (1975), in a 40-year longitudinal study of 140 people in the Berkeley-Oakland longitudinal studies, who were measured in their thirties and again in their seventies, also found substantial evidence for personality style continuity. They used various sources of data, including an extensive interview dealing with numerous life domains such as parenthood, marriage, occupation, friendship, activities, health concerns, and death, as well as measures of self-concept and life satisfaction.

These authors derived four different personality types for women and three distinct types common to men (see Table 8.4). They observed more continuity among the women than among the men. For both the fearful-ordering and autonomous women, consistency was observed across the 40-year time span, while more discontinuity, specifically more ego disorganization, was found in the anxious-asserting women later in life.

TABLE 8.4

PERSONALITY STYLES FOR MEN AND WOMEN

	Features Common Early and Late in Adult Life	Differences Early and Late in Adult Life
Fearful-ordering mothers	Depressed mood and activity level Low adaptive capacity Low sense of self-worth Health and economic disadvantage	More anxiety in old age More positive family life in early adult life
Anxious-asserting mothers	Anxiety and tension assertiveness and restlessness Low satisfaction High self-doubt Need to share Health disadvantage Interpersonal conflict	More ego disorganization in late life
Autonomous mothers	Aloofness High mental capacity Positive sense of self Cheerfulness Criticalness Interpersonal distance	
Person-oriented mothers	Warm, close, nonconflictual interpersonal relations	
Person-oriented fathers		More unrewarding career and financial strain in young adulthood
Active-competent fathers	High capacity Positive sense of self Interpersonal directness	More irritability and worry in young adulthood More charm and nonconformity in late life
Conservative-ordering fathers		Shyer and less demonstrative in young adulthood More relaxed and even-tempered in young adulthood More controlled and conservative in late life

Source: From H. Maas & J. Kuypers. (1974). *From thirty to seventy.* San Francisco: Jossey-Bass, p. 198.

For men, the picture was somewhat more complicated. Active-competent fathers both changed and remained similar in both a positive and negative sense. Less positive personality change (e.g., more career strain) was observed in the person-oriented fathers. Those men who were termed conservative-ordering evidenced the most change; they became less relaxed and more overcontrolled in later life.

In some respects, these findings bear out the personality-style consistency found by Neugarten and her colleagues for both men and women. However, substantial evidence for change, and for sex differences in personality change, was also observed.

While it is important to keep in mind that Maas and Kuypers's longitudinal research ignored subjects who were young adults (less than 30 years old), it nevertheless covers a greater time frame than does the Neugarten research. On the other hand, one could argue that historical-cultural changes, such as economic fluctuations and alterations in family patterns, are in part responsible for many of the changes that were interpreted as occurring with age. However, the personality changes Maas and Kuypers observed in their sample of men do resemble what Levinson observed regarding changes in the life structure.

Age Differences in Coping Styles

Despite the evidence for stability of distinct personality styles, a few cross-sectional studies do suggest age differences in coping styles. For example, McCrae (1982) utilizing a cognitive framework to examine the relationship between stress and coping, found younger adults to more frequently use hostility or fantasy to cope with significant life events, compared to middle-aged adults. For the most part, however, the similarities across age in coping styles, such as taking rational action, seeing advice, denial, or isolation, outweighed the differences. McCrae (1989), using cross-sectional, longitudinal, and sequential data analyses, found moderate relationships with age in the use of a number of very diverse coping mechanisms. The most consistent cross-sectional finding was that older individuals used less interpersonal aggression to deal with stress than younger ones. Older people were more forgiving and less likely to take out their frustrations on others (Costa et al., 1991). However, the authors suggest that the situation one is in dictates use of coping skills, rather than age. Not all studies agree, but most findings suggest a consistent pattern in coping styles which is maintained into late adulthood (Costa et al., 1991).

The Parental Imperative

Neugarten found that patterns of adjustment did indeed differ between men and women. While "older men seemed more receptive than younger men of their affiliative, nurturant, and sensual promptings; older women were more receptive than younger women of aggressive and egocentric impulses" (Neugarten, 1973, p. 320).

For men, Guttman (1975, 1977) found a trend from **active** to **passive mastery** with increased age; for women, a shift from passive to active mastery has been found.

Active mastery, which is an instrumental-productive style, means one attempts to change the world rather than oneself to meet one's needs, obligations, and/or the requirements of others. On the other hand, passive mastery, a passive-receptive style, suggests that one changes or is changed, rather than the environment, to deal with demands made by others in the real world. These changes seem similar to Whitbourne's identity styles.

Guttman (1975, 1977), whose cross-cultural findings agree with those of Neugarten (1973), explains this shift in terms of the **parental imperative.** Young boys and girls are socialized differently, and they develop stereotypically sex-role–related skills, abilities, and characteristics. Consequently, the response by men to the "chronic emergency" of parenthood is that they are forced to assume greater responsibility and become more dominant and aggressive in the service of their own and their family's welfare. Women develop their nurturant, caring, supportive skills out of the necessity of being physically close to their children. When the demands of parenthood decrease, men and women are both free to revert back to the side of themselves they repressed in the service of being parents. Guttman argues that out of both parents' inability to simultaneously meet both the physical and emotional needs of their children, fathers become the providers of food and physical security, whereas the mothers provide emotional security by staying within sight and sound of their offspring.

These sex differences, according to Guttman, are to a certain extent innate and evolutionary and are predominantly shaped and strengthened by culture. A study by Helson and Moane (1987) confirmed Guttman's findings. They found that, during their late twenties, women showed an increase in femininity and self-discipline. However, later in life, femininity decreased and was replaced by an increase in confidence, dominance, and coping skills.

HOW PERSONALITY IS ASSESSED—STABILITY VERSUS CHANGE

You must realize that whether certain dimensions of personality show stability or change is partly influenced by how personality is assessed. Projective tests, for example, often show change (e.g., interiority), while structured interviews and standardized personality inventories often portray a picture of stability.

Whether personality appears to change with age also depends on whether one's data were gathered cross-sectionally or longitudinally. Cross-sectional studies sometimes show age effects as a function of sample homogeneity, and in cross-sectional research, age differences are confounded by cohort differences (Costa et al., 1983). Longitudinal evidence, however, often demonstrates age changes in personality but is potentially confounded by time-of-measurement effects (see Moss & Sussman, 1980).

The accurate measurement of personality can pose some unique problems for the adult developmental researcher. Many personality measures have not been normed on elderly people, suggesting misleading conclusions about individuals' standings relative to others. A notable exception is the widely used self-report personality measure called the Minnesota Multiphasic Personality Inventory (MMPI) (Butcher et al., 1991).

Individual differences among older people may make norms difficult to use meaningfully. Moreover, items on many personality scales were originally developed for the purpose of assessing psychopathology, so that their value in understanding normal or less pathological forms of personality functioning may be limited (Schaie & Schaie, 1977). In addition, long batteries of tests may be fatiguing, and small print or paper that creates glare may be difficult to read. Some individuals who are poorly educated or not test-wise may feel threatened by being assessed. Instructions may be difficult to follow for those who have attentional deficits or are sensorially impaired. On many personality inventories, people may not realize that, for example, "wanting to join clubs and organizations" and "not wanting to be around others" require two different responses that may mean the same thing. Last, if items do not pertain to the everyday circumstances of many adults (e.g., dating, career goals, parental relations), they may not be taken seriously.

Self-report personality inventories may also be subject to the effects of **response set,** such as guessing, choosing extreme responses or neutral responses, or answering in socially desirable unduly positive terms (Carstensen & Cone, 1983; Kozma & Stones, 1986). For example, agreeing with a statement such as "I have never lied to anyone," or "I always vote for the candidate I truly believe in," would define a socially desirable response set. Response set may be especially important when dealing with personal issues (Lawton et al., 1980).

Schaie and Schaie (1977) suggest it is important to first decide for what purpose such assessments are to be made to enhance their usefulness on an individual basis. There are advantages and disadvantages to both objective methods (McCrae & Costa, 1990) and clinical tools for assessment such as projective techniques (Hayslip & Lowman, 1986). The use of either depends on the availability of appropriate, current norms and evidence for the measure's reliability and validity with the population of interest (Kaszniak, 1990). In addition, the test administrator's interpersonal skills such as honesty, supportiveness, eye contact, sensitivity to fatigue, and competence in administering and interpreting personality measures all influence results. Moreover, the adult's reactions to being assessed are important considerations, as defensiveness or anxiety may, say, influence response set.

All personality test data gathered from adults should be used cautiously, considering the consequences of decisions based on such data. In this way, information gathered from each person can be used to his or her best advantage in vocational, educational, or counseling situations.

MORE SPECIFIC ASPECTS OF THE ADULT PERSONALITY

So far, we have attempted to answer the basic questions of what we mean by personality, whether personality varies with age, and how personality affects the experience of aging. However, much research in more specific areas of personality functioning has been conducted, and some of this is also of interest to the adult personality theorist. We discuss two areas: self-concept (Breytspraak, 1984; Hayslip, 1985; Suls, 1982) and locus of control (Baltes & Baltes, 1986: Garber & Seligman, 1980; Langer, 1983; Lefcourt, 1981; Seligman, 1975).

The study of these more specific aspects of personality has definite implications for the adult personality theorist. For example, it may be important to understand the effects of a stressful life transition such as divorce or a normative life event such as retirement on self-concept or one's sense of personal control over the environment.

These aspects of personality may play a central role in understanding how individuals deal with their aging and, thus, relate to the personality-aging issues discussed earlier. For example, those with positive self-concepts experience greater life satisfaction and less anxiety, and enjoy more control over events in their lives (George, 1981; Larson, 1978; Lawton, 1983). They also have more positive views of their own development and aging (Brubaker & Powers, 1976).

Self-concept

Positive self-concept has been seen as pivotal in defining the aging experience (Atchley, 1982; Brubaker & Powers, 1976; Bultena & Powers, 1978) and contributing to longevity (see Bell et al., 1972). Having a positive self-concept can also help reduce the negative effects of relocation from one's home to a nursing home (Bennett & Eckman, 1973; Lieberman, 1975). Moreover, self-concept has been identified as an important predictor of change in the assessment of counseling interventions with adults of all ages (Levy et al., 1980).

Markus and Herzog (1991) and Wells and Stryker (1988) feel that self-concept is dynamic. Our self-concept influences what we know about ourselves—our goals, hopes, preferences, values, and relationships. It is social in nature, influenced by the many interpersonal and societal factors we all encounter. Self-concept is composed of many domain-specific **self-schemas**, or areas of the self such as family self or work self, that include past, current, and future selves (Cross & Markus, 1991). With age, self-schemas are bolstered and strengthened; our knowledge about ourselves is increased with experience. This is particularly true for family, work, and personal self-schemas (Atchley, 1989). Our roles as workers, parents, spouses, and friends are influenced by the self-schemas we bring to them,

A healthy self-concept is essential to development in adulthood.

and these same schemas are in turn influenced by how successful we are in carrying out these roles (Markus & Herzog, 1991). If these roles confirm our self-knowledge, then self-schemas are strengthened. If they do not, our self-schemas may need to be redefined. In these respects, changes in self-schemas resemble Whitbourne's ideas about identity style discussed earlier.

Some theorists feel that self-concept is constructed out of experience (Breytspraak, 1984; Lewis, 1979; Smith, 1979). In other words, our self evolves out of, yet shapes, our feelings about ourselves as adults and our relationships with others. This approach is more consistent with the dialectical approach to personality discussed earlier.

Others, however, feel that self-concept develops in distinct stages (Dickstein, 1977). According to this view, the self develops through five distinct stages: (1) the dynamic self, characteristic of infancy, or the coordination of others' demands with those of one's conscience or those stemming from biological drives, (2) the self as object, characteristic of childhood, or self-awareness via interaction with others, (3) the self as knower, typical of adolescence, or the self as real or unique, (4) the self as an integrated whole, or a balance between unique needs and abilities and the demands of the environment, and (5) the selfless self, or self as perpetually changing and striving toward increased acceptance and improvement. According to Dickstein (1977), the last two levels in the development of the self are characteristic of adulthood.

Mortimer and associates (1982) assessed the stability of a number of dimensions of self-concept over a 14-year period in a sample of college students. They used a self-rating technique known as the semantic differential (Osgood et al., 1957), where people rate themselves along a number of bipolar continua (e.g., happy-sad). The dimensions of self-concept derived from these self-ratings were well-being, sociability, competence, and unconventionality.

In many ways, these dimensions were quite stable over time: (1) they retained their meaning (structure), (2) individuals maintained their relative order on each dimension, (3) intraindividual rank ordering of importance was constant, and (4) levels of each were similar across the 14-year period. Interestingly, however, Mortimer et al. (1982) found differences between individuals' responses to various life events, such as work and career progress, marriage, and life as a whole, depending on whether their self-ratings had increased or decreased over the 14-year period. Those who were classified as stable lows or decreasers responded less positively to these life events.

The investigators concluded that the relationship between the experience of life events and self-concept is reciprocal—each affects and is influenced by the other. This reciprocal relationship is consistent with both the cognitive and dialectical approaches to personality discussed earlier.

Comparisons of adults regarding self-concept have yielded inconsistent results, with some cross-sectional studies reporting declines with age (Bloom, 1961) and others reporting no differences or slight increases (Hess & Bradshaw, 1970; Nehrke, 1974; Nehrke et al., 1980). Some studies have found some aspects of the self (e.g., assertiveness) to be more variable than others (e.g., amiability) over time (Monge, 1975; Pierce & Chiriboga, 1979). These conflicting findings are most likely artifacts of cohort or sampling differences, different measures of self-concept, or differential life events interacting with and changing the individual's sense of self.

In light of the fact that our self-concepts are complex and change with experience (Breytspraak, 1984; Grant, 1969; Lorr, 1978; Monge, 1975; Pierce & Chiriboga, 1979), studies comparing different components across age are bound to yield findings that are confusing and inconsistent. Most recently, however, Costa et al. (1986) found no longitudinal evidence for changes in psychological well-being, which is closely related to general self-concept and life satisfaction.

Locus of Control

A number of researchers and practitioners have observed that it can be important to maintain a sense of personal control over events such as being relocated from one's home to an institution (Langer, 1980; Langer & Rodin, 1976; Solomon, 1982; Weisz, 1983).

Locus of control is domain-specific; it has intellectual and health dimensions (Lachman et al., 1982; Lachman, 1986; Lefcourt, 1981; Wallston & Wallston, 1978). Each dimension is distinct from generalized locus of control, where only distinctions between internal (I have control over my life) and external (other people or events control my life) locus of control are generally made (Levinson, 1975).

While general locus of control seems to show adequate differential stability (Gatz et al., 1986; Lachman, 1986b), some studies suggest that, with age, individuals generally become less internal and more external. Other studies do not support this (Lachman, 1983, 1985). The change toward more externality with age is stronger for domain-specific locus of control, such as intellectual and health locus of control (Lachman, 1986a).

People's feelings about the control they can exert over events in their daily lives may make the transition to retirement either easier or more difficult (Abel & Hayslip, 1986, 1987). Also, older people who are institutionalized or depressed may have distorted ideas about their ability to control their own lives which interferes with their functioning (Kennelly et al., 1985; Langer, 1982; Maiden, 1986; Weisz, 1983). Fortunately, interventions designed to restore accurate assessments of self-control (competence) have been successful, leading to improved morale, better health, and less helplessness (Langer & Rodin, 1976; Rodin & Langer, 1977; Schulz & Hanusa, 1979).

The study of these more specific areas of personality functioning may help us to understand more fully the process by which personality changes or remains consistent throughout adulthood. It may be that individuals who can maintain positive views of themselves in the face of change and can retain a sense of personal control not only live longer, happier lives, but also show more stability of personality over time.

SUMMARY

This chapter dealt with personality stability and change as well as with how personality affects the aging process to influence how people cope with changes in their lives. Personality can be understood along a *continuum* of emphasis, from a focus on unobservable processes to one using observable behaviors as the unit of personality. Using Maddi's *core* versus *periphery* model, one can understand the role that development plays in differentiating individuals (at the peripheral level) who also share some characteristics (the core of personality).

Stability can be defined in many ways, such as *absolute, differential,* and *ipsative,* as well as in terms of personality *coherence.*

Several factors affect the stability of personality in adulthood. Major views about adult personality, by Gould, Erikson, Levinson, Whitbourne, Riegel, and Costa and McCrae, were discussed, each of which predicts either stability or change in personality with age. One's biases about *activity/disengagement,* the level at which personality is studied, how one goes about measuring it (e.g., using psychometric versus projective methods), and the particular *developmental design* (e.g., cross-sectional, longitudinal) all affect whether individuals appear to change as they age.

While developmental stages provide us with a convenient framework within which to study adult personality, they must be viewed as *descriptive* attempts to represent intraindividual change. Riegel's *dialectical* theory and both Thomae's and Whitbourne's cognitive theories of personality are consistent with the mediating role that personality plays in affecting and being affected by life events. Cognitive approaches stress the *interpretation* or *appraisal* of life events and experiences as critical to adaptation and coping.

Relying on data such as those from the *Berkeley-Oakland* studies and *Kansas City* studies, one can conclude that, while most individuals may face age-graded sets of tasks or events, they cope with these tasks at a *socioadaptational level,* in ways that are more or less adaptive but *consistent* with their established life histories. At an *intrapsychic level,* there is much evidence for increased *interiority* with age. Guttman's research dealing with sex differences in coping suggests that patterns of personality change are specific to either men or women, and grow out of the cultural *imperative* to perform the *parental roles.*

While cross-sectional data often present a picture of apparent age change, studies of adult personality reveal that cohort differences do exist for many psychological traits. Longitudinal studies paint a clear picture of personality stability with age, relying on psychometric scales to measure personality *traits.* Personality change and stability in the adult years is, thus, a complex issue, subject to the effects of many influences.

KEY TERMS AND CONCEPTS

Personality
Trait
Periphery
Psychosocial crises
Personality types
Disengagement theory
Socioadaptational
Parental imperative
Genotypic continuity
Self-concept
Q-sort
Life structure
Primary appraisal
Secondary appraisal
Tertiary appraisal
Illusion of absolute safety
Self-efficacy
Core
Transformations
Dialectics
Life satisfaction
Activity theory
Interiority
Intrapsychic
Phenotypic persistence
Learned helplessness
Mentor
Identity style
Accommodation
Assimilation
Active mastery
Passive mastery
Absolute stability
Differential stability
Ipsative stability
Coherence
Self-schemas
Locus of control

REVIEW QUESTIONS

1. What approaches have been used to define and study personality? Is one better than another?
2. Does personality change with aging? What factors govern whether the answer to this question is yes or no?
3. What do the views of Erikson, Levinson, and Gould have to say regarding change and consistency in adult personality?
4. What does Freudian theory have to say about adult personality development? In what ways are Gould's transformations similar to a Freudian approach?
5. What is meant by the life structure? In what manner is it changed throughout adulthood? What are its limitations?
6. What are psychosocial crises? What objections have been raised regarding psychosocial crises as a way of understanding adult personality change?
7. Are adult developmental stages descriptive or prescriptive? What does dialectical theory say about this issue?
8. What is the cognitive view of personality? How are Thomae's and Whitbourne's views similar?
9. What are the Berkeley-Oakland studies and the Kansas City studies? What do they say about the question of personality and its effects on aging? What do the findings of Maas and Kuypers suggest regarding the role of personality in adjustment to aging?
10. What are psychological traits? What do data from psychological tests measuring traits suggest regarding the stability of personality with age?
11. What are self-concept and locus of control? In what ways is each multidimensional and complex?

CHAPTER 9

Work, Retirement, and Leisure

C H A P T E R   O U T L I N E

INTRODUCTION

Most of us spend a great deal of our time working behind a desk, at a machine, or in the home rearing children. We may work eight to 10 hours per day, five to six days a week. Moreover, we probably have spent a good deal of our high school and/or college careers thinking about and preparing for our life's work. Our work role is often critical to our identities as adults, and, indeed, we are socialized into a work role relatively early in our lives. After we have worked for 20 to 30 years, we may begin to think about retirement.

Assuming that life expectancy will increase in the future, odds are we will spend at least 40 years of our lives as employed people. For many individuals, what they have done occupationally helps them structure their lives in retirement. Others never retire in a formal sense. In other words, the world of work has a pervasive influence on many aspects of our lives, throughout our lives. Levinson (1986), among other theorists, attaches a great deal of importance to work as an organizing principle in understanding adult development.

The focus of this chapter is to discuss the continuum of occupational selection, work, retirement, and leisure. For organizational reasons, we will discuss these topics separately, but their interdependence and relationships to other areas of our lives, such as our marriage and roles as parents, are a reality. For example, Super (1980), a prominent occupational theorist, has suggested that roles people play in various "theaters"—home, community, church, school, or club—help to define, and are influenced by, their roles in the workplace. Since roles in these "theaters" change with age, in many cases, the work role will also change. Rebok et al. (1986) feel that work is an important influence on our beliefs about our intellectual adequacy.

OCCUPATIONAL ROLES AND THEIR SELECTION

The selection of an occupation is one of the most important decisions made by individuals during their lives. To some extent, our occupation determines how our time is spent, who our friends will be, where we will live, our attitudes and values, as well as our life-style (Tolbert, 1974).

Work often occupies a central position in our adult lives, serving as a basis for our self-concept, self-esteem, and often our very identity (Chown, 1977; Coleman & Antonucci, 1983; Havighurst, 1982; Marshall, 1983). For example, in young adulthood, both men and women who are either working or going to school have higher self-esteem than do those who are unemployed or hold part-time jobs. For young women as well as women in mid-life, being employed contributes to feelings of well-being (Adelmann et al., 1989; Stein et al., 1990). This is particularly true for women whose children have left home and who begin work thereafter, even if they did not plan to do so when they got married (Adelmann et al., 1989).

These studies indicate that work produces intrinsic satisfaction for the individual beyond that derived from economic returns (Cohn, 1979). People low in self-efficacy may choose more traditional, less risky occupations (Hackett & Betz, 1981; Subich et al., 1986). This suggests that feelings about ourselves as viable, productive people both influence and are influenced by work.

Because self-efficacy and occupational choice are related, the occupation one selects is very important. However, career choices are often made with little thought or assistance. Because we are aware of this, there has been an increasing emphasis on career guidance and placement (Osipow, 1987). Moreover, decision-making about careers is no longer limited to adolescence but continues throughout the life cycle (Osipow, 1983).

Although selecting an occupation is an organized series of choices, many extraneous and unpredictable factors are also involved in this process (Whitbourne & Weinstock, 1979). For example, economic factors, the accessibility of educational and training opportunities, and supply-and-demand market conditions all affect an individual's occupational choice. In addition, individuals often get "locked in to" jobs by accident, or take jobs they thought were only temporary, only to end up spending their entire lives in these jobs.

Moreover, many people who thoughtfully choose their careers find out that these they "plateau" in young and middle adulthood. For men, a plateauing career can be particularly frustrating (Bardwick, 1986). Not only are their new career choices severely restricted, but they also feel less marketable, less interested in being promoted, and more desirous of leaving their present position.

Many people are never able to enter the career of their first choice (Sarason et al., 1975). This is one of the primary reasons individuals attempt mid-career life changes or pursue entirely new careers after retirement. More than likely, this is due to the fact that attitudes toward work have changed dramatically in the last several decades, from those valuing materialism to those emphasizing self-fulfillment and self-actualization.

Occupational Development

Perhaps the major means of socialization during young and middle adulthood is through work. Your occupation will affect, and in part result from, your identity, life-style, socioeconomic level, and friendship patterns. It will also help determine what society expects of you regarding behavior and performance in your **occupational role** (Osipow, 1983; Whitbourne & Weinstock, 1979). Such expectations include manner of dress, activities, code of conduct, values, and standard of housing. Most occupations have an expected role associated with them; and how well we conform to these expectations often determines how we are viewed by society in general and by our occupational peers.

Sarason et al. (1975) believe that, through making a career choice, we first become aware of the aging process, because the decision will determine how most of the rest of our lives will be occupied. According to the United States Bureau of Labor Statistics (1983), the average male can expect to work 38 years, and the average female 28 years, of their respective life spans. If anything, these estimates will increase in the next decade.

When we use the terms *career development* or **occupational development,** we are describing a semiorganized, coherent pattern of jobs that lead us to some implicit (subjective) or explicit standard level of performance or goal. Career development implies a variety of decisions made, versus a more or less random, unrelated series of jobs held just to get by financially. For example, many of you have worked at various jobs in the summer while full-time students. However, others work at a variety of jobs because they lack the requisite skills or educational background to pursue a career. Because we believe occupational development to be a continuous process, let us examine several theories of career choice, emphasizing those ideas with a life-span focus.

Holland One major theory of occupational choice is that of Holland (1973, 1985). Holland's theory is considered a trait-factor approach, since it predicts that vocational selection and satisfaction will be determined by *congruence* or fit between an individual's attributes and vocational interests. According to Holland, individuals' vocational interests are viewed as extensions of their personalities. Occupations are categorized by the interpersonal settings in which the individual must function, as well as associated life-styles. Holland views these personal-social factors as more important to occupational selection than the performance requirements of the occupation per se.

This theory predicts individuals will choose an occupation that is a fit, or congruence, among their personalities, the types of interpersonal setting in which they function, and the life-styles associated with their occupations. By doing this, we can express ourselves, best apply our skills as we believe them to be, and take on work roles that are compatible with our personalities.

Holland's theory predicts that congruence between an individual and an occupation is the major factor responsible for vocational choice, stability, and satisfaction. Thus, dissatisfaction is the result of an incongruence—mismatch—among these factors. Research by Spokane (1985) has supported the positive relationship between congruence and career choice, career persistence, career stability, and work satisfaction.

Holland's theory is somewhat limited for our purposes, for two reasons. First, there is usually a difference between an individual's perceived and actual abilities in adulthood (Kidd, 1984; Panek & Sterns, 1985). Perceived abilities are at the core of Holland's theory. Second, Holland's theory does not have a definite life-span focus. For example, Adler and Aranya (1984) studied career stages in accountants and found personality type–occupation congruence to vary with life stage (see Vondracek et al., 1986).

Super Super's (1953, 1957, 1969, 1990) theory is an example of a self-concept approach to occupational development. That is, the individual selects an occupation that allows for the expression of self-concept. This theory is presented within a life-span framework. Crook et al. (1984) suggest that so-called career maturity is facilitated by self-concept, which in turn promotes achievement.

Super describes occupational development as a series of career stages that result from modification of the individual's self-concept and adaptation to an occupational role. Individuals can thus be located along a continuum of **vocational maturity** throughout their occupational lives. The more consistent are individuals' vocational behaviors with what is expected of them at different ages, the more vocationally mature they are (Super, 1980, 1990).

As proposed by Super, vocational development progresses through five distinct stages. These are the (1) implementation stage, (2) establishment stage, (3) maintenance stage, (4) deceleration stage, and (5) retirement stage.

The implementation stage, characteristic of later adolescence, is when individuals take on a number of temporary positions (trial occupations) in which they begin to learn behaviors related to the work role. Such experimentation may begin in high school, or even earlier, is referred to as the *trial work period*, and may be very unstable (Havighurst, 1982).

Grotevant and Cooper (1988) have discussed the central role the family plays in helping an adolescent to choose a career. Parents can serve as models for career choices, and their work attitudes and behaviors can exert a powerful influence on career choices. It is worth noting, however, that when new or interesting career paths are opened to students in high school, their parents' career development may be influenced as well!

Family influence and individual factors such as self-esteem and perceived ability must also be understood in light of cultural influences. Cultural attitudes and expectations varying by gender, socioeconomic status, or ethnicity may well modify the family's influence on an adolescent's choice of career (Grotevant & Cooper, 1988). In addition, historical changes in what careers are "hot" influence occupational choice. For example, engineering and teaching have been desirable at different times in the past 20 years, while social service and high-tech careers are highly sought after at present.

As an individual's self-concept becomes more definite, he or she begins to move toward a specific occupational choice and enters the establishment stage. This usually occurs during young adulthood and is characterized by stability in occupation, productivity, and advancement. Although individuals may change jobs or positions, they rarely change vocations. Also during this stage, greater congruence is achieved between the individual's self-concept and occupational role.

Following the establishment stage is a period of transition that usually occurs during late middle adulthood (ages 45 to 55 years), called the maintenance stage. This is the time when individuals prepare to decrease their occupational activity, since they either feel they have already attained their occupational goals or realize they will never attain these goals. This is referred to as a career "plateau," and it means maintaining but no longer striving and achieving. People in this situation are occupationally stable, yet they may be frustrated by the realization that some of their goals are unattainable.

By the mid-fifties, individuals begin to enter the deceleration stage, during which they begin to prepare for retirement, more actively consider what leisure activities are important to them, and begin to separate themselves from the job. This period is quite difficult for those to whom work has been the most important part of their lives.

Finally, there is the retirement stage, in which individuals formally divorce themselves from the work role.

Ginzberg Another life-span theory of occupational choice is that of Ginzberg (1971). Ginzberg's theory also suggests that individuals progress through a series of occupational periods or stages. In this case, there are three stages: the fantasy period, tentative period, and realistic period. This theory integrates personal interests, values, and abilities as all being important in occupational choice.

Since the fantasy and tentative periods correspond to childhood and adolescence, respectively, they will not be addressed in detail here. The realistic period corresponds to the period between age 17 and the end of young adulthood, but Ginzberg believes the process of occupational choice and development is actually life-long and open-ended, where the individual constantly reaches compromises in occupational selection based on external factors such as job requirements, educational opportunities, and certain personal factors such as abilities and interests.

CAREER PATTERNS AMONG MEN AND WOMEN

While we have defined careers as more or less stable, in reality stability is only an ideal. As early as 1951, Miller and Form (see Havighurst, 1982) identified several career patterns for men varying in terms of orderliness or stability. These are as follows:

1. *Conventional*—a typical career path from trial (trying out several jobs) to stable employment; characteristic of managerial, skilled, and clerical workers
2. *Stable*—common among professionals (e.g., managers, physicians, dentists, lawyers, and college professors), whether one goes directly from college or graduate school to a profession
3. *Unstable*—characterized by trial-stable-trial career patterns; common among domestic, semiskilled, and clerical workers
4. *Multiple-trial*—characterized by frequent job changes, with no one job type predominant; also characteristic of clerical, semiskilled, and domestic workers

While most (73%) white-collar workers had stable or conventional career patterns, only 46 percent of blue-collar and 29 percent of unskilled workers had stable or conventional work histories (Miller & Form, 1951). The occupations defining these patterns most likely have changed, and the number of people in each has (and will) changed, but there is little reason to believe that the patterns themselves have changed.

Slocum and Cron (1985) found that, in a sample of nearly 700 salespeople aged 21 to 60, the distinct career phases of trial, stabilization, and maintenance did seem to exist, in part supporting the career paths for men discussed above.

Women's Career Development Attention to women's occupational development is comparatively recent (Fitzgerald & Betz, 1983). This is due to previous assumptions that (1) a woman's primary roles were as housewife and mother, and (2) career concerns were important primarily only to single women. The process of career development is more complex for women than for men because of the differences in socialization and in the combination of attitudes, role expectation, behavior, and sanctions that constitute it (Diamond, 1988).

Societal values about men's and women's roles have changed, as has the diversity among women's career patterns. Fitzgerald and Betz (1983) suggest that, because women may not have the variety of career choices open to men and often are not able to fulfill their goals, theories of occupational development based on men simply do not fit women. For example, a woman may have to decide whether she even wants to pursue a career, a choice that most men do not have to make. She may also feel pressure to choose between a career and being a mother or wife, again a choice that few men must make. While cultural shifts in career opportunities seem to influence women's career development, that of men is most influenced by their parents' career aspirations for them (King, 1989).

A comparatively recent model of women's career development is that of Astin (1984). Astin bases her approach to women's vocational choice on motivation for a career, such as needs for pleasure, survival, or contribution; expectations concerning alternative forms of work to satisfy her needs; sex-role socialization (family vs. work), and perceived opportunities in the work world (i.e., discrimination, job distribution, and economic constraints).

Astin's (1984) career model for women has been criticized as giving too little attention to individual differences and the force of the Women's Movement as factors in career choice (Fitzgerald & Betz, 1983). For example, Osipow (1983) suggests that career-oriented women have higher achievement needs, while homemakers have higher needs for acceptance and affection. Also, in addition to ability, attitude toward sex roles (work versus family), confidence in making decisions, and tendency to engage in solving mathematics problems have all been found to predict career choice (Fassinger, 1990).

The topic of career patterns in women has naturally been of interest as women's roles have changed and more women have entered the work force, often in positions earlier thought to be appropriate for men (Havighurst, 1982). Although they still lag behind men in earnings, fewer women are unemployed, and more women are pursuing chosen careers (Harmon, 1983: Havighurst, 1982).

Women's career paths appear to be more complex than those of men. Wolfson (1976) studied the career patterns of college women and found that seven patterns emerged, varying along the dimension of span of participation (high, medium, or low), degree of participation (male- versus female-dominated occupations), and employment history (never worked or employed). More recently, Betz (1984) followed up with nearly 500 college women 10 years after graduation, classifying them as:

1. Never worked
2. Low career commitment, traditional occupation
3. Low career commitment, pioneer (nontraditional)
4. Moderate career commitment, traditional
5. Moderate career commitment, pioneer

6. High career commitment, traditional
7. High career commitment, pioneer

Betz found that most women (about two-thirds) were highly committed to their careers and that about 70 percent were employed in traditionally female occupations. Most had worked continuously since graduation, and only 1 percent had been full-time homemakers over the 10-year period. Most (79%) had successfully combined careers and homemaking. Women in traditional careers, however, were less likely to change careers and more likely to make downward (horizontal) career shifts than were pioneer women. Older women were more likely never to have worked. Relative to earlier studies, Betz found that nontraditional career patterns, considered "unusual" earlier, were no longer seen this way. This study supports the optimistic yet varied picture that women's careers are taking.

While women's careers vary over time, they do so in a way that is different from men. Moreover, women's commitment to their employers, feelings about changing jobs, and desire for promotion all vary by age (Arnstein & Isabella, 1990). For example, while job satisfaction does not vary by age, the intention to change jobs is greatest for women in their late teens, early twenties, and early thirties. For women over 45, desire for promotion is lowest. Thus, while stage theories of career development, such as Super's, may hold up for men, they do not relate to women equally well (Ornstein & Isabella, 1990).

Women now define their lives in terms of home, career, and continued education. Despite discrimination, the demands of dual-career marriages, and less income, they seem to be highly committed to their chosen career paths. Some women may experience what is termed *multiple-role strain* due to stress from their various roles (Repetti et al., 1989). That is, stress arises when the demands of one role (e.g., worker) interfere with the fulfillment of another role (mother). Multiple-role strain is greatest for mothers of young children, those employed full-time, and married women whose husbands contribute relatively little to household labor and child care. Also, Greenglass (1988) found that women experienced greater job stress than men in similar managerial positions. As interest in women's career development continues to grow, research will explore more fully the process in career decision-making for women (Osipow, 1983).

The Women's Movement The Women's Movement has contributed greatly to the diversity we see in women's career paths. Harmon (1989) studied two groups of women, those who were 18 in 1968 who were reassessed at age 30 in 1981, and a separate group of 18-year-olds in 1983. College freshmen and adult women of the 1980s were similar in terms of their career aspirations, and were more specific than those in 1968 regarding desirable occupations. Historical changes in women's roles seem to have produced women who are more aware of the need for women to be employed and who are more likely to consider nontraditional careers than their age peers in the 1960s.

Jenkins (1989) found that, among both college-bound and business-oriented women, a substantial number (59–72%) experienced major changes in their careers over a 14-year period. For some, for example non-college teachers, involvement with family became more important, while others (professors, businesswomen) were more involved in being successful and in managing their careers.

Tangri and Jenkins (1992) found that three major women's career types could be described: *role innovators, traditionals,* and *moderates.* Role innovators came from more privileged backgrounds, and were the most autonomous and individualistic. They seemed to be the most highly motivated to do their very best in their careers. They also had the most doubts about their ability to succeed and their identity, having made more ambiguous and difficult academic choices. Traditionals were more likely to displace their concerns about achievement onto their husbands, to choose people-oriented occupations, and to feel confident about their ability to succeed in a career. However, although their careers should promise security, they should not interfere with running a household or raising children. Over the 14-year period (1967–1981), four career trajectories were found: (1) those that were continuously role-innovative, (2) those that were continuously traditional, (3) those that became more role-innovative over time, and (4) those that became more traditional over time.

Diversity and flexibility in career choice are important for both men and women, whether one's career is homemaking or management. Reflecting this approach, Chiswick (1982) has calculated the market value of a homemaker's time on a par with her peers employed outside the home.

Havighurst (1982) advocates **flexible careers,** where people actually change careers, for a small number of people in middle adulthood and prior to retirement. As individuals age, employers might utilize such people's experience in different positions in the event that pregnancy, physical/sensory changes, or health problems prevent them from doing the jobs they held for many years. Such flexibility could be beneficial for both employee and employer.

OCCUPATIONAL DEVELOPMENTAL TASKS

Havighurst (1982) suggests that there are distinct **occupational developmental tasks,** similar to those espoused by life-stage theorists such as Holland and Ginzberg. The first of these development tasks is preparing for an occupational career (adolescence), perhaps by entering an apprenticeship or attending a specific vocational training school or university. While many test their ability to function independently of their parents at this point, others may hold various part-time jobs or simply remain unemployed. Depending on the marketplace, specific job skills needed, or availability of career options, the "right way to go" is clearer for some people than it is for others.

Even for college-bound middle-class individuals, especially for women, career options may be narrow or individuals may suffer from **ca-**

reer indecision (Holland & Holland, 1977; Solomone, 1982). They may vacillate between alternatives, refuse to seek out new information, or make no commitment at all. While some colleges may forbid students to commit themselves to a given major until after they have completed two years of course work, which contributes to career indecision, individual personality characteristics such as indecisiveness, fear of success, anxiety, submissiveness or dependency, or the tendency to avoid risks may also foster it. Dysfunctional family relationships may also influence (and be influenced by) career indecision (Lopez, 1983). Career indecision is also affected by sex-role stereotypes, pressures from a family or spouse to "get established," or subcultural—that is, racial or socioeconomic—norms regarding "adulthood." For young adults who are making career choices, greater confidence seems to relate to less career indecision and greater feelings of mastery and control (Taylor & Popma, 1990).

Ironically, once one has invested in a given career path, these same factors may prevent an individual from switching careers. Many people need a period of *moratorium* (Erikson, 1963; Marcia, 1966) to allow themselves to find out what occupational path is best for them. Many times we feel pressure to become instant successes. Perhaps to avoid failing to please others, we pursue what our parents did. Marcia (1966) calls this pattern a *foreclosed* one. In other words, there are a great number of pushes and pulls to decide, or not to decide, on a given occupation at this point in our lives. Later on, similar choices may confront us when our wives or husbands decide to switch careers, return to school, retire early, or not to retire at all. Thus, career indecision applies to all phases of the occupational cycle. Different cohorts of individuals, based on distinct occupational histories and patterns of occupational socialization, may be more or less prone to such indecision (Gordon, 1981). Thus, Crites (1981) found the percentage of "undecided" occupations to vary between 5 and 61 percent over a span of 50 years.

Havighurst's second occupational developmental task is getting started in an occupation. People in this phase are learning the ropes, so to speak. They are being socialized into the job role regarding what skills they are expected to maintain or develop, how they are expected to dress, how much time they are to spend at working, as well as how they are to relate to peers and people in positions of authority (Newman & Newman, 1986). Depending on how realistic their preconceptions about a career are, they may experience a certain degree of "reality shock." Things may not be as they expected them to be!

If one's job is embedded in a career pattern, is subject to the obsolescence of skills, or is highly complex and technical, this may influence whether more time and effort will be needed to devote to this occupational phase. This time and effort is often to the detriment of one's relationships with a spouse, children, or friends. Consequently, such decisions, while occupationally justifiable, may nevertheless have repercussions, ranging from problems with one's health to emotional difficulties.

These same conflicts may reemerge when a woman decides to enter or return to the work world, forcing her to balance the demands of work and family. Two-career couples must balance their available time with work-task demands and minimize work-role conflicts if family conflict is to be avoided (Greenhaus et al., 1989). Jobs that are varied and/or permit some autonomy seem to produce less stress between partners. However, work roles that are ambiguous, overly taxing, or conflicting lead to more interpersonal conflict, tension, stress, and fatigue (Greenhaus et al., 1989). Even when both partners work, the responsibility for housework, marriage, and parenthood unfortunately continues to rest with women. Men are still seen as primarily responsible for earning income (Thompson & Walker, 1989).

For women, commitment to a career may be influenced by factors such as stability of the marriage, whether she and her husband jointly planned their careers, and if she earned 20 percent more than her husband (Steffy & Jones, 1988). Moreover, whether she had developed coping skills to deal with multiple role demands and whether she had support from relatives who lived close by also influenced a woman's career commitment (Steffy & Jones, 1988). Women who are dedicated to their careers are able to allocate their energy, withdrawing from community activities to deal with the demands of work, parenting, and marriage. Indeed, the challenges dual-career couples face underscore the delicate relationship between work and family (see Chapter 7).

Havighurst (1982) suggests that the third occupational developmental task is reaching and maintaining satisfactory performance in one's occupational career, which applies mostly to people in middle adulthood.

Osipow et al. (1985) feel that the pressures of work and one's response to these pressures varies across the life span. Such pressures, of course, affect work performance. These researchers studied over 300 employed men and women in five age ranges: below 25, 25 to 34, 35 to 44, 45 to 54, and 55+. While gender did not influence occupational stress, strain, or coping, younger people under 25 experienced the most psychological and interpersonal strain. For people over 25, strain in general declined consistently with age. Perhaps older people are better at coping with strain or have left jobs that are stressful. Younger people also reported distinct types of stresses at work, such as having unchallenging work, experiencing conflict between the values or objectives of different people at work, or being in an aversive physical environment. Older people reported that work overload and being responsible for others at work were more stressful to them. With increased age, people tended to change coping styles to those that were more effective, such as recreation, better self-care, and more effective use of time. With increased age, people also made better use of social support to cope with job stress.

Changing Careers in Mid-life

The above research does not single out middle adulthood as a time of **career crisis** (see Costa & McCrae, 1980a). Yet, middle-aged individuals seem to be most vulnerable to **job loss** (Lajer, 1982). Murphy and Burck (1976) have suggested that middle adulthood can be especially pivotal occupationally. Rather than being upwardly mobile, some individuals seem to focus on the stable, fulfilling aspects of their careers (Levinson, 1978). For others, the mid-career phase is a largely negative one, characterized by dissatisfaction and restlessness followed by a stable period; this is presumably based on the notion of a male mid-life crisis (Osipow, 1983).

Costa and McCrae (1980a) found little evidence for mid-life career disruption. Some people do not experience a crisis or even a period of occupational transition; and there are individual differences in how people respond to dissatisfaction if it is experienced at all. Given that career development cannot be understood in isolation from the rest of life, emphasis on the inevitability of mid-career crisis seems an oversimplification.

However, some people do change careers in middle adulthood. Such changes may be **horizontal,** from one career to another, or **vertical,** to a higher level of responsibility (Osipow, 1983). Many people experience several vertical career changes in their lives. Both types of changes come about for a variety of reasons (Driskel & Duaw, 1975; Heddescheimer, 1976; Wright & Hamilton, 1978). Family changes such as divorce, widowhood, adult children leaving home; a desire for more income, status, or security; philosophical differences with one's employer; and dissatisfaction with how one's skills are used are common reasons for career changes.

Individuals who hold jobs that are less responsive to economic changes or more complex, and those who have been in a career for many years are less likely to change careers (Gold, 1979; Gottsfredson, 1977). By contrast, Vaitenas and Weiner (1977) found that such factors as lack of interest, incongruity with one's occupation, lack of consistent and diversified interests, fear of failure, or history of emotional problems—but not age—predicted career change. This suggests that some people are more likely to change careers than others, whether or not such changes occur in middle adulthood. At present, it clearly would be premature and inaccurate to state that mid-life is necessarily a period of occupational upheaval for men.

While studies of women in mid-life are comparatively rare, Abush and Burkhead (1984) found that a Type A personality, relatively little autonomy and feedback at work, less significance in one's job, and fewer friendships were all associated with greater job stress. While the empty nest may be an important stressor for some women, it is not a universal one that relates to job dissatisfaction or personal unhappiness (Black & Hill, 1984). Eadwins and Mellinger (1984) found that personality characteristics, such as affiliation, maturity, or locus of control, influence job stress among different role groups of women aged 30 to 55, but age was not correlated with job stress in this study. As is the case for men, there appears to be little evidence for a mid-life occupational crisis in women.

The Loss of One's Job

Almost 11 million people lost their jobs between 1981 and 1988 (Fraze, 1988). Changes in our economy brought about by inflation, competition within industries, or undercutting (regarding price or quality of products) of industries in the United States by countries such as Japan or China can

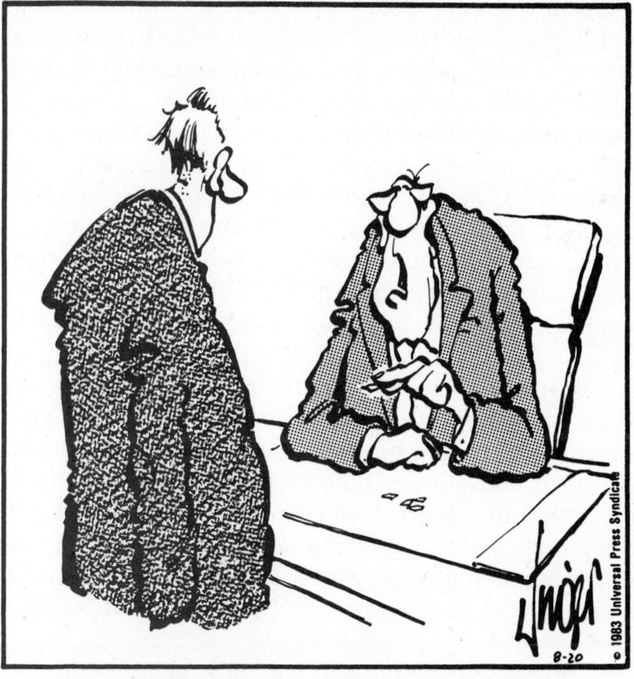

"I'm sorry, Wilson. After 16 years of loyal service, you're being replaced by this microchip."

Source: HERMAN by Jim Unger, *Charleston Times-Courier* (1983, August 20). HERMAN copyright 1983 Universal Press Syndicate. Reprinted by permission. All rights reserved.

disrupt careers, even those that are stable. College professors, middle-level managers, and research scientists can find themselves unemployed or laid off indefinitely just as easily as those who are not formally trained or who hold blue-collar skilled or semiskilled positions. In any event, loss of self-esteem, feelings of alienation and depression, family discord and abuse, alcoholism, and, in some situations, even suicide are the result of such unforeseen "wrinkles" in people's careers. Many individuals even feel they are responsible for losing their jobs, contributing to depression and feelings of failure.

DeFrank and Ivancevich (1986) suggest that the personal impact of job loss and/or unemployment on individuals can be quite debilitating: declines in physical health and self-esteem, depression, anxiety, or suicide. Moreover, job loss has potential psychological, economic, and social effects on all members of the family (McLloyd, 1989). Estes and Wilensky (1978) found that these effects are a function of resulting financial stress and stage of the family life cycle (Duvall, 1971). More specifically, childless couples and couples with school-age children suffered the most. In contrast, morale was higher when children were independent, had left home, or when the couple was alone again. These couples probably had more social support from their adult children. Lajer (1982) found that individuals were at greater risk for admission to a psychiatric unit if they were older than 45 and/or had been unemployed for a longer period of time (e.g., 1 year).

According to DeFrank and Ivancevich (1986), many factors influence individuals' responses to the loss of their jobs. While loss of a job means loss of both income and status, age is a more important predictor of responses to job loss, with middle-aged men being more vulnerable than older or younger men. In addition, how people perceive this loss, their degree of social support, their existing coping skills, and how long they are unemployed all contribute to how they respond to job loss (Mallinckrodt & Fretz, 1988).

While job loss does not seem to be particularly devastating for young individuals, it can contribute to criminal behavior (Allen & Staffensmeir, 1989). Yet, at least efforts can be made to seek another position.

For most middle-aged and older people who lose their jobs, life is disrupted in many ways (Kuhert, 1989). If we can understand what it is about working and not working (e.g., returning to school or retiring) that has an impact, as well as determine what outcomes individuals expect in each case, long-term damage from job loss can be minimized (Kinicki, 1989).

For older, poorly educated persons who have low self-esteem, job loss seems to be most devastating; they also have the lowest expectation of finding a new job (Kinicki, 1989). Merriam (1987), however, surveyed over 200 workers aged 20 to 65 who had lost their jobs regarding their expectations of being retrained in a new job-skills program. Middle-aged participants were especially concerned about their ability to do the work, felt they were too old, and found retraining more difficult than they expected. In contrast, people aged 50 and above found the learning more meaningful to them personally. This suggests that middle-aged people's job-related expectations are most severely affected by job loss.

When people lose their jobs, they must find ways of reorganizing their nonwork lives, assessing themselves realistically yet positively. Ultimately, they must distance themselves from the job loss and remind themselves that there is more to life than work (Kinicki & Latack, 1990).

Those who are left behind at work are not untouched, either. If people feel they have been able to express their opinions about decisions being made at work, they are more likely to survive someone else's job loss and see the decision (e.g., a layoff) as a fair one (Davy et al., 1990). If they feel otherwise, they generally end up liking their jobs less and are more likely to consider quitting or changing jobs (Davy et al., 1990).

The last major occupational developmental task is adjusting to retirement and reduced income (Havighurst, 1982). Health or other physical changes may force some people to consider retirement, but, in any case, retirement has varying effects on individuals, depending on their motives for and satisfaction with their work, relationship with their spouse (Brubaker, 1983), and attitude toward retirement (Glamser, 1976, 1981). We will discuss retirement in more depth shortly.

We have emphasized that occupational development must be viewed as a lifelong process and as one influenced by cultural, familial, and individual factors. As noted above, most theories of career development are limited because they focus primarily on men. Although statistics indicate that over 50 percent of women between the ages of 16 and 64 are currently in the work force, they suffer discrimination on the job, as reflected in discrepancies in their pay compared to men performing the same job (*Sex Equity in Education Bulletin,* 1983). Furthermore, the largest group of individuals now entering the work force are women over 40 years of age and married women with young children.

Since our occupation and work roles are related to our self-concept, identity, and friendship patterns, there is an obvious need to study in greater detail the processes involved in career decision-making—and career indecision—particularly among those who have not attended college. We often make career choices by accident or impulse, on the basis of inaccurate information, or due to pressure to make a decision—any decision. In order to deal with such problems, school systems, colleges, and state and local agencies are implementing career-planning programs for people of varying ages. These programs can be quite successful in facilitating appropriate career decision-making for individuals at all age levels. For example, Franklin-Panek (1978) found that participation in a career life-span planning program could increase both self-concept and career decision-making ability in adults. Stonewater and Daniels (1983) have developed a career decision-making course for students, also reporting much success. Fountain (1986) and Baxter (1986) have developed specific modules for use in the classroom to aid individuals in understanding the economics of the labor market, the economy, and career choice.

INDUSTRIAL GERONTOLOGY

The United States and other industrialized nations are currently experiencing what is called the **"graying" of the American work force.** Due to economic factors, increased longevity, and federal legislation, more individuals are remaining in the work force for a longer time than before. In the years between 1985 and 2000, the number of workers between the ages of 45 and 65 is expected to grow by 41 percent, whereas the number in the 16-to-35 age group will decline slightly (Johnston, 1987). By the end of this century, the median age of the labor force will increase from about age 36 to age 39 (*Report of the Secretary of Labor,* 1989). For these reasons, business and industry would do well to consider the needs and abilities of the older worker as important (Johnson & Johnson, 1982; Meier & Kerr, 1976; Rhodes, 1983).

The study of the older worker is referred to as *industrial gerontology.* Our goal will be to make you aware of attitudes in business and industry towards the older worker, to summarize the literature regarding the abilities of older workers, and to present some suggestions for dealing with older workers.

Who is the older worker? According to the Work in America Institute (1980), the United States Bureau of Labor Statistics considers anyone, regardless of occupation, aged 55 years or above to be an **older worker,** describing those between the ages of 25 and 54 as **prime age** (Sheppard & Rix, 1977). However, the term *older worker* is often applied at age 40 (Barnes-Farrell, 1983). It should be noted that this designation is a general one and varies substantially from one occupation to another. For instance, 35 may be considered old for a professional athlete but relatively young for a surgeon.

Discrimination Against Older Workers

Business and industry, as well as many younger workers, have numerous negative attitudes and stereotyped images of older workers. They are often characterized as (1) less productive than younger workers, (2) slow doers, slow thinkers, slow to adjust to change compared to younger workers, (3) lacking physical strength and endurance, (4) set in their ways and more stubborn, (5) difficult to train and slow to learn, (6) lacking drive and imagination, (7) having less education, and (8) having learned to get by with less effort. The most widely accepted negative stereotype of the older worker is that job productivity and performance decline with age (Rhodes, 1983; Sparrow & Davies, 1988). Many of these negative beliefs are unfounded and generally stem from lack of knowledge and understanding about the aging process.

Because of this age bias, individuals tend to "age-type" occupations, and this age classification is strongly influenced by job level (Barnes-Farrell, 1983). It is also affected by the number of older people who apply for a particular job (Cleveland et al., 1988). Occupations that require a high

BOX 9.1

CHANGES IN WOMEN'S EMPLOYMENT

Early in America's history, women worked long, hard hours, primarily within their own homes or farms. By the turn of this century, around 20 percent of women were working outside the home. However, these women were usually single or widowed, and very few were in career paths. During World War II, many women were recruited into the work force due to the shortage of men. Since World War II, the numbers of working women have continued to increase. Labor force participation for women between the ages of 29 and 64 was approximately 20 percent in 1900, 30 percent in 1940, 67 percent in 1988, and is expected to be 80 percent by the year 2000.

As more and more women enter the labor force, they will be exposed to factors in the workplace that require adaptation and adjustment. To the extent that these work-related factors will be perceived as stressful, it has been predicted that stress-related illnesses such as coronary heart disease will increase, perhaps approximating the rates for men.

Source: Adapted from: Matthews, K.A. & Rodin, J. (1989). Women's changing work roles: Impact on health, family, and public policy. *American Psychologist, 44,* 1389–1393.

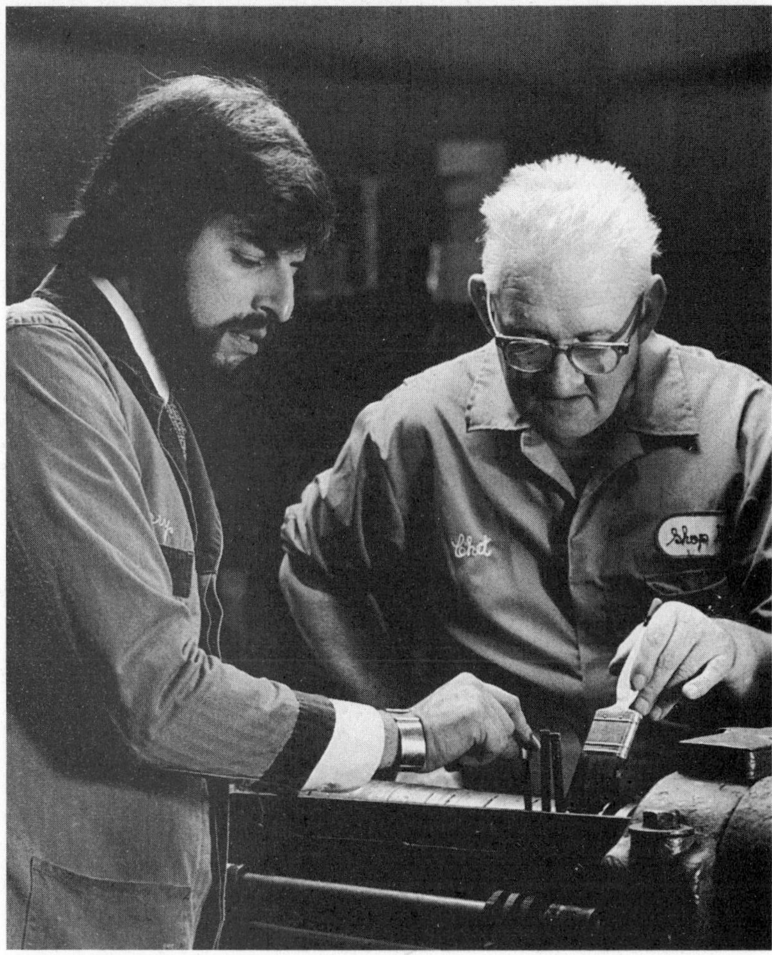

In many job situations, performance remains unaffected by age. The older employee has many skills that can be relied upon and taught to younger, less experienced workers.

degree of training and experience such as dentist, college professor, and physician, are generally associated with being older.

Ageism in Employment

Before we examine the truth of the above assumptions, it is important to realize that implicit and explicit **ageism in employment** occurs for both sexes in all types of jobs, though it is against the law (Rosen & Jerdee, 1976; Sheppard, 1976). Indeed, complaints about age discrimination on the job filed with the Equal Opportunity Commission doubled from 1981 to 1987, according to the American Association of Retired Persons in 1991. For older minorities, employment problems are especially severe (Freeman & Williams, 1987). Ageism refers to the process of systematic stereotyping of and

BOX 9.2

STUDY CHALLENGES FIRMS' POLICIES ON OLDER WORKERS

MIAMI BEACH, Fla. (AP)—Long-held beliefs that older workers are harder to train, cost more, are inflexible and don't work as efficiently are wrong, according to a study released recently about employees 55 and older.

The Commonwealth Fund, a philanthropic foundation which commissioned the report, noted that its economic findings challenged conventional corporate wisdom and policies.

"Until now, corporations have had to make policies about older workers based on hunches and impressions," said Thomas Moloney, the foundation's senior vice president. "These studies for the first time provide numerical results from real companies that have hired older workers."

Consultants examined the success of programs emphasizing older workers at Days Inns of America Inc., The Travelers Corp. and B&Q PLC, Britain's largest home-improvement store chain.

"The interesting thing about the three case studies is that in no instance were these companies motivated by compassion or social justice," Moloney said. "These were motivated by profitability and the availability of skilled workers."

At Days Inns, older workers in the company's 24-hour computerized telephone reservation center in Atlanta were trained in the same time as younger workers, cost much less to train over time because of significantly lower turnover and generated more bookings, the report said.

At Travelers, an in-house job-bank set up to replace temporary hires saved $871,000 in one year, capitalized on company familiarity and improved morale by conveying the idea that the company takes care of it own, the study found.

B&Q was confronted with complaints that younger employees often showed little interest in customer contact and had little product knowledge. But store managers initially thought older workers couldn't do the job.

When a new store was staffed entirely by workers 50 and older, profits were 18 percent higher, turnover nearly six times lower, absenteeism 39 percent less and losses to theft and damage less than half than that at five comparison stores, the report said.

The older workers at Days Inns worked all three shifts, and employees at the B&Q store in Macclesfield, England, worked an average of eight overtime hours a month.

Changing demographics and the aging of American society already are encouraging employers to look to older workers to fill some voids.

"Let's all hope that the labor-force shortages materialize," Moloney said. "It's how society defines who's too old to work."

Pressure to find skilled workers will make age discrimination the issue of the '90s as sex discrimination was in the '70s and racial discrimination in the '60s, he predicted.

"Managers will no longer be able to afford to discriminate against competent, skilled older Americans," Moloney said. "A marketplace that's been trained to believe older workers are of little value" will be forced to re-evaluate its attitudes.

Source: The Advocate, Newark, Ohio, Tuesday, June 4, 1991, page 11.

discrimination against people because they are old, just as racism and sexism do on the basis of skin color and gender (Butler, 1969).

Avolio and Barrett (1987) found evidence for ageism in a simulated interview even when it was made explicit that the young and old job applicants were equally qualified. Similarly, Craft et al. (1979) reported that, in a simulated hiring study, managers evaluating résumés believed older candidates to be more likely to be opinionated, less serious, and less ambitious.

The unemployment rate for adult males 55 to 64 years of age is higher than for those aged 25 to 54 years, a trend that has been common for the past 20 years (Barrow & Smith, 1983). Moreover, once out of work, older workers are likely to remain unemployed much longer than younger workers (Quinn & Burkhauser, 1990). When reemployed, they often find jobs at lower pay, requiring less skill, and at lower occupational levels (Barnes-Farrell, 1983; Love & Torrence, 1989).

Sheppard (1976) studied laid-off professional men, engineers, and scientists and found age to be the most significant variable related to employment status. Wachtel (1966) studied 2000 hard-core unemployed individuals in Detroit and found age to be the major reason for their unemployment. In a study of the impact of a plant closing and subsequent move, Love and Torrence (1989) found the median length of unemployment for those age 55 and over to be 27 weeks, compared to 13 weeks for workers under age 45.

Since older adults experience more prolonged unemployment, they are also more likely to become discouraged and drop out of the work force altogether (Hansson et al., 1990). Discouraged unemployed older workers are different in many ways from unemployed older workers who are actively searching for a job. Discouraged unemployed older workers tend to have significantly lower job-search self-efficacy expectations, more disorderly work histories, longer periods of current unemployment, and higher reported levels of depression, social isolation, and psychological discouragement (Rife & Kilty, 1989–90).

Older workers tend to be laid off or unemployed earlier than younger workers, and there are several reasons for this. First, due to the fact that they have seniority, they tend to remain in declining industries and occupations until the jobs finally disappear as a result of economic or technological change (Johnson & Johnson, 1982). A good example is the U.S. automotive industry, which suffered dramatically during the late 1970s. At this time, there were many layoffs and plant closings. When the plants reopened, many of the assembly-line positions no longer existed, having been replaced by industrial robots. Second, older workers tend to have lower levels of formal education and, therefore, are excluded from positions with higher requirements. Third, they have less mobility, due to greater responsibilities and obligations, compared to younger workers (Johnson & Johnson, 1982). Finally, they have less well-developed job-seeking attitudes and skills compared to younger workers, due to the fact that they may not have interviewed for a job in 10 or 15 years (Johnson & Johnson, 1982). Contributing to the problem is that many current personnel selection tests and interview procedures may be unfairly discriminating against older job applicants (Arvey & Mussio, 1973; Salvendy, 1974; Stagner, 1985). Selection tests may not have norms for older workers, or may measure abilities that decline with age but have nothing to do with actual job performance (Stagner, 1985).

Discrimination against workers as a function of age may even begin at age 30 in some occupations. In a widely publicized incident that occurred in 1983, a woman aged 38 brought a lawsuit against a television station at which she was co-anchor of the news. She was apparently demoted because some viewers considered her "too old."

AGE DISCRIMINATION IN EMPLOYMENT ACT (ADEA)

The problem of age discrimination was so severe that federal laws had to be enacted to prohibit it. The legislation was titled the **Age Discrimination in Employment Act (ADEA),** and it was originally passed in 1967 but amended in 1974 and 1978 to provide more comprehensive coverage. This legislation protects workers between the ages of 40 and 70 years and prohibits: (1) failing to hire someone between 40 and 70 years because of age, (2) discharging a person because of age, (3) discriminating in pay or benefits because of age, (4) limiting or classifying an individual to his or her disadvantage because of age, (5) instructing an employment agency not to refer someone to a job, or to only certain kinds of jobs, because of age, and (6) placing any advertisements that show preference based on age or specify an age bracket. However, this legislation is not universal; it does not cover all employees in all occupational settings. Exempt from this legislation are the federal government, employers of less than 20 people, and jobs where age is a **bona fide occupational qualification (BFOQ).** Overall, although age discrimination is against the law, it still exists today.

ADULTS SPEAK

AGE DISCRIMINATION IN THE WORKPLACE: ONE MAN'S STORY

Vic is 59 years old. He is married, and has two children and three grandchildren. He is unassuming and pleasant to be around, and works extremely well with people. After getting out of school, he worked for over 20 years in the computer hardware and software industry, installing, scheduling, and maintaining systems. After working for Xerox for 12 years, he decided to go into business for himself. He acquired a printing business and handled all aspects of computerized billing, graphics, and delivery for over five years.

When the economy worsened in the 1980s, he was forced to sell his business, but his troubles had just begun. He sought work for six months then finally landed a position installing new printing-franchise businesses. He was laid off after six months because he had the least seniority.

Over the next four years, he repeatedly applied for positions for which he was highly qualified and was passed over for someone younger. In many cases, he was more qualified than the individuals with whom he had an initial interview! Once he was told, "With your background and experience, you're more qualified than I am. I bet you could really tell some war stories!" Finally, Vic was forced to accept a position as a car salesman, and eventually worked for the Census Bureau in data processing. One day, he injured his shoulder lifting a box of computer paper, and was awarded a permanent partial disability from the government. After that, he looked for jobs in the computer industry. Many interviews went like this one: "Aren't you Mr. White? Something's come up since we talked earlier today. Just leave your application with receptionist, and we will get back with you." When Vic told the interviewer he had only filled out his name and address and hadn't completed the portion of the application pertaining to his background and training, he was told, "Don't worry, that's not im-

Continued

Research on the Older Worker

Exactly what do we know about older workers? The following is a summary of findings on specific issues involving the older worker.

JOB SATISFACTION

Concerning job satisfaction, there is a positive and linear relationship between age and overall satisfaction until at least 60 (Rhodes, 1983). That is, as age increases, the individual's overall satisfaction with the job increases. Interestingly, this relationship holds for both blue-collar and white-collar jobs, and both males and females.

JOB PERFORMANCE

The crucial issue in industrial gerontology concerns the relationship between age and actual job performance. The general belief in business and industry is that older people in the workplace are less capable, less effi-

continued

portant." When he insisted on telling the interviewer about himself, she went to her desk but refused to sit down, standing as far away from him as she could. When he called later in the week about the position, he was told, "Oh, that was filled by someone more qualified."

In another situation he was told, "Oh, your gray hair won't hurt you here." He was then sent to a subordinate in his thirties, who looked at the résumé and said, "You have some real heavy experience here." He never once asked about any of Vic's previous jobs. He did not get this job either; the company hired someone who was 25. Vic feels that his experience as well as his gray hair caused him to be discriminated against, that he was simply paid "lip service." In many cases, when being interviewed by someone in his own age bracket, it appeared the interviewer felt threatened by his background. In fact, Vic says that "hiring a 25- or 30-year-old made the guy feel safe."

When he applied for a printing managerial position he was told, "You're 58? Well, I guess the best we can count on you for is seven years, right?" The younger man the company hired had to be replaced in 6 months! The last example of age discrimination is when he applied for another position, casually mentioning that he had had an operation within the last six months. After this, things went downhill fast. No questions were asked about the nature of his injury or whether it was work-related. Vic felt that this was an excuse to turn him down because he was older.

He is now, finally, employed in a home-security business monitoring alarms via a computer terminal. Over the past four years, he figures he has been turned down for jobs he was highly qualified for at least 30 times. He was often told, "You're really overqualified for this job. You would be bored and the pay would be an insult to you." Even though Vic really wanted these jobs, he felt that these were simply excuses to reject him because of his age.

Vic concluded by saying, "These years have probably been the worst period of my life. I had lost my mother, then my father. I told a friend one day, 'You really get to the point where you say, is there ever going to be an end to this?' It was a devastating experience."

Many older people, despite having retired, continue to practice their trades with enthusiasm and skill.

cient, and less productive (Stagner, 1985). Does performance really decrease as a function of age? Although this is a most important question, it is difficult to answer and findings often vary as a function of a number of factors, such as type of occupation studied and performance criteria employed. For example, in occupations where physical strength is required for job performance, such as manual labor, older workers may show performance decrements due to changes or declines in physical functioning (see Chapter 3). However, in other occupations, where these abilities are not highly related to successful performance, such as college professor, little age decrement in performance is observed (Sheppard & Rix, 1977).

Although physical strength may decrease with age, most jobs today have physical demands well below the capabilities of most normal aging workers (Meier & Kerr, 1976). Studies of skilled and semiskilled jobs, using data derived from production records, generally fail to show negative relationship between age and performance (Sparrow & Davies, 1988). In fact, the relationship between age and productivity may vary, depending on the way performance is evaluated, whether by supervisors' ratings, production speed, or another method (Waldman & Avolio, 1986). But the belief that job performance declines with age has endured for over 30 years without substantial evidence and support (McEvoy & Cascio, 1989).

As noted in Chapter 4, research is somewhat supportive of an age decrement in performance on tasks where speed is a major component (Panek et al., 1979). The age-speeded performance relationship has been quite difficult to study in real-life situations, for a number of reasons. First, with advancing age and job tenure, individuals tend to be promoted to supervisory positions. Therefore, it is difficult to compare speed of performance of young and old workers on the same job. Second, when older workers are employed in positions where speed is important, they are often able to compensate effectively for any decrease in speed through experience with the job. For example, they may know shortcuts and use more efficient methods of doing their jobs (Johnson & Johnson, 1982). For these reasons, we are unable to generalize from laboratory studies of psychomotor reaction time (see Chapter 4) or job simulations to real-life job performance.

Due to the many confounding factors and the difficulty in developing reliable and valid criteria for job performance, we still know very little that is conclusive regarding the actual relationship between age and speeded job performance. In many industries and occupations, there may be very little or no age-related decline in productivity. Although we have discussed the fact that there are clear age-related changes in physical capacity, certain aspects of cognitive functioning, hearing, vision, and psychomotor speed, it is not yet clear if these changes or decrements actually

BOX 9.3

DOES AGE MAKE A DIFFERENCE TO YOU?

When asked, most of us might state that a person's age makes no difference to us in our personal relationships, but we often "think twice" about older people in specific occupational contexts. Consider the following list of individuals in specific occupations. Ask yourself, "Would I feel differently about this person if I learned that he or she was older than I thought, say, 60, 65, or 70?" If your health or well-being, or that of your family, were "on the line," would you feel safer with someone younger? Honestly evaluating your reactions may make you more aware of your own ageistic biases!

Your family doctor

Your dentist

Your barber or beautician

The person driving the school bus your children take every day

The salesperson or checkout clerk at the store you shop at

Your therapist

The lab technician doing your blood work

The receptionist or secretary in your office

Your surgeon

The airline pilot flying the plane you or your family are on

Your children's teacher

Your pharmacist

Your mechanic

Your lawyer

Your congressional representative

The electrician rewiring your house

The nurse in your doctor's office

The telephone operator taking your message

affect job performance (Barnes-Farrell, 1983). Yet, age discrimination has as its very foundation the belief that because of these changes, the job performance of the older employee must suffer. Unfortunately, overgeneralizations about the relationship between age, specific abilities and skills, and job performance simply strengthen the bias against older employees, who in some cases are as young as 30.

JOB TURNOVER AND ABSENTEEISM

There is a negative relationship between age and job turnover. That is, as age increases, individuals are less likely to leave their current positions (Rhodes, 1983). As for absenteeism, the relationship is partially a function of type of absence—avoidable or unavoidable—and gender. Avoidable absences are those where an employee is absent without prior approval, such as just not showing up for work. Unavoidable absences are those that are due to sickness or accidents.

For males, as age increases, avoidable absences decrease, while for females, the relationship does not change as a function of age (Rhodes, 1983). It is unclear why there are sex differences in the age–avoidable-absence relationship, but one possible explanation centers on the assumption that working females still serve as the primary caretakers of the family. Therefore, when a child is ill or needs to go to the doctor, it may be the mother who misses work to take care of the child.

In terms of unavoidable absences, for males, a higher rate of unavoidable absences occur for younger and older workers. The fewest unavoidable absences occur for middle-aged workers. This might be because younger and older workers tend to have the most time lost due to accidents. For females, the pattern is similar to that for avoidable absences. Although age and work absence are related for men, salary and health insurance costs for older workers in most companies are not higher than those of younger workers (AARP, 1986). Nor is increased age associated with a greater number of accidents or illnesses (Rhodes, 1983).

VALUES, NEEDS, AND JOB PREFERENCES

There seems to be a relationship between an employee's values, needs, and job preferences and job satisfaction, occupational level, and work behavior in numerous settings. Therefore, it is important for management to know if the employee's needs, values, and job preferences change as a function of age.

Regarding the value of work, although findings are somewhat mixed, they tend to support the assumption that older workers have a stronger belief in the **Protestant work ethic** than do younger workers (Aldag & Brief, 1977; Johnson & Johnson, 1982).

In addition, age is positively related to factors such as job satisfaction, job involvement, internal work motivation, and organizational commitment. Furthermore, with increasing age, workers tend to have higher needs for security and affiliation and lower needs for self-actualization and growth (Rhodes, 1983).

Concerning the motivational aspects of pay, older workers value the financial rewards of work more than younger workers (Johnson & Johnson, 1982). In addition, both male and female older workers are motivated more by monetary compensation. Older workers of both sexes often report that they continue to work in order to (1) remain active and engaged, (2) enhance meaningful life experiences, and (3) socialize (Johnson & Johnson, 1982). Regarding the job itself, younger workers often respond very unfavorably to jobs they see lacking in significance or meaning; older workers do not. But older workers do not like jobs with a high degree of complexity.

JOB TRAINING

Due to the fact that we live in a highly technological, rapidly changing world, both on and off the job, training and retraining are important issues for workers of all ages (Sterns & Hayslip, 1990). Although we know that older adults are capable of learning and acquiring new skills, industry, for the most part, has held to the belief that older adults cannot learn or be retrained—"You cannot teach an old dog new tricks" (see Chapters 5 and 6). Reflecting this bias, Parnes and Meyer (1972) found skill obsolescence to be a major factor in the voluntary withdrawal of middle-aged men from the work force.

While there is a noticeable absence of training research on the older worker, those studies that exist do not support the myth that older workers cannot acquire new skills (Meier & Kerr, 1976). Indeed, training is an important mediating variable between age and job performance (Sparrow & Davies, 1988). That is, training can enhance and improve the performance of older workers in some occupations, particularly where experience, judgment, and maturity are important.

The American Association of Retired Persons has developed some excellent suggestions to facilitate the learning and training of older workers (AARP, 1988). These are presented in Box 9.4. The effects of training and retraining older workers will be a rapidly increasing area of interest as the "graying" of the American work force continues.

Capabilities of the Older Worker: Conclusion

We hope this discussion has convinced you that beliefs regarding the older worker, for the most part, are not valid! In fact, as Johnson and Johnson (1982), Rhodes (1983), and Meier and Kerr (1976) suggest, older workers have the work attitudes and behaviors that are valued by business and industry. They have experience, are loyal to the company, and value the work ethic. They are reliable, have good work habits, less absenteeism and turnover, and satisfactory job performance (see Table 9.1). Therefore, it would appear to make sense for industry to actively attempt to recruit and retain older workers, rather than directly or indirectly avoid them.

BOX 9.4

MEETING THE NEEDS OF THE OLDER WORKER

The American Association of Retired Persons (AARP) (1988) advocates retraining mid-career and older employees, based on the philosophy of the aging worker as a resource to the employer. To be used effectively, this resource must be properly conserved and managed, but can yield an employee who is productive and happy on the job throughout his or her career. This is in contrast to the philosophy of the employee as an asset that decreases in value with time. As a result of this philosophy, training older employees is not cost-effective as their value lessens the longer they stay on the job.

Employees who are mid-career and beyond face several problems: (1) career burnout, (2) career plateauing, and (3) career obsolescence. AARP suggests several solutions to each career difficulty:

Problem: Career Burnout
Solutions:

1. Look for signs such as absenteeism, poor job attitudes, lower quality of work, complaints about being overworked
2. Job redesign or rotation
3. Special temporary assignments
4. Reassignment as mentors or trainers
5. Stress-management training

Problem: Career Plateauing
Solutions:

1. Assign projects that use the employee's special skills
2. Give more frequent feedback about performance
3. Provide alternative career paths
4. Provide training and development opportunities

Problem: Career Obsolescence
Solutions:

1. Retrain to sharpen current skills or learn new ones
2. Encourage involvement in professional organizations
3. Encourage continuing professional education to keep up with new developments
4. Establish a career-planning system
5. Encourage older employees to consider career options and career contingency plans
6. Hold career-planning workshops
7. Start a career-information center

In designing a training program, AARP recommends the following:

1. Build a long-range plan. In this way, each employee's skills can be best used and developed so that both employee and company benefit.
2. Use performance appraisals as a source of training and development planning. Knowing what strengths and weaknesses employees have enables an employer to design training to best help each develop new skills or maintain skills that have deteriorated.
3. Survey training needs and develop a list of priorities based on input from employees.
4. Develop flexible ideas about training. Training can be skill-specific, interpersonally-oriented, formal, or informal in nature, and can even involve retirement planning. It might include alternatives to total retirement such as temporary work assignments, part-time work, or consulting.

Source: American Association of Retired Persons (1988). *How to train older workers* (pp. 5–10).

In fact, business and industry are beginning to address the demands of the changing and aging work force. For example, the Volvo plant in Uddevalla, Sweden, is being ergonomically designed to accommodate a work force in which 25 percent will be over age 45 and 40 percent are women; this means that tools must be less demanding physically.

McFarland reports that, during the labor shortages of young men during World War II, it was necessary to reemploy large numbers of retired

TABLE 9.1

ATTITUDES TOWARD OLDER WORKERS

About 400 randomly selected U.S. companies of various sizes were surveyed by the American Association of Retired Persons to find out what the companies rated as "excellent" or "very good" about workers 50 and older. The highlights:

Higher Ratings	**Percent**
Good attendance and punctuality	86
Commitment to quality	82
Loyalty and dedication to company	79
A great deal of practical not just theoretical knowledge	76
Solid experience in job and/or industry	74
Solid/reliable performance record	71
Someone to count on in a crisis	70
Ability to get along with co-workers	60
Emotional stability	59
Lower Ratings	
Physical agility	22
Desire to get ahead	18
Good educational background	17
Ability to learn new skills quickly	17
Feeling comfortable with new technology	10

Source: Dallas Times Herald, May 3, 1991.

older workers in industry (McFarland, 1973). This served as the major impetus for investigations of the capabilities of older workers.

McFarland and others have suggested that instead of judging workers by their chronological age, it is of more value to judge them in terms of *functional age,* that is, in terms of what they can do (see Chapter 1). The concept of functional age has led to attempts to derive measures of functional ability required for each job and to place individuals, regardless of age, in jobs that best match their abilities (Meier & Kerr, 1976).

Although this approach is commendable and makes good sense, research has not been overly supportive of the functional-age approach in industry. The major difficulty is that for the skills investigated, declines or decrements with age are assumed. Individual differences, which we have repeatedly pointed out as important sources of variability in performance and behavior, are overlooked. Furthermore, approaches to functional age have attempted to use a global measure of a person's functional age or ability. This does not take into account different performance levels on different abilities in adulthood. As pointed out in Chapter 1, individuals tend to become more different from one another on many abilities throughout adulthood and old age. For these and other reasons, the courts have generally upheld chronological age as a valid criterion for retirement decisions (Avolio & Panek, 1981).

Despite these difficulties, various alternative strategies have been suggested that may be more helpful. For example, Arthur et al. (1990), using a sample of petroleum-transport drivers, investigated relationships among performance on an information-processing–based test battery, job performance, and age. These researchers found that when age differences in job performance occur, they can be better explained by performance on the information-processing tasks rather than by age per se.

Although there has been an overall shift toward less ageism in employment, attitudes toward older workers among hourly workers and supervisors have shown no improvement in the last 30 years (Bird & Fisher, 1986). Before we give up on changing attitudes toward the older worker, we must realize that these attitudes are multidimensional and influenced by a number of different factors. For example, in an investigation of managerial-skill requirements in the mining industry, Avolio and Waldman (1989) found that ratings of skill importance were correlated with the age of the person being rated, years of experience, and the age of the rater. That is, correlations with rated age varied across different skill dimensions. These findings have implications for fair-employment practices. To the extent that a rater's perceptions of a job are due to factors such as the age of the employee or his or her own age, raters may have difficulty in arriving at fair and appropriate decisions regarding which skills are required for a job.

RETIREMENT

It is quite likely that most of you reading this text will eventually retire, withdrawing from the work force either voluntarily or involuntarily. Since most of us will experience **retirement,** it is important that we be aware of the issues and factors that will affect us at that time, in order to plan appropriately for both the event and the role associated with being retired (Atchley, 1988).

The extent to which we make decisions about retirement as young adults, as in selecting a company with a pension plan or considering its retirement package, suggests that, like career development, retirement is a process. For example, Dobson and Morrow (1984) found that among nonfaculty college employees, career orientation—that is, job satisfaction, work commitment, and endorsing the work ethic—was related to retirement attitudes and retirement planning. Abel and Hayslip (1986), who studied both blue-collar and white-collar industrial workers, obtained the same results. In both studies, age was not related to retirement attitudes.

The process of retirement may begin in early adulthood and have an effect on the retiree, his or her family, and society in general. Our goal is to present the reasons behind retirement from a historical perspective and then to discuss the factors related to the retirement process and its effects on the individual.

Rationales for Retirement

There appear to be two basic rationales for the original development of the concept of retirement. One rationale suggests that it allows individuals to enjoy their remaining years in pursuit of hobbies or leisure activities, after having spent the major portion of their lives producing goods and services for society and/or a particular organization. In this sense, retirement is a thank-you for a job well done.

A second rationale for retirement is that it allows for a constant, predictable, and orderly flow of workers through the work force. Retirement makes possible the replacement of older workers with younger ones who are considered more productive and efficient.

Regardless of one's bias, the fact is that the number of retired individuals has been increasing dramatically in the industrialized nations in the past 100 years. In 1900, approximately 70 percent of American men over age 65 were employed. By 1960, the figure had dropped to 35 percent, and by 1975, to 22 percent. In 1984, only about 11 percent of older adults were still in the work force; and by 1988, this figure had dropped again, to less than 10 percent (AARP, 1990). Interestingly, while labor-force participation has decreased steadily since 1900 for men, the participation rate for women has increased during this same period (Robinson et al., 1985).

Why has the percentage of older adults who are retired continued to increase? A number of factors might explain this trend. First, since the beginning of this century, the United States has progressively shifted from an agricultural to an industrial base (Havighurst, 1982). Moreover, the United States has shifted from a nation where the majority of individuals were self-employed (e.g., as farmers and craftsmen) to one where most people work for others. When individuals were self-employed or involved in a family business, they worked until they died or became disabled. Therefore, the decrease in the number of older adults who are still in the work force is a reflection of the shift in the percentages who work for themselves versus those who work for others.

Second, life expectancy has increased substantially in this century; more individuals are alive to retire today than in previous years. The logic supporting this belief is as follows: Before 1900, very few individuals lived to be 65 years or older. Those who lived longer tended to be those who were in the best health. Therefore, they were able to remain on the job longer. While, with improved health care and medical technology, life expectancy has increased, some (but not all) individuals' abilities and capacities may nevertheless decline in old age. Therefore, although individuals live longer, some are not physically able to continue to work, so they leave the work force. So the decrease in the percentage of older adults in the work force is a reflection of the fact that more individuals are living longer.

The third reason is the continued development of formal retirement systems and pensions, as well as legal factors. Since individuals tend to work to support themselves and their families financially, if no provision is made to do so when they retire, they will continue to work. Note that the United States was one of the last Western industrialized nations to provide retirement benefits for older adults. It wasn't until 1935 that the Social Security Act was passed, mandating that people over 65 who had worked a certain length of time were eligible for benefits. By contrast, some form of retirement system was in place in Germany in 1889 and in the United Kingdom in 1908. Each year, additional financial plans, including pensions, tax shelters, IRAs, and so forth, become available, allowing individuals to prepare for their economic security during retirement. For this reason, more and more individuals are covered under some form of pension or retirement plan, and a greater percentage of individuals are able to leave the work force (Quinn & Burkhauser, 1990).

In addition, since the law specifies at what age one is eligible for retirement benefits, organizations and institutions can then "legally" set mandatory retirement ages and force individuals from the work force when they reach that age.

A fourth reason for the decrease in the number of older workers is increasing productivity due to technological advancements. That is, advanced technology, such as computers and industrial robots, is taking over many of the jobs originally performed by humans. This results in an oversupply of labor in many occupations. Since older workers are often viewed as unproductive, they are considered expendable and are encouraged to retire early. Again, the net result is a decrease in the overall number of older adults in the work force (Robinson et al., 1985).

Finally, during this century, there has been a change in attitudes toward work, the meaning of work, and the support of nonworking members of society (Havighurst, 1982). Individuals have moved farther away from the belief that the major purpose in life is to work and be active. This has been replaced by the belief that the purpose of work is to attain self-actualization and/or obtain the money necessary to pursue other interests. In this light, Havighurst (1982) reports that job satisfaction has declined since 1973, reflecting changing values on the meaning of work. It is interesting to observe that older people are more likely to be self-employed than younger adults, and if an older individual works at all, it is more likely to be on a part-time basis (Quinn & Burkhauser, 1990).

In addition, traditional American philosophy was based on self-sufficiency and independence—taking care of yourself. Gradually, American society has adopted the philosophy that the government has some responsibility for the care and support of its citizens. While early findings suggested that people who retired early did so involuntarily, current data suggest that individuals now do so voluntarily (Quinn & Burkhauser, 1990). In fact, they have more to lose than to gain by continuing to work. Therefore, with successive cohorts, greater percentages of Americans have

BOX 9.5

DO WE WORK TOO HARD?

Many persons are committed to the Protestant Work Ethic which suggests that one must work hard in order to be successful. In contrast, we are bombarded by messages from professionals as well as by the media that say we must enjoy life, relax, and not get too caught up in work.

A study by the Economic Policy Institute in Washington, D.C. suggests that we are losing the battle with work. Compared to two decades ago, the average American worker puts in 140 more hours per year on the job and is less willing to take paid days off. Relative to 20 years ago, paid time off—vacations, sick leave, personal days, and holidays—fell by 15%. Of course, with more expensive health care and housing, all signs of a not-so-rosy economic picture driven by inflation, workers may feel that they must work harder. Yet, they face increasing job stress, fatigue and pressure due to the "joint demands of work and family life." Economists Juliet Schor and Laura Leete-Guy also found that Americans spend more time getting to and from work, adding another 20 hours to the total. This means that we are working nearly a month more per year than we were 20 years ago. Perhaps more than ever, we need to enjoy what little leisure time we have!

Source: Dallas Times Herald, February 24, 1992.

felt that, rather than continue to work to support themselves in old age, they should retire and let others support them through Social Security and pension plans (Quinn & Burkhauser, 1990).

Adjustment to Retirement

The process of postretirement adjustment may be a gradual one, even in the best of circumstances (Ekerdt et al., 1985). Ekerdt et al. (1985) suggest that individuals progress through several phases of retirement adjustment: the *honeymoon* phase, the *disenchantment* phase, and the *stability* or *reorientation* phase. The euphoric honeymoon stage occurs immediately after retirement and lasts roughly six months. Retirees are very enthusiastic and look forward to doing things they have not had time to do. They might begin new projects and look forward to what the future will bring. Often, individuals become very involved in a variety of physical activities such as golf, bowling, tennis, or jogging. In the second phase, disenchantment, 13 to 18 months after retirement, there is less involvement in physical activities, and people experience an emotional letdown. They find that their expectations of retirement have been unrealistic or that they have underestimated the change that retirement brings. In this phase, they also come to terms with the loss of structure that working gave their daily lives. They see less of their working friends, often feel lost or bored, and tend to focus on the past.

This second adjustment phase may be difficult for some men. Cohen and Gans (1978) offer the following example:

> It really doesn't matter whether or not a man enjoyed the work he did for forty years. In fact, he built his existence around it. It was his job that routed him out of bed and forced him to get dressed each morning. It gave him a place

to go and people to see all day. It demanded the biggest part of his time and energy. And it not only defined his importance in the world but also permitted him to feel that he was successfully providing for his family. If a man believes that he *is* what he does for a living, the day he retires may leave him feeling that he no longer exists at all. He has lost any reason to get up and go out of the house five days a week. There are no more familiar people who count on seeing him during the day. His family does not depend on his energy or skills anymore. Social Security benefits and pension funds will provide for his family whether he rises at the crack of dawn or sleeps until noon.

For many elderly men the need to work goes far beyond any thought of a paycheck.

> Peter Hutchinson is a seventy-six-year-old man who in the 1930s turned a small department store into a giant business. It made him a millionaire many times over before he was fifty. If he chose to do so, Peter could spend his retirement in ways that the rest of us can merely fantasize about. Yet every morning he puts on his shirt and tie and takes his place in the office at a desk assigned to the chairman emeritus. Ed, his middle-aged son, actually runs the business and makes all the important decisions. His father's presence is really in no way essential to the company's day-to-day operations. In fact there was a time several years ago when Ed was very close to asking his father to leave altogether, for Peter's way of doing business had long since become obsolete. The decisions he insisted upon making were cutting into the firm's profits. But Ed finally came to the conclusion that his father's sense of well-being was so bound up with the company that it was better to respect his father's feelings and accept what small business losses might result from what he did (pp. 171–172).

Most retired people eventually find activities and life-styles that are satisfying and meaningful.

The last phase, 19 months and up, is characterized by stability, or a reorientation to the day-to-day realities of being retired. In this phase, the retiree finds a predictable and satisfying daily routine and life-style. A new circle of friends is established, and choices and decisions about the future can be made with confidence (Ekerdt et al., 1985).

Preretirement training that is effective should lessen unrealistic expectations of the retirement experience. These unrealistic expectations are likely responsible for the honeymoon and disenchantment phases of adjustment.

Not everyone who retires fully disengages from the work force. Quinn et al. (1990) found that among those who left career jobs, more than one-fourth did something other than retire altogether. Myers (1991) found that there are actually four different postcareer paths: (1) part-time employment on the career job, (2) either part-time or (3) full-time employment on a new job, and (4) full-time retirement. In this study, which path people chose was influenced by economic factors such as existing wealth, pension, and Social Security benefits, as well as the availability of training or job opportunities.

BOX 9.6

JAPANESE LOVE OF WORK A LIFELONG AFFAIR

Older workers in Japan represent the norm rather than the exception. In 1982, 74.9 percent of Japanese men between the ages of 60 and 64 were working, in contrast to 67.5 percent in Great Britain, 56.4 percent in the United States, and 39.7 percent in France. For the age group 65 to 69 years, Japan's labor force includes 38.9 percent of these individuals, compared to the 17.1 percent rate in the United States and single-digit percentages in Great Britain, Germany, and France. These percentages are even more striking due to the fact that more than 95 percent of Japanese firms have a mandatory retirement age of 60 or under.

Despite the prevailing mandatory retirement age in Japan, three out of four Japanese firms rehire retired workers or continue their employment beyond the official retirement age. As a rule, these rehired or retained workers step down from managerial or supervisory positions to posts of lesser responsibility. Japanese employers, with government encouragement, also actively help new retirees search for new jobs if this is necessary.

Japanese employers generally are willing to make work adjustments to maintain older workers' productivity and interest in the job. Approximately 55 percent of firms have a formal policy to help older workers remain healthy and productive through job transfers, reduced working hours, or changes in work operation and physical environment. Many more firms use these measures informally. Changes from demanding jobs such as assembly line work to less physically stressful positions often occur as early as their late forties for Japanese workers.

Toyota, Nissan, and Matsushita Electric (Panasonic) are among the many corporations engaged in job redesigning for an aging labor force. In doing so, employers are responding to current and anticipated labor shortages, government pressure to increase older workers' labor force participation, and the need to heighten morale among workers.

Source: Adapted from Japanese love of work a lifelong affair (1988). *Working Age,* Vol. 3, No. 5, March/April.

Factors Related to the Decision to Retire

It is not easy to state conclusively why people retire; the decision is often a personal one and due to a number of factors. These factors should not be considered independent; many are highly related to each other (Parnes et al., 1985).

Major factors influencing the decision to retire are health, occupational level, financial situation, age, gender, work satisfaction, and personal attitudes. These factors have been separated into personal ones (health, economic situation, attitudes toward work/retirement, and degree of social support) and institutional ones (workplace conditions, employer policy, public policy, economic conditions, and societal values) (Robinson et al., 1985).

HEALTH

One of the most important factors influencing individuals' decisions to retire is their health status (Colsher et al., 1988). In fact, the main reason often given for retiring by both men and women is "poor health" (Sammartino, 1987). Health status plays a very important role both for individuals who are subject to mandatory retirement rules and those who are not. Poor health makes working burdensome and difficult.

As noted in Chapter 3, Type A personalities tend to be stress-prone and to cope with it less well. Assuming that retirement is somewhat stressful, do Type A individuals view retirement positively? Indeed, Type A individuals seem to adjust to both voluntary and involuntary retirement equally well (Swan et al., 1991).

Clark and Spengler (1980) report that there appear to be two types of individuals who choose to retire early (62 years of age or earlier). These are (1) individuals in good health, with financial resources, who desire additional leisure time, and (2) individuals in poor health. Once individuals with poor health retire, they often find that their health affects the plans they had made for themselves for retirement. In some cases, however, their health may improve as they are relieved of the burden and responsibility of working.

While some individuals who retire early due to poor health do so voluntarily, others do so involuntarily (Sammartino, 1987). These people are forced to retire abruptly because they do not have the option of working part-time, or cannot "phase out" of work gradually by reducing the hours they work overtime (Quinn & Burkhauser, 1990). They cannot support themselves on a part-time income because their expenses remain fixed (Quinn & Burkhauser, 1990). Thus, they retire because they have no other alternative.

OCCUPATIONAL LEVEL

An individual's occupational level plays a very important role in the decision to retire, be it voluntarily or due to mandatory retirement policies. As discussed in Chapter 3, occupational level is highly correlated with socioeconomic status and level of education, each of which is related to a number of other factors such as life expectancy and intelligence.

Individuals at the highest occupational levels, such as doctors, lawyers, senior executives, and other professionals, usually continue to work in some capacity; they very seldom retire completely (Hayward et al., 1989; Palmore et al., 1982). These individuals usually continue to work at a reduced level, as consultants or summer replacements, or they may work on special assignments and cases. As they usually have high levels of expertise and commitment, they may choose or be encouraged to continue working in some capacity in their profession. When individuals in this occupational category do retire, it is primarily due to poor health, though this is not a common reason for retirement (Hayward et al., 1989).

At the second occupational level are individuals who are lower-level executives and middle managers within organizations. These people are usually forced to retire due to mandatory-retirement policy. Often such individuals retire at 60 rather than waiting until the mandatory retirement age of 65 or 70. People at the second occupational level often choose early retirement for two reasons. First, they may realize their careers have reached a plateau, and they will not likely advance any higher. They choose to leave early since they have nothing to gain by staying on. Moreover, they are still young enough and may be in good enough health to enjoy retirement activities. Second, companies often offer an attractive retirement package to those in target positions who retire early. For example, maximum retirement benefits for retirement at age 65 result in a pension of 45 percent of base salary. Individuals may be encouraged to retire at age 60, at which point they will receive a pension of 42 percent of the baseline plus free insurance until age 68. Therefore, the individual has little to gain financially by staying on the job. In tough economic times, it may actually be to both the company's and the employee's advantage to retire early. Younger, less senior employees can be paid less. For some people, however, good retirement income cannot replace the feeling of doing a good job and of being needed and depended on.

Early retirement is, unfortunately, quite common in positions where younger workers are viewed as more productive than older ones, or when younger workers can perform the same duties for significantly lower pay than older ones. The company's rationale in this case is higher productivity for lower cost.

The majority of workers in the United States fall into the categories of skilled (e.g., tool-and-die maker), semiskilled (e.g., electrician's assistant), and unskilled (e.g., farm laborer). Individuals in these three categories usually retire as a function of the mandatory-retirement rules of the organization, regardless of their health status and attitudes toward work.

FINANCIAL SITUATION

The decision to continue to work or retire is also affected by one's financial situation. Since individuals obviously need money to maintain their life-styles after retirement, those who are enrolled in pension plans or know they have a secure income when they retire tend to have a more positive attitude toward retirement (Quinn & Burkhauser, 1990). Those who do not feel secure often experience stress and anxiety.

It is the individuals at the lower occupational levels who tend to have the lowest retirement benefits—benefits are related to earnings. These are the very individuals who are subject to mandatory-retirement rules. Given their relatively low earnings while working, these individuals, in most cases, have not had extra money to put aside for retirement. It is this group that is usually adversely affected by retirement, especially in terms of financial resources (Verdi & Hayslip, 1991).

AGE

As one would expect, individuals are more likely to retire the older they are (George et al., 1984). Age 65 is commonly thought of as the "normal" retirement age. However, almost two-thirds of older workers retire before age 65 (U.S. Senate Special Committee on Aging, 1987–1988). There are many reasons why age affects the decision to retire. Some of these include poor health, job boredom, and mandatory-retirement rules. Thus, it is not age per se that influences the decision to retire but factors usually associated with aging and deteriorating health.

GENDER

In general, women seem to hold more positive expectations of retirement, as do individuals who are married and whose children live close to them (Anson et al., 1989). Moreover, predictors or reasons for retirement are somewhat different for males and females. For example, George et al. (1984) found six predictors of retirement for males and only one for females.

Specifically, for males, George et al. (1984) found: age (the older, the more likely to retire); education level (the lower, the more likely to retire); occupational status (the lower, the more likely to retire); health condition (the more health limitations, the more likely to retire); financial situation (those enrolled in pension programs are more likely to retire); and job tenure (the longer employed, the more likely to retire).

For females, the only predictor of retirement found was age, with the older more likely to retire. For some women, the decision to retire may be related to her husband's health, pension earnings, leisure activities, and so forth. For instance, a woman may retire early in order to care for a sick and infirm husband.

WORK SATISFACTION

It is not surprising that many individuals enjoy working and wish to work as long as they can, particularly if they are in good health. Therefore, when one retires, one gives up not only the economic advantages but these additional benefits as well.

For this reason, individuals who are satisfied with their jobs continue to work longer than individuals who are dissatisfied. Because those in higher occupational levels have higher work satisfaction, it is difficult to discuss job satisfaction without keeping in mind its relationship to occupational level.

Cohn (1979) found that, just prior to retirement, work satisfaction begins to decrease in relation to overall life satisfaction. This may be because individuals are beginning to disassociate themselves from their jobs. They may also anticipate adequate income in retirement by this time (Burkhauser & Turner, 1980). Adequate income in retirement via Social Security benefits does seem to influence the decision to retire (Reynolds et al., 1987). This is particularly true for those in relatively poor health (Quinn, 1977).

PERSONAL ATTITUDES TOWARD RETIREMENT

Often, regardless of the factors discussed above, the individual's personal attitude toward retirement plays a very important role in the decision to retire (Glamser, 1976, 1981). For example, McGee et al. (1979) investigated attitudes toward retirement in male middle- to upper-level managers ranging in age from 28 to 61 years. They found that managers anticipating a change in life-style in retirement were more likely to have negative attitudes toward it than those anticipating continuity of life-style. Interestingly, no relationship was found between attitude toward retirement and present commitment to work. This indicates that individuals with a high degree of commitment to the job can have a positive attitude toward leaving the job (retirement) and vice versa (Abel & Hayslip, 1986).

McPherson and Guppy (1979) studied men ranging in age from 55 to 64 years and investigated preretirement attitudes and decision-making. These researchers found that socioeconomic status (i.e., occupation, income, and educational level), perceived health, organizational involvement (e.g., clubs), job satisfaction, and level of leisure activities were all positively related to preretirement attitudes and decision-making. Moreover, the higher one's income, the more involvement in leisure and organizational activity was found. This was accompanied by better perceived health and more positive preretirement attitudes. Similar results have been found by Abel and Hayslip (1986). While the study by McPherson and Guppy was limited to men, it highlights the importance of many of the factors we have discussed in the decision to retire.

Research by Fletcher and Hansson (1991) suggests that anxiety about the social aspects of retiring can be objectively measured. They found that retirement anxiety was composed of four dimensions: (1) social integration and identity, (2) social adjustment/hardiness, (3) anticipated social exclusion, and (4) lost friendships. The social aspects of retirement anxiety predicted fear of retirement and were strongest for people who were shy, lonely, and who expected to have little control over their lives after retirement (Fletcher & Hansson, 1991).

Retirement Preparation

Atchley (1979) suggests that individuals anticipating retirement engage in a decision-making process where they compare their financial and social situation while working to that anticipated after retirement. Attitudes toward work and retirement, degree of preretirement planning, support of a spouse, one's job situation, financial inducements by government or employer to remain employed or retire, availability of flexible work options, and the general economic climate—all are considered to determine if someone should retire. Dorfman (1989) found that after health, planning for retirement was the strongest predictor of retirement satisfaction for men.

The significance of preparation for retirement, one's financial situation, and other variables has been reported in a study by Ekerdt and associates (1989). These researchers found that workers were more likely to retire if they foresaw a good pension awaiting them, if they held positive retirement attitudes, if they engaged in informal and formal retirement preparation, and if their retirement occurred at older ages.

To avoid financial crises and other retirement-related problems among retirees, many companies are now implementing preretirement-planning programs for workers of all levels and ages. Preretirement training is also viewed as desirable by workers themselves (Kalb & Kohn, 1975). Ekerdt (1989) indicates that there are two major types of information common to all preretirement programs. First is information regarding the company's financial benefits and Social Security. Second is advice, counseling, and suggestions concerning such topics as health care and services, leisure activities, legal matters, and changes in life-style.

WHO PREPARES FOR RETIREMENT?

The expectation that preparation programs will fully prepare one for retirement depends on one's ideas regarding retirement and retirement planning. Is retirement an ongoing process, perhaps beginning in one's twenties or thirties, or is it a discrete event whose salience increases the closer one is to retirement age?

The more highly educated and better off financially one is, the more flexibility one is likely to enjoy. For example, one might be in better health and have better health-care benefits (Verdi & Hayslip, 1991). For those who are less highly skilled and more poorly educated, retirement preparation activities are less frequent (Campione, 1988; Ekerdt, 1989; Ferraro, 1990; Verdi & Hayslip, 1991). This suggests that for those who cannot afford to retire—that is, those who have held the lowest-paying jobs and consequently contributed less to company pension plans and Social Security—special efforts may be needed to induce anticipation and planning for retirement (Verdi & Hayslip, 1991).

The majority of Americans do not report engaging in any systematic, self-initiated retirement preparation (Ekerdt, 1989). Moreover, there seems to be some misunderstanding about retirement provisions among even those who have company-sponsored pensions (Ekerdt, 1989). Indeed, more recent cohorts seem to be preparing for retirement less actively (Ferraro, 1990).

Data on the prevalence of retirement-preparation programs are difficult to assess. Ekerdt (1989) suggests that the figures vary. From 15 to 88 percent of firms report offering some type of planning assistance, depending on how such programs are defined and the extensiveness of what is offered.

Ekerdt suggests that programs should encompass both planning and counseling. If we view retirement as a process, programs with multiple goals are likely to be most effective (Ekerdt, 1989).

One of the difficulties in evaluating both the prevalence and efficacy of retirement planning lies in the fact that not everyone who could enroll in a formal program does so (Campione, 1988). In this light, Turner et al. (1990) found that, among nearly 2800 university employees, only a few had engaged in any more than financial planning, a problem especially common among those less well-off financially. Higher education, greater family income, being male, and increased age related to more financial planning (Turner et al., 1990). People who are experiencing job burnout and for whom leisure activities are important may also choose to retire earlier (Rowe, 1990) and may, therefore, engage in both formal and informal planning to a greater extent.

For those who do not prepare, fear or ignorance of retirement is a likely explanation (Research and Forecasts, 1980). However, poor program quality may also explain nonparticipation (Palmore, 1982). Given the diversity in how programs are defined, and in what constitutes participation, however, one should be somewhat cautious about concluding that available data are accurate.

CONTENT AND DELIVERY OF RETIREMENT-PLANNING PROGRAMS

It should not be surprising that there is some diversity in programs regarding content, design, and implementation. Most programs, however, tend to focus on the following issues: income and finances, health and maintenance, living arrangements, relationships, leisure-time use, and aging and development (i.e., widowhood, postretirement life) (Ekerdt, 1989). There probably needs to be more flexibility in content depending on local resources and the needs of those to be served (Ekerdt, 1989).

There is much controversy about how such programs should be delivered (Ekerdt, 1989). The distinction between information and counseling, discussed above, will influence the extent to which a lecture or discussion format is used, whether an audience or participant mode of presentation is employed, and whether planning is done individually or in groups. Given the diversity of goals, target audiences, and resources, it would be premature to argue that one method or approach is more effective than another. It seems clear, however, that there should be some effort to match those who deliver retirement-preparation programs with their audiences so that individuals of lesser authority, rank, or power are not being taught or led by persons of greater authority, rank, or power; that is, women by men, nonsupervisory by supervisory personnel, or blue-collar by white-collar workers (Ekerdt, 1989).

IS RETIREMENT PLANNING EFFECTIVE?

Retirement preparation seems to have many advantages. In that workers can and do retire unexpectedly, the anticipatory socialization that accompanies early planning could be viewed positively; that is, one is not caught unprepared. The later planning begins, the greater the risk of making costly and potentially irreversible decisions (Ekerdt, 1989). Preparing for retirement should encourage attention to the future, for example, health maintenance and income security, rather than a focus solely on the present, that is, career advancement. Retirement planning should also be beneficial because one's identity and circle of friends will not revolve around work.

In reality, retirement preparation is both advantageous and disadvantageous (Ekerdt, 1989). In addition to benefiting individuals, preparation can also help companies test new methods for educating and training employees, as well as lessening turnover by increasing morale. Other, perhaps more controversial objectives of retirement planning involve acceptance of retirement and willingness to retire, as well as cutting pension costs for the employer (Ekerdt, 1989).

While early retirement may be beneficial for those with viable work alternatives, good health, and sufficient interpersonal and emotional resources, many people choose to work longer, especially if they anticipate a drop in income and enjoy their work. For such individuals, adopting a retirement-oriented mind-set as a function of a retirement-preparation program may actually be counterproductive!

Retirement preparation may also reduce a company's financial obligation to an employee (Ekerdt, 1989). Underwood (1984) argues that through retirement planning, employers can facilitate early private investment decision-making, which may not only prove to be more financially advantageous to the employee but also cause a shift in the attitude that government and employer should bear the principal burden for the employee's retirement security.

Whether retirement planning is effective depends on the criteria one uses to measure program efficacy. Those programs whose intent is simply to convey information probably should be evaluated differently from those whose focus is on individual counseling, attitude change, and well-being. Moreover, employers may use different criteria from those used by individuals to evaluate the worth of a program.

In spite of the importance of this issue, there is surprisingly little research speaking to the question of program efficacy (Ekerdt, 1989).

Often, samples are small, use of random assignment to treatment versus control groups is overlooked or simply impossible, and self-selection of participants biases results, as does selective attrition of participants. Moreover, goals may be ill defined, and measures to evaluate the extent to which stated or implied goals are met may be poorly designed or lacking altogether. Post hoc studies may obscure real programmatic gains.

Available data suggest that while programs can facilitate short-term attitude change, long-term change in attitudes and their translation into actual retirement-planning behaviors is minimal (Abel & Hayslip, 1987; Glamser, 1981). Those who enroll in such programs and who benefit to the greatest extent may be more likely to engage in retirement planning anyway. That is, their participation is itself a form of planning (Glamser, 1981).

For all of these reasons, definite conclusions about whether programs are effective in a long-term sense cannot be reached. Indeed, the realities of retirement may force people to redefine what is desirable or even attainable, undermining styles of adaptation and/or goals they may have established in the program years earlier (Abel & Hayslip, 1987).

There is very little data regarding retirement among women (Quinn & Burkhauser, 1990). What is available is often ambiguous. Now that more women are entering the work force, we need to learn more about women's decision to retire.

In the next section, we will discuss the effects of retirement on the individual, the organization or industry, others, and society as a whole.

Effects of Retirement

THE INDIVIDUAL

One's life-style in retirement is often characterized by lower income, fewer required activities, and more free time (McGee et al., 1979; National Council on Aging, 1981; Streib & Schneider, 1971). Some people do experience a loss of self-esteem or depression, since one's self-concept may revolve around the work role. If retirement causes extreme stress in men, it is because a significant part of their identity lies in their jobs (Havighurst, 1982). If we view retirement as an ongoing process, however, such a negative view seems unjustified.

Studies fail to support such a loss-oriented view of retirement (Robinson et al., 1985). For example, Streib and Schneider (1971) suggest that only 30 percent of people encounter difficulties in adjusting to retirement. Of these individuals, 40 percent stated that the major reason they were having difficulty was financial problems, 28 percent claimed difficulties due to health reasons, 22 percent missed their jobs, and 10 percent were lonely due to the death of their spouse.

Research findings are often inconsistent with our common-sense assumptions regarding the negative aspects of retirement (George et al., 1984; Gratton & Haug, 1983). For example, poor health may be the cause rather than the result of retirement; and health may even improve for some individuals after retirement.

Indeed, retirement may have little effect on the individual, and what changes do occur may be positive as well as negative for both men and women (Gratton & Haug, 1983; George et al., 1984). For instance, George et al. (1984) found that retirement had no adverse effects on life satisfaction for either men or women. Furthermore, individuals see retirement differently as a function of factors such as gender, health status, income, and marital status (Hooker & Ventis, 1984; Robinson et al., 1985; Rowland, 1977). Therefore, it is difficult to discuss the effects of retirement in general terms. Simply put, some individuals experience difficulties in retiring, while others do not.

Bosse and associates (1991) suggest that retirement is a stressful event for individuals for whom retirement has negative implications. It will be stressful, for instance, for those who are forced to retire unexpectedly for reasons of health, plant closings, or the like, and for those who experience health or financial declines after retirement. Lee and Shehan (1989) and Ekerdt and Vinick (1991) found little evidence for a negative effect of retirement on marital satisfaction, except for concerns over division of labor at home when the wife was still working.

One of the major positive aspects of retirement is that it may allow increased time for social and leisure activities, especially if the individual has adequate money and is in good enough health to engage in these activities (Glamser & Hayslip, 1985). In fact, self-worth may increase after retirement if an individual is able to transfer the self-esteem derived from the previous job to current activities. It appears that the most important condition for an individual to adjust well to retirement is activity—doing something. Thus, after retirement, many individuals begin or resume their education, as by obtaining a college degree or enrolling in a program such as Elderhostel (see Chapter 5).

On the negative side, two major aspects of retirement are: (1) increased psychosomatic complaints and (2) decreased income (George et al., 1984). The increase in psychosomatic complaints can be attributed to stress resulting from worry over one's economic situation, health, lack of satisfying interpersonal relationships, and missing one's previous job. A study by Aldwin et al. (1987) suggests that even when physical health is accounted for, retirees report more negative psychological symptoms than do those working, with older workers reporting the fewest symptoms. Moreover, those who retired either early or late reported more symptoms than those who retired at age 65. Since these findings are adjusted for the effects of physical health, this study suggests that retirement may pose problems for many men. That older workers reported the fewest mental health difficulties suggests that they may underestimate the impact retirement will have on them, highlighting the importance of preretirement education as a means of identifying potential problems in adjustment.

Often, reasons for adjustment problems after retirement are a function of previous occupational level. For example, Riley and associates (1968) found that former managers and executives have difficulty in adjusting to retirement at first, because they feel a significant loss of power and status. On the other hand, even though blue-collar workers report a greater readiness to retire since they are not emotionally tied to their jobs, they are less likely to want to retire and therefore have more difficulty in adjusting to it. There are two primary reasons for this: (1) their income while working generally does not allow them to save large amounts of money for later use, and (2) they do not often develop hobbies and leisure activities during adulthood.

Retirement can create a number of other difficulties. While working in retirement may be satisfying and increase income, people are penalized for earning extra income up to a certain point, depending on income level and age, if they receive Social Security benefits. On the other hand, some people are not financially able to *not* work in retirement. Such pressures force people to keep working while retired or to delay retirement altogether, particularly if they are self-employed or hold lower-paying jobs (Boaz, 1987).

Robinson et al. (1985) note that people who are unemployed—more common among blacks and other minorities—become discouraged and often "retire" from this unemployed state rather than from jobs. This may apply to as many as 20 percent of all early retirees (Lauriant & Rabin, 1976; Reno, 1976; Robinson et al., 1985).

In conclusion, responses to retirement vary as a function of a number of factors, such as the importance of work for the person, whether retirement was chosen or forced, the extent of psychological and economic preparation, and occupational level (Cowling & Campbell, 1986; Solomon, 1984).

SOCIETY

Retirement can also affect society, which, in this case, refers to other workers in one's company, other individuals in general, and society's institutions.

One of the major effects retirement has on society pertains to the allocation of economic resources. In general, retirees draw on pension systems, they do not contribute to it (Reynolds et al., 1987). Furthermore, retired individuals have needs for goods and services such as senior centers, recreational facilities, and housing that often require reallocation of goods and services from other age groups or programs.

Another societal aspect of retirement is that it affects one's industry or company both positively and negatively. On the positive side, it gives the company a somewhat objective yet arbitrary method—chronological age—of replacing higher-paid, older employees with lower-paid, younger employees (Robinson et al., 1985). Furthermore, chronological age as the sole criterion for retirement affects all workers equally, since they will all eventually reach that age. This provides the company with a practical administrative procedure that is objective and avoids potential charges of discrimination, favoritism, and bias (Donahue et al., 1960).

On the negative side, organizations must provide economic support—contributions to a pension plan, medical insurance, and life insurance—for individuals who are no longer producing for the company. From the company's perspective, retirees are taking from the system but are not contributing to it. Employers may offer early retirement programs, but they can be costly. Companies may also be faced with the need to retrain workers whose skills have become obsolete, yet feel pressure from other workers to eliminate such programs (Robinson et al., 1985).

For other employees in the retiree's company, retirement allows for upward mobility in positions and pay increases, and for orderly and planned progression of workers throughout all levels of the organization. At the same time, the younger workers who occupy the positions vacated by retirees now have the greater responsibility and demands of these higher positions. They must contribute to the pension and benefits system in order to support retirees. The same can be said of most workers; that is, since they are working, they are contributing to the support of individuals who are not working. Because our population is "graying," there are more and more retirees to be supported by fewer and fewer workers.

A good exercise to stimulate discussion might be to list all possible implications, advantages, and disadvantages of your own eventual retirement for others and society in general. Then have the entire class discuss everyone's ideas. Perhaps we should abolish retirement . . . or should we?

As mentioned earlier, many assume that when one retires, leisure activities become more important to help "fill up" one's time. This is clearly inaccurate, as we will see.

LEISURE

One of the major consequences thought to result from retirement is a dramatic increase in the amount of time for leisure pursuits and activities (Burrus-Bammel & Bammel, 1985; Glamser & Hayslip, 1985; Robinson et al., 1985). Indeed, a discussion of leisure is part of many companies' retirement-preparation programs.

Definition of Leisure

Defining **leisure** adequately is difficult, since one person's leisure activity may be an occupation to another (Burrus-Bammel & Bammel, 1985). Leisure may be a state of mind—relaxation. For example, let us suppose someone's primary occupation is bank management and hobby or leisure activity is coin-collecting and -dealing. Should this be considered a leisure activity, since it is related to one's occupation and involves making money? Or, consider a lawyer, who during nonwork time travels around the country visiting law schools—is this leisure? Leisure satisfaction may be **intrinsic,** or it may lead to the attainment of some other goal, in which case it is **instrumental.**

For our purposes, we will define leisure activity as any activity in which individuals engage during free time (Kubanoff, 1980). These activities may or may not involve relaxation in an obvious sense. This definition does not distinguish between activities that are related to a job and those that are not, nor whether the activity involves purely self-enjoyment (intrinsic) or earning money (instrumental). Moreover, this definition does not distinguish between choosing to have leisure time, as when taking time off from work or spending weekends or evenings engaged in an activity, and having leisure time imposed on the individual, as when laid off or forcibly retired. As work becomes more intrinsically meaningful, the distinction between leisure and work is more difficult to make. Indeed, because work structures our lives, its impact on and relationship to leisure is substantial (Cutler & Hendricks, 1990) (see Box 9.4).

Types of Leisure Activities

Although almost any activity can be considered a leisure activity, researchers generally group leisure activities into four major categories (Bosse & Ekerdt, 1981; Glamser & Hayslip, 1985; Gordon et al., 1976). These are (1) cultural, such as attending sporting events, church and religious meetings, clubs, and the movies; (2) physical, including bowling, camping, fishing, golf, hunting, and odd jobs around the home; (3) social, such as playing cards, drinking with friends at a bar or club, visiting with family and relatives, visiting with friends and neighbors, and going to parties; and (4) solitary, including reading books, magazines, and newspapers, listening to the radio, and watching television.

Learning to Live with Leisure

Americans have generally subscribed to what is often described as the Protestant work ethic, which views work as sacred and something to be enjoyed. Basically, one is expected to be a working and contributing member of society. For this reason, leisure and leisure activities have generally been equated with idleness, something to be engaged in by only the young and retirees. For example, Hooker and Ventis (1984) found a commitment to the work ethic to relate negatively to life satisfaction in retirees. Indeed, we have been made to feel guilty about actively engaging in leisure activities, that is, not working and enjoying ourselves. In fact, many Americans do not know how to relax when they are not working at their jobs. On their days off, they mow the lawn, paint the house, and so forth.

It is important to recognize that leisure is contextual in nature. How it is defined, how we experience it, and whether it is satisfying are relative to many factors—family life-style, work values, sex roles, and relationships with others (Cutler & Hendricks, 1990).

Leisure Competence

Leisure competence means understanding the meaning of leisure for you personally, as well as acting on that understanding through your involvement in meaningful leisure activities. As with retirement, it is perhaps best to state that the development of leisure competence is a learning process (Peacock & Talley, 1985). That is, people do not suddenly become aware of leisure in retirement. A process approach has the advantage of reframing retirement more positively, rather than seeing it as leading to the "problem" of developing leisure activities.

YOUNG ADULTHOOD

During young adulthood, leisure activities are important because they provide a means of relaxation from daily pressures experienced on the job, at home, and in the family. Consider an individual who works as a stockbroker in a high-pressure situation for eight or more hours a day, followed by a one-hour commute home every evening through heavy traffic. This individual may enjoy getting away from those pressures by engaging in fishing at a quiet pond.

Another reason leisure is important is because it may permit one to feel self-actualized or fulfilled. Since individuals often enter fields or jobs they are not interested in, leisure activities may serve as compensation for the lack of self-fulfillment attainable on the job. For example, an individual might want to be an artist but constantly be told he or she cannot earn a living in that endeavor. This individual, in order to achieve some economic security, may obtain a degree in accounting or engineering, yet spends his or her leisure time painting.

Leisure activities also provide a social outlet for meeting others with similar interests, such as stamp collecting, flying, bowling, and dancing. This aspect may be especially important for women, because in most instances women outlive their husbands. As young adults, women would be wise to develop leisure activities and friendship networks indepen-

Developing leisure competence is a skill that all adults, regardless of age, should work toward acquiring.

dently of their husbands, which can be maintained after the death of their spouse.

MIDDLE ADULTHOOD

During middle adulthood, leisure activities begin to assume roles in addition to those that are important during young adulthood. Leisure activities may now fill in time and allow for the development of other roles, if activities related to the job are lessening (Kelly et al., 1986). Leisure may also provide opportunities for meaningful activities in the middle-aged years if work and family commitments have lessened. For instance, rather than having to take children to Little League, ballet class, or Cub Scouts, individuals now have the time to pursue their own activities. Leisure activities may also provide an outlet where social relationships can be developed and maintained.

As we will discuss later in this chapter, finding fulfilling leisure activities can lead to greater life satisfaction and better adjustment to retirement in older adults (Palmore, 1979). Thus, it is important to at least begin to develop leisure activities in adulthood that can be continued into retirement.

LATE ADULTHOOD

In order to understand leisure during late adulthood, we must briefly discuss three theories having different views regarding activity level during old age. These are **disengagement theory, activity theory,** and **continuity theory.**

Disengagement Theory This theory, which was formulated by Cummings and Henry (1961), proposes that as individuals approach and enter later maturity, there is a natural tendency to psychologically and socially withdraw or disengage from the environment. This withdrawal is stimulated by increased awareness of our own mortality. In a sense, individuals begin to prepare for the ultimate disengagement, death.

Cummings and Henry assumed this tendency to withdraw or disengage was natural and mutual—society also withdraws from the aging individual—and resulted from changes in certain internal processes that were inherent to aging, implying that disengaging is almost intrinsic. Moreover, they assumed that in order to successfully age, one must disengage from others. Disengagement was assumed to begin for females with the departure of the last child from the home and for males with retirement. Since its original formulation, the theory has been redefined somewhat to accommodate individual differences in extent of disengagement.

Activity Theory Activity theory stands in direct contradiction to disengagement theory and assumes that there is a positive relationship between activity and life satisfaction. That is, while aging individuals confront inevitable physiological changes, their social-psychological needs remain essentially unchanged. Therefore, the older individual who manages to resist withdrawing from the social world and maintains activities for as long as possible will experience greater life satisfaction. Activity theory assumes that all individuals have the ability to construct or reconstruct their lives by substituting new roles and activities for lost ones.

According to Howe (1988), for both substantive and methodological reasons, neither disengagement nor activity theory is sufficient by itself to explain fully the many and complex patterns of adjustment to aging. Each theory appears too simplistic, filled with tacit assumptions and accompanied by many ideological overtones.

Continuity Theory Continuity theory, which was proposed by Kelly (1982), provides a dialectical consideration of leisure as well as a framework to examine the relationship between leisure activities in early and later life (Howe, 1988). In some respects, it builds on activity theory but incorporates individual identity as a central issue in the continuity of activity. This theory proposes that optimal or successful aging is characteristic of those individuals who are able to maintain and continue their roles, activities, habits, or associations in retirement, or to find meaningful substitute pursuits.

Since our identity during adulthood is based on a number and variety of roles, the loss of one particular role, such as the work role, will not necessarily result in an identity crisis. Thus, according to continuity theory, there is identity continuity through substituting or increasing leisure roles for lost roles such as those that are family- or work-related.

Leisure Activities in Adulthood

FACTORS THAT AFFECT LEISURE ACTIVITIES

The factors that affect leisure activities are complex and varied (Kelly et al., 1986). We will first highlight some of the major factors affecting choice of and ability to engage in leisure activities across the life span.

Because leisure activities vary according to age, it should not be surprising to find that they are related to a number of factors. The major factors affecting leisure behavior are income level, personality, interest, health, ability level, transportation, education, and a number of social characteristics (Burrus-Bammel & Bammel, 1985; J. R. Kelly, 1975, 1983a, 1983b). Each of these factors can play an important role in the selection of and participation in leisure activities. You may wish to spend your spring break at the seashore, but if you cannot afford the plane fare, or do not have a car, you're likely to be stuck at home!

Although often overlooked, transportation has a profound impact on an individual's quality of life, life-style, and participation in a variety of activities, especially for older adults. Adequate transportation allows the individual access to shopping facilities, medical services, social contacts with others, and participation in activities of all types. Lack of available transportation affects a large percentage of older adults (Carp, 1970).

In adulthood, leisure activities change according to the current needs, abilities, and health of the individual (Burrus-Bammel & Bammel, 1985). While there are individual differences in the choice of leisure activities in adulthood, the three most important factors in determining leisure activities appear to be health, economic resources, and time constraints (Kaplan, 1975). Having someone to do something with and viewing leisure positively are also very important.

There appear to be common types of leisure activities adults engage in which vary with age (Gordon et al., 1976; Kaplan, 1975; Moran, 1979). There are other forms of leisure activities common to all adults (Kelly, 1983a).

During adulthood, the majority of leisure activities tend to be **active** and focus outside the home. These include exercising, jogging, playing sports, and going to movies, bars, and restaurants. The primary focus of these leisure activities is active "doing" and/or participation. Many adults also spend time in **passive** leisure activities such as reading, watching television, or just relaxing.

Adults report that they engage in leisure activities for various reasons. These include personal interest, a means of coping with pressure and stress, and meeting individuals with similar interests. Overall, adults stress the importance of interest and meaningfulness in the selection of their leisure activities (Kelly, 1983a).

Middle age serves as a transition between the active leisure orientation of young adulthood and the passive leisure style of later adulthood. Individuals begin reducing the frequency of action-oriented activities such as participation in sports, and increasing the frequency of passive-oriented activities such as reading.

There are two primary reasons for this change. First, declining health may limit participation in action-oriented activities for some people. Second, individuals begin to select activities that they can continue into later adulthood. Often, these new activities are somewhat related to the activities of young adulthood. For example, instead of playing softball, the individual now spends leisure time being an umpire. Instead of long-distance jogging, the individual now takes up walking or biking.

Middle-aged people also often participate in leisure activities by becoming involved in civil organizations, joining clubs, or enrolling in adult education courses that deal with topics they have always had an interest in but have never had the time or opportunity to explore. These topics range from academic areas to genealogy and astrology (see Chapter 5).

Although some older adults engage in active leisure activities, the majority are involved in passive leisure activities (Gordon et al., 1976). These include watching television, reading, or socializing with friends (Glamser & Hayslip, 1985). In many instances, older adults must develop new leisure activities because of economic and physical health factors reducing the opportunity for former leisure activities (Moran, 1979).

For many older people, being involved in some form of activity is critical to feeling positive about themselves (Cottrell, 1962). This implies that leisure competence is itself an important construct in understanding adulthood.

Leisure Research in Adulthood

Although adults participate in similar types of leisure activities, the overall frequency of participation decreases with age. As mentioned above, there is a shift from action-oriented activities to passive-oriented ones with age.

Glamser and Hayslip (1985) conducted a six-year longitudinal investigation of the impact of retirement on participation in leisure activities. One hundred and thirty-two male workers aged 60 and older who were employed in semiskilled positions were surveyed regarding the types and frequency of their leisure activities. Activities were arranged into one of four major categories (see above): (1) cultural, (2) physical, (3) social, or (4) solitary. They found that, during the six-year period, the overall level of leisure activity declined. However, there was a substantial amount of individual change in leisure activity and substantial social disengagement following retirement. The greatest decline was in social activities, followed by cultural, then physical activities. Interestingly, stability across time was found for physical activities—the most common pattern was continued *non*participation.

Similar results were reported by Mobily et al. (1986) in a cross-sectional study of rural elderly people. However, these researchers found that there were also gender differences in activity participation. Females engaged primarily in home-centered activities such as baking or sewing; males tended to report outdoor activities such as fishing and hunting.

Kelly et al. (1986) investigated leisure activities in four age groups—40 to 54 years, 55 to 64 years, 65 to 74 years, and 75 years and older—in a small midwestern city. These researchers assessed overall activity level and identified 28 kinds of leisure, which were reduced to eight major types. These types were cultural, travel, exercise and sport, family leisure, outdoor recreation, social activities, community organizations, and home-based activities.

Kelly et al. (1986) found both consistency and differences in leisure activities with age. In terms of differences with age, there was a decline in overall activity level, sport and exercise, and outdoor recreation. There was continuity in a number of core activities such as family, social, and home-based activities. Results also indicated that for the 40-to-54 and 55-to-65 age groups, travel and cultural activities were important. For the 65-to-74 age group, social and travel activities predominated, and for the oldest age group (75 years plus), the most common leisure activities were family- and home-based activities.

While these studies all support, to some extent, the basic tenets of disengagement theory, we must reemphasize that there are individual differences in the degree of disengagement among older adults.

McGuire and associates (1986) identified *limiting* factors and *prohibitory* factors in a study of outdoor recreational activities across the life span. Limiting factors reduce participation, while prohibiting factors prevent it altogether. Most people, regardless of age, stressed that lack of time, people, and poor health were major constraints both limiting and prohibiting activities, with health taking on more importance with age. Interestingly, constraints of income, safety, access to transportation, and lack of information did not change across age levels. While lack of money seemed to affect most people, lack of time was an important issue, especially to middle-aged people, and not having a companion increased as a barrier among older adults.

Patterns of Leisure During Retirement

Recently, there has been interest in studying the life-styles of individuals during retirement, since a number of investigations have documented that later-life adaptation is strongly related to activity and social context outside the home (Palmore, 1979). These life-styles are often referred to as **leisure life-styles.**

TYPES OF LEISURE LIFE-STYLES

One of the most extensive studies of life-styles among retired persons was conducted by Osgood (1983), who examined the patterns of retirement life-styles among residents of three age-segregated retirement communities in Florida and Arizona. Data were obtained from in-depth interviews in three retirement communities: blue-collar mobile-home residents in Florida, upper-middle-class condominium dwellers in Florida, and a self-sufficient community of private homeowners in Arizona.

Six major types or patterns of residents were found in these communities (see Table 9.2). Osgood found the majority of residents to be joiners, socializers, humanitarians, or recreationalists.

Although results of this study might vary as functions of geographic region and socioeconomic status, they begin to build an important data base for future leisure programming, of which there is great need (Burrus-Bammel & Bammel, 1985). Information regarding the life-styles and interests of residents of retirement communities is also important because, as more people live to advanced old age and move to them, planners and developers will need information about what types of services and activities should be available to residents.

Comparatively speaking, little research has been conducted regarding leisure activities in adulthood. Most of what is available is cross-sectional and focuses on level of leisure activities versus their meaningfulness. One major reason for this lack of research is that leisure tends to be in opposition to the traditional work ethic in our society.

SUMMARY

The focus of this chapter was on *occupational choice* and *career development.* To think that we select an occupation, spend our adult years in that occupation, and eventually retire from that occupation is overly simplistic. Occupational selection, retirement, and leisure are quite complex and affected by many factors, such as *personality, health, education, attitudes toward work and retirement,* and *sex-role expectations.*

The major theories of occupational choice are those of *Super, Holland,* and *Ginzberg.* While available research in this area has little to say

TABLE 9.2

LEISURE LIFE-STYLES IN THREE AGE-SEGREGATED RETIREMENT COMMUNITIES

Pattern/Type	Approximate Percentage	Characteristics
Organizers	10–15%	1. Devote all their time and energy to formally organizing various clubs, organizations, activities, projects, classes, and meetings 2. Extremely dedicated to community and want to make the community the kind of place they can be proud of and enjoy living in 3. Busy and active all day 4. Usually healthier and younger members of the community
Joiners	70–80% (Joiners, Socializers, Humanitarians, Recreationalists)	1. Join and take part in formal activities developed by the "organizers" 2. Very active; plan their day around preferred activities, clubs, meetings, etc.
Socializers		1. Gregarious, friendly, spend days informally socializing with friends and neighbors 2. Not active in formal clubs, activities, and organizations 3. Respected for their friendliness and helpfulness
Humanitarians		1. Constantly assisting and helping others in the community, usually older and in worse health 2. Overall, devote all their time and energy to helping the less fortunate
Recreationalists		1. Constantly engaging in numerous and various leisure-time activities such as golf, swimming, fishing, etc. 2. Primarily associated with others who share similar recreational interests 3. Recreation is the central focus around which their time is organized
Retirees	10–15%	1. Retired from active participation in the community 2. Characterized by lack of any social role 3. Usually older and in worse health than other members of the community 4. With advancing age and failing health, individuals who were once in other patterns; withdrawn

Source: From N. J. Osgood. (1983). Pattlerns of aging in retirement communities: Typology of residents. *Journal of Applied Gerontology, 2,* 28–43.

about the career development of women, a notable exception is the theory of *Astin* and the work of Tangri and Jenkins.

Men and women differ in their career patterns, but each is highly *complex* and subject to the influence of *opportunity, economic constraints, family influences,* and *decision-making skills.* While many advocate *occupational developmental tasks* particular to distinct life stages, occupational/career development—defined as a coherent pattern of jobs—is a life-long process, influencing and being influenced by events in other areas of one's life. Young adulthood is often an upwardly mobile occupational period, but middle adulthood may or may not be occupationally stable. Some people are more likely to change careers than are others; *flexibility* is common among some.

The capabilities of older workers were discussed. Biases regarding older workers abound, most of which lack consistent support or are weakly related to job performance.

While *retirement* usually implies *disengagement* from the work role, individuals seem to go through distinct phases of adjustment to retirement—*honeymoon, disenchantment,* and *stabilization.* As with occupational development, the decision to retire and the impact of retirement are influenced by a number of factors, the most important of which are health status and retirement preparation.

Retirement—withdrawal either voluntarily or involuntarily from the work force—was discussed from both a theoretical and practical perspective. The major factors influencing the *decision to retire* voluntarily are both *personal* and *institutional* in nature: *health status, occupational level, retirement preparation, economic climate, personal financial situation, age, gender, work satisfaction,* and *personal attitudes.* There are *individual differences* in reasons for retirement, and such differences mediate the effects of retirement on the individual and society.

Leisure was defined as any activity in which individuals engage during free time, though defining leisure clearly is difficult. Developing *leisure competence* is a life-long process. There are numerous ways to classify leisure activities, and the selection of and participation in them is affected by many factors, such as personal interest, health, and economic resources.

Participation in leisure activities during adulthood seems to be important to well-being. Research indicates there are certain types of leisure activities that are characteristically engaged in by people of different ages. Moreover, with increasing age, there is a general decrease in the overall frequency of participation in activities, with a shift away from *active* to more *passive activities.* These patterns of leisure activity, as well as *leisure life-styles,* seem to be influenced by numerous factors.

KEY TERMS AND CONCEPTS

Occupational role
Occupation development
Retirement
Leisure
Disengagement theory
Activity theory
Continuity theory
Active leisure activity

Job loss
Career crisis in mid-life
Horizontal versus vertical career moves
Institutional versus personal factors in the decision to retire
Intrinsic versus instrumental leisure activities

Passive leisure activity
Leisure life-styles
Flexible careers
Career indecision
Leisure competence
"Graying" of the American work force
Age Discrimination in Employment Act (ADEA)
Occupational developmental tasks
Protestant work ethic
Career
Vocational maturity
Older worker
Prime age
Ageism in employment
Bona fide occupational qualification (BFOQ)
Functional age

REVIEW QUESTIONS

1. How is a person's occupational selection important in adulthood? What factors contribute to career patterns that are different for men and women?
2. What are the major theories of occupational choice? What are some of the advantages and disadvantages of each?
3. What are some of the basic rationales for retirement? Are these reasons logical?
4. What are the effects of retirement on the individual and society?
5. What are some of the major reasons why leisure activities are important for adults? How do such activities vary by age?
6. What is career indecision? How does it relate to occupational choice?
7. What is the Age Discrimination in Employment Act (ADEA)?
8. Are the myths held by business and industry regarding the older worker accurate? What seem to be the bases for such attitudes?
9. What are the advantages and disadvantages of retirement preparation? Is preparing for retirement effective?
10. What is the impact of job loss on the individual?

CHAPTER 10

Mental Health and Psychopathology

CHAPTER OUTLINE

INTRODUCTION

One in five Americans suffers from some form of mental illness in any one month, according to the National Institute of Mental Health (NIMH) (Myers et al., 1984; Regier et al., 1988). Yet, only a fifth of these seek help for their problems, and most of the time they go to physicians (Robins et al., 1984). Moreover, one third of all people will face mental illness or substance abuse difficulties some time in their lives. These sobering figures suggest that mental illness is a substantial problem in our society and, therefore, deserves serious attention. Indeed, most of us have felt depressed from time to time. We may also have used or abused drugs to cope with our feelings or stresses in our lives.

As the proportion of middle-aged and older individuals increases, the number experiencing some form of mental illness will likely also increase. Current estimates suggest that between 14 and 25 percent of older people suffer from mental illness (Fleming et al., 1986), though diagnosable disorders in late life vary in frequency. They range from 26 percent for serious cognitive impairment to 1 percent for schizophrenia (Anthony et al., 1992).

Recent NIMH findings, based on detailed interviews with over 20,000 adults, suggest that major depression peaks in early adulthood (ages 20–25) and declines thereafter through age 60, only to increase again, with the highest rates of depression being in very late life (age 80 and beyond) (Burke et al., 1990). Perhaps due to the stressfulness of American life, more positive attitudes toward admitting to feeling distressed, or greater availability of help, the incidence of depression has increased over the last decade (Klerman & Weissman, 1989; Wickramaratne et al., 1989).

For anxiety disorders, including panic disorders, obsessive-compulsive disorders, and phobias, findings are similar, except that compared to depression, their relative incidence is greater for the very old than the young.

These figures indicate that, among adults, emotional difficulties are likely to continue to be a serious concern requiring the help of mental health professionals (Roybal, 1988).

While depression is a common problem for younger and older adults, it appears that certain mental disorders, such as schizophrenia and substance abuse, may be less common for middle-aged and older adults. We cannot dismiss this information entirely, but it should be viewed cautiously, for several reasons. First, older people may need to be diagnosed by different means than younger ones. For example, we might understand more about older people's problems if we relied on observations of behavior rather than test scores of formal interviews. Second, reporting symptoms (e.g., sleeplessness) versus diagnoses (e.g., depression) may yield different findings (Blazer et al., 1987). Third, clinicians' biases about the elderly or women may cause them to misdiagnose (Rodenheaver & Datan, 1988). In addition, the source of our data affects our findings about mental health and mental illness across the life span. For example, one might rely on actual chart reviews, referrals from mental health personnel, reports of frequency of symptoms, or self-administered questionnaires. Each source might yield a different answer! For this reason, it is important to realize that how our data are gathered affects our conclusions regarding the prevalence of mental illness in adulthood. Recall that this was also the conclusion we reached in Chapter 2 in discussing research methods in adulthood.

This chapter focuses on the continuum of **mental health–mental illness,** with particular emphasis on late adulthood. Although some forms of mental illness are less common among middle-aged and elderly people, if we assume that older adults are less likely to seek help for their problems, then we could easily argue that they are more vulnerable to most types of psychological disorders. Either they are less prone to see themselves in need of help, or they are regarded as less likely to benefit from help (see Chapter 11). While a comprehensive discussion of abnormal behavior is beyond the scope of this chapter, you may consult Carson and Butcher (1991), or Davison and Neale (1990), for a thorough review of all its forms.

Studies do not always agree, but the information they provide can be helpful in supplying a rough estimate of the incidence of disorders across age, which is important for research and planning purposes. Such information can also be valuable in alerting mental health personnel to the disorders older or younger persons are especially prone to, and helpful in affecting the design and implementation of mental health services specifically designed for individuals who are "at risk" psychologically (e.g., those who are ill or isolated).

The terms *mental health* and *mental illness* mean many things; we will first define them so you can understand how these concepts relate to adulthood. Other goals in this chapter are to delineate what factors contribute to good mental health in elderly people, and to make recommendations about how we can best facilitate a positive sense of oneself in old age.

Mental health in late adulthood is often particular to the life situation of the older person.

DEFINING MENTAL HEALTH AND ABNORMALITY IN ADULTHOOD

What Is Abnormal? What Is Healthy?

It is probably accurate to say that we know more about what mental health is *not* than about what qualities positively define it in adulthood.

The terms *normal* and *abnormal* are difficult to define precisely, because the criteria for each change with time and with society's expectations (Birren & Renner, 1980; Carson & Butcher, 1991). Thus, as society's standards for acceptable, "normal" behavior change, so, too, do our ideas about normal or abnormal behaviors particular to the aged. This is because once a behavior is labeled abnormal or deviant, it immediately becomes the concern of a qualified professional—a psychologist, psychotherapist, or psychiatrist—and assumed to be disruptive, unlawful, or harmful to oneself or others (Ullman & Krasner, 1975). It is at this point that our attitudes toward older people as individuals and as consumers of psychological services come into play.

Birren and Renner (1979, 1980) suggest that mental health is very difficult to define, regardless of whether we are referring to young adults or to the aged. Jahoda (1958) suggests that mentally healthy people possess the following characteristics: (1) a positive self-attitude, (2) an accurate perception of reality, (3) environmental mastery, (4) autonomy, (5) personality balance, and (6) psychological growth or self-actualization. Do you think these are reasonable criteria?

We might argue that behaviors that are harmful to individuals and/ or take away from their sense of well-being are best considered abnormal (Carson & Butcher, 1991). Thus, behaviors that bring one into conflict with others and are perceived as distressing or disruptive to one's well-being are often deemed maladaptive.

However, behaviors that most laypeople and professionals would define as abnormal by this standard are often quite adaptive for many aged individuals. Indeed depression, aggressiveness, obsessive-compulsive behavior, isolation, passivity, and anxiety can all be reasonable responses to threat, loss, or aggression by others (Birren & Renner, 1979; Gurland, 1973; Lieberman, 1975). For example, feeling depressed at the death of one's spouse or because of serious illness are perfectly normal reactions. Likewise, feeling anxious about being relocated to a nursing home, or being resistant to expectations by nursing-home staff to behave "appropriately" by taking medicine or generally being a "good patient" may seem quite natural, given the circumstances. Consider the following case history:

> Mr. Gibson, a successful businessman and the "Don Juan" of the small community in which he lived, was diagnosed at the age of 70 as suffering from cancer of the prostate gland. He had ignored the symptoms of increased difficulty in urination for two years prior to the diagnosis. When he suffered an acute blockage of urination, he was forced to seek consultation in the emergency room, where the cancer was discovered. A team of specialists determined that the cancer had spread to surrounding tissues. Nevertheless, the blockage of urination was severe enough that surgery was required to remove a portion of the prostate gland, which was followed by radiation therapy to the surrounding tissues. Surgery was successful, and hormone therapy was prescribed. Therapy was successful, and Mr. Gibson could urinate without difficulty and suffered no pain from the cancer in the other tissues.
>
> The family of Mr. Gibson was puzzled yet pleased with his response to the therapy. He appeared to have accepted his illness philosophically and seemed more open and concerned about his wife and two children than he had been for many years. He began to make plans for his oldest son to assume responsibility for the family business. He apologized profusely to his wife for the many years of infidelity and, in her presence, asked the forgiveness of God for his sins. The woman with whom he had an affair for ten years was telephoned by Mr. Gibson, the situation explained, and financial support was arranged for her. Mr. Gibson, although he had shown little recent interest in his faith, asked that the Catholic chaplain visit him daily. He confessed his sins repeatedly, noting that he was now being repaid for a lifetime of sin, deceit, and manipulation.
>
> Mr. Gibson also believed it necessary to endure penance for his sin. A life-long smoker, he forced himself to quit, although the doctors had assured him that quitting would not affect his current condition or prognosis. Withdrawal from tobacco was extremely difficult, and Mr. Gibson often returned to smoking, only to repeatedly quit for a few days, a week, or sometimes a month. He gave large financial gifts to the local Catholic church, gifts so large that the priest contacted Mr. Gibson's physician, expressing concern that he might be acting irrationally. The chaplain attempted to assure Mr. Gibson that he was having difficulty forgiving himself.
>
> Throughout the early months of diagnosis, surgery, and hormonal therapy for carcinoma of the prostate, the attending physician felt it important for Mr. Gibson to be seen regularly by a psychiatrist. Mr. Gibson was more than pleased to speak with the consulting psychiatrist, yet did not perceive

anything unusual about his lack of concern about his illness coupled with his excessive penance. Four months following surgery, growth of the cancer was identified in x-rays of the bone, yet Mr. Gibson appeared unconcerned (Blazer, 1990).

Do you feel Mr. Gibson handled his illness well? Do you think his denial helped or hindered his adjustment? How did his belief system influence his behavior? Do you think he should have sought professional help?

As a general rule, if our behaviors interfere with relationships with others or our work, and cause our health to deteriorate, one should suspect a problem. For example, not eating or sleeping, failing to take or abusing medications, "blowing up" and hitting someone for no reason, or secluding oneself might all be reasons for concern, particularly if these behaviors persist over weeks or months. We might be especially worried about a family member or friend if these behaviors all occur together rather than in isolation.

Cohen (1990) suggests that most older adults are in good mental health, that only a minority of older people suffer from significant mental disorders. Marked intellectual or memory declines, changes in sleeping patterns, sexual disinterest or activity, or preoccupation with death may indicate a mental health problem that should be evaluated (Cohen, 1990). Moreover, vague physical decline or multiple somatic (body) complaints may mask depression, suicidal thoughts, or represent profound despair and giving up (Cohen, 1990). Careful attention to each individual's current life circumstances, family support system, and life history can lead to the identification of behaviors that may signal emotional distress. Being sensitive to these factors may also enable us to understand how a given person's behaviors or feelings are a legitimate response to stress, loss, or change.

Gurland (1973) notes that misinterpreting certain behaviors as abnormal is especially a problem if behaviors are considered singly rather than in combination. Moreover, when the environment or society is perceived to be the cause of the behavior, it is less likely to be judged as abnormal since the individual is not at fault (Gurland, 1973).

Given the above discussion, you should conclude that applying rigid standards to aged people, therefore, presents some difficulties. Due to decreased income, poor health, isolation, retirement, widowhood, or the effects of prescription drugs, many older individuals simply do not have the opportunity to be autonomous or master their environments (Gurland, 1973). They may be legitimately depressed or hostile, and may turn away from what appears to them a bleak future to focus on the past. They may not have the financial or interpersonal resources to make decisions about their lives or to plan ahead. Thus, for some individuals, in some situations, denial, depression, anxiety, or hostility may actually help in adjusting to events over which they have little control, such as terminal illness or being isolated from others due to illness, forced retirement, or institutionalization (Gurland, 1973).

There is merit in stating that everyone behaves "abnormally" in certain situations, while in others the same behavior may clearly be inappropriate. An example is yelling at a ball game versus yelling in class. For this reason, it is important to realize that in looking for abnormality, we should not forget that adults have strengths as well (Cohen, 1992).

For some people, specific life events evoke pathological reactions (see Figures 10.1, 10.2, and 10.3). For those who do not experience these life changes, life moves more smoothly. Even among people who experience the same life event, some will likely respond by becoming depressed,

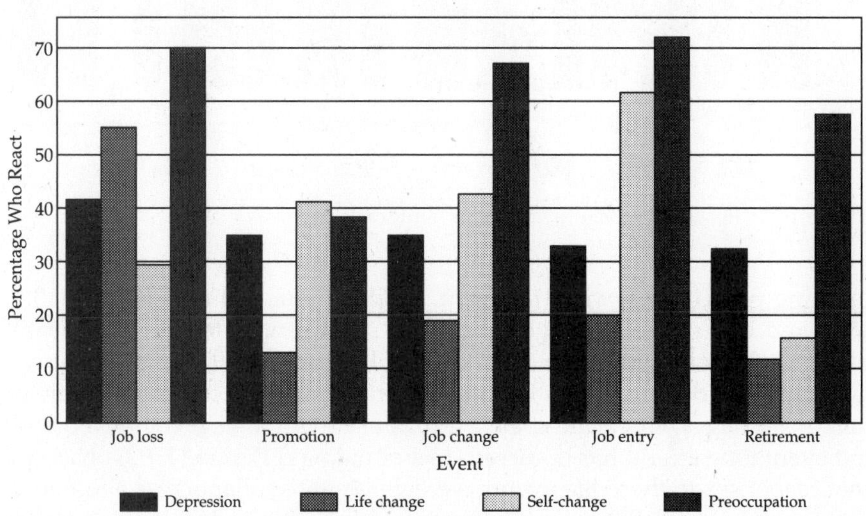

Figure 10.1 Reactions to occupational life events.

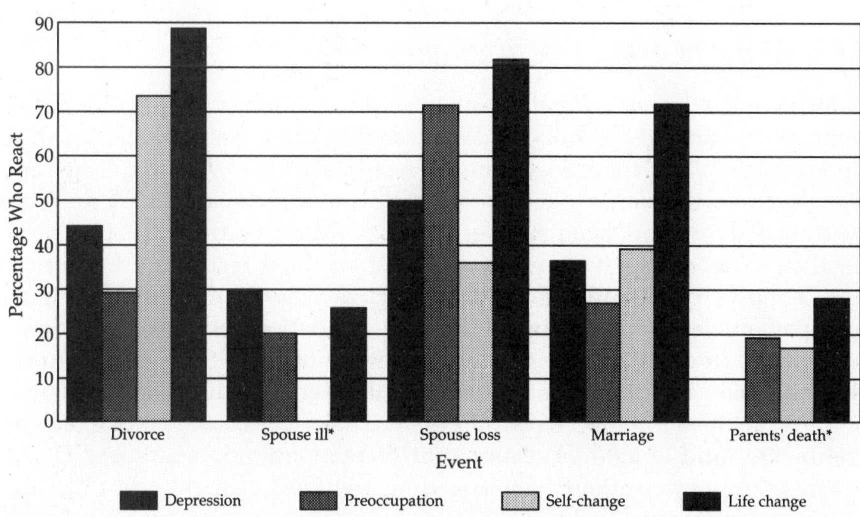

Figure 10.2 Reactions to marital life events. *Information not available.

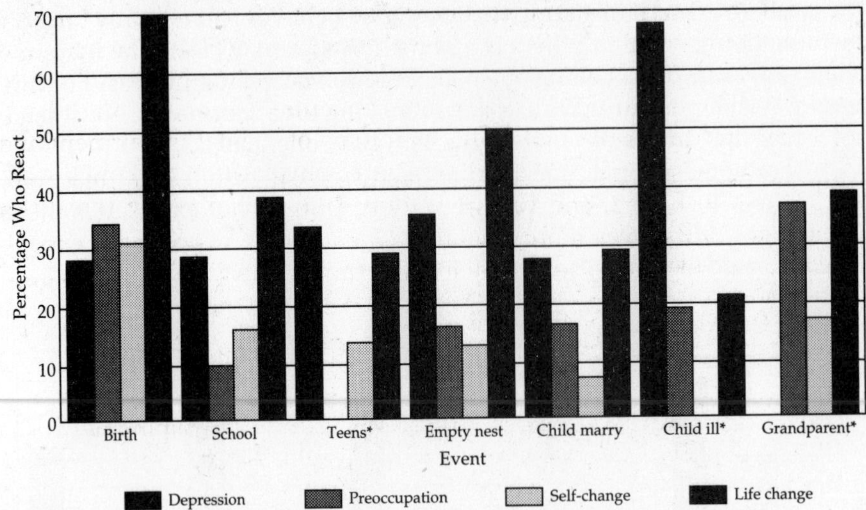

Figure 10.3 Reactions to family life events. *Information not available.

or being preoccupied with the event, while others will not. Figures 10.1, 10.2, and 10.3 show the range of responses to various life events in a sample of 2300 adults aged 18 to 65 (Pearlin & Lieberman, 1979). Depression is a negative response to such events, but they may also transform individuals' self-images, create life changes, or cause them to be preoccupied with the event long after it has occurred. Lieberman and Peskin (1992) observed that responses to these life events were generally similar across age. However, with increased age, people perceived less change in their self-image after experiencing family, marital, or family life events (Lieberman & Peskin, 1992).

THE INFLUENCE OF MENTAL HEALTH SERVICES

Older people's use of mental health services also helps to define what is mentally healthy in adulthood. Older people often see themselves in a more positive light than do younger ones (Harris and Associates, 1975). However, ageistic biases that mental-health service providers may hold toward the elderly work against older clients (Ford & Sbordone, 1980). These negative expectations have many roots: unresolved conflicts about one's own aging or one's parents', and about death. Lack of experience with aged patients leads to even more negative evaluations of their prognoses.

In addition to negative attitudes toward older clients, many physical-emotional problems are often mistakenly seen as a direct consequence of aging, such as isolation from others, inadequate income, poor access to health care, and limited educational or recreational opportunities. These factors work against older people getting the kind of mental health care they want and need.

We will discuss many of the problems associated with mental health services for the aged more fully in Chapter 11. But until the many barriers are dealt with, what we know about mental health and aging is likely to continue to be very limited and based on a biased sample of potential clients, perhaps those with the fewest resources and in the poorest health. Surveys often sample only community residents, and adults often inadvertently or deliberately misreport symptoms of mental impairment and mental illness (Barbee & McLaulin, 1990; Murphy et al., 1988; Pollitt et al., 1989; Waxman, 1986). Some people simply do not report symptoms they do not consider serious enough to warrant attention (Brody, 1985).

Lawton (1978) has suggested that the use of mental health services will increase as future cohorts of elderly people become more educated and, thus, more psychologically sophisticated. Current services might be more fully used if they were less traditional in nature (Lieberman, 1978; Sargent, 1980). That is, help could be provided by paraprofessionals, nurses, friends and volunteers, or those in the "natural helping network" of the aged, such as druggists, beauticians, mail carriers, custodians, and peers.

It should be clear that one's ideas about the mental health of older people versus younger people are heavily influenced by one's beliefs and attitudes regarding aging and development (see Chapters 1 and 9). A service provider's lack of contact with older clients may be both a cause for and result of his or her ideas about mental health and mental illness in adults.

DSM-III-R

As with mental health, defining pathology in the aged is complex. In many cases, signs and symptoms of pathology in old age are *not* the same as those in the young. Moreover, individual and situation-specific differences are substantial (Gurland, 1973).

At present, however, the diagnosis of mental illness in adulthood is made using the *Diagnostic and Statistical Manual of Mental Disorders,* or **DSM-III-R,** of the American Psychiatric Association (1987, 4th ed.). It defines mental disorders and enables clinicians, researchers, and practitioners to communicate about abnormality using the same language. Thus, DSM-III-R provides not only a working set of definitions that aid diagnosis and treatment, but also, in some cases, information about etiology and specific criteria for making a diagnosis.

DSM-III-R uses a multiaxial, or multidimensional, system so that each individual can be comprehensively evaluated for the purposes of either planning a treatment program or predicting therapeutic outcome.

Axes I and II encompass all of the mental disorders. Axis II deals with personality disorders and specific developmental disorders, and axis I includes all other mental disorders. Axis III includes physical disorders and conditions. Each axis forms a dimension that refers to a unique bit of information about the individual. Each individual is assessed along each axis, and the first three axes represent the official diagnostic assessment.

Axes IV and V supplement the first three and are useful in arriving at a more complete understanding of the individual for treatment purposes. Axis IV deals with severity of psychosocial stresses, and Axis V focuses on highest level of adaptive functioning in the past year. Multiple diagnoses within axes are possible.

The clinician, using DSM-III-R, reaches a principal diagnosis (usually on Axis I), which refers to the condition for which the individual was recommended for assessment or admitted to care. Each entry within the five axes is accompanied by information about its (1) essential features, (2) associated (sometimes but not always present) features, (3) age of onset, (4) cause, (5) expected impairments in functioning, (6) complications, (7) predisposing factors, (8) prevalence, (9) sex ratio, (10) familial pattern, and (11) characteristics that distinguish it from other disorders. Following this information is specific diagnostic criteria for the disorder.

Relative to DSM-I (1952) and DSM-II, DSM-III (1980) and DSM-III-R represent major improvements as aids in diagnosis with the aged (see Butler et al., 1990; Gatz et al., 1980). Despite these improvements, however, we recommend its use with caution; it must be used conservatively. Diagnoses utilizing DSM with other age groups have proven somewhat unreliable (see Davison & Neale, 1990). While practitioners need to refer to DSM-III-R for hospital diagnoses or insurance forms, they should evaluate the definitions and classifications carefully, since these may not always clearly reflect reality for the older person. This is not to imply that DSM-III-R is useless, but it does suggest that we not let it blind us to what clinical experience, psychological tests, interviews with family, and so forth, have to tell us about the older person we are treating.

DSM-IV is currently being developed and should be complete by 1993 (Frances et al., 1989, 1990). Rather than change the criteria for diagnosis, DSM-IV will be more explicitly documented and therefore be more empirically based. It should also be clearer, simpler, and more clinically useful. Thus, the potential for misdiagnosis should be lessened (Frances et al., 1990). It is designed to be more compatible with the 10th edition of World Health Organization's *International Classification of Diseases* (ICD-10), also to be published in 1993. All of these changes should make DSM-IV more useful for the diagnosis of mental illness in elderly adults.

Current Models of Abnormal Behavior in Old Age

Aside from cataloging the varieties of abnormal behavior, in what general terms can we see psychopathology in the aged? Zarit (1980) and Eisdorfer (1983) have discussed several: the medical model, aging-as-illness model, and the behavioral model. In addition, they note the legal, statistical, humanistic, and social-deprivational models.

Briefly, the **medical model** assumes an underlying cause, usually of a physical or structural nature (a disease state), to be responsible for one's behavior. The outward symptoms are simply a manifestation of this disease. Alleviation of the symptoms via some form of treatment assumes that the disease process has been reversed. The **aging-as-illness model** stems from the medical model and assumes that the underlying illness is the aging process itself. The **behavioral model** focuses on the learning history of the person and those factors in the environment, or a person's perception of those factors, that cause and maintain behaviors, which, due to their consequences, are seen as maladaptive. This model is problem- or symptom-oriented, rather than attributing difficulties to some unobserved process or state.

While each approach has its advantages and disadvantages, we must remember that, strictly speaking, they cannot be compared in that they rest on entirely different assumptions, that is, what causes abnormal behavior (Reese & Overton, 1970). The medical model, on one hand, leads us to focus on a single internal disease state exclusive of the environment. It implies a single, best treatment for each disorder that is organic in nature. On the other hand, it has led to a more finely tuned approach to the identification of organic disorders in aged people (Zarit, 1980). The application of a behavioral strategy to defining abnormal behavior can be used to identify and change those aspects of the environment responsible for the maintenance of maladaptive behavior. However, it does not rely on judgment about the presence of what may be a vaguely defined condition.

Legal criteria for mental illness rest on assumed competence. *Humanistic* ideas about abnormality stress lack of individual growth and self-actualization. *Statistical* criteria imply that differences from others, expressed in behaviors that are rare in their frequency, create difficulties for people. The *social-deprivation* approach suggests that factors such as stress and isolation in and of themselves create pathology in the aged.

Zarit (1980) suggests that each of these models, taken singly, is a problem when applied to older individuals. How should competence be defined? How is one to evaluate departures from "optimal growth"? Are behaviors that are infrequent necessarily abnormal? Who is to define what stress is? Is stress necessarily bad? Are events generally seen as stressful, such as retirement, always viewed as such? When we attribute pathology to factors such as isolation, we are confusing the "problem" with the person (Cohen, 1980). For example, while some elderly individuals are isolated or in ill health, they are not necessarily abnormal simply *because* they are isolated, ill—or older, for that matter!

Many of those who hold the most negative attitudes toward the aged also believe in the aging-as-illness model. The central issue here is what we mean by anything being caused by old age. We generally do not view chronological age as being causal (see Chapter 1). Instead, age-related changes in behavior are dependent on other factors, such as cardiovascular status, life-style, and the number and spacing of individual stressors.

When people approach later adulthood, they do not suddenly, by virtue of being 65 or 70, become more abnormal. For example, it is one thing to say that age and depression are related; it is quite another to say *how* and *why* they are related. An older person may be depressed over factors that have nothing to do with aging per se, such as marital difficulties. Nevertheless, the aging-as-illness view contributes to the use of such nondescript terms as *senility,* which are of little value diagnostically. Moreover, they encourage a we-cannot-treat-this-person-because-he-or-she-is-old approach, which is, at worst, no effort at treatment, and at best, custodial care in an institution (Zarit, 1980).

It is likely that none of models discussed by Zarit is sufficient to define abnormal behavior in the aged adequately. But each contributes a piece of the puzzle. Thus, it is important to recognize how the models differ and that they may be combined in a meaningful way to aid in understanding maladaptive behavior in adulthood (Carson & Butcher, 1991).

SPECIFIC FORMS OF PSYCHOPATHOLOGY AMONG THE AGED

Here, we concentrate on the manifestations of the major forms of psychopathology that are *unique* to older people. We must not forget, however, that many of the factors contributing to these syndromes are *not* age-related. This awareness is perhaps the most important issue in best deciding how to treat a disturbed elderly person (see Gallagher et al., 1979).

Organic Disorders

ALZHEIMER'S DISEASE

Mr. Jones, 77 years old and a successful farmer in North Carolina for most of his adult life, was asked by his family to consult with a psychiatrist because they were concerned that his judgment had deteriorated. He retired from active farming at age 67, and after many years of intensive labor, enjoyed his rest and relaxation. Three sons and two tenant farmers continued growing tobacco, corn, and soybeans on his fertile 200 acres. He had negotiated an arrangement by which they would provide him a monthly portion of their income based on the success of the crop during the year. Never believing in banks, Mr. Jones received the payment in cash, as he had done most of his life, and kept it secured in his farmhouse.

Mr. Jones and his wife had few needs, and, therefore, most of the income was saved. Neither his wife nor family became concerned about his banking habits until one day he could not account for much of the income accumulated over the past two years. The money had been secured somewhere in the 12-room farmhouse (not in the usual hiding place), and Mr. Jones could not remember where he had put the money. About $25,000 had evidently been stuffed into books, dressers, cans, and other "banks."

On questioning, Mr. Jones was concerned that he had difficulty placing his hands on the money as quickly as he might like but did not see this as a major problem since he continued to receive regular income. Because he was increasingly distrustful of his sons, he was not inclined to tell them where he kept the money, nor was he willing to let them care for it. He believed his wife would give it to their sons and could not trust her with the money, either. Otherwise, Mr. Jones had no complaints. He slept well, ate well, and spent most of his day sitting on the porch or occasionally watching television. He expressed satisfaction with his life and little desire to do more than he was doing. Only with encouragement would he walk with his wife, yet he did not feel any decrease in his energy.

During an examination of his mental functioning, Mr. Jones knew his name, that he had been brought to a doctor, and that it was the fall of the year (harvest time). He was confused, however, as to the year, the month, and the day of the month but did not feel that this was important, given that he no longer was forced to keep up with such things. He was given a screening examination in the office, the Mini-Mental State Examination (a mental-status exam). His score suggested borderline severe cognitive impairment.

Despite being disoriented, Mr. Jones denied any memory problems other than "what would be expected at my age." In fact, he was not aware that the family had encouraged him to seek this examination for memory difficulties. He believed his major problem was back pain, and he complained of this only occasionally. Throughout the interview, Mr. Jones was pleasant, showed symptoms of neither anxiety nor depression, and could follow questions without difficulty, although his answers tended to be brief and provided little information beyond what was asked. (Blazer, 1990)

As the above example suggests, the diagnosis of **dementia** can be very disruptive for older individuals and their families. We use the term *dementia* to refer to a cluster of disorders that produce both cognitive and emotional changes in the older adult. The causes of dementia receiving the most attention at present are **multi-infarct dementia** and **Alzheimer's disease.**

The dominant feature of true, organically based dementia is brain-cell (neuronal) loss or impairment (see Chapter 3). It is important to note that, in dementia, brain-cell losses are correlated with a number of behavioral changes. For the most part, however, definitive answers of why brain cells degenerate have yet to be discovered. Once the exact cause of dementia is identified, treatments can be developed.

Whitbourne (1985) discusses several possible theories to explain the loss of brain cells with age. It may be that, while many neurons may serve overlapping functions, only when (1) certain critical connections between neurons, termed *synapses*, are severed through the loss of certain neurons, or (2) neuronal loss reaches a certain threshold, do people evidence changes in their behavior such as memory loss or learning difficulties.

Recent discoveries have isolated a specific group of proteins, called *beta-amyloids*, that kills brain cells and is particular to Alzheimer's disease (Selkoe, 1991). These proteins are located in certain areas of the brain and not others. In addition to the discovery of specific proteins that destroy brain cells, we have also learned that, for the form of Alzheimer's disease that occurs before the age of 60, there is a genetic mutation that seems to run in families. At present, however, there are also a number of genetic possibilities involving alterations in DNA that might produce the familial form of early-onset Alzheimer's disease. Although it can occur as early as age 30 (Selkoe, 1991), this form of Alzheimer's disease is relatively infrequent, affecting only a small percentage of Alzheimer's victims.

The classic global symptoms associated with Alzheimer's disease include disorientation to time and place, short-term and sometimes long-term memory loss, eye-hand coordination disturbances, impairment of intellect—specifically, deficits in calculation, learning new material, and abstraction—and impaired judgment (Gilhooly et al., 1986). Mental slowing is also frequently present (Nebes & Madden, 1988). Different forms of dementia manifest themselves somewhat differently, however. For example, people with Alzheimer's have more difficulty in recalling objects than in remembering locations (National Institute on Aging, 1989).

Alzheimer's disease affects between 4 and 6 percent of those 65 and older (Zarit & Zarit, 1983); and 20 percent of those age 80 or older exhibit signs of dementia. At present, 4 million Americans suffer from a specific form of dementia (Alzheimer's Disease Association, 1991). As age increases, the prevalence of Alzheimer's disease also increases, especially after age 75 (Evans et al., 1989). There is some reason to believe that, due to increased diagnostic sensitivity, even these figures may be underestimates, with the true prevalence far exceeding earlier figures of 2.5 million (Evans et al., 1989).

Alzheimer's is a disease of brain dysfunction named for its discoverer, Alois Alzheimer, in 1907. Many adults of normal intelligence become afflicted with Alzheimer's disease, which causes changes in their thinking and behavior, from accustomed patterns to bizarre and disoriented confusion. Forty-five to 50 percent of all dementias are due to Alzheimer's disease (Heston & White, 1991).

Individuals with Alzheimer's disease may act confused, paranoid, drunk, tired, or depressed, depending on their personality. Their judgment will be poor, and they may compensate for their inabilities for a period of time, when they can still realize their shortcomings. Sometimes, however, they appear quite normal, and in the early stages of the disease, they often deny they are experiencing any problem whatsoever.

Long known as senility and considered inevitable if one lived long enough, we now know that Alzheimer's disease is a specific disorder, *not* simply normal aging. There are other types of dementia, and careful diagnosis must be sought, though this is difficult to do in many cases, particularly in the early stages of the disease. Some people have mental-function problems that are reversible, but true Alzheimer's patients—if they have been diagnosed correctly—usually do not.

A diagnosis of Alzheimer's disease can be verified only by a histological exam. Early-onset dementia of the Alzheimer's type is more rapid and progressive than late-onset Alzheimer's disease (Heston & White, 1991).

Currently, DSM-III-R puts Alzheimer's disease in the category of primary degenerative dementia that is a late-onset (senile) type. In practice, the presence of higher than normal concentrations of senile plaques (clusters of dead or dying neurons) and neurofibrillary tangles (bundles of twisted neural fibers) in the cerebral cortex are adequate to identify Alzheimer's disease (see Chapter 3). People with Down syndrome who survive into adulthood also have elevated concentrations of plaques and tangles, again suggesting a genetic basis for Alzheimer's.

There are a variety of biochemical, electrophysiological, and neural changes associated with Alzheimer's disease that are often, on analysis after death, confounded by vascular damage associated with multiple cerebral infarcts (Bondareff, 1986; Gilhooly et al., 1986). However, since certain structures of the brain (hippocampus, amygdala, and brain stem) seem especially affected by plaques and tangles, postmortem diagnosis is relatively easy to make. In addition, people with Alzheimer's disease commonly show decreased levels of cortical neurotransmitters (acetylcholine and norepinephrine) (Bondareff, 1986). There is also a suspected link between increased levels of aluminum and the formation of tangles (Bondareff, 1986). Many people believe that there are distinct subtypes of Alzheimer's disease as well (American Psychiatric Association, 1987).

Often, individuals who are injured and taken to the emergency room, are in jail, or are in intensive-care units—particularly if they have been drinking or are on medication—act confused and have difficulty answering questions. This contributes to falsely diagnosed dementia of the Alzheimer's type.

Personality changes such as depression and withdrawal, anxiety, agitation, loss of interest in work, inability to concentrate, or denial of any problem may act as the first signals of the onset of Alzheimer's disease. Memory loss is the major symptom and may be the cause of many behavior and personality changes that coincide with early development of the disease. Patients are generally somewhat puzzled, if not unconcerned, about their memory loss and errors in judgment as the disease worsens. From occasional absentmindedness, Alzheimer's disease worsens to the point where individuals lose memory of all remembered and learned routines, facts, and information, including their names and the names of spouses and other family members.

Many everyday activities depend on memory, so daily life becomes chaotic and confusing when one cannot remember how to put on a jacket, tune a TV, or brush one's teeth. Personality and behavioral changes may involve disregard for habitual manners and morals, unforeseen, senseless mood swings from laughter to tears, or a sudden turnabout from love to hate. As noted above, the individual may not recognize those whom he or she has loved deeply for years.

Controls over physical functions also become impaired. Walking becomes an unsteady shuffle. Posture sags, and appetite decreases. Hallucinations of sight and sound occur. Bowel and bladder control is lost. Disorientation in space and time is pervasive. The individual may wander aimlessly and eventually become unable to communicate. The Alzheimer's patient becomes increasingly difficult for others to relate to, understand, and care for. Finally, the patient may fall into a coma, which results from secondary infections such as pneumonia.

As this discussion suggests, the symptoms of Alzheimer's disease are often most obvious in the early stages of the disorder, when people are still intact enough to realize that they are not as functional as they once were. It is at this point that they try to compensate for their failings and perhaps persist in denying that they are even ill. They may write notes to themselves to help them remember things, and they might make excuses to others when they lose their way. For example, they might say they had to work late to conceal the fact that they got lost on the way home from work.

Family members may reinforce this denial, preferring to see the patient's memory difficulties as just a part of the aging process (Pollitt et al., 1989). As time passes, however, the symptoms worsen, eventually leading to incontinence, complete disorientation, loss of overlearned information such as one's name, total dependence on others for care, and eventual death (see Table 10.1). People with Alzheimer's disease may live up to 20 years after diagnosis (Heston & White, 1991).

The severity of impairment in Alzheimer's disease varies with chronicity and diffusion of damage to the cerebral cortex (Pfeiffer, 1977). Those with the fewest personality resources (e.g., the fewest existing coping skills) and the least support from others, whose damage is diffuse and whose onset of symptoms is sudden, decline the most quickly.

In many cases, the primary, cognitive features of Alzheimer's disease are impossible to separate from those that are secondary (emotional) to structural losses in brain cells. For example, anxiety and depression are common reactions to Alzheimer's disease. And a true functional disorder—one that creates difficulties in everyday functioning for an individual despite intact brain function—may coexist with dementia. We will have more to say about functional disorders shortly.

TABLE 10.1

ALZHEIMER'S DISEASE—TYPICAL COURSE AND RANGE OF SYMPTOMS

Age of onset:	45 years of age or older
Premorbid history:	Usually unremarkable for emotional and physical health
Initial symptoms:	Psychiatric: depression, anxiety, agitation, withdrawal, hallucinations, paranoia, jealousy Memory: forgetfulness, i.e., "losing things," forgetting names, commitments; disorientation in new surroundings, i.e., getting "lost" in a store, or while driving
Middle stage symptoms:	Language: difficulty finding words in conversation or in naming objects; loss of verbal and behavioral spontaneity Withdrawal, i.e., no longer wants to go out or be with people (including friends and family) Purposeless overactivity, i.e., cleaning and re-cleaning the house Inability to handle professional and financial responsibilities Poor judgment and insight Social indiscretions; i.e., making loud demands in a restaurant or store, inappropriate verbalizations in public Lack of concern for the future
Late stage symptoms:	Decreased language skills; significant word finding problems; poor verbal comprehension; decreased reading, writing, and math skills Difficulty performing simple gestures Inability to use common objects such as stove, washing machine Gross disorientation in time and place, i.e., may become lost easily even in own home
Very advanced symptoms:	Total dependency on caretaker for simple tasks, i.e., dressing, eating, toilet functions Inability to comprehend or communicate with people No awareness of past or future
Death usually occurs 5–10 years after diagnosis of disease	

Source: Ware & Carper (1982).

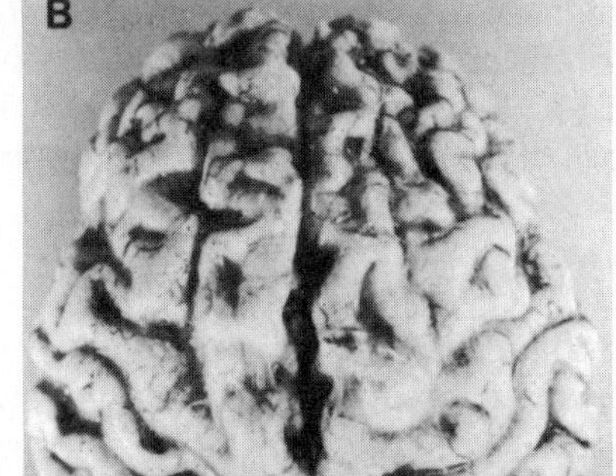

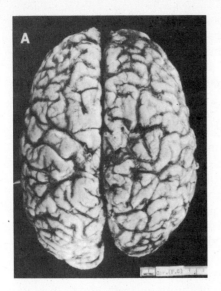

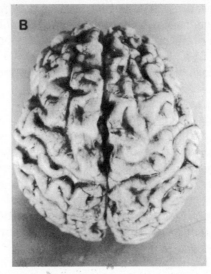

Relative to a normal aged brain (A), the brains of people suffering from Alzheimer's disease (B) are disproportionately small, and have alterations in both the fissures and sulci of the cerebral cortex.

After death, in addition to evidence of organic deterioration due to senile plaques and neurofibrillary tangles, the brain may appear small, with convolutions being smaller and fissures being wider than normal (see photos). Research in this area continues, specifically in studies of deficits in certain neurotransmitters inhibiting communication between neurons (i.e., acetylcholine and norepinephrine) and toxic accumulations of aluminum contributing to the formation of neurofibrillary tangles among those who have shown dementia symptoms (National Institute on Aging, 1989). And while we know that beta-amyloid proteins contribute to plaques and tangles, how and why such proteins are formed is still a mystery (Selkoe, 1991).

A diagnosis of Alzheimer's disease is best viewed descriptively. That is, it is based on symptoms and tells us little about etiology, or the underlying cause. Moreover, a diagnosis of Alzheimer's does not suggest any specific treatment. Complicating matters is the fact that many forms of dementia—Alzheimer's disease and *Pick's* disease, for example—are virtually indistinguishable, although there is some disagreement on this point (Sloan, 1980). Pick's disease is much rarer than is Alzheimer's. Strub and Black (1981) suggest that those with Pick's disease are socially inappropriate, slovenly, and unconcerned, despite cognitive intactness. Common symptoms are overeating, hypersexuality, and euphoria, and there is a unique type of neuronal loss distinct from that of Alzheimer's disease. In contrast, Alzheimer's patients are neat and quite social but have substantial intellectual loss. Pick's disease may be genetic in origin.

Usually, a diagnosis of Alzheimer's disease is made only after other causes for the individual's difficulties in concentration, memory, or abstract reasoning have been ruled out (Gilhooly et al., 1986). It is, therefore, a "diagnosis of exclusion." Clinically, the symptoms of all forms of dementia are similar and overlap with those of the normal aging process (see Chapter 3) (Gilhooly et al., 1986). However, as noted above, dementia is *not* an inevitable consequence of the aging process.

MULTI-INFARCT DEMENTIA

In addition to dementia of the Alzheimeı's type is repeated *multi-infarct dementia,* consisting of gradual yet somewhat progressive intellectual impairment brought on by a series of strokes of varying intensity. In many cases, abrupt changes in movement or memory function occur, followed by periods of mild recovery. Senile plaques and neurofibrillary tangles are typically absent (Bondareff, 1986). Multi-infarct dementia comprises 10 to 20 percent of all dementias (Bondareff, 1986; Heston & White, 1991; Zarit & Zarit, 1983). Its onset is somewhat earlier and more irregular than that of Alzheimer's disease. Definite cerebrovascular lesions (infarcts), the loss of brain tissue that results in softening of the brain from impaired blood flow, are present. In multi-infarct dementia, personality and insight into one's behavior are relatively unimpaired until late in the disorder, and emotional lability is common (Heston & White, 1991; Sloan, 1980). Memory loss is thought to be "spotty," and high blood pressure is often present.

In many cases, cerebral blood vessels are completely blocked, producing major damage to the brain, termed *strokes.* Strokes often are quite severe, leaving the patient paralyzed, with severely impaired speech, and impaired intellectual functioning. In other cases, strokes are fatal. A variety of other symptoms, such as limb weakness and acalculia (inability to perform calculations), are often present. Wernicke's aphasia, or loss of ability to comprehend language and inappropriate language; and agnosia, inability to recognize objects, may accompany multi-infarct dementia.

Multi-infarct dementia is considerably less common than often believed. And there are even those who doubt the role that impaired blood flow to the brain plays in accounting for its symptoms (Marsden, 1978). With hypertension medication, and/or surgery, vascular disorders leading to multi-infarct dementia can be prevented. Moreover, changes in diet and exercise, treatment of diabetes mellitus, and discouraging use of alcohol and tobacco can be quite helpful (Bondareff, 1986).

Among the other dementias that have been defined symptomatically are *Huntington's Chorea,* which is comparatively rare and thought to be genetic in origin. It is accompanied by peculiar writhing movements that are easily identified by a physician. *Parkinson's* disease is a degenerative neuromuscular disease involving progressive loss of motor control. It may also produce dementia. Normal-pressure hydrocephalus is a treatable accumulation of cerebrospinal fluid producing dementialike symptoms. In some cases, too, AIDS can produce dementia, and there is a rare, viral form of dementia termed *Creutzfeldt-Jacob disease.* Its onset is, in contrast to Alzheimer's, usually well defined, and death occurs relatively quickly, within two months.

The diagnosis of Alzheimer's disease and its distinction from other forms of dementia require a thorough physical, neurological, and cognitive evaluation by an interdisciplinary team of professionals. In addition to a complete physical and neurological exam, a detailed family history, psychological testing to assess cognitive and personality functioning, as well as assessment of any drug regimen the individual may be on are all essential. But again, it is only through an autopsy of brain tissue at death that a definitive diagnosis of Alzheimer's disease can be made (Heston & White, 1991). When other causes of Alzheimer's are ruled out, a probable diagnosis can be confirmed by reassessing the individual over a period of three to six months to observe progressive changes in intellectual functioning.

Helping Alzheimer's Patients and Their Families

Managing the symptoms of Alzheimer's disease is critical to the well-being of both the patient and his or her family. Indeed, families have been termed "secondary victims" of the disease because of the hopelessness of its prognosis, as well as its progressive, unrelenting nature—much like a diagnosis of AIDS (Gatz & Peason, 1988).

Managing the cognitive, physical, and behavioral consequences of Alzheimer's disease is a skill that must be acquired. For this reason, family members must be educated about the nature of the disease, its course and progression, aspects of daily life, as well as self-care. Many such programs exist for this purpose; a typical one is illustrated in Table 10.2.

Families must be aware of the changing cognitive skills of the Alzheimer's victim, because errors in judgment can have many consequences. Some of them are relatively minor, while others can be catastrophic—auto accidents, explosions (leaving the gas on after cooking), injury (falls, cuts, or burns from cooking), or financial hardship (not being able to pay bills or balance a checkbook).

Surprisingly, giving up a job or household responsibilities is easy, relatively speaking—people become quite anxious when they realize they can no longer work as they once did. However, some individuals, especially men, may resist giving up driving, as it permits them some autonomy and may be the last vestige of pride in one's skills. Not being able to drive safely, getting lost, and injuring oneself or others become real possibilities. In some cases, car keys must be hidden—suspending the Alzheimer's victim's driver's license may not be sufficient.

As the disease progresses, keeping things on an even keel in all respects becomes increasingly important. Individuals are easily overwhelmed by sudden changes in a room's physical appearance or everyday routines, as well as new people in their home environment. Even changes in the volume or tone of a family member's voice, as might occur when a wife yells at her afflicted husband, can evoke a great deal of anxiety accompanied by crying, withdrawal, acting-out behavior, or increased mental incompetence (Heston & White, 1991; Mace & Robbins, 1991). Attention to the patient's level of fatigue, wandering, bowel and bladder hygiene, as well as household safety, is essential. For example, constipation or incon-

TABLE 10.2

CAREGIVERS EDUCATION: PROGRAM AWARE*

I. Week 1: Nature and history of Alzheimer's disease
   A. "Forgetfulness" vs. sustained memory loss
   B. Diagnostic evaluation: exclude reversible causes
   C. Related disorders
   D. Pathology and consequent behavior
   E. Theories of causation
   F. Course, individuality
   G. Management of symptoms

II. Week 2: Stresses of caring for the A.D. patient
   A. Psychological responses of caregivers
   B. Impact of behavioral difficulties on caregiver
   C. Means of managing behaviors
   D. Means of modifying caregiver stress
   E. Communication techniques

III. Week 3: Daily care of A.D. patients
   A. Assessing functional abilities
   B. Potentiating preserved skills
   C. Simplifying tasks
   D. Providing meaningful, "failure-free" activities
   E. Managing behavioral difficulties
   F. Involving home health care
   G. Adapting the environment

IV. Week 4: Nutrition and the A.D. patient
   A. Nutritional changes throughout the aging process
   B. Meal management
   C. Management of nutritional problems
   D. Recipes

Continued

tinence must be regularly monitored, especially since incontinence often leads to institutionalization (Heston & White, 1991). Family members should make sure to check that smoke alarms are working, remove dials and knobs from stoves, and be certain that house keys and car keys can always be found. Dangerous areas such as attics, basements, garages, or swimming pools should be locked. Identity bracelets or identifying labels on clothes can be quite helpful.

All of these adjustments demand patience and compassion. Families, especially spouses (who are most likely to be caregivers), need to realize that a diagnosis of Alzheimer's disease need not be cause for shame. In fact, relatives and neighbors may need to be told, if only to help the family handle such problems as wandering or acting out. Perhaps most difficult are the "many deaths" families experience. Realizing that the person to whom you have been married for 30 years no longer recognizes you, can no longer remember your birthday or anniversary, can no longer tie

Continued

V. Week 5: Community services and long-term care
   A. Available programs
   B. Alternative living arrangements
   C. Legal assistance
   D. Medicare and Medicaid
   E. Information agencies (Alzheimer's Association)

VI. Week 6: Current research
   A. Describing the disease process
   B. Identifying possible causes
   C. Methods of treatment
   D. Caregiver studies

VII. Week 7: Changing family roles and relationships
   A. Family structure
   B. Role changes
   C. "New" responsibilities
   D. Recognizing negative feelings about caregiving
   E. Identifying caregiver concerns and goals

VIII. Week 8: Coping and caregiving: Living with A.D.
   A. Easing the burden
   B. Caring for yourself
   C. The future

*Each caregiver is provided with a detailed booklet that supplements and expands on each week's discussion topics.

Source: Joseph M. Foley. Elder Health Center, University Hospitals of Cleveland.

his or her shoes, bathe, shave, or go to the toilet independently, can be quite painful. Not being able to be sexually intimate can be particularly disheartening (Wright, 1991).

The many losses that the family endures take time to adjust to. With appropriate help and support, however, most families come to terms with the illness and the demands it makes on them physically, emotionally, and financially (Whitlatch et al., 1991). In this respect, it is important to see that the caregiver has his or her own limits and needs relief from providing care to an impaired husband, wife, father, or mother. For many loved ones, caring for themselves becomes as much a problem as does caring for the impaired loved one. They feel tired, angry, and then guilty about their feelings or not fulfilling their responsibilities well enough.

Being able to share feelings, find sources of support, and learn new caregiving skills are the focus of Alzheimer's support groups, often sponsored by one of over 200 chapters of the Alzheimer's Association. Such support can be crucial to the caregiver's survival. For example, in one case, a wife had been caring for her impaired husband for 10 years. He was a counselor in private practice, very proud and protective of his wife, yet he refused to acknowledge that he could no longer manage his business affairs—the couple had filed for bankruptcy twice. When questioned, his wife admitted to having thoughts of killing herself. She had little access to help, and she was unable to express her anger at her husband. When asked if she had made any close friends to whom she could turn in the 10 years they had lived in the city, she broke down, crying. "I have no one," she said.

Even in the best of circumstances, caregivers, who are more often than not wives but also daughters or daughters-in-law, do experience feelings of burden. Depression, impaired health, feelings of helplessness and isolation, and loss of satisfaction with life are often negative consequences of caregiving (Chenoweth & Spencer, 1986; Colevick & George, 1986; Gallagher et al., 1989: Haley et al., 1987; Lawton et al., 1989).

What seems to be critical is how the demands of caregiving are interpreted (Deimling & Bass, 1986) as well as the impact of the disease on the family as a whole (Gatz et al., 1990; Pearlin et al., 1990). For example, how are symptoms interpreted? Are they seen as manageable? Is there help with caregiving? What are the likely outcomes for the caregiver? the impaired family member? the family network? How are caregiving responsibilities handled? As the patient's condition worsens, will family members, friends, and neighbors be there to help? If arguments about caregiving arise, how are they resolved? If necessary, whose decision is it to institutionalize the elder? How will such care be paid for? Table 10.3 illustrates many of the common concerns caregivers express, many of which can be dealt with by either individual or family therapy (Smith et al., 1991).

Anger and frustration often characterize feelings of burden in family members who must care for a loved one with dementia.

TABLE 10.3

COMMON CAREGIVER CONCERNS

Improving coping skills

Time management Includes problems of the caregiver not having enough time for personal activities. Problems inferring an inability to manage time or to be organized also belong here.

Dealing with stress Includes problems regarding coping with stress and anxiety, especially from caregiving.

Other coping mechanisms Includes problems that emphasize caregiver's realization of the need to develop/use various coping mechanisms such as forbearance, assertiveness, sharing feelings and concerns over caregiving with others, enhancing personal control, and modeling peers.

Family issues

Regarding husband Includes problems regarding such concerns as lack of time to spend with husband, motivating him to become more involved in caregiving and impact of caregiving on marriage.

Regarding siblings Includes problems having to do with both getting siblings to assume more responsibility in caregiving and caregiver's feelings of anger and resentment toward siblings.

Regarding caregiver's children Includes problems focused on the impact or issues that caregiving has raised for caregiver's children.

Responding to elder's care needs

Emotional behavioral Includes problems involving issues that are primarily psychological or behavioral in nature, such as dealing with elder's affect, cognitive problems, motivation, involvement in daily living tasks, and relationships with people other than the caregiver.

Physical safety Includes problems focused on elder's physical well-being and overall safety such as handling medical emergencies, concern over elder's physical limitations, etc.

Legal financial Includes problems involving elder's legal and financial affairs.

Quality of relationship with elder

Includes problems of caregiver's feelings toward elder: the wish to avoid conflict with elder: elder's inability to respond to caregiver's needs: being the central figure in elder's life; and having quality communication with elder.

Eliciting formal and informal support

Includes problems involving caregiver's recognition of the need for or attempt to get assistance with caregiving duties from sources including relatives other than spouse, respite services, and community services.

Guilt and feelings of inadequacy

Guilt Includes problems regarding any expression of "guilt" whatsoever by the caregiver.

Feelings of inadequacy Includes problems over caregiver's feelings relating to low self-esteem, lack of confidence, and lack of self-acceptance.

Long-term planning

Includes problems focused on planning for elder's future. Including such issues as considering or applying for nursing homes, and discussions with elder or other family members about future arrangements.

Description of pressing problem categories. These categories were generated from the over 100 problems listed by the entire sample of 51 clients in the study.

Source: Smith et al. (1991).

It is important to recognize that caring for a loved one with Alzheimer's can have its positive side. Caregivers derive a great deal of satisfaction in doing everything that they can (Gatz et al., 1990; Lawton et al., 1989). Families can be drawn closer together, and in some cases, the quality of a marriage may actually improve (Gatz et al., 1990).

While some forms of dementia are commonly believed to be irreversible, to suggest that such memory loss is beyond help would be incorrect (see Box 10.1). A decrement-with-compensation approach (see Chapter 1) can be quite helpful in designing a supportive environment that can lessen the effects of such losses. This perspective is illustrated in a study by Zarit et al. (1982), who used a cognitive training approach (didactic visual imagery, practical problem solving) to facilitate memory performance in a group of community living elderly with memory impairments characteristic of Alzheimer's disease. The gains they observed were small, however, and not specific to training. Some individuals benefited more than did others. The authors state that, while caregivers (family) were, on average, more depressed after the training, the sessions illuminated the extent of their loved ones' memory loss to them.

ADULTS SPEAK

CAREGIVING AND COPING

"I feel that something has been snatched from me," said one older woman who had looked forward to retirement with her husband. He had been diagnosed with Alzheimer's disease and could no longer manage the family business. Moreover, his inability to manage it made it even less marketable. She became angry at him because he could no longer function. He screamed back at her, "You're not my wife. My wife has crow-black hair." Indeed, she did, decades ago. His daughter said, "I feel about my father and the tragedy of the disease the way I felt about Beethoven going deaf. The thing that was greatest about him, his mind, he lost."

A man talking eight years after placing his mother in a nursing home: "Sometimes when there is a real good soprano in the church choir, I choke up. You see, mother sang at weddings and funerals, and she always sang the 'Star-spangled Banner' at local events. So when I hear a really good soprano, I feel that I am witnessing the prolonged, living death of a person who was once one thing and now is nothing. And in witnessing her living death, I end up being a weekly mourner. I sometimes resent that I can't go to church without crying."

The daughter-in-law of an afflicted woman talked about the dark feelings she had had over the years about caring for a person who, after all, "isn't even my mother": "Every one of these people walking into that nursing home on Sunday afternoon is there out of guilt. . . . They certainly don't look happy . . . I think to myself, 'I hope my kids never put me in one.'"

A caregiver who had lost 40 pounds, and whose hair had fallen out to such an extent that she had to wear a wig, went to her doctor, who told her her problems were the result of stress and advised her to forget everything for an hour a day: "Now how can you forget an 85-year-old woman lying in bed calling, 'Flo, come here. Flo. Flo?' How can you forget that? How can you hear it and not go see what's wrong? Of course, there's never anything wrong, but how can you just sit and say, 'I'm gonna ignore you'?"

A professional social worker was surprised at some of her emotions when she became caregiver to her mother: "There was a sort of gleeful maliciousness in some of my reactions to her, particularly in terms of my being more competent than she was. . . . All my life, my mother was 'in charge.' And I always had to struggle, somehow, to find my place in the sun. As bad as it was, there was something about this situation that, at times, I secretly relished."

The same social worker reflected on the Alzheimer's child's nightmare: "Of course, everytime I forget something—and I do forget—I think, what's going to happen? I have visions of myself in my mother's painful condition. Maybe it's one of the reasons it's so painful to be with my mother. I see myself there. It's just overwhelming. It's times like that when I really do believe it would be nice if we could work out some system when, at a given point, a committee or somebody says, 'Here, drink this, Honey.' And that's the end of that."

Source: Alzheimer's Association.

BOX 10.1

CAN A PERSON WITH ALZHEIMER'S DISEASE STILL LEARN?

Camp and his colleagues have demonstrated that after as few as two brief training sessions, memory-impaired elderly people could remember the name of a staff person using the *spaced-retrieval technique* (Camp, 1990; Camp & McKitrick, 1991; Camp & Schaller, 1989). This technique initially involves presenting the client with the name to be learned and the client's repeating the name. Sixty seconds later, the client's inability to remember the name was verified. Subsequently, this process was repeated, with the staff member seated across from the older client. A correct answer caused the interval to the next test trial to increase; an incorrect answer caused it to decrease. Between trials, client and examinee engaged in social conversation as a distractor. Intervals between trials increased from 5 seconds to 120 seconds. One week later, the process was repeated, with trial intervals increasing from 120 seconds to 240 seconds. Between trials, musical notes prompted the client's recall. One week later, the client was able to spontaneously recall the name of the staff member; this was maintained 6 months later. The advantages of this technique are that clients can experience immediate success at remembering and that it is less cognitively demanding than other, more elaborate memory enhancement techniques (Camp & Schaller, 1989) such as the method of loci (see Chapter 5). The entire technique is social—talking and playing music or games between trials. Thus, it is less threatening and more enjoyable to the memory-impaired elder, who may already be sensitized to his or her memory deficits and failures (Camp & Stevens, 1990).

These findings suggest that even some severely impaired elderly can use memory-improvement strategies but that individual differences in this capacity are great. In the Zarit et al. (1982) study, it may be that these impaired elders' lessened expectations of themselves or their unwillingness to use the imagery techniques provided for them accounted for the limited success of memory training (see Chapter 5). While most studies evaluating the success of caregiver interventions do not strongly support their impact (Gatz et al., 1990), they can be helpful in many respects (Smith et al., 1991).

As discussed above, the burdens experienced by the families of those with dementia are great. Zarit et al. (1980) found that feelings of burden were greater when the aged person was not visited by other relatives. Interestingly, they found also that the severity of behavior problems accompanying dementia (e.g., memory loss, mood swings, lessened ability to care for oneself) was not related to family caregivers'—primarily spouses'—feelings of stress due to providing care. Deimling and Bass (1986) reported the same results. These findings highlight the importance of social support being available in the community to lessen feelings of helplessness, anger, and depression that family members often experience in caring for an aged relative (Burtz, Eaton, & Bond, 1988).

Lazarus and associates (1981) found that family members of an individual with Alzheimer's disease became more knowledgeable about the course of the illness and were able to be more realistic and accepting about what they could and could not expect from the elder. As a consequence, they were able to cope with their own feelings of ambivalence about the ill relative. Similar success has been reported by Hausman (1979) in dealing with feelings about (1) the dependence of an elderly parent on an adult, and (2) the children's fears of their own (and their parents') aging and death brought about by the realities of having to care for an elderly parent. In small discussion groups, issues such as their parents' grief, self-centeredness, and communication problems involving the adult children and other relatives and professionals were successfully brought out in the open, shared, and solutions reached. Hausman (1979) suggests that these children learned to be more in touch with their parents' feelings, helping them cope with their own (as well as their parents') feelings precipitated much later on by institutionalization, retirement, ill health, or death. A "coming together" can be brought about by such changes. However, the task of coping with these events is made easier if preestablished patterns of relating to one another in an open, honest, and supportive manner are available to both parent and child.

Note that a study by Reifer et al. (1981) found that aged people with dementia or depression tended to underestimate the extent of their illnesses. For this reason, family members are often a valuable source of information. As discussed above, such denial can be adaptive; it may represent an attempt to cope with a situation over which the elder has no control, or a response to the family's lessened expectations of him or her as an older person. More extensive discussions of interventions for caregivers of people with dementia can be found in Cicirelli (1986), Gatz et al. (1990), Gwyther and George (1986), Zarit and Anthony (1986), Haley et al. (1987), Smith et al. (1991), and Zarit et al. (1987).

While at present we cannot reverse Alzheimer's disease, behavioral interventions, reality orientation, and individual and group therapy (see Chapter 11) can be helpful to both the Alzheimer's victim and the caregiver. Moreover, relatively straightforward changes in furniture arrangement, carefully defining areas within an institution to lessen random wandering, and orienting people via signs are all things that can make life more predictable for the caregiver and alleviate feelings of anxiety and agitation in the patient (Zarit & Anthony, 1986). Relaxation and imagery training can lessen confusion and increase self-care skills by helping dementia patients to focus their attention on the environment (Weldon & Yesavage, 1982).

We will have more to say about interventions for caregivers as a form of family therapy in Chapter 11.

Disorders That Mimic Dementia

In addition to distinguishing among the several types of dementia, one must be sensitive to those conditions that symptomatically mimic irreversible organicity but are treatable and reversible (Butler et al., 1990; Heston & White, 1991).

This distinction has tremendous importance for the elderly. Writing these disorders off as senility or organic may overlook a variety of conditions that, if left untreated, can deteriorate to the point where they become irreversible. To avoid such errors, diagnosis should be based on a comprehensive exam. Such an examination should include a complete physical, drug history, CAT scan, careful personal history from the older person and the family, and a psychometric evaluation of cognitive functioning. If the exam reveals the absence of such dementialike conditions, then the elderly person can be treated for the symptoms that are truly characteristic of organically based dementia. But reversible dementialike conditions may be caused by prescription-drug toxicity, side effects of drugs such as sedatives or anti-agitation drugs (LaRue et al., 1985), polypharmacy (drug interactions) (LaRue et al., 1985), infections, neurosyphilis, cerebral tumors, metastatic cancerous tumors, especially those that have spread to the brain from the lungs, and alcohol or drug abuse (Heston & White, 1991).

DELIRIUM

Mrs. Bishop was an 80-year-old woman, living alone, who fell while walking down the steps after church on Sunday morning. She fractured the upper bone in her left leg near its attachment to the pelvis—a femoral neck fracture. Following evaluation by an orthopedic surgeon, it was decided that the fracture was not severe enough to require surgery but could be treated with traction and immobility. She improved over the next few days and appeared to adjust to the hospital without difficulty, although she did require a sedative at night—flurazepam (Dalmane) 30 mg—for five days after being hospitalized.

Bored in the hospital, Mrs. Bishop typically requested the Dalmane at 8 P.M. and immediately fell asleep. She would sleep well until 2 A.M., when she became agitated and frightened and did not know where she was. This happened four nights after she first took Dalmane. The nurses could not understand this dramatic change in her behavior. When their attempts to calm her failed, they called the intern on call. The doctor frightened her even more, for she perceived him to be "a man in a white coat coming to take me away." He gave her the tranquilizer haloperidol (Haldol) by injection, and after the second dose she went to sleep. She became agitated again the next morning, but the agitation lasted only 30 minutes or so, and she calmed down and seemed to do well during the day.

She had little memory of what had occurred during the previous night. The sleeping medication was discontinued. Although she had considerable difficulty sleeping during the next two or three nights, she improved dramatically, and three days later, when she was discharged from the hospital, she was sleeping well; the fear and agitation had disappeared. Two weeks later, she returned to see the orthopedic surgeon for an evaluation and reported the confusion she had experienced in the hospital (Blazer, 1990).

Was this woman suffering from dementia? Probably not. Instead, she experienced delirium, which is dementialike but treatable. Treated delirium is generally short-lived (less than a week), but if left untreated it can result in permanent cerebral damage and death (Raskind & Peskind, 1992; Sloan, 1980). It may result from drug toxicity, simple exhaustion, a blow to the head, heart disease, malnutrition, anemia, diabetes, fluid-electrolyte disturbances, hepatitis, fever, and acute alcoholic intoxication (Blazer, 1990; Butler et al., 1990; Teri & Reifer, 1987). Symptoms such as agitation, paranoia, depression, disorientation, incontinence, lethargy, and sleeplessness have been documented as consequences of drug toxicity or drug interactions in the aged, particularly with barbiturate use (Bressler, 1987;

Gray & Hayslip, 1990; Heston & White, 1991; Hicks et al., 1980). Such problems can easily be misinterpreted as reflecting organicity or a functional disorder.

ALCOHOLISM AND DEMENTIA

Alcoholism can play a central role in the misdiagnosis of dementia in the aged (Zimberg, 1987). But with alcoholism, cognitive losses are much less severe, as is disorientation; emotional lability is often present. Delirium tremens (DTs) and hallucinations are common during withdrawal. Treatment is definitely possible but may take up to two years. If left untreated, a so-called "alcoholic dementia," characterized by memory loss and falsification to fill in gaps (Korsakoff's syndrome), which is indistinguishable from other dementias, usually appears if alcohol abuse has been chronic (Carson & Butcher, 1991; Raskind & Peskind, 1992). The symptoms of barbiturate use and withdrawal are similar to those of alcohol abuse over a long length of time (Sloan, 1980).

Common Functional Disorders

In discussing **functional disorders** in the aged, we will confine our discussion to depression and suicide, paranoia, schizophrenia, and anxiety. Sleep disturbances and hypochondriasis are more properly thought of as outgrowths of these functional problems.

DEPRESSION

Mrs. Sawyer, 70 years old and "without a care," complained to her family physician that she had lost much of her motivation and interest. The symptoms were not severe, yet she noticed that they had begun to interfere with her activities and dampened much of the pleasure she previously derived from her busy schedule. Her feelings were unexplained, though she believed "I should feel better than ever," for many former family problems had been resolved, financial struggles had been overcome, and her good health continued. Although she loved her grandchildren, she found herself dreading their visits. Hobbies she previously pursued had been discarded. At times, she would stare into space for many minutes before she realized that her mind had wandered. An avid jogger, she had neglected her exercise program as well.

Mrs. Sawyer also reported difficulty sleeping. She awakened two or three times during the night and, for the last time, a couple of hours before her husband in the morning. Her appetite had decreased, and she had lost five pounds over three months. She perceived a decrease in her energy, though when forced to respond in a situation, she could manage her household responsibilities and social engagements. On occasion, she would find herself crying for no apparent reason. Yet, what disturbed her the most was her loss of interest in virtually everything she did. Even when she accompanied her husband on a trip or was invited to a close friend's house for an evening meal, she had to force herself and found little pleasure from her efforts. These feelings were not acceptable to Mrs. Sawyer, for she had previously been a happy and secure woman (Blazer, 1990).

The above older person is depressed. Depression is the most common functional disorder in the aged (Burke et al., 1990; Cohen, 1990), with estimates as high as 15 percent. We must be careful to separate transient depressive reactions from prolonged, dysfunctional depression in aged people, which is often referred to as complicated or pathological bereavement. By this we mean that the response of depression is out of proportion to the loss. It is unrealistic, self-destructive, and harmful to oneself and others.

Older people are often reluctant to admit to feeling depressed and may mask their depression through a variety of ego defense mechanisms. They may use denial, counterphobic defenses (overcompensation), or express symptoms through somatic complaints and hypochondriasis (Salzman & Shader, 1979). For this reason, it is important to separate depression-related somatic (bodily) disturbances from genuine physical illnesses. In addition, sleep disturbances may or may not be symptomatic of depression or anxiety (Blazer, 1990; Salzman & Shader, 1979; Stenback, 1980). Depression may precede or result from a serious illness or pain (Parmalee et al., 1991), or it may be a byproduct of drug effects (Blazer, 1990; Gray & Hayslip, 1990).

It is also very important to separate the normal depression accompanying loss and grief (see Chapter 12) from that which is pathological. For those who (1) are in poor health, (2) have the fewest or most limited range of coping skills, (3) are isolated from others, or (4) are in situations they feel are beyond their control, such as being institutionalized or forcibly retired, pathological depression as a response to loss is more likely (Stenback, 1980; J. A. Peterson, 1980).

Depression in both younger and older people has many common features. In a study of over 4,500 adults aged 50 and older, Lewinsohn et al. (1991) found that depression tends to be associated with everyday stress, less support from and interaction with others, fewer interpersonal skills, and fewer pleasurable activities. Moreover, depressed individuals typically think less rationally, have more negative expectations of themselves and about the future, and tend to externalize success (Lewinsohn et al., 1991). Major life events, alcohol use, and the tendency to internalize failure did not relate to depression. What was unique to older people who were depressed was poor health. In general, however, complaints about memory, sleep difficulties, and low self-esteem all correlated with depression independent of age.

In late-life depression, it is crucial to understand that it involves *narcissistic* losses—that is, valued aspects of oneself. For example, loss of one's health, a significant person, status at work or in the community, cognitive abilities, or part of one's body through illness or surgery are all terribly central to most of us, let alone to an older person. What is critical is not the loss per se but the perception that this loss cannot be replaced.

Older people who are depressed manifest two major symptoms (Blazer, 1990; Stenback, 1980): *depressive mood* (sadness, guilt, hopelessness, helplessness) and *reduced behavior* (giving up, apathy). Those who are depressed often feel excessively guilty or anxious or are aggressive. Negativism and other cognitive disturbances such as limited attention, disorganized thought, and short-term memory loss, and a variety of physical complaints such as indigestion or sleeplessness and suicidal ideas are also often present.

Recently, Newmann et al. (1991) have discovered that individuals aged 65 to 92 expressed their depression in terms of *depletion*. They felt worthless, lost interest in daily activities, lost their appetites, and felt hopeless. They frequently thought about death and dying. Younger elders, in contrast, expressed their depression in terms of depressive moods.

Gallagher and Thompson (1983) have defined major depression in terms of five major components, according to *Research Diagnostic Criteria* (RDC) (Spitzer et al., 1978), which they maintain are more discriminating regarding types of depression and more stringent than those specified by DSM-III-R. According to these standards, the following components must be present for a major depressive episode to be diagnosed:

1. Mood disturbance
2. Five of eight related symptoms: psychomotor agitation, recurrent thoughts of suicide, weight loss, sleep difficulty, loss of energy, loss of interest in pleasurable activity, feelings of worthlessness/guilt, and diminished concentration
3. Duration of two weeks or more
4. No evidence of schizophrenia
5. Evidence of impaired functioning (e.g., at work, school, home, taking medication)

While estimates of depression have ranged as high as 15 percent based on less stringent criteria, when using the RDC, the true prevalence among the aged of depression is closer to 4 to 6 percent (Gallagher & Thompson, 1983). Reflecting their perspective of depression as the "final common pathway" for a number of more narrowly defined disorders, Gallagher and Thompson (1983) recommend a comprehensive multidimensional assessment procedure to positively diagnose depression in the aged, similar to that used in the diagnosis of dementia.

Biological factors (biochemical disturbances) and social/cultural factors (loss, cultural views regarding the worth of the aged, isolation, death, retirement, institutionalization) can contribute to depression in older people (Butler et al., 1990; Cohen, 1990; LaRue et al., 1985).

Psychological factors such as reactions to physical change, perceived loss of sexuality and material possessions, failure, inability to replace the loss of others—all contribute to depression in the older person. Depression can be mild (transient, reactive) and characterized by hypochondriacal preoccupation; it may also be neurotic, representing an attempt to cope with early childhood conflicts (Stenback, 1980). In addition to hypochondriasis, severe depressions are characterized by excessive guilt, a great deal of anxiety, delusions, excessive fatigue, dysphoria (a general feeling of not being well), excessive use of alcohol, and suicidal thoughts. When manic behavior accompanies depression, it is termed **bipolar;** if no mania is present, depression is termed **unipolar** (Carson & Butcher, 1991).

Depression seems to feed on itself. One might think that depressed people would want to learn new techniques for coping with their problems. However, Foster and Gallagher (1986) compared older people who were being treated for major depressive disorder and nondepressed aged in terms of perceived helpfulness of new techniques in coping with various life events and feeling "down." These authors found that depressed elders made less use of information seeking (finding out more, seeking advice from others) and problem solving (taking specific action) than did younger depressives (Billings et al., 1983). Elderly depressed people were more likely to use emotional discharge (verbal outbursts, drug use, eating, smoking) as coping techniques than nondepressed ones. Despite the fact that depressed and nondepressed aged used similar types of coping strategies, the depressed aged individuals rated these efforts as less helpful. Perhaps they had already decided that the situation was beyond hope (Foster & Gallagher, 1986). Maiden (1987) found elderly depressed women to experience *personal helplessness* ("I will fail at this task"), while nondepressed women expressed a more generalized and less devastating *universal helplessness* ("Everyone would fail at this task"). Depression can be treated in therapy or with antidepressants (see Chapter 11), though exercise may also be effective (McNeil et al., 1991).

PSEUDODEMENTIA

Mrs. Johnson was 70 years old when her husband died in April, after a protracted illness. Her two daughters noticed, even at the funeral, that their mother was "not herself." Over the next month, she virtually stopped eating: she would eat only at the insistence of her daughters, who attended her throughout a meal. She would neither dress nor bathe herself, usually staying in nightclothes during the day. She sat around most of the day staring into space and rarely spoke unless spoken to. When her daughters attempted to converse with her, she responded with irrelevant and "crazy-sounding" remarks. In May, she was taken to a neurologist, for her primary-care physician believed her to be severely demented. Had she possibly suffered a stroke? Her daughters protested. She was doing well until the death of their father. "How could she lose her mind so quickly?"

When she was evaluated by a psychiatrist, Mrs. Johnson said virtually nothing. The psychiatrist immediately suspected she was suffering a severe, psychotic depression. He placed her in the hospital and started medications. Since she refused to eat, a nasogastric tube was placed into her stomach for feeding. Finally, the psychiatrist prescribed electroconvulsive therapy (ECT). After he discussed the necessity of the treatment and the expected outcome with both the patient and her family, all agreed to proceed with the treatments. Nine treatments later, Mrs. Johnson had returned to her former self. She left the hospital on a low dose of lithium carbonate and was doing well three years after hospitalization (Blazer, 1990).

In order for accurate diagnosis and treatment of depression to occur, physical causes must be ruled out. Often, physical and mental illness go hand in hand (see Box 10.2). In these cases, the treatment of depression may consist of providing support in time of loss and drug therapy with lithium or tricyclics, though illness may alter the body's response to drugs

BOX 10.2

EXAMPLES OF RELATIONSHIPS BETWEEN MENTAL AND PHYSICAL HEALTH IN OLDER ADULTS

The Impact of Psychogenic Stress That Leads to Physical Health Consequences
Example: Anxiety → gastrointestinal symptoms
The accurate diagnosis of gastrointestinal (GI) symptoms can be very difficult in the elderly, with research showing that as many as 5 of 9 older persons with GI trouble may experience psychogenic problems that lead to their physical discomfort.

The Effect of Physical Disorder That Leads to Psychiatric Disturbance
Example: Hearing loss → onset of delusions
More than 25% of the elderly have a hearing impairment; a sensory-deprivation phenomenon may lead to psychotic symptoms in certain vulnerable individuals; an increased frequency of hearing loss has also been identified in older adults with late-onset schizophrenia.

The Interplay of Coexisting Physical and Mental Disorders
Example: Congestive heart failure + depression → further cardiac decline
Cardiac disorder and depression are two of the most common health problems of the elderly. A covert depression could bring about indirect suicidal behavior acted out by failure on the part of the patient to follow a proper schedule of medication; the resulting clinical picture could then be one of further deterioration in overall cardiac capacity.

The Impact of Psychosocial Factors on the Clinical Course of Physical Health Problems
Example: Diabetic with infected foot, living in isolation → increased risk of losing foot in absence of adequate social supports to help with proper medical management and followup
(More than two in five older women and nearly one in six older men live alone.)

Source: Cohen (1992).

(Salzman & Nevis-Olsen, 1992). In addition, individual psychotherapy, cognitive restructuring of the environment, and reducing isolation can be most helpful in treating depression (see Chapter 11) (Gallagher & Thompson, 1983).

Depression, where affective symptoms predominate, must also be separated from dementia, where cognitive symptoms are most characteristic. Misdiagnosed depression has been termed **pseudodementia** (Salzman & Shader, 1979) (see Table 10.4). Depression may or may not accompany cognitive impairment, and depression can coexist with dementia (see Figures 10.4 and 10.5). While those who are depressed often complain of memory problems, testing does not bear out memory deficits (O'Connor et al., 1990).

Depressive equivalents are also important in the diagnosis of depression (Blazer, 1990; Cohen, 1990; Pfeiffer, 1977; Salzman & Shader, 1979; Stenback, 1980). In these cases, the depression is "masked" by physical complaints such as fatigue, loss of appetite, constipation, or sleeplessness. Anger and guilt are turned inward instead of being expressed overtly. The symptoms help people deny the fact that they are depressed

TABLE 10.4

MAJOR CLINICAL FEATURES DIFFERENTIATING PSEUDODEMENTIA (DEPRESSION) FROM DEMENTIA

Clinical Features	Pseudodementia	Dementia
1. Onset of illness	Usually specific	Determined only within broad limits
2. Duration	Brief duration before requesting help	Usually long duration
3. Progression	Symptoms develop rapidly	Symptoms develop slowly through course of illness.
4. History	Prior psychiatric problems are common	Psychiatric dysfunction uncommon
5. Complaints	Frequent and detailed complaint of cognitive loss Disability is emphasized; failures are highlighted	Infrequent and vague complaint of cognitive loss. Disabilities are overlooked or concealed. Satisfaction with accomplishment is frequently noted, however trivial.
6. Efforts	Minimal effort on even simple tasks	Patients usually struggle to perform tasks.
7. Affect	Change often pervasive, with strong sense of distress	A frequent lack of concern with labile and shallow affect.
8. Social skills	Notable loss, usually early in course of illness	Often retained in early stages
9. Nocturnal dysfunction	Uncommon	Often accentuated
10. Attention and concentration	Often intact	Usually faulty
11. Memory loss	Occurs equally for recent and remote events, but "memory gaps" for specific periods are common	Loss for recent events usually more severe than remote, but "gaps" for other specific periods are infrequent.
12. Variability in performance	Usually marked	Consistently poor

Source: From D. Gallagher & L. Thompson. 1983. Cognitive impairment. In P. Lewisohn & L. Teri (Eds.), *Clinical geropsychology: New directions in assessment and treatment* (p. 12). Elmsford, NY: Pergamon Press. Adapted from C. Wells. (1979). Pseudodementia. *American Journal of Psychiatry.*

yet permit them to legitimately ask for help. Again, social or interpersonal factors, or real physical losses, may bring about this process. Ironically, because these symptoms serve a useful function in "protecting" the person, they often resist treatment (Pfeiffer, 1977).

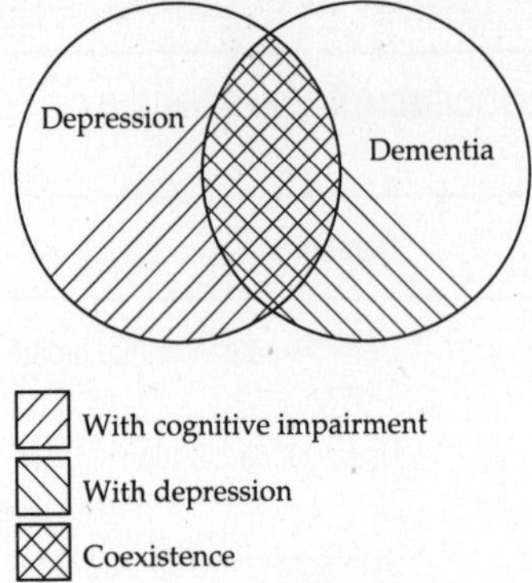

Figure 10.4 Illustration of diagnostic categorization of dementia and depression with coexistence. *Source:* Teri & Reifer (1987).

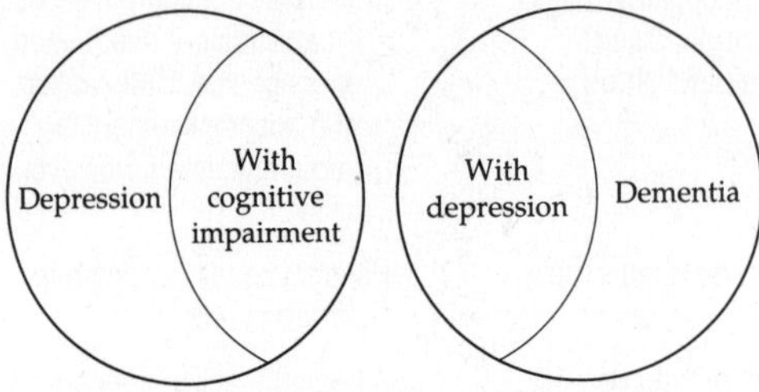

Figure 10.5 Illustration of diagnostic categorization of depression and dementia as mutually exclusive disorders. *Source:* Teri & Reifer (1987).

SUICIDE

Suicide is more common in older people than in any other age group and is particularly prevalent in elderly white males (Cohen, 1990; Koenig & Blazer, 1992). This is despite the fact that suicide rates increased for all age groups over the last decade (Cohen, 1990). There appear to be cohort differences in suicide rates (Blazer et al., 1986).

It is important to realize that our picture of the prevalence of suicide varies by age, time of measurement, and cohort, as well as whether our data are cross-sectional or longitudinal. While cross-sectional data suggest that suicide rates for the aged are higher, longitudinal data suggest otherwise (Koenig & Blazer, 1992). However, elderly suicides declined until 1980, but since then they have increased by 25 percent (Koenig & Blazer, 1992; Meehan et al., 1991).

Depression is the single most common element in suicide, regardless of age (Carson & Butcher, 1991). Most people attempt suicide following a depressive episode. Suicide rates for teenagers are increasing; and while the relative frequency is low, suicide among young children has also gained increasing attention (Peek, 1984; Pfeffer, 1984).

Depression is a common element in suicide among adults of all ages.

In addition to age, marital status, occupation, and gender are correlated with the incidence of suicide (Carson & Butcher, 1991). Those who live alone, are divorced or separated, are male (regarding successful attempts), or are lawyers, psychologists, dentists, or physicians seem to be most at risk. Women who are middle-aged also seem to be vulnerable (Humphrey & Palmer, 1990–91), as do individuals in the Baby Boom generation due to economic pressures and competition for jobs (Koenig & Blazer, 1992).

Seiden (1985–86) suggests that nonwhite suicide rates are lower than those of whites because nonwhites are less vulnerable to the loss of status that accompanies aging, having had less all their lives. However, Robins et al. (1977) did not find such racial differences. Boldt (1982) and Blazer

(1986) have found a cohort effect in acceptance of suicide; younger generations were more positive than were older ones. Moreover, even older cohorts reported being more accepting of it than when they were young. If such generational shifts exist, they pose special challenges for those in the field of suicide prevention.

To evaluate the seriousness of suicide potential, the Los Angeles Suicide Prevention Center uses a so-called Lethality Scale. This scale evaluates suicide risk using data about the caller. Though it is not always accurate, it does help hotline workers understand whom they are dealing with in a crisis situation. And perhaps callers see such detailed questioning as an indication that someone is indeed interested in whether they live or die.

Many skills are important in dealing with potential suicides (Osgood, 1990). Providing support and alternatives to suicide, and making people aware of how their distress is impairing their ability to realistically assess and solve their problems, are very important. Moreover, being assertive and directive, when necessary, and simply being with those who are at risk are the most important elements in averting a suicide attempt (Hipple, 1986).

One should not misinterpret the statistics above as an indication that younger people or females just want attention, or that older people or males do not want to be prevented from killing themselves. Regardless of the moral and ethical issues of whether people have the right to take their own lives, the fact is that if someone truly wishes to kill him- or herself, he or she can do so without ever communicating the intent to anyone. Many people who leave notes or contact suicide prevention programs do want help. Consequently, *all* references to suicide should be taken seriously—the costs of not doing so are too great (Carson & Butcher, 1991; Miller, 1979).

What are some of the reasons older adults commit suicide? Research indicates some of the major correlates are poor or failing health, widowhood, diminishing social roles, loss of friends, social isolation, and depression (Kastenbaum, 1985; Koenig & Blazer, 1992; Miller, 1978, 1979; Osgood, 1985, 1990). We recommend that you exercise caution here in drawing conclusions about their causal importance in suicide, however. While the importance of living alone is paramount among the widowed, particularly elderly widowers, widowed elderly are not more prone to suicide within the first year of bereavement (Stenback, 1980). Those who attempt suicide, however, are more likely to have suffered the loss of a close relative through death or divorce in the past than otherwise. It is important to note that it is not being divorced or widowed per se, but the *inability to replace* confidant relationships that makes loss pivotal (Stenback, 1980).

Retirement is often considered a crisis for elderly men, but there is little evidence to support the notion that it is causally linked to suicide. Many elderly people who enjoy good health and have adequate retirement income may in fact see retirement positively; particularly for men, the benefits of being released from work commitments can be very positive aspects of retirement (see Chapter 9).

For some elders, ageism, poor health, isolation, or marital conflict accompanying withdrawal from the work force, not retirement per se, may contribute to lower self-esteem and depression (Osgood, 1985). Koenig and Blazer (1992) emphasize that poor health, especially if it is accompanied by protracted, severe pain, often predicts suicide. Much depends on the value attached to the retirement by the older person (see Chapter 9). Not surprisingly, in light of the above, alcoholism and suicide seem to be highly related (Osgood, 1990).

In contrast to retirement, relocation may predict suicide among the elderly, particularly the less competent (Nirenberg, 1983). Miller (1979) states that the mere prospect of being institutionalized was enough to precipitate suicide for some elderly men.

When overt, quick means of taking one's life are not available, many elderly people resort to other methods: starving themselves, refusing to follow physicians' orders, voluntary isolation, behaving dangerously, excessive drinking or drug abuse, or smoking. These behaviors may be regarded by staff and other residents as problems in themselves.

Suicide in institutions such as nursing homes, mental hospitals, and geriatric wards is commonplace for many elderly (Osgood & Brant, 1990). Such institutions are seen, accurately or not, by many aged as depersonalizing, dehumanizing, lonely places.

Nelson and Faberow (1975, 1980) have termed covert methods of suicide that often occur in nursing homes *indirect self-destructive behavior (ISDB)*. According to these authors, ISDB differs from suicide in that it does not have immediate fatal consequences but is thought to ultimately lead to an individual's premature death. While these behaviors may have a self-destructive component and stem from isolation or depression, they may also serve to alleviate feelings of powerlessness or low self-esteem. At present, research suggests that institutionalization clearly has the potential for eliciting suicidelike behavior in those older people who do not see relocation in a positive light, or who are already depressed or feel hopeless. As alternatives to nursing home care become more available, and when residents perceive themselves to be in better control of their lives, it is likely that the relationship between institutionalization and ISDB will decrease.

For many individuals, both young and old, committing suicide may be the final expression of the wish to control the little they have that is valued. Elderly suicides have been described by Stenback (1980) as **egoistic**. Egoistic suicides involve few commitments to interpersonal or cultural values, often resulting in or stemming from social isolation (see Durkheim, 1897). Hence, for some elderly people, the suicide act is highly individualistic and very serious in its intent. This makes it particularly difficult to mobilize effective support on which the older person can rely in a crisis due to stress and/or loss (Miller, 1979). This, in turn, unfortunately frequently encourages a we-can't-do-anything-about-the-problem approach to treatment (Miller, 1979). And this attitude, in turn, may reinforce the older person's sense of isolation and hopelessness. One sees him- or herself as someone whose life is in fact worthless if no one seems to want one to *not* take it. This attitude may also foster ignorance of both the scope and seriousness of suicidal threats by older people. Often, greater efforts are made to save the lives of those who are perceived to have a life that is "worth saving," i.e., the person is young (see Blauner, 1966; Sundow, 1967).

The diversity among the aged as well as the variety and potential for interaction among the many factors correlated with—but not necessarily causing—elderly suicides would seem to argue against the construction of suicide-proneness or lethality scales for use with elderly clients. While theories about suicide-prone elderly are attractive, it is, again, the recognition of each aged person as a unique individual that best facilitates the prevention of suicide.

Nevertheless, perhaps the most intensive study of the older white male, who is most at risk relative to other elderly people, has been carried out by Miller (1978, 1979). Miller conducted a systematic examination of 301 white, elderly male suicides in Arizona during 1970 to 1975, also interviewing the widows of 30 of these men. His analyses suggest that a profile of the suicide-prone older man could be constructed. According to Miller's data, the typical older white male who takes his life:

1. Seldom attended church
2. Was not visited by, or did not visit, friends or relatives at least once a week
3. Left a suicide note for someone
4. Left a will
5. Was experiencing chronic sleeping problems the year before his death
6. Was addicted to, or had a strong reliance on, drugs
7. Had a relative with an emotional or mental illness
8. Killed himself in the bedroom of his house

In addition, the elderly suicide victim was described as a loner who had few close friends, had suffered the death of a friend or relative who served as a confidant within the last two years of his life, used a firearm (usually a pistol) that was purchased a month prior to his death, saw his physician a month prior to his death, and suffered a serious, painful physical illness during the last year of his life. He also frequently was described as seeing himself as inadequate or useless, being unhappy or depressed (Robins et al., 1977), and gave verbal or behavioral clues of his impending suicide.

While this profile is purely descriptive, not prescriptive, it seems to present viable diagnostic possibilities for those working with elderly people. However, it should never be taken as evidence of a guarantee that someone who is older will or will not commit suicide.

Conclusions about causative factors in elderly suicides are often based on interviews with survivors, or research that lacks control groups (see Miller, 1979). Client confidentiality makes evaluation of suicide-prevention efforts difficult. It is also important to note that the motivations of those who attempt suicide, regardless of age, in fact may differ from those who are successful.

As mentioned above, Miller (1979) noted that aged men who committed suicide visited their physicians a month prior to their deaths. Perhaps these physicians were not skilled in "picking up on" the cues the men were providing. What would have happened had the physicians been more skillful in confronting these men about the reasons for their visits? Simply being able to acknowledge suicidal thoughts could have been vitally important to these elderly men, whose value systems often stressed self-reliance and independence.

In this regard, Miller (1979) found 60 percent of his sample to have given a clue to their impending suicides. Over a third of their families admitted to acknowledging such clues! Twenty-three percent did not recognize any clues; but many did nothing even when they were given advance notice!

> In one case, the deceased told his wife and daughter every night for two weeks that he wanted to take his life, yet his family failed to secure the professional attention he so desperately needed. . . . In at least two of the cases, . . . wives found suicide notes in advance of the men's deaths—one, one week in advance and the other the day before—but totally discounted the credibility of the notes (p. 294).

Miller speculates that it is possible that the wives in these cases were implicitly cooperating with the husbands who wanted to end their lives.

Miller (1979) states regarding suicide prevention, "Although they [the research team] emphasized that outreach services are imperative to reach depressed people who may have become withdrawn and isolated, they felt the *ultimate answer would be for old age itself* to offer the elderly something worthwhile for which to live" (p. 19).

It is important to note that such factors as retirement, widowhood, divorce, or institutionalization must be interpreted by people in such a way that taking one's own life is seen as the only solution. Some people become overwhelmed by a loss; others, who have more positive coping skills, react to the same loss with resilience and are able to "bounce back."

Miller (1979) discusses the balance between the quality and quantity of life. According to this view, each person forms a personal equation whereby, when the **line of unbearability** is crossed, he or she determines that quality of life is more important than quantity. Individuals' evaluation of what it takes to push them beyond their lines of unbearability are likely to differ from one another. For some, this invisible line is defined by the mere prospect of growing old and dying in an institution (Miller, 1979). For others, it may be living in pain; loss of a girlfriend or boyfriend, husband or wife; loss of one's work affiliation with retirement; having failed in school or as a spouse or parent; feeling unloved by one's parents or children; or simply feeling alone.

Obviously, more attention needs to be given to education about suicide and directed at the elderly, their families, physicians, and the general public (Osgood, 1990). Suicide is preventable.

Mrs. Jensen was a 77-year-old woman who came to visit her primary-care physician at the insistence of her daughter. For 20 years, she had suffered from "nerves," dating approximately to the time that she had retired from her work as a cashier in a supermarket. Although always the nervous type, worry and anxiety had increased gradually since her retirement. She had seen a physician five years before, who had prescribed the nerve medicine diazepam (Valium), and she had taken the medicine intermittently when she felt especially anxious.

During the months prior to seeing the doctor, she had suffered more symptoms of dizziness. When the dizzy spells occurred, her heart would race and she would feel prickling around her lips, pain in her chest, and shortness of breath. Although the dizzy episodes only lasted for a few seconds, she began to worry that her heart was failing. She felt as if her heart was about to jump out of her chest. On one occasion, she even imagined that she had suffered a small stroke. When examined in the physician's office, he found no evidence of disease in her heart or in her blood pressure. Her neurologic examination was normal. He suggested she continue to take the Valium when needed. She returned a few months later, saying that she had continued to take Valium in about the same amount as she had in the past but she could feel no evidence that the medicine was of benefit. She finally chose to stop taking Valium, and had discontinued the drug for a month before the return visit. She suffered no increase in her symptoms and the dizziness was not as much of a problem as previously (Blazer, 1990).

We have all felt anxious from time to time. However, people who are chronically anxious often appear tense and hyperactive and are apprehensive and vigilant about what terrible thing might happen next. These symptoms must exist for a month, and other disorders such as depression or schizophrenia must be ruled out, for a diagnosis of **anxiety** to be made (American Psychiatric Association, 1987). While we know comparatively little about chronic anxiety in later adulthood, Himmelfarb (1984) found, in a sample of over 2000 adults aged 55 to 90, that scores on a self-report measure of anxiety generally decreased with age up to 69 and increased rapidly thereafter. Women were more anxious than men. Similar findings regarding anxiety have been found by Burke et al. (1990).

Sheikh (1992) suggests that anxiety may be expressed either cognitively, via difficulty in sleeping and concentration or nervousness, or somatically, through gastrointestinal symptoms, shortness of breath, or rapid heartbeat. Some studies have found that cognitive anxiety varies little with age, but somatic anxiety increases with age (Gaitz & Scott, 1972). Other studies have found an increase in cognitive anxiety with age (Gurin et al., 1963).

Sheikh (1992) groups anxiety disorders into several types: generalized anxiety, phobias, panic disorders, and obsessive-compulsive behaviors. In each case, frequency decreased with age (Sheikh, 1992).

For many people, physical illness is often accompanied by anxiety. More specifically, cardiovascular illness, drug toxicity, endocrine-system imbalance, anemia, central nervous system tumors, injuries or infection, and lung disease can all lead to any one of the above forms of anxiety (Sheikh, 1992).

Collectively, studies suggest that poor health, relocation stress, isolation, or fears about loss of control may precipitate anxiety reactions that may be dysfunctional among the very old (75+), who are predominantly women. Estimates for transient anxiety reactions run as high as 20 percent in some studies (Blazer, 1990). In Himmelfarb's study, when the relationship between age and anxiety, as well as the relationship between gender and anxiety, were adjusted statistically for factors such as perceived health, quality of housing, and social support, these relationships were lessened considerably or eliminated altogether.

PARANOID REACTIONS

Paranoid symptoms, that is, delusional or hallucinatory persecutory ideas, may accompany dementia, coexist with severe depression, or simply be a response to isolation or to sensory/cognitive losses. Examples are accusations of being talked about, one's food being poisoned, or mail being stolen (Blazer, 1990; Post, 1980). In these cases, paranoid reactions must be viewed in light of older people's attempts to make sense of their everyday environment via projection of hostile or persecutory intent onto others, rather than random, wildly bizarre delusions. Such accusations can be somewhat logical. Providing cues for forgetfulness, such as a system to keep track of when a "forgotten" letter was written; treating sensory deficits, with more seasoning on food or a hearing aid; explaining major changes like relocation before they occur; and communicating clearly with those who are sensorily impaired often improve matters greatly (Kermis, 1986) (see Chapter 3). Paranoia in such cases certainly should not be interpreted as a reason for institutionalizing an older individual.

Older paranoiacs are obviously difficult to treat because of their intense distrust of others. In many cases, older people with delusional ideas live their lives out in isolated, undisturbed fashion and may simply seem odd to others.

These simple paranoid-psychotic types are distinct from those suffering schizophrenialike illnesses such as paranoid schizophrenia. In the latter cases, delusions are more systematic, organized, and bizarre. Examples are being convinced one is being plotted against by the police or that poisonous gasses are being pumped into one's room. Neither severe speech disturbances nor catatonic behaviors are common in older paranoiacs, though paranoid reactions sometimes accompany dementia (Blazer, 1990; Crook, 1987).

Kermis (1986) notes that if one accepts the irrationality of the paranoid's initial delusions, subsequent delusional ideas often make sense logically. Older paranoiacs have delusions of grandeur (superiority), reference (others are following them), or persecution. Paranoid reactions must last for at least a week, and schizophrenia and organicity must be ruled out, before a diagnosis can be made (American Psychiatric Association, 1987).

Paranoid reactions may also be acute, short-term responses to being hospitalized or transferred to a nursing home (Kermis, 1986). Paranoid reactions in older people appear to be exaggerations of existing personality characteristics, for example, as when a normally withdrawn person develops delusions of influence by others (Kermis, 1986).

SCHIZOPHRENIA

Schizophrenia, like the paranoid reactions discussed above, is comparatively rare in late adulthood and, thus, has not received a great deal of attention (Blazer, 1980; Cohen, 1990; Rabins, 1992). Older schizophrenics were most likely diagnosed much earlier in life and simply grow old in an institution. Older chronic paranoid schizophrenics, while more upset by their symptoms, actually seem to make better social adjustments than when they were younger (Kermis, 1986).

Schizophrenics have a well-developed, severe delusionary system, loosely strung-together thinking, and bizarre speech and hallucinations (American Psychiatric Association, 1987). In addition, catatonic (frozen) or maniclike behavior may be present, accompanied by withdrawal into a private world that severely interferes with relationships with others and makes functioning on an everyday basis impossible. Schizophrenics typically do not react emotionally to their symptoms. If they have grown old in an institution, they often have a characteristic "burned-out" appearance: they walk around in a stupor or simply lie on the floor. They may utter incoherent, animallike sounds or be mute; they may smack their lips, grimace, or drool like infants. They show little or no evidence of cognitive activity, stemming from years of medications to control outbursts of anger brought on by delusions or the dull sameness of institutional life. They often have a fixed stare, with dark circles under their eyes, and a plodding gait (Carson & Butcher, 1991). We know as little that is definitive about what causes schizophrenia developing in late life, termed **paraphrenia,** as we do about the disorder starting in early adulthood or childhood.

Extensive schizophrenialike paranoid delusions sometimes accompany dementia. The aged schizophrenic often manifests delusions of reference (e.g., others are looking at or talking about him or her), severe hypochondriacal delusions (e.g., cancer or syphilis), or manic behavior (i.e., having extraordinary amounts of energy that must be released). When the disease is organic—and again, this is rare—they may be delusionally jealous, but the classic symptoms of dementia often predominate (Post, 1980, 1987).

The underlying organic degeneration typical of dementia has little to do with paraphrenia; they simply coexist. Cognitive losses are usually minimal in these cases, and paranoia, which often precedes the illness, is easily observed in the early stages of dementia. Those with more interpersonal problems earlier in life tend to be the worst off in this regard; their delusions are more severe. Elderly people with paranoid delusions that are narrower in scope than those of younger paranoiacs can be treated with tranquilizing drugs (Post, 1980; 1987).

Simon (1980) and Sadavoy and Fogel (1992) have discussed personality or character disorders and neuroticism in later life. Personality disorders are diverse and include paranoids, antisocial personalities, narcissistic personalities, as well as those who are psychologically dependent on others (Sadavoy & Fogel, 1992). Comparatively little is known about these topics, except that aging tends to intensify dominant patterns established early on in life, including those typical of the character disorder. That is, the dependent personality becomes more so; and the same is true of many other character disorders (Simon, 1980). They seem to be brought on by chronic stress and often appear in mid-life (Sadavoy & Fogel, 1992). Interpersonal loss, physical incapacity, role loss, or losses in self-definition often are responsible, and many individuals with personality disorders somaticize their illness, have difficulties with relationships, or simply withdraw and become depressed as they age (Sadavoy & Fogel, 1992).

Symptoms such as transient, acute anxiety not accompanied by dementia or psychosis and not chronic (see above discussion), alcoholism exclusive of organic loss brought on by excessive use, and drug misuse may all be seen as attempts by the aged person to cope with loss, stress, physical illness, or disfigurement. They may also represent attempts to manage grief at the death of a spouse or child (see Chapter 12).

Transient or acute depression and anxiety may also define what has been termed *relocation shock* (Aldrich & Mendkoff, 1963; Butler et al., 1981; Miller & Lieberman, 1965). This sometimes occurs when an older person is moved, often involuntarily, from his or her home to an institution or from one institution to another. The older person may no longer be able to care for him- or herself, the family may no longer be able to care for the aged person, or the nursing home may close for economic reasons. Depression or anxiety, in this case, is often a reaction to abandonment, loss of control over one's life, the inability to care for oneself, or a sense that the move is a permanent one. These feelings can be lessened or avoided altogether by sharing information about the move beforehand, involving the elderly person to the greatest extent possible in decision making and planning, and continuing to visit regularly. Most important, older people in these situations must feel that they are still human beings. Each family must continue to be loving and supportive and communicate these feelings clearly to the older family member. Acute depression or anxiety in older people may accompany serious illness, injury, or impending surgery in addition to relocation (Blazer, 1990; Butler et al., 1990; Stenback, 1980).

Drug Use and Abuse Among Older Adults

Data from the National Disease and Therapeutic Index (NDTI) indicated that, in 1982, people aged 60 and older comprised 16 percent of the U.S. population but accounted for 30 percent of the total patient visits to private-practice physicians and for 38 percent of the drug prescriptions made by these physicians (Ostrom et al., 1985). Older people also account for almost half of all deaths from either adverse drug reactions or misuse of prescription medications.

Compared to younger age groups, elderly people not only take many more drugs but also consume a wider variety of them. This is partially a result of the numerous chronic physical conditions increasing with age for which drugs are prescribed, such as hypertension, congestive heart failure, and ischemic heart disease. The elderly are also more likely to have multiple prescriptions for these chronic conditions (Glantz & Backenheimer, 1988).

Aged individuals are also the largest consumers of over-the-counter (OTC) drugs. Specifically, the 1981 Panel on Aging and the Geochemical Environment found that while only 10 percent of the general population regularly used OTC drugs, 60 percent of people over the age of 65 habitually used such drugs (cf. Glantz & Backenheimer, 1988). Indeed, 75 percent of all older people regularly use some type of medication, of which a third are OTC drugs (Whanger, 1984).

The use and misuse of OTC medications, prescription drugs, and psychoactive drugs, as well as alcohol, have numerous implications for practitioners working with older adults. In recent research in this area, for example, Folkman and associates (1987) have indicated that elderly drug use is a complex issue involving both metabolic/physiologic and psychosocial factors. Consequently, attention to the multiple facets of this problem underscores an awareness of its impact on the lives of older people and their families.

As people age, there are a number of physiological changes that impact how the body responds to drugs. These changes are expressed in terms of the initial absorption of a drug from the gastrointestinal tract, distribution of a drug in the circulatory system, metabolism of a drug into a different form that can be used by the body, and elimination of a drug from the body (see Cherry & Morton, 1989).

In particular, decreases in lean body mass and water content, and increases in adipose tissue, all influence how a drug is initially absorbed, distributed, and later metabolized (see Bressler, 1987; Cherry & Morton, 1989). The length of time it takes for half a drug to be eliminated from an individual's system is referred to as the drug's *half-life*. For the aged, the half-life of most drugs is greater than for younger people, especially for protein-bound drugs. Normally, those drugs with a longer half-life will be bound to a protein to a greater extent, leading to greater concentrations of the unbound drug in the bloodstream. Thus, the unbound or free fraction of the drug is circulated by the blood to a greater extent, leading to altered and more intense action at the receptor site. Eventually, the drug will be metabolically transformed by the liver and then excreted by the kidneys. As the free portions of the drug are excreted, the bound portions are released into the bloodstream over time, to be eventually metabolized and excreted. Overall, greater levels of the active portion of the drug remain in the body, which is equivalent to receiving a higher dose of the drug and can lead to altered drug reactions and toxicity (Cherry & Morton, 1989).

For people with chronic or acute illness, the likelihood of polypharmacy is greater, and the presence of the illness itself undermines the body's ability to absorb, metabolize, and excrete drugs, further contributing to drug toxicity and/or more polypharmacy. Consequently, dosages must be individualized.

DEFINING DRUG MISUSE

Whanger (1984) specifies the criteria for substance abuse:

1. Pathologic pattern of use—pathological use includes the lack of ability to alter one's pattern of use, regular use to maintain adequate functioning, and complications (blackouts or overdose)
2. Impairment of social or cognitive functioning due to substance abuse (e.g., work difficulties, accidents, violent behavior)
3. Duration of use over a month.

When people think of drug abuse there is a tendency to first think of the abuse of illegal substances such as marijuana, LSD, heroin, or crack cocaine. But older people rarely abuse illegal drugs, though such abuse is not unheard of. However, there may be a dramatic rise in the use of illegal drugs with their increased availability, particularly as younger aged individuals who were exposed to and addicted to illegal drugs themselves age.

Currently, the drugs that older adults abuse most often are prescription and OTC medications. This occurs by obtaining multiple psychotropic drug prescriptions, obtaining these drugs in other nonmedically sanctioned ways (e.g., from friends or family members), or combining various drugs or drugs and alcohol, which may produce psychoactive effects such as hallucinations, confusion, anxiety, or paranoia. There has also been some concern about the abuse of OTC medications, such as sedatives and laxatives, and the possible consequences of this abuse for the older person's health, such as excessive weight loss and chronic intestinal inflammation.

Darnell and associates (1986) found that only half (49.3%) of aged individuals complied with prescription directions; 5.6 percent shared medications with others, and 7.5 percent took additional doses of their medications. Other authors have found that 50 percent of their sample misused prescription drugs and that this misuse was related to the number and kinds of drugs they were taking (Memmink & Heikkila, 1975). Underused drugs included those prescribed for symptom relief rather than cure, drugs with side effects, and drugs that were quite expensive, whereas prescription drugs that were overused related to sleep, appetite, and mood.

Tragically, many elderly people may be inadvertently endangering their health and even their lives. Sadly, too, in many cases, medication-related problems are the reason for institutionalization (Johnson et al., 1989). Recent evidence suggests that even after entrance into a long-term care facility, excessive or at least moderate prescription drug use by aged people occurs. Such use is related to their lower functional status, physical health, and emotional well-being (Cooper & Ratner, 1989; Horgas et al., 1989).

While some data suggest a decline in alcohol use up to age 65 and an increase thereafter (Zimberg, 1987), this may be influenced by cohort differences, with older cohorts expressing more temperance and being less permissive or condoning in their attitudes toward its use (Benshoff & Roberto, 1987). Recent data tend to reject this conclusion, however (Adams et al., 1989).

Despite the apparent age-related decline, alcohol abuse is a serious problem among the aged, particularly men. Zimberg (1987) and Wood (1978) separate those who have been chronic alcohol abusers for an extended period of time (early-onset alcoholics) from those whose increased use of alcohol is reactive and of late onset.

In reliably ascertaining alcohol use, direct questions regarding extent of use are likely to be avoided by the aged person, or simply answered untruthfully (Olsen-Noll & Bosworth, 1989). Similar queries of family and friends may yield more accurate answers. Because alcohol abuse often creates social and interpersonal problems for the older person, Zimberg (1987) recommends asking questions regarding the extent of change in recent behavior and personality, as well as issues regarding isolation or conflict with others, deficits in self-care and in routine, everyday transactions (e.g., meeting appointments, income management), troubles with the law, and episodes of memory loss or confusion.

Excessive alcohol consumption may spontaneously remit in later adulthood, often due to the unpleasant physical, behavioral, and emotional side effects on the aged person and his or her family (Zimberg, 1987). Because of this, it is important to understand why some people continue to drink heavily into old age and why others begin to drink later in life. In many cases, depression, as well as inability to cope with losses associated with retirement, spousal bereavement, illness, marital discord, or loneliness, contributes to both patterns. Indeed, the psychosocial stresses some people experience in later life outweigh the negative effects of the use of alcohol itself (Cantor & Koretzky, 1989; Folkman et al., 1987).

Folkman et al. (1987) found that misusers felt more threatened and overwhelmed, and were less satisfied with the manner in which they coped with everyday hassles. Thus, feelings, rather than behaviors, were associated with all types of drug misuse in the aged. Those aged people who have more health problems and who are more emotionally distressed want or need to use drugs more and are, in turn, more vulnerable to drug misuse, which, in turn, heightens the perception that they are (dis)stressed and not coping well (Barbre, 1989; Folkman et al., 1987). Health care professionals and practitioners should be sensitive to anxiety, social withdrawal, low self-esteem, dissatisfaction with one's coping skills, and lessened self-efficacy as possible indicators of extensive drug (mis)use.

Especially critical is knowledge pertaining to the disastrous effects of the interaction between alcohol and sedatives, cardiovascular medications, or antihistamines. Ignorance or denial of such issues simply provides the elderly alcoholic with another means by which to avoid treatment. Moreover, alcoholic symptoms, such as slurred speech, atoxic gait, sleep disturbances, or confusion, can be misinterpreted as symptoms of dementia, often thought to be untreatable, or even due to normal aging (see above). In extreme cases, Korsakoff's syndrome and alcohol-induced dementia can be brought on by years of hard drinking, as can cirrhosis of the liver and cardiovascular, pancreatic, and kidney disorders. On the other hand, alcohol abuse can reflect dementia in some cases (Benshoff & Roberto, 1987).

The complicated array of symptoms that the elderly often present make it difficult to accurately diagnose their illnesses. Often, physical illnesses may incorporate symptoms that mimic mental illness. One common set of symptoms that can result from a number of mental or physical problems is a decrease in cognitive functioning, including memory loss, confusion, or disorientation. A careful examination must be made to obtain an accurate diagnosis because such symptoms may be a result of any number of ailments, notably drug effects but also depression, hypothyroidism, vitamin deficiencies, or delirium, to name just a few (Eisdorfer & Cohen, 1978; Gilhooly et al., 1986). If an accurate diagnosis is not made, it may lead to more serious misspecifications of drug treatment, complicating matters further.

For those aged alcoholics who seek treatment, that is, detoxification, followed by inpatient or outpatient care of both a medical and psychosocial nature, the outlook is good (Benshoff & Roberto, 1987; Zimberg, 1987), especially for the unimpaired client (Cantor & Koretzky, 1989). Peer support (Alcoholics Anonymous), education of caregivers, as well as family or couples therapy may also be helpful in maintaining a relationship with one's family and friends. A closely monitored aftercare program, especially for those who are alone, is essential (Cantor & Koretzky, 1989).

FACILITATING DRUG ADHERENCE IN OLDER PEOPLE

It is clear that practitioners should routinely question elderly people about their drug use, getting information about what drugs they are taking (including OTC medications), how much they are taking, and how often. All current and outdated prescriptions should be carefully examined. For many aged, this requires active supervision by and involvement of family, friends, neighbors, or service providers.

Once a proper drug regimen has been established, wherein "drug holidays" may be declared and polypharmacy minimized by the permanent elimination of some medications, monitoring drug adherence by aged individuals is critical. Older people often willfully fail to comply with a physician's prescriptions in a variety of ways: (1) by taking drugs *not* prescribed, (2) failing to take drugs that are prescribed, (3) not knowing the proper schedule of drugs to be taken at a specified dose, and (4) knowing but failing to take proper dosages at correct intervals (Hulka et al., 1976). Of course, when older patients are unable to clearly read medicine labels, fail to remember where bottles of pills or capsules are stored or where more than one drug with varying dosages is involved, noncompliance is a seri-

BOX 10.3

ALCOHOL ABUSE AND OLDER ADULTS

Alcohol Abuse Among Older People Presents a Growing Problem

Most older drinkers are not alcoholics. But if alcohol interferes with daily life or relationships, it's time to seek help.

Statistics show that approximately 10 percent of the senior population in America (around 2,500,000) over the age of 60 have alcohol problems. Two types of "problem drinkers" surface in their later years.

First, there are the "early-onset alcoholics." These people have used alcohol excessively throughout their lives. The majority of this group does not live long enough to reach their senior years. Those who do survive a lifetime of heavy drinking comprise about two-thirds of older alcoholics.

The second group consists of older people who first use alcohol as a temporary relief to their problems and later evolve into problem drinkers. They comprise the "late-onset alcoholic" group.

Why Older People Sometimes Turn to Excessive Drinking

Most people adjust readily to the aging process. They are healthier and more active today than ever before, and lead happy, productive retirement years. Older people who turn to excessive drinking do so because of several contributing factors.

They sometimes begin to drink heavily because of a **dramatic change in their lives,** such as **boredom with retirement.** After many years of employment, they may **lose a sense of identity** because their role in society has drastically changed.

Some turn to alcohol for comfort because they **do not have enough money.** Living on a fixed income can cause stress. But spending money on alcohol further strains the budget.

The **loss of a spouse, family member, or friend** is not easy for anyone to handle, and it is sometimes more difficult for seniors. Excessive drinking might seem to ease their grief and feelings of loneliness.

A **lack of any spiritual or religious affiliation** can also lead to alcoholism. Because some older people feel they have no one or nowhere to turn, they turn to what they conceive as their "only true friend," the bottle.

Older citizens play a vital role in society.

What Makes Senior Citizens So Susceptible to Alcohol?

Natural changes in the body make older people less resistant to the powerful effects of alcohol. As people age, their bodies take longer to process alcohol. Even moderate drinking can sometimes cause intoxication. Serious damage to health may also occur more quickly in older drinkers.

Our population of people over age 65 takes 25% of all prescription and nonprescription drugs. The **use of medication, combined with alcohol,** can dangerously, and often tragically, multiply the effects of these substances.

Loved Ones Should Be Aware of the Psychological Causes That Trigger Alcohol Abuse

Children grow up and leave home. **Family changes** leave a void that some senior adults cannot face. Their **feelings of abandonment** can lead to isolation and depression. Some older alcoholics think they can "drink away" their negative feelings. A sense of worthlessness is only reinforced by alcohol, a depressant drug.

Friends and Family Must Be Supportive

Everyone needs encouragement. Friends and loved ones can help older people build self-esteem by taking an interest in their activities and offering praise along the way.

Express understanding and concern for the alcoholic's situation without being judgmental. Be patient! Recovery takes time.

Most important . . . believe that your loved one can recover!

Recognizing Alcoholism . . . A Giant Step Toward Recovery

The older alcohol abuser, as well as family and friends, often ignore the signals of alcoholism as only signs of aging or senility. Don't make that same mistake! Be alert to physical and mental changes.

Appearance

- Pallid, yellowish skin and yellow or bloodshot eyes.
- Swelling of hands, ankles or feet and body bruises.

Continued

Box 10.3 continued

Health

- Chronic gastric problems, such as heartburn, indigestion, ulcers, and diarrhea.
- Constant fatigue and headaches.
- Frequent injuries, such as broken bones or sprains.

Behavior

- Hangovers, blackouts, memory loss, and confusion.
- Anxiety, nervousness, and insomnia.
- Hand tremors, loss of appetite, and prolonged periods of isolation.
- Mood swings, depression, and belligerence.
- Denial and/or hostility when drinking is discussed.

Source: Ohio Department of Liquor Control in cooperation with the Governor's Office of Advocacy for Recovery Services and the Ohio Department of Aging.

ous problem. Doctor-patient communication is vital in this respect. The nurse, social worker, or pharmacist often assumes critical roles in educating the older person regarding the side effects of drugs, proper dosages, intervals between dosages, as well as ascertaining the older person's faith in the drug's effects on his or her illness (Skolnick et al., 1984). Pacing of teaching efforts in drug education, the use of both written and oral teaching aids, ensuring comprehension, and education and support in the use of written memory aids to ensure compliance are especially important (Skolnick et al., 1984). For some elderly, self-taught aids, facilitated by computer software designed to remind the individual to take medication, may even be possible.

Regardless of the age of the client, but especially with the aged, one should always have an extensive drug history and an accurate record of what drugs he or she is taking, in what dosage, and how often. An extensive list of commonly prescribed medications and psychoactive drugs for the aged, including total dosage levels in milligrams per day, can be found in Bressler (1987), Benshoff and Roberto (1987), and Whanger (1984), who suggest that the best rule of thumb is to "start low and go slow."

Assessment

A comprehensive discussion of all forms of assessment with adults clearly is beyond our scope here. However, thorough discussions of the assessment of mental health (Gurland, 1980), depression (Gallagher & Thompson, 1983), organicity/cognitive functioning (Blazer, 1990; Crook, 1987; Kaszniak, 1990; Miller, 1980; Sloane, 1980; Zarit & Zarit, 1983), and personality functioning (Lawton et al., 1980; Hayslip & Lowman, 1986) are available. Assessments generally vary in terms of the level of skill being assessed. Examples of this continuum of functional skills are presented in Figure 10.6 (Kemp & Mitchell, 1992).

As a general rule, before conducting an assessment, one should be clear in defining for what purpose an interview, questionnaire, psycholog-

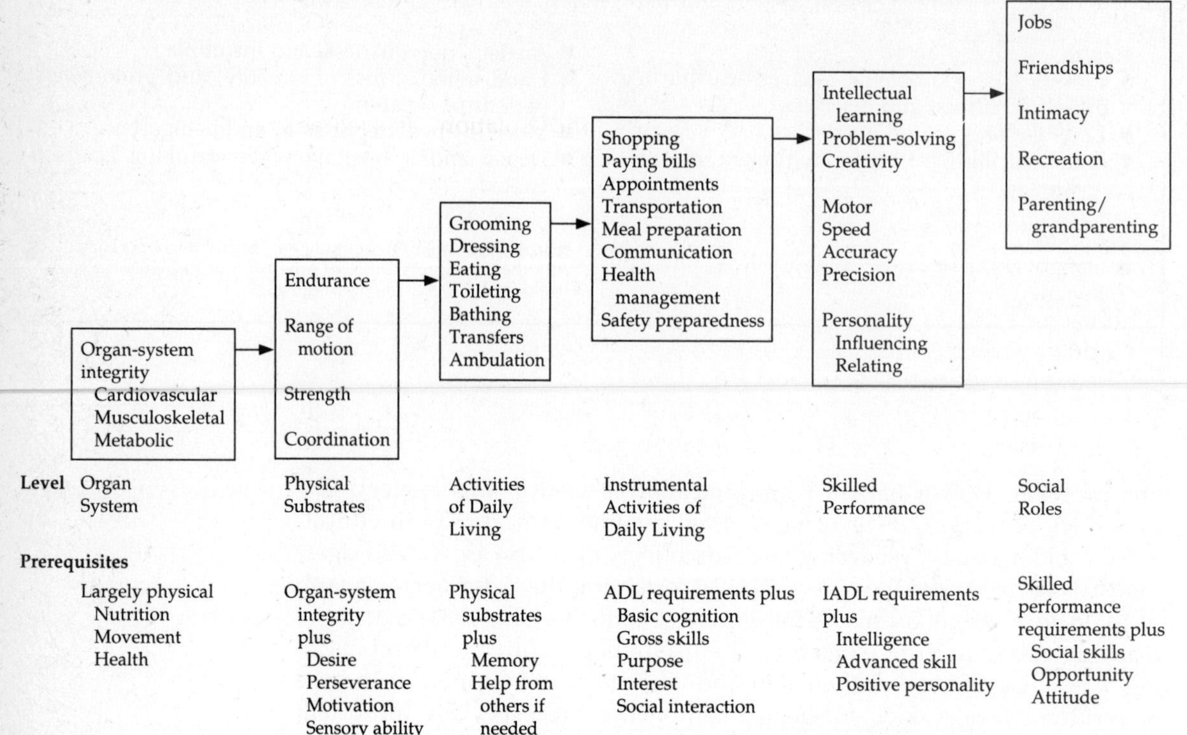

Figure 10.6 Levels of skill in assessment. *Source:* Kemp & Mitchell (1992).

ical test, or clinical examination is being done (Schaie & Schaie, 1977). For example, assessments might be used to measure the effects of a given intervention to aid a counselor in reaching a decision about an individual's adjustment to changed life roles such as the viability of retirement. Assessment might also be used to establish job-related competence/retraining, or to determine levels of competence or self-care as it relates to relocation.

Whatever the specific assessment technique utilized, its purpose should be clearly explained to the older individual and the family. The pace of the interview or test procedure should be relatively slow, and the materials should reflect the existing level of sensory-motor capacities of the individual (see Chapter 4).

Wherever possible, as an adjunct to standard nonage-related assessments, techniques especially developed for the aged and/or for which current age (cohort) norms exist should be relied on. For example, **mental-status questionnaires** for the assessment of cognition (Gurland, 1980) and the **Geriatric Depression Scale** to assess depression (see Gallagher & Thompson, 1983; Sheikh & Yessavage, 1986) can each be utilized to screen individuals. In most mental-status questionnaires, skills regarding orientation to time and place, short-term memory for details, ability to do mental calculations, comprehension of relationships, and visual-spatial skills are typically assessed (Heston & White, 1991). In the Geriatric Depression Scale, straightforward questions regarding mood state are asked, including changes in satisfaction with life, daily activities, apprehension about the future, feelings of hopelessness, helplessness, and isolation, as well as memory complaints (Sheikh & Yessavage, 1986). With these scales, we must be cautious about adhering rigidly to cutoff scores. As measures of a person's relative competence or pathology, cutoff scores should be avoided given the variability among elderly people (Schaie & Schaie, 1977).

In general, scales with demonstrated reliability and validity should be utilized (Anastasi, 1988; Cronbach, 1991). This is no less true for older individuals. Briefly, a scale is reliable—stable—if it yields scores that correlate highly with one another on two occasions for a given individual. A test's reliability may also be ascertained by correlating scores from odd-numbered items with those from even-numbered ones, or scores from the first half of the scale with scores from the second half. The extent to which a scale consistently measures some quality associated with the person and is not a function of random error indicates whether it is a reliable scale.

A valid scale measures what it intends to measure when judged against some external criterion of that quality. The scale may correlate highly with some accepted measure of that quality, differentiate among individuals who are presumed to possess varying levels of that quality, or accurately predict future performance of individuals who possess that quality to a certain degree. In general, measures that are valid are almost always reliable, but the opposite need not be the case. A measure can be quite reliable (i.e., we know it measures *something* consistently) but not valid (i.e., the "something" the scale is designed to measure cannot be identified).

Age-corrected norms based on cross-sectional studies are unlikely to be of help in the absence of reliability and validity data for an assessment technique (Kaszniak, 1990; Schaie & Schaie, 1977). Scales that possess adequate norms for elderly people are rare and, when available, need to be supplemented with reliability and validity data (see Chapter 8).

Above all, assessments should be comprehensive. Such assessments are quite thorough, thereby providing the examiner with information from a variety of sources on which to make a judgment regarding functional status or candidacy for intervention. Ideally, assessments should be conducted at least twice by different examiners. At a minimum, broad-based assessments in the areas of neurological functioning, learning, memory, intelligence, personality, psychopathology, self-care, morale, social/interpersonal skills, stress, and coping should be given, then interpreted in light of the individual's health, level of education, and family history. These factors assume a great deal of importance in influencing older people's responses to psychological tests and assessments. Thorough familiarity with the individual's goals, interests, family, and other factors will aid in not only the selection of which scales to administer but also their interpretation and intelligent use. Obviously, we should be as interested in what individuals are capable of—their **functional skills**—as in the assessment of decline.

Assessment of older people in the above domains may be accomplished via standardized testing, though such procedures relying on well-defined instructions and alternatives may obscure the true range of the elder's function or personality resources (Hayslip & Lowman, 1986). Self-ratings or interviews as single sources of information should be viewed with caution due to the influences of current health, medications, or tendencies to deny or represent symptoms more positively.

Extensive functional behavioral assessment procedures involving structured interviews have been developed and used productively for some time (Older Americans Resources and Services questionnaire; Fillenbaum, 1990; Pfeiffer, 1976), as has the Comprehensive Assessment and Referral Evaluation (Gurland et al., 1977). These interviews (1) identify the problem, and (2) explore its history and relationship to the older person's current social, occupational, or familial situation (Kemp & Mitchell, 1992).

Older people may not interpret self-rated items as they were intended, or may endorse items that are confounded by health status such as sleeplessness or changes in eating habits. Acknowledging such symptoms may lead to a diagnosis of depression that may or may not be accurate (see Addington & Fry, 1986).

ERRORS IN DIAGNOSIS

When a diagnosis of, for example, depression or dementia is falsely made, it is termed a **false-positive** error. When such conditions are assumed not to exist when they are in fact present, a **false-negative** error has been made. False negatives are especially critical if the disorder is one that will cause the individual to deteriorate further and irreversibly harm him or her if left untreated.

Depending on what effects a false-positive diagnosis may have, the error in judgment can result in serious consequences for older individuals and their families. For example, diagnosing someone as depressed rather than demented makes it more likely that the individual will receive treatment. On the other hand, falsely diagnosing someone as having dementia (Alzheimer's disease, multi-infarct dementia) may overlook a disorder that, if left untreated, produces irreversible damage, or worse still, leads to death (as with depression). Interestingly, Perlick and Atkins (1984) found clinicians to be more likely to make a diagnosis of dementia than depression, given the same symptoms, if the hypothetical patient was described as old. Diagnoses based on quantitative scores may miss important qualitative changes in individuals' responses to test items such as those in a mental-status questionnaire (see Zarit et al., 1985).

Personal interviews supplemented by interviews with family and friends, as well as judicious use of individualized personality assessment techniques called projective techniques (see Chapter 8), may prove invaluable in understanding a particular older individual in the context of his or her unique life situation (Hayslip & Lowman, 1986; Zarit et al., 1986).

Whenever possible, instructions should be personalized, and care should be taken to first establish trust and rapport in order to allay the person's fears and anxiety about the assessment itself or the consequences of the assessment. Particular care should be taken to use materials and techniques that are concrete, clear, and easily seen and heard. Preferably, assessments would be done in a relaxed, nonthreatening, familiar atmosphere. If possible, they should not be so long as to needlessly fatigue or irritate the individual.

Due to the influence of such noncognitive factors on performance (see Chapter 5), we should be especially cautious about relying too heavily on performance or structured-interview data to the extent that our own common sense and observations tell us something else may be wrong. Things may not really be as bad as our assessments indicate. Simply put, we should strive for a balanced yet realistic assessment of the elder's behavioral skills, abilities, or personality characteristics in light of what we know about that person's reaction to being depressed, background, family, daily living situation, and health. As Zarit et al. (1985) note, gerontological assessment is not developed to the extent that "a cookbook that can sort out the multiple influences on test behavior" is available (p. 733). Mounds of information do not compensate for common sense, good clinical judgment, sensitivity, experience, and interpersonal skills.

MENTAL HEALTH IN LATER LIFE

Birren and Renner (1980) suggest that mental health at any age involves "the ability to respond to other individuals, to love, to be loved, and to cope with others in give-and-take relationships" (p. 29). They add that the mentally healthy elder "should have the essential quality of being able to cope with loneliness, aggression, and frustrations without being overwhelmed" (p. 29), since they are likely to encounter the death of a spouse or friend, physical decline, and so forth, as part of the normal aging process. Again, coping with these changes can involve a whole range of responses. Those qualities Birren and Renner discuss that are especially pertinent to mental health in later adulthood are the five *R*s: (1) relevance to a set of values, (2) reverence, or self-esteem for one's own values, (3) life review, and (4) a release from stress in that one's life accomplishments and values are (5) reconciled with one's ideals.

It was stated at the outset of this chapter that we probably know more about what mental health in adulthood is not than what it is. Consequently, we are drawn to the problems older people sometimes experience (e.g., depression, paranoia, organicity, hypochondriasis, and suicide). This often leads to the development of mental health services that are remedial rather than preventative. That is, they encourage us to find out what is wrong so we can make a diagnosis, rather than encourage a positive orientation toward wellness.

Optimally Mentally Healthy Aged People

Hellebrandt (1980) has written about those characteristics associated with what are called the *advantaged aged*. This term refers to the well-educated, reasonably healthy, financially secure, independent-living elderly person. Hellebrandt talks of these individuals as not feeling old, accepting their physical/health-related limitations, and being occupied with meaningful activities of their own choosing. Moreover, they hold very individualistic feelings about work and retirement, and religion or a personally meaningful set of values. Also, they exhibit a notable lack of fears about death.

While we do not want to imply that reviewing one's life cannot be helpful (see Chapter 11), advantaged aged rarely reminisce about the past. But what transcends all of these qualities is what we might call "sitting loose in the saddle." In other words, they express an attitude of flexibility about life in general as well as about aging. While the specific qualities listed above are not important in and of themselves, flexibility in adapting to life's pleasures and problems is important to being mentally healthy at any age.

Institutionalized aged people can experience positive mental health like other elderly people. Noelker and Harel (1978) found that nursing home residents who had the highest morale and life satisfaction (1) had more favorable attitudes about entry into a long-term care situation, (2) held more positive perceptions of the facility and its staff, (3) had their preferences met regarding visitors, (4) saw their life there as permanent, and (5) had higher self-rated health. They also lived the longest! We see here the importance of perceived control as a factor contributing to positive mental health among older people who are institutionalized (Solomon, 1982) (see Chapter 8).

Harel and associates (1982) found that if rural elderly had ample social resources (e.g., not lonely, having someone to depend on), felt that financial resources were adequate, and saw themselves as healthy or active, they enjoyed good mental health.

It is only when poor health, social isolation, inadequate income, and substandard housing are experienced *simultaneously* that older individuals report low morale; seriously chronically ill aged may have the most difficulty (Birren & Renner, 1980; Felton & Revenson, 1987).

Why are some elders more adaptive than others? A longitudinal study by Mussen et al. (1982) suggests that the seeds for positive mental health in old age may have been sown years earlier. They found that women who were life-satisfied at age 70 were described at age 30 as "mentally alert, cheerful, satisfied with their lives, self-assured, and neither worrisome nor fatigued" (p. 321). Strong concerns of husbands for their wives' health, the quality of their marriages, and both income and leisure time were also important predictors of life satisfaction in women at age 70. For men, physical and emotional well-being and their wives' personality characteristics predicted life satisfaction at age 70.

Valliant and Valliant (1990) tested over 200 healthy college students in the early 1940s and reinterviewed them four times over the next 40 years. People who enjoyed positive mental health in their fifties had come from intact homes and had trusting relationships with their parents that permitted some autonomy and initiative. In a word, these students had developed mature yet flexible ego defenses to help them cope with stress and change. These served them well later in life. Interestingly, people with the poorest mental health later in life were most likely to have used mood-altering drugs before the age of 50. These individuals had very rigid ways of coping and consequently used drugs to deal with feelings of fragility and threat. In these studies, we see what part developing a flexible yet adaptive attitude toward life in young adulthood plays in contributing to mental health in later life.

An emotional bond to a "significant other," whether sibling, spouse, or friend, also seems to contribute to emotional stability in old age (Snow & Crapo, 1982). People who are ill or isolated often lack this special person, who serves as a buffer or confidant (Botwinick, 1984).

It is important to note that research on positive mental health in old age through identification of its correlates and causal factors provides the basis for changing either the environment and/or some aspect of the person, making it more likely that he or she will continue to prosper throughout life. The counseling we would provide as a result is of a preventative rather than remedial nature (see Chapter 1); that is, skills can be developed and changes made early on in life. Often, what appears to be a consequence of old age, on close scrutiny, really emerges as an individualized life-long pattern of coping. And this pattern of adjustment may be very adaptive, or it may be very ineffective.

Increased self-confidence and self-reliance, healthy attitudes about one's strengths and weaknesses, learning and maintaining effective coping skills, and an active approach toward the environment are prerequisites for mental health in both young and elderly people (Valliant & Valliant, 1990). By contrast, unrealistic expectations of self, narrowness of experience, emotional fragility, resistance to criticism, and a restrictive environment encourage unhealthy styles of coping in both the young and the old.

In closing our discussion of mental health and psychopathology, we again point out the importance of looking at these topics as opposite ends of a single continuum, whose definition is, therefore, relative rather than absolute. Under these conditions, we can interpret both our own and others' behavior in a realistic, flexible manner. Moreover, assessment procedures, therapeutic efforts, and design of mental health services for both mentally healthy and pathological adults can more fully be geared to the needs of the individual in light of current circumstances, unique life history, and personal experiences.

Blazer (1990) suggests that successful aging is a combination of many factors: personal vitality, resilience, adaptive flexibility, realistic autonomy and control, integrity, and a good person-environment "fit." People who have aged successfully take care of themselves both physically and mentally. They get regular physical and mental exercise and find a way to get the most out of whatever life brings them—good or bad. Perhaps they were much like this as younger people. Maybe it's not too late to start?

SUMMARY

Information about *mental health* and mental illness across the adult life span must be viewed with caution, for a number of reasons. Mental health and mental illness are best thought of as ends of a *continuum.* This is particularly important in that mental health has rarely been defined, especially in the aged, and has been traditionally seen as the absence of mental illness. A variety of models have been proposed to understand this continuum with the aged; each has strengths and weaknesses that must be kept in mind in defining mental illness and in planning mental health interventions with the aged.

Of major importance is separating *reversible* and *irreversible* forms of *dementia,* as well as separating *dementia* and *depression* in the aged. The confusion of these categories, termed *pseudodementia,* often leads to improper treatment of, or no treatment at all for, aged individuals and their families. *Drug use* and *abuse,* especially alcohol, can also mimic dementia.

Indeed, caregivers often suffer as much as do dementia victims, leading to feelings of helplessness and burden in caregivers, most of whom are women. Access to support and information as well as developing good coping skills are very important in maintaining caregiver well-being. While forms of dementia such as *Alzheimer's disease, multi-infarct* dementia, and *depression* have received the most attention, other disorders such as *anxiety, paranoia,* and *schizophrenia* are less well understood.

Depression is, in some respects, unique in older persons, yet in other ways it is expressed universally. As depression is a key element in suicide, its assessment should be done carefully, especially since suicides in late life are often difficult to prevent.

The *assessment* of mental health–mental illness should be *purposeful* and as *comprehensive* as possible in order to make as *reasonable* an interpretation as possible in light of an older person's goals, needs, resources, and capabilities. While mental illness does occur, particular attention should be paid to optimally mentally healthy persons who are older. They have much to teach us about successful aging.

KEY TERMS AND CONCEPTS

Mental health–mental illness	False positives
Abnormal behavior	False negatives
Medical model	DSM-III-R

Aging-as-illness model
Behavioral model of mental illness
Dementia
Alzheimer's disease
Multi-infarct dementia
Reversible versus irreversible dementia
Pseudodementia
Functional disorders
Bipolar versus unipolar depression
Depressive equivalents
Schizophrenia
Paranoia
Anxiety
Mental-status questionnaire
Geriatric Depression Scale
Reliability
Validity
Egoistic suicide
Drug use and abuse
Half-life
Optimal mental health
Successful aging
Caregiver burden
Pick's disease
Paraphrenia
Functional skills
Senile plaques
Neurofibrillary tangles
Personal versus universal helplessness
Spaced retrieval technique
ISDB
Line of unbearability
Drug misuse
Polypharmacy

REVIEW QUESTIONS

1. What are some of the problems in getting an accurate picture of abnormal behavior across adulthood?
2. What is mental health? How can it be defined for the aged?
3. What seem to be prerequisites for positive mental health among the aged?
4. What models of mental illness does Zarit use in understanding abnormal behavior among the aged? What are each model's strengths and weaknesses?
5. What is dementia? Of what value is its diagnosis?
6. What is the distinction between irreversible and reversible organic conditions? Why is this distinction important?
7. What is pseudodementia? How is it different from dementia?
8. What guidelines need to be kept in mind in assessing elderly people?
9. What are some of the difficulties in caring for a family member with Alzheimer's disease? How can caregivers be helped?
10. How common is drug abuse among older people? How can drug adherence be improved among the aged?

C H A P T E R 11

Intervention and Therapy

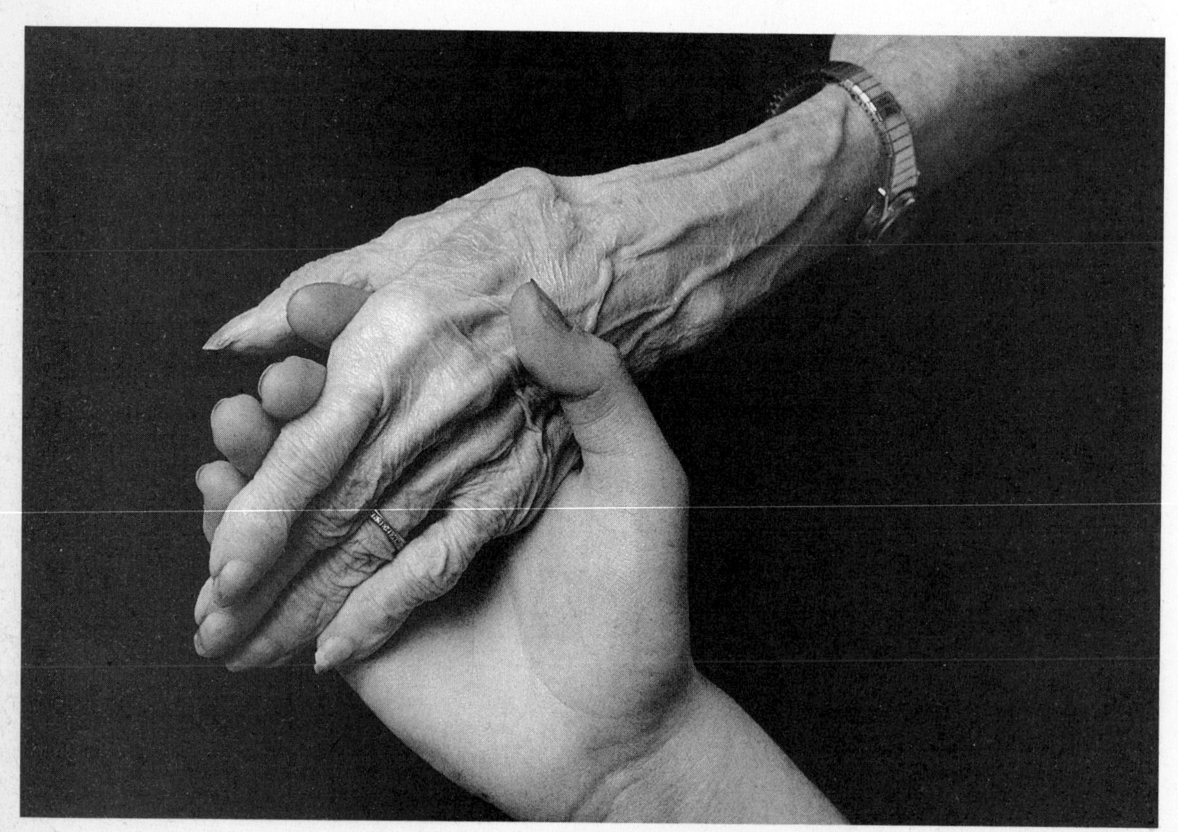

C H A P T E R   O U T L I N E

INTRODUCTION

Most of us rely on others in times of need or severe stress, and it is the mental health professional to whom we often turn when we experience emotional problems that are beyond our own resources to handle effectively. In this chapter, we will examine the psychological treatment of adults as well as more specific questions dealing with the importance of chronological age in treating mental illness. In addition, we will discuss interventions designed to help adults handle difficulties in everyday life whether or not they are longstanding in nature.

MENTAL HEALTH SERVICES—EQUALLY HELPFUL FOR ALL ADULTS?

According to the National Institute of Mental Health, nearly 30 million Americans require professional treatment for mental illness during any six-month period (Sullivan, 1987). Currently, direct costs of mental illness are estimated to exceed $20 billion per year (Roybal, 1988). The problem has now reached the point where "the personal and social costs of mental illness are similar in scale to those for heart disease and cancer" (Sullivan, 1987).

Indeed, many have argued that the elderly are especially vulnerable to mental health problems (see Chapter 10). For this reason, they are particularly in need of improved mental health services (Roybal, 1988). Services are currently very scattered and difficult to access in many areas (Lebowitz & Niederehe, 1992). Since between 15 and 25 percent of the 28 million older Americans suffer from mental health problems, this means that as many as 7 million of them may need professional mental health services (Fleming et al., 1986). If middle-aged people are included in these figures, the need for help increases still further. Yet, very few of these people are receiving the treatment they need. There are many reasons for this, as we will see.

Although the situation is problematic for elderly individuals, data indicate that minority aged men and women are statistically more likely to experience psychological problems than are the elderly as a whole (Roybal, 1988; Rodenheaver & Datan, 1988). The situation is made worse by the fact that women and racial and ethnic minorities are much less likely to have the psychological and social resources to deal with mental health problems (Roybal, 1988; Rodenheaver & Datan, 1988). They may be discriminated against, living in poverty, or isolated from others.

Reports by the President's Commission on Mental Health (1978) and the White House Conference on Aging (1981) have documented the relatively high prevalence of mental health disorders in older people (see Chapter 10). Nevertheless, there is meager support for mental health care. For example, in 1984, 1.5 percent of funds for mental health went to potential elderly clients for access to mental health services directed to older adults. Older people comprised 6 percent of all clients at community mental health centers, 3 percent of all clients seen in private practice, and 1 percent of clients seen by psychologists working in nursing homes (American Psychological Association, 1984). The very low incidence of mental disorders among people in nursing homes is due to regulations limiting the number that can receive a primary psychiatric diagnosis (Lebowitz, 1988).

A recent survey by Knesper and associates (1985) confirmed this trend. These authors surveyed over 9000 mental health service providers and found older people to be underrepresented; more elderly were seen by primary care physicians than by other mental health personnel such as psychologists, psychiatrists, or social workers. These physicians often did not refer their patients to mental health personnel (George et al., 1988). In addition, people who could not pay for services were less likely to receive private help. Unfortunately, those who are poor are also, statistically speaking, more likely to have more severe mental health problems. Recent discussions of mental health care for adults suggest that the situation has not changed a great deal over the last five to ten years (Lasoski, 1986; Lebowitz & Niederehe, 1992; Smyer et al., 1990).

A discussion of all possible forms of treatment with adults of all ages is beyond our scope here, but see Garfield and Bergin (1986) for in-depth treatments of the major approaches to psychotherapy and counseling. We will focus on the variety of treatment approaches for older adults, taking into account age bias in treatment and referral (Carstensten & Edlestein, 1987; Smyer et al., 1991; Gatz et al. 1985). In many respects, therapy and other interventions with aged people is, in principle, much like those with young and middle-aged adults (Myers, 1991).

Fortunately, a great deal of research arising from the life-span tradition (see Chapter 1) has demonstrated that older adults are equally amenable to change (Baltes et al., 1980; Birren et al., 1983). Ideally, this should provide additional impetus for professionals to actively treat elderly clients by focusing on their potential for change in the context of the relationship with a counselor or therapist (Steenbarger, 1991).

Well-being and Mental Health Services

In perhaps the most comprehensive study dealing with mental health services to date, Veroff and associates (1981a, 1981b), in 1976, asked over 2500 adults a wide variety of questions regarding their mental health, where they sought help for emotional problems, as well as how effective this help was. These individuals were compared with a similar sample of adults who had been interviewed in 1957. While comparisons within individuals were not possible, intracohort estimates of age changes (see Chapter 2) in the use of mental health services were obtained based on data from individuals ranging in age from 21 to 65+ over a 20-year period of time.

Not only were these investigators able to determine age effects both in how people viewed their mental health and in their use of mental health services, but they were also able to examine the role that cultural changes played in this process. Understanding the relationships between mental health, well-being, and help-seeking can lead to a better understanding of the reasons why adults of all ages do, or do not, seek help for mental/emotional problems.

AGE EFFECTS IN WELL-BEING: RELATIONSHIP TO HELP-SEEKING

Regarding well-being, younger people were found to differ from older people in four major ways. First, younger people focused on interpersonal joys and sorrows in their lives, while older ones tended to focus on the more spiritual or community-oriented sources of happiness and well-being. Rather than being caught up in how their lives might be, older people tended to appreciate things for what they actually were. While the bases for feelings of well-being differed, older and younger individuals seemed equally happy overall. Second, younger people reported being more overwhelmed by life. Third, older people were most past-oriented, in that the past was more often seen as a source of happiness; the future was seen less often as a time for positive change. Fourth, younger people were more diverse in how they defined well-being.

In both 1957 and 1976, fewer older people reported having problems for which they could have used professional help. For this reason, it is not surprising to find that in these years, older people less often reported feeling "overwhelmed" when "bad things" happened to them. Because they had confronted illness and death, they were able to put other problems into perspective.

COHORT DIFFERENCES IN HELP-SEEKING

In Chapter 2, we discussed cohort or generational influences on development. Because value systems about seeking help might vary with one's generation, we might also expect to see cohort or historical influences in seeking help for mental health concerns. For example, those interviewed in 1976 were more than likely to see talking with others as sources of help when they were worried; thus, more intimate means of solving personally distressing problems were being used than earlier. Institutional sources of help, such as churches, were sought less often than in 1957. This implies that older cohorts will be less likely to deal with their problems by seeking out a mental health professional. By contrast, what are considered personal or family matters by the old are dealt with in a more "outside" help-seeking manner by younger people. These 20-year differences also suggest that future cohorts of older adults will be more likely to turn to others in times of trouble, because a historical shift toward more professional help-seeking seems to have occurred. Several other findings emerged from the same study:

1. In general, people in 1976 were more prone to seek expert help, and less likely to deny their problems.
2. Within cohorts, there was a great deal of consistency in help-seeking. Those who were younger in 1957 were just as likely to seek informal help versus those who were middle-aged and older in 1976. Likewise, those who were middle-aged in 1957 and elderly in 1976 were consistent in their tendency to seek out a mental health professional.

IMPLICATIONS FOR HELP-SEEKING

These results imply that it is those who are younger who are more likely to be more positive about receiving professional help. Thus, younger people tended to be more psychological in their orientation toward assistance from someone who is professionally trained, that is, a psychologist, social worker, clergy, doctor, lawyer, or psychiatrist. While a third of the 1976 adult sample could not see themselves as ever having difficulties requiring professional assistance, those who did seek help in 1976 were more likely to select a specialized mental health professional, such as a psychologist, psychiatrist, or counselor, over a general help source, such as a doctor or lawyer.

While the national surveys of Veroff et al. are revealing, we must be cautious in interpreting the findings because different people were interviewed in 1957 and 1976. Thus, we have no longitudinal information dealing with age changes in well-being and help-seeking, and the effects of age

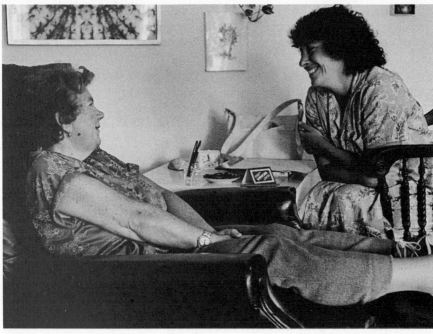

Older people are equally viable candidates for successful counseling interventions.

on help-seeking are undoubtedly influenced by the gross cultural shifts noted above. When results of comparisons of similar-aged people in 1957 versus 1976 do not overlap, they are best interpreted as cohort or historical effects (see Chapter 2).

Barriers to Mental Health Services

Many have expressed great concern about the underutilization of available mental health services by elderly adults. In some cases, services that exist are based on the irreversible decrement model of aging (see Chapter 1) that, until recently, has dominated gerontological research and practice (Kastenbaum, 1978). Unfortunately, despite a more positive outlook about adulthood and aging supported by research findings, negative expectations about older people continue to influence mental health services. For example, people who are disabled or mentally retarded may be denied continued eligibility to community-based services because they are too old, and people may be refused admission to a nursing home if the reason for their disability is a mental disorder. Thus, age and diagnosis, not people's functional abilities, may determine the type of help they can get (Lebowitz & Niederehe, 1992). In addition, rehabilitation services often have a strong job component to them; their goal is to provide the disabled individual with job skills as well as everyday living skills. Older adults who may be suffering from both chronic physical illness and mental disorder and who may not want or need job-skill training often have no rehabilitation services designed with them in mind. Moreover, meal services, housing, senior centers, and day care services are not designed for people with more serious mental disorders. For these reasons, older adults often "fall through the cracks" of available community services (Lebowitz & Niederehe, 1992). These dilemmas present challenges to mental health services planners who want to serve all adults equally.

EXTERNAL BARRIERS

External barriers to mental health services are the objective, observable aspects of the mental health system itself. Felton (1982) points out that, while many older adults seek basic services such as housing, meals, or income assistance, what are offered are often life-enhancing services such as socialization, growth experiences, and activity programs (Estes, 1979). Clearly, this suggests that mental health service providers need to more carefully design and implement their programs so that they will be perceived as acceptable by potential older clients.

Brim and Phillips (1988) argue that intervention works best when it is understood in terms of the principles of life-span development (see Chapter 1). These principles are (1) the continued malleability of the person throughout life, (2) the substantial differences between individuals in adulthood, and (3) the multidimensionality and multidirectionality of change. Taking this point of view enables one to plan interventions at many levels. For example, when, where, and with whom to intervene are all issues that the therapist should consider. Should services be inpatient or outpatient in nature? Is therapy to be preventative or remedial? Should the focus be on children or adults? Should the target be men or women? seriously or mildly impaired populations? What skills should the individual develop? Considering all of these questions simultaneously allows us to make more informed decisions about therapy and intervention, and we can provide help that is effective and timely.

Many types of services could be provided at multiple levels depending on the individual's need in a variety of settings (Danish, 1981). For example, we could treat individuals, families, or even change cultures or societies to enhance individual adjustment. Services could be provided by professionals, paraprofessionals, and peers (Myers & Salmon, 1984; Sargent, 1980; Waters, 1984). While paraprofessionals may not substitute for professionals, they can supplement care nicely (Smyer et al., 1990).

Coordination of services (Smyer & Gatz, 1979) of the community-based, institutional, and individual types is essential (Felton, 1982; Lebowitz & Niederehe, 1992; Myers & Salmon, 1984; Smyer & Gatz, 1979). But in many cases, health care providers and community agencies do not make timely referrals (Smyer et al., 1990). The end result is that the adult

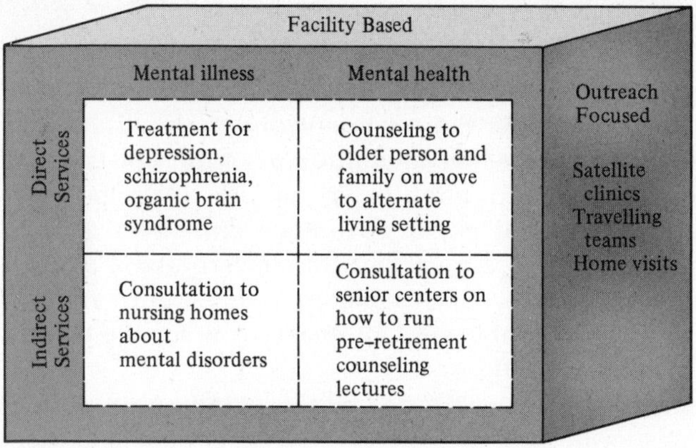

Figure 11.1 Organization of mental health services for adults and older people. *Source: Issues in Mental Health and Aging* (1979). NIMH.

goes from one agency to another, with no real purpose or satisfaction. We have all probably experienced trying to get answers from service providers and felt like "we got the runaround." Figure 11.1 illustrates how mental health services might be organized to solve many of these problems.

Transportation to where services are offered may be a problem for older people who cannot drive or afford cars. Mass transit may not be available; and the older person who lives alone or in a rural area may be isolated from others.

The cost of services is also a major barrier to their use by older adults. Reimbursing for mental health services on a par with treatment for physical illness would make such help more feasible financially (Roybal, 1988). Raising Medicare ceilings on reimbursement for mental health services provided by any professional qualified to deliver them would also help matters greatly (Hagebak & Hagebak, 1983; Santos et al., 1984). This situation has recently improved since psychologists' services are now reimbursable under Medicare.

Santos and associates (1984) point out that existing services may be already overburdened, personnel may be poorly trained, and services may not be geared to deal with elderly patients. For example, making home visits and offering services in other contexts such as senior centers, churches, or at public housing would improve access to existing mental health services by older people.

In sum, poorly designed services, lack or coordination, cost, ignorance of the potential of psychological interventions, and services that are narrow in scope emerge as major external barriers interfering with the use of mental health services by older people.

INTERNAL BARRIERS

Internal barriers primarily reflect client or therapist attitudes and biases and contribute to lack of interest in the treatment of elderly adults. For example, we might question the feelings and attitudes of therapists about treating the aged patient, which are often based on lack of professional experience with elders and limited personal contact with them as well (Goodstein, 1982). In fact, there is a great deal of concern about ageism (see Chapter 1) among professionals which sometimes pervades treatment, often resulting in no care at all or, at best, poor quality care for the elderly (Butler et al., 1991; Gatz et al., 1980).

Gatz and Pearson (1988) have expanded on these findings of professional bias, discovering specific misconceptions about older people in therapy. For example, belief in the pervasiveness of Alzheimer's disease, wherein nothing can be done, leaves many professionals helpless. Likewise, thinking that memory difficulties are a normal sign of aging and do not require professional intervention, or that only drugs and not psychotherapy can be effective in treating depression, ultimately discourages professional helping efforts for middle-aged and older individuals. Unfortunately, some middle-aged and older adults may also hold such beliefs.

Another factor behind the lack of mental health care elderly people sometimes receive is **countertransference** (Blum & Tallmer, 1977; Goodstein, 1982). This means that the therapist projects his or her own negative feelings about aging, death, or loss onto the elderly client, interfering with diagnosis and treatment. Caring for both one's elderly parents and for one's children can intensify a therapist's countertransference, leading to (1) unrealistic demands for a cure, (2) a parental "know-it-all" attitude, or (3) hostility, pity, or sympathy toward elderly people as individuals who cannot care for themselves (Goodstein, 1982).

Sometimes complicating this situation is the older person's transference to the counselor. He or she may see the therapist as a parent or child figure. Transference may cause the client to see the helper as someone to be taught, an authority figure, or a long-lost sexual object. Because of transference, when therapy ends, breaking off the relationship with the therapist may be difficult (Thompson et al., 1986).

Recognizing and handling these feelings requires both honesty and objectivity. Goals for therapy must be set and adhered to in light of the client's needs, abilities, and resources, but with a large measure of empathy for both the physical and interpersonal losses the older person may have experienced (Knight, 1986; 1992).

Respecting people as individuals, encouraging independent decision-making, and knowledge of community resources are all important (Lawton & Gottesman, 1974; Smyer & Gatz, 1979). Ultimately, the individual's dignity and self-respect must be preserved throughout the course of therapy. These factors are especially important given the suspicion and distrust with which some older clients may approach therapy. Many elderly people prefer to help themselves rather than turn to others, which is based on a work ethic emphasizing independence at all costs (Butler et al., 1979).

It may also be that middle-aged and older individuals do not think in psychological terms. Instead, they may see their distress or symptoms as indications of physical illness or consequences of normal aging. Such bias or ignorance appears to explain why families do not seek professional help for a member who may be suffering from some form of dementia (Pollitt et al., 1989). However, once one labels a problem as psychological, the decision that professional help is appropriate must still be made. One must also decide to seek that help, assuming it is available. Thus, the process of getting help is a complex one, and solutions to this problem, by necessity, should be flexible to reflect this complexity.

Narrow ideas about older people as "crazy, senile, or depressed," limited experience with elderly people, and professional backgrounds that are conceptually narrow also work against the development of interventions with the elderly (Eisdorfer, 1983). A flexible approach not only is more likely to succeed in helping middle-aged and older clients, but also generates more knowledge about the processes of development and aging (Baltes & Danish, 1980). This, in turn, provides an even broader basis for future treatment efforts.

Quite often, younger individuals "fit the mold" for the ideal patient/client who can be helped. They are more likely to fulfill our expectations of being "YAVIS"—*y*oung, *a*ttractive, *v*erbal, *i*ntelligent, and *s*uccessful—and are therefore seen as having more therapeutic potential. Thinking of older adults evokes images of decline, loss, or death, issues that many of us would just as soon ignore (see Chapter 1).

In many cases, mental health services are organized around age-related themes or life events such as widowhood, death, retirement, disability, or illness (Smyer, 1984). These services, unfortunately, ultimately increase ageistic notions of what older people's problems really are (Lieberman, 1978; Neugarten, 1983). They may also intensify the effects of being isolated or institutionalized (Zarit, 1980). These programs provide structure and a source of identity for many adults and are easily identified as sources of support (Danish et al., 1980). However, they may "turn off" other older people, leading to more age segregation. Programs that are age-heterogenous or issue-oriented (e.g., coping with loss or change, career counseling, maintaining decision-making and independence) may be more beneficial to participants. They can lessen age segregation and remove the stigma of seeing a mental health professional (Sargent, 1982; Smyer et al., 1990). Table 11.1 summarizes the barriers to mental health services we have discussed.

Gottesman and associates (1973) note that, with older clients, one's choice of treatment should always involve (1) the capacities (physical, emotional, and cognitive) of the individual, (2) expectations of significant others, and (3) what the elderly person expects of him or herself. These are important issues for not only elderly people but adults of all ages (see Table 11.2).

TABLE 11.1

BARRIERS TO MENTAL HEALTH SERVICES

External Barriers	Internal Barriers
Nature of services available	Lack of therapist experience in treating adults
Narrowness of services	Specific misconceptions about adults and aged people
Lack of coordination	Countertransference
Lack of transportation	Transference
Costly services or lack of reimbursement by Medicare	Lack of psychological-mindedness in older adults
Poorly trained personnel	YAVIS syndrome
Cultural ignorance of adults' potential for change	Fear of being stigmatized as crazy
Understaffed facilities	Self-help mentality

TABLE 11.2

LEVELS OF INTERVENTION: SOME POSSIBLE THERAPIES

	Site of the Disorder					
	Self		Significant Other		Society	
Treater	**Physical Capacity**	**Expectation**	**Family/Friend**	**Therapist**	**Institution**	**Real World**
Self	Adapt, medicate, use appliances	Adapt	Support, help	Teach	Reform	Initiate, support, agitate change
Family/friend	Medicate, understand, ignore	Support, model, punish, understand	Model, advise, communicate	React, complain, compliment	Compliment, complain, investigate	Initiate, agitate, support change
Therapist	Medicate, use protheses	Medicate, understand, therapy	Group therapy	Schooling, introspection	Organizational development	Initiate, agitate, support change
Institution	Contain, care for, medicate	Support, punish, understand	Inform; share care, help	Hire; train, assign	Administer, plan change	Lobby, meet, lead
Real world	Laws, social support, assistance programs	Norms	Support, limit	Support, limit	Laws; assistance programs	Legislation, evolution, revolution

Source: Gottesman et al. (1973).

APPROACHES TO THERAPY AND COUNSELING WITH OLDER ADULTS

Freud contended that middle-aged and older adults were not good candidates for therapy:

> On the one hand, near or above the fifties the elasticity of the mental processes, on which the treatment depends, is as a rule lacking—older people are no longer educable—and, on the other hand, the mass of material to be dealt with would prolong the duration of the treatment indefinitely (Freud, 1905, pp. 258–259).

Yet, in fact, research does not bear out age as a predictor of therapeutic success (Garfield, 1986; Knight, 1988). However, this conclusion is partly due to the small numbers of older people studied (Dusk et al., 1983). Because client age fails to predict who can be helped, we should be primarily concerned with improving quality of life, not necessarily just its quantity, regardless of our client's age (Eisdorfer, 1983).

More specific goals in therapy with adults and older persons are:

1. Insight into one's behavior
2. Symptom (anxiety or depression) relief
3. Relief to relatives
4. Delaying deterioration (psychic or physical)
5. Adaptation to the present situation
6. Improving self-care skills
7. Encouraging activity
8. Facilitating independence
9. Becoming more self-accepting
10. Improving interpersonal relationships (Gotestam, 1980; Wellman & McCormack, 1984).

We want to emphasize that these are therapeutic goals for adults of all ages! Each goal will be more or less important depending on the individual's physical health, strengths and resources, as well as the therapist's own biases. But relying on a single approach virtually guarantees an unsatisfying helping experience for *both* the counselor and the client (Eisdorfer & Stotsky, 1977).

Many treatment approaches are commonly used with younger and middle-aged adults. However, we are unsure whether a given approach works better with younger versus older adults. Gatz et al. (1985) highlight the importance of diagnosis (organicity, chronicity, situationality) and patient types (community-living versus institutionalized) as factors in evaluating outcome research with adults and elderly people. For these reasons, different therapies may work better with different types of older individuals. However, whether certain approaches are more effective for younger versus older adults, or for older adults versus younger ones with certain mental disorders, is unknown at this time.

Wherever possible, we should try to put all the approaches to treatment into an adult developmental perspective—they seem to share a number of features. However, many therapeutic approaches have been especially developed for older people (life review) and for those who reside in certain environments such as nursing homes (reality orientation).

Since many therapies are closely derived from a particular theory of personality, we recommend rereading Chapter 8 on personality development, in addition to perhaps examining a comprehensive text on personality and psychotherapy (Hall & Lindzey, 1985; Maddi, 1990). Doing so will enable you to achieve a fuller understanding of the relationship between personality theory and psychotherapy/counseling.

In addition to what might be termed *generalized approaches* to helping middle-aged and older people (e.g., individual psychoanalytic therapy, behavioral approaches), more specific techniques geared to the aged person's capabilities and environment have also become popular in recent years. Milieu therapy and, as mentioned above, reality orientation are examples of these more specialized techniques. While it is tempting to focus on these narrower approaches, serious consideration must be given to the therapeutic options open to the aged individual in distress. Unfortunately, since the field of clinical gerontology is relatively new, use of these specific treatment modalities with the older adults has, in most cases, preceded evaluation of their effectiveness. The array of counseling and intervention approaches used with the aged is presented in Table 11.3.

Individual Psychotherapy—Psychoanalysis

Psychoanalysis is based on the assumption that through insight, which is aided by the guidance of a therapist, one may come to grips with troublesome emotions that have been repressed via unconscious defense mechanisms (Freud, 1924). While such defenses ordinarily operate very efficiently, a breakdown in one's defenses leads to anxiety. Anxiety is a sign that control exercised by the ego (i.e., reality orientation) over both the id (i.e., instincts, wishes, drives) and the superego (i.e., morals, ideals) is weakening. Through free association, conflicts between the ego, id, and superego, normally unconscious, are made conscious, and their meaning interpreted to the client by the therapist (Hall & Lindzey, 1985).

Unfortunately, Freud saw very few older clients—even in their forties and fifties—and, as noted above, was quite skeptical about his technique's success with the elderly. He assumed that the effect required to change people whose defenses had been overused for years was not worth the limited time left to them. This skepticism is still shared by some modern-day therapists (Brammer, 1984). Gotestam (1980), however, notes such Freudian therapists as Abraham and Goldfarb as instrumental in pioneering changes in psychoanalytic therapy with the aged. For example, the therapist may be supportive and make use of the aged person's defense mechanisms. The older person's need to be dependent on the therapist—transference—would instead be encouraged.

TABLE 11.3

BEGINNING COUNSELING APPROACHES WITH OLDER PEOPLE

Model	Strategies	Uses	Strengths	Weaknesses
Psychiatric/ psychological	Drug therapy, psychoanalysis	Physical illness, organic problems, behavior difficulties	Psychoactive drug therapy helpful in some cases	Difficult to document objectively; treatment is usually very long; only certain aged can benefit
Milieu	Change physical environment of institution to one more like residential setting	Listless, withdrawn, and psychiatric-medically infirm, generally more regressed patients	Promotes resocialization, improves general environment	Very general, not specific for one-to-one or one-to-family treatment; designed for use in institutional settings only; efficacy limited
Reality	Continual stimulation by presentations of fundamental data, such as date, day of week, year, weather, next meal, next holiday	Memory loss, confusional states, general disorientation	Stimulates active mental processes	Designed for use in early treatment stages and for the disoriented; efficacy limited
Cognitive	Alter thinking strategies and problem-solving/ coping skills	Adjustment to life change, stress reduction, cognitive change	Easily used by most older people	Real-life environment may not support new thinking skills; not all aged can benefit
Behavioral	Define undesirable and desirable behavior in behavioral terms; reinforce desired behavior; withdraw reinforcers from undesired behavior	All types of general behavioral problems	Easily learned; results usually quick if the process is used correctly	Does not address itself to the social context that influences behaviors, ethical concerns
Ecological/ social	Same as with behavior modification, plus examination of effect on social environment	All types of general behavioral dysfunction	Focus on specific behaviors and social context of behavior	Not enough known about linkages between individual behavior and the social environment
Family	Encourage redefinition of family interaction patterns	Enhances problem-solving and communication, adaptation to life change	Involvement of entire family; dysfunctional patterns are changed	Difficult to carry out when all family do not actively participate
Group	Support and feedback by others in context of group leader support	Enhance social adjustment; life review and reminiscence	Facilitates interpersonal skills in a safe environment	Efficacy limited; excludes impaired, disruptive elders

Adapted from Keller & Hughston (1981).

As noted above, much of the skepticism about older individuals as clients is based on a biological-decline model of aging. Not only are older people's biological drives thought to be weaker, but their ego strength is thought to be weaker as well (based on their preoccupation with loss), impairing their ability to respond to therapy (see Birren & Renner, 1979). Some, however, advocate brief psychoanalytic therapy with the aged, where the more realistic goals of reducing anxiety and restoring the person to a more functional state can be achieved (Silberschatz & Curtis, 1991).

Silberschatz and Curtis (1991) term this variation on classic psychoanalysis *time-limited psychodynamic therapy.* Clients spend 3 to 4 months rather than years, in therapy. Pathogenic (abnormal, destructive) beliefs about oneself rooted in childhood can be dealt with through therapy by clearly defining goals for the client. Middle-aged and older clients may believe they are too old to change, or simply unworthy of help. To "test" the therapist, they may be hostile, late for appointments, argue with the therapist, or be very passive. All of these maneuvers are designed to find out if the destructive beliefs about oneself formed in childhood, which can be quite painful, need to be maintained or whether they can be challenged. Silberschatz and Curtis (1991) emphasize that these "tests" should be understood as an outgrowth of painful experiences early in life. They should not be interpreted as evidence for the adult's rigidity or resistance to therapy—a "lost cause."

Another interesting theme that emerges in time-limited therapy with adults is *survivor guilt* (Silberschatz & Curtis, 1991). As adults grow older and witness the physical decline and death of friends and family, they become increasingly prone to experience guilt over outliving these loved ones. Adults may also feel this guilt if their children or grandchildren experience difficulties. It may even explain why some adults allow themselves to be abused at the hands of their grandchildren or children (see Chapter 7). Because they feel guilty about past failures as parents, or because they have outlived a spouse, they may feel that they "deserve" to be abused. Such guilt also causes many adults to set few goals for themselves, to feel depressed, or to believe in the many myths of aging. But by drawing on the experiences adults have accumulated, or the many roles they have played, insight into their behavior may be attained. Since painful childhood experiences are quite distant, they may be easier to discuss. Ironically, because they have limited time left to live, this enables many adults to work through childhood trauma. The older client has less time to waste and, thus, is more willing to use this time wisely in therapy (Silberschatz & Curtis, 1991).

Despite their potential, psychoanalytic approaches do not work well with severely confused and/or disturbed aged. In these cases, behavioral or life review (reminiscence) approaches are perhaps more effective, according to some authors (Lesser et al., 1981).

Reports of classic psychoanalysis are rare with older clients (Newton et al., 1986), and the studies are often poorly designed and documented (Gotestam, 1980; Wellman & McCormack, 1984). However, recent well-controlled studies have revealed that psychoanalytic therapy can indeed be quite helpful, leading to fewer distressing symptoms such as anxiety or depression, greater self-esteem, and more functional behavior (Lazarus et al., 1987).

For people who are not highly motivated or are disorganized psychologically, therapists, in order to be effective, must be more supportive and less active. For others who are more highly motivated and better organized, the therapist can play a more active role (Horowitz et al., 1984). Short-term analytic interventions have also been effective in the treatment of late-life depression (Thompson et al., 1987).

Good candidates for psychoanalysis should have some insight into their unconscious motives, be committed to changing, be able to tolerate very strong emotions, and have had some success in relating to others (Myers, 1991). Certainly, psychoanalysis should not be dismissed, but perhaps reserved for highly verbal, insightful older clients.

LIFE REVIEW THERAPY

An extension of psychoanalytic thought is **life review** therapy. As Butler and associates (1991) point out, life review therapy is more than a simple recall of the past, although reminiscence is important in this approach. Butler et al. (1991) also point out that obtaining extensive autobiographies from elderly clients is important, allowing them the opportunity to put their lives in order. Thus resolving internal conflict, improving relationships with one's family, making decisions about success and failure, resolving guilt, clarifying one's values, and simply "getting out" feelings about painful experiences in the past are all benefits to be gained from the life review (Newton et al., 1986).

The use of music, art, photographs, or even a trip to a memorable place in one's past can help clients focus on themselves (Calarusso & Nemiroff, 1991). Constructing one's genealogy or family tree can also bring the positive and negative aspects of the past to the present. Life review and reminiscence help the client gain a sense of continuity in life; past and present make more sense. Moreover, one's inner feelings and outer experiences and relationships can be better understood and interconnected. In a sense, one can be more "in synch" with his or her past and with others through reminiscence or life review therapy.

Life review therapy may be successfully conducted either individually or in a group setting. Either way, the life review can be a frustrating, painful experience for many aged, who require emotional support from a counselor for an extended period of time in order to deal with the byproducts of this process. Many older people have led hard, frustrating lives that forced them to make choices they later regretted, such as not finishing high school. Many lack someone with whom such confidences may be shared.

Despite its potential for some types of people, Brammer (1984) suggests that life review therapy falsely assumes that problems in adulthood rest on childhood experiences. Moreover, Romaniuk and Romaniuk (1981) have pointed out that reminiscence is not unique to older people, but is triggered by many events throughout the adult life cycle. While Butler et

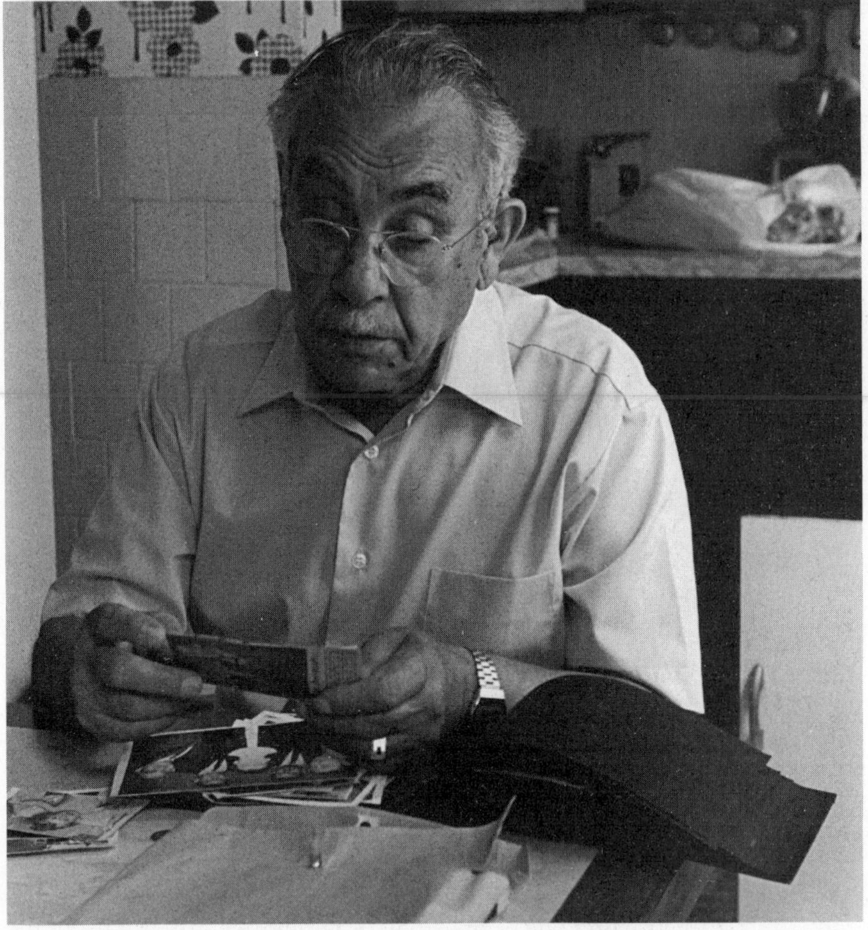

The life review can be an enriching experience for adults of all ages.

al. (1991), Birren (1982), Lesser et al. (1981), and Wheeler and Knight (1981) have reported life review/reminiscence therapy to be successful—that is, resulting in less depression and fewer memory complaints—more structured versions of life review work best with relatively intact elderly persons. However, objective evidence supporting the effectiveness of life review therapy is scarce (Kastenbaum, 1987).

Group Therapy

The distinguishing feature of **group therapy** with aged people is that dependency needs can be used to their best advantage (Hayslip & Kooken, 1982). Since many older people are isolated, group therapy may be especially suited to them (Finkel, 1991). It may also be quite helpful for adult caregivers, who often must shoulder the burden of caring for an ill or dying family member (Smyer et al., 1990). In many cases, simply being with others evokes a feeling of safety. Problems, fears, and hidden emotions can be shared with others. These may range from relationship difficulties, to illness, retirement, or simply feeling alone or unworthy. Face-to-face contact, touching another person, and sharing experiences are quite important to many middle-aged and older adults (Finkel, 1991). This is in contrast to younger adults, for whom making and breaking relationships is more common and touching is less comforting (Finkel, 1991). Group therapy for younger people seems a bit less personal and intimate.

Group therapy can take many forms. These range from issue-oriented, or life-event, discussion groups, to groups designed to stimulate interaction among group members (Finkel, 1991; Smyer, 1984; Smyer et al., 1991; Waters, 1984). Groups can also be designed to promote independence and a positive sense of self. Common themes are social losses, independence, illness, sensory loss, death, and loneliness (Finkel, 1991).

Groups are typically short-term when used in institutions, and informal in nature. They may be self-help, educational, or more formally therapeutic. Both self-help and educational groups may not carry the stigma of being "in therapy." Group therapy is often used in a variety of settings in combination with art therapy, dance therapy, or music therapy for elderly people (Hartford, 1980).

Waters (1984) stresses that, while basic helping skills may be a bit more difficult to accomplish with aged people without special training, the skills necessary to conduct group therapy are similar for clients of all ages. These skills are: (1) communicating clearly, (2) establishing trust, (3) openness to thoughts and feelings, (4) goal-setting, (5) confrontation, when necessary (6) empathy, (7) respect for the client's wishes, and (8) knowing when to make decisions (Waters, 1984).

In working with older adults, however, one needs to realize that physical or sensory losses may dictate slower paced and shorter counseling sessions. Moreover, using properly designed written materials (e.g., large, clear, bold print; nonglare paper) and having adequate lighting are very important. Sessions must be held at locations that are easily accessible for those who have difficulty walking. Conducting sessions in areas without background noise that would interfere with hearing is also essential. Groups may also need to be smaller than for younger people, to lessen the elder's confusion and fatigue; and plans need to be made with each group member as to what he or she will do when the group ends. Group work may not be advisable for older adults who are severely disturbed, aggressive, extremely introverted, or disoriented (Burnside, 1984).

All forms of group therapy provide many benefits for older individuals. These benefits include:

1. Enabling people to see that their problems are not unique, which can alleviate their sense of isolation
2. Providing individuals with the opportunity to learn new social and communication skills
3. Being able to give support, guidance, or insight to others
4. Allowing airing of feelings about being old, ill, or alone.

Finkel (1991) and Parham and associates (1982) note that well-designed research demonstrating the effectiveness of group therapy with older people is lacking. Its effectiveness seems to rest on accurate assessment (see Chapter 8) of each prospective member to identify those who may interfere with the sharing process or fail to profit from feedback from the group leader as well as from one another. Group leaders may facilitate discussion, provide structure, define goals, clarify what is being said, or simply be supportive.

Wellman and McCormick (1984) suggest that group therapy, in its many forms, has been effective, but that research results are clouded by methodological shortcomings such as lack of control groups and disabilities among group members as impediments to group progress. Although it is limited, there is evidence that some forms of group therapy—self-help, psychoeducational, and formally therapeutic—can indeed accomplish the goals listed above (Smyer et al., 1990).

Family Therapy

Family therapy is another attractive alternative in treating older people whose difficulties are communicative in nature (Hayslip & Kooken, 1982). Family therapy can aid in adjustment to roles such as retirement or grandparenthood, and help resolve problems accompanying caring for an ill spouse, institutionalizing one's parent(s) or spouse, or conflicts arising from an older parent being cared for at home by a middle-aged child. Each family member can be involved in setting up clear expectations for behavior, improving communication, decreasing distrust and guilt, or dealing with hostility and anxiety.

Family therapy may be especially effective in reestablishing communication.

Family therapy with middle-aged and older couples has been of some interest to mental health professionals. As couples age together, they may face several developmental tasks: the exit (or reentry) of children, retirement, physical health decline, disability of either husband or wife, and death (Smyer et al., 1990). Family therapy can help couples reestablish intimacy, learn to enjoy life without being preoccupied with illness, nurture and let go of children, and grieve over losses of loved ones.

While some couples come to therapy with long-standing conflicts that are intensified by the demands of working, child-rearing, retirement adjustment, or illness, others face such transitions with few previous difficulties in their relationships. For long-term conflicted couples, more confrontive therapy may be necessary to force them into changing their patterns of communication and behavior. Couples without long-standing problems may benefit from education and information, problem-solving, or simply providing access to resources (Patterson, 1987; Smyer et al., 1990). For some couples dealing with their sexuality, education and instruction in sexual techniques can be helpful in reestablishing sexual intimacy and lessening marital tension (Kaplan, 1991; Knight, 1992; O'Donahue, 1987; Whitlatch & Zarit, 1989).

Family therapy is also appropriate for dealing with parent-child conflicts centering around remarriage, struggles for power in the home, or restrictions on the aged person brought about by ill health or the divorce of an adult child. In these cases, allowing each person to express his or her feelings, explore options, and increase sensitivity to others' points of view are the major benefits of family therapy.

As discussed in Chapter 7, a family systems approach now characterizes views of the family. In dealing with families, both parents and children need to be understood as developing individuals. However, interactions among dyads in the family—parent-child, sibling-sibling, husband-wife—each of which is also changing, are also important in understanding how families cope with life transitions or crises (Parke, 1988). It is for this reason that family therapy must involve all members of both the nuclear and extended family.

Herr and Weakland (1979) have applied family systems theory (Haley, 1971) to work with families where there is an elder. Systems theory treats the family as a working system of relationships between family members. Each set of relationships is influenced by and influences every other. This approach, then, stresses the here-and-now nature of interaction among family members. The therapist concentrates on how a problem is being handled by the family as a whole, often intervening when the family is in crisis, under the assumption that they are most amenable to change at this time. The primary objective is to effect a structural change in family communication patterns, and secondarily, to change behavior (Weeks & Wright, 1985).

Several problematic interactions involving elder family members may exist, according to Herr and Weakland:

1. Scapegoating the older person—e.g., the elder is blamed for the family's problems

2. Parent-child role reversal—the elder is forced into the role of child
3. Dyadic alliances—e.g., mother and daughter join forces against father
4. Symbiotic relationships—older parents cannot "let go" of their adult children
5. Incongruencies between what the older person expects and that which his adult children expect from him or her
6. Role inversion—e.g., due to a husband's illness, his wife assumes his former duties
7. Fearful withdrawal of the older person from younger family members.

These difficulties may be brought on by events such as illness, death, retirement, or institutionalization, or they may be long-standing in nature.

Herr and Weakland (1979) specify the framework within which the family-counseling process takes place as follows:

1. Establishment of initial contact with the client(s)
2. Inquiry and definition of the problematic interaction
3. Inquiries into the handling of the problem by family members
4. Goal-setting
5. Perceptions of the problem by the family
6. Analysis of how the problem is being maintained and construction of a strategy for its avoidance in the future
7. Further interventions and their evaluation
8. Termination of the therapeutic relationship.

Keller and Hughston (1981), who also take a systems approach, emphasize that opportunities for communication and sharing must be "scheduled." Other techniques, such as reminiscence and contracting (defining and agreeing on the consequences of a behavior pattern), can be used to deal with many types of unproductive behavior within the family: attention-gaining, bossiness, counter-hurting (striking back), and disablement (not taking responsibility).

It may also be very important for the therapist to relabel problems so that they can be more effectively solved. For example, the therapist might *relabel* a problem in terms of the relationship rather than characteristic of specific individuals. Specific directives can also be used to set ground rules for resolving conflict with family members. In such cases, the therapist may use straightforward direction—changing who is responsible for certain tasks. Or the therapist may *paradoxically* direct the family to continue engaging in the behavior that brought them to therapy, for example, to keep fighting over who is to care for an elderly parent (Gilewski et al., 1985; Zarit, 1980).

FAMILY THERAPY WITH CAREGIVERS

Recently, Cicirelli (1986), Cohen (1982), and Zarit and Anthony (1986) have successfully used family therapy to solve a number of problems and choices families with older members often face, such as deciding whether to institutionalize an elderly parent or selecting alternatives to institutionalization such as day care or home care. Family therapy can also help children cope with the terminal illness of an older family member or help them care for a parent who has been diagnosed with Alzheimer's disease (see Chapter 10). For example, Zarit and Anthony (1986) suggest that giving information, active problem-solving, support, and one-on-one counseling can help families make decisions about caring for a family member with dementia. When feelings of isolation and burden can be dealt with, the stress of coping with the death of a loved one or caring for a family member who has Alzheimer's disease can be relieved (Gwyther & George, 1986; Robins et al., 1986; Zarit et al., 1986). Moreover, feelings of guilt, which often accompany the decision to institutionalize an older parent, can be lessened, leaving the family intact. If properly handled, such issues can actually strengthen the family's feelings of closeness, love, and interdependence. Moreover, the elder need not give up control over his or her life, yet can accept help from others without feeling dependent on them. Thus, families can avoid feeling overwhelmed by guilt, anger, hopelessness, or helplessness.

Sterns and associates (1984) suggest that family therapy can be more effective if it is supplemented by individual counseling, depending on the level of functioning of the family as a whole and the individuals in it. These levels of functioning range from panic to mastery. Depending on how effectively the family is functioning, different methods of treatment may be necessary. For example, for highly functional families, education may be sufficient, while for families in pain, individual, group, or family therapy may be necessary.

Behavioral Interventions

As with psychodynamic psychotherapy and both group and family therapy, use of behavioral methods of intervention is not unique to older people (see Garfield & Bergin, 1978). Unlike psychodynamic approaches, however, **behavior therapy** focuses on the immediate, observable consequences of stimulus-response contingencies in the environment (Hoyer, 1973).

Behavior therapy is most often used in an inpatient institutional setting, where control over reinforcers (rewards) and behaviors one wants to change is more likely. According to this approach, application of a behavioral strategy requires that three primary tasks be carried out:

1. Definition and assessment, prior to intervention, of the desired target behavior
2. A reinforcer, defined as a stimulus whose impact makes the desired behavior more frequent or of longer duration, must be identified; this reinforcer may be self-administered or administered by the therapist
3. Establishment of specific behavior-reinforcer contingencies.

Positive stimuli, leading to pleasurable events; negative stimuli, which provide relief from aversive events; or reinforcing stimuli, which decrease the frequency of a behavior by providing unpleasant consequences, may all be used for the purpose of defining such contingencies.

A variation on this process is the token economy, where patients can earn tokens for desired behaviors, which can later be exchanged for appropriate rewards (Zarit, 1980). Another technique that can be utilized by the behavior modifier involves positively reinforcing a behavior that competes with the unwanted target behavior. An example is rewarding self-care behaviors that compete with aggressive behaviors.

Contracting is a form of behavior modification that deserves mention. In contracting, the client and therapist arrive at a mutually agreed-on, clearly specified goal. Being able to jointly define this goal may in itself promote a sense of control and independence for some elderly (Hayslip & Kooken, 1982).

Extensive discussions of behavioral techniques with the aged can be found in Hussian (1986, 1987), Levy et al. (1980), and Rosenstein and Swenson (1980). Of all the forms of intervention discussed in this book, it is perhaps the easiest to document, and there is ample well-designed research to support its efficacy in dealing with a variety of behavior problems (Smyer et al., 1990). For example, overly dependent interactions with other elderly people and nursing home staff, incontinence, aggressive behavior, withdrawal, inappropriate sexual behavior, wandering, anxiety, and self-care can all be treated behaviorally (Smyer et al., 1990). Many of these behaviors are a consequence of being institutionalized and have been termed *excess disabilities* (Kahn & Miller, 1978). Note that behavioral methodologies have also been utilized to successfully modify staff attitudes toward elderly patients (Hussian, 1981; LaRue et al., 1985; Richards & Thorpe, 1980).

Behavioral technology, whether with younger or older people, has a number of advantages. It can be readily measured and its effects easily assessed, goals can be objectively defined, and it can be carried out and understood by staff at all levels of training. Relative to drug therapy and aversive behavioral interventions (e.g., time-out procedures), positive behavioral interventions, such as reinforcing the individual if an inappropriate behavior does not occur, are more acceptable to older people (Burgio & Sinnott, 1990).

Behavior therapy can also be tailored to the individual patient, and behavioral procedures are relatively brief and economical. However, though it can be taught, it requires a great deal of experience to use effectively, and its use can create some ethical questions, particularly when used with impaired, institutionalized, or isolated older adults.

Hoyer (1973) and Levy et al. (1990) have raised a number of these ethical issues in behavioral work with the aged:

1. The long-term effects of such interventions, which may be harmful when the techniques are discontinued, should be considered.
2. Whether the reinforced behavior is actually within the person's

capacities (e.g., withdrawal of staff control over daily activities) or will be supported by the immediate environment/staff should be evaluated.

3. Careful selection of the target behavior itself should occur. For example, discouraging someone from eating foreign objects via negative reinforcement may generalize to eating food, which might lead to malnutrition or death.

Intervention with a client for intervention's sake is not always in the older person's best interests (Hayslip, 1985). In many cases, it may be more feasible to change the environment or to leave things as they are. These alternatives should be given consideration if one is unsure of the consequences of a particular treatment (Baltes & Danish, 1981; Danish, 1980).

Cognitive Therapies

Closely related to behavioral approaches is **cognitive behavior therapy** (Ellis, 1962; Meichenbaum, 1977; Beck, 1976). While Ellis and Beck focus on rational analysis of the client's belief system, Meichenbaum alters the "inner dialogue" of the individual. In general, however, cognitive behavior therapists believe that the way a person thinks largely determines the way he or she feels. In other words, thought causes emotion.

Thus, cognitive behavior therapy is an attempt to help the client change his or her maladaptive thinking habits to relieve emotional disturbances such as depression, anger, and anxiety. Ellis (1962) views this process in an *A-B-C* fashion. *A* is designated as the event the client thinks is causing the anxiety, depression, or the like. The emotional disturbance lies at point *C*. A client might believe that, for example, her depression (*C*) is being caused by her getting old (*A*). Ellis insists that age (*A*) is not causing the depression (*C*). Instead, the depression (*C*) is attributed to the woman's belief (*B*) about her own aging; the belief is the culprit. In this case, the woman might erroneously believe that being old means that she is a person unworthy of respect or love (Hayslip & Kooken, 1982).

Elderly people, perhaps lacking feedback about themselves from others, often make "thinking errors" that are not realistic (Hayslip & Caraway, 1989). For example, irrational assumptions about one's age or loss of one's skills may lead to feelings of self-depreciation in many aged individuals. These feelings can lead to anger, guilt, and depression. Cognitive techniques instruct the elder to substitute more rational thoughts for these irrational ones (Caraway & Hayslip, 1989). Specific techniques are available for this purpose and are presented in Table 11.4 (Thompson et al., 1991).

While the age similarities outweigh differences, there are a few aspects of cognitive behavior therapy that are unique to older adults (Thompson et al., 1991). For example, the therapist must be more flexible, special attention should be given to cohort differences in education and interests, an assessment of physical history must be made, and a conference with the client's physician and family should be arranged. In addition, the therapist may have to be more active with older clients to keep them focused

TABLE 11.4

COGNITIVE AND BEHAVIORAL TECHNIQUES PARTICULARLY USEFUL WITH ELDERS

Cognitive
- Dysfunctional Thought Record (DTR) (Describing the situation, one's emotions and thoughts in the situation)
- Generating alternative thoughts (see below)
- Vertical arrow technique (see below)
- Evaluating the evidence (see below)

Behavioral
- Daily mood monitoring
- Older Person's Pleasant Events Schedule (Identifying pleasurable daily activities)
- Journal writing (activities, events, or thoughts)
- Assertiveness training
- Relaxation training

*Partial listing of convenient cognitive distortions**

1. *All-or-nothing thinking*: Seeing things in terms of black and white, with no gray areas.
2. *Mental filter*: Selectively attending to certain classes of events; "negative scanning."
3. *Jumping to conclusions*: Includes "mindreading," or acting as if one knows what others are thinking, and "fortune telling," or predicting future calamities.
4. *Emotional reasoning*: Believing something is true because you feel it is so ("I feel like a failure, so I must be one").
5. *Should and implied should statements*: Making opinions into absolute rules using words like "should," "must," and "ought," or beliefs that imply such a process.

Generating alternative thoughts

Therapist: Are those helpful thoughts to have? Could you have said something different to yourself?
Client: No, they upset me. I could have said, "Just because he didn't call doesn't mean he doesn't care. He may be busy today. He does have that big project at work."
Therapist: Okay, and what happens to your anger when you think that?
Client: Well, it's true, I do feel less angry, only about 50%. But it seems like he never calls me!

Evaluating the evidence

Therapist: Okay, well, we're not finished. You've said that this could be overgeneralization, but it sounds like it's hard for you to believe it. Let's examine the evidence for your thought that he "never" calls. When was the last time he called?
Client: Don't know. Been so long I can't remember.
Therapist: Think a moment. (Pause)
Client: Well, he called last week to see how I was doing. That was Thursday, from work. And he called last Sunday, too. I guess he calls, but he doesn't like to talk very long. He doesn't like the phone. I still feel angry and hurt.

Vertical arrow technique

Therapist: It seems like there is more to this. You can't seem to let go of the hurt and anger. What does it mean about you if your son doesn't talk to you or call you enough? What does it mean about you as a person?
Client: About me? Well, it must mean he doesn't love me.
Therapist: Uh-huh. And if he doesn't love you, then what?
Client: Well, if he doesn't love me, I've done something wrong. But that's personalizing, isn't it?
Therapist: That's correct, but let's not work on distortions right now. What do you believe about yourself if he doesn't love you?
Client: If he doesn't love me . . . if he doesn't love me, his own mother, then I must be a terrible person. I am a complete failure!

Continued

Therapist: It sounds like you believe that if you don't have your son's complete love, you are nothing in life, a complete failure. This seems to be a deeper belief you have. Perhaps that has something to do with why you moved closer to him. This thought is one we'll have to work on for awhile, until you can believe that your self-worth has nothing to do with your son's love for you.

Source: Thompson et al. (1991). *Adapted from Burns (1980), pp. 40–41.

on the issue at hand, and should expect the pace of therapy to be slower, due to fatigue or resistance to giving up long-held assumptions about oneself or others (Hayslip & Caraway, 1989; Thompson et al., 1991).

Cognitive behavior approaches to therapy have been successfully utilized to treat a variety of cognitive and emotional problems in the aged, including depression (Gallagher & Thompson, 1982; Thompson & Gallagher, 1983), memory loss, test anxiety, performance on intellectual tasks, and response speed (Labouvie-Vief & Gonda, 1976; Richards & Thorpe, 1978; Reidl, 1981). Kooken and Hayslip (1984) and Hayslip (1989) have used a cognitive-behavioral approach emphasizing both stress inoculation (cognitive) and relaxation training to modify test anxiety and intellectual performance in older people. Puder (1988) used cognitive behavior therapy to successfully treat the side effects of medication use for chronic pain and coping ability in older people.

While cognitive-behavioral research has recently begun to catch on with geropsychologists, much of the work is limited to groups, not individuals (Wellman & McCormack, 1984). A notable exception is the work of Toseland and Smith (1990). These authors found that individual cognitive behavior therapy emphasizing stress management, problem-solving, and coping was effective in enhancing well-being and reducing distress in women caring for frail aged parents. However, sampling issues, placebo (expectancy) effects, measurement problems, and attrition (loss of participants) remain as problems be addressed in this area of research (Hayslip & Caraway, 1989).

The studies by Thompson and Gallagher (1983) and Gallagher and Thompson (1982) are perhaps the best examples of the potential of cognitive behavior interventions with elderly individuals dealing with depression. As the name suggests, they use both cognitive and behavioral approaches to treat the client (see Table 11.4). These authors qualify their support for this method, however, noting that it works best with people whose depression is exogenous—a reaction to recent stress—rather than endogenous, or life-long (Thompson et al., 1987). And while people who are suffering from mild dementia can benefit, suicidal or severely depressed clients do not seem to respond to cognitive behavior techniques (Thompson et al., 1991).

Specialized Treatments for Elderly People

In addition to life review therapy, reality orientation (Folsom, 1968), remotivation therapy, pet therapy, and milieu therapy have become popular treatment alternatives for the institutionalized aged (see Brink, 1990).

REALITY ORIENTATION

Reality orientation (RO) stresses the lessening of confusion/disorientation, primarily within an institution. It may be highly structured, focusing on orientation to time, place, and person. Studies of RO tend to be primarily descriptive, and generalized improvement or discharge from the institution have been the goals of choice (Sherwood & Mor, 1980). Research investigating the impact of RO is equivocal and flawed in many respects, for example, by not controlling for staff expectancy of improvement or failing to use a control group (Smyer et al., 1990).

Zeplin and associates (1981) found that RO is effective in reducing disorientation, but that this effectiveness is limited to those who are not severely disoriented and those who are younger. The authors conclude that "the limited effectiveness of RO notwithstanding, it is useful as a vehicle to organize attention to the disoriented, thereby guarding against unjustified custodial policies" (p. 77). Waters (1984), Wellman and McCormack (1984), and Gatz et al. (1985) review the evidence for the effectiveness of RO and conclude that, while it does temporarily improve orientation to time and place, more permanent, deeper changes in mood and cognitive status do not follow from reality orientation.

Storandt (1978) points out that adherence to a rigid treatment regimen often limits the effectiveness of RO. Its use should be flexible and probably limited to those aged who are not profoundly deteriorated (Gatz et al., 1985). Plus, the less disoriented patient may become hostile if needlessly exposed to RO, consequently requiring more staff time and effort to deal with this anger (Storandt, 1983).

REMOTIVATION THERAPY

A similar but more intensive approach is **remotivation therapy** (RT), which is designed to improve the individual's reality contact and social skills.

Remotivation, which can be employed by nursing aides, assumes that the "healthy" portions of the person's personality can be activated (Storandt, 1978). Remotivation therapy stresses acceptance by the therapist and other group members, who act as "bridges" from the client to reality and foster rediscovery of previously satisfying activities. Increased social competence, self-care skills, and greater levels of activity are the goals of RT. Remotivation therapy may be moderately effective, but its effectiveness varies with the patient, favoring those who are more deteriorated (Waters, 1984; Wellman & McCormack, 1984). Like RO, remotivation therapy is very popular, despite inconsistent evidence of its effectiveness (Storandt, 1983).

BOX 11.1

VALIDATION THERAPY: HELP FOR DISORIENTED OLDER PEOPLE

Validation therapy was developed by Naomi Feil, a social worker, to help restore some measure of functioning to severely impaired older people. In contrast to reality orientation, whose goal is to keep the disoriented older person attuned to reality—today's date, where one is living, time of day—validation therapy accepts the disoriented older person as he or she is at present (Feil, 1989). Validation also helps us understand the reason behind a disoriented older person's feelings, whether anger, sadness, fear, or happiness.

Feil feels that in the disoriented old, early learned emotional memories replace intellectual thinking, preventing them from functioning in the world as it is now. To validate is to acknowledge the feelings of the old person, who has returned to the past to survive (Feil, 1989). In a sense, the validation therapist helps the old person replace intellect with feelings to restore a sense of self-worth. This enables him or her to reduce the stress of living in a world that may no longer be meaningful, to justify continuing to live and, of course, to feel happier. Validation therapy also enables the helper to become comfortable with the disoriented old.

Instead of labeling as demented those who may appear to be mindlessly preoccupied with past memories or any emotionally significant past experience, validation therapy tries to understand such behavior as a coping mechanism the elder uses to survive—to deal with losses in the face of a limited, or at least emotionally barren, existence.

Feil contrasts the struggle to keep living in the present, which she calls *malorientation,* with the wisdom of disorientation. This concept is very similar to Erikson's despair, which leaves the individual depressed, frustrated, angry, and hopeless. Integrity is recaptured, not by trying to live in the present or by denying or distorting losses, but by reliving old experiences and feelings. Present-day fears trigger old fears, which must be reexperienced.

According to Feil, the failure to resolve the past leads to vegetation. However, through validation therapy, the disoriented person can experience resolution. Feil defines resolution via the following case of an elderly woman who is in a nursing home struggling to survive:

> Disoriented old-old lose the capacity to think intellectually. They forget how to classify people and objects. They forget dictionary meanings of words. They forget how to compare things. They forget how to analyze things that are different. They forget the "as if." A hand feels soft, as if it were a baby. The hand *becomes* the baby. They lose metaphoric thinking. They return to early thinking. "Tapes" from early childhood return. Later learned intellectual thinking goes. A woman whose whole existence was her motherhood caresses her hand. She longs to be useful. She sees in her mind's eye, with her vivid (eidetic) image, her baby. Her retina is damaged, but her image is clear. She begins to talk to her hand—her baby. Her sensory cells do not inform her that her hand is in front of her. She restores her motherhood—her dignity—by recreating her baby through using a body part. She has *wisdom to create in old-old age* (Feil, 1989, p. 17).

As one might imagine, validation therapy is somewhat controversial and has yet to be independently documented as effective with severely disoriented older people. Yet, it may offer hope to family caregivers or staff who must deal with the confused oldest-old person suffering from dementia.

Zarit (1980) even suggests that techniques such as RO and RT are designed to stimulate patients who are understimulated due to institutionalization. Such techniques are therefore designed to correct deficits that may not have otherwise occurred, according to Zarit. Remotivation may have its greatest impact early on, when enthusiasm for remotivation groups is highest among the staff and patients (Storandt, 1983).

MILIEU THERAPY

Milieu therapy involves the creation of a so-called therapeutic community, where all aspects of the elderly patient's interactions with the staff are redesigned to benefit the patient. Milieu therapy makes three assumptions:

1. Patient care will be humane and noncustodial.
2. Its use enhances ward management.
3. It relies on the immediate interpersonal resources of the environment in which it is utilized (Sherwood & Mor, 1980).

Therapeutic goals may be increased social skills, greater responsibility for one's actions, more involvement in structured activities, or greater self-esteem (Barnes et al., 1973). New skills can be learned in a relatively safe environment. Milieu therapy also relies on peer support to achieve its goals. Milieu therapy varies from one environment to another and is often used in combination with other approaches, such as behavior therapy or group therapy.

While milieu therapy has several drawbacks, such as minimal responsibility being placed on patients themselves for change and patient-staff discrepancies in goals, it may nevertheless benefit those elderly who have become very apathetic and unresponsive (Storandt, 1983). It is not recommended for hostile, acting-out elderly individuals.

In addition to the milieu approach, a number of what may be termed *environmental manipulations* may be appropriate in some situations (Waters, 1984). Many of these changes can be helpful, especially for individuals suffering from dementia. Simply clarifying or highlighting certain aspects of the environment may reduce anxiety, disorientation, and confusion in elderly people (Fozard & Popkin, 1978). Moreover, there are many positive benefits to older people, such as improved physical health and morale, and enhanced self-esteem, when they are given control over certain aspects of their everyday environment (Schulz & Hanusa, 1978). Being able to set one's own visiting hours, to have plants in one's room, and to choose from a variety of food for dinner can all be quite beneficial to people who are institutionalized or otherwise lack control over their everyday lives (Hayslip & Caraway, 1989; Langer, 1980). While these approaches do not seem to be "therapy" in a traditional sense, they show a great deal of promise as environmental approaches to treatment.

PET THERAPY

Pet therapy is not unique to the elderly; it is used with many individuals, such as abused children, the physically handicapped, and the mentally retarded. However, a great deal of interest has developed in the therapeutic use of pets in the treatment of older persons who are institutionalized, isolated, or cognitively impaired (Angier, 1983; Arkow, 1982). While studies of pet therapy are few in number, they indicate some short-term benefits to be gained. For example, people have more positive feelings about themselves, increase their interaction with others, feel less depressed, and

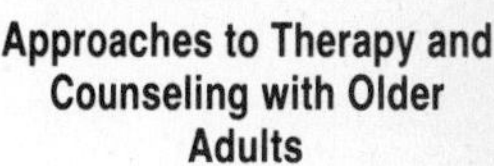

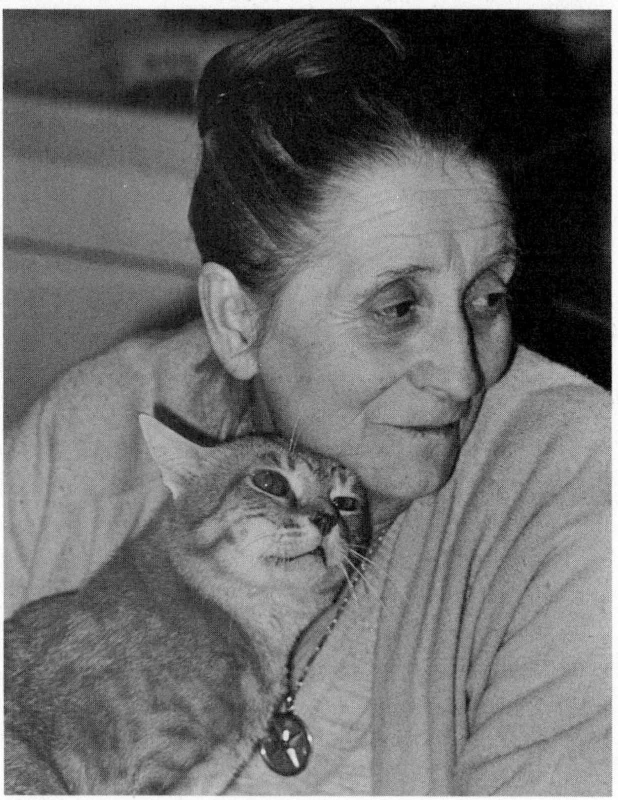

Pet therapy is a viable option for many older people who are isolated or institutionalized.

improve their cognitive functioning. Dogs, cats, birds—even turtles!—are not only lovable and affectionate, but need care that demands a certain amount of responsibility. This allows people to shift focus from their own anxieties or dissatisfactions with life to the welfare of an animal who wants and needs love and care. As a result, older people may gain a sense of control over their own feelings and the immediate situation as well.

Pets can also be used to elicit life-history information that may be of importance, for example, childhood experiences with pets (Brickel, 1984). Such information can be obtained in a nonthreatening way. Feelings about one's past, such as life events where a pet was present, or present feelings of depression can be discussed in a situation where the animal provides a sense of security and both psychological and tactile comfort. In addition, caring for a pet often lessens isolation from others; and it is very difficult to pout or be grumpy with a lovable dog or cat!

Obviously, some common-sense decisions need to be made regarding the responsibility of an older person for care of a pet. Caring for gerbils is less demanding than is caring for a dog. Pets may not be able to be kept in a nursing home. In some cases, an animal is too active or can bring on allergies. Nevertheless, these are minor problems compared to the therapeutic gains that can be achieved. In addition to live pets, Francis (1984) has advocated the use of plush animals, with similar positive results. While most of us react positively to small animals, their use with aged people, who often have no one to whom they feel close, can be quite beneficial.

Rogers's Self-therapy

Rogerian self-therapy is a popular framework for therapists working with the aged, in that it provides insight into the world of the older person (Grammer, 1984). He or she can experience what Rogers has termed *unconditional positive regard;* that is, his or her feelings of self-worth are affirmed by the therapist. Especially for those who are lonely, dependent, or isolated, simply being listened to can be very important.

A person-centered approach challenges the age bias of the counselor, and it may be difficult to implement with noncommunicative elderly or those who have multiple sensory deficits (Brammer, 1984). Despite these difficulties, simply being with the older person, making eye contact, and touching and expressing support and empathy for him or her as an individual is the essence of Rogerian therapy. In view of older people's frequent skepticism of counseling, counselors who display these qualities can perform a truly valuable service.

Psychopharmacological (Drug) Treatments

Drug treatment for adults has been a clear option in the cases of schizophrenia, anxiety, and depression (Coleman et al., 1984). But its use with other older people has been criticized, though psychotropic medications are widely used with the aged (Hicks & Davis, 1980). While some have abandoned drug treatment as too risky (Gallagher & Thompson, 1982, 1983; Roose, 1991), others advocate the psychopharmacological treatment of the aged (Bressler, 1987; Crook et al., 1983). Perhaps we should not abandon drug treatment of older people entirely, but instead see it as an intervention to complement individual and/or group counseling (Cohen, 1984).

Several major categories of drugs have been used with the aged to date. They include:

1. Antidepressants (tricyclics, MAO inhibitors, lithium carbonate, electroconvulsive therapy, estrogens)
2. Antipsychotic agents and anti-Parkinsonian drugs (chlorpromazine)
3. Antimanics (antipsychotics, lithium carbonate)
4. Antianxiety agents/hypnotics (barbiturates, chloral hydrate, meprobamate, benzodiazepines, chlordiazepocids, propranolol)
5. Cognitive-acting drugs (cerebral vasodilators, CNS stimulants, gerovital, anabolic substances, cholinomimetic agents) (Kapnick, 1978; Hicks et al., 1980; Roose, 1991).

Antipsychotic drugs are commonly used to treat agitation, violent or irrational behavior, and perceptual disturbances (hallucinations) accompanying paranoid state or late-life schizophrenia. Predictable side effects include extrapyramidal motor signs (tremors), for which anti-Parkinson (anticholinergic) medication is then often incorrectly prescribed to remedy. Other side effects include tardive dyskinesia (involuntary facial, mandibular, or finger movements) with prolonged use, and akathisia (uncontrolled restlessness/agitation). Occasionally, glaucoma, constipation, and retention of urine are seen as side effects of antipsychotic medications in the aged.

Major tranquilizers used to treat psychosis produce similar side effects. Most often, reduced dosage levels and/or "drug holidays" are recommended in these cases. Antidepressant drugs (tricyclics, MAO inhibitors) often interact with a variety of foods, including cheese and caffeine. Tricyclics can create many problems, such as arrhythmia, stroke, myocardial infarction, and tachycardia, for those aged with cardiovascular disorders. Doxepin, amitriptyline, and imipramine are the recommended antidepressant compounds for use with the aged (Roose, 1991). Antimanics (lithium) often produce the side effects of nausea, central nervous system toxicity, and confusion.

Antianxiety drugs (barbiturates) often produce paradoxical symptoms—excitement—and negatively affect enzyme action. Other minor tranquilizers (benzodiazepine) can be both physiologically and psychologically addictive.

A variety of cognitive-acting drugs (e.g., hydrergine) are used to reverse cognitive impairment, though their use in this way has been questioned (see Hicks et al., 1980).

More generally, older people are particularly sensitive to drug effects. And there are substantial individual differences in response to psychopharmacological agents among older people (Gray & Hayslip, 1990; Hicks & Davis, 1980). Polypharmacy, the use of and interaction among many drugs, is a pervasive problem with the aged (Gray & Hayslip, 1990). Furthermore, older people are not as capable of metabolizing and excreting drugs (e.g., lithium carbonate) as are the young (Bressler, 1987). Most drugs, prescription or not, have a longer half-life in older individuals; they build up in concentration when fixed-dosage intervals are used, due to age-related changes in fat-to-muscle tissue ratio. Thus, portions of the drugs are not being used by the body, and the drug is ineffective. This, in addition, makes interaction with other drugs, medicines such as anticoagulants and antacids, and many foods more likely, which then produces a variety of side effects that may not only be harmful but also intensify other health problems such as impairment of renal, liver, or cardiovascular functioning (Bressler, 1987).

Drug interactions and side effects may also be misdiagnosed as dementia, since they can produce symptoms of confusion, memory loss, agitation, depression, paranoid delusions, or hallucinations. These may be viewed as distinct conditions by the unsuspecting clinician, who often prescribes more drugs to deal with these side effects. Drug treatment may also produce a variety of side effects that produce health management problems in themselves, ranging from mild confusion, depression, and urinary or cardiac dysfunction, to hallucinations or seizures (Bressler, 1987; Gray & Hayslip, 1990) (see Chapter 10).

Societal Intervention as Therapy

In addition to changing the individual, we might also want to alter the environment or context in which that person functions. As mentioned above, this is common to many specialized interventions with older people, such as milieu therapy. Interventions at the physical/social environment level can be quite effective, in place of or in combination with treatment at the individual or family level (Gatz et al., 1985; Smyer, 1984). In societal interventions, attention needs to be given to both the microenvironment (home or institution, including activities programs and rehabilitation) and the macroenvironment (neighborhood, community, or subculture) as targets for intervention. The adult-in-context approach presented in Chapter 1 is very consistent with the idea of societal intervention as therapy.

Earlier in this chapter, we discussed numerous cultural forces that affect adults' adjustment and mental health (see also Chapter 10). For example, intergenerational relationships (see Chapter 7) affect older people's sense of independence, and demographic shifts (the "graying" of America) influence both worker-retiree ratios and the experience of retirement. For example, enhancing intergenerational relationships in light of these demographic shifts is a likely target for societal change (see Chapters 1 and 9). Also, the increase in divorce may create in older parents a sense of failure in raising their children. In addition, the changing involvement of women in work affects how they define their roles (see Chapter 9) as well as decisions the couple may make regarding child care and parenting (see Chapter 7).

Clearly, these broader social influences will affect future cohorts of older people. Not only will their role commitments and relationships to younger people change, but what they expect of themselves as well as what others expect of them will be altered as our culture changes (see Cohen, 1992). Counselors and therapists need to be aware of these influences, much as they need to be skilled in various therapeutic techniques in order to facilitate the "fit" (Lawton & Nahemow, 1973) between the older person and his or her micro- and macroenvironments.

Intervention at a broader societal level may indeed be helpful and necessary (Lowy, 1980). Altering attitudes toward middle-aged and older adults, therefore enabling them to increase their reliance on the community, family, and friends are examples of such intervention. Moreover, the development of services geared to older people (such as home-based care, outreach, hospice care, foster grandparent programs, and widow-to-widow programs) may prove to be as effective as intervention at the individual level. The counselor will often utilize societal resources and many of the available treatments in combination to achieve a more effective solution for the patient and family or institutional staff. He or she thus acts not only as a counselor but also as advocate and psychosocial care planner (Lawton & Gottesman, 1974).

PREVENTION AS INTERVENTION

As we become aware of the role many factors play in the development difficulties for which professional help is warranted, our concern has increasingly shifted toward prevention as a form of intervention (Kastenbaum, 1987; Smyer et al., 1990).

Prevention that is timely, properly targeted, and strategic—flexible and individualized—is most likely to be effective (Kastenbaum, 1987). Those who are now old, families of impaired adults, and the general public are all common targets of prevention (Gatz, 1985). The level at which prevention is targeted is important as well. For example, we might choose to focus on the individual, the family, the reference (peer) group, or society.

Prevention may be most useful for those who value self-help (Sargent, 1982). Self-help, on both individual and group levels, is very popular among older people and can be very effective (Smyer et al., 1990). One major advantage of self-help is that it need not occur in a therapist's office; it can take place in nontraditional settings (therapeutically speaking), such as senior centers and community centers.

Among adults, domains of prevention include self-care of a physical and/or psychological nature, social support and relationships, and self-management of health problems (Kastenbaum, 1987). The timing of prevention may dictate its effectiveness, referring to whether education, advocacy, seeking support, or consultation is initiated earlier or later in the development of a problem. For example, changing to proper diet and exercise regimens can be important to one's health in adulthood depending on when one begins to exercise regularly and restrict one's fat intake. For those who do so early, before they become obese or suffer a cardiovascular illness (e.g., stroke or heart attack), making these changes can be quite effective. In order for preventive interventions to work, of course, they must be acceptable to the individual. For example, if one is convinced that weight loss or developing communication skills will enhance the quality and quantity of one's life, then chances are greater that preventive behavior changes will be begun and maintained over the long haul (Kastenbaum, 1987).

CONCLUDING REMARKS ABOUT THERAPY AND INTERVENTION

In light of the issues about development and aging raised in Chapter 1, counselors who deal with adults of all ages should come to terms with what they expect from younger versus older clients. What kinds of assumptions do they make about adults of varying ages? Are clients dealt with on an age-related basis, or are other factors taken into account in assessment and therapy? Clearly, counselors' views about human development based on comparisons of the young and the old, as well as their own recollections of youth, all play an important role in how effective they will be with clients of all ages. Moreover, beliefs about personality change (see Chapter 8) are likely to have an important bearing on whether one chooses to work with adults of all ages, or with older clients at all. They also influence which approaches are selected for use with a particular client. As noted in Chapter 8, while many feel existing personality theory has little to offer the gerontological counselor, one's beliefs about "what makes people tick" will certainly influence his or her choice of therapy with adults and the elderly.

In light of the questions raised at the beginning of this chapter, we recommend striking a balance between acquiring specialized knowledge about the assessment and therapy of adults of a given age range, and developing a more flexible, individualized approach with basic competences in assessment, therapeutic approaches, and community psychology. Such a philosophy has characterized our discussion of adulthood throughout this text.

The adult counselor should be prepared to call on other professionals, such as social workers and physicians, when necessary, and to intervene at multiple levels—individual, family, societal—simultaneously (Gottesman et al., 1973). Of course, therapy could be both preventive and remedial. Perhaps many of the difficulties adults of all ages experience could be headed off by a dual emphasis on prevention and remediation.

Above all, the integrity and individuality of the person must be maintained to ensure that, regardless of the quantity of the years the individual has lived, the quality of his or her life can be improved. We can learn new skills, gain insight into ourselves, improve our relationships with others, and express our innermost feelings (Gatz et al., 1985). Most of us can benefit in these ways from help of many kinds. Since growth and change are realities for all adults, professional helpers can facilitate this personal growth and development throughout the adult years.

SUMMARY

A number of individual and cultural factors have converged to create more interest in the treatment of older clients. Despite this interest, a variety of barriers currently exist to the older adult's access to the mental health system, including beliefs in untreatability, cost, and resistance to help due to ignorance or pride. Evidence does not suggest age as a factor in the efficacy of various therapies.

Several therapeutic options currently exist for elderly people who decide to see a therapist. These include *psychodynamic, behavioral, cognitive, group, family,* and *pharmacological* treatment. More specialized approaches include *life review, remotivation, reality orientation, milieu,* and *pet therapy.*

One not only should examine the feasibility of different approaches with different types of older clients, but establish their efficacy. Recently, many have advocated *self-help* or psychotherapy in nontraditional settings as alternatives to more formal types of intervention with the aged. Regardless of the nature of the help provided, it should be directed at *multiple levels*—individual, family, community, and subcultural. It should also be geared to the needs, interests, capabilities, and goals of the individual. To be most effective, such help should be preventive in nature.

KEY TERMS AND CONCEPTS

Mental health system
Well-being
Countertransference
Transference
Psychodynamic therapy
Behavior therapy
Cognitive behavior therapy
Group therapy
Life review
Remotivation therapy
Survivor guilt
Levels of intervention
Barriers to mental health services
Reality orientation
Pet therapy
Family systems theory
Relabeling
Paradoxical directives
Psychopharmacological treatment
Milieu therapy
Prevention as intervention
Family therapy
Time-limited psychodynamic therapy
Remediation
Unconditional positive regard
Internal versus external barriers
Polypharmacy

REVIEW QUESTIONS

1. How important is age in the treatment of psychological disorders?
2. What barriers exist to older adults' access to treatment?
3. What factors need to be taken into account when designing a treatment plan, according to Gottesman et al. (1973)?
4. What objections to the treatment of older clients did Freud have? What changes in psychodynamic therapy with the aged have taken place since Freud's time?
5. What are the advantages and disadvantages of group therapy with aged clients?
6. What is family systems theory? How might it be used with the aged?
7. What are the advantages and disadvantages of behavioral interventions with the aged?

8. What is cognitive behavior therapy? In what ways has it been successfully used with older people?
9. What are the principal drawbacks to psychopharmacological treatment? What guidelines have been proposed for its use?
10. What specialized treatment techniques have been developed for elderly people? Are they successful? For what types of elderly people are they best suited?
11. What is meant by the concept of levels of intervention? How might it be applied to older individuals?
12. How can prevention as an intervention strategy be effective?

C H A P T E R 12

Death and Dying

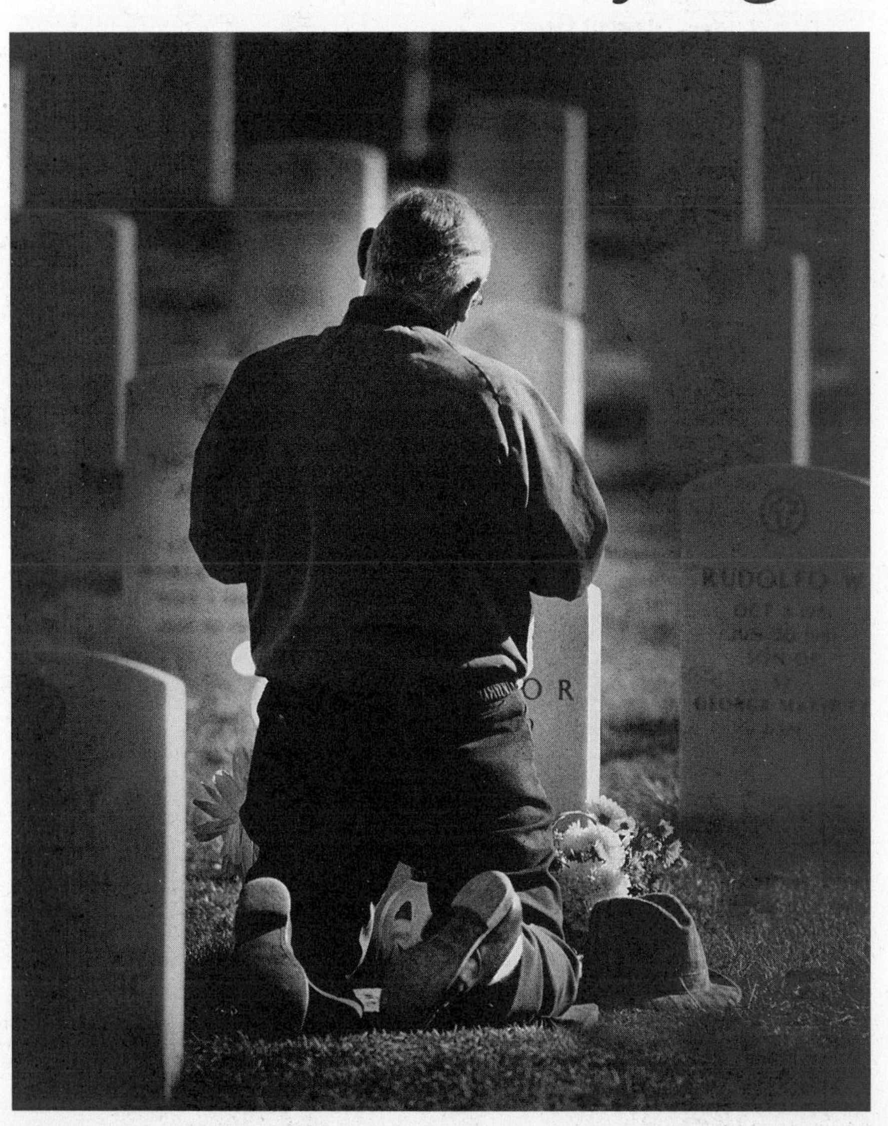

CHAPTER OUTLINE

INTRODUCTION

"We all have to go sometime!" "There are only two things for certain in this life—death and taxes!" "Drop dead!" "I'm dying to go." "He kicked the bucket." "She bit the dust."

Most of us have made these statements at one time or another. In some cases, we may have been vaguely serious about death, while in others, we may have been angry, depressed, or apprehensive. Or perhaps we were trying to be humorous.

All of these statements, and others like them, reflect the simultaneous curiosity and repulsion we feel at the thought of death. This ambivalence can be likened to what we will call the "wet-paint phenomenon." We want to touch the paint to find out if it is really wet—but without getting our hands dirty or sticky. Likewise, many of us want to touch or see death, but without getting too close. For example, we may slow down to get a good look at an accident, or be curious about what happens to the body at the moment of death or thereafter. The popularity of such films as *Flatliners* and recent interest in near-death experiences reflects the curiosity about death we all have.

By confronting dying and death on a personal level, we can face our feelings about our own or another's death. Moreover, we can better understand the role death plays in our daily lives (DeSpelder & Strickland, 1992; Kalish, 1985a, 1985b; Kubler-Ross, 1969).

We may be literally forced to confront death as a reality of life daily—on radio and TV, in the newspaper. It is this basic fact of our existence, that we know we will die because we are human, that argues for getting in touch with how we feel about our own and others' deaths. There is much value in not only reading and talking about dying and death, but also simply feeling or contemplating it. In spite of the fact that we ultimately have no control over the timing of our death, coming to terms with our feelings about its certainty in our lives and in the lives of those we love may gain us a measure of comfort.

For many of us, the thought of our own death seems distant. Indeed, it is comparatively rare for young adults to die, unless their deaths are violent. Yet, as young adults, we must face the inevitable loss of important people in our lives, especially our parents and grandparents. Their deaths leave a void in our daily lives, and they remind us that we, too, will not live forever.

For those who are middle-aged, the physical realities of aging (see Chapter 3), as well as the increased likelihood of losing our parents or age peers due to debilitating illness, bring death closer. Perhaps these losses remind us of the harshness and finality of death.

For older people, death is almost a fact of daily life. In seeing loved ones die, many of whom are people we have shared our lives with, the reality of our own death is perhaps most evident.

Yet, it is important to realize that we live throughout our adult lives with the knowledge that we will die. For this reason, coming to terms with our own death and the loss of people important to us is best thought of as an ongoing process.

Although it is probably difficult to "live every day as if it were our last," acknowledging death's ongoing presence in our lives is healthy. It helps us treasure who and what we have. It helps us keep things in perspective. It keeps us from taking life for granted. While we cannot predict when we will die, we know of death's certainty. This death-awareness can help us personally, but being preoccupied with death or being death-denying is often self-defeating and emotionally damaging. An 83-year-old woman perhaps said it best: "I know that my death will come soon, but I still love life."

With these thoughts in mind, let us first discuss what death is. Being able to define death is important to understanding age differences in people's reactions to death and underscores very real concerns about the quality and quantity of life. Life and death go hand-in-hand; one cannot exist without the other. All living things die. As adults, we can shrink in horror from death's certainty, or we can grow from it emotionally, spiritually, and interpersonally.

DEFINITIONS OF DEATH

Clinical, Brain, Social, and Psychic Death

What is death? This seems an obvious enough question. Yet, it is a difficult definition to "pin down." Death means different things to different people, and approaches to defining it do not always agree. By one standard an individual may be dead, and by another, the person is still considered alive!

The most widely held definition of death in the United States is broadly known as the legal-medical definition. This approach is the one used by many courts of law today pertaining to whether a person is dead or alive, and encompasses two types of death. **Clinical death** is one variety. The criteria for clinical death are having one's heart and breathing cease spontaneously, and there are no reflexes. In clinical death, however, resuscitation is possible.

The second type of death is called **brain death,** where one's brain cells die, which is reflected in a flat EEG for a certain period of time, often 24 hours (Wass, 1989). Veatch (1979) uses the term to refer to the brain's inability to integrate bodily systems due to the central nervous system's loss of functioning.

By other criteria, death can occur in the absence of changes in the brain or vital organ systems. In this light, Pattison (1977) has discussed **social death.** This type of death occurs when a person is abandoned by or isolated from others. Often, the individual who is expected to die is talked about as if he or she were not present. For many critically ill adults and older people who are severely impaired, social death reflects the fact that their lives are seen as finished even though they are quite alive by other criteria.

What often follows social death is **psychic death** (Pattison, 1977). Here, individuals accept their fate and regress, a very severe and personal form of withdrawal. In a sense, they will or think themselves to death. Perhaps the best example of this form of death is *voodoo death.* It is an extreme form of **learned helplessness** (Seligman, 1975) where the individual is thought to bring about his or her own death by giving up on life. He or she is helpless to prevent it. Severe feelings of depression and lack of control are common in those who are psychically dead.

Implications of Varying Criteria for Death

The multiple classifications of death lead to some perplexing legal and moral issues, as evidenced by a number of cases presented in the newspapers and on television. Most notable is that of Karen Ann Quinlan who, as a result of a mix of drugs and alcohol, was brain-dead yet was being supported via a respirator. Even after she was disconnected, she continued to breathe on her own for some time before she "died." These details of the legal and moral issues are beyond the scope of this text, but they suggest some complex value judgments about who is dead and who is not. At the very least, they should cause us to question what that primary quality (or qualities) is that defines life.

The principal difficulties created by the many definitions are that the criteria for death obviously do not provide any objective or agreed-upon basis for a scientific decision about death, or a decision about when one is declared dead by a coroner. Moreover, the criteria vary by state: some states have adopted brain death as a criterion, while others have not. Death may also be interpreted differently by different people, such as physicians, lawyers, and family members. Take the example of a person with irreversible brain damage who is in a coma. This person might be revived; the coma could be drug-induced. Someone who is in a coma can also breathe independently. By one standard, brain death, the individual is dead. By another, clinical death, the person is alive. In 1968, the Harvard Ad Hoc Committee to Examine the Definition of Brain Death was formed, and defined death to include (1) unresponsivity, (2) no movements or breathing, (3) no reflexes, and (4) a flat EEG for 24 hours. By these standards, a person who is in a deep coma could be considered dead!

The multiple definitions of death also raise the issues of who should make the decision about when a life has ceased to exist. Given that death is not an all-or-none phenomenon, the point at which death is defined as occurring is a moral decision, not a technical or scientific one (Veatch, 1979). It is at this point that the value of a person's life comes into play. When has the individual's life reached the point where he or she is not worth reviving by extraordinary means? Who should—or could—decide on the value of an individual's life? That these dilemmas are on our minds is evidenced by several recent events. For example, in 1991 in Washington state, an amendment to the state constitution permitting physician-assisted suicide for those who are hopelessly terminally ill was placed on the November ballot (it was defeated at the polls). Moreover, the best-selling book for many months in 1991 was *Final Exit*, by Derek Humphrey, which discusses rational suicide.

While most of us would agree that life is worthwhile, questions regarding the quality versus quantity of life immediately come into play when we make such a judgment. In practice, some lives are valued more highly than others in our society. The lives of the young, the powerful, and the productive are valued; those of the old, the powerless, and the nonproductive are seen as less worthy (DeSpelder & Strickland, 1992).

When we sentence people to die a social death by avoiding those who are dying or grieving, we, in effect, force death out of our lives. Sadly, social death can in fact cause some to give up on life and thus, die a psychic death. In these circumstances, what people who are dying are thinking and feeling is a mystery to us. Do people near death look forward to it? Would they sooner live than die? What do life and death mean to them?

PERSONAL MEANINGS OF DEATH

What death means to us personally dictates how we live our lives as well as how we react to death. Death is often seen as the ultimate loss in our lives. What does one lose through death?

Death as Loss

As Kalish (1976, 1985) has observed, death may mean losses of several kinds to different people:

1. Loss of ability to have experiences
2. Loss of ability to predict subsequent events
3. Loss of our bodies
4. Loss of ability to care for people who are dependent on us
5. Loss of a loving relationship with our family
6. Loss of opportunity to complete treasured plans and projects
7. Loss of being in a relatively painless state

Death as Punishment and Release

In addition to seeing death in terms of loss, Kalish (1976, 1985) discusses several other meanings death may take on, for elderly people in particular. Punishment for one's sins is one of these, and this is presumably linked to one's beliefs about an afterlife.

Reynolds and Kalish (1976) found that while older people generally equated moral goodness with a longer life span, a majority of those surveyed saw death, particularly accidental death, as retribution, rather than seeing a long life as a reward. Thus, premature death per se need not be viewed as punishment. Viewed in another way, it is possible that a long life could in fact be seen as punishment, if one fears he or she will be judged at death or if a loved one has died earlier in one's life. Moreover, when the person who is dying has suffered a great deal, sudden death may be seen as a release from unbearable or protracted pain (Kalish & Reynolds, 1976).

Death as Transition

Death as transition means that the person sees death as a stopping-off point. What may or may not happen afterwards is really more important.

Reynolds and Kalish (1976) found that older people, relative to the young, expected and wanted to live longer, possibly indicating that their feelings about the afterlife were negative. Perhaps their feelings were influenced by their religious views. It may be that those elderly individuals who are more religious experience less death anxiety (Wass, 1989). Before we jump to this conclusion, however, it is important to realize that religiosity–fear of death relationships are often influenced by people's views about the value or purpose of life.

What is meaningful about life is highly subjective and varies by age. This was illustrated in a study by Reker and associates (1987), who compared five groups of younger, middle-aged, and older adults in terms of the purpose they saw in life. In general, older people reported more purpose in life than did the young and were more death-accepting. Yet, the oldest-old (75+ years) and the young (16–29 years) experienced the most meaninglessness in life, most lacked goals, and felt the most free-floating anxiety. People who saw their lives as having the most meaning also expressed the greatest sense of well-being. Interestingly, people whose lives were most goal-oriented expressed the least happiness, joy, and peace of mind. Findings such as these should alert us to what it is about life that people find meaningful as an important factor in interpreting their views and feelings about death.

If we are highly religious, we may fear death as an anticipated punishment for sin, or see death as a reward for a good life. While those of us who are not religious presumably have nothing to fear in this sense, the fact that we will not exist at all after death may cause a great deal of anxiety. Again, much seems to depend on what life and death mean to us.

Death and the Use of Time

Death is an event that makes the dimension of time meaningful, as well as helping us to order our lives (Kalish, 1976). Without such orderliness, nothing would be any more important than anything else! Thus, our goals and accomplishments, our sense of the past, present, and future, as well as our relationships with others become meaningful to the extent that we know we will not live forever. As many of us have learned, it is often only when we nearly lose someone that we truly appreciate how special he or she is to us.

For some people, simply living life on a day-to-day basis may become more important than being preoccupied with future goals and plans. We often are prone to look forward to the future, especially when our lives seem to stretch out before us. However, many aged people seem to be able to balance the past-future aspects of their lives (Stevens-Long, 1984). While Peterson (1980) speculates that a sense of time pressure creates a great deal of stress for many middle-aged individuals, Bascue and Lawrence (1977) have found that older people turn away from the future, which they interpret as a means of coping with fears about impending death. Similarly, Reker et al. (1987) found that older people were less likely to see life in terms of reaching goals and thinking about the future.

RESPONSES TO DEATH

Fear of Death

As mentioned above, what life and death mean to us is likely to influence how we respond to death. When you think of death, how do you feel? Anxious? Peaceful? Depressed? How we respond to death is of central concern to researchers and laypeople alike, reflected in the simple statement "I am afraid of death." While fear and anxiety are not the only ways in which we respond to our death (Kastenbaum & Aisenberg, 1976), they have received considerable research attention over the last 20 years. Fear is certainly a response to death that psychologists and counselors have invested a great deal of time and energy in understanding.

What might people mean when they say they are fearful of death? While some might express anxiety over the variety of losses accompanying death (see above), others may fear the loss of control over their everyday lives that may come about as a function of dying. People who are dying are often isolated from others in an institutional setting such as a nursing home or hospital (Marshall & Levy, 1990). While institutionalizing an older family member may be the only option for some families, dying in such situations can be very depersonalizing, and everyday decisions people are accustomed to making on their own may no longer be possible. For example, how one's time is spent, when one eats, and what possessions one is permitted to keep are decisions often made by others. This issue of control has important implications for the development of alternatives to traditional hospital care for dying persons, as we will see later.

MULTIPLE DEATH FEARS

Research on the meaning of death, as well as responses to death, suggests that both are multidimensional. Thus, death concerns must be separated from those relating to the dying process. Furthermore, fears about one's own death may differ from those surrounding significant others. Moreover, we may or may not be consciously aware of our fears about death or dying. Not feeling particularly death-anxious may simply reflect a person's success at denial, in which case such fears may lie at a covert, unconscious level (Hayslip & Stewart-Bussey, 1986). The death-anxious individual may have many physical complaints, difficulty sleeping, change his or her eating habits, have difficulty in completing a task, or show overconcern with the welfare of others. In such cases, individuals do not report being anxious or concerned about death or dying but inexplicably experience some of these difficulties (Wass, 1989).

In addition to physical complaints, concerns over death may be observed as a change in an individual's personality, for example, if an easy-to-get-along-with person becomes difficult to relate to. As noted above the individual may give away valued personal possessions, be unable to complete everyday tasks, or be excessively concerned over the welfare of others (Kastenbaum, 1985). What may underlie many of these behaviors in older people is awareness that death is near (Kastenbaum, 1978). Such feelings may create inner turmoil and often lead to behavior designed to finish "unfinished business" (Kubler-Ross, 1974).

Quite possibly, the individual's inability to explain these symptoms can create other difficulties, themselves secondary to death but nonetheless disturbing. For example, physical complaints and sleeplessness can be of course interpreted as symptoms of genuine physical illness (Eisdorfer & Stotsky, 1977). In this case, symptoms ironically resist treatment because they fulfill a psychic function—they allow one to express concerns or fears in an acceptable manner to oneself or others. While it is OK to be physically ill, many individuals have great difficulty in admitting that they are indeed afraid.

Contrary to what we might expect, elderly people do not report fearing death per se. They do, however, fear—to a great degree—the dying process: dying in pain, dying alone, or the loss of control over everyday events or bodily functions. Where these fears are clearly justified, ending one's own life or wanting to die may be seen as preferable to suffering a painful, lonely death for some individuals.

While the older person's desire to die may indeed reflect intense physical pain and suffering, however, it can also be an expression of feeling unloved and rejected by the family (Montalvo, 1991). For some people who are able to make life-and-death decisions and demonstrate their competence in the face of insurmountable odds, letting go of life is easier. For

BOX 12.1

THE DYING PERSON'S BILL OF RIGHTS

I have the right to be treated as a living human being until I die.

I have the right to maintain a sense of hopefulness, however changing its focus may be.

I have the right to be cared for by those who can maintain a sense of hopefulness, however changing this might be.

I have the right to express my feelings and emotions about my approaching death in my own way.

I have the right to participate in decisions concerning my care.

I have the right to expect continuing medical and nursing attention even though "cure" goals must be changed to "comfort" goals.

I have the right not to die alone.

I have the right to be free from pain.

I have the right to have my questions answered honestly.

I have the right not to be deceived.

I have the right to have help from and for my family in accepting my death.

I have the right to die in peace and dignity.

I have the right to retain my individuality and not be judged for my decisions, which may be contrary to beliefs of others.

I have the right to discuss and enlarge my religious or spiritual experiences, whatever these may mean to others.

I have the right to expect that the sanctity of the human body will be respected after death.

I have the right to be cared for by caring, sensitive, knowledgeable people who will attempt to understand my needs and will be able to gain some satisfaction in helping me face my death.

Source: A. Barbus. (1975). *American Journal of Nursing, 1,* 99.

others, concerns about pain and suffering simply mask deeper feelings of loneliness and rejection—such individuals have suffered a social death. What they want and need is to be cared about.

Findings on the complex nature of death-fear support the view that fear of death may reflect many concerns. Hayslip and associates (1981) and Fiefel and Nagy (1981) have found that while older and younger people did not differ in consciously expressed death-fear, there were substantial age differences in covert (unconscious) death concerns, such as fears of losing others, pain/suffering, loss of goals/achievements, or loss of control. These age differences suggested that older people experienced more covert death-fear than did the young, but reported less overt fear. Hayslip and associates (1991) found that, while men with AIDS and healthy men expressed similar degrees of conscious death-fear, terminally ill men experienced more covert death-fear. It may be that in the face of imminent death, individuals need to consciously deny their fears about dying in order to continue functioning on a daily basis (Pattison, 1977).

Conte and associates (1982) constructed an easily administered, short measure of death anxiety. They found no age differences in items that were straightforward in their intent (e.g., "Do you worry about dying?" "Do you worry that you may be alone when you are dying?"). Assuming that fears about death are complex and may not be expressed in an open manner, one must view such attempts to get at death-fear with some suspicion.

The question of whether we can truly understand how people feel about death seems to revolve around how threatening death and dying actually are, and how able people are in acknowledging their feelings about death. Whether we are able to consciously accept our own mortality is not an easy question to answer and reflects a belief in the influence of unconscious processes on our behavior. If one's conscious fears about death and dying cannot be admitted, they may be denied altogether and show up somewhere else—that is, be displaced—by wanting things to be in order, for example, or by having many physical complaints.

FACTORS THAT INFLUENCE DEATH ANXIETY

Rather than age per se, factors such as health status or anxiety may play a more important role in explaining death concerns in adults (Kastenbaum, 1985; McCrae et al., 1986; Neimeyer, 1989). While a variety of other factors in addition to health and anxiety interact with the age–death anxiety relationship, findings do not always present a consistent picture. People who are alone and/or institutionalized, living in an urban setting, have poor mental health, are female, and are poorly educated are all more likely to report fearing death (Neimeyer, 1989). However, many other studies do not report a relationship between death fears and such factors as retirement, life satisfaction, religiosity, socioeconomic status, and gender (Neimeyer, 1989). Moreover, ethnic variations in the expression of death fears have been found by Kalish and Reynolds (1976) and by Bengtson et al. (1977).

It may also be that one's feelings about death are an outgrowth of specific life experiences, such as being relocated to a nursing home, being forcibly retired, having failing health, or experiencing the death of one's spouse. These events may sensitize one to loss in general; and of course, the loss of one's own life is the ultimate loss people experience.

We can conclude from the above discussion that interpreting self-reported fears of death is not as straightforward as it may at first seem. Much seems to depend on how death is interpreted; that is, what does death mean to each individual? Fears about death must also be understood in light of current life circumstances (health, whether one is alone), the individual's value systems, and what it is about death and dying that the individual is actually fearful of. Regardless of whether older people are fearful, death seems to be more of a fact of life in the lives of most aged people, according to Kalish (1985).

Overcoming and Participating

One's feelings about death are thought by many to determine the quality of life left to live. One response to death or dying may be termed **overcoming** (Kastenbaum & Aisenberg, 1976). Overcomers see death as the enemy, as external, or as a personal failure. Others may show a **participatory** response to death. Participators see death as internal, as an opportunity to be reunited with a loved one, and as a natural consequence of having lived. While these styles of reacting to death may be life-long, it appears that, as one approaches death, he or she shifts from an overcoming to a participatory mode (Kastenbaum & Aisenberg, 1976).

In our culture, it may be very difficult to adopt a participatory response to death. Death is often violent in nature, and we literally may not see it, as it often occurs in institutions such as hospitals and nursing homes. At the same time, life and death have been "technologized"; medical science can now cure diseases and extend lives that would have ended 20 years ago. Indeed, we have come to expect that medicine can cure anything, and so the inability of medical science to triumph over death is seen as a failure. All these factors push us in the direction of attempting to overcome death.

DEATH AND DYING IN YOUNG ADULTHOOD

For young adults, death comes, for the most part, unexpectedly. Rather than dying because of disease, when young adults die it is often by accident or through violence. While it is the rare younger person who dies of cancer or heart disease, fatal illnesses such as AIDS are increasing among young adults (Cook & Oltjenbruns, 1989). In most cases, death is due to homicides, auto or motorcycle accidents, and in some cases war (Cook & Oltjenbruns, 1989).

Regardless of the cause of death, the process of dying disrupts relationships with parents, children, and spouses; interferes with future goals and plans; and often undermines one's sense of attractiveness and sexuality. Understandably, a terminal illness or a sudden death leaves family and friends feeling frustrated, angry, and lonely. Because death in young adulthood is nonnormative (see Chapter 1), individuals feel angry and cheated that personal or career goals they have set for themselves are never going to be reached. If individuals have children, they must experience the sadness of not seeing their children grow up, marry, and raise their own children (Rando, 1984).

Terminal Illness

If young adults are suffering from AIDS or cancer, they face many difficulties. As we are all painfully aware, at present AIDS has no cure, leaving the individual with no hope whatsoever for a long life. AIDS victims and their families are often isolated and feel both shame and guilt over contracting a disease that many people inaccurately associate with homosexuality. AIDS sufferers are often discriminated against at work, have difficulty getting insurance coverage, and even have problems getting adequate medical care. As a result, they often deny their diagnosis or hide their symptoms from others. This sometimes results in not getting appropriate medical care and the spread of the disease via unsafe sexual practices.

In addition, AIDS victims who keep to themselves inadvertently deny others the opportunity to offer support. At present, isolation is the AIDS victim's major enemy. Being physically isolated from others because of medical treatment magnifies this sense of social isolation (Price et al., 1986). Both AIDS sufferers and their families grieve over the many losses

ADULTS SPEAK

TERMINAL ILLNESS

Being faced with a terminal illness forces us to reevaluate our lives. A 27-year-old woman dying of cancer, with perhaps two weeks to live, talks about the impact of her illness on her values and relationships:

> I now see things in a much different light. Even though I will probably die young, I don't just sit around and wait for it. Actually, no one is given any more time than I am. We wake each morning to a new day, and that is all. No one is promised ahead of time that they will be here for spring vacation, for the wedding in August, or even for the dentist appointment next Thursday. We are all equal in that we have one day to fill with anything we please. The quality of life lived each day is more important than how long we live. . . . I am not the only one in the boat but no one else can do my living or dying for me.

Source: Rosenbaum (1980), p. 19.

that death brings. Yet, ironically, they are not permitted to grieve as others do because they are blamed for this illness. We might term this special sense of loss *unsanctioned grief*, because individuals who die of AIDS are often held responsible for their illness. Both those with AIDS and their survivors are stigmatized, making adjustment both before and after death more difficult (Herck, 1990).

While young adults with cancer are also isolated and are often discriminated against at work, even if they are in remission, they nevertheless face unique problems. They may have to cope with seemingly endless visits to physicians, painful diagnostic procedures, disfiguring surgery, and either chemotherapy or radiation therapy. Moreover, there is no guarantee that these treatments will be effective, or if the cancer is in remission, that it will not return.

Despite their illness, young adults' needs for intimacy, autonomy, and dignity must be met. In many cases, they must find a way to pay for treatment and still make ends meet at home. A semblance of a family and social life must be maintained, which can be difficult for those who are weak, have lost weight, or whose appearance has changed due to surgery, chemotherapy, or radiation therapy.

Loss of a Child

Young adults who lose children through death, particularly if those children die at a relatively young age, grieve for a long time (Miles, 1984). Just as children are often protected from death because we assume they should not and could not understand its nature, parents of young children who have died are often forced to be physically and emotionally separated from the dead child, especially if he or she has died during childbirth or shortly thereafter. The mother may be sedated, or the father may be given the "job" of telling his wife that their child has died (Hildebrand & Schreiner, 1980). Funerals may be avoided because it is assumed they would be too upsetting, further interfering with the couple's healthy expression of feelings.

Many times, parents assume that they are responsible. They might feel they did not prepare themselves adequately; they should have done something to prevent their child's death, even though they may not know what this "something" may be (Share, 1978). They often feel alone—isolated from friends, family, and one another. They may feel angry and resentful toward others—family, friends, and medical staff. They also may be disappointed in one another (Share, 1978). Ultimately, perhaps, a child's death challenges feelings of "parental omnipotence"—the feeling that because they are parents, they should be able to "fix" everything in their child's life.

The feelings of having failed as a parent and having lost a part of oneself when an infant dies are intensified by the fact that, in many cases, miscarriage, stillbirth, or the neonatal or infant death referred to as Sudden Infant Death Syndrome (SIDS) cannot be prevented or predicted (Davidson, 1984; Donnelly, 1982; Naeye, 1980). In spite of the tremendous publicity SIDS has received, researchers are still unable to explain why infants stop breathing without warning (see Davidson, 1984; Nakushian, 1976). At best, parents might purchase a respiratory monitor to keep them aware of an infant's breathing.

In any case, one's greatest fear as a young parent is that his or her child may die suddenly and that he or she will be powerless to prevent it. The death of a very young child can have serious consequences for the family as a whole (Davidson, 1984; Osterweis et al., 1984; Share, 1978). It may lead to school difficulties, divorce, or physical/mental illness.

Bohannon (1990–1991) conducted a study of husbands and wives whose child had died in a one-year period. She found that husbands seemed to grieve with less intensity than did their wives. It may be, however, that they were simply less willing to report feeling anger, guilt, or a loss of control than were their wives. And while wives became less angry over time, husbands' anger increased. Men were more likely to use denial as a coping mechanism than were women, and they also saw others as less supportive than did their wives.

Men do grieve for the loss of a child, yet it may take them longer to admit this to themselves and others. Instead, they may argue over minor issues, plunge themselves into exercise or work, or withdraw (DeFrain et al., 1990–1991). One husband said, "I took up jogging. I feel an aggressiveness that took or takes over, and I run it out and cry the whole way." Another man stated, "My wife always said the death did affect her more. But this wasn't really true, because men can't show their feelings as a woman can. They keep it inside, and that was my situation" (DeFrain et al., 1990–1991).

Bohannon (1990–1991) also found that couples who saw their marriages as less satisfying had higher levels of grief after their child's death. For families where an atmosphere of open communication between husband and wife and parents and children exists, grief work is easier to accomplish. Parents can communicate their feelings to one another without feeling that they must "put up a front" for the sake of their remaining children (Share, 1978; Osterweis et al., 1984). In these cases, information and communication are not something to be managed, but instead are shared with all family members in an atmosphere of love, caring, and respect for one another's feelings, whether those feelings are usually acceptable (e.g., sadness, sorrow) or not (e.g., anger, guilt, jealousy, relief) (Furman, 1984; Kubler-Ross, 1969; Share, 1978).

Understanding why their child died, and that it was not their fault, is very important—it helps to make sense of a death that "doesn't make sense." Kotch and Cohen (1985–1986), for example, have found that sharing the autopsy report with bereaved parents was helpful in assisting them to cope with the loss of their infant. Some families seek professional help to assist them in working through their grief. For others, community support is very important. One such self-help group is the Compassionate Friends, where parents who have lost children can come together to share

BOX 12.2

THE COMPASSIONATE FRIENDS: SUPPORT FOR BEREAVED PARENTS

Despite the fact that a child's death is extremely traumatic, many families have nowhere to turn when a child dies. The pain of losing a child to an accident, a suicide, a homicide, an illness, or in childbirth is far-reaching, intense, and lonely.

Parents often simply need to be in the presence of others who understand and acknowledge the pain of their loss, who have felt the emotions they are feeling. Others need to talk openly about their loss, and it is important for them to share their feelings with others. These emotions may range from extreme sadness to guilt, anger, self-doubt, and hopelessness. Some parents who have suffered and learned to live with and grow from the loss of their child can offer support, and serve as sounding boards, confidants, or even "psychological punching bags." They offer hope and compassion to those parents who have suffered a loss so devastating that it is too terrible to discuss with anyone. While many find their faith to be a source of strength, no religious creed or affiliation is involved. Ideally, parents can get beyond the hurt and remember their children with love, yet with a touch of sadness. A parent expressed her feelings in a poem she entitled "Remembrance."

Remembrance

I see your smile in the brightness of the summer
sun
A gentle breeze is the touch of your hand on mine
A wave breaks softly on the shore, and I hear you
whisper,
"Remember me."

A winged bird begins its flight into the distant sky.
The sound of children's laughter fills the air.
The evening stars become your eyes, and I reply—
"You are ever near."

Priscilla D. Kenney
TCF, Kennebunk, ME
(*Compassionate Friends*, 1991)

their feelings as well as to help one another cope with the death of a loved son or daughter (see Box 12.2).

ABORTION AS LOSS

A woman who decides to have an abortion faces a unique sense of loss. Even if she freely chooses abortion, she may nevertheless experience psychological difficulties. If, for example, she feels conflict about having an abortion, has an abortion relatively late in her second trimester or pregnancy, or has an abortion because of her child's malformation, she may experience more anger, guilt, or depression (Harris, 1986; Pepper, 1987). Of course, she may also face rejection from, or be judged by, family or friends who feel that abortion is morally wrong.

This may cause others to hold the individual responsible for the abortion, as they might when one dies of AIDS, which can lead to feelings of extreme guilt or anger toward others in the woman. Because they are often avoided by friends or family, such women are sometimes caught between their negative feelings toward these people and their need for support in the face of loss. For these reasons, it may take some time for the individual to come to terms with her abortion and to fully resolve her grief over the loss (Kesselman, 1990).

DEATH IN MIDDLE ADULTHOOD

For adults who are in their forties and fifties, the possibility of their own death becomes real. Cancer, heart disease, stroke, heart attacks, and rarer diseases such as amyotrophic lateral sclerosis (ALS) and multiple sclerosis (MS) are the major killers of middle-aged adults (see Chapter 3). For men, lung, colorectal, and prostate cancer become major concerns, while for women, lung, breast, and colorectal cancer are the most common (American Cancer Society, 1991).

It is commonly believed that individuals in mid-life engage in reevaluating their lives, though such "stock-taking" is not unique to middle-aged people (see Chapter 8). For individuals facing a terminal illness, however, reevaluating life and its meaning are likely consequences. The quality of one's relationships, as well as one's achievements and goals, are assessed with a finality that was never present before. With such musings comes mourning over goals that can never be achieved or relationships that can never be fulfilled.

For these reasons, it may be especially important for the dying person to continue to carry out the roles of father, mother, spouse, mentor, friend, or worker. Plans for the future must be made. Unfinished business must be settled (Kubler-Ross, 1969). One's affairs must be put in order; the security of a business must be ensured, a child's college education must be paid for. For these reasons, discussing one's obligations and responsibilities, so that they are not left unmet after death, is critical. Perhaps special attention must be given to an inheritance, will, or funeral arrangements. Since children, spouse, aging parents, and employees are often dependent on the middle-aged person, it is important that the individual be able to feel as if his or her obligations have been met (Rando, 1984). Then personal peace can be made, and good-byes can be said in good conscience.

Life-threatening Illness

Physical illnesses that are life-threatening constitute a major life crisis for most individuals (Moos & Tsu, 1977). While individuals who die suddenly of a stroke or heart attack obviously cannot adjust to their illness, those who survive face a sometimes difficult and prolonged period of rehabilitation and adjustment, as do their families, especially if recovery is not complete. One's life-style, parental and work roles, and even very identity are altered, and fears about a recurrence are common (Cook & Oltjenbruns, 1989). Despite these concerns, nearly half the families surviving a heart attack feel that they have emerged from it stronger and more closely knit (Dhooper, 1983).

As with young adults, middle-aged people face a series of adjustments in the face of cancer. Mages and Mendelsohn (1979) have described the particular series of adjustments individuals and their families must make after a diagnosis, listed in Table 12.1.

TABLE 12.1

ISSUES AND TASKS RELATED TO COPING WITH CANCER

I. Issue: Discovery of cancer.
Adaptive task: To seek appropriate treatment.

II. Issue: Primary treatment.
Adaptive task: To recognize and cope with the situation and one's emotional reactions and to integrate the experience of illness with the rest of one's life.

III. Issue: Damage to one's body from the cancer and/or treatment.
Adaptive task: To mourn the loss, replace or compensate for lost parts or functions, and maximize other potentials in order to maintain a sense of self-esteem and intactness.

IV. Issue: Returning to normal activities and maintaining continuity in life roles.
Adaptive task: To understand and communicate one's changed attitudes, needs, and limitations in a way that permits functioning within one's social and physical environment with a minimum of constriction of one's life.

V. Issue: Possibility of recurrence and progression of the disease.
Adaptive task: To learn to cope with this uncertainty and to continue appropriate medical follow-up.

VI. Issue: Persistent or recurrent disease.
Adaptive task: To exercise freedom of choice when possible and accept one's dependence on others when necessary, while continuing appropriate treatment.

VII. Issue: Terminal illness.
Adaptive tasks: To prepare for the final separation from family and friends, to put one's affairs in order, to use medical and personal resources to minimize pain, and to retain as much self-sufficiency and personal dignity as possible.

Source: Cook, A. S., & Oltjenbruns, K. A. (1989). *Dying and Grieving: Life span and family perspectives* (p. 338). New York: Holt, Rinehart, and Winston.

If the individual's cancer is incurable, then the rights and obligations of the person as a dying individual come into play. (See Box 12.1 for more about the rights of dying individuals.)

The other major ways in which death affects middle-aged individuals is through the loss of one or both parents, and the loss of a spouse through divorce (Cook & Oltjenbruns, 1989).

Death of a Parent in Mid-life

As individuals age, the aging and eventual death of their parents are more likely. And when a parent dies, the likelihood of one's own death becomes greater. Thus, the fact that a parent is still alive serves as a "psychological buffer" against death (Moss & Moss, 1983). As long as a parent is alive, one can still feel protected, cared for, approved of, and even scolded. Stripped of this "protection," one must acknowledge that he or she is now a senior member of the family and that death is a certainty. The orderliness of life and death—that those who are older should die first—is reinforced when a parent dies.

There is some indication that the death of a mother has more of an impact than that of a father (Osterweis et al., 1984). While children certainly mourn and grieve over the loss of their fathers, mothers may represent the last evidence of one's family of origin, as women typically outlive men.

The death of a parent may also have special significance for men versus women. For an adult male, the death of his father may represent the loss of a trusted friend, role model, and valued grandparent, especially if he has male children of his own, as his identity is, in part, tied to that of his father. An important part of raising his own son may be telling stories about his father and encouraging his son to feel closer to a grandfather. For an adult woman, her mother's death may heighten her own feelings as a mother, particularly if she and her mother have remained close over the years and have shared child-raising experiences.

Over and above the unique impact on adult men and women, adults grieve deeply for both parents, and their death signals the loss of one's childhood. The adult will never again experience the unconditional love that only parents can provide (Cook & Oltjenbruns, 1989).

Douglas (1990–1991) studied patterns of adjustment in 40 middle-aged adults whose parent(s) had died. Men reported less emotional upheaval at the death of their fathers, while both men and women reacted strongly to their mothers' deaths. These results may be due, in part, to men having more difficulty in acknowledging their emotions, and the fact that the mother's death represented the loss of both parents, given that women often die later than do men. A parent's death symbolizes many things: one's own mortality, independence from authority, attachment, and love. For those whose childhood relationships with their parents were more positive, reactions to death were stronger. In addition, for many middle-aged individuals, a parent's death coincided with personal, marital, or work crises; in some cases, the loss of a parent seemed to intensify a couple's marital difficulties (Douglas, 1990–1991). Quite often, the death of a parent causes adult children to reevaluate the quality of their own relationships as well as where their lives are headed.

Divorce is, in many respects, as much of a death as is the actual death of a spouse (Raphael, 1983). Divorce signals the end of a marital relationship, yet the spouse is still alive. Consequently, the surviving spouse is often ambivalent about the breakup of the relationship, particularly if the couple has children. There may be a remote chance that they will remarry. What complicates matters is that both spouses often feel rejected by others and have difficulty accepting the fact that they have "failed." They may have problems reestablishing themselves financially, especially if they are women. If the former spouse then dies, grief can be intense, particularly if feelings about the divorce have not been fully resolved (Doka, 1986). In this case, too, support or understanding from other family members, especially one's current spouse, may be lacking (Doka, 1986). Individuals may not know what to say, or may not consider the ex-spouse a family member.

We have stated that death affects the family as a whole. Thus, the death of a parent or grandparent can have short- and long-term consequences for a child, including emotional and school (interpersonal, academic) difficulties, physical illness, and an influence on the choice of mate later on, based on the image of the dead parent (Furman, 1984; Wass, 1989). Moreover, children who have not been able to grieve over the loss of a parent suffer from loss of self-esteem and experience a sense of loneliness as young adults (Murphy, 1986–1987).

Furman (1984) stresses the supportive, accepting role that the surviving parent must play in helping a grieving child, and the importance of assuring the child that he or she will be cared for in a continuing relationship with the surviving parent or grandparent. Questions about the death (how? why? where?) should be answered openly, and reactions to the feelings about the loss observed in an accepting home atmosphere. The distinction between temporary and permanent absences should be made clear to the child.

Divorce, as well as death, often has severe, long-term effects on children (see Chapters 8 and 9). Children of divorce mourn and express grief over the loss of the relationship with their parents, just as they might if one or both parents were to die. They may become depressed, angry, or experience guilt, assuming that the break-up was somehow their fault. They may express fears about the future, as well as about who will care for them, and be generally anxious about what will happen to them (Heatherington, 1979). Divorced parents, in turn, may have more difficulty in communicating with their children, caring for and supporting them, and are often less consistent in their demands. In spite of the divorce, they also need to hold down jobs and satisfy their needs for intimate companionship and contact.

While the immediate effects of divorce on both parent and child seem to lessen after approximately two years, it seems logical to assume that long-term effects may exist for some children, and for some parents as well, in terms of relationships with the opposite sex, later marital quality, and personal happiness. Longitudinal data (two years +) bear out the long-term negative effects of divorce on children's emotional health and school performance (Heatherington, 1989; Guidubaldi et al., 1983; Guidubaldi & Perry, 1985). Murphy (1991) has also found that there may be long-term consequences for children whose parents have divorced: children who mourned the loss of their parents' relationship were lonelier as young adults.

DEATH AND AGING

Late adulthood is often a period that we, unfortunately, come to think of in terms of loss. Many, for example, tend to assume that with aging comes giving up those things we value in our culture—good health, relationships with others, and status in the community as independent and productive people (Kastenbaum, 1985). But perhaps the most important losses thought to accompany getting older are those of one's spouse, and, ultimately, one's own life.

It may be said that much of the neglect or avoidance of older people in our society has as its basis the link between aging and death (Kastenbaum, 1985). This association poses an interesting problem for many of us. As Kastenbaum (1978, p. 1) has pointed out, "Together they have posed for many a classic ambivalence: one does not want to die, yet one does not want to grow old."

Kalish (1985) suggests that a number of aspects of death awareness increase as one ages. Older people are likely to have had more death experiences (parents, siblings, friends) than are younger people. This has several consequences: (1) the future seems more definite, rather than seeming infinite (when we are very young, being 60 seems a long way off!), (2) older people may see themselves as less worthy because their future is more limited, (3) desirable roles are closed off to them, and (4) not knowing what to do with one's "bonus time" on earth, one may think that he or she has already used up what years were available. Also, as more friends and relatives die, older people become more attuned to sadness and loneliness, and to signals from their bodies that say death is near (Kalish, 1985).

Keith (1979) examined the relationship between life changes, such as marital status, health, church involvement, and informal family or friendship contacts, and elderly people's response patterns toward life and death. People were classified as (1) positivists, those whose life goals were fulfilled and for whom death was not to be feared; (2) negativists, those who feared death and saw it as something that cut short their time on earth; (3) activists, who saw death as a foreclosing on ambition even though valued goals had been achieved; and (4) passivists, who saw death as a respite from life's disappointments, for whom death was actually a positive adjustment to life.

Keith (1979) found those experiencing the most discontinuity in their lives to more frequently be negativists or passivists. Women tended to be more accepting of death than were men. Changes in marital status and health tended to elicit negativism in men only. Religiosity tended to produce positivistic responses in women. Those with higher incomes tended to be positivists, whereas those with lower incomes tended to be passivists (especially when the spouse was ill) or negativists. Less formal and informal activity was associated with passivism. Given that a substantial proportion of older people favor euthanasia (Wass, 1989; Mathieu & Peterson, 1970), a passive orientation may reflect the value they place on ending their own lives.

Sill (1980) found that, in an institutionalized sample of aged people, those who were more aware of the limited time they had left withdrew from others to a greater extent. Marshall and Levy (1990) have described this last phase of life as the "legitimization of one's biography" (p. 249). That is, with an awareness of imminent death, older people are, in effect, writing the last chapters of their life stories (Marshall & Levy, 1990). The goal of this last process is not only to make sense of one's life, but also to understand death itself.

Kastenbaum (1985) suggests that younger people may adopt the **principle of compensation** to preserve a sense of continuity and fairness about life and death. This principle suggests that, just as we may have been left a penny (or perhaps with inflation, a dollar) to compensate for a lost tooth as children, older or terminally ill people are compensated for losses of health and, ultimately, life by the promise of eternity. Near death, individuals are assumed to acquire a kind of spiritual wisdom that lets them view death more positively.

This approach can have many psychological advantages for the dying, older people, and survivors. For example, it may enable survivors and a dying person to share a common view about the afterlife, and later reduce guilt about not "having done right by" the deceased person or minimize the social disruption of death by lessening the sadness of grieving by assuming that someone is "so much happier now" (Kastenbaum, 1985, p. 624). The principle of compensation also reinforces the practice of **regressive intervention**—doing little in the belief that there is nothing more that can be done for the old person. Interestingly, however, older people who are dying rarely say that the afterlife is a compensation for death (Kastenbaum, 1985).

While the principles of compensation and regressive intervention coexist with negative attitudes toward the aged in general, both principles have a similar impact on dying individuals. The assumption that "old means incompetent" has simply been replaced by "old means wise." Both are means of control that serve the interests of those who believe in them, who have the "knack of ignoring individual reality in favor of generalized expectancies" (Kastenbaum, 1985, p. 625).

If ours is a death-denying culture (Kubler-Ross, 1969), it may make sense to many to avoid those experiences or people that threaten or disturb us most. We live in a culture that tends to sensationalize death by focusing on mass death, the deaths of famous people, and crime and violence. Our culture also dissociates us from natural death, death on an everyday level, and the deaths of specific people, particularly if they are old (DeSpelder & Strickland, 1992; Kastenbaum, 1978). It is the very belief that death is more appropriate for the aged and, by inference, less so for the young (Wu, 1990–1991) that forces us to rely on our own experiences (or lack of them) and our own biases in dealing with issues regarding death and dying and adults of all ages. These biases may be especially destructive if the person is older or dying. We may feel prepared to deal with the death of someone who is older, whereas we are caught off guard when someone young dies. As Kastenbaum (1985) suggests, this expectation has been strengthened by lower infant and childhood mortality in recent decades.

Kastenbaum (1978, p. 3) states, "So long as we can believe that old people are ready for death and that it is high time for them to leave the scene, we can also hold our emotional responses and professional services within acceptable limits. . . . If we just *know* that death is appropriate for old people, then there is little need to explore precisely what this old man or woman is thinking or feeling."

Integrity and Death

Many prominent, apparently well-accepted ideas about aging tend to reinforce the association between older people and death, leading to the conclusion that death and dying are "more natural" or "more appropriate" for older people than for the young.

The term *integrity* suggests a sense of completeness and is said to result in acceptance of death, while *despair* implies a fear of death as a premature end to an unsatisfying life. According to Butler (1963), realizing one's mortality brings about the process of life review—pulling together one's life's experiences, righting wrongs, and reaching closure about relationships with significant others (see Butler et al., 1990). What integrity and life review have in common is the process of *introspection* (looking inward) (Newman & Newman, 1986). While introspection can be very satisfying, it can also have serious consequences for the older person who is unable or unwilling to attempt a reintegration or reinterpretation of life's successes, failures, joys, and disappointments. For these individuals, introspection can precipitate a depressive crisis, anxiety, anger, or, ultimately, the decision to end their lives.

Disengagement and Death

Perhaps the most widespread idea about the aging-death relationship is disengagement, originally proposed by Cumming and Henry (1961). Disengaging from others (who are also thought to withdraw from the aged person) should permit one to prepare for death. Thus, older people, al-

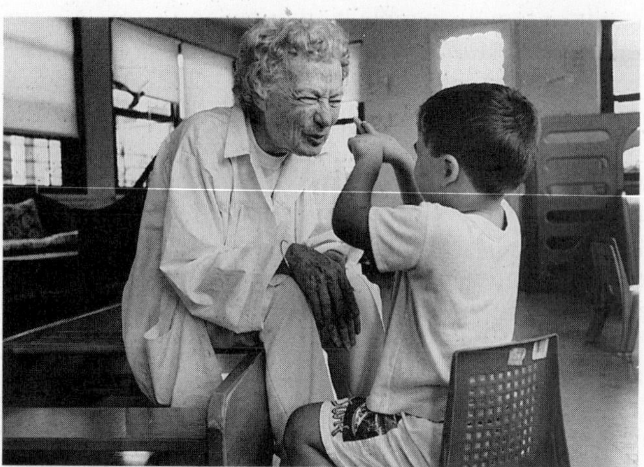

Appreciating the continuity of the life cycle is one of the hallmarks of integrity.

though very much biologically alive, are treated as if they were dead, under the assumption that they wish to be alone. They die what we discussed earlier as a social death. Simply put, they may be written off by others; and this may be expressed in the form of hostility or avoidance, or worse still, involve physical abuse or emotional cruelty by others.

Sill (1980) and Kalish (1985) concluded that institutionalized elderly who estimated that they had less time to live disengaged from others more. It is possible, however, that others in the immediate environment—staff—implicitly socialize elders to withdraw from others, who then, in turn, focus on their own deaths (Sill, 1980). Nursing home care need not be a death sentence, however. Stein and associates (1990), in measuring the anticipation of stress in nursing home care, argue that if proper interpersonal support is available to the elder, adjustment and survival are more likely. Vickio and Cavanaugh (1985) found that increased contact with death among nursing home staff lead to less death anxiety and more comfort in talking about it.

In conclusion, instead of seeing disengagement or integrity/life review as characteristic of all elderly, we might instead view these processes as being characteristic of some people more than others irrespective of age but consistent with personality traits or specific life experiences.

BEREAVEMENT—SURVIVING DEATH

Regardless of age, the loss of a child, parent, sibling, spouse or grandparent is likely to be one of the most disruptive life events that we experience (Holmes & Raye, 1967; Rowland, 1977). Kastenbaum and Costa (1977) suggest that referring to someone as "bereaved" simply indicates that he or

Grief is very personal. Grief work is often very painful to those who lose a loved one.

she has survived someone's death. *Grief* is the term we use to refer to the manner in which one deals with and responds to this loss. *Mourning* indicates a socially condoned way of expressing one's grief or acknowledging that a life has ended, for example by holding a funeral. While we might assume that older people are especially prone to negative effects after losing a significant other (most likely a husband or wife), research does not consistently bear this out.

Statistics suggest that older people clearly must deal more frequently with the loss of a spouse. By the age of 65, 50 percent of women have lost their husbands; by the age of 75, two-thirds are widowed (Osterweis et al., 1984). Anyone who has to deal with several closely spaced deaths might not have the opportunity to do the grief work necessary to "work through" each loss (Kastenbaum, 1978). These people may be literally overwhelmed by grief, suffering from **bereavement overload,** and may appear depressed, apathetic, or experience physical problems (Kastenbaum, 1978). Since deaths are often sudden, the people who are left behind suffer from *acute grief,* commonly believed to be more difficult to cope with than *anticipatory grief.* Not only are older people likely to experience bereavement overload, but those who lose family through accidents or violence, as well as professionals who must deal with the dying (e.g., police, firefighters, and EMTs), can also suffer from the burden of losing many people at once.

Are Bereaved People at Risk?

Perhaps the most common loss older people face is the loss of a spouse. Is losing a spouse harmful to the survivor? Schulz (1978) concludes that the aged are at risk, both physically and psychologically, as a consequence of widowhood but questions the assumption that such negative effects are a consequence of widowhood per se. In other words, what exactly is it about being widowed that makes death or illness more likely? Does the pain of widowhood cause people to become ill?

There are many reasons why widows and widowers die more frequently than those who are not widowed. These include:

1. Those who are in better health tend to remarry, leaving those who are in poorer health behind.
2. Those who are fit tend to marry those who are also fit.
3. Both widows and their spouses lived in the same high-risk environment.
4. The loss of a spouse creates a sense of hopelessness and depression, leading to lowered resistance to disease and/or stress.
5. The death of one's spouse robs one of the support and/or cues required to take medicine on time, eat balanced meals, keep doctor's appointments, and the like (Schulz, 1978).

Rowland (1977) concludes that widows have a greater chance of developing either a physical or psychological illness. They also are more likely to die within six months to a year after the deaths of their husbands than are nonwidows, according to Rowland. This risk was even higher when the spouse's death was sudden.

If, however, a woman has advance knowledge of her husband's impending death due to illness, she may be able to psychologically prepare herself and adjust more easily to life without him (O'Bryant, 1990–1991). The wife can discuss her emotional, social, and financial future with her husband, facilitating her adjustment and allowing him to feel that his wife will survive after he dies. Thus, whether loss is harmful seems to depend on whether other concurrent losses or stresses must be coped with and whether support from others is available (Levav, 1989–1990).

Relative to widows, we know comparatively little about how widowers cope with the loss of their wives. Since women generally outlive men, widowers are less common than widows. For this reason, support from other men who have lost their wives is likely to be scarce.

Contrary to what we might expect, Carey (1979–1980) concluded that widowers were significantly better adjusted than were widows during the first year of bereavement. While being forewarned, allowing one to grieve in an anticipatory way, seems important for widows, it is not for widowers, according to Carey's research. Widows who were more highly educated, had higher incomes, and lived alone (with no children to care for or live with) made better adjustments after their spouses' death; but this was not the case for widowers. Interestingly, those with stable, happy marriages and those with constant, pervasive marital problems appeared to be better adjusted. Not facing the death and/or deterioration prior to death, and uncertainty about what life would be like after the death, were the major problems to be overcome by the widows and widowers in this study.

It seems that uncertainty about or denial of impending death is negatively related to postdeath adjustment for older people. A two-year longitudinal study by Lund and associates (1986) suggested that widows and widowers tended to face common problems in bereavement, suggesting that the loss of one's spouse is a universal adjustment for both men and women.

Lund and associates (1986–1987) have also found that elderly people who had difficulty coping with a death two years later differed from those who were "good copers." Poor copers expressed lower self-esteem prior to bereavement, and had more confusion and a greater desire to die, cried more, and were less able to keep busy shortly after the death. This suggests that elderly individuals who experience particularly strong emotions and have poor self-images are likely to have problems in adjusting to death later on.

Moss and Moss (1980) have discussed the impact that investing oneself emotionally in a marital relationship has on subsequent remarriage among those elderly who were widowed. Many older women attempt to relate to their new husbands in terms of their former relationships with deceased husbands (Lopata, 1973). In many cases, this "**sanctification**" of the deceased spouse can interfere with the new relationship, and in order to move on, ties with the first spouse must be worked through by both parties.

Relocation stress (see Parkes, 1987–1988; Schulz & Brenner, 1977) or loss of support, even if that support falls into the category of nagging (e.g., "Have you taken your medicine yet?"), also seem to be associated with increased probability of death in elderly people who are widowed (Rowland, 1977). Nirenberg (1983) found that, while relocation stress was greatest for less competent older individuals, being able to acquire appropriate behavioral skills and gradual exposure to the physical and spatial aspects of a nursing home predicted postmove adjustment after three months.

In evaluating the impact of loss, it is important to realize that people may not be accurate in reporting how they feel, and that not everyone who is bereaved participates in bereavement research (Stroebe & Stroebe, 1989–1990).

Grieving in Young and Elderly Adults

LOSS OF A SPOUSE

Whether older people grieve in different ways than the young is a matter of some disagreement. Some authors discuss stages of grief: (1) initial shock/disbelief, (2) working through feelings and review of the relationship with the deceased, and (3) restructuring phase, where life moves on, all of which may last for varying periods of time (Kalish, 1976; Schulz, 1978). Research by Barrett and Schneweis (1980–1981), however, does not support the notion that reactions to being bereaved change consistently with the passage of time widowed.

It is commonly believed that, in general, younger people have a more difficult time adjusting to the loss of a spouse than do older individuals. In this case, a spouse's death may force the young person into child care or work responsibilities for which he or she is unprepared. Too, since widowhood in young adulthood is relatively uncommon, other men and women may not be available as models for how to survive alone.

Sanders (1979–1980) found the younger widow to initially experience intense grief reactions—denial, anger, guilt, feelings of aloneness, physical illness or sleep disturbances, and preoccupation with the death—followed by decrease of these reactions 18 months later. The reverse was true for older widows and widowers. Being able to anticipate one's feelings in order to prepare oneself for a spouse's death may have beneficial effects on later adjustment over the short term, but the long-term effects of the loss were clearly evident. Loneliness was, for all bereaved, the chief long-term problem (Sanders, 1979–1980).

While some have found younger people who are widowed to make poorer adjustments than do older people (Carey, 1979–1980; Williams-Conway et al., 1991), others do not. For example, Thompson et al. (1989) discovered that older bereaved spouses were initially more distressed than nonbereaved spouses but that two years later there were few differences between the groups. This suggests that while older people are emotionally affected by a spouse's death, they come to grips with their loss within two years. Similarly, Sable (1991) found that, within three years, older women's grief subsides.

Given the strong emotional bond that years of marriage can create, we must not fail to realize that the *broken-heart syndrome* probably accounts for a certain degree of illness or difficulty in adjustment experienced by widows.

While some older women eventually move on with their lives, others do not seem to be able to do so. They remain forlorn. In Sable's (1991) study of bereaved women, 78 percent thought they would never get over their loss; they simply learned to live with it. Moreover, older women adjusted to loss less well than did younger women. This is contrary to the myth that says because older women are more prepared for their husbands' eventual deaths, they will adjust more quickly and more completely. But for some individuals, the pain of losing a spouse or a child never goes away. As a 76-year-old woman said, when asked about her life after her husband's death, "I always feel sad . . . I'm not doing well. I'm not able to function very well. . . . Lately I can't join in the living. . . . No one needs me. No one seems to care" (Sable, 1991, p. 136).

A 73-year-old woman summed up this sense of longing after her husband's death: "Time doesn't heal if you have a great love. It doesn't

ADULTS SPEAK

LOSING A SPOUSE IN YOUNG ADULTHOOD

The grief that young adults feel at losing a spouse lingers for a long time. Three years after losing his wife of two years to a car accident at the age of 25, this young widower wrote:

> The experience of grief and healing is not magical, and it doesn't leave you immune to the pain of loss. Many people have said to me, "You have really become a strong person by surviving Becky's death." Maybe it's true that I am more capable of handling life's crises than I was before widowhood. Maybe my grief has inspired me not to give up when I try to meet other challenges in life. The pain of grief, however, is one that seared me, and one that can quickly rise within me. One day when I was at a lake with my cousin, we became a part of a search party to find a five-year-old girl. On the third cross, my cousin located the child and pulled her from the lake. She was dead from drowning. I stood by the shore and stared at this child while the medics worked on her. Like Becky, she looked so alive and yet was dead. In the background her mother screamed, "Oh my God, not my baby, please don't take my baby." I watched and felt helpless. Later, when I cried in the shower that evening my tears were for the child and for her mother. There were also tears for myself. I cried for losing the someone I loved so early in my adult years, so suddenly and so completely. (Lichtenberg, 1990, p. 89)

He writes, "I learned you cannot grieve alone; grief is frightening due to its immense range and the intensity of feelings it provokes; and even when healing occurs, there remains a heightened sensitivity to loss" (p. 83).

Source: Lichtenberg (1990). Remembering Becky. *Omega, 21,* 83–89.

lose the loss. We loved each other. I miss him terribly" (Sable, 1991, p. 136).

Remember that in families where an older spouse dies, both the surviving spouse and adult children have suffered a loss. Bass et al. (1990) found that spouses were more negatively affected by the death of an aged spouse than were their children, yet they tended to become more socially active afterward than their children, perhaps in an effort to rebuild support from others that was lacking prior to the spouse's death. Children were more likely to expect the death, to realize sooner that death was imminent, and to discuss the parent's feelings about dying in this study. While children tried to emotionally prepare themselves for their parent's death, this seemed to make adjustment more difficult.

Findings such as these should alert us to our own biases about anticipatory grief. They should also help us recognize the tremendous psychological burden spouses carry in caring for a dying husband or wife.

LOSS OF AN ADULT CHILD

Approximately 10 percent of adults over the age of 60 experience the death of a grown child (Moss et al., 1986–1987). Not only is the death of an adult child untimely, but a life-long parent-child bond is severed forever. Because this loss is comparatively rare, others who have experienced such a loss are most likely unavailable to provide needed emotional support (Moss et al., 1986–1987). If a son or a daughter had children, grandparents may have to raise these children and be faced with caring for themselves at the same time. Moreover, they may have had to face the losses of friends, spouse, and their own parents as well. Since their child is not alive to provide them with support and assistance, they may be at additional risk for being institutionalized should they become ill, frail, or otherwise dependent (Moss et al., 1986–1987).

When an adult child dies, the entire family's relationships are affected. Surviving siblings must deal with their own loss, which influences their relationships with one another as well as with older parents. Guilt, anger, and depression may cloud family relationships, impede communication, and disrupt family helping patterns and family rituals. Family reunions, for example, are never the same once an adult child has died, especially if this person "held the family together." As a result, surviving adult children and parents may not see one another as often. Christmas, Thanksgiving, New Year's, or birthdays can never be celebrated as they were before.

For the surviving parent, hope for the future may be eroded. As adults, we look forward to a lifetime with our children. When a child dies, our own mortality (and immortality) is shaken; we can no longer share in the joy of their lives.

When the death of a grown child is experienced by elderly parents, grief reactions are often very intense and prolonged (Markussen, 1983; Sanders, 1979–1980). Indeed, death of a child has replaced death of a spouse as the single most stressful event adults may experience. Older people who lose adult children through death experience a particular sense of failure that is difficult to deal with. As noted above, being a parent involves a sense of omnipotence about one's ability to care for a child that is formed very early in the child's life (Miles, 1984; Osterweis et al., 1984; Stevens-Long, 1984). Very few adults expect to bury their own children.

Grief Work

As many of those who have lost a loved one know, grief is a very complex and private experience. Grief is considered work because acknowledging and working through our feelings, as well as reorganizing our lives, takes great effort. While we often grieve anticipatorily, before a person actually dies, some of our grief can also be experienced at a funeral or memorial service honoring the life of the person who has died. Funerals and other forms of ritual serve to structure our emotions at a time when we might otherwise be overwhelmed. We may busy ourselves making funeral arrangements or entertaining relatives, with little or no time to be alone and reflect on how we are really feeling.

Funerals' major functions are (1) to provide a socially acceptable, healthy means to prepare the body for burial—its **secular** function—and (2) to provide a symbolic rite of passage from the state of living to the state of being dead—its **sacred** function (Schulz, 1978). Funerals can also provide psychological support to the bereaved family and others who have suffered the loss.

In a sense, funerals are a final symbol of the fact that a person has lived, and they, as well, reaffirm the group identity of survivors so that they can continue to function after the death (Lopata, 1973). Thus, funerals can help those who mourn to work through their grief immediately after a death. Whether funerals are helpful in this sense in the long run, however, has yet to be explored. Funerals, as rituals marking death, have changed in many ways (see Box 12.3), perhaps indicating that they fulfill their function of supporting bereaved people more adequately than in the past (Irion, 1990–1991).

Grief may take years to be fully resolved, or it may never be worked through. But *should* grief be worked through? The answer to this question is complex. If "working through" implies taking away what little is left of the deceased in someone's life—memories of a relationship—then the answer to this question is definitely No. It is often out of our own wish to avoid pain that we prevent others from experiencing the pain necessary to do grief work. But avoiding talking about the obvious, "managing" communication by changing the subject, or denying the physical and emotional aspects of grief can only serve to make the loss more hurtful, and most likely will make postdeath adjustment more difficult (Share, 1978). This may be especially important when death is sudden, as acute grief accompanying sudden death is believed to be more difficult to cope with (Thompson & Range, 1990–1991).

Since bereaved individuals, regardless of age, may have built their lives on a primary relationship with a significant other, extreme caution

BOX 12.3

THE CHANGING FUNERAL

Irion (1990–1991) has made an intensive study of funerals as cultural rituals that symbolize our feelings about losing a loved one. He contends that, because we are more aware of the psychological aspects of grief, funerals as rituals to facilitate grief work have changed in many ways. For example:

1. *Pastoral funeral orders to instruct clergy are now more sensitive to the needs of mourners.* These needs may be psychological or spiritual, and they clearly go beyond where to stand or what gestures to make. Being aware of the mourner's need to express grief, get support from others, and accept the reality of death is now important.
2. *New funeral orders recognize that the funeral is a community function, not a private exercise.* Funerals bring people together. Death signals the loss of a part of the community. Active participation by the community is encouraged. Recognizing ethnicity, race, family, and regional customs is now essential to the extent that community values as well as individual ones are reflected at the funeral.
3. *New funeral services show awareness of the importance of facing the reality of death.* The reality of the death of a loved one and its pain are brought home by viewing the body. The funeral involves a separation from the body of the deceased person. It communicates a sense of finality.
4. *The funeral is set within the context of the mourning process.* Funerals acknowledge that grief is an extended process that takes time. The survivors must not be forgotten after the funeral and will require extended pastoral support.
5. *Funerals are now responsive to the dynamics of pluralism.* Funerals now recognize the needs of people of different faiths and ethnic backgrounds. One "standard" funeral cannot serve everyone.
6. *New funerals recognize that there are ministries other than that of the clergy.* Laypeople and funeral directors are acknowledged as playing an important, emotionally supportive role in ministering to bereaved family members.

These changes in the rituals of funerals can make them more responsive to the needs of mourners, helping them to better cope with grief and loss.

Source: Irion, P. E. (1990–1991). Changing patterns of ritual response to death. *Omega, 22,* 159–172.

needs to be exercised in judging extended grief reactions as abnormal (Jackson, 1979) (see below). Indeed the immediate expression of feelings, as well as support from others and acknowledging the wish to be alone, seem to be helpful in grief resolution (Hafer, 1983; Kubler-Ross, 1982; Parkes & Weiss, 1983).

When the surviving spouse has no other source of emotional support (is isolated from others), or has children to support with few financial and psychological resources, bereavement seems more difficult (Bankoff, 1983; Raphael, 1983; Rowland, 1977; Silverman & Coopersmith, 1984). Individuals who are psychologically "hardy"—committed to their goals in the face of adversity, with a sense of control over their lives—adjust better to the loss of a spouse than those who are less hardy (Campbell et al., 1991).

Grief is often composed of many different types of responses—affective, behavioral, physical—and seemingly contradictory emotions. For example, one can simultaneously experience an intense desire to hold on to the image or memory of the dead spouse, along with guilt, anger, and/

or relief (Jackson, 1979). Accepting such emotions seems to positively predict bereavement outcome (Parkes & Weiss, 1983; Worden, 1982).

Remaining in touch with a bereaved person is a crucial element in his or her ultimate survival (Morgan, 1989). This is important because those who are bereaved are often avoided and treated as if they are sick (Kalish, 1985).

It seems that people who are not themselves bereaved have a difficult time understanding how bereaved individuals think or feel. For example, Williams-Conway and associates (1991) found that professionals attributed more emotional distress and difficulty in adjusting to husbands' deaths than did the widows themselves, while widows yearned more strongly for their husbands and felt more isolated than professionals judged them to feel. However, when other people were asked to imagine bereavement, and their responses were compared to those who had lost a loved one to a variety of causes, perceptions were surprisingly similar (Thompson & Range, 1990–1991). The one exception was that people could not predict the experience of bereavement from suicide, specifically regarding the amount of helpfulness of contact with others. For most be-

ADULTS SPEAK

A WIDOW'S GRIEF

"Widow" is a harsh and hurtful word. It comes from the Sanskrit and it means "empty." I have been empty too long. I do not want to be pigeon-holed as a widow. I am a woman whose husband has died, yes. But not a second-class citizen, not a lonely goose. I am a mother and a working woman and a friend and a sexual woman and a vital woman. I am a person. I resent what the term widow has come to mean. I am alive. I am part of the world.

After my husband died, I felt like one of those spiraled shells washed up on the beach. Poke a straw through the twisting tunnel, around and around, and there is nothing there. No flesh. No life. Whatever lived there is dried up and gone.

But what of love? The warmth, the tenderness, the passion I had for Martin? Am I rejecting that, too?

Ah, that is the very definition of bereavement. The love object is lost. And love without its object shrivels like a flower betrayed by an early frost. How can we live without it? Without love? Without its total commitment? This explains the passionate grief of widowhood. Grief is as much a lament for the end of love as anything else.

Acceptance finally comes. And with it comes peace. Today I carry the scars of my bitter grief. In a way I look upon them as battle stripes, marks of my fight to attain an identity of my own. I owe the person I am today to Martin's death. If he had not died, I am sure I would have lived happily ever after as a twentieth-century child wife never knowing what I was missing.

But today I am someone else. I am stronger, more independent. I have more understanding, more sympathy. A different perspective. I have a quiet love for Martin. I have passionate, poignant memories of him. He will always be part of me.

Source: Caine, L. (1974). *Widow.* New York: William Morrow.

reaved individuals, feelings of isolation and separateness from others are the major obstacles to asking for and receiving help.

It is common to observe in those who are grieving a desire for a certain amount of time alone. However, the extent to which anyone, but especially an older widowed male, becomes isolated from others robs him or her of an important source of support and feedback about emotions such as anger, guilt, sadness, anxiety, or depression. Self-imposed isolation over an extended period of time may indicate that the person is experiencing difficulty in coping with his or her loss, if it arises out of a desire to deny that the death has occurred. What is crucial is the quality of one's behavior (e.g., harmful, self-destructive, unrealistic), not its quantity (length of time grieving), in judging whether the grief is abnormal (Lindemann, 1943).

Abnormal or maladaptive grief frequently involves a long-term change in the individual's typical behaviors, that is, chronic depression, extended denial of the death, self-abusive or self-destructive behavior, and isolation from others (Jackson, 1979). Normal, adaptive grief may or may not last for an extended time period (e.g., two to three years), depending on a number of factors, such as personality, health, relationship with the deceased person, and support from others. If, after two years, people continue to feel sad from time to time about a loved one's death, this does not necessarily mean they are having trouble completing the grief process. Balkwell (1985) and Stevenson (1985) have found that widowers are more likely to be socially isolated and less apt to express their feelings, perhaps indicating that men may have a more difficult bereavement than do women, though there are wide individual differences in grieving among widows (Bankoff, 1983; Silverman & Cooperband, 1984). And note that even the loss of a beloved pet can evoke intense feelings that take time to resolve (Cook & Oltjenbruns, 1989; Weisman, 1990–1991).

THE WORK OF ELIZABETH KUBLER-ROSS

If we assume that people who are terminally ill are ready to die, we may, tragically, deny them the opportunity to deal with what was referred to above as unfinished business, a term coined by Kubler-Ross (1974). Quite often, discussions about death and dying are seen as depressing or sad, and consequently avoided with those who are dying, regardless of age. But acknowledging any and all needs is the key to helping those adults who are struggling with their mortality or who are dying (Kubler-Ross, 1969, 1974).

Since the publication in 1969 of *On Death and Dying,* where Kubler-Ross's stages through which people progress in reacting to their impending deaths were first outlined, her theories have been overinterpreted (Kastenbaum, 1975). These stages consist of (1) *denial* (no, not me), (2) *anger* directed at doctors, nurses, or those who will go on living, (3) *bargaining* with others (God) in order to prolong life, (4) *depression* in reaction to one's worsening symptoms or deterioration, knowing that death will follow, and (5) *acceptance,* a sense of readiness for death, but without loss of hope that life could be prolonged if a cure were found.

However, emotions people express near death seem to vary with a number of factors. Wu (1990–1991) found that family support and age determined how dying people felt about life and death. Younger terminally ill patients expressed more bargaining and anger, while older patients expressed more depression and acceptance. Those with immediate family support felt more fearful but were less depressed than people without family support. Moreover, younger people who lacked support were more angry than those with meaningful family ties, while levels of support were not important for older individuals (Wu, 1990–1991).

Whether people are aware of their terminal diagnosis and impending death also seems to influence their emotions. In general, people who are close to death but are not aware of it are more likely to mention religion less often than other sources (Baugher et al., 1989–1990). In contrast, those who are aware of impending death seem to be equally likely to see others, religion, the afterlife, and oneself as sources of strength. Overall, Baugher et al. (1989–1990) found little evidence for increased withdrawal from others as nearness to death increased, as might be predicted from Kubler-Ross's theory, which has been interpreted to mean that people at this time are either depressed or accepting.

Using Kubler-Ross's Stage Theory Productively

Kubler-Ross's ideas have been interpreted to mean that every person should experience the five stages, and in the given order. Thus, staff or family may feel compelled to push a dying person through each stage until he or she has reached acceptance; anything else is seen as a failure. But prolonged reactions of denial or anger can have positive emotional consequences for many terminally ill people even though they may make others uncomfortable. Plus, in reality, there is a great deal of moving back and forth among the stages (Kalish, 1976; Kastenbaum, 1975; Peterson, 1980; Rodabough, 1980). Despite this variability, research demonstrates that depression seems to be a common experience for those who are dying (Wass, 1989).

Dismissing someone's behavior as "just anger" may ignore very important external reasons (family conflicts, poor quality of care) for that anger. A patient's purported denial may also reflect a mutual pretense by the medical staff and/or family that the patient's death is not impending (Peterson, 1980). This may reinforce the family's or staff's needs to deny both their own and the individual's death, but it robs the dying person of the opportunity to draw others closer. It also prevents finishing unfinished business, especially making up for past sins and hurts, and saying the unsaid. In addition, it denies those who are in a position to help the dying person the opportunity to learn about life from someone else.

Funerals, despite the positive result of helping to structure the grieving process (Schaie & Geiwitz, 1982), may reinforce denial rather than acceptance of death by the use of such terms as *passed on* and *slumber room,* reconstructive efforts to make the deceased look "alive," or ceremonies that do not reflect the real values of the person when he or she was alive. Quite often, the immediate family are physically separated from others who attend the funeral, further isolating them from people as well as from their own feelings about the death. They may feel that they must maintain an air of respect or an image of strength in the face of their loss. For example, anger is often a perfectly legitimate response to death and loss (Kalish, 1985), but if anger or sadness is suppressed or internalized, as might be appropriate at a funeral, it often shows up as depression (Lindemann, 1943), further complicating adjustment and making communication more difficult later on.

We can conclude from this discussion of Kubler-Ross's work that, whatever its deficiencies, it teaches us to deal with dying individuals "where they happen to be at the moment (emotionally speaking)". The same can certainly be applied to those who are experiencing anticipatory grief prior to a loved one's death.

If we fail to recognize that every person's feelings about his or her own or someone else's impending death are unique, we deny that person the right to make (or not make) decisions about life as well as death. These may be decisions that someone desperately wants and needs to make in order that he or she, or a loved one, may die "an **appropriate death**" (DeSpelder & Strickland, 1992; Kalish, 1985); in other words, one dies in the manner one wishes to, with loved ones and with little pain.

Relating to those who are bereaved and grieving demands that we recognize that grief is very personal, and that widows and widowers may grieve in various ways consistent with their personal feelings about the death. Consequently, it might be useful to explore whether the grieving person believed the death was preventable, evaluate the strength of his or her relationship to the deceased, and take stock of what interpersonal and emotional resources the survivor has available (Bugen, 1979; Robbins, 1990–1991).

PSYCHOTHERAPY WITH DYING PEOPLE

Levy (1990) discusses therapy with terminally ill people in the context of "humanizing death" (p. 189). For most individuals who are terminally ill, it is when they are most healthy, relatively speaking, that they can benefit to the greatest extent from formal psychotherapy. Thus, the earlier they can begin therapy, the better. As long as the patient is alive, the goal of all forms of therapy is simply to enhance the quality of life for both patient and family and to help them cope with the disease. People have more energy to devote to therapy at this point, and new coping skills are more likely to be learned.

However, a major problem for dying patients is that treatable psychological dysfunction is often overlooked. Some maintain that depressed patients have low self-esteem but that those who are terminally ill retain positive feelings of self-worth (Dabratz, 1990). In contrast, Levy (1990) suggests that depression and anxiety are common and are treatable disorders in the terminally ill. While organic factors (e.g., neurochemical changes) can contribute to depression, it is also a common reaction to the knowledge that one's illness is terminal. Moreover, feelings of abandonment by friends, coworkers, one's physician, and even one's family can contribute to depression in those who have lost all hope in a long life, or even an abbreviated life. But, while hopes to live until spring, or until a birthday or graduation, eventually fade, the object of one's hope shifts to others or to simply having a peaceful death and/or eternal life (Levy, 1990).

Learning to cope with fears of losing control and being dependent, and adapting to the physical losses that accompany dying, are also issues that can be addressed in therapy. People who withdraw from others near death may not be depressed; they may be withdrawing from others naturally as preparation for death (Levy, 1990).

Since people who are depressed often entertain thoughts of suicide, the therapist must inquire as to what the dying person is actually thinking about. For example, the therapist might ask, "I wonder if you're becoming very discouraged. Do you find yourself having crying spells? What sort of thoughts go through your mind at these times? Have you thought that rather than going on like this, life may not be worth living? Have you actually thought of what you might do to end your life?" (Goldberg, 1981, p. 376). If suicidal thoughts are uncovered, then treatment of the underlying depression can proceed. If treatment is successful, the cognitive, affective, and especially somatic symptoms of depression may lessen. For those who are severely depressed, antidepressants may be prescribed. These can alleviate crying spells, sleeplessness, and withdrawal (Katon, 1982).

When individual therapy is recommended, spouses and family members need also to be involved, since dying affects the whole family. Communication patterns can be observed and, if necessary, changed, and couples can explore other ways of sharing innermost feelings when their physical expression is muted by the disease process (Levy, 1990). Group therapy is also an option for some dying people, who receive valuable support from other group members.

Levy (1990) suggests that therapy with dying individuals does not aim to rework the entire person by uncovering latent conflicts. Instead, patients' denial is supported so long as it does not impede communication. People can learn to rely on coping skills that have worked in the past. Also, while they are still competent, patients can discuss their wishes regarding funeral arrangements, wills, and their desires pertaining to the termination of treatment. Living wills can be written. Decisions can be made regarding a surrogate—usually a family member—who, in the event that choices regarding euthanasia become necessary, can act on the patient's behalf. The psychologist can also help the patient and family make a choice as to where to die, at home or in the hospital.

Since the dying patient's emotional well-being is intimately linked to that of the family and vice versa, family therapy can help both the patient and the family (see Chapter 11).

The therapist's role does not end when the patient dies. For the next 18 to 24 months, surviving family members need support in ventilating feelings, and in dealing with guilt, anger, or grief as well as going on with their lives. Talking about the details of the death, actively discussing the lost family member, and confronting one's needs for intimacy (for the spouse) are issues that the therapist can explore with the family after death (Levy, 1990).

For those who are near death themselves, the therapist's primary roles are to remain emotionally supportive, encourage the patient to remain active in decision-making, and help the patient combat side effects of the disease itself and of drugs by using techniques such as relaxation or self-hypnosis (Levy, 1990). The therapist can become quite close to the dying person—as close as family. Thus, the patient's death leaves a void that the therapist must fill, just as grieving spouses, parents, or children must.

Communicating with Others About Death and Dying

Because of the abhorrence of death in our culture, we may avoid discussing the very things that some people have a real need to confront, under the assumption that these issues are either already settled, private, or simply too terrible to talk about (DeSpelder & Strickland, 1992; Kastenbaum, 1985). These issues may involve making funeral arrangements, writing a will, reviewing a treasured relationship, or talking out one's own fears surrounding death itself, the dying process, or the afterlife.

While loss is equated with death for some, it is important to realize that for others, death may actually be positive (Keith, 1979). Young people who have many plans for the future may fear death because it represents an end to valued goals and achievements, whereas the elderly may feel sorrow over the loss of their ability to care for others (Kastenbaum, 1985). Some may be concerned over the impact of their death on others, while still others fear the loss of their bodies or what may happen to the body after death. As noted above, each person's feelings are unique. Unfortunately, there are no easy solutions as to what to say, or when to say it. In most cases, going with "what is in your gut" may be best—a look, a hug, or a squeeze may be more comforting than anything you can say.

It is commonly assumed by the young that, given the closeness of the aged to death, elderly people must be more fearful of it. The young often see death as something that happens to others; if young people die at all, it is often perceived to be violently (Kalish, 1976). They often project these feelings about their own deaths onto aged people. These behaviors are encompassed by the term *countertransference* (Wilensky & Weiner, 1977). We have a tendency to deny our feelings about death, but we can also view it as an opportunity to get to know ourselves as well as others.

The needs of each person are better served by exploring what death means to him or her. This approach is particularly important because chronological age is a poor predictor of death concerns (Kastenbaum,

1985). What in life does this individual value? How important are such things as family, health, religion, or work? What does the individual expect the future to bring? How important are friends?

While preoccupation with death can be harmful, it can also have positive benefits, facilitating funeral planning and writing a will, and encouraging the sharing of feelings essential to open communication. Kalish (1976) and Kastenbaum and Aisenberg (1976) have noted that older people *personalize* death more often than do the young. This personalization may take the form of wanting to be reunited with a departed loved one, for example. Such behavior may reflect religious beliefs or simply represent a wish to be with those with whom one has shared a long life. It almost goes without saying that family, professionals, and others interested in helping adults of all ages should develop those skills that facilitate the expression of each individual's feelings about such issues (Wass & Corr, 1984).

What are the skills we are referring to? Perhaps most importantly, they involve openness to others' experiences and points of view. Regardless of one's own convictions or beliefs, both allowing the person to express the feelings or ideas most important to him or her and listening in a nonjudgmental way provides what Carl Rogers (1956) termed *unconditional positive regard*. Here, what we mean by this is that anything is permissible to talk about—or to not talk about! As discussed earlier in the book, it also means that someone will be listened to in an empathetic, uncritical manner. For many people, young and old, simply being taken seriously and listened to is a long-forgotten experience. Such an open attitude can provide the dying person with the opportunity to make choices at a very important moment, and give a sense of dignity, control, and importance to his or her decisions and opinions (Kastenbaum, 1978).

Individual Differences in Responses to Death

One of the major themes implicit in this discussion is the recognition of individual differences in views about death, dying, and adjusting to loss. Imposing a number of "shoulds" on someone can only discourage healthy coping responses. For example, wanting to share concerns about one's own or another's death, writing a will, planning a funeral, wishing to die at home, discussing the possibility of euthanasia, and arranging for bodily disposal and the welfare of survivors may be vitally important to both the dying person and his or her family. It is important to communicate that you are able to accept the person on his or her own terms, as an individual.

Being aware of available family or community resources (e.g., Compassionate Friends, Widow to Widow programs) is also an invaluable skill. While some feel that these programs may have a stigmatizing impact on the bereaved, they appear to be a valuable source of comfort and support at a time when such support is scarce. In fact, informal support may be more acceptable than professional help to people who value family or neighborhood ties.

HOSPICE CARE

Within the past decade, **hospice** care for the terminally ill has emerged as a viable alternative to hospital deaths, which are often depersonalizing, lonely, painful experiences for both the dying people and their families.

While the term *hospice* originally referred to a way station for travelers on journeys, today it has come to represent an approach, a concept, or an attitude toward making terminally ill people's lives as full as possible until they die (Kubler-Ross, 1978; Rinaldi & Kearl, 1990). Thus, individuals who are still living can avoid the social death we discussed earlier.

Hospice care, originally popularized in England by Cecily Saunders at St. Christopher's Hospice in London, spread to the United States in the early 1970s, first at New Haven Hospice in New Haven, Connecticut. Since then, literally thousands of hospices have sprung up around the country. While hospices can take on many forms—home-care-based, hospital-based, freestanding units, wholly volunteer—many are set up to care specifically for elderly patients, most of whom have cancer.

Characteristics of hospice care include (1) pain and symptom control, (2) alleviating isolation, (3) physician-directed services, (4) treatment on a 24-hour-per-day basis, for both patient and family, (5) involvement of an interdisciplinary team, (6) bereavement follow-up for the family after death, (7) use of volunteers, and (8) opportunities for staff support of one another, to lessen burnout and facilitate their own grief when a patient dies (Davidson, 1978; Dubois, 1980; Wass, 1989).

While most hospice personnel agree on the philosophical basis of this approach to care, there is less consensus on issues such as the extent of a patient's control over his or her life, the origins of hospice, and the suitability of hospice for all terminally ill patients (Rinaldi & Kearl, 1990). Perhaps this lack of agreement underscores the importance of treating

ADULTS SPEAK

WHAT IS HOSPICE?

What is it about hospice care that is so special? A 29-year-old woman dying of cancer, with perhaps two weeks to live, talked about it:

> Here I am treated as a person. I have a sense of my dignity. Well, I don't mean that, it sounds so proud, but here I am simply myself, and no one minds. I am glad to live each day now, one at a time. I like to nap in the afternoons, but I am so busy here, it is actually hard for me to fit that in. So many people—friends I didn't know cared for me, people I used to work with—have written to me, come to visit me and so forth, now that I am here, and it is all right to say what is happening. (Stoddard, 1980, pp. 4–5)

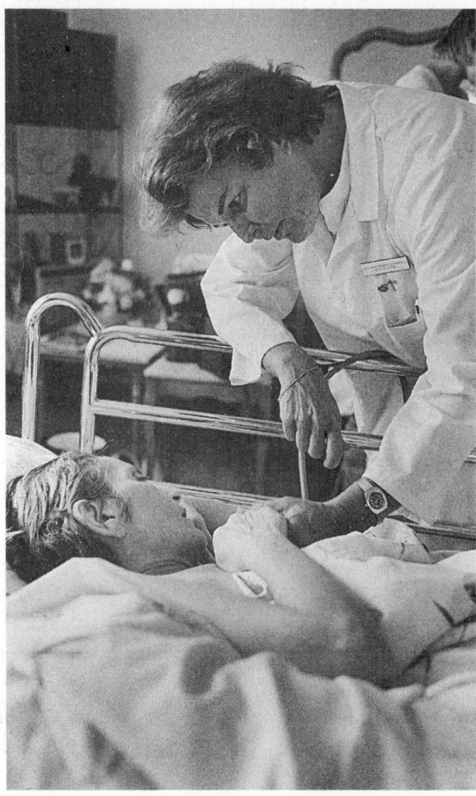

Hospice care emphasizes the quality of life.

every dying patient as an individual. Patients in hospice care have the same rights to quality care (see Box 12.1, above) as do those receiving care in a hospital.

Most important, hospice permits those who are dying to make decisions and exercise control over their lives in a warm, caring, and comparatively pain-free atmosphere. Thus, hospice, in many cases, simply supports each patient and family in making all types of decisions related to family matters, funeral planning, wills, grieving, where death will occur, and most important of all, with whom, under what conditions, and how death will happen.

For the many individuals who value personal control or wish to be close to their loved ones, hospice care is a viable alternative. For others, who perhaps need the security of a hospital or have always depended on others to make decisions for them, hospice would likely be inappropriate. In spite of its emphasis on the dignity and self-worth of the dying person, it is not a panacea for the many problems he or she faces on a daily basis. Furthermore, as Hine (1979–1980) has discussed, the responsibilities associated with hospice home care are not those that all families wish or are able to bear. Hospice deals only with dying people and their families, but perhaps its real value is to teach us all to cherish and nurture our relationships with others while we can.

EUTHANASIA

Euthanasia, literally translated, means "good death" (DeSpelder & Strickland, 1992). Given comparatively recent advances in medical technology that allow for the extension of human life almost indefinitely, concerns about fatal illnesses such as AIDS, Alzheimer's disease, and certain forms of cancer, as well as serious birth defects, have become heightened. The dying person, family members, and physicians may agonize over whose wishes are to be respected if the dying person is near death, in pain, or on life-support machinery. If that person is in a coma or is a newborn, he or she cannot speak up. So, who decides what is to be done? What if the person were to recover from a "fatal" illness or were to come out of a coma? What if a cure were found?

The ethical issues of euthanasia are complex (Hafen & Frandsen, 1983). Some object to **active euthanasia,** defined as taking active measures to end someone's life to relieve needless suffering or to preserve individual dignity. **Passive euthanasia,** defined as failing to use life-saving measures that might prolong someone's life, may be more acceptable. But all forms of euthanasia are equally repulsive to some people, depending on their philosophical or religious beliefs. Yet, terminal care is costly: a family's finances and insurance coverage can be completely sapped over an extended period of time. Furthermore, caring for a dying family member who is suffering can be excruciating.

It is interesting to note that Ward (1980) did not generally find elderly people to favor euthanasia. Those who did tended to be in poorer health, more dissatisfied with their lives, and more anomic—feeling estranged from others. Those who had less formal education and were more religious tended to reject active euthanasia most strongly. Ward postulated that age differences, and thus nearness to death, contributed to fears of death (though they were not measured in his study), while cohort effects influenced acceptance of euthanasia. Older people were less likely to favor it, as were women and nonwhites (Ward, 1980).

The individual who supports euthanasia can state his or her right to die by writing a **living will.** A living will is a directive that impels the physician to cease using artificial means of prolonging life when there is no realistic hope for recovery and allows the individual to die naturally. However, in California, where living wills first became legal in 1976, if more than two weeks have passed since the signer was diagnosed as terminally ill, then the physician is not legally bound to execute the document. In the absence of terminal illness, it may be in force for five years after signing. Should one become terminally ill after this five-year period, and if there is no current living will, the physician can exercise his or her best professional judgment. In such cases, the living will should be reexecuted. It is arranged this way because one might change his or her mind when death is imminent.

Individuals write a living will for many reasons—due to financial pressures and out of the wish to make death and grieving easier or more predictable for oneself or one's family, among others. But fear of prosecution or legal action may cause a physician to refuse to support a patient's wishes or discourage a living will altogether. On the other hand, wanting to speed up the dying process and end suffering, a physician could take matters into his or her own hands. What is dignified or merciful to one person may not be acceptable to another. So, while livings wills are not legally binding in all states, frank, open discussion with one's physician and family can increase the chances of one's wishes being carried out.

Euthanasia is obviously a moral, ethical, and legal-medical gray area. As we discussed at this chapter's outset, what constitutes the legal criteria for death varies from state to state. Thus, no legal penalties await the physician who fails to carry out the patient's wishes, which may conflict with those of the family.

As Hafen and Frandsen (1983) suggest, the arguments for and against euthanasia are many. Several problems complicate each point of view: death isn't usually instantaneous, medical ethics is not well defined, conflicts of interest are inevitable, and ultimately, decisions about the quality, value, or worth of human life are involved. What if euthanasia got out of hand and were used to eliminate "inferior" people? Who decides when to end a life? These issues will continue to be debated, probably for years to come.

A FINAL WORD

Klopfer and David (1977), in a discussion of psychotherapy with the aged, note that "too many [therapists] . . . are seeking for *something to do to their clients,* rather than being concerned about how *to be somebody with them*" (p. 345). It is, perhaps, this essential aloneness, the inability to communicate, that prevents helpers, families, and friends from "getting in touch" with the person who faces life without a husband or wife or who is coping with a terminal illness. This is certainly true for the aged, but it is no less true for younger adults. A respect for the individuality of every life is perhaps the most important quality to recognize and develop in dealing with adults of all ages.

To be permitted to make choices, unhampered by the biases of others, to be told that one's life still counts, is all that many people ask. Being sensitive to these wishes is perhaps the most essential skill we can nurture in helping adults deal with their own deaths, and in counseling those who are coping with the loss of a significant other.

The issues discussed here are those we all face at any age: desiring control over our lives, wanting to be loved and cared for, needing to be treated with respect and dignity as individuals, and perhaps most importantly, appreciating the intertwining of life and death. As Wass and Corr (1981) have so cogently stated,

> We cannot grasp or evaluate the proportions and the significance of life if we do not bring death into the picture. Just as death must be construed through life, so also life must eventually be seen in the context of death. Certainly death is not the only perspective from which to understand life, but . . . it is indispensable as a constitutive element of human existence (p. 7).

SUMMARY

This chapter dealt with a variety of issues pertaining to *death* and *dying* in adulthood. Death can mean many things, and defining death is a complex process that depends on a number of criteria. The understanding of what one means when *fear of death* is stated is also multifaceted. Fear of death is multidimensional and can exist at both conscious and unconscious levels of awareness. Fears about *death* need to be separated from those about the *dying process* or the *afterlife*. In addition to fear, *overcoming* and *participating* are common responses to death among adults.

Death, for the most part, is foreign to the lives of young adults, though terminal illness and loss of a child do affect some young individuals. For middle-aged people, the real possibility of their own deaths and the loss of their parents are the major aspects of death that are confronted. Older people think about death more often than do younger ones, and personalize it more frequently as well. Their responses to death are highly variable but seem to be related to a number of factors, most notably, health status and institutionalization. Loss of a spouse and/or an adult child are the most common ways in which death affects older people.

While *grief* and *bereavement* are distinct from one another, research does not support the notion that older people are more prone to physical or emotional illness or death simply because they are bereaved. Rather, it seems more important to examine factors that influence whether surviving individuals interpret their losses as replaceable. While older widows and widowers may cope with different short- and long-term issues from those of younger ones, loneliness remains the chief problem for all those who are bereaved.

As *Kubler-Ross's* stage theory implies, it is most important, when working with grieving people, to recognize each person's feelings as unique and to deal with each individual in a nonjudgmental manner.

Hospice care has provided many terminally ill individuals and their families with an alternative to dying in an institution. Its chief characteristics are pain/symptom control, 24-hour care, treatment of the patient and family as a unit, and bereavement follow-up.

Euthanasia is a highly controversial area regarding the quality versus quantity of life. Distinctions between *active* and *passive* euthanasia can be made, and there are age, sex, and racial differences regarding its acceptance. While *living wills* have helped structure decisions regarding euthanasia, there remain numerous issues complicating their utility in many situations.

Most important in talking with adults about death is the recognition that each person is a *unique individual.* Open, honest communication that reflects an appreciation for the needs and values of both the dying person and his or her family seems to work best.

KEY TERMS AND CONCEPTS

Clinical death
Brain death
Cerebral death
Social death
Psychic death
Death as loss
Death anxiety
Death versus dying
Overcoming
Participating
Integrity
Life review
Grief versus bereavement
Anticipatory versus acute grief
Regressive intervention
Living will
Unconditional positive regard
Husband sanctification
Secular versus sacred function of funerals
Countertransference
Bereavement overload
SIDS
Denial
Anger
Bargaining
Depression
Acceptance
Personalization of death
Hospice
Grief work
Death as punishment
Death as transition
Disengagement
Principle of compensation
Passive versus active euthanasia
Right to die
Death with dignity
Broken-heart syndrome
Unfinished business
Appropriate death
Unsanctioned grief

REVIEW QUESTIONS

1. What is the basis for the presumed association between aging and death? What are some of the consequences of this association?
2. What approaches have been taken in defining death?
3. When someone says he or she is fearful of death, what might that person mean? What factors are associated with death anxiety? How else might someone respond to death?
4. What are the various meanings of death? What experiences influence them?

5. What is the distinction between grief and bereavement?
6. Are widows and widowers at greater risk as a consequence of being bereaved? What explanations for the phenomenon have been proposed?
7. What are the unique problems bereaved individuals experience? Are there different sets of problems for the young adult versus the older adult?
8. How has Kubler-Ross's work helped us in communicating with the dying? Has it impeded such communication?
9. What skills might one develop in working with others where death and dying are issues?
10. What is hospice care? In what ways does it differ from the hospital in the care of the terminally ill?
11. What are the advantages and disadvantages of a living will?
12. What is the distinction between active and passive euthanasia? Is euthanasia morally wrong?

EPILOGUE

You have now completed your introduction to adulthood and aging. What should you make of all of the information you have gathered? Perhaps we can provide you with a few guideposts to help you organize what you have read. Because each chapter dealt with a somewhat different aspect of adult development, it would be easy for you to lose sight of the fact that changes in each area of our lives are interwoven with changes in other areas. As we discussed in Chapter 1, it would be unusual to observe that what happens to us as young adults is completely independent of events we experience as middle aged or older persons. Likewise, development in certain areas of our lives does have an impact on other aspects of our existence. Our physical development (Chapter 3), for example, influences our relationships with others (Chapter 7) as well as our intellectual and cognitive skills (Chapters 4, 5, 6) and our personality and self image (Chapter 8). Moreover, having a supportive network of family and friends (Chapter 7) is crucial to our well being (Chapter 10), and our well being is often influenced by our experiences in the context of work and retirement (Chapter 9). How we sense and process what happens to us (Chapter 4) is the foundation for most of our experiences and relationships. Of course, we all live with the knowledge that our skills, relationships, careers, and, indeed, all that is important to us will be changed forever when our lives come to an end (Chapter 12). The point we want to make is that our adult lives are quite dynamic and, while we have discussed these various aspects of adult development as if they were separate from one another, in reality we should try to understand our own development as adults as something that is amazingly complex. Rarely do decisions and choices that we make, or fail to make, fail to impact on us in many different ways.

We also want to stress that how your life will play itself out in all its complexity will likely be different from that of your friends, siblings, parents, and grandparents. Each person travels his or her own unique path. As adults, we are constantly being bombarded with what is "normal," and we often forget that what is normal for one person may not necessarily be so for the next. Moreover, what was normal for our parents or grandparents may not apply to us, or to our children, for that matter! There are individual differences in how our lives progress; let us learn from these differences so that we can lead happy, fulfilling, and productive lives.

Last, we want to remind you that although younger and older adults are different in many ways, they nevertheless have much in common. This is especially important because we live in a culture that often pits the young and the old against one another. Kuhn and Bader (1991) have expressed this sense of commonality nicely in the following ways:

1. Both younger and older persons are not often taken seriously.
2. Many younger and older persons are either physically or emotionally dependent and need to be taken care of.
3. Both younger and older adults have trouble in the job market.
4. Both younger and older persons experience significant body changes.
5. Because of our biases about age changes in competence, both younger and older persons are likely to be denied input into decisions that may affect them.
6. Both younger and older persons have a wealth of learning and experience before them . . . and behind them.
7. Both younger and older persons can make a difference in their world. Both are free to initiate social change.

To this we add that both younger and older persons are, will be, or have been: parents, children, workers, caregivers, citizens, lovers, learners, and grievers. Most important, younger and older persons are people with good and bad qualities, strengths and weaknesses, and goals and accomplishments that are important to them. Each lives life as he or she sees it.

Recognizing that our lives are complex, that we do differ from others, yet realizing that we share much in common with those who are younger or older than ourselves can help us to age well. We can set realistic goals for ourselves, learn to cope with stress and change, enjoy our relationships with others, and, perhaps most importantly, be happy.

A P P E N D I X

What Is Your Life Expectancy?

Your life-style choices play a significant role in your overall health and longevity. They are often the key factors in determining whether you develop heart disease, cancer, diabetes, osteoporosis or some other life-threatening condition. If you answer this test honestly, and if you have no obvious symptoms of heart disease, cancer, or diabetes, your answers will give you a fairly good evaluation of your expected longevity. If you don't like what the test predicts about your health, you can take charge and help lower your risks.

Circle the score for each characteristic that applies to you. Total the score, then check your risk category.

FAMILY HISTORY

Choose any that apply.

- −2 Both mother and father were free of cancer and heart disease and lived beyond age 75
- −1 Only one parent was free of cancer and heart disease and lived beyond age 75
- +2 Coronary heart disease before age 50 in one or both parents
- +3 Coronary heart disease before age 40 in one or both parents
- +2 High blood pressure before age 50 in only one parent
- +3 High blood pressure before age 50 in both parents
- +1 Diabetes mellitus before age 60 in one or both parents
- +2 Cancer in a parent or sibling
- +2 Stroke before age 60 in only one parent
- +3 Stroke before age 60 in both parents

WEIGHT

Choose one.

- 0 Normal or within 10% of normal
- +2 Overweight by 20 to 29%
- +3 Overweight by 30 to 39%
- +4 More than 40% overweight

BLOOD PRESSURE

Systolic

Choose one.
−1 100 to 120
0 121 to 140
+1 141 to 170
+2 171 to 190
+3 Over 190

Diastolic

Choose one.
−1 60 to 70
0 71 to 85
+1 86 to 100
+2 101 to 110
+3 111 to 120
+4 Over 120

CHOLESTEROL

Total

Choose one.
−2 150 to 170
−1 171 to 190
0 191 to 210
+1 211 to 240
+2 241 to 280
+3 281 to 320
+4 Over 320

HDL

Choose one.
−2 66 to 80
−1 51 to 65
0 41 to 50
+1 31 to 40
+2 25 to 30
+3 Below 25

SMOKING

Choose any that apply.
−1 Never smoked
−1 Quit over 5 years ago
0 Quit 1 to 5 years ago
+1 Quit within the past year
+2 Smoke less than 1 pack of cigarettes a day
+3 Smoke 1 pack of cigarettes a day
+4 Smoke about 1½ packs of cigarettes a day
+5 Smoke 2 packs of cigarettes a day
+1 Smoke a pipe or cigars
+3 Began smoking as a teenager
+5 Have smoked for more than 20 years
+1 Smoke marijuana 1 or 2 times a week
+2 Smoke marijuana daily
+1 Live *or* work in heavily air-polluted area
+2 Live *and* work in heavily air-polluted area

ALCOHOL USE

Choose any that apply.
−1 Drink no more than 1½ ounces of hard liquor, 12 ounces of beer, or 5 ounces of wine once or twice a week

0 Drink almost every day but not more than 1½ ounces of hard liquor, 12 ounces of beer, or 5 ounces of wine a day
+1 Drink two drinks each day totalling 3 ounces of hard liquor, 24 ounces of beer, or 10 ounces of wine
+2 Drink more than two drinks each day
+5 Smoke cigarettes, pipe, or cigar, *and* drink alcohol at least several times a week

PERSONALITY AND STRESS EVALUATION

Choose any that apply.
+1 Intense desires to get ahead
+2 Constant driving need for success
+2 Easily irritated, annoyed, or frustrated
+2 Angry and hostile if losing in competition
+2 Fiercely competitive; must win
+3 Angry and hostile, even if successful
+1 Have many projects going on at once
+1 Constantly bothered by incomplete work
+2 Don't express anger; hold feelings inside
+2 Work hard without feeling satisfaction
+2 Frequent stress symptoms—knot in stomach, heart palpitations, headaches, poor sleep, intestinal symptoms, constipation
+2 Hardly laugh; depressed often
+2 Rarely discuss problems or feelings with others
+2 Constantly strive to please others rather than yourself
−1 None of the above

EXERCISE

Choose one in each group, then calculate your score for this section as indicated.

Frequency of exercise:
+5 Daily or almost daily
+4 3 to 5 times a week
+3 1 to 2 times a week
+2 2 to 3 times a month
+1 Less than 3 times a month

Duration of each exercise period:
+4 More than 45 minutes
+3 20 to 40 minutes
+2 10 to 20 minutes
+1 Less than 10 minutes

Intensity of each exercise period:
+5 Sustained vigorous exercise
+4 Intermittent vigorous exercise

+3 Moderately vigorous exercise
+2 Moderately non-vigorous exercise
+1 Light, leisurely activity

To determine your fitness rating, multiply your score for each section.

$$\underset{\text{Intensity}}{\underline{\qquad}} \times \underset{\text{Duration}}{\underline{\qquad}} \times \underset{\text{Frequency}}{\underline{\qquad}} = \underset{\text{Score}}{\underline{\qquad}}$$

For example: $3 \times 4 \times 3 = 36$. The maximum is 100. Use your answer to determine your physical fitness rating below.

PHYSICAL FITNESS RATING

Choose one.
−2 81–100 is very active, high fitness
−1 61–80 is active and healthy
0 41–60 is acceptable and good
+1 31–40 is not good enough
+2 21–30 is inadequate
+3 20 and below is sedentary, poor fitness

DIETARY HABITS

Choose any that apply.
+2 Use salt freely, without tasting food first
+2 Eat cabbage, broccoli, or cauliflower less than 3 times a week
+3 Eat high-fiber grains, such as whole-wheat bread, brown rice, and bran cereal, less than once a day
+3 Eat fewer than 3 fruits and vegetables a day
+1 Follow a fad weight-loss diet once or twice a year

Eat heartily at meals, and snack between meals:
+3 Daily or almost daily
+2 4 days a week
+1 2 days a week

Eat beef, bacon, or processed meats:
+3 5 to 6 times a week
+2 4 times a week
+1 2 times a week

Eat eggs, alone or in other foods:
+3 12 eggs a week
+2 8 eggs a week
+1 6 eggs a week

Eat ice cream, cake, or rich desserts:
+2 Almost every day
+1 Several times a week

Eat butter, cream, cream cheese, and cheese:
+3 Every day
+2 Almost every day
+1 2 to 3 times a week

SEX AND PHYSICAL BUILD

Choose one.
0 Male, with slim build
+1 Male, heavily muscled, with stocky build
+3 Female, take birth-control pills, and smoke
+1 Female, post-menopausal, and take estrogen
0 Female, take birth-control pills, and don't smoke
0 Female, post-menopausal, and don't take estrogen

INTERPRETING YOUR SCORE

To determine your score, add all scores from the categories. Check your total score below to see if your health and your life are at risk.

−15 **Lowest Risk**—This is the best possible score. You should enjoy a long, healthy life free of cancer, heart disease, stroke, or diabetes.

−14 to +6 **Low Risk**—You are in very good health; odds are in your favor of continued good health and a long, productive life free of cancer, heart disease, diabetes, and stroke. If you wish to improve your odds, check the test to see where you gained points. If possible, work on improving those areas.

7 to 11 **Moderate Risk**—You are at some risk of developing ill health and can expect to live an average life span. Try to correct conditions or habits for which you scored a 2, 3, or 4, and you may help add years to your life. Stop smoking, if you smoke, and follow the risk-reducing nutrition plan and risk-reducing exercise plan. These will help lower your risks.

12 to 20 **High Risk**—Your risk of developing a life-threatening illness early in life and dying sooner than you should is considerable. You can help lower your risks by correcting conditions for which you scored a 2, 3, or 4. Stop smoking, if you smoke, and follow the risk-reducing nutrition plan and the risk-reducing exercise plan to help lower your risks.

21+ **Very High Risk**—Your health is at dangerous risk, and you may die prematurely if you don't change your ways immediately to begin to correct your unhealthy habits. Seek medical advice and psychological therapy to help you change your habits. Stop smoking, if you smoke, and follow the risk-reducing nutrition plan and the risk-reducing exercise plan to help lower your risks.

Source: Howard, E. J. (1986). *Health Risks.* Tucson, AZ: Body Press, pp. 7–12.

G L O S S A R Y

Abnormal behavior Behavior that is at odds with reality or injurious to oneself or others.

Absolute stability Stability of means or averages over time.

Absolute threshold The minimum level of stimulus energy/intensity required for the individual to detect stimulation.

Accommodation The process whereby the eye adjusts itself to attain maximal image resolution (clarity).

Accommodation versus assimilation Piagetian styles of interacting with the environment. Accommodation involves changing one's behavior to fit the environment, while assimilation involves changing the environment to suit one's behavior.

Active euthanasia Doing something to cut life short for those who are in pain or suffering. Failing to do something (passive) that would otherwise extend life.

Active leisure activity Refers to activities such as exercising, jogging, playing sports, or going to restaurants. The primary focus of these leisure activities is active "doing" and/or participation.

Active mastery A style of relating to the environment that changes with age in different ways for men and women, according to Guttman. Imposing oneself on the environment to change it.

Active versus passive role of the organism Developmental issue concerned with whether the developing organism plays an active or a passive role in its own developmental process.

Activity theory Theory that suggests that the older individual who manages to resist withdrawal from the social world and remains active will maintain life satisfaction.

Adaptation The change in sensitivity of the eye as a function of change in illumination. There are two types: dark adaptation—improvement in sensitivity to light in a dark environment; and light adaptation—increased sensitivity to light in a light environment.

Adaptation level The process whereby individual receptor processes (hearing, vision) tend to function at a comfortable level relative to the external stimulation, so that a stimulus of a given magnitude is perceived as neither strong nor weak.

Age credit Adding IQ points to the score of an older person under the assumption of age decline to equate that person's average score with that of someone younger.

Age debit Subtracting IQ points from the score of a younger person under the assumption of age decline to equate that person's score with that of someone older.

Age Discrimination in Employment Act (ADEA) Federal law enacted in 1967 to prohibit age discrimination in employment. Amended in 1974 and 1978 to provide more comprehensive coverage.

Age function A statement of the relationship between a given variable and chronological age.

Ageism Discrimination or bias against persons due to their age.

Ageism in employment Discrimination against workers on the basis of their age.

Age-normative influences Factors that are general to development, are highly related to chronological age, and are presumed to affect everyone of a given chronological age range similarly.

Aging The biological, psychological, and sociological aspects of growth and development across the life span.

Aging as illness model A variation of the medical model ascribing aging-related changes (decrements) to physical causes.

Aging process The process of aging emphasizing change. The aging process is complex and affected by many biological, psychological, sociological, and environmental factors.

Alzheimer's disease A form of dementia characterized by a higher than normal incidence of senile plaques and neurofibrillary tangles in brain tissue.

Androgyny Refers to a change in the traditional gender roles associated with males and females toward the integration of the characteristics, traits, and behaviors of both genders.

Anticipation interval The time interval taken to encode and rehearse a paired-associate prior to the next item-pair.

Anticipatory grief Preparation or rehearsal for death prior to its actual occurrence.

Anxiety A sense of impending dread or apprehension that is amorphous in character.

Arteriosclerosis Progressive hardening of blood vessel walls with age.

Atherosclerosis Progressive narrowing of blood vessel walls with age.

Attachment An emotional bond that develops between children and their parents. Often viewed as the foundation upon which other interpersonal relationships are built.

Audition The hearing sense.

Auditory training A procedure used by individuals with hearing impairments to comprehend what others are saying. Involves attending to certain key sounds and words in the conversation while at the same time watching the speaker's lips move.

Baby boom period The period from approximately 1940 to 1957 during which there was a high birthrate in the United States.

Beck Depression Inventory A widely used test for the diagnosis of depression in adulthood.

Behavior therapy Form of therapy where rewarding and punishing stimuli in the environment are manipulated to bring about a desired behavior(s).

Behavioral model Approach to personality and mental illness emphasizing behavioral responses to distinct situations that vary in their requirements for adaptive behavior.

Bereavement overload The inability to work through the deaths of loved ones that occur close to one another in time.

Bifactorial designs Baltes's two factor (age and cohort) approach to describing developmental change.

Biographical life events One of Buhler's dimensions of change that is experiential and stable.

Biological age Biological age has two aspects. It can be considered to be the relative age or condition of the individual's organ and body systems. Also, it refers to individuals' present position relative to their potential life span, which varies from species to species.

Biological death The cessation of function or irreversible damage to certain critical organs or organ systems.

Biological life events One of Buhler's dimensions of change that is independent of experience and declines with age.

Bipolar vs. unipolar depression Depression characterized by mood swings (bipolar) versus predominately sad affect (feeling low) (unipolar).

Bona fide occupational qualification (BFOQ) An ability, trait, or factor that is considered to be related to job performance.

Brain death Death via the cessation of higher order brain activity.

Brain plasticity The capacity of the brain to regenerate or compensate for losses in brain cells.

Career A planned, coherent, organized sequence of positions that have meaning for the individual.

Career crisis in midlife During midlife a number of individuals become dissatisfied with their current occupation, which often leads to stress.

Career indecision The inability to choose a particular occupation, or difficulty in deciding whether to change occupations or remain in the same occupation.

Cautiousness Being conservative in decision making and with respect to many aspects of behavior.

Central explanations for RT slowdown Central (brain and spinal cord) explanations for reaction time (RT) view the slowdown in behavior/performance with age as being due to some higher level internal process.

Cerebral death The cessation of brain activity for a given period of time (e.g., 24 hrs.), often termed brain death.

Childless marriage A marriage in which both partners decide not to have children. This decision can be based on a number of reasons such as personal concerns, economic costs, and career demands.

Clinical death The cessation of spontaneous heart and respiratory activity.

Cognitive behavior therapy Form of therapy emphasizing internal cognitions or ideas about oneself or the environment as key concepts in bringing about behavior change.

Cognitive personality theory Approach to personality emphasizing one's perceptions or cognitions about experiences or events.

Cognitive versus noncognitive influences Referring to the distinction between factors (noncognitive) that influence performance on tests of learning or memory (e.g., fatigue) and those processes that the tests are designed to reflect (i.e., cognition [learning, memory]).

Cohort A group of individuals sharing a common set of experiences (e.g., individuals born at a given point in history who, by virtue of their birth data, experience certain sets of events at roughly the same time in their development).

Cohort/generation effects Sociocultural influences that are particular to a group of persons sharing a common set of experiences due to being born at a certain point in history.

Cohort sequential Developmental design permitting the separation of age and cohort effects, where time of measurement is confounded.

Collagen A fibrous protein present in connective tissue (ligaments, muscles, joints, bones).

Colleague marriage In the colleague marriage, the partners recognize role and responsibility differences. Each partner assumes responsibility and authority for specific duties and tasks within the family, and these are generally stable, rather than constantly changing.

Color vision The faculty by which colors are perceived and distinguished.

Companionship marriage A marriage in which there is no differentiation between male and female roles. Each partner can take on the rights, obligations, and duties of the other. In fact, each may exchange duties and responsibilities with the other on some prearranged agreement (e.g., each week or month).

Competition at recall When old S-R associations interfere with the learning of new associations.

Complementarity Theory of mate selection that suggests that opposites attract.

Complexity explanation for RT Central theory used to explain response slowing with age. Views the psychomotor slowdown with increasing age as due to the increased difficulty of older adults to respond as tasks become more complex.

Confidant One with whom intimate moments, secrets, etc., can be shared, who provides emotional support through life.

Confounding When the effects of at least two factors cannot be disentangled, they are said to be confounded.

Convoy Personal network of friends and family members who accompany us throughout the life cycle.

Core Core constructs are central overriding ideas or assumptions about personality, according to Maddi.

Correlation vs. causation The distinction between relationships among variables that descriptively covary with one another (correlation) versus statements that explain the influence of one variable on another (causation).

Countertransference The difficulties experienced by a younger therapist who is treating an older client (e.g., feelings about one's parents may be projected upon the older client).

Crossover effect The fact that for more recent cohorts black females' life expectancy will exceed that of white males.

Cross-sectional Design in which the behavior or performance of several groups of persons who differ in age, sex, etc., are compared at one point in time.

Cross-sectional sequences A design within P. B. Baltes's bifactorial model where at least two independent cross-sectional age samples are drawn at each level of cohort.

Cross sequential Developmental design permitting the separation of time of measurement and cohort effects, where age is confounded.

Crystallized ability Acculturated skills that build upon one another and remain stable across most of adulthood.

Cult of the adult Refers to the period of the 1980s in the United States during which society believed that you could be over 30 and still enjoy life.

Cult of the aged Refers to the Colonial period in America during which it was considered acceptable and positive to be old. Older adults were viewed with respect and occupied places of honor, prestige, and leadership in society and business.

Cult of the young Refers to the period of the 1960s in America when being young was considered good and positive, and being old was considered bad and negative.

Cultural ethics Prevailing attitudes of a society at a particular point in time that determine how individuals view their relationship with society and others at all points in the life span.

Custodial grandparents Grandparents who have assumed parental responsibility for a grandchild.

Death anxiety Fear of death, dying, or the afterlife that may or may not be consciously expressed.

Death versus dying The moment of death versus the process of days' or weeks' duration leading up to death.

Death with dignity Death that is "appropriate" (of the individual's choosing) and that preserves the person's sense of respect and honor.

Decision making The ability to make or the process of making decisions—may be affected by personal characteristics or task demands.

Decision/premotor time In a perceptual-motor reaction time task, the time lapsed from the onset of the stimulus to the initiation of the response to that stimulus.

Decrement with compensation model Model of aging emphasizing interventions that can compensate for age-related declines in functioning.

Deep friendships Friendships based on intimate feelings between individuals.

Deep processing Material that is encoded at the meaning level is deeply processed.

Dementia A cluster of behaviors or characteristics (e.g., disorientation) common to many diagnostic entities ranging from depression to Alzheimer's disease.

Depressive equivalent A form of depression whereby persons complain of physical ailments, etc., yet consciously deny that they feel depressed.

Determinism versus nondeterminism The issue of whether one's behavior is dictated by various factors (e.g., heredity, past experience) or whether behavior is independent (free) of these controlling factors.

Developmental stages Developmental issue that revolves around the question of whether higher order behaviors and activities, such as motor skills or cognitive skills, develop in a qualitative manner, incorporating earlier (preceding) and simpler forms of behavior (stages of development).

Developmental tasks Behaviors, activities, skills, or milestones that individuals are expected to accomplish by their culture during specific stages of the life cycle. For instance, in our culture these include activities for the adult such as obtaining a driver's license and voting.

Developmental versus nondevelopmental research Developmental research seeks to explore relationships between age (or age-related factors) and some variable of interest. Nondevelopmental research, on the other hand, explores relationships between variables that are age-irrelevant.

Deviation IQ A method of computing an intelligence quotient based upon deviations from the mean.

Dialectical operations Theory of Riegel that suggests internal factors (genetically preprogrammed instinctual behaviors, traits, characteristics, physiological state) and external factors (aspects of the physical environment, cultural components) continuously influence and are influenced by each other.

Difference threshold The degree to which a stimulus (e.g., sound, light) must be louder or brighter to be perceived as such.

Differential stability Stability of individual differences over time.

Differentiation of abilities The hypothesis that the relationship between distinct abilities becomes more differentiated or spreads out (lessens) with age.

Disengagement theory Theory that suggests that with increasing age individuals withdraw (disengage) from society and society withdraws (disengages) from the individual. There are two types of disengagement, psychological and social. The theory has been reformulated to account for individual differences.

Double jeopardy The notion that the black aged suffer a dual cultural disadvantage because they are both old and black.

DSM-III-R The *Diagnostic and Statistical Manual* of the American Psychiatric Association. It serves as the major framework for the classification and treatment of mental disorders in the United States today.

Ecological validity Refers to the ability of tasks or tests to reflect everyday requirements (e.g., the real-life ecology of learning).

Ecology of mental health Applying real-world criteria in defining mental health for adults of varying ages.

Elder abuse Psychological, physical, or financial neglect or active harm of older persons by others.

Empty nest Refers to the time when all the children have left the home. Its impact may be positive or negative.

Encoding The interpretation or giving of meaning to information so that it may be stored and retrieved.

Errors of omission versus errors of commission On numerous real-world and laboratory tasks the performance of older adults is marked by more errors of omission (omitting an answer) than errors of commission (giving an incorrect answer). Often interpreted as an indication of cautiousness.

Everyday intelligence Intelligence applied to everyday cognitive functioning that is adaptive.

Exchange theory Theory that has been adapted to help explain negative attitudes toward aging. Suggests individuals attempt to maximize rewards and reduce costs in interpersonal relationships.

Exercised versus unexercised abilities Denny's notion that abilities maintain themselves with age if they are used; those that are not used (unexercised) decline.

Existential questioning Self-examination of the meaning of one's existence.

Expectancy/set theory Central theory used to explain response slowing with age. Views the slowdown in responding with age as the result of older individuals' inability or difficulty in preparing their response to a stimulus.

Experimental versus control group The experimental group is typically the one that is the object of a treatment program or manipulation. The control group generally lacks such a treatment and serves as a baseline against which the effects of the treatment can be measured.

Experimental versus correlational approach Two approaches to research, one of which emphasizes control and the manipulation of independent-dependent variable relationships (experimental), while the other emphasizes corelationships between variables, where inferences about causality are not possible (correlational).

Explicit versus implicit memory Explicit memory requires purposeful effort to recall information while implicit memory involves the casual if not unintentional acquisition of seemingly irrelevant information in the process of learning a task.

Exposure factor Term used in the study of accidents. Refers to amount of time individual is in a situation when an accident can occur—for example, number of miles driven or number of hours worked.

Extended family Close relatives such as aunts, uncles, cousins, and grandparents. See *kinship network.*

External validity The extent to which the results of a study generalize to other samples, tests, procedures, etc.

Extrinsic factors related to sexual behavior External, environmental, and/or social factors that affect an individual's sexual behavior. These include factors such as religious beliefs and cultural attitudes.

Factor analysis Statistical technique to reduce a matrix of intercorrelations among variables down to fewer factors that are more interpretable.

False negatives Error of diagnosis where a disorder is diagnosed as absent when it is, in fact, present.

False positives Error of diagnosis where a disorder is falsely diagnosed as present when it is not (false positive).

Family systems theory An approach to understanding and treating families that emphasizes the entire family as a system of interrelating individuals.

Field dependence/independence A construct developed to explain individual differences in perception. Persons who are field dependent make judgments that are heavily influenced by the surrounding, immediate environment, while field independent persons' judgments are not influenced by the immediate environment.

Filial maturity When adult children no longer view their parents as only parents but as real people who need their help.

Filial responsibility Refers to the perceived obligation (frequently determined by law, custom, or personal preference) with regard to the various types of services and social support that children should provide for their older parents.

Filter theory of mate selection Theory of mate selection that suggests that in selecting a mate people do so via the use of a hierarchical set of "filters." The person who passes through each of these filters is the person we marry.

Flexible careers Careers or occupations that allow the individual flexibility in working hours, working days, etc.

Fluid ability Cognitive skills that are independent of acculturated influences and that decline with increased age.

Functional ability An individual's ability to care for himself/herself or the ability to cope in a given situation.

Functional age (industrial) Judging workers on their ability to function or perform a job adequately as opposed to their chronological age.

Functional analysis An analysis of an individual's behavior in relation to the function it serves in managing the environment.

Functional (definition of age) An index of a person's level of capacities or abilities relative to those of others of similar age.

Functional disorders Behavioral changes that are problematic, whose causes can be attributed to psychogenic versus organic factors. Functional disorders can coexist with organicity.

Gender roles Those behavior patterns (culture specific) that are considered appropriate and often specific to each gender, which are formed (acquired) early in life and are maintained until death.

General adaptation syndrome Selye's notion of the body's three-phase reaction to stress or illness (alarm, resistance, exhaustion).

Generalizability The dimension(s) along which the results of a study might be externally valid (e.g., generalization to other samples, tasks, or procedures).

Genetic biological theories of aging Theories of aging that emphasize the formation of genetic structures as explanations for the aging process.

Genotypic continuity Genotypic continuity suggests that persons with certain clusters of traits change in certain ways.

Glare sensitivity Sensitivity to bright light that results in unpleasantness or discomfort and/or that interferes with optimum vision.

Global perception Perception based on a response to the "whole" stimulus rather than the separate parts of the stimulus.

Grandparental styles Modes of interacting with one's adult children and grandchildren (e.g., formal versus involved styles) and the meaning attached to the grandparent role.

"Graying" of the American work force Refers to the fact that more and more individuals are remaining on the job for a longer time. Therefore, the average age of the average worker is increasing.

Grief versus bereavement Grief refers to the expression of feelings about a loss, while bereavement simply indicates that one has experienced a loss.

Group marriage A marriage in which a number of couples are legally married in a traditional manner (a husband and a wife), but these individuals share living arrangements, duties, responsibilities, and sexual partners.

Group therapy A form of therapy where individuals in a group setting share experiences under the guidance of a group leader.

History-normative influences Factors or events that occur at a specific point in time (day, year, month) and theoretically impart upon everyone in that society or culture.

Homogeneous versus heterogeneous samples Persons who are to a large extent like one another define a homogeneous sample; heterogeneous samples are composed of persons who are very different from one another.

Homosexual partnership A relationship where two gay individuals make a personal commitment to each other to live together as married partners. Each partner shares or takes individual responsibility for specific roles and duties within the relationship.

Horizontal career move A move from one career to another.

Hospice A philosophy of caring for the terminally ill and their families emphasizing individualized care over cure and bereavement counseling.

Hypothetical constructs Ideas, definitions, and concepts that only have meaning and relevance within a particular theory. They do not have any physical or material existence outside the theory.

Identity style One's style of interacting with others that influences self-concept and self-esteem.

Illusion of absolute safety Gould's concept stressing the false myth of safety learned during childhood, that one eventually gives up in adulthood.

Implicit versus explicit theories of intelligence Implicit theories of intelligence refer to ideas about what intelligence is, while explicit theories refer to the abilities we use when we behave intelligently.

Independent versus dependent samples In a cross-sectional study, persons in different age-groups are selected independently of one another. In a longitudinal study, however, samples at later points in time are dependent upon those with which the study began.

Independent versus dependent variables Independent variables are those that are manipulated by the experimenter. Dependent variables' effects depend upon some manipulation of the independent variable.

Indirect self-destructive behavior (ISDB) Taking one's life covertly or indirectly within an institution by becoming combative, not taking medication, not eating, etc.

Individual differences Refers to differences between persons on any trait, behavior, ability, or performance skill at any given point in time. See *interindividual differences.*

Informal role types According to Rosow, informal role types assume no institutional status but have definite roles attached to them. These include family scapegoat, heroes, criminals, etc.

Information overload Central theory used to explain response slowing with age. Assumes that as stimulus information from the environment increases, the individual's information processing systems may be overloaded and consequently will not be able to perform quickly and correctly.

Information processing approach to aging A framework within which to structure the implications of age changes in various abilities. This approach suggests that once a person has received stimulation from the environment, this stimulation (information) must pass through four distinct information processing stages before a response in the form of observable behavior occurs. A breakdown in function in any of these stages can affect the relationship between stimuli (input) and responses (output).

Informed consent The process by which a research participant voluntarily agrees to participate in a study, having been fully informed of the risks and benefits associated with such participation.

Inspection intervals In a paired associates task, the inspection interval is the lapse of time taken to inspect (read) the item pair.

Institutional role types According to Rosow, an institutional role type assumes a given status for a person who has defined roles. These include such factors as social class, gender, race, and age.

Instrumental leisure activity Leisure activity that is in the service of attaining a goal or producing a result.

Integrity A sense of completeness about one's life characterized by an acceptance of death (Erikson).

Intellectual plasticity The view that suggests older adults' intellectual skills are quite plastic or malleable with training or intervention.

Intelligence General index of an individual's ability to behave intelligently in situations or in tests designed to elicit such behaviors.

Interdependence Referring to the interrelatedness of events in our lives. Each influences and is influenced by the other.

Interest-related friendships Friendships that are based on some similarity of life-style or interest. These may include plants, pets, hobbies, or sports.

Interference The process by which learning or memory is interfered with via unlearning (new associations interfere with already learned ones) or competition at recall (where new and old associations compete or interfere with one another).

Interindividual differences Refers to differences between persons on any trait, behavior, ability, or performance skill at any given point in time. See *individual differences.*

Interiority Neugarten's term for the tendency to become preoccupied with one's inner experiences (intrapsychic level) with increased age.

Internal validity Validity as it applies to independent-dependent variable relationships (i.e., that only the independent variable is casually related to the dependent variable).

Interpersonal relationships Relationships with others. These include friends, spouse, family members, and so forth.

Intraindividual changes Refers to changes within an individual over time on any trait, behavior, ability, or performance skill.

Intraindividual differences Refers to differences between traits, behaviors, abilities, or performance levels within a person at any one point in time.

Intrapsychic Refers to internal personality dynamics.

Intrinsic factors related to sexual behavior Biological-physiological changes in the body structures and organ systems that are part of the normal aging processes and are related to sexual behavior.

Intrinsic leisure activity Intrinsic leisure activities are those that are inherently satisfying to the individual.

Intrinsic (primary) versus extrinsic (secondary) influences on life expectancy Intrinsic factors (e.g., genetic inheritance, race) contribute directly to life expectancy, while extrinsic factors' (smoking, exercise) influence on life expectancy is indirect.

IQ An index of an individual's ability to perform on a test of intelligence, relative to age peers.

Irreversible decrement model Model of aging emphasizing the parallel between biological decline and social-psychological change.

Job loss The loss of one's position due to a number of factors. These include factory closing, a position being phased out, or being replaced by industrial robots, etc.

Kinship network The extended family—aunts, uncles, and cousins. See *extended family.*

Knowledge acquisition components Aspects of intelligence that help us gain new knowledge.

Learned helplessness The perception that the correlation between one's behavior and desired outcomes is minimal.

Learning Learning is the acquisition of information and facts via experience.

Legal age The age, defined by law, governing certain behaviors or responsibilities (e.g., drinking, voting, service in the military, being legally responsible for damages one might cause).

Leisure Typically refers to a person's activities during free time. Leisure can include work or may simply be a state of mind.

Leisure competence The development of satisfying leisure activities—implies understanding the meaning of leisure for you personally.

Leisure life-styles Patterns of activity among retirees. Researchers classify these individuals into categories on the basis of their primary leisure activities.

Lethality scale A method of assessing potential suicide risk via gathering information about age, sex, etc.

Life expectancy How long on the average one is expected to live; it is species specific.

Life review The internal process by which the individual comes to terms with crises, problems, conflicts, etc., in an effort to make sense out of personal life experiences via reminiscence.

Life satisfaction Overall perception or feeling about the quality of one's life.

Life-span developmental model A view that sees development as the result of an interdependence between internal and external factors throughout the course of the life span.

Life structure Levinson's concept emphasizing the overall plan of one's life, composed of many interrelated aspects (e.g., work vs. family).

Life tendencies Buhler's set of motivating forces that organize behavior at various points in one's development.

Line of unbearability One's personal equation governing suicide as an end to life where life's quality is emphasized over its quantity.

Lipofuscin Aging pigment that accumulates in certain organ systems with age.

Living will A provision by which the individual directs the physician or family not to needlessly sustain that individual's life if such acts would prolong suffering.

Locus of control Our orientation to the environment in terms of the extent of control we expect to have over it.

Longevity The theoretical upper limit of the life span; it is species specific.

Longitudinal design Study in which the changes in behavior or performance of a group of persons is studied by repeatedly assessing them at several points in time.

Longitudinal sequences A design within P. B. Baltes's bifactorial model where at least two dependent samples of cohorts are followed at several (at least two) levels of age.

Maturational ground plan The biologically determined sequence one progresses through, according to Erikson's psychosocial stages.

Mechanics versus pragmatics of intelligence Distinction by P. B. Baltes emphasizing basic fundamental intellectual skills (mechanics) versus the use of intellectual skills that are more applied or adaptive (e.g., wisdom) (pragmatics).

Mechanistic model Stimulus-response or behavioral models of development. Human development is seen as progressive, continuous, quantitative improvement in the levels of abilities and behavior.

Medical model Model of abnormal behavior emphasizing distinct diagnostic categories with presumed physical causes.

Memory The storage and retrieval of facts over time. May also be defined functionally.

Menopause The cessation of menstruation and the ability to bear children. Usually occurs in one's late forties or early fifties.

Mental age An index of an individual's having accumulated a certain degree of age credits (in months) relative to chronological age to yield an IQ.

Mental health/mental illness The concept of adjustment lying on a continuum emphasizing the presence of adaptive qualities (mental health) or their absence, implying the presence of maladaptive qualities (mental illness).

Mental-health system The system of inpatient, outpatient, formal, and informal mental-health service providers.

Mental status questionnaire Screening instrument composed of questions regarding orientation to time and place (e.g., one's residence, month, day, year, etc.) designed to identify individuals who may have some form of organicity.

Mentor One who guides or advises another in terms of either occupational or personal goals, behaviors, etc.

Metacomponents Aspects of intelligence that help us make decisions and adapt to the environment.

Metamemory One's memory for what is in one's memory, to include self-assessment or self-estimates of one's memory capacity or efficiency.

Midlife crisis A personal sense of upheaval experienced by some men and women in their forties, fifties, and sixties.

Milieu therapy A form of therapy often used within institutions where all aspects of the interpersonal environment are changed to facilitate the individual's adaptation or adjustment (e.g., interactions with staff).

Mnemonic devices Referring to a variety of techniques by which learning and memory performance may be improved.

Motor-cognitive rigidity Refers to the degree to which an individual can shift without difficulty from one activity to another.

Motor time In a perceptual-motor reaction time task, the time lapse from the initiation of the response to the stimulus to the completion of that response. Sometimes called *movement time.*

Multidimensional change Refers to numerous changes in different types of ability, skill, and behavior simultaneously within an individual over time.

Multidirectional change Numerous behaviors and traits that exhibit different types of change (e.g., increases and decreases in functioning) along the course of development.

Multi-infarct dementia Dementia produced by small strokes producing clusters of dead neurons or infarcts that create disturbances in the flow of blood to the brain.

Myth A belief based more on fiction or imagination than fact.

Nature versus nurture Developmental issue concerned with whether development is the result of genetically determined hereditary forces (nature), or of learning and/or other environmental influences (nurture).

Negative versus positive transfer Negative transfer occurs when two tasks interfere with each other's learning or recall, whereas positive transfer occurs when each task facilitates the other.

Neural noise Central theory used to explain response slowing with age. It is thought to be either random background neural activity or irregularities in the action of the cells carrying the signals that interfere with information passing from one part of the brain to another.

Neurofibrillary tangles Intertwined nerve fibers that interfere with brain cell function.

Neurotransmitter substances Various chemicals (e.g., acetylcholine) that make possible communication across synapses between brain cells.

Noise Background interference. Stimuli that interfere with the individual's ability to detect a relevant signal or stimulus.

Nongenetic biological theories of aging Theories of aging that emphasize changes in cells and tissues with age after they have been formed.

Nonnormative influences Factors that are not related to age or history and that affect specific individuals during the life cycle. These factors cannot be attributed to the normal process of development or to the impact of environmental, cultural-societal events.

Nontraditional student Student who is older than the "traditional" 18 to 22-year-old, often involved in very diverse forms of adult education.

Normal versus pathological aging Normal aging occurs in the absence of disease, while pathological aging is caused by disease. This distinction is similar to that between primary and secondary aging.

Nuclear family The traditional nuclear family in American society is one in which there is a husband, wife, and children.

Occupational development Refers to the selection and choice of an occupation during the life course. Often called *career development.*

Occupational developmental tasks The particular goals, activities, or skills associated with a specific occupation.

Occupational role The behaviors, status, and traits associated with a specific occupation. Occupations vary in terms of the expectancies of society and others with regard to behaviors and activities.

Old age dependency ratio The ratio of older persons who are receiving retirement or health care benefits relative to the number of younger person whose earnings support such funds.

Older worker Designation varies substantially as a function of specific occupation. It can be applied as early as age 40.

Open marriage A marriage that is based on a legally sanctioned union between a husband and a wife, but in which partners feel it is perfectly acceptable to have intimate and/or sexual relations with other partners.

Organic brain syndrome General term implying that some structural organic change is responsible for one's behavior. Often termed *dementia.*

Organismic model Views the course of development as being genetically programmed. Development is seen as qualitative and progresses through a series of discontinuous stages.

Orthogenetic principle Suggests that the perception of shapes, forms, objects, and stimuli follows a specific and predictable life-span trend. Early in life children perceive the world in a diffuse or global manner; as they get older, they learn to integrate the parts of the stimulus pattern with the whole stimulus pattern simultaneously in relation to each other.

Osteoporosis The process of our bones hardening or becoming brittle with age, linked to a reduction of bony material. This results in greater fragility, and is related to a deficit in calcium.

Outer, middle, inner ears Sections of the ear (see Chapter 4). Changes in the inner ear, and to a lesser extent in the middle ear, are responsible for losses in hearing with age.

Overcoming A style of dealing with death that emphasizes death as failure.

Paired associates task Task where the learner is to associate and recall certain stimuli (S) that have been paired with specific responses (R).

Paradoxical directives Suggestions by the therapist to the client not to engage in a behavior designed to reveal its self-defeating nature and establish control over that behavior.

Paranoia Feelings of persecution or suspiciousness.

Paraphrenia Term given to schizophrenia when it appears for the first time in later life.

Parental imperative The notion that biological and cultural factors cause men and women to suppress certain behaviors or characteristics. When the demands of parenthood cease, these suppressed characteristics can surface.

Participating A style of dealing with death that emphasizes the interrelatedness of life and death as natural partners.

Passive euthanasia Failing to do something that would otherwise extend the life of a terminally ill person.

Passive leisure activity Refers to activities such as reading or watching television in the home.

Passive mastery A style of coping that emphasizes the molding of oneself to the environment that varies by age and sex, according to Guttman.

Pattern recognition Involves recognizing a specific stimulus pattern from a group of stimulus patterns or displays.

Perception The interpretation of sensory stimulation.

Perceptual inference Theory that suggests that older adults do not utilize incomplete information as effectively as young adults.

Perceptual information processing model Model of driving behavior that suggests the abilities of perceptual style, selective attention, and perceptual motor reaction time are related to behavior or performance.

Perceptual information processing tasks Laboratory tasks that serve as a method of accurately determining the condition and efficiency of our perceptual processes. These include tasks such as geometric illusions.

Perceptual-motor reaction time A reaction time task.

Perceptual noise theory Central theory used to explain response slowing with age. Views slowdown in performance as due to an age decrement in ability to suppress irrelevant stimuli.

Performance components Various mental operations such as making comparisons, which help us to solve problems.

Peripheral explanations for RT slowing View the loss of response speed with age as due to decrements in the sense organs and/or peripheral nervous system.

Peripheral field The outer areas of the visual field. The visual field is the extent of physical space visible to an eye in a given position—that whole area you see.

Periphery That aspect of personality that is situational and behavioral, according to Maddi.

Personal/subjective age The age that one privately feels.

Personal versus universal helplessness Personalized, idiosyncratic feelings about helplessness versus generalized ideas about helplessness that apply to all people.

Personality Cohesive organization of traits or qualities that give behavior meaning or consistency.

Personality-perceptual rigidity Refers to an individual's ability to adjust readily to new surroundings and changes in cognitive and environmental patterns.

Personality "types" Neugarten's clusters of personalities whose styles differ and who vary regarding life satisfaction.

Personalization of death Giving death a personal meaning (e.g., death means being reunited with loved ones).

Person-environment interaction Theory that suggests that all aspects of behavior and performance can be conceived of as a result of the interaction or transaction between the individual and the environment.

Pet therapy Form of therapy using real or plush animals as aids in reestablishing caring relationships with others.

Phenotypic persistence Stability of certain traits over time.

Physiological theories of aging Theories of biological aging that emphasize breakdown of certain organs or organ systems.

Pick's Disease A form of dementia that is genetic in origin.

Pitch discrimination The ability to detect changes in the pitch of sounds.

Pluralism Refers to the fact that development takes on many forms.

Poverty level index A dollar figure set by the government to officially designate individuals as living below the poverty line, for purposes of eligibility for federal assistance.

Practice effects The fact that individuals typically improve with practice, independent of the effects of aging.

Premature presbycusis The damaging effects of repeated exposure upon hearing in adults and the middle-aged.

Presbycusis The most common hearing disorder of older adults. It is characterized by a progressive bilateral loss of hearing for tones of high frequency due to degenerative physiological changes in the auditory system as a function of age.

Presbyopia The progressive decline with age in the eye's ability to focus on near objects. Results mainly from a loss of elasticity in the lens.

Primary appraisal An initial evaluation of an event as stressful or not.

Primary memory Memory for material whose limit is five to seven bits of information.

Primary mental abilities Theory of intelligence hypothesizing seven major abilities—the focus of Schaie's work on the aging of intelligence.

Prime age Designation varies substantially as a function of specific occupation. The United States Bureau of Labor Statistics considers the ages between 25 and 54 to be "prime age" for a worker.

Principle of compensation The perception that terminally ill persons are compensated for the loss of life by the promise of eternity.

Progeria A disease process that rapidly accelerates the physical signs and symptoms of aging.

Projective techniques Unstructured techniques for personality assessment that tap unconscious processes.

Prospective memory Memory for facts or actions to be performed in the future.

Protestant work ethic Traditional work value that views work as sacred and something to be engaged in and enjoyed.

Pseudodementia The misdiagnosis of depression as dementia in older persons.

Psychic death Extreme withdrawal from others, often characterized by giving up.

Psychoanalytic model Views development as instinctual and biologically based, progressing through a series of discontinuous psychosexual stages that are quantitatively different.

Psychodynamic therapy Freud's psychoanalytic therapy emphasizing free association, insights provided by the therapist, and the uncovering of unconscious material embedded in one's childhood experiences.

Psychological age Refers to the adaptive capacities of the individual, such as coping ability or intelligence.

Psychometric tradition Perspective emphasizing the construction of empirically derived tests with established reliability and validity to assess intelligence or personality.

Psychomotor speed rigidity Refers to the individual's rate of emission of familiar cognitive responses.

Psychopharmacological therapy Drug therapy. Often contraindicated with elderly persons due to unwanted side effects of many medications. Can be used with other forms of therapy.

Psychosocial crises Erikson's sequence of individual-social choices that face all persons at various points in their lives (e.g., intimacy vs. isolation).

Q-sort A method of personality assessment where individuals sort statements about themselves along a continuum of "most to least like me."

Qualitative versus quantitative change Developmental issue concerned with the question of whether behavior change is the result of the continuous accumulation of small improvements in similar behaviors or processes (quantitative), or the acquisition of new processes or behaviors (qualitative).

Random assignment Procedure by which subjects have an equal chance of being assigned to a treatment versus a control group; a means of experimental control to equate the groups at an experiment's outset.

Reality orientation (RO) Form of therapy stressing reorientation of self to time and place on a daily basis.

Recognition versus recall Methods of studying memory processes (retrieval, encoding), presenting tasks where cues for the information exist (recognition) versus those where such cues must be generated (recall).

Reductionist versus holist approach to development Developmental issue concerned with whether all aspects of development and behavior can be reduced to an observable stimulus-response connection (reductionist), or whether to understand behavior and development, we must view the total situation (holist).

Registration The process of taking in information or stimulation so that it may be processed.

Regression to the mean The fact that individuals whose scores place them at the extremes of the sample distribution will become less extreme upon retesting, independent of any genuine developmental change.

Regressive intervention Doing little or nothing for someone who is terminally ill because that person is beyond all help.

Relabeling A technique frequently used in cognitive or family therapies where the "problem" is redefined so as to enable the client to see things from a new perspective.

Reliability The repeatability or internal consistency of a scale or test.

Reminiscence The process of looking back on one's life, central to the life review.

Remotivation therapy A form of therapy assuming that the healthy portion of the person's personality can be activated via restructuring the real environment with the help of the therapist and others.

Response bias Term used in laboratory investigation of cautiousness. Refers to the particular response characteristics of individuals—their criteria for making a response.

Retirement Voluntary or mandated withdrawal from an occupation or the work force.

Retrieval The "getting out" of information from memory storage.

Reversible (acute) versus irreversible (chronic) dementia Referring to the distinction between dementias whose cause can be identified and whose symptoms can be reversed (e.g., malnutrition) versus those whose causes are organic and presumed irreversible (e.g., brain cell loss).

Rigidity hypothesis Assumption that as we become older we become more rigid or less flexible in our behavior, attitudes, habits, and personality.

Rites of passage Rites, rituals, or milestones that mark the transition from one stage of the life cycle to another. For example, a "rite of passage" from the stage of adolescent to adulthood might be obtaining a job or getting married. These rites vary from culture to culture.

Role change A role shift that involves the complete shifting from one type of role to another. An example would be a change from student to teacher.

Role transition A role shift that involves the evolution of one form of a specific role to another form of that same role. An example would be a shift from mother to grandmother.

Roles Roles are the behaviors, traits, and characteristics expected by others for individuals who occupy a specific social position in society.

Rote versus mediated learning Rote learning is learning via simple repetition, whereas mediated learning relies on a scheme or mnemonic (e.g., *i* before *e* except after *c*). Some tasks and some persons tend to favor one type of learning over the other.

Schizophrenia General term suggesting symptoms that imply a break with reality (e.g., delusions or hallucinations).

Secondary appraisal Deciding upon one's available options in coping with change.

Secondary memory Memory for material whose span exceeds the capacity of primary memory (5–7 digits). Often referred to as short-term memory. Requires active rehearsal.

Secular versus sacred function of funerals Secular aspects of funerals refer to their function in disposing of the body, while their sacred function refers to the memorialization of life and transition to death.

Selective attention The control of information processing so that a particular source of information is processed more fully than any other simultaneous sources of information.

Selective dropout The fact that certain individuals are not available or choose not to participate in retesting due to illness, schedule conflicts, lack of interest, etc., producing a biased sample of retestees.

Selective exposure The formulation of a belief or attitude on the basis of limited information—not having observed all possible instances.

Selective sampling The fact that not all persons who are contacted for a study choose to volunteer, often producing a biased sample of individuals that may not generalize to nonvolunteers.

Selective survival The fact that not all members of a given cohort survive into adulthood, yielding a sample that is no longer representative of its original cohort.

Self-concept Our view of ourselves, often defined to include self-esteem (what we think of this view of self).

Self-efficacy The sense of one's ability to succeed or accomplish a task.

Self schemas Views of ourselves as complex, changing individuals.

Semantic differential Technique of personality assessment where individuals rate themselves along a continuum defined by opposites (e.g., happy-sad).

Semantic versus episodic memory Refers to the distinction between the recall of general information (e.g., what a plane is) and the recall of specific details (e.g., dates, places; for instance, the date and destination of your last plane trip).

Senile plaques Clusters of dead or dying neurons that interfere with brain function and that are especially present in the brains of persons with Alzheimer's disease.

Sensation The reception of physical stimulation and the translation of this stimulation into neural impulses.

Sensory information processing tasks Laboratory tasks that serve as a method of accurately determining the condition and efficiency of our sensory system. These include tasks such as critical flicker fusion and click fusion.

Sensory memory Memory that is preattentive—it requires no conscious effort or attention. Material is processed solely in terms of its physical (visual, aural) features.

Sensory receptors Structures that receive and register stimulation from the environment. Each primary sense has specific receptors.

Serial learning task Task where the learner is required to learn and recall items in a given order (e.g., as presented).

Shallow processing Material that is processed at the sensory level (visually, aurally).

Shifting roles As we progress along the life span we are constantly shifting roles. Role shifts may occur in two ways, via role transitions or role changes.

Signal A specific cue or stimulus that the individual must respond to, observe, or detect.

Similarity Theory of mate selection that suggests that individuals who are similar on a number of factors are attracted to each other.

Social age Refers to the social habits and roles of the individual relative to the expectations of society.

Social clock Expectations about the timing of various events, behaviors, and activities along the life cycle with regard to their being "on" or "off" time.

Social death Death via the cessation of interpersonal relationships, i.e., being treated as if one were dead.

Social learning theory Personality theory that emphasizes the role of models who serve as guides for the construction of internal standards of behavior.

Socialization The process that molds each of us into a member of a particular society or subculture through our acquisition of the roles appropriate to our age, gender, social class, or ethnic group.

Socioadaptational Refers to adaptation at the level of roles and relationships with others.

Somesthesis Our sensitivities to touch, vibration, temperature, kinesthesis, and pain are collectively referred to as "somesthesis" since they arise from normal and intensive stimulations of the skin and viscera.

Spearman's two-factor theory Theory of intelligence specifying a general ability factor (G) complemented by several test-specific ability factor(s).

Speechreading Another name for lipreading. A procedure used by individuals with hearing impairments to comprehend what others are saying.

Speed versus accuracy trade-off Accuracy is stressed at the expense of speed in performing a psychomotor task; often characteristic of older persons.

Stability versus change The issue of whether personality remains stable or changes with increased age.

Stage theory of dying Kübler-Ross's notion that dying patients go through discrete stages (denial, anger, bargaining, depression, acceptance) in their reactions to impending death.

Stage theory of intellectual development The notion that the quality or function of intelligence changes with age, according to such theorists as Schaie or Piaget.

Stage theory of mate selection The process by which individuals are attracted to one another, fall in love, and marry. This process is defined in terms of discrete stages corresponding to the deepening and stability of the relationship, and in part by stimulus variables and social role expectations.

Stanford-Binet intelligence test Major test of intelligence applying to children and adults; yields an IQ via the accumulation of mental age credits.

Status The relative position of a person within society. This status is often affected by factors such as age, gender, occupation, education level, and so forth. Often considered social position.

Stereotype Beliefs, attitudes, or expectations about individuals from a specific group that are presumed solely on the basis of the individual's membership in that group.

Stimulus persistence theory A theory based on the assumption that stimulus traces persist longer in the nervous systems of older people than in those of younger ones, accounting for slowness of behavior.

Storage Memory process whereby information is organized in some fashion—storehouse of information that has been encoded and that will be retrieved.

Structure-function versus antecedent-consequent Developmental issue concerned with whether a theory analyzes behavior and development in terms of structure-function (organism) or antecedent-consequent relationships (mechanism).

Structure of intellect Guilford's theory of intelligence hypothesizing 120 separate abilities.

Styles of child rearing Distinct patterns of relating to, disciplining, and educating one's children, yielding very different personality patterns (e.g., authoritarian, permissive).

Styles of grandparenting Different approaches taken by middle-aged and elderly persons toward defining the role of grandparent (e.g., reservoir of family wisdom, parent surrogate).

Sudden infant death syndrome (SIDS) The spontaneous cessation of breathing via a cerebral shutdown among infants from birth through approximately a year of age.

Survivor guilt Feelings of guilt over having survived a loved one's death.

Sustained and transient visual channels Relates to the assumption that different types of visual stimuli are processed by different neural channels in the visual system. Sustained channels detect stable high spatial frequency stimuli, with little contrast, and respond more slowly yet more persistently over a longer span of time. Transient neural channels, on the other hand, respond to low spatial frequency stimuli that are moving and respond more quickly for shorter periods of time.

Synchrony Referring to the coordination of events in our lives so that they complement one another.

Task pacing The slowing down of presentation rates so that learning and memory can be improved.

Tenuous role types According to Rosow, tenuous role types reflect persons in definite social positions (status) who do not have well-defined functions or roles. These include the aged and the unemployed.

Terminal change (drop) The decline in functioning that precedes death by three to five years.

Tertiary appraisal Reevaluating one's actions as successful or not in coping with change.

Tertiary memory Memory for overlearned, meaningful material that is relatively permanent and whose capacity is unlimited. Often termed long-term memory.

Time lag Study in which the effects of cultural change are assessed by comparing at least two samples of persons who are of similar ages.

Time of measurement effects Influences that affect all persons, regardless of age or cohort, at a given point in time.

Time perspective A shift in one's definition of life in terms of time since birth versus time left to live.

Time sequential A sequential design separating the effects of age and time of measurement where the cohort is confounded. The replication of a cross-sectional design at another time of measurement.

Traditional marriage A relationship between a husband and a wife. In the classic traditional marriage, the husband is considered the head of the family and the decision maker. The wife's role is usually limited to child care and household matters. This type of marriage relationship is decreasing in relative frequency.

Trait An internal quality or characteristic reflected in behavior that is consistent across situations.

Transactional model Point of view stressing the individual's interaction or transaction with the environment, as a means of understanding how persons adapt to or cope with change.

Transference The attribution to the therapist of positive or negative qualities by the client.

Transformations Gould's notion that through experience we are transformed into adults, having shed several myths about the world, ourselves, and our parents collective referred to as the *myth of absolute safety*.

Trifactorial designs Schaie's three-factor (age, cohort, time of measurement) scheme for measuring and explaining developmental change.

Type A versus Type B individuals Type A individuals are hard driving and achievement oriented, whereas Type B individuals are more relaxed, less hurried, and less preoccupied with success.

Types of widows Research by Lopata indicating that there are a number of types of widows; each type has a specific set of characteristics. These types include liberated women, merry widows, working women, widow's widows, traditional widows, and grieving women.

Unconditional positive regard Rogers's concept emphasizing uncritical acceptance of another person.

Unfinished business Feelings of not having said or did what was important after a loved one dies, leading to feelings of guilt or regret.

Universals of aging Factors identified by Cowgill and Holmes that are assumed to be present and similar in all cultures/societies regarding the aged.

Unlearned When new S-R associations interfere with the maintenance of previously learned associations.

Unsanctioned grief Grief over the loss of a loved one that is not condoned by others due to the nature of death, as in suicide or AIDS.

Validation therapy A form of therapy with extremely impaired elders where the authenticity of the person's feelings and experiences is acknowledged rather than challenged.

Validity The extent to which a test or scale measures what it purports to measure.

Variations of aging Variations or differences between cultures/societies in terms of the aging experience, identified by Cowgill and Holmes.

Vertical career move A move to a higher level of responsibility within a specific career.

Vigilance The ability to maintain attention to a task for a sustained period.

Visual acuity The eye's ability to resolve detail. It is most often equated with accuracy of distance vision compared to the "hypothetical normal person."

Visual search behavior How an individual searches, scans, or processes a visual scene.

Vocational maturity Super's index of the congruence between one's vocational behaviors and societal expectations. Varies by stage of the occupational life cycle.

Wechsler Adult Intelligence Scale (WAIS) Major test of adult intelligence yielding both verbal and performance IQs; termed a point scale.

Well-being Referring to the subjective state of being well (i.e., self-esteem, morale, life satisfaction).

Wisdom factor The use of one's experience or life perspective to aid in adaptation to the aging process.

REFERENCES

APA Monitor. (1991, July). Women's expectations are menopause villains (p. 14). Washington, DC: American Psychological Association.

Abel, B. J., & Hayslip, B. (1986). Locus of control and attitudes toward work and retirement. *Journal of Psychology, 120*, 479–488.

Abel, B. J., & Hayslip, B. (1987). Locus of control and preparation for retirement. *Journal of Gerontology, 42*, 162–165.

Abrahams, J. P. (1976). Health status as a variable in aging research. *Experimental Aging Research, 2*, 63–71.

Abramson, L., Seligman, M., & Teasdale, J. (1978). Learned helplessness in humans: Critique and reformulation. *Journal of Abnormal Psychology, 87*, 49–74.

Abush, R., & Burkhead, E. J. (1984). Job stress in mid-life working women: Relationships among personality type, job characteristics, and job tension. *Journal of Counseling Psychology, 31*, 36–44.

Achenbach, T. M. (1978). *Research in developmental psychology: Concepts, strategies, methods*. New York: Free Press.

Adams, B. N. (1968). *Kinship in an urban setting*. Chicago: Markham.

Adams, D. L. (1969). Analysis of a life satisfaction index. *Journal of Gerontology, 24*, 470–474.

Adams, R. D. (1980). The morphological aspects of aging in the human nervous system. In J. E. Birren and R. B. Sloane (Eds.), *Handbook of mental health in aging* (pp. 149–160). Englewood Cliffs, NJ: Prentice-Hall.

Adams, W., Garry, P., Rhyne, R., Hunt, W. C., & Goodwin, J. S. (1989, November). Alcohol use in healthy elderly. Paper presented at the Annual Scientific Meeting of the Gerontological Society of America. Minneapolis, MN.

Addington, J., & Fry, P. S. (1986). Directions for clinical-psychosocial assessment of depression in the elderly. In T. L. Brink (Ed.), *Clinical Gerontology* (pp. 97–118). New York: Haworth Press.

Adelman, M. (1990). Stigma, gay life-styles, and adjustment to aging: A study of later-life gay men and lesbians. *Journal of Homosexuality, 20*, 7–32.

Adelman, R. K., Antonucci, T. C., Crohan, S. E., & Coleman, L. M. (1989). Empty-nest cohort and employment in the well-being of mid-life women. *Sex Roles, 20*, 173–189.

Adler, S., & Aranya, N. (1984). A comparison of the work needs, attitudes, and preferences of professional accountants at different career stages. *Journal of Vocational Behavior, 25*, 574–580.

Aging and Vision News. (1990). Aging and visual function (pp. 1–4). New York: Lighthouse National Center for Vision and Aging.

Ahammer, I. M. (1973). Social learning theory as a framework for the study of adult personality development. In P. B. Baltes & K. W. Schaie (Eds.), *Life-span developmental psychology: Personality and socialization* (pp. 253–284). New York: Academic Press.

Ainlay, S. C. (1981). Intentionality, identity, and aging: An inquiry into aging and adventitious vision loss. *Dissertation Abstracts International, 42*, 1810A.

Aisenberg, R., & Treas, J. (1985). The family in late life: Psychosocial and demographic considerations. In J. E. Birren & K. W. Schaie, *Handbook of the psychology of aging* (2nd ed.) (pp. 169–189). New York: Van Nostrand Reinhold.

Albrecht, G. L., & Gift, H. C. (1975). Adult socialization: Ambiguity and adult life crises. In N. Datan & L. Ginsburg (Eds.), *Life-span developmental psychology: Normative life crises* (pp. 237–251). New York: Academic Press.

Aldag, R. J., & Brief, A. P. (1977). Age, work, values, and employee relations. *Industrial Gerontology, 4*, 192–197.

Alder, A. G., Adam, J., & Arenberg, D. (1990). Individual differences assessment of the relationship between change and initial level of adult cognitive functioning. *Psychology and Aging, 5*, 560–568.

Aldrich, C., & Mendkoff, B. (1963). Relocation of the aged and disabled: A mortality study. *Journal of the American Geriatrics Society, 11*, 185–194.

Allan, E. A., & Steffensmeier, D. J. (1989). Youth, employment, and property crime: Differential aspects of job availability and job quality on juvenile and young adult arrest rates. *American Sociological Review, 54*, 107–123.

Allen, S., & Hayslip, B. (1990, November). A model

for predicting bereavement outcome. Paper presented at the Annual Convention of the Gerontological Society. Boston.

Allison, P., & Furstenberg, F. (1989). How marital dissolution affects children: Variations by age and sex. *Developmental Psychology, 25,* 540–549.

Allport, G. W. (1961). *Pattern and growth in personality.* New York: Holt, Rinehart, and Winston.

Alpert, J. L., & Richardson, M. S. (1980). Parenting. In L. Poon (Ed.), *Aging in the 1980s: Psychological issues* (pp. 441–454). Washington, DC: American Psychological Association.

Ambert, A. M. (1982). Differences in children's behavior toward custodial mothers and custodial fathers. *Journal of Marriage and the Family, 44,* 73–83.

American Association of Retired Persons. (1984). How well do you hear? Washington, DC: Author.

American Association of Retired Persons. (1985). A profile of older Americans: 1985. Washington, DC: Author.

American Association of Retired Persons. (1986). A profile of older Americans: 1986. Washington, DC: Author.

American Association of Retired Persons. (1986). Staying well: Healthy activities for healthy older persons. Washington, DC: Author.

American Association of Retired Persons. (1986). Workers over 50: Old myths, new realities. Washington, DC: Author.

American Association of Retired Persons. (1987). Divorce after 50: Challenges and choices. Washington, DC: Author.

American Association of Retired Persons. (1988, March/April). Japanese love of work: A life-long affair. *Working Age, 3* (pp. 6–7). Washington, DC: Author.

American Association of Retired Persons. (1990). A Profile of Older Americans: 1990. Washington, DC: Author.

American Psychiatric Association. (1987). *Diagnostic and statistical manual of mental disorders* (4th rev. ed.). Washington, DC: Author.

American Psychological Association. (1982). Ethical principles in the conduct of research with human participants. Washington, DC: Author.

American Psychological Association. (1984). Mental health added to Older Americans Act. *APA Monitor, 19,* 121–128.

Anastasi, A. (1988). *Psychological testing.* New York: Macmillan.

Anastasi, A. (1988). *Psychological testing* (6th ed.). New York: Macmillan.

Anderson, C., Porrata, E., Lore, J., Alexander, S., & Mercer, M. (1969). A multidisciplinary study of psychogenetic patients. *Geriatrics, 23,* 105–113.

Angier, N. (1983, November). Four-legged therapists. *Discover,* 87–89.

Anschultz, L., Camp, C. J., Markley, R. P., & Kramer, J. J. (1985) Maintenance and generalization of mnemonics for grocery shopping by older adults. *Experimental Aging Research, 11,* 157–160.

Anschultz, L., Camp, C. J., Markley, R. P., & Kramer, J. J. (1987). A three-year follow-up on the effects of mnemonic training in elderly adults. *Experimental Aging Research, 13,* 141–143.

Ansello, E. F., & Hayslip, B. (1979). Older-adult higher education: Stepchild and Cinderella. In H. Sterns, E. Ansello, B. Sprouse, & R. Layfield-Faux (Eds.), *Gerontology in Higher Education* (pp. 262–273). Belmont, CA: Wadsworth.

Anson, L., Antonovsky, A., Sagy, S., & Adler, I. (1989). Family, gender, and attitudes toward retirement. *Sex Roles, 20,* 355–369.

Anthony, J. C., & Aboraya, A. (1992). The epidemiology of selected mental disorders in later life. In J. E. Birren, R. B. Sloane, & G. D. Cohen (Eds.), *Handbook of mental health and aging* (pp. 27–73). New York: Academic Press.

Antonucci, T. C. (1985). Personal characteristics, social support, and social behavior. In R. Binstock & E. Shanas (Eds.), *Handbook of aging and the social sciences* (pp. 94–128). New York: Van Nostrand Reinhold.

Antonucci, T. C., & Akiyama, H. (1991, Winter). Social relationships and aging well: How do they exert their salubrious effects? *Generations,* 39–45.

Arena, J. G., Hightower, N. E., & Chong, G. C. (1988). Relaxation therapy for tension headache in the elderly: A prospective study. *Psychology and Aging, 3,* 96–98.

Arenberg, D. (1967). Regression analyses of verbal learning on adult age differences at two anticipation intervals. *Journal of Gerontology, 22,* 411–414.

Arenberg, D. (1976). The effects of input condition on free recall in young and old adults. *Journal of Gerontology, 31,* 551–555.

Arenberg, D. (1982). Learning from our mistakes in aging research. *Experimental Aging Research, 8,* 73–75.

Arenberg, D., & Robertson-Tchabo, E. (1977). Learning and aging. In J. E. Birren & K. W. Schaie (Eds.), *Handbook of the psychology of aging* (p. 482). New York: Van Nostrand Reinhold.

Arkow, P. (1982). Pet therapy: A study of the use of companion animals: Selected therapies. Colorado Springs: Humane Society of Pikes Peak Region.

Arlin, P. K. (1984). Adolescent and adult thought: A structural interpretation. In M. L. Commons,

F. A. Richards, & C. Armon (Eds.), *Beyond formal operations: Late adolescent and adult cognitive development* (pp. 258–271). New York: Praeger.

Arthur, W., Jr., Fuentes, R., & Doverspike, D. (1990). Relationships among personnel tests, age, and job performance. *Experimental Aging Research, 16,* 11–16.

Arvey, R. D., & Mussio, S. (1973). Test discrimination, job performance, and age. *Industrial Gerontology, 16,* 22–29.

Ashley, P. K. (1985). Deafness in the family. In H. Orlans (Ed.), *Adjustment to hearing loss* (pp. 71–82). San Diego, CA: College-Hill Press.

Astin, H. S. (1984). The meaning of work in women's lives: A sociopsychological model of career choice and work behavior. *Counseling Psychologist, 12,* 117–126.

Atchley, R. C. (1975). The life course, age grading, and age-linked demands for decision-making. In N. Datan & L. Ginsburg (Eds.), *Life-span developmental psychology: Normative life crises* (pp. 261–278). New York: Academic Press.

Atchley, R. C. (1979). Issues in retirement research. *Gerontologist, 19,* 44–54.

Atchley, R. C. (1982). The aging self. *Psychotherapy: Theory, Research, and Practice, 19,* 388–396.

Atchley, R. C. (1989). A continuity theory of normal aging. *Gerontologist, 29,* 183–190.

Atchley, R. C. (1989). *The social forces and aging* (5th ed.). Belmont, CA: Wadsworth.

Austin, D. R. (1985). Attitudes toward old age: A hierarchical study. *Gerontologist, 25,* 431–434.

Avolio, B. J., & Barrett, G. V. (1987). Effects of age stereotyping in a simulated interview. *Psychology and Aging, 2,* 56–63.

Avolio, B. J., & Panek, P. E. (1981, November). Assessing changes in levels of capacity and preferences across the working life span [paper]. 34th annual meeting of the Gerontological Society, Toronto.

Avolio, B. J., & Panek, P. E. (1983, August). Automobile accidents characteristic of young and old female drivers [paper]. 91st annual meeting of the American Psychological Association, Anaheim, CA.

Avolio, B. J., & Walman, D. A. (1989). Ratings of managerial skill requirements: Comparison of age- and job-related factors. *Psychology and Aging, 4,* 464–470.

Balkwell, C. (1985). Transition to widowhood: A review of the literature. In L. Cargan (Ed.), *Marriage and family: Coping with change* (pp. 312–322). Belmont, CA: Wadsworth.

Baltes, M. M., & Baltes, P. B. (1986). *The psychology of control and aging.* Hillsdale, NJ: Erlbaum.

Baltes, P. B. (1968). Cross-sectional and longitudinal sequences in the study of age and generation effects. *Human Development, 11,* 145–171.

Baltes, P. B. (1987). Theoretical propositions of life-span developmental psychology: On the dynamics between growth and decline. *Developmental Psychology, 23,* 611–626.

Baltes, P. B., & Danish, S. (1980). Intervention in life-span development and aging. In R. R. Turner & H. W. Reese (Eds.), *Life-span developmental psychology: Intervention* (pp. 49–78). New York: Academic Press.

Baltes, P. B., & Schaie, K. W. (1976). On the plasticity of intelligence in adulthood and old age: Where Horn and Donaldson fail. *American Psychologist, 31,* 720–725.

Baltes, P. B., & Willis, S. L. (1982). Plasticity and enhancement of intellectual functioning in old age: Penn State's Adult Development and Enrichment Program (ADEPT). In F. I. M. Craik & S. E. Trehub (Eds.), *Aging and cognitive processes* (pp. 353–389). New York: Plenum.

Baltes, P. B., Dittman-Kohli, F., & Dixon, R. (1984). New perspectives on the development of intelligence in adulthood: Toward a dual process conception and a model of selective optimization with compensation. In P. Baltes & O. Brim (Eds.), *Life-span development and behavior* (Vol. 6, pp. 33–76). New York: Academic Press.

Baltes, P. B., Nesselroade, J. R., Schaie, K. W., & Labouvie, G. V. (1972). On the dilemma of regression effects in examining ability-related differentials in ontogenic patterns of intelligence. *Developmental Psychology, 6,* 78–84.

Baltes, P. B., Reese, H., & Nesselroade, J. R. (1986). *Life-span developmental psychology: Introduction to research methods.* Hillsdale, NJ: Erlbaum.

Baltes, P. B., Reese, H. W., & Lipsitt, L. P. (1980). Life-span developmental psychology. *Annual Review of Psychology, 31,* 65–111.

Baltes, P. B., Schaie, K. W., & Nardi, A. (1971). Age and experimental mortality in a seven-year longitudinal study of cognitive behavior. *Developmental Psychology, 5,* 18–26.

Baltes, P. B., Smith, J., Standinger, U., & Sowarka, D. (1990). Wisdom: One facet of successful aging? In M. Perlmutter (Ed.), *Late life potential* (pp. 63–82). Washington, DC: Gerontological Society.

Baltes, P. B., Sowarka, D., & Kleigl, R. (1989). Cognitive training research on fluid intelligence in old age: What can older adults achieve by themselves? *Psychology and Aging, 4,* 217–221.

Banaji, M., & Crowder, R. (1989). The bankruptcy of

everyday memory. *American Psychologist, 44,* 1855–1863.

Bandura, A. (1977). Self-efficacy: Toward a unifying theory of behavioral change. *Psychological Review, 84,* 191–215.

Bandura, A. (1981). Self-referent thought: A developmental analysis of self-efficacy. In J. Flavell & L. Ross (Eds.), *Social cognitive development: Frontiers and possible futures* (pp. 200–239). Cambridge: Cambridge University Press.

Bandura, A. (1982). The self and mechanisms of aging. In J. Seils (Ed.), *Psychological perspectives on the self* (pp. 3–39). Hillsdale, NJ: Erlbaum.

Bandura, A. (1986). *Social foundations of thought and action: A social cognitive theory.* Englewood Cliffs, NJ: Prentice-Hall.

Bandura, A. (1989). Regulation of cognitive processes through self-efficacy. *Developmental Psychology, 25,* 729–735.

Bankoff, E. A. (1983). Social support and adaptation to widowhood. *Journal of Marriage and the Family, 45,* 827–840.

Bardwick, J. M. (1986). *The plateauing trap.* Toronto: Bardam Books.

Barnes, E. K., Sack, A., & Shore, H. (1973). Guidelines to treatment approaches. *Gerontologist, 13,* 513–527.

Barnes-Farrell, J. L., & Piotrowski, M. (1989). Workers' perceptions of discrepancies between chronological age and personal age: You're only as young as you feel. *Psychology and Aging, 4,* 376–377.

Barnes-Farrell, J. L. (1983). Perceptions of age-typed occupations: A preliminary investigation [Interim report N00014-82-K-0449]. West Lafayette, IN: Purdue University Department of Psychological Sciences.

Barr, R. A., & Giambra, L. M. (1990). Age-related decrement in selective auditory attention. *Psychology and Aging, 4,* 597–599.

Barrett, C., & Schneweis, K. (1980–1981). An empirical search for stages of widowhood. *Omega, 11,* 97–104.

Barrett, G. V. (1976, October). Task design, individual attributes, work satisfaction, and productivity [paper]. Comparative Administration Research Institute Conference, Berlin.

Barrett, G. V., & Depinet, R. L. (1991). A reconsideration of testing for competence rather than for intelligence. *American Psychologist, 46,* 1012–1024.

Barrett, G. V., & Thornton, C. L. (1978). Relationship between perceptual style and driver reaction to an emergency situation. *Journal of Applied Psychology, 52,* 169–176.

Barrett, G. V., Alexander, R. A., & Forbes, J. B. (1977). Analysis of performance measurement and training requirements for driving decision-making in emergency situations. *JSAS Catalogue of Selected Documents in Psychology, 7,* (Ms. No. 1623), 126.

Barrett, G. V., Thornton, C. L., & Cabe, P. A. (1969). Relation between embedded-figures test performance and simulator behavior. *Journal of Applied Psychology, 53,* 253–254.

Barrow, G. M., & Smith, P. A. (1983). *Aging, the individual, and society* (2nd ed.). New York: West.

Baruch, G., Barnett, R., & Rivers, C. (1983). *Lifeprints: New patterns of love and work for today's woman.* New York: McGraw-Hill.

Bascue, L. O., & Lawrence, R. (1977). A study of subjective time and death anxiety in the elderly. *Omega, 8,* 81–89.

Bass, D. M., Noelker, L. S., Townsend, A. L., & Deimbing, G. T. (1990). Losing an aged relative: Perceptual differences between spouses and adult children. *Omega, 21,* 21–40.

Baugher, R. J., Burger, C., Smith, R., & Wallston, K. (1989–1990). A comparison of terminally ill persons at various time periods to death. *Omega, 20,* 103–116.

Baumagin, V. E., & Hirn, K. F. (1982). Observations on changing relationships for older married women. *American Journal of Psychoanalysis, 42,* 133–142.

Baxter, N. (1986). Career information in the classroom. *Occupational Outlook Quarterly, 30,* 32–33.

Baylor, A. M., & Spiduso, W. W. (1988). Systematic aerobic exercise and components of reaction time in older women. *Journal of Gerontology: Psychological Sciences, 43,* P121–P126.

Beck, A. (1976). *Cognitive therapy and the emotional disorders.* New York: International Universities Press.

Beck, P. (1982). Two successful interventions in nursing homes: The therapeutic effects of cognitive activity. *Gerontologist, 22,* 378–383.

Beder, H. (1989). Purposes and philosophies of adult education. In S. B. Merriam & P. M. Cunningham (Eds.), *Handbook of adult and continuing education* (pp. 37–50). San Francisco: Jossey-Bass.

Bell, B., Rose, C., & Damon, A. (1972). The normative aging study: An interdisciplinary and longitudinal study of healthy aging. *International Journal of Aging and Human Development, 3,* 5–17.

Belmont, J., Epperson, J., & Anderson, N. (1989, November). Simple reaction time as problem-solving: Relations to fluid and crystallized intelligence [paper]. Annual Meeting of the Gerontological Society, Minneapolis.

Bem, S. (1981). Gender scheme theory: A cognitive

account of sex typing. *Psychological Review, 88,* 354–364.

Bengtson, V., & Troll, L. (1978). Youth and their parents: Feedback and intergenerational influence in socialization. In R. Lerner & G. Spanier (Eds.), *Child influences on marital and family interaction: A life-span perspective* (pp. 215–240). New York: Academic Press.

Bengtson, V., Kasschau, P. L., & Ragan, P. K. (1977). The impact of social structure on aging in individuals. In J. E. Birren & K. W. Schaie (Eds.), *Handbook of the psychology of aging* (pp. 327–353). New York: Van Nostrand Reinhold.

Bengtson, V., Rosenthal, C., & Burton, L. (1990). Families and aging: Diversity and heterogeneity. In R. Binstock & L. George (Eds.), *Handbook of aging and the social sciences* (pp. 263–287). New York: Academic Press.

Bengtson, V. L., Cuellar, J. B., & Ragan, P. K. (1977). Stratum contrasts and similarities in attitudes toward death. *Journal of Gerontology, 32,* 76–78.

Benjamin, B. J. (1981). Frequency variability in the aged voice. *Journal of Gerontology, 36,* 722–726.

Benjamin, B. J. (1982). Phonological performance in gerontological speech. *Journal of Psycholinguistic Research, 11,* 159–167.

Bennett, K. C., & Thompson, N. L. (1991). Accelerated aging and male homosexuality: Australian evidence in a continuing debate. *Journal of Homosexuality, 20,* 65–76.

Bennett, R., & Eckman, J. (1973). Attitudes toward aging: A critical examination of recent literature and implications for future research. In C. Eisdorfer & M. P. Lawton (Eds.), *Psychology of adult development and aging* (pp. 575–597). Washington, DC: American Psychological Association.

Benshoff, J. J., & Roberto, K. A. (1987). Alcoholism in the elderly: Clinical issues. *Clinical Gerontologist, 7,* 3–14.

Bensman, J., & Lilienfeld, R. (1979, October). Friendship and alienation. *Psychology Today,* 56–66.

Bentler, P. M., & Newcomb, M. D. (1978). Longitudinal study of marital success and failure. *Journal of Consulting and Clinical Psychology, 46,* 1053–1070.

Berg, C. A., & Sternberg, R. J. (1985). A triarchic theory of intellectual development during adulthood. *Developmental Review, 5,* 353–389.

Bergman, C. S., Plomin, R., McClearn, G., Friberg, L., & Pederson, N. L. (1988). Genotype-environment interaction in personality development: Identical twins raised apart. *Psychology and Aging, 3,* 399–406.

Bergman, M. (1971a). Changes in hearing with age. *Gerontologist, 11,* 148–151.

Bergman, M. (1971b). Hearing and aging: Implications of recent research findings. *Audiology, 10,* 164–171.

Bergman, M. (1980). *Aging and the perception of speech.* Baltimore: University Park Press.

Betz, N. E. (1984). A study of career patterns of women college graduates. *Journal of Vocational Behavior, 24,* 249–263.

Bifora, F. A., & Longino, C. F., Jr. (1990). Elderly Hispanic migration in the United States. *Journal of Gerontology: Social Sciences, 45,* S212–S219.

Biller, H. B. (1982). Fatherhood: Implications for child and adult development. In B. Wolman (Ed.), *Handbook of developmental psychology* (pp. 702–725). Englewood Cliffs, NJ: Prentice-Hall.

Billings, A., Cronkite, R. C., & Moos, R. H. (1983). Social-environmental factors in unipolar depression: Comparisons of depressed patients and nondepressed controls. *Journal of Abnormal Psychology, 92,* 119–133.

Binstock, R. (1983). The aged as scapegoat. *Gerontologist, 23,* 136–143.

Binet, A. (1905). Review of C. Spearman: The proof and measurement of association between two things; General intelligence objectively defined and measured. *Année Psychologie, 11,* 623–624.

Bird, C. P., & Fisher, T. D. (1986). Thirty years later: Attitudes toward the employment of older workers. *Journal of Applied Psychology, 71,* 515–517.

Birren, J. E. (1964). *The psychology of aging.* Englewood Cliffs, NJ: Prentice-Hall.

Birren, J. E. (1982, November). A review of the development of self [paper]. Annual meeting of the Gerontological Society, Boston.

Birren, J. E., & Cunningham, W. (1985). Research on the psychology of aging: Principles, concepts, and theory. In J. E. Birren & K. W. Schaie (Eds.), *Handbook of the psychology of aging* (2nd ed., pp. 3–34). New York: Van Nostrand Reinhold.

Birren, J. E., & Morrison, D. F. (1961). Analysis of WAIS subtests in relation to age and education. *Journal of Gerontology, 16,* 363–369.

Birren, J. E., & Renner, V. J. (1979). A brief history of mental health and aging. In *Issues in mental health and aging: Research* (Vol. 1, pp. 1–26). Washington, DC: National Institute of Mental Health.

Birren, J. E., & Renner, V. J. (1980). Concepts and issues of mental health and aging. In J. E. Birren & R. B. Sloane (Eds.), *Handbook of mental health and aging* (pp. 3–33). Englewood Cliffs, NJ: Prentice-Hall.

Birren, J. E., & Schaie, K. W. (1977). *Handbook of the psychology of aging.* New York: Van Nostrand Reinhold.

Birren, J. E., & Woodruff, D. S. (1973a). Academic and professional training in the psychology of aging. In C. Eisdorfer & M. P. Lawton (Eds.), *The psychology of adult development and aging* (pp. 11–36). Washington, DC: American Psychological Association.

Birren, J. E., Cunningham, W., & Yamamoto, K. (1983). Psychology of adult development and aging. *Annual Review of Psychology, 34*, 543–576.

Birren, J. E., Woods, A. M., & Williams, M. V. (1980). Behavioral slowing with age: Causes organization, and consequences. In L. W. Poon (Ed.), *Aging in the 1980s: Psychological issues* (pp. 293–308). Washington, DC: American Psychological Association.

Bischman, D. A., & Witte, K. L. (1990, August). Food identification, taste complaints, and depression in the elderly [paper]. Convention of the American Psychological Association, Boston.

Black, S. M., & Hill, C. E. (1984). The psychological well-being of women in their middle years. *Psychology of Women Quarterly, 8*, 282–292.

Blackburn, J. A., & Papalia, D. (1992). The study of adult cognition from a Piagetian perspective [unpublished manuscript]. University of Wisconsin: Madison, WI.

Blackburn, J. A., Papalia-Finlay, D., Foye, B. F., & Serlin, R. C. (1988). Modifiability of figural-relations performance among elderly adults. *Journal of Gerontology, 43*, P87–P89.

Blakely, A. E. (1979). OAA amendments remember the forgotten Americans. *Perspective on aging, 8*, 4–5.

Blanchard-Fields, F. (1986). Reasoning in adolescents and adults on social dilemmas varying in emotional saliency. *Psychology and Aging, 1*, 325–333.

Blauner, R. (1966). Death and social structure. *Psychiatry, 28*, 378–394.

Blazer, D. (1980). Epidemiology of mental illness in late life. In E. Busse & D. Blazer (Eds.), *Handbook of geriatric psychiatry* (pp. 249–272). New York: Van Nostrand Reinhold.

Blazer, D. (1986). Depression. *Generations, 10*, 21–23.

Blazer, D. (1990). *Emotional problems in late life.* New York: Springer.

Blazer, D. (1991, Winter). Spirituality and aging well: A framework for meaning. *Generations*, 61–67.

Blazer, D., Bachar, J. R., & Manton, K. G. (1986). Suicide in late life: Review and commentary. *Journal of the American Geriatrics Society, 34*, 519–525.

Blazer, D., Hughes, D. C., & George, L. K. (1987). The epidemiology of depression in an elderly community population. *Gerontologist, 27*, 281–287.

Blenkner, M. (1965). Social work and family relationships in later life with some thoughts on filial maturity. In E. Shanas & G. Streib (Eds.), *Social structure and the family: Generational relations* (pp. 46–59). Englewood Cliffs, NJ: Prentice-Hall.

Block, J. (1962). *The Q-sort method in personality assessment and psychiatric research.* Springfield, IL: Thomas.

Block, J. (1971). *Lives through time.* Berkeley, CA: Bancroft Books.

Bloom, B. L., Hodges, W. F., & Caldwell, R. A. (1983). Marital separation: The first eight months. In E. J. Callahan & K. A. McCluskey (Eds.), *Life-span developmental psychology: Nonnormative life events* (pp. 217–239). New York: Academic Press.

Bloom, K. L. (1971). Age and the self-concept. *American Journal of Psychiatry, 118*, 534–538.

Blum, J., & Tallmer, M. (1977). The therapist vis-à-vis the older patient. *Psychotherapy: Theory, Research, and Practice, 14*, 361–367.

Blumenthal, H. T., & Birns, A. W. (1964). Autoimmunity and aging. In B. L. Strebler (Ed.), *Advances in Gerontological Research* (Vol. 1, pp. 289–342). New York: Academic Press.

Blumenthal, J. A., Emery, C. F., Madden, D. J., Georger, L. K., Coleman, R. E., Riddle, M. W., McKee, D. C., Reasoner, J., & Williams, R. S. (1989). Cardiovascular and behavioral effects of aerobic-exercise training in healthy older men and women. *Journal of Gerontology: Medical Sciences, 44*, M147–M157.

Boaz, R. F. (1987). Work as a response to low and decreasing real income during retirement. *Research on Aging, 9*, 428–440.

Bohannon, J. R. (1990–1991). Grief responses of spouses following the death of a child: A longitudinal study. *Omega, 22*, 109–122.

Boldt, M. (1982). Normative evaluation of suicide and death: A cross-generational study. *Omega, 10*, 145–158.

Bolla-Wilson, K., & Bleecker, M. L. (1989). Absence of depression in elderly adults. *Journal of Gerontology: Psychological Sciences, 44*, P53–P55.

Bond, J. B., & Harvey, C. D. (1988). Intergenerational perceptions of family interactions [paper]. Annual Meeting of the Canadian Association of Gerontology. Halifax, NS.

Bondareff, W. (1980). Neurobiology of aging. In J. E. Birren & R. B. Sloane (Eds.), *Handbook of mental health and aging* (pp. 75–99). Englewood Cliffs, NJ: Prentice-Hall.

Bondareff, W. (1985). The neural basis of aging. In

J. E. Birren & K. W. Schaie (Eds.), *Handbook of the psychology of aging* (pp. 157–176). New York: Van Nostrand Reinhold.

Bondareff, W. (1986). Biomedical perspective of Alzheimer's disease and dementia in the elderly. In M. Gilhooly, S. Zarit, & J. E. Birren (Eds.), *The dementias: Policy and management* (pp. 1–24). Englewood Cliffs, NJ: Prentice-Hall.

Borges, M. A., & Dutton, L. J. (1976). Attitudes toward the aging: Increasing optimism found with age. *Gerontologist, 16,* 220–224.

Bornstein, R., & Smircina, M. (1982). The status and support for the hypothesis of increased variability in aging populations. *Gerontologist, 22,* 258–260.

Bosse, R., & Ekerdt, D. J. (1981). Change in self-perception of leisure activities with retirement. *Gerontologist, 21,* 650–654.

Bosse, R. A., Aldwin, C. M., Levenson, M. R., & Ekerdt, D. J. (1987). Mental health differences among retirees and workers: Findings from the normative aging study. *Psychology and Aging, 2,* 383–389.

Bosse, R., Aldwin, C. M., Levenson, M. R., & Workman-Daniels, K. (1991). How stressful is retirement? Findings from the normative aging study. *Journal of Gerontology: Psychological Sciences, 46,* P9–P14.

Botwinick, J. (1967). *Cognitive processes in maturity and old age.* New York: Springer.

Botwinick, J. (1970a). *Aging and cognitive processes.* New York: Springer.

Botwinick, J. (1972). Sensory-perceptual factors in reaction time in relation to age. *Journal of Genetic Psychology, 121,* 173–177.

Botwinick, J. (1973). *Aging and behavior.* New York: Springer.

Botwinick, J. (1977). Intellectual abilities. In J. E. Birren & K. W. Schaie (Eds.), *Handbook of the psychology of aging* (pp. 580–605). New York: Van Nostrand Reinhold.

Botwinick, J. (1978). *Aging and behavior* (2nd ed.). New York: Springer.

Botwinick, J. (1984). *Aging and behavior* (3rd ed.). New York: Springer.

Botwinick, J., & Siegler, I. (1980). Intellectual ability among the elderly: Simultaneous cross-sectional and longitudinal comparisons. *Developmental Psychology, 16,* 49–53.

Botwinick, J., West, R., & Storandt, M. (1978). Predicting death from behavioral test performance. *Journal of Gerontology, 33,* 755–762.

Boucouvalas, M., & Krupp, J. (1989). Adult development and learning. In S. B. Merriam & P. M. Cunningham (Eds.), *Handbook of adult and continuing education* (pp. 183–200). San Francisco: Jossey-Bass.

Bowlby, J. (1969). *Attachment and loss: Attachment* (Vol. 1). New York: Basic Books.

Bramel, D. (1969). Interpersonal attraction, hostility, and perception. In J. Mills (Ed.), *Experimental social psychology* (pp. 1–120). New York: Macmillan.

Brammer, L. M. (1984). Counseling theory and the older adult. *Counseling Psychologist, 12,* 29–38.

Breslau, L., & Haug, M. (1983). *Depression and aging: Causes, care, and consequences.* New York: Springer-Verlag.

Bressler, R. (1987). Drug use in the geriatric patient. In L. Carstensen & B. Edelstein (Eds.), *Handbook of clinical gerontology* (pp. 152–176). Elmsford, NY: Pergamon.

Bretschneider, J., & McCoy, N. (1988). Sexual interest and behavior in 80- to 102-year-olds. *Archives of Sexual Behavior, 17,* 109–129.

Breytspraak, L. (1984). *The development of the self in later life.* Boston: Little, Brown.

Brickel, C. M. (1979). The clinical use of pets with the aged. *Clinical Gerontologist, 2,* 72–74.

Brim, O. G. (1966). Socialization through the life cycle. In O. G. Brim & S. Wheeler (Eds.), *Socialization after childhood: Two Essays.* New York: Wiley.

Brim, O. G., & Phillips, D. A. (1988). The life-span intervention cube. In E. M. Hetherington, R. M. Lerner, & P. B. Baltes (Eds.), *Child development in life-span perspective* (pp. 270–300). Hillsdale, NJ: Erlbaum.

Brim, O. G., & Ryff, C. (1978). On the properties of life events. In P. Baltes & U. Brim (Eds.), *Life-span development and behavior* (pp. 368–387). New York: Academic Press.

Brink, T. (1990). *Mental health in the nursing home.* Beverly Hills, CA: Sage.

Brockner, J. (1983). Low self-esteem and behavioral plasticity. In L. Wheeler & P. Shaver (Eds.), *Review of personality and social psychology, 4,* 237–271.

Broderick, C. B. (1982). Adult sexual development. In J. Wolman (Ed.), *Handbook of developmental psychology* (pp. 726–733). Englewood Cliffs, NJ: Prentice-Hall.

Brody, E. M. (1979). Aging parents and aging children. In P. K. Kagan (Ed.), *Aging parents* (pp. 267–287). Los Angeles: University of Southern California Press.

Brody, E. M., Johnson, P. T., & Fulcomer, M. C. (1984). What should adult children do for their elderly parents? Opinions and preferences of three generations of women. *Journal of Gerontology, 39,* 736–746.

Brody, J., Brock, D., & Williams, T. (1987). Trends in

the health of the elderly population. In L. Breslow, J. Fielding, & L. Lave (Eds.), *Annual Review of Public Health, 8,* 211–234.

Brubaker, T. (1983). *The family in later life.* Beverly Hills, CA: Sage.

Brubaker, T. H., & Powers, E. A. (1976). The stereotype of "old": A review and alternative approach. *Journal of Gerontology, 31,* 441–447.

Bruce, D. (1991). Mechanistic and functional explanations of memory. *American Psychologist, 46,* 46–48.

Bruck, P., Coyne, A., & Botwinick, J. (1982). Adult age differences in metamemory. *Journal of Gerontology, 37,* 354–357.

Buck, P. (1966). *The people of Japan.* New York: Simon & Schuster.

Bugen, L. R. (1979). *Death and dying: Theory, research and practice.* Boston, MA: Little, Brown.

Bultena, G. L., & Powers, E. (1978). Denial of aging: Age identification and reference group orientations. *Journal of Gerontology, 33,* 748–754.

Bumpass, L. L., & Sweet, J. A. (1989). National estimates of cohabitation. *Demography, 26,* 615.

Burg, A. (1967). Light sensitivity as related to age and sex. *Perceptual and Motor Skills, 24,* 1279–1288.

Burgio, L. D., & Sinnott, J. (1990). Behavioral treatments and pharmacotherapy: Acceptability ratings by elderly individuals in residential settings. *Gerontologist, 30,* 811–816.

Burke, D. M., & Light, L. L. (1981). Memory and aging: The role of retrieval processes. *Psychological Bulletin, 90,* 513–546.

Burke, K. C., Burke, J. D., Regier, D. A., & Rae, D. S. (1990). Age at onset of selected mental disorders in five community populations. *Archives of General Psychiatry, 47,* 511–518.

Burkhauser, R. V., & Turner, J. A. (1980). The effects of pension policy through life. In R. L. Clark (Ed.). *Retirement policy in an aging society* (pp. 12–31). Durham, NC: Duke University Press.

Burnside, I. M. (1984). *Working with the elderly: Group processes and techniques.* Belmont, CA: Wadsworth.

Burnside, I. M. (1991, Winter). From one who is chronologically gifted: Not growing old quietly. *Generations,* 19–21.

Burrus-Bammel, L., & Bammel, G. (1985). Leisure and recreation. In J. E. Birren & K. W. Schaie (Eds.), *Handbook of the psychology of aging* (2nd ed., pp. 848–863). New York: Van Nostrand Reinhold.

Burtz, M. P., Eaton, W. O., & Bond, J. B. (1988). Effect of respite care on dementia and nondementia patients and their families. *Psychology and Aging, 3,* 38–42.

Buskirk, E. R. (1985). Health maintenance and longevity: Exercise. In C. E. Finch & E. L. Schneider (Eds.), *Handbook of the biology of aging* (2nd ed., pp. 894–931). New York: Van Nostrand Reinhold.

Buss, A. (1979). Dialectics, history, and development: The historical roots of the individual-society dialectic. In P. B. Baltes & O. G. Brim (Eds.), *Life-span development and behavior* (pp. 313–333). New York: Academic Press.

Buss, D. M. (1989). Conflict between the sexes: Strategic inference and the invocation of anger and upset. *Journal of Personality and Social Psychology, 56,* 735–747.

Busse, E. W. (1991, Winter). A gerontologist looks at his own retirement and aging: Theory applied to oneself. *Generations,* 55–57.

Butcher, J. N., & Graham, J. R. (1989). The MMPI restandardization project. Tampa, FL: University of Minnesota Continuing Education Project.

Butler, R. N., Lewis, M., & Sunderland, A. (1991). *Aging and mental health: Positive psychosocial and biomedical approaches.* New York: Springer.,

Butler, R. N. (1963). The life review: An interpretation of reminiscence in the aged. *Psychiatry, 26,* 65–76.

Butler, R. N. (1969). Ageism: Another form of bigotry. *Gerontologist, 9,* 243–246.

Butler, R. N. (1983, July/August). A generation at risk. *Across the Board,* 37–45.

Cahen, G. D. (1990). Psychopathology and mental health. In J. E. Birren & K. W. Schaie (Eds.), *Handbook of the psychology of aging* (pp. 359–371). New York: Academic Press.

Calarusso, C. A., & Nemiroff, R. A. (1991). Impact of adult developmental issues on treatment of older patients. In W. Myers (Ed.), *New techniques in the psychotherapy of older patients* (pp. 245–264). Washington, DC: American Psychiatric Press.

Calasanti, T. M. (1988). Participation in a dual economy and adjustment to retirement. *International Journal of Aging and Human Development, 26,* 13–27.

Calhoun, R., & Gounard, B. (1979). Meaningfulness, presentation rate, list length, and age in elderly adults' paired-associate learning. *Educational Gerontology, 4,* 49–56.

Callahan, D. (1987). *Setting limits.* New York: Simon & Schuster.

Cameron, P. (1972). Stereotypes about generational fun and happiness vs. self-appraised fun and happiness. *Gerontologist, 12,* 120–123.

Cameron, P. (1975). Mood as an indicant of happiness: Age, sex, social class, and situational differences. *Journal of Gerontology, 30,* 216–224.

Camp, C. C. (1989). Facilitation of new learning in Alzheimer's disease. In G. Gilmore, P. Whitehouse, & M. Wykle (Eds.), *Memory, aging, and de-*

mentia: Theory, assessment, and treatment (pp. 212–225). New York: Springer.

Camp, C. C., & McKittrick, L. A. (1991). Memory interventions in Alzheimer's-type dementia populations; Methodological and theoretical issues. In R. L. West & J. D. Sinnott (Eds.), *Everyday memory and aging: Current research and methodology* (pp. 155–172). New York: Springer.

Camp, C. C., & Schaller, J. R. (1989). Epilogue: Spaced-retrieval memory training in an adult day care center. *Educational Gerontology, 15,* 641–648.

Camp, C. C., & Stevens, A. B. (1990). Spaced retrieval: A memory intervention for dementia of the Alzheimer's type (DAT). *Clinical Gerontologist, 10,* 58–61.

Campanelli, P. A. (1968). Audiological perspectives in presbycusis. *Eye, Ear, Nose, and Throat Monthly, 47,* 3–9, 81–86.

Campbell, A. J., Barrie, M. J., & Spears, G. F. (1989). Risk factors for falls in a community-based prospective study of people 70 years and older. *Journal of Gerontology: Medical Sciences, 44,* M112–M117.

Campbell, D. T., & Stanley, J. C. (1963). *Experimental and quasiexperimental designs for research.* Chicago: Rand McNally.

Campbell, J., Swank, P., & Vincent, K. (1991). The role of hardiness in the resolution of grief. *Omega, 23,* 53–66.

Campione, W. A. (1988). Predicting participation in retirement-preparation programs. *Journal of Gerontology, 43,* 591–595.

Canestrari, R. E. (1963). Paced and self-paced learning in young and elderly adults. *Journal of Gerontology, 18,* 165–168.

Canestrari, R. E. (1968). Age changes in acquisition. In G. A. Talland (Ed.), *Human aging and behavior* (pp. 169–187). New York: Academic Press.

Cantor, M. (1979). Effect of ethnicity on life-styles of the inner-city elderly. In A. Monk (Ed.), *The age of aging* (pp. 241–264). Buffalo, NY: Prometheus Books.

Cantor, M. (1991). Family and community: Changing roles in an aging society. *Gerontologist, 31,* 337–346.

Cantor, M., & Little, V. (1985). Aging and social care. In R. Binstock & E. Shanas (Eds.), *Handbook of aging and the social sciences* (pp. 745–781). New York: Van Nostrand Reinhold.

Cantor, W. A., & Koretzky, M. B. (1989). Treatment of geriatric alcoholics. *Clinical Gerontologist, 9,* 67–70.

Carey, R. (1979–1980). Weathering widowhood: Problems and adjustments of the widowed during the first year. *Omega, 10,* 163–175.

Carlson, N. R. (1986). *Physiology of behavior.* Boston: Allyn & Bacon.

Carlson-Jones, D., & Vaughn, K. (1990). Close friendships among senior adults. *Psychology and Aging, 5,* 451–457.

Carp, F. M. (1970). The mobility of retired people. In E. J. Cantilli & J. Shmelzer (Eds.), *Transportation and aging: Selected issues.* Washington, DC: U.S. Government Printing Office.

Carroll, J. B. (1979). How shall we study individual differences in cognitive abilities? In R. Sternberg & D. Detterman (Eds.), *Human intelligence: Perspectives on its theory and measurement* (pp. 3–31). Norwood, NJ: Ablex.

Carson, R. C., & Butcher, J. N. (1991). *Abnormal psychology and modern life* (9th ed.). New York: HarperCollins.

Carstensen, L., & Cone, J. (1983). Social desirability and the measurement of well-being in elderly persons. *Journal of Gerontology, 38,* 713–715.

Carstensen, L., & Edelstein, B. (1987). *Handbook of clinical gerontology.* New York: Praeger.

Carter, B., & McGoldrick, M. (1988). Overview: The changing family life cycle—a framework for family therapy. In B. Carter & M. McGoldrick (Eds.), *The changing family life cycle: A framework for family therapy* (pp. 1–25). Boston: Allyn & Bacon.

Caspi, A., & Bem, D. J. (1990). Personality continuity and change across the life course. In L. A. Pervin (Ed.), *Handbook of personality: Theory and research* (pp. 549–575). New York: Guilford Press.

Caspi, A., & Elder, G. (1986). Life satisfaction in old age: Linking social psychology and history. *Psychology and Aging, 1,* 18–26.

Caspi, A., Bem, D., & Elder, G. (1989). Continuities and consequences of interactional styles across the life course. *Journal of Personality, 57,* 375–406.

Cater, J., & Easton, P. (1980, May 3). Separation and other stress in childhood. *Cancel,* 972–974.

Cattell, R. B. (1950). *Personality: A systematic, theoretical, and factual study.* New York: McGraw-Hill.

Cavanaugh, J. C., Grady, J. G., & Perlmutter, M. P. (1983). Forgetting and the use of memory aids in 20- and 70-year-olds' everyday life. *International Journal of Aging and Human Development, 19,* 149–158.

Cavanaugh, J. C., & Poon, L. W. (1989). Metamemorial predictors of memory performance in young and elderly adults. *Psychology and Aging, 4,* 365–368.

Ceci, S. J., & Brofenbrenner, U. (1991). On the demise of everyday memory: "The rumors of my death are much exaggerated" (Mark Twain). *American Psychologist, 46,* 27–31.

Cerella, J., & Lowe, D. (1984, November). Age deficits and practice: 27 studies reconsidered [paper]. Annual meeting of the Gerontological Society, Washington, DC.

Cerella, J., Poon, L. W., & Williams, D. M. (1980). Age and the complexity hypothesis. In L. W. Poon (Ed.), *Aging in the 1980s: Psychological issues* (pp. 332–340). Washington, DC: American Psychological Association.

Chalke, H. D., & Dewhurst, J. R. (1957). Accidental coal-gas poisoning. *British Medical Journal, 2,* 915–917.

Chase-Landsdale, P. L., & Hetherington, P. M. (1990). The impact of divorce on life-span development: Short and long-term effects. In P. Baltes, D. Featherman, & R. Lerner (Eds.), *Life-span development and behavior* (Vol. 10, pp. 107–151). Hillsdale, NJ: Erlbaum.

Chatters, L. M., & Taylor, R. J. (1989). Age differences in religious participation among black adults. *Journal of Gerontology: Social Sciences, 44,* S183–S189.

Chatters, L. M., & Taylor, R. J. (1990). Social integration. In Z. Harel, E. A. McKinney, & M. Williams (Eds.), *Black aged: Understanding diversity and service needs* (pp. 82–90). Newbury Park, CA: Sage.

Chen, Y. P. (1985). Economic status of the aging. In R. Binstock & E. Shanas (Eds.), *Handbook of aging and the social sciences* (pp. 641–665). New York: Van Nostrand Reinhold.

Chenoweth, B., & Spencer, B. (1986). Dementia: The experience of family caregivers. *Gerontologist, 26,* 267–272.

Cherlin, A. C., & Furstenberg, F. (1986). *The new American grandparent.* New York: Basic Books.

Cherlin, A. C. (1990, January 23). Future of stepfamilies depends on the stepchildren of today. *Dallas Times Herald.*

Cherry, K. E., & Morton, M. R. (1989). Drug sensitivity in older adults: The role of physiologic and pharmacokinetic factors. *International Journal of Aging and Human Development, 28,* 159–174.

Chiriboga, D. A., Catron, L. S., & Associates. (1991). *Divorce: Crisis, challenge, or relief?* New York: New York University Press.

Chiswick, C. (1982, Summer). The value of a housewife's time. *Journal of Human Resources,* 413–425.

Chown, S. M. (1977). Morale, careers, and personal potentials. In J. E. Birren & K. W. Schaie (Eds.), *Handbook of the psychology of aging* (pp. 672–691). New York: Van Nostrand Reinhold.

Cicirelli, V. G. (1985). The role of siblings as family caregivers. In W. J. Sauer & R. T. Coward (Eds.), *Social support networks and the care of the elderly* (pp. 93–107). New York: Springer.

Cicirelli, V. G. (1986). Family relationships and care/management of the demented elderly. In M. Gilhooly, S. Zarit, & J. E. Birren (Eds.), *The dementias: Policy and management* (pp. 89–103). Englewood Cliffs, NJ: Prentice-Hall.

Cicirelli, V. G. (1989). Feelings of attachment to siblings and well-being in later life. *Psychology and Aging, 4,* 211–216.

Clark, J. E., Lanphear, A. K., & Riddick, C. C. (1987). The effects of videogame-playing on the response selection processing of elderly adults. *Journal of Gerontology, 42,* 82–85.

Clark, L. E., & Knowles, J. B. (1973). Age differences in dichotic listening performance. *Journal of Gerontology, 28,* 173–178.

Clark, R., & Spengler, J. (1980). *The economics of individual and population aging.* Cambridge: Cambridge University Press.

Clarke-Stewart, K. A. (1989). Infant day care: Maligned or malignant? *American Psychologist, 44,* 266–273.

Clayton, V. (1975). Erikson's theory of human development as it applies to the aged: Wisdom as contraindicative cognition. *Human Development, 18,* 119–128.

Clayton, V., & Birren, J. E. (1980). The development of wisdom across the life span: A reexamination of an ancient topic. In P. B. Baltes & O. G. Brim (Eds.), *Life-span development and behavior* (pp. 104–135). New York: Academic Press.

Cleveland, J., Festa, R., & Montgomery, L. (1988). Applicant pool composition and job perceptions: Impact on decisions regarding an older applicant. *Journal of Vocational Behavior, 32,* 112–125.

Clingempeel, W. G., & Reppucci, N. D. (1982). Joint custody after divorce: Major issues and goals for research. *Psychological Bulletin, 91,* 102–127.

Clingempeel, W. G., & Segal, S. (1986). Stepparent–stepchild relationships and the psychological adjustment of children in stepmother and stepfather families. *Child Development, 57,* 474–484.

Cobb, S. (1976). Social support as a moderator of life stress. *Psychosomatic Medicine, 38,* 300–314.

Cockburn, J., & Smith, P. T. (1991). The relative influence of intelligence and age on everyday memory. *Journal of Gerontology: Psychological Sciences, 46,* P31–36.

Cockerham, W. C., Sharp, K., & Wilcox, J. A. (1983). Aging and perceived health status. *Journal of Gerontology, 38,* 349–355.

Cohen, C. I., & Rajkowski, H. (1982). What's a friend? Substantive and theoretical issues. *Gerontologist, 22,* 261–266.

Cohen, G. (1979). Language and comprehension in old age. *Cognitive Psychology, 11,* 412–429.

Cohen, G. (1980). Prospects for mental health and aging. In J. E. Birren & R. B. Sloane (Eds.), *Handbook of mental health and aging* (pp. 971–993). Englewood Cliffs, NJ: Prentice-Hall.

Cohen, G. (1984). Counseling interventions for the late-twentieth-century elderly. *Counseling Psychologist, 12,* 97–100.

Cohen, G. (1985). Toward an interface of mental and physical health phenomena in geriatrics: Clinical findings and questions. In C. Gaitz & T. Samorijski (Eds.), *Aging 2000: Our health care destiny, biomedical issues* (pp. 233–299). New York: Springer.

Cohen, G. D. (1990). Psychopathology and mental health in the mature and elderly adult. In J. E. Birren & K. W. Schaie (Eds.). *Handbook of the psychology of aging* (pp. 375–404). New York: Academic Press.

Cohen, G. (1992). The future of mental health and aging. In J. E. Birren, R. B. Sloane, &. G. D. Cohen (Eds.), *Handbook of mental health and aging* (pp. 893–914). New York: Academic Press.

Cohen, J. (1957). The factorial structure of the WAIS between early adulthood and old age. *Journal of Consulting Psychology, 21,* 283–290.

Cohen, M. M. (1982). In the presence of your absence: The treatment of older families with a cancer patient. *Psychotherapy: Theory, Research, and Practice, 19,* 453–460.

Cohen, S. Z., & Gans, B. M. (1978). *The other generation gap.* Chicago: Follett.

Cohn, R. M. (1979). Age and the satisfaction from work. *Journal of Gerontology, 34,* 264–272.

Colarusso, C. A., & Nemiroff, R. A. (1981). *Adult development: A new dimension in psychodynamic theory and practice.* New York: Plenum.

Colavita, F. B. (1978). *Sensory changes in the elderly.* Springfield, IL: Thomas.

Cole, S. (1979). Age and scientific performance. *American Journal of Sociology, 84,* 958–977.

Coleman, J. C. (1976). *Abnormal psychology and modern life.* Glenview, IL: Scott, Foresman.

Coleman, J. C., Butcher, J. N., & Carson, R. C. (1984). *Abnormal psychology and modern life* (7th ed.). Glenview, IL: Scott, Foresman.

Coleman, L. M., & Antonucci, T. C. (1983). Impact of work on women at mid-life. *Developmental Psychology, 19,* 290–294.

Colerick, E. J., & George, L. K. (1986). Predictors of institutionalization among caregivers of patients with Alzheimer's disease. *Journal of the American Geriatric Society, 34,* 493–498.

Colsher, P. L., Dorfman, L. T., & Wallace, R. B. (1988). Specific health conditions and work-retirement status among the elderly. *Journal of Applied Gerontology, 7,* 485–503.

Comfort, A. (1964). *Aging: The biology of senescence.* New York: Holt, Rinehart, and Winston.

Comfort, A. (1980). Sexuality in later life. In J. E. Birren & R. B. Sloane (Eds.), *Handbook of mental health and aging* (pp. 885–892). Englewood Cliffs, NJ: Prentice-Hall.

Coni, N. K. (1991). Ethical dilemmas faced in dealing with the sick aged. In F. Ludwig (Ed.), *Lifespan extension: Consequences and open questions* (pp. 68–80). New York: Springer.

Connidis, I. A., & Davies, L. (1990). Confidants and companions in later life: The place of family and friends. *Journal of Gerontology: Social Sciences, 45,* S141–149.

Conte, H., Weiner, M., & Plutchik, R. (1982). Measuring death anxiety: Conceptual, psychometric, and factor-analytic aspects. *Journal of Personality and Social Psychology, 43,* 775–785.

Conway, M. (1991). In defense of everyday memory. *American Psychologist, 46,* 19–26.

Cook, A. S., & Oltjenbruns, K. A. (1989). *Dying and grieving: Life-span and family perspectives.* New York: Holt, Rinehart, and Winston.

Cooper, S., & Ratner, E. (1989, November). Patterns of medication use among elderly upon admission to nursing homes. Paper presented at the Annual Scientific Meeting of the Gerontological Society of America. Minneapolis, MN.

Corby, N., & Solnick, R. (1980). Psychosocial and physiological influences on sexuality in the older adults. In J. E. Birren & R. B. Sloane (Eds.), *Handbook of mental health and aging* (pp. 893–921). Englewood Cliffs, NJ: Prentice-Hall.

Cornelius, S. W., Caspi, A., & Harnum, J. (1983, November). Intelligence adaptation [paper]. Annual meeting of the Gerontological Society, San Francisco.

Cornelius, S. W. (1990). Aging and everyday cognitive abilities. In T. Hess (Ed.), *Aging and cognition: Knowledge, organization, and utilization* (pp. 411–444). Amsterdam: North Holland.

Cornelius, S. W., & Caspi, A. (1987). Everyday problem-solving in adulthood and old age. *Psychology and Aging, 2,* 144–153.

Corso, J. F. (1971). Sensory processes and age effects in normal adults. *Journal of Gerontology, 26,* 90–105.

Corso, J. F. (1977). Auditory perception and communication. In J. E. Birren & K. W. Schaie (Eds.), *Handbook of the psychology of aging* (pp. 535–553). New York: Van Nostrand Reinhold.

Costa, J. J. (1984). *Abuse of the elderly.* Lexington, MA: Heath.

Costa, P. T., Jr. (1991). The use of the five-factor model: An introduction. *Journal of Personality Assessment, 57,* 393–398.

Costa, P. T., Jr., & McCrae, R. (1978). Objective personality assessment. In M. Storandt, I. Siegler, & M. Elias (Eds.), *The clinical psychology of aging* (pp. 119–143). New York: Plenum.

Costa, P. T., Jr., & McCrae, R. (1980a). Still stable after all these years: Personality as a key to some issues in adulthood and old age. In P. Baltes & O. Brim (Eds.), *Life-span development and behavior* (pp. 66–103). New York: Academic Press.

Costa, P. T., Jr., & McCrae, R. R. (1980b). Functional age: A conceptual empirical critique. In S. G. Haynes and M. Feinleib (Eds.), *Second Conference on the Epidemiology of Aging* (Publication No. 80–969, pp. 23–46). Washington, DC: U.S. Government Printing Office, National Institutes of Health.

Costa, P. T., Jr., & McCrae, R. (1986). Cross-sectional studies of personality in a national sample: 1. Development and validation of survey measures. *Psychology and Aging, 1,* 140–143.

Costa, P. T., Jr., & McCrae, R. R. (1989). Personality continuity and the changes of adult life. In M. Storandt & G. VandenBos (Eds.), *The adult years: Continuity and change* (pp. 45–77). Washington, DC: American Psychological Association.

Costa, P. T., Jr., McCrae, R., & Arenberg, D. (1983). Recent longitudinal research on personality and aging. In K. W. Schaie (Ed.), *Longitudinal studies of adult psychological development* (pp. 222–265). New York: Guilford Press.

Costa, P. T., Jr., Zonderman, A., McCrae, R., Coroni-Huntley, J., Locke, B., & Barbano, H. (1986). Longitudinal analyses of psychological well-being in a national sample: Stability of mean levels. *Journal of Gerontology, 42,* 50–55.

Cottrell, L. (1962). The adjustment of the individual to his age and sex roles. *American Sociological Review, 7,* 617–620.

Courtney, S. (1989). Defining adult and continuing education. In S. B. Merriam & P. M. Cunningham (Eds.), *Handbook of adult and continuing education* (pp. 15–25). San Francisco: Jossey-Bass.

Covey, H. C. (1989). Old age portrayed by the ages-of-life models from the middle ages to the 15th century. *Gerontologist, 29,* 692–698.

Cowgill, D. (1986). *Aging around the world.* Belmont, CA: Wadsworth.

Cowgill, D. O., & Holmes, L. D. (1972). *Aging and modernization.* New York: Appleton-Century-Crofts.

Cowley, M. (1982). *The view from 80* (pp. 3–6). New York: Penguin.

Cowling, W. R., & Campbell, V. G. (1986). Health concerns of aging men. *Nursing Clinics of North America, 21,* 75–83.

Cox, H. G. (1990). Roles for aged individuals in post-industrial societies. *International Journal of Aging and Human Development, 30,* 55–62.

Cox, H. G., & Hammonds, A. (1988). Religiosity, aging, and life satisfaction. *Journal of Religion and Aging, 5,* 1–21.

Craft, J. A., Doctors, S. I., Shkop, Y. M., & Benecki, T. J. (1979). Simulated management perceptions, hiring decisions, and age. *Aging and Work, 2,* 95–100.

Craik, F. I. M. (1977). Age differences in human memory. In J. E. Birren & K. W. Schaie (Eds.), *Handbook of the psychology of aging* (pp. 384–429). New York: Van Nostrand Reinhold.

Craik, F. I. M., & Lockhart, R. S. (1972). Levels of processing: A framework for memory research. *Journal of Verbal Learning and Verbal Behavior, 11,* 671–684.

Crane, D. P. (1986). *Personnel: The management of human resources.* Boston: Kent.

Crites, J. O. (1981). *Career counseling.* New York: McGraw-Hill.

Cronbach, L. J. (1991). *Essentials of psychological testing.* New York: HarperCollins.

Crook, R. H., Healy, C. C., & O'Shea, D. W. (1984). The linkage of work achievement to self-esteem, career maturity, and college achievement. *Journal of Vocational Behavior, 25,* 70–79.

Crook, T. (1987). Dementia. In L. Carstensen & B. Edelstein (Eds.), *Handbook of clinical gerontology* (pp. 96–111). New York: Praeger.

Crook, T. H., Ferris, S. H., & Bartus, R. T. (1983). *Assessment in geriatric psychopharmacology.* New Canaan, CT: Mark Powley Associates.

Crook, T. H., Bartus, R. T., Ferris, S. H., Whitehouse, P., Cohen, G. D., & Gershon, S. (1986). Age-associated memory impairment: Proposed diagnostic criteria and measures of clinical change [report of an NIMH work group]. *Developmental Neuropsychology, 2,* 261–276.

Crooks, R., & Bauer, K. (1980). *Our sexuality.* Reading, MA: Benjamin/Cummings.

Cross, S., & Markus, H. (1991). Possible selves across the life course. *Human Development, 34,* 230–255.

Cruikshank, M. (1991). Lavender and gray: A brief survey of lesbian and gay aging studies. *Journal of Homosexuality, 20,* 77–88.

Cuellar, J. (1978). El Senior Citizens Club. In B.

Myerhoff & A. Simic (Eds.), *Life's career: Aging* (pp. 207–230). Beverly Hills, CA: Sage.

Cumming, E. (1963). Further thoughts on the theory of disengagement. *International Social Science Journal, 15,* 377–393.

Cumming, E. (1975). Engagement with an old theory. *International Journal of Aging and Human Development, 6,* 187–191.

Cumming, E., & Henry, W. E. (1961). *Growing old: The process of disengagement.* New York: Basic Books.

Cummings, S. R., & Nevitt, M. C. (1989). A hypothesis: The causes of hip fractures. *Journal of Gerontology: Medical Sciences, 44,* M107–111.

Cunningham, W. R., Sepkowski, C., & Opel, M. (1978). Fatigue effects on intelligence-test performance in the elderly. *Journal of Gerontology, 33,* 541–545.

Cunningham, W. R., & Tomer, A. (1991). Intellectual abilities and age: Concepts, theories, and analysis. In E. Lovelace (Ed.), *Aging and cognition: Mental processes, self-awareness, and interventions.* Amsterdam: North Holland.

Cusack, O., & Smith, E. (1984). *Pets and the elderly: The therapeutic bond.* New York: Haworth Press.

Cutler, N. E., & Gregg, D. W. (1991, Winter). The human "wealth span" and financial well-being in older age. *Generations,* 45–49.

Cutler, S., & Hendricks, J. (1990). Leisure and time use across the life course. In R. Binstock & L. George (Eds.), *Handbook of aging and the social sciences* (pp. 169–185). New York: Academic Press.

Cutrone, C., Russell, D., & Rose, J. (1986). Social support and adaptation to stress in the elderly. *Psychology and Aging, 1,* 47–54.

Dabratz, M. E. (1990). The life-closure scale: A measure of psychological adaptation in death and dying. *Hospice Journal, 6,* 1–15.

Dancy, J., Jr. (1977). *The black elderly: A guide for practitioners.* Ann Arbor: University of Michigan.

Daniel, D., Templin, R., & Shearon, R. (1977). The value orientations of older adults toward education. *Educational Gerontology, 2,* 33–42.

Danish, S. (1981). Life-span development and intervention: A necessary link. *Counseling Psychologist, 9,* 40–43.

Danish, S., Smyer, M., & Nowak, C. (1980). Developmental intervention: Enhancing life-event processes. In P. B. Baltes & O. G. Brim (Eds.), *Life-span development and behavior* (pp. 340–366). New York: Academic Press.

Darnell, J., Murray, M., Martz, B., & Weinberger, M. (1986). Medication use by ambulatory elderly: An in-home survery. *Journal of the American Geriatrics Society, 34,* 1–4.

Davenport, J. (1986). Learning style and its relationship to gender and age among Elderhostel participants. *Educational Gerontology, 12,* 205–217.

Davidson, G. W. (1978). *The hospice: Development and administration.* Washington, DC: Hemisphere.

Davidson, G. W. (1984). Stillbirth, neonatal death, and sudden infant death syndrome. In H. Wass & C. Corr (Eds.), *Childhood and death* (pp. 243–257). Washington, DC: Hemisphere/McGraw-Hill.

Davidson, M. J., & Cooper, C. L. (1986). Executive women under pressure. *International Review of Applied Psychology, 35,* 301–326.

Davis, K. (1985). Health care policies and the aged: Observations from the United States. In R. Binstock & E. Shanas (Eds.), *Handbook of aging and the social sciences* (pp. 727–744). New York: Van Nostrand Reinhold.

Davis-Friedmann, D. (1981). Retirement and social welfare programs for Chinese elderly: A minimal role for the State. In C. Nusbert & M. Osako (Eds.), *The situation of the Asian/Pacific elderly.* Washington, DC: International Federation on Aging.

Davis-Friedmann, D. (1983). *Chinese elderly and the Communist revolution.* Cambridge, MA: Harvard University Press.

Davison, G. C., & Neale, J. M. (1990). *Abnormal psychology* (4th ed.). New York: Wiley.

Davy, J. A., Kinicki, A. J., & Scheck, C. L. (1991). Developing and testing a model of survivor responses to layoffs. *Journal of Vocational Behavior, 38,* 302–317.

DeFrain, J. (1990–1991). The psychological effects of a stillborn on surviving family members. *Omega, 22,* 81–108.

DeFrank, R. S., & Ivancevich, J. M. (1986). Job loss: An individual-level review and model. *Journal of Vocational Behavior, 28,* 1–20.

Deimling, G., & Bass, D. (1986). Symptoms of mental impairment among elderly adults and their effects on family caregivers. *Journal of Gerontology, 41,* 778–784.

Dennis, W. (1966). Cognitive productivity between the ages of 20 and 80 years. *Journal of Gerontology, 21,* 1–8.

Denny, N. (1974). Clustering in middle and old age. *Developmental Psychology, 10,* 471–475.

Denny, N. (1982). Aging and cognitive changes. In B. Wolman (Ed.), *Handbook of developmental psychology* (pp. 807–827). Englewood Cliffs, NJ: Prentice-Hall.

Deshler, D., & Hogan, N. (1989). Adult education research: Issues and directions. In S. B. Merriam

& P. M. Cunningham (Eds.), *Handbook of adult and continuing education* (pp. 183–200). San Francisco: Jossey-Bass.

DeSpelder, L. A., & Strickland, A. L. (1992). *The last dance: Encountering death and dying*. Palo Alto, CA: Mayfield.

DeVos, S. (1990). Extended-family living among older people in six Latin American countries. *Journal of Gerontology: Social Sciences, 45*, S87–94.

Dhooper, S. S. (1983). Family coping with the crisis of a heart attack. *Social Work in Health Care, 9*, 15–31.

Dial, D. W. (1988). Prime-time television portrayals of older adults in the context of family life. *Gerontologist, 28*, 700–706.

Diamond, E. E. (1988). Women's occupational plans and decisions: An introduction. *Applied Psychology: An International Review, 37*, 97–102.

Dickens, W. J., & Perlman, D. (1981). Friendship over the life cycle. In S. Duck & R. Gilmour (Eds.), *Personal relationships: 2. Developing personal relationships* (pp. 91–122). New York: Academic Press.

Dickstein, E. (1977). Self and self-esteem: Theoretical foundations and their implications for research. *Human Development, 20*, 149–150.

Dion, K. K., & Berscheid, E. (1972). What is beautiful and is good. *Journal of Personality and Social Psychology, 24*, 285–290.

Dirken, J. M. (1972). *Functional age of industrial workers*. Groningen, Sweden: Wolters-Moorhoff.

Dixon, R. A., Simon, E., Nowak, C., & Hultsch, D. F. (1982). Text recall in adulthood as a function of level of information, input modality, and delay interval. *Journal of Gerontology, 37*, 358–364.

Dixon, R. A., & Hultsch, D. F. (1983). Structure and development of metamemory in adulthood. *Journal of Gerontology, 38*, 682–688.

Dobbs, A. R., & Rule, B. G. (1990). Adult age differences in working memory. *Psychology and Aging, 4*, 500–503.

Dobson, C., & Morrow, P. C. (1984). Effects of career orientation on retirement planning. *Journal of Vocational Behavior, 24*, 73–83.

Doherty, W. J., & Jackson, N. S. (1982). Marriage and the family. In J. Wohlman (Ed.), *Handbook of developmental psychology* (pp. 667–680). Englewood Cliffs, NJ: Prentice-Hall.

Doka, K. J. (1986). Loss upon loss: The impact of death after divorce. *Death Studies, 10*, 441–449.

Donahue, W., Orback, H., & Pollack, O. (1960). Retirement: The emerging social pattern. In C. Tibbitts (Ed.), *Handbook of social gerontology* (pp. 330–406). Chicago: University of Chicago Press.

Donaldson, G. (1981). Letter to the editor. *Journal of Gerontology, 36*, 634–638.

Donnelly, K. (1982). *Recovering from the loss of a child*. New York: Macmillan.

Doppelt, J. E., & Wallace, W. L. (1955). Standardization of the Wechsler Adult Intelligence Scale for older persons. *Journal of Abnormal and Social Psychology, 51*, 312–330.

Dorfman, L. T. (1989). Retirement preparation and retirement satisfaction in the rural elderly. *Journal of Applied Gerontology, 8*, 432–450.

Dorrell, B. (1991). Being there: A support network of lesbian women. *Journal of Homosexuality, 20*, 89–98.

Douglas, J. D. (1990–1991). Patterns of change following parents' death in mid-life adults. *Omega, 22*, 123–139.

Douglas, K., & Arenberg, D. (1978). Age changes, age differences, and cultural change on the Guilford-Zimmerman Temperament Survey. *Journal of Gerontology, 33*, 737–747.

Dowd, J. J., & Bengtson, V. (1978). Aging in minority populations: An examination of the double-jeopardy hypothesis. *Journal of Gerontology, 33*, 427–436.

Drachman, D. A. (1980). An approach to the neurology of aging. In J. E. Birren & R. B. Sloane (Eds.), *Handbook of mental health and aging* (pp. 501–519). Englewood Cliffs, NJ: Prentice-Hall.

Driskill, T., & Dauw, D. C. (1975). Executive mid-career job change. *Personnel and Guidance Journal, 54*, 562–567.

Duberman, L. (1974). *Marriage and its alternatives*. New York: Praeger.

Dubois, P. M. (1980). *Hospice way of death*. New York: Human Sciences Press.

Dunham, C. C., & Bengtson, V. (1986). Conceptual and theoretical perspectives on generational relations. In N. Datan, A. L. Greene, & H. Reese (Eds.), *Life-span developmental psychology: Intergenerational relations* (pp. 1–27). Hillsdale, NJ: Erlbaum.

Dusk, D., Hiat, M., & Schroeder, H. (1983). Self-statement modification with adults: A metaanalysis. *Psychological Bulletin, 94*, 408–422.

Duvall, E. (1971). *Family development*. Philadelphia: Lippincott.

Eadwins, C. J., & Mellinger, J. C. (1984). Mid-life women: Relationship of old age and role to personality. *Journal of Personality and Social Psychology, 47*, 390–395.

Einstein, G. O., & McDaniel, M. A. (1990). Normal aging and prospective memory. *Journal of Experimental Psychology: Learning, Memory, and Cognition, 16*, 717–726.

Eisdorfer, C. (1960). Rorschach rigidity and sensory

decrement in a senescent population. *Journal of Gerontology, 15,* 188–190.

Eisdorfer, C. (1968). Arousal and performance: Experiments in verbal learning and a tentative theory. In G. A. Tolland (Ed.), *Human aging and behavior* (pp. 189–216). New York: Academic Press.

Eisdorfer, C. (1983). Conceptual models of aging: The challenge of a new frontier. *American Psychologist, 39,* 197–202.

Eisdorfer, C., & Cohen, D. (1978). The cognitively impaired elderly: Differential diagnosis. In M. Storandt, I. C. Siegler, & M. F. Elias (Eds.), *The clinical psychology of aging* (pp. 7–42). New York: Plenum.

Eisdorfer, C., & Stotsky, B. (1977). Intervention, treatment, and rehabilitation of psychiatric disorders. In J. E. Birren & K. W. Schaie (Eds.), *Handbook of the psychology of aging* (pp. 724–748). New York: Van Nostrand Reinhold.

Eisdorfer, C., & Wilkie, F. (1973). Intellectual changes with advancing age. In L. F. Jarvik, C. Eisdorfer, & J. Blum (Eds.), *Intellectual functioning in adults* (pp. 102–111). New York: Springer.

Eisdorfer, C., & Wilkie, F. (1979a). Stress and behavior in the aging. *Issues in mental health and aging: Research* (Vol. 3). Rockville, MD: Department of Health, Education, and Welfare.

Eisdorfer, C., & Wilkie, F. (1979b). Research on crisis and stress in aging. In H. Pardes (Ed.), *Issues in mental health and aging: Research* (Vol. 3). Rockville, MD: Department of Health, Education, and Welfare.

Eisner, D. A. (1972). Life-span differences in visual perception. *Perceptual and Motor Skills, 34,* 857–858.

Ekerdt, D. J. (1989). Retirement preparation. In M. P. Lawton (Ed.), *Annual review of gerontology and geriatrics* (Vol. 9, pp. 321–356). New York: Springer.

Ekerdt, D. J., & Bosse, R. (1985). An empirical test for phases of retirement: Findings from the Normative Aging Study. *Journal of Gerontology, 40,* 95–101.

Ekerdt, D. J., & Vinick, B. H. (1991). Marital complaints in husband-working and husband-retired couples. *Research on Aging, 13,* 364–382.

Ekerdt, D. J., Vinick, B. H., & Bosse, R. (1989). Orderly ending: Do men know when they retire? *Journal of Gerontology: Social Sciences, 44,* S28–35.

El-Baradi, A. F., & Bourne, G. H. (1951). Theory of tastes and odors. *Science, 113,* 660–661.

Elder, G. H. (1979). Historical change in life patterns and personality. In P. B. Baltes & O. G. Brim (Eds.), *Life-span development and behavior* (pp. 117–159). New York: Academic Press.

Elder, G. H. (1986). Military times and turning points in men's lives. *Developmental Psychology, 22,* 233–245.

Elder, G. H., Jr. (1991, Winter). Making the best of life: Perspectives on lives, times, and aging. *Generations* 12–19.

Elias, M., Elias, J., & Elias, P. (1990). Biological and health influences on behavior. In J. Birren & K. Schaie (Eds.), *Handbook of the psychology of aging* (pp. 80–102). New York: Academic Press.

Elias, M. F., & Streeten, D. H. P. (Eds.). (1980). *Hypertension and cognitive processes.* Mount Desert, ME: Beech Hill.

Elias, P. K., Elias, M. F., Robbins, M. A., & Gage, P. (1987). Acquisition of word-processing skills by younger, middle-aged, and older adults. *Psychology and Aging, 2,* 340–348.

Elliott, L. (1987). Attitudes toward hearing loss. *Center on Aging McGaw Medical Center Newsletter, 3,* 4–5.

Ellis, A. (1962). *Reason and emotion in psychotherapy.* New York: Lyle Stuart.

Emery, C. F., & Blumenthal, J. A. (1990). Perceived change among participants in an exercise program for older adults. *Gerontologist, 30,* 516–521.

Emmerich, W. (1973). Socialization and sex role development. In P. B. Baltes & K. W. Schaie (Eds.), *Life-span developmental psychology: Personality and socialization* (pp. 123–144). New York: Academic Press.

Engen, T. (1977). Taste and smell. In J. E. Birren & K. W. Schaie (Eds.), *Handbook of the psychology of aging* (pp. 554–561). New York: Van Nostrand Reinhold.

Engen, T. (1982). *The perception of odors.* New York: Academic Press.

Engle, M. (1990). Little old ladies are much maligned: Diversity reconsidered. *Educational Gerontology, 16,* 339–346.

Erikson, E. H. (1959). Identity and the life cycle. *Psychological Issues, 1.*

Erikson, E. H. (1963). *Childhood and society* (2nd ed.). New York: Norton.

Erikson, E. H. (1982). *Adulthood.* New York: Norton.

Estes, C. L. (1979). *The aging enterprise.* San Francisco: Jossey Bass.

Estes, R. J., & Wilensky, H. L. (1978). Life-cycle squeeze and the morale curve. *Social Problems, 25,* 277–292.

Estes, W. K. (1975). The state of the field: General problems and issues of theory and metatheory. In W. Estes (Ed.), *Handbook of learning and cognitive processes* (Vol. 1, pp. 1–24). Hillsdale, NJ: Erlbaum.

Evans, D. A. (1989). Prevalence of Alzheimer's disease in a community population of older persons. *JAMA, 262,* 2551–2556.

Evans, L. (1988). Older driver involvement in fatal and severe traffic crashes. *Journal of Gerontology: Social Sciences, 43,* S186–193.

Farrimond, T. (1989). Accident and illness rates for younger and older workers when employment is based on medical examination. *Psychological Reports, 65,* 556–558.

Fassinger, R. E. (1990). Causal models of career choice in two samples of college women. *Journal of Vocational Behavior, 36,* 225–248.

Featherman, D. L. (1983). Life-span perspectives in social science research. In P. B. Baltes & O. G. Brim, Jr. (Eds.), *Life-span development and behavior* (Vol. 5). New York: Academic Press.

Feifel, H., & Nagy, V. T. (1981). Another look at fear of death? *Journal of Counsulting and Clinical Psychology, 49,* 278–286.

Feil, N. (1989). *Validation: The Feil method.* Cleveland, OH: Author.

Felton, B. J. (1982). The aged: Settings, services, and needs. In L. R. Snowden (Ed.), *Reaching the underserved* (pp. 23–42). Beverly Hills, CA: Sage.

Felton, B. J., & Revenson, T. A. (1987). Age differences in coping with chronic illness. *Psychology and Aging, 2,* 164–170.

Ferraro, K. F. (1987). Double jeopardy to health for black older adults? *Journal of Gerontology, 42,* 528–533.

Ferraro, K. F. (1990). Cohort analysis of retirement preparation, 1974–1981. *Journal of Gerontology: Social Sciences, 45,* S21–31.

Field, D. (1991). Continuity and change in personality in old age: Evidence from five longitudinal studies. *Journal of Gerontology: Psychological Sciences, 46,* P271–274.

Field, D., & Milsap, R. E. (1991). Personality in advanced old age: Continuity or change? *Journal of Gerontology: Psychological Sciences, 46,* P299–308.

Field, T. M., & Widmayer, S. M. (1982). Motherhood. In B. Wolman (Ed.), *Handbook of developmental psychology* (pp. 681–701). Englewood Cliffs, NJ: Prentice-Hall.

Fillenbaum, G. G. (1990). *Multidimensional functional assessment of older adults.* Hillsdale, NJ: Erlbaum.

Filsinger, E., & Sauer, W. (1978). An empirical typology of adjustment to aging. *Journal of Gerontology, 33,* 437–445.

Finch, C. E., & Hayflick, L. (Eds.). (1977). *Handbook of the biology of aging.* New York: Van Nostrand Reinhold.

Finkel, S. I. (1991). Group psychotherapy in later life. In W. Myers (Ed.), *New techniques in psychotherapy of older patients* (pp. 223–244). Washington, DC: American Psychiatric Press.

Finley, N. J., Roberts, M. D., & Banahan, B. F. (1988). Motivators and inhibitors of attitudes of filial obligation toward aging parents. *Gerontologist, 28,* 73–78.

Fischer, D. H. (1977). *Growing old in America.* New York: Oxford.

Fitzgerald, J. M., & Mellor, S. (1988). How do people think about intelligence? *Multivariate Behavioral Research, 23,* 143–157.

Fitzgerald, L. F., & Betz, N. E. (1983). Issues in the vocational psychology of women. In W. B. Walsh & S. H. Osipow (Eds.), *Handbook of vocational psychology: Foundations* (Vol. 1, pp. 83–160). Hillsdale, NJ: Erlbaum.

Fitzgerald, L. S., & Crites, J. O. (1980). Toward a career psychology of women: What do we know? What do we need to know? *Journal of Counseling Psychology, 27,* 44–68.

Flanagan, J. C., & Russ-Eft, D. (1976). *An empirical study aid in formulating educational goals.* Palo Alto, CA: American Institutes for Research.

Fleming, A. S., Rickards, L. D., Santos, J. F., & West, P. R. (1986). *Report on a survey of community mental health centers* (Vol. 3). Washington, DC: Action Committee to Implement the Mental Health Recommendations of the 1981 White House Conference on Aging.

Fletcher, W. L., & Hansson, R. O. (1991). Assessing the social components of retirement anxiety. *Psychology and Aging, 6,* 76–85.

Flicker, C., Ferris, S. H., Crook, T., & Bartus, R. T. (1989). Age differences in the vulnerability of facial-recognition memory to proactive interference. *Experimental Aging Research, 15,* 189–194.

Folkman, S., Lazarus, R. S., Pimley, S., & Novacek, J. (1987). Age differences in stress and coping processes. *Psychology and Aging, 2,* 171–184.

Folsom, J. (1968). Reality orientation for the elderly mental patient. *Journal of Geriatric Psychiatry, 1,* 291–307.

Fontana, A. (1977). *The last frontier: The social meaning of growing old.* Beverly Hills, CA: Sage.

Ford, C., & Sbordone, R. (1980). Attitudes of psychiatrists toward elderly patients. *American Journal of Psychiatry, 137,* 571–577.

Foseland, R., & Smith, G. (1990). Effectiveness of individual counseling by professional and peer helpers for family caregivers of the elderly. *Psychology and Aging, 5,* 256–263.

Foster, J., & Gallagher, D. (1986). An exploratory study comparing depressed and nondepressed elders' coping strategies. *Journal of Gerontology, 41,* 91–93.

Fountain, M. (1986). Matching yourself with the world of work: 1986 edition. *Occupational Outlook Quarterly, 30,* 2–12.

Fox, C. F. (1979). A cross-sequential study of age changes in personality in an aged population [unpublished doctoral dissertation, University of Florida]. *Dissertation Abstracts International, 4,* 4461.

Fozard, J. L. (1980). The time for remembering. In L. Poon (Ed.), *Aging in the 1980s: Psychological issues* (pp. 273–287). Washington, DC: American Psychological Association.

Fozard, J. L. (1990). Vision and hearing in aging. In J. Birren & K. Schaie (Eds.), *Handbook of the psychology of aging* (pp. 150–171). New York: Academic Press.

Fozard, J. L., & Popkin, S. (1978). Optimizing adult development: Ends and means of applied psychology of aging. *American Psychologist, 33,* 975–989.

Fozard, J. L., Nuttal, R. J., & Waugh, N. C. (1972). Age-related differences in mental performance. *Aging and Human Development, 3,* 19–43.

Fozard, J. L., Wolf, E., Bell, B., McFarland, R. A., & Podolsky, D. (1977). Visual perception and communication. In J. E. Birren & K. W. Schaie (Eds.), *Handbook of the psychology of aging* (pp. 497–534). New York: Van Nostrand Reinhold.

Frances, A. J., Pincus, H. A., Widiger, T. A., Davis, W. W., & First, M. B. (1990). DSM-IV: Work in progress. *American Journal of Psychiatry, 147,* 1439–1441.

Frances, A. J., Wideger, T. A., & Pincus, H. A. (1989). The development of DSM-IV. *Archives of General Psychiatry, 46,* 373–375.

Francis, G. M. (1984). Plush animals as therapy in a nursing home. *Clinical Gerontologist, 2,* 75–76.

Franklin-Panek, C. E. (1978). Effects of personal-growth groups on the self-concept and decision-making ability of normal adults. *Psychology: A Quarterly Journal of Human Behavior, 15,* 25–29.

Fraze, J. (1988, January). Displaced workers: Oakies of the 80s. *Personnel Administrator, 33,* 42–51.

Freedman, J. L., Sears, D. O., & Carlsmith, J. M. (1981). *Social psychology.* Englewood Cliffs, NJ: Prentice-Hall.

Freeman, F. M., & Williams, C. L. (1987, September–October). Minorities face stubborn inequalities. *Perspective on Aging* (National Council on Aging), *32,* 15–17.

Freud, S. (1924). *On psychotherapy. Collected papers of Sigmund Freud* (Vol. 1, pp. 249–263). London: Hogarth Press.

Friedman, M., & Rosenman, R. H. (1974). *Type A behavior and your heart.* New York: Knopf.

Friedrich, D. (1972). *A primer of developmental methodology.* Minneapolis: Burgess.

Friend, R. A. (1991). Older lesbian and gay people: A theory of successful aging. *Journal of Homosexuality, 20,* 99–111.

Fries, J. F., & Crapo, L. M. (1981). *Vitality and aging.* San Francisco: Freeman.

Furman, E. (1984). Children's patterns in mourning the death of a loved one. In H. Wass & C. Corr (Eds.), *Childhood and death* (pp. 185–203). New York: Hemisphere.

Furry, C., & Baltes, P. B. (1973). The effect of age differences in ability-extraneous performance variables on the assessment of intelligence in children, adults, and the elderly. *Journal of Gerontology, 28,* 78–80.

Furstenberg, F. F. (1982). Conjugal succession: Reentering marriage after divorce. In P. B. Baltes & O. G. Brim, Jr. (Eds.), *Life-span development and behavior* (Vol. 4, pp. 107–146). New York: Academic Press.

Gaitz, C. M., & Scott, J. (1972). Age and the measurement of mental health. *Journal of Health and Social Behavior, 13,* 55–67.

Gallagher, D., & Thompson, L. (1982). Treatment of major depressive disorder in older adult outpatients with brief psychotherapies. *Psychotherapy: Theory, Research, and Practice, 19,* 482–490.

Gallagher, D., & Thompson, L. (1983). Depression. In P. Lewisohn & L. Teri (Eds.), *Clinical geropsychology: New directions in assessment and treatment* (pp. 7–37). Elmsford, NY: Pergamon Press.

Gallagher, D., Thompson, L., & Levy, S. (1980). Clinical psychological assessment of older adults. In L. Poon (Ed.), *Aging in the 1980s: Psychological issues* (pp. 19–40). Washington, DC: American Psychological Association.

Gallagher, D., Breckenridge, J. N., Thompson, L. W., & Peterson, J. A. (1983). Effects of bereavement on indicators of mental health in elderly widows and widowers. *Journal of Gerontology, 38,* 565–571.

Gallagher, D., Wrabetz, A., Lovett, S., Del Maestro, S., & Rose, J. (1989). Depression and other negative effects on caregivers. In E. Light & B. Lebowitz (Eds.). *Alzheimer's disease treatment and family stress: Directions for research* (pp. 218–244). NIMH: Rockville, MD.

Garber, J., & Seligman, M. E. P. (1980). *Human helplessness.* New York: Academic Press.

Gardner, H. (1983). *Frames of mind: The theory of multiple intelligences.* New York: Basic Books.

Garfield, S. L. (1986). Research on client variables in

psychotherapy. In S. L. Garfield & A. E. Bergin (Eds.), *Handbook of psychotherapy and behavior change* (pp. 271–298). New York: Wiley.

Garfield, S. L., & Bergin, A. E. (1986). *Handbook of psychotherapy and behavior change* (3rd ed.). New York: Wiley.

Garn, S. M. (1975). Bone loss and aging. In R. Goldman and M. Rockstein (Eds.), *The physiology and pathology of aging* (pp. 39–57). New York: Academic Press.

Gatz, M., & Peason, C. (1988). Ageism revised and the provision of psychological services. *American Psychologist, 43,* 184–188.

Gatz, M., Bengtson, V., & Blum, M. (1990). Caregiving families. In J. Birren & K. Schaie (Eds.), *Handbook of the psychology of aging* (pp. 404–426). New York: Academic Press.

Gatz, M., Popkin, S., Pino, C., & VandenBos, G. (1985). Psychological interventions with older adults. In J. E. Birren & K. W. Schaie (Eds.), *Handbook of the psychology of aging* (pp. 755–788). New York: Van Nostrand Reinhold.

Gatz, M., Siegler, I., George, L. K., & Tyler, F. B. (1986). Attributional components of locus of control: Longitudinal, retrospective, and contemporaneous analyses. In M. M. Baltes & P. B. Baltes (Eds.), *The psychology of control and aging* (pp. 237–263). Hillsdale, NJ: Erlbaum.

Gatz, M., Smyer, M., & Lawton, M. P. (1980). The mental health system and the older adult. In L. Poon (Ed.), *Aging in the 1980s: Psychological issues* (pp. 5–18). Washington, DC: American Psychological Association.

Gekoski, W. L., & Knox, V. J. (1983, November). Identifying age stereotypes in adolescents: An attributional approach [paper]. Annual meeting of the Gerontological Society, San Francisco.

Gelfand, D. (1982). *Aging: The ethnic factor.* Boston: Little, Brown.

Gentry, M., & Schulman, A. D. (1988). Remarriage as a coping response for widowhood. *Psychology and Aging, 3,* 191–196.

George, L. K. (1981). *Role transitions in later life.* Monterey, CA: Wadsworth.

George, L. K. (1990). Social structure, social processes, and social-psychological states. In R. Binstock & L. K. George (Eds.), *Handbook of aging and the social sciences* (pp. 186–204). New York: Academic Press.

George, L. K., & Clipp, E. C. (1991, Winter). Aging well is ultimately what gerontology is all about. *Generations,* 5–7.

George, L. K., & Clipp, E. C. (1991, Winter). Subjective components of aging well: Researchers need to reconsider. *Generations,* 57–61.

George, L. K., & Weiler, S. J. (1981). Sexuality in middle and late life: The effects of age, cohort, and gender. *Archives of General Psychiatry, 38,* 919–923.

George, L. K., Blazer, D. G., Winfield-Saird, I., Leaf, P. J., & Fishback, R. L. (1988). Psychiatric disorders and mental-health-service use in later life: Evidence from the Epidemiological Catchment Area Program. In J. Budy & G. Maddox (Eds.), *Epidemiology and Aging* (pp. 189–219). New York: Springer.

George, L. K., Fillenbaum, G. G., & Palmore, E. (1984). Sex differences in the antecedents and consequences of retirement. *Journal of Gerontology, 39,* 364–371.

Gerber, J., Wolff, J., Klores, W., & Brown, G. (1989). *Lifetrends: The future of baby boomers and other aging Americans.* New York: Macmillan.

Gerson, L. W., Jarjoura, D., & McCord, G. (1987). Factors related to impaired mental health in urban elderly. *Research on Aging, 9,* 356–371.

Giambra, L. M., & Martin, C. E. (1977). Sexual daydreams and quantitative aspects of sexual activity: Some relations for males across adulthood. *Archives of Sexual Behavior, 6,* 497–505.

Giambra, L. M., & Quilter, R. E. (1988). Sustained attention in adulthood: A unique, large-sample, longitudinal, and multicohort analysis using the Mackworth Clock-Test. *Psychology and Aging, 3,* 75–83.

Gibb, G. D., & Bailey, J. R. (1983). Attitude toward equal-rights-amendment scale: An objective-measurement look at attitudes toward equal rights legislation. *Psychological Reports, 53,* 804–806.

Gilewski, M. J., Kuppinger, J., & Zarit, S. H. (1985). The aging marital system: A case study in life changes and paradoxical intervention. *Clinical Gerontologist, 3,* 3–15.

Gilewski, M. J., & Zelinski, E. M. (1986). Questionnaire assessment of memory complaints. In L. Poon (Ed.), *Handbook for clinical memory assessment of older adults* (pp. 93–105). Washington, DC: American Psychological Association.

Gilford, R. (1984). Contrasts in marital satisfaction throughout old age: An exchange-theory analysis. *Journal of Gerontology, 39,* 325–333.

Gilhooly, M., Zarit, S., & Birren, J. E. (1986). *The dementias: Policy and management.* Englewood Cliffs, NJ: Prentice-Hall.

Ginzberg, E. (1971). *Career guidance.* New York: McGraw-Hill.

Gittings, N. S., & Fozard, J. (1986). Age changes in visual acuity. *Experimental Gerontology, 21,* 423–434.

Glamser, F. D. (1976). Determinants of a positive attitude toward retirement. *Journal of Gerontology, 31*, 104–107.

Glamser, F. D. (1981). The impact of preretirement programs on the retirement experience. *Journal of Gerontology, 36*, 244–250.

Glamser, F. D., & Hayslip, B. J. (1985). The impact of retirement on participation in leisure activities. *Therapeutic Recreation Journal, 19*, 28–38.

Glantz, M. D., & Backenheimer, M. S. (1988). Substance abuse among elderly women. *Clinical Gerontologist, 8*, 3–26.

Glenn, N. D., & McLanahan, S. (1981). The effects of offspring on the psychological well-being of older adults. *Journal of Marriage and the Family, 43*, 409–421.

Glenn, N. D., & Supancic, M. (1984). The social and demographic correlates of divorce and separation in the United States: An update and reconsideration. *Journal of Marriage and the Family, 46*, 563–575.

Glenn, N. D., & Weaver, C. N. (1978). A multivariate, multisurvey study of marital happiness. *Journal of Marriage and the Family, 40*, 269–282.

Glick, R. C. (1977). Updating the life cycle of the family. *Journal of Marriage and the Family, 39*, 5–15.

Golan, N. (1986). *The perilous bridge: Helping clients through mid-life transitions.* New York: Free Press.

Gold, A. R. (1979). Reexamining barriers to women's career development. *American Journal of Orthopsychiatry, 48*, 690–702.

Gold, D., & Arbuckle, T. (1990). Personality, cognition, and aging. In E. Lovelace (Ed.), *Aging and Cognition* (pp. 351–378). Amsterdam: North Holland.

Goldberg, R. J. (1981). Management of depression in the patient with advanced cancer. *JAMA, 245*, 373–376.

Goldenberg, I., & Goldenberg, H. (1991). *Family therapy: An overview.* Pacific Grove, CA: Brooks/Cole.

Goodstein, R. K. (1982). Individual psychotherapy and the elderly. *Psychotherapy: Theory, Research and Practice, 19*, 412–418.

Gordon, C., Gaitz, C. M., & Scott, J. (1976). Leisure and lives: Personal expressivity across the lifespan. In R. Binstock & E. Shanas (Eds.), *Handbook of aging and the social sciences* (pp. 310–400). New York: Van Nostrand Reinhold.

Gordon, V. W. (1981). The undecided student: A developmental perspective. *Personnel and Guidance Journal, 59*, 433–439.

Gotestam, K. (1980). Behavioral and dynamic psychotherapy with the elderly. In J. E. Birren & R. B. Sloane (Eds.), *Handbook of mental health and aging* (pp. 775–805). Englewood Cliffs, NJ: Prentice-Hall.

Gottesman, L. E., Quarterman, C., & Cohn, G. (1973). Psychosocial treatment of the aged. In C. Eisdorfer & M. P. Lawton (Eds.), *The psychology of adult development and aging* (pp. 378–427). Washington, DC: American Psychological Association.

Gottsdanker, R. (1980). Aging and the maintaining of preparation. *Experimental Aging Research, 6*, 13–27.

Gottsfredson, G. D. (1977). Career stability and redirection in adulthood. *Journal of Applied Psychology, 62*, 436–445.

Gould, R. (1972). The phases of adult life: A study in developmental psychology. *American Journal of Psychiatry, 129*, 521–531.

Gould, R. (1975, February). Adult life stages: Growth toward self-tolerance. *Psychology Today*, 74–78.

Gould, R. (1979). Transformations in mid-life. *New York University Education Quarterly, 10*, 2–9.

Goulet, L. (1972). New directions in research on aging and retention. *Journal of Gerontology, 27*, 52–60.

Goulet, L., & Baltes, P. (Eds.) (1970). *Life-span developmental psychology: Research and theory* (p. 463). New York: Academic Press.

Granick, S., Kleban, M. H., & Weiss, A. D. (1976). Relationships between hearing loss and cognition in normally hearing aged persons. *Journal of Gerontology, 31*, 434–440.

Grant, C. R. H. (1969). Age differences in self-concept from early adulthood through old age. *Proceedings of the American Psychological Association, 7*, 717–718.

Gratton, B., & Haug, M. R. (1983). Decision and adaptation: Research on female retirement. *Research on Aging, 5*, 59–76.

Gray, G. R., & Hayslip, B. (1990). Drug use and abuse among older adults and their implications for practitioners. *Southwestern, 6*, 33–52.

Greenblatt, C. (1983). The salience of sexuality in the early years of marriage. *Journal of Marriage and the Family, 45*, 289–299.

Greenglass, E. R. (1988). Type A behavior and coping strategies in female and male supervisors. *Applied Psychology: An internal review, 37*, 271–288.

Greenhaus, J. H., Paraseeraman, S., Grannose, C., Rabinowitz, S., & Beutell, N. J. (1989). Sources of work-family conflict among two-career couples. *Journal of Vocational Behavior, 34*, 133–153.

Gribben, K., & Schaie, K. W. (1978, November). Performance factors and age-group ability differences: Practice in the face of fatigue [paper]. Annual meeting of the Gerontological Society, Dallas.

Griew, S., & Davies, D. R. (1962). The affects of aging on auditory vigilance performance. *Journal of Gerontology, 17*, 88–90.

Grotevant, H. D., & Cooper, C. R. (1988). The role of family experience in career exploration: A life-span perspective. In P. B. Baltes, D. L. Featherman, & R. L. Lerner (Eds.), *Life-span development and behavior* (Vol. 8, pp. 231–258). Hillsdale, NJ: Erlbaum.

Guidubaldi, J., & Perry, J. (1985). Divorce and mental health sequelae for children: A two-year follow-up of a nationwide sample. *Journal of the American Academy of Child Psychiatry, 24*, 531–537.

Guidubaldi, J., Cleminshaw, H. K., Perry, J. D., & McLoughlin, C. S. (1983). The impact of parental divorce on children: Report of the nationwide NASP study. *School Psychology Review, 12*, 300–323.

Guilford, J. P. (1959). *Personality*. New York: McGraw-Hill.

Gurin, G., Veroff, J., & Field, S. (1963). *Americans view their mental health*. New York: Basic Books.

Gurland, B. J. (1973). A broad clinical assessment of psychopathology in the aged. In C. Eisdorfer & M. P. Lawton (Eds.), *The psychology of adult development and aging* (pp. 343–377). Washington, DC: American Psychological Association.

Gurland, B. J. (1980). The assessment of mental health status in older adults. In J. E. Birren & R. B. Sloane (Eds.), *Handbook of mental health and aging* (pp. 671–700). Englewood Cliffs, NJ: Prentice-Hall.

Gurland, B. J., Kuriansky, J., Sharpe, L., Simon, R., Stiller, P., & Birkett, P. (1977). The comprehensive assessment and referral evaluation (CARE): Rationale, development, and reliability. *International Journal of Aging and Human Development, 8*, 9–42.

Guttman, D. (1975). Parenthood: A key to the comparative study of the life cycle. In N. Datan & L. Ginsburg (Eds.), *Life-span developmental psychology: Normative life crises* (pp. 167–184). New York: Academic Press.

Guttman, D. (1977). The cross-cultural perspective: Notes toward a comparative psychology of aging. In J. E. Birren & K. W. Schaie (Eds.), *Handbook of the psychology of aging* (pp. 302–326). New York: Van Nostrand Reinhold.

Gwyther, L., & George, L. K. (1986). Introduction: Symposium on caregivers for dementia patients. *Gerontologist, 26*, 245–247.

Haan, N. (1972). Personality development from adolescence to adulthood in the Oakland growth and guidance studies. *Seminars in Psychiatry, 4*, 399–414.

Haan, N., Millsap, R., & Hartka, E. (1986). As time goes by: Change and stability in personality over 50 years. *Psychology and Aging, 1*, 220–232.

Habib, J. (1985). The economy and the aged. In R. Binstock & E. Shanas (Eds.), *Handbook of aging and the social sciences* (pp. 479–502). New York: Van Nostrand Reinhold.

Hackett, G., & Betz, N. (1981). A self-efficacy approach to the career development of women. *Journal of Vocational Behavior, 3*, 326–329.

Hafen, B. Q., & Frandsen, K. J. (1983). *Faces of death: Grief, dying, euthanasia, and suicide*. Englewood, CO: Morton.

Hafer, W. K. (1981). *Coping with bereavement*. Englewood Cliffs, NJ: Prentice-Hall.

Hagebak, J. E., & Hagebak, B. R. (1983, January–February). Meeting the mental health needs of the elderly: Issues and action steps. *Aging*, 26–31.

Hagestad, G. O. (1978). Patterns of communication and influence between grandparents and grandchildren [paper]. World Conference of Sociology, Helsinki, Finland.

Hagestad, G. O., & Neugarten, B. L. (1985). Age and the life course. In R. Binstock & E. Shanas (Eds.), *Handbook of aging and the social sciences* (pp. 35–61). New York: Van Nostrand Reinhold.

Haley, J. (1971). Family therapy. *International Journal of Psychiatry, 9*, 233–242.

Haley, W. E., Levine, E. G., Brown, S. L., & Bartolucci, A. A. (1987). Stress, appraisal, coping, and social supports as predictors of adaptational outcome among dementia caregivers. *Psychology and Aging, 2*, 323–330.

Hall, B. L. (1989). The hospitalized elderly and intergenerational conflict. *Journal of Applied Gerontology, 8*, 294–306.

Hall, C., & Lindzey, G. (1985). *Theories of personality*. New York: Wiley.

Hall, G. S., & Lindzey, G. (1985). *Introduction to theories of personality*. New York: Wiley.

Hamon, R. R., & Blieszner, R. (1990). Filial responsibility expectations among adult child–older parent pairs. *Journal of Gerontology: Psychological Sciences, 45*, P110–121.

Hanson, J. C. (1988). Changing interests of women: Myth or reality? *Applied Psychology: An International Review, 37*, 133–150.

Hanson, S. L., Sauer, W. J., & Seelbach, W. C. (1983). Racial and cohort variations in filial responsibility norms. *Gerontologist, 23*, 626–631.

Hansson, R. O., Briggs, S. R., & Rule, B. L. (1990). Old age and unemployment: Predictors of control, depression, and loneliness. *Journal of Applied Gerontology, 9*, 230–240.

Harel, Z., Aollod, R., & Bognar, B. (1982). Predictors of mental health among semirural aged. *Gerontologist, 22*, 499–504.

Harkins, S. W., Price, D. D., & Martelli, M. (1986). Effects of age on pain perception: Termonociception. *Journal of Gerontology, 41*, 58–63.

Harlan, W. H. (1968). Social status of the aged in three Indian villages. In B. Neugarten (Ed.), *Middle age and aging* (pp. 469–485). Chicago: University of Chicago Press.

Harmon, L. W. (1983). Testing some models of women's career development with longitudinal data [unpublished address]. College Park: University of Maryland.

Harmon, L. W. (1989). Longitudinal changes in womens' career aspirations: Developmental or historical? *Journal of Vocational Behavior, 35*, 46–63.

Harmon, R. R., & Blieszner, R. (1990). Filial responsibility expectations among adult child–older parent pairs. *Journal of Gerontology: Psychological Sciences, 45*, P110–112.

Harris, B. G. (1986). Induced abortion. In T. Rando (Ed.), *Parental loss of a child* (pp. 241–256). Champaign, IL: Research Press.

Harris, D. K., & Cole, W. E. (1980). *Sociology of Aging*. Boston: Houghton Mifflin.

Harris, L., & Associates. (1975). *The myth and reality of aging in America*. Washington, DC: National Council on Aging.

Harris, R. L., Elliott, A. M., & Holmes, D. S. (1986). The timing of psychosocial transitions and changes in women's lives: An examination of women aged 45 to 60. *Journal of Personality and Social Psychology, 51*, 409–416.

Harris, W. (1952). Fifth and seventh cranial nerves in relation to the nervous mechanism of taste sensation: A new approach. *British Medical Journal, 1*, 831–836.

Hartford, M. E. (1980). The use of group methods for work with the aged. In J. E. Birren & R. B. Sloane (Eds.), *Handbook of mental health and aging* (pp. 806–826). Englewood Cliffs, NJ: Prentice-Hall.

Hartley, J. T. (1986). Reader and text variables as determinants of discourse memory in adulthood. *Psychology and Aging, 1*, 150–158.

Hartley, J. T. (1989). Memory for prose: Perspectives on the reader. In L. W. Poon, D. C. Rubin, & B.A. Wilson (Eds.), *Everyday cognition in adulthood and late life* (pp. 135–156). Cambridge: Cambridge University Press.

Hartley, J. T., Harker, J. O., & Walsh, D. (1980). Contemporary issues and new directions in adult development of learning and memory. In L. Poon (Ed.), *Aging in the 1980s: Contemporary issues* (pp. 239–252). Washington, DC: American Psychological Association.

Hartup, W. W. (1989). Social relationships and their developmental significance. *American Psychologist, 44*, 283–292.

Hausman, C. (1979). Short-term counseling groups for people with elderly parents. *Gerontologist, 19*, 102–107.

Havighurst, R. J. (1952). *Developmental tasks and education*. New York: McKay.

Havighurst, R. J. (1972). *Developmental tasks and education* (3rd ed.). New York: McKay.

Havighurst, R. J. (1973). History of developmental psychology: Socialization and personality development through the life-span. In P. B. Baltes & K. W. Schaie (Eds.), *Life-span developmental psychology: Personality and socialization* (pp. 4–24). New York: Academic Press.

Havighurst, R. J. (1982). The world of work. In J. Wolman (Ed.), *Handbook of developmental psychology* (pp. 771–787). Englewood Cliffs, NJ: Prentice-Hall.

Havighurst, R. J., & Albrecht, R. (1953). *Older people*. New York: Longmans, Green.

Hayflick, L. (1965). The limited in vitro lifetime of human diploid cell strains. *Experimental Cell Research, 37*, 614–636.

Hayflick, L. (1977). The cellular basis for biological aging. In L. E. Finch & L. Hayflick (Eds.), *Handbook of the biology of aging* (pp. 159–186). New York: Van Nostrand Reinhold.

Hayflick, L. (1988). Biological aging theories. In G. Maddox (Ed.), *Encyclopedia of Aging* (pp. 64–68). Englewood Cliffs, NJ: Prentice-Hall.

Hayghe, H. (1984, December). Working mothers reach record numbers in 1984. *Monthly Labor Review*, pp. 21–34.

Hayslip, B. (1985). Idiographic assessment of the self in the aged: A case for the use of the Q-sort. *International Journal of Aging and Human Development, 20*, 293–311.

Hayslip, B. (1988). Personality-ability relationships in aged adults. *Journal of Gerontology: Psychological Sciences, 43*, P74–84.

Hayslip, B. (1989). Alternative mechanisms for improvements in fluid-ability performance in aged persons. *Psychology and Aging, 4*, 122–124.

Hayslip, B. (1989b). Fluid-ability training with aged persons: A past with a future? *Educational Gerontology, 16*, 573–596.

Hayslip, B., & Caraway, M. (1989). Cognitive therapy with aged persons: Implications of research design for its implementation and evaluation. *Journal of Cognitive Psychotherapy, 3*, 255–271.

Hayslip, B., & Kennelly, K. (1982). Short-term memory and crystallized-fluid intelligence in adulthood. *Research on Aging, 4*, 314–332.

Hayslip, B., & Kennelly, K. (1985). Cognitive and noncognitive factors affecting learning among older adults. In B. Lumsden (Ed.), *The older adult as learner* (pp. 73–98). Washington, DC: Hemisphere.

Hayslip, B., & Kooken, R. (1982). Therapeutic interventions—mental health. In N. Ernst & H. Glazer-Waldman (Eds.), *The aged patient: A sourcebook for the allied health professional* (pp. 282–303). New York: Yearbook Medical Publishers.

Hayslip, B., & Lowman, R. (1986). The clinical use of projective techniques with the aged: A critical review and synthesis. *Clinical Gerontologist, 5,* 63–94.

Hayslip, B., & Maloy, R. (1991). The interface between cognitive abilities and everyday cognitive functioning. In R. L. West & J. D. Sinnott (Eds.), *Everyday memory and aging* (pp. 190–200). New York: Springer-Verlag.

Hayslip, B., & Sterns, H. (1979). Age differences in relationships between crystallized and fluid intelligences and problem-solving. *Journal of Gerontology, 34,* 404–414.

Hayslip, B., & Stewart-Bussey, D. (1986). Locus of control–death anxiety relationships. *Omega, 17,* 41–50.

Hayslip, B., Fish, M., Wilson, M., & Haynes, J. (1989). The Kendrick Battery: Sensitivity to survival effects. *International Journal of Aging and Human Development, 28,* 225–235.

Hayslip, B., Kennelly, K., & Maloy, R. (1990). Fatigue, depression, and cognitive performance among aged persons. *Experimental Aging Research, 16,* 111–115.

Hayslip, B., Luhr, D., & Beyerlein, M. (1991). Levels of death anxiety in terminally ill men: A pilot study. *Omega, 24,* 13–20.

Hayslip, B., Panek, P., & Stoner, S. (1990). Cohort differences in Hand Test performance: A time-lagged analysis. *Journal of Personality Assessment, 54,* 704–710.

Hayslip, B., Pinder, M., & Lumsden, B. (1981). The measurement of death anxiety in adulthood: Implications for counseling. In R. Pacholski & C. Corr (Eds.), *Proceedings of the forum for death education and counseling* (pp., 201–211). Arlington, VA: Forum for Death Education and Counseling.

Hayward, M. D., Hardy, M. A., & Grady, W. R. (1989). Labor-force withdrawal patterns among older men in the United States. *Social Science Quarterly, 70,* 425–448.

Heckhausen, J., Dixon, R. A., & Baltes, P. B. (1989). Gains and losses in development throughout adulthood as perceived by different adult age groups. *Developmental Psychology, 25,* 109–121.

Heddescheimer, J. (1976). Modal motivations for mid-career changes. *Personnel and Guidance Journal, 55,* 109–111.

Hellebrandt, F. (1980). Aging among the advantaged: A new look at the stereotype of the elderly. *Gerontologist, 20,* 404–417.

Helson, H. (1964). *Adaptation level theory.* New York: Harper & Row.

Helson, R., & Moane, G. (1987). Personality change in women from college to mid-life. *Journal of Personality and Social Psychology, 53,* 176–186.

Herck, G. M. (1990). Illness, stigma, and AIDS. In G. Herck, S. Levy, S. Maddi, S. Taylor, & D. Wertleib (Eds.), *Psychological aspects of serious illness* (pp. 103–150). Washington, DC: American Psychological Association.

Herr, J., & Weakland, J. (1979). *Counseling elders and their families: Practical techniques for applied gerontology.* New York: Springer.

Hertzog, C. (1989). The influence of cognitive slowing on age differences in intelligence. *Developmental Psychology, 25,* 636–651.

Hertzog, C., Dixon, R. A., & Hultsch, D. F. (1990). Relationships between metamemory, memory predictions, and memory task performances. *Psychology and Aging, 5,* 215–223.

Hertzog, C., Schaie, K. W., & Gribbin, N. (1978). Cardiovascular disease and changes in intellectual function from middle to old age. *Journal of Gerontology, 33,* 872–883.

Hertzog, C., Williams, C. V., & Walsh, D.A. (1976). The effects of practice on age differences in central perceptual processing. *Journal of Gerontology, 31,* 428–433.

Herzog, A. R., & House, J. S. (1991, Winter). Productive activities and aging well: Meaningful but flexible opportunities are needed. *Generations,* 49–55.

Hess, A., & Bradshaw, H. L. (1970). Positiveness of self-concept and ideal self as a function of age. *Journal of Genetic Psychology, 117,* 56–57.

Hess, B. B., & Waring, J. M. (1978). Parent and child in later life. In R. M. Lerner & G. B. Spanier (Eds.), *Child influences on marital and family interaction: A life-span perspective* (pp. 241–273). New York: Academic Press.

Heston, L. L., & White, J. A. (1991). *The vanishing mind.* New York: Freeman.

Hetherington, E. M. (1979). Divorce: A child's perspective. *American Psychologist, 34,* 851–858.

Hetherington, E. M., Cox, M., & Cox, R. (1985). Long-term effects of divorce and remarriage on the adjustment of children. *Journal of the American Academy of Child Psychiatry, 24,* 518–530.

Hetherington, E. M., Stanley-Hagan, M., & Anderson, E. R. (1989). Marital transitions: A child's perspective. *American Psychologist, 44,* 303–312.

Hickey, T. (1980). *Health and aging*. Monterey, CA: Brooks/Cole.

Hickey, T., & Douglass, R. L. (1981). Neglect and abuse of older family members: Professionals' perspectives and case experiences. *Gerontologist, 21,* 171–176.

Hicks, R., & Davis, J. M. (1980). Pharmacokinetics in geriatric psychopharmacology. In C. Eisdorfer & W. E. Fann (Eds.), *Psychopharmacology of aging* (pp. 169–212). Jamaica, NY: Spectrum.

Hicks, R., Funkenstein, H., & Dysken, J., & Dovis, M. (1980). Geriatric psychopharmacology. In J. E. Birren & R. B. Sloane (Eds.), *Handbook of mental health and aging* (pp. 745–774). Englewood Cliffs, NJ: Prentice-Hall.

Hiemstra, R. (1976). Older adult learning: Instrumental and expressive categories. *Educational Gerontology, 1,* 227–236.

Hiemstra, R. (1985). The older adult's learning projects. In D. B. Lumsden (Ed.), *The older adult as learner* (pp. 165–196). Washington, DC: Hemisphere.

Hildebrand, W. L., & Schreiner, R. L. (1980). Helping parents cope with perinatal death. *American Journal of Pediatrics, 22,* 121–125.

Hill, C. T., & Stuhl, D. E. (1981). Sex differences in effects of social and value similarity in same-sex friendship. *Journal of Personality and Social Psychology, 41,* 488–502.

Hill, R. (1965). Decision-making and the family cycle. In E. Shanas & G. Streib (Eds.), *Social structure and the family: Generational relations.* Englewood Cliffs, NJ: Prentice-Hall.

Himmelfarb, S. (1984). Age and sex differences in the mental health of older persons. *Journal of Consulting and Clinical Psychology, 52,* 844–856.

Hine, V. (1979–1980). Dying at home: Can families cope? *Omega, 10,* 175–187.

Hipple, J. (1986). Suicide: The preventable tragedy [unpublished manuscript]. University of North Texas: Denton, TX.

Hoffman, L. W. (1989). Effects of maternal employment in the two-parent family. *American Psychologist, 44,* 283–292.

Holland, J. L. (1973). *Making vocational choices.* Englewood Cliffs, NJ: Prentice-Hall.

Holland, J. L. (1985). *Making vocational choices: A theory of vocational personalities and work environments* (2nd ed.). Englewood Cliffs, NJ: Prentice-Hall.

Holland, J. L., & Holland, J. E. (1977). Vocational indecision: More evidence and speculation. *Journal of Counseling Psychology, 24,* 404–414.

Holliday, S. G., & Chandler, M. J (1986). *Wisdom: Explorations in adult competence.* Basel, Switzerland: Karger.

Holmes, J. H., & Rahe, R. H. (1967). The social readjustment rating scale. *Journal of Personality and Social Psychology, 11,* 213–218.

Holstein, M. (1991, Winter). Lois Swift: Growing old in San Francisco's Tenderloin. *Generations,* 11–12.

Hooker, K., & Ventis, D. G. (1984). Work ethic, daily activities, and retirement satisfaction. *Journal of Gerontology, 39,* 478–484.

Hooper, F. H., Hooper, J. O., & Colbert, K. (1984). Personality and memory correlates of intellectual functioning: Young adulthood to old age. Basel, Switzerland: Karger.

Horn, J. L. (1970). Organization of data on life-span development of human abilities. In L. Goulet & P. Baltes (Eds.), *Life-span developmental psychology: Research and theory* (pp. 424–466). New York: Academic Press.

Horn, J. L. (1975). Gf-Gc Sampler [mimeo]. Denver: University of Denver.

Horn, J. L. (1978). Human ability systems. In P. Baltes (Ed.), *Life-span development and behavior* (Vol. 1, pp. 211–256). New York: Academic Press.

Horn, J. L. (1982). The aging of human abilities. In B. B. Wolman (Ed.), *Handbook of intelligence: Theories, measurements, and applications* (pp. 267–300). New York: Wiley Interscience.

Horn, J. L., & Cattell, R. B. (1966). Refinement and test theory of fluid-crystallized general intelligence. *Journal of Educational Psychology, 53,* 253–270.

Horn, J. L., & Cattell, R. B. (1967). Age differences in fluid and crystallized intelligence. *Acta Psychologica, 26,* 107–129.

Horn, J. L., & Donaldson, G. (1976). On the myth of intellectual decline in adulthood. *American Psychologist, 31,* 701–719.

Hornblum, J. N., & Overton, W. F. (1976). Area and volume conservation among the elderly: Assessment and training. *Developmental Psychology, 12,* 68–74.

Horne, H. L., Lowe, J. D., & Murry, P. D. (1990, August). Anxiety of young adults over expected caregiver role [paper]. Annual meeting of the American Psychological Association, Boston.

Horowitz, M. J., Marmar, C., Weiss, D. S., DeWitt, K. N., & Rosenaum, R. (1984). Brief psychotherapy and grief reactions. *Archives of General Psychiatry, 41,* 439–448.

Hotaling, G. T., & Sugarman, D. B. (1986). An analysis of risk markers in husband-to-wife violence: The current state of knowledge. *Violence and Victims, 1,* 101–124.

Hotvedt, M. (1983). The cross-cultural and historical

context. In R. Weg (Ed.), *Sexuality in the later years.* New York: Academic Press.

Howath, T. B., & Davis, K. L. (1990). Central-nervous-system disorders in aging. In E. Schneider & J. Rowe (Eds.), *Handbook of the biology of aging* (pp. 306–329). New York: Academic Press.

Howe, C. Z. (1988). Selected social gerontology theories and older adult leisure involvement: A review of the literature. *Journal of Applied Gerontology, 6,* 448–463.

Hoyer, W. J. (1973). Application of operant techniques to the modification of elderly behavior. *Gerontologist, 13,* 18–22.

Hoyer, W. J. (1974). Aging and intraindividual change. *Developmental Psychology, 10,* 821–826.

Hoyer, W. J., & Plude, D. J. (1980). Attentional and perceptual processes in the study of cognitive aging. In L. W. Poon (Ed.), *Aging in the 1980s: Psychological issues* (pp. 227–238). Washington, DC: American Psychological Association.

Hoyer, W. J., Labouvie, G., & Baltes, P. B. (1973). Modification of response-speed deficits and intellectual performance in the elderly. *Human Development, 16,* 233–242.

Hoyer, W. J., Raskind, C., & Abrahams, J. (1984). Research practices in the psychology of aging: A survey of research. *Journal of Gerontology, 39,* 44–48.

Hudson, F. (1991). *The adult years: Mastering the art of self-renewal.* San Francisco: Jossey-Bass.

Hudson, R. B., & Strate, J. (1985). Aging and political systems. In R. Binstock & E. Shanas (Eds.), *Handbook of aging and the social sciences* (pp. 554–585). New York: Van Nostrand Reinhold.

Hulicka, I. (1967). Age changes and age differences in memory functioning. *Gerontologist, 7,* 46–54.

Hulicka, I., & Grossman, J. (1967). Age-group comparisons for the use of mediators in paired-associate learning. *Journal of Gerontology, 22,* 46–51.

Hulka, B., Cassel, J., Kupper, L., & Burdette, J. (1976). Communication, compliance, and concordance between physicians and patients with prescribed medications. *American Journal of Public Health, 66,* 847–853.

Hulse, S., Egeth, H., & Deese, J. (1980). *The psychology of learning.* New York: McGraw-Hill.

Hultsch, D. F. (1969). Adult age differences in the organization of free recall. *Developmental Psychology, 1,* 673–678.

Hultsch, D. F. (1971). Adult age differences in free classification and recall. *Developmental Psychology, 4,* 338–342.

Hultsch, D. F. (1974). Learning to learn in adulthood. *Journal of Gerontology, 29,* 302–308.

Hultsch, D. F. (1975). Adult age differences in retrieval: Trace-dependent and cue-dependent forgetting. *Developmental Psychology, 11,* 197–201.

Hultsch, D. F., & Dixon, R. A. (1984). Memory for text materials in adulthood. In P. Baltes & O. Brim (Eds.), *Life-span development and behavior* (Vol. 6, pp. 77–108). New York: Academic Press.

Hultsch, D. F., & Dixon, R. A. (1990). Learning and memory in aging. In J. E. Birren & K. W. Schaie (Eds.), *Handbook of the psychology of aging* (pp. 258–274). New York: Academic Press.

Hultsch, D. F., & Hickey, T. (1978). External validity in the study of human development: Theoretical and methodological issues. *Human Development, 21,* 76–91.

Hultsch, D. F., & Plemons, J. (1979). Life events and life-span development. In P. B. Baltes & O. Brim (Eds.), *Life-span development and behavior* (pp. 1–36). New York: Academic Press.

Hultsch, D. F., Hickey, T., Rakowski, W., & Fatula, B. (1975). Research on adult learning: The individual. *Gerontologist, 15,* 424–430.

Hummert, M. L. (1990). Multiple stereotypes of elderly and young adults: A comparison of structure and evaluations. *Psychology and Aging, 5,* 182–193.

Humphrey, J. A., & Palmer, S. (1990–1991). The effects of race, gender, and marital status on suicides among young adults, middle-aged adults, and older adults. *Omega, 22,* 277–286.

Hussian, R. (1981). *Geriatric psychology: A behavioral perspective.* New York: Van Nostrand Reinhold.

Hussian, R. (1986). Severe behavioral problems. In L. Teri & P. Lewinsohn (Eds.), *Geropsychological assessment and treatment* (pp. 121–143). New York: Springer.

Hussian, R. (1987). Wandering and disorientation. In L. Carstensen & B. Edelstein (Eds.), *Handbook of clinical gerontology* (pp. 177–188). New York: Praeger.

Hyde, J. S. (1982). *Understanding human sexuality* (2nd ed.). New York: McGraw-Hill.

Ikels, C. (1982). Final progress report on cultural factors in family support for the elderly [mimeo]. Cited in J. Keith (1985). Age in anthropological research. In R. Binstock & E. Shanas (Eds.), *Handbook of aging and the social sciences* (p. 247). New York: Van Nostrand Reinhold.

Ingersoll-Dayton, B., & Antonucci, T. C. (1988). Reciprocal and nonreciprocal social support: Contrasting sides of intimate relationships. *Journal of Gerontology: Social Sciences, 43,* S65–73.

Inglis, J., & Caird, W. K. (1963). Age differences in successive responses to simultaneous stimulation. *Canadian Journal of Psychology, 17,* 98–105.

Irion, P. E. (1990–1991). Changing patterns of ritual response to death. *Omega, 22,* 159–172.

Jackson, E. (1979). Bereavement and grief. In H.

Wass (Ed.), *Dying: Facing the facts* (pp. 279–298). Washington, DC: Hemisphere.

Jackson, J. J. (1985). Race, national origin, ethnicity, and aging. In R. Binstock & E. Shanas (Eds.), *Handbook of aging and the social sciences* (pp. 264–303). New York: Van Nostrand Reinhold.

Jacques, E. (1965). Death and the mid-life crisis. *International Journal of Psychoanalysis, 46,* 502–514.

Jahoda, M. (1958). *Current concepts of positive mental health.* New York: Basic Books.

Jahoda, M. (1961). A social-psychological approach to the study of culture. *Human Relations, 14,* 23–30.

Janson, P., & Ryder, L. K. (1983). Crime and the elderly: The relationship between risk and fear. *Gerontologist, 23,* 207–212.

Jarvik, L. F., & Blum, J. E. (1971). Cognitive declines as predictors of mortality in twin pairs: A twenty-year longitudinal study of aging. In E. Palmer & F. Jeffers (Eds.), *Prediction of life-span* (pp. 144–211). Lexington, MA: Heath.

Jarvik, L. F., & Falek, A. (1963). Intellectual stability and survival in the aged. *Journal of Gerontology, 18,* 173–176.

Jarvik, L. F., Blum, J. E., & Varma, O. (1972). Genetic components and intellectual functioning during senescence: A 20-year study of aging twins. *Behavioral Genetics, 2,* 159–171.

Jenkins, J. J. (1979). Four points to remember: A tetrahedral model of memory experiments. In L. S. Cermal & F. I. M. Craik (Eds.), *Levels of processing in human memory* (pp. 429–446). Hillsdale, NJ: Erlbaum.

Jenkins, S. R. (1989). Longitudinal predictors of women's careers: Psychological, behavioral, and social-structure influences. *Journal of Vocational Behavior, 34,* 204–235.

Jensen, A. R. (1969). How much can we boost IQ and scholastic achievement? *Harvard Education Review, 39,* 1–123.

Johnson, C. L. (1988). Active and latent functions of grandparenting during the divorce process. *Gerontologist, 28,* 185–191.

Johnson, C. L., & Troll, L. (1992). Family functioning in late life. *Journal of Gerontology: Social Sciences, 47,* S66–72.

Johnson, D. R., & Johnson, J. T. (1982). Managing the older worker. *Journal of Applied Gerontology, 1,* 58–66.

Johnson, R., Cooper, C., Malikowsky, C., & Hawkins, R. (1989, November). Medication use by residents of a board and lodging facility. Paper presented at the Annual Scientific Meeting of the Gerontological Society of America. Minneapolis, MN.

Johnston, W. B. (1987). *Workforce 2000: Work and workers for the 21st century.* Indianapolis, IN: Hudson Institute.

Jourard, S. (1987). *The transparent self* (2nd ed.). New York: Van Nostrand Reinhold.

Kahana, B., & Kahana, E. (1983). Stress reactions. In P. Lewisohn & L. Teri (Eds.), *Clinical geropsychology: New directions in assessment and treatment* (pp. 139–169). New York: Pergamon Press.

Kahana, E., & Kahana, B. (1970, August). Theoretical and research perspectives on grandparenthood [paper]. Annual meeting of the American Psychological Association, Miami.

Kahana, E., & Midlarsky, E. (1982, November). Is there help beyond exchange? Contributory options in late-life adaptation [paper]. Annual meeting of the Gerontological Society, Boston.

Kahn, R., & Antonucci, T. (1980). Convoys over the life course: Attachment, roles, and social support. In P. B. Baltes & O. G. Brim, Jr. (Eds)., *Life-span development and behavior* (Vol. 3, pp. 254–286). New York: Academic Press.

Kahn, R., & Miller, N. (1978). Assessment of altered brain function in the aged. In M. Storandt, I. Siegler, & M. Elias (Eds.). *The clinical psychology of aging* (pp. 43–69). New York: Plenum.

Kahneman, D. (1973). *Attention and effort.* Englewood Cliffs, NJ: Prentice-Hall.

Kalb, N., & Kohn, M. (1975). Preretirement counseling: Characteristics of programs and preferences of retirees. *Gerontologist, 15,* 179–181.

Kalish, R. (1976). Death and dying in a social context. In R. Binstock & E. Shanas (Eds.), *Handbook of aging and the social sciences* (pp. 483–507). New York: Van Nostrand Reinhold.

Kalish, R. (1985a). The social context of death and dying. In R. Binstock & E. Shanas (Eds.), *Handbook of aging and the social sciences* (pp. 149–172). New York: Van Nostrand Reinhold.

Kalish, R., & Reynolds, D. (1976). *Death and ethnicity: A psychocultural study.* Los Angeles: University of Southern California Press.

Kaplan, H. S. (1974). *The new sex therapy.* New York: Brunner/Mazel.

Kaplan, H. S. (1975). *The illustrated manual of sex therapy.* New York: Quadrangle.

Kaplan, H. S. (1991). Sex therapy with older patients. In W. Myers (Ed.), *New techniques in psychotherapy with older patients* (pp. 21–38). Washington, DC: American Psychiatric Press.

Kaplan, M. (1975). *Leisure: Theory and policy.* New York: Wiley.

Kapnick, P. (1978). Organic treatment of the elderly. In M. Storandt, I. Siegler, & M. Elias (Eds.), *The clinical psychology of aging* (pp. 225–251). New York: Plenum.

Kastenbaum, R. (1985). Dying and death: A life-span approach. In J. E. Birren & K. W. Schaie (Eds.), *Handbook of the psychology of aging* (pp. 619–643). New York: Van Nostrand Reinhold.

Kastenbaum, R. (1987). Prevention of age-related problems. In L. Carstensen & B. Edelstein (Eds.), *Handbook of clinical gerontology* (pp. 122–134). New York: Praeger.

Kastenbaum, R., & Aisenberg, R. (1976). *The psychology of death.* New York: Springer.

Kastenbaum, R., & Costa, P. (1977). Psychological perspectives on death. *Annual Review of Psychology, 28,* 225–249.

Kaszniak, A. W. (1990). Psychological assessment of the aging individual. In J. E. Birren & K. W. Schaie (Eds.). *Handbook of the psychology of aging* (pp. 427–445). New York: Academic Press.

Katon, W. (1982). Depression, somatic symptoms, and medical disorders in primary care. *Comprehensive Psychiatry, 23,* 274–287.

Kausler, A. (1991). *Experimental psychology and human aging* (2nd ed.). New York: Springer-Verlag.

Kausler, D. H. (1990). Motivation, human aging, and cognitive performance. In J. E. Birren & K. W. Schaie (Eds.), *Handbook of the psychology of aging* (pp. 172–183). New York: Academic Press.

Kaye, L., Stuen, C., & Monk, A. (1985). The learning and retention of teaching skills by older adults: A time-series analysis. *Educational Gerontology, 11,* 113–125.

Keating, D. (1982). The emperor's new clothes: The new look in intelligence research. In R. J. Sternberg (Ed.), *Advances in the psychology of human intelligence* (Vol. 2, pp. 1–46). Hillsdale, NJ: Erlbaum.

Keith, J. (1985). Age in anthropological research. In R. Binstock & E. Shanas (Eds.), *Handbook of aging and the social sciences* (pp. 231–263). New York: Van Nostrand Reinhold.

Keith, P. (1979). Life changes and perceptions of life and death among older men and women. *Journal of Gerontology, 34,* 870–878.

Keith, P. M., Hill, K., Goudy, W. J., & Powers, E. A. (1984). Confidants and well-being: A note on male friendships in old age. *Gerontologist, 24,* 318–320.

Keller, J., & Hughston, G. (1981). *Counseling the elderly: A systems approach.* New York: Harper & Row.

Kelly, G. A. (1955). *The psychology of personal constructs.* New York: Norton.

Kelly, J. B. (1982). Divorce: The adult perspective. In J. Wolman (Ed.), *Handbook of developmental psychology* (pp. 734–750). Englewood Cliffs, NJ: Prentice-Hall.

Kelly, J. R. (1975). Life styles and leisure choices. *Family Coordinator, 24,* 185–190.

Kelly, J. R. (1983a). Leisure identities and interactions. London: Allen and Unwin.

Kelly, J. R. (1983b). Leisure styles: A hidden care. *Leisure Sciences, 5,* 321–328.

Kelly, J. R. (1988). Leisure in later life: Roles and identities. In N. J. Osgood (Ed.), *Life after work: Retirement, leisure, and the elderly.* New York: Praeger.

Kelly, J. R., Steinkamp, M. W., & Kelly, J. R. (1986). Later-life leisure: How they play in Peoria. *Gerontologist, 26,* 531–537.

Kemp, B. J., & Mitchell, J. (1992). Functional assessment in geriatric mental health. In J. E. Birren, R. B. Sloane, & G. D. Cohen (Eds.), *Handbook of mental health and aging* (pp. 672–698). New York: Academic Press.

Kendig, H. L., Coles, R., Pittelkow, Y., & Wilson, S. (1988). Confidants and family structure in old age. *Journal of Gerontology, 43,* 31–40.

Kennedy, G. F. (1990). College students' expectations of grandparent and grandchild role behaviors. *Gerontologist, 30,* 43–48.

Kennelly, K. J., Hayslip, B., & Richardson, S. K. (1985). Depression and helplessness-induced cognitive deficits in the aged. *Experimental Aging Research, 8,* 165–173.

Kenshalo, D. R. (1977). Age changes in touch, vibration, temperature, kinesthesis, and pain sensitivity. In J. E. Birren & K. W. Schaie (Eds.), *Handbook of the psychology of aging* (pp. 562–579). New York: Van Nostrand Reinhold.

Kenshalo, D. R. (1979). Aging effects on cutaneous and kinesthetic sensibilities. In S. Han & D. Coons (Eds.), *Special senses in aging* (pp. 189–217). Ann Arbor: Institute of Gerontology, University of Michigan.

Kermis, M. (1984). *The psychology of aging: Theory, research, and practice.* Newton, MA: Allyn & Bacon.

Kermis, M. (1986). *Mental health in late life: The adaptive process.* Boston: Jones & Bartlett.

Kesselman, I. (1990). Grief and loss: Issues for abortion. *Omega, 3,* 241–248.

Kidd, J. M. (1984). The relationship of self and occupational concepts to the occupational preferences of adolescents. *Journal of Vocational Behavior, 24,* 48–65.

Kimmel, D. C. (1978). Adult development and aging: A gay perspective. *Journal of Social Issues, 34,* 113–130.

Kimmel, D. C. (1988). Ageism, psychology, and public policy. *American Psychologist, 43,* 175–178.

King, S. (1989). Sex differences in a causal model of career maturity. *Journal of counseling and development, 68,* 208–215.

Kinicki, A. J. (1989). Predicting occupational role

choices after involuntary job loss. *Journal of Vocational Behavior, 35,* 204–218.
Kinicki, A. J., & Latack, J. C. (1990). Explication of the construct of coping with involuntary job loss. *Journal of Vocational Behavior, 36,* 339–360.
Kinsbourne, M., & Berryhill, J. (1972). The nature of the interaction between pacing and the age decrement in learning. *Journal of Gerontology, 27,* 471–477.
Kite, M. E., & Johnson, B. T. (1988). Attitudes toward older and younger adults: A metaanalysis. *Psychology and Aging, 3,* 233–243.
Kivasic, K. C. (1981, April). Studying the "hometown advantage" in elderly adults' spatial cognition and spatial behavior [paper]. Annual Convention of the Society for Research in Child Development, Boston.
Kivasic, K. C. (1989). Acquisition and utilization of spatial information by elderly adults: Implications for day-to-day situations. In L. W. Poon, D. C. Rubin, & B. A. Wilson (Eds.), *Everyday cognition in adulthood and late life* (pp. 265–283). Cambridge: Cambridge University Press.
Kivett, V. R. (1985). Consanguinuity and kin level: Their relative importance to the helping network of older adults. *Journal of Gerontology, 40,* 228–234.
Kivnick, H. Q. (1985). Grandparenthood and mental health: Meaning, behavior, and satisfaction. In V. L. Bengtson & J. F. Robertson (Eds.), *Grandparenthood* (pp. 49–88). Beverly Hills, CA: Sage.
Kleemeier, R. W. (1962). Intellectual change in the senium. *Proceedings of the Social Statistics Section of the American Statistical Association, 1,* 290–295.
Klerman, G. L., & Weissman, M. M. (1989). Increasing rates of depression. *JAMA, 261,* 2229–2235.
Kline, D. W., & Scheiber, F. (1985). Vision and aging. In J. E. Birren & K. W. Schaie (Eds.), *Handbook of the psychology of aging* (2nd ed., pp. 296–331). New York: Van Nostrand Reinhold.
Klisz, D. (1978). Neuropsychological evaluation in older persons. In M. Storandt, I. C. Siegler, & M. F. Elias (Eds.), *The clinical psychology of aging* (pp. 71–95). New York: Plenum.
Klopfer, B., & Davis, R. (1977). Issues in psychotherapy with the aged. *Psychotherapy: Theory, research, and practice, 14,* 343–348.
Knesper, D. J., Pagnucco, D. J., & Wheeler, J. (1985). Similarities and differences across mental-health-services providers and practice settings in the United States. *American Psychologist, 40,* 1352–1369.
Knight, B. (1986). *Psychotherapy with older adults.* Newbury Park, CA: Sage.
Knight, B. (1992). *Older adults in psychotherapy.* Newbury Park, CA: Sage.
Koenig, H. G., & Blazer, D. G. (1992). Mood disorders and suicide. In J. E. Birren, R. B. Sloane, & G. D. Cohen (Eds.), *Handbook of mental health and aging* (pp. 380–409). New York: Academic Press.
Koenig, H. G., Kvale, J. N., & Ferrel, C. (1988). Religion and well-being in later life. *Gerontologist, 28,* 18–28.
Kogan, N. (1973). Creativity and cognitive style: A life-span perspective. In P. B. Baltes & K. W. Schaie (Eds.), *Life-span developmental psychology: Personality and socialization* (pp. 145–178). New York: Academic Press.
Kogan, N. (1990). Personality and aging. In J. E. Birren & K. W. Schaie (Eds.), *Handbook of the psychology of aging* (pp. 330–346). New York: Academic Press.
Kohlberg, L. (1966). A cognitive-developmental analysis of children's sex-role concepts and attitudes. In E. E. Macoby (Ed.), *The development of sex differences* (pp. 48–64). Stanford, CA: Stanford University Press.
Kohlberg, L. (1973). Continuities in childhood and adult moral development revisited. In P. B. Baltes & K. W. Schaie (Eds.), *Life-span developmental psychology: Personality and socialization* (pp. 180–207). New York: Academic Press.
Kohn, M. L., & Schooler, C. (1983). *Work and personality: An inquiry into the impact of social stratification.* Norwood, NJ: Ablex.
Kolodny, R. C., Masters, W. H., & Johnson, V. E. (1979). *Textbook of sexual medicine.* Boston: Little, Brown.
Kooken, R. A., & Hayslip, B. (1984). The use of stress inoculation in the treatment of text anxiety in older students. *Educational Gerontology, 11,* 39–58.
Kosberg, J. I. (1988). Preventing elder abuse: Identification of high-risk factors prior to placement decisions. *Gerontologist, 28,* 43–50.
Kosnik, W., Winslow, L., Kline, D., Pasinki, K., & Sekular, R. (1988). Visual changes in daily life throughout adulthood. *Journal of Gerontology: Psychological Sciences, 43,* P63–70.
Kotch, J. B., & Cohen, S. R. (1985–1986). SIDS counselors' reports of own and parents' reactions to reviewing the autopsy report. *Omega, 16,* 129–139.
Kozma, A., & Stones, M. (1986). Social desirability in measures of subjective well-being: A systematic evaluation. *Journal of Gerontology, 42,* 56–57.
Krauss, I. (1980). Between- and within-group comparisons in aging research. In L. Poon (Ed.), *Aging in the 1980s: Psychological issues* (pp. 542–551). Washington, DC: American Psychological Association.
Krauss, I., Awad, Z., & McCormick, D. (1981, April). Learning, remembering, and using spatial

information as an older adult [paper]. Annual Convention of the Society for Research in Child Development, Boston.

Kryter, K. (1970). *The effects of noise on man.* New York: Academic Press.

Kubanoff, B. (1980). Work and nonwork: A review of models. *Psychological Bulletin, 88,* 60–77.

Kubler-Ross, E. (1969). *On death and dying.* New York: Macmillan.

Kubler-Ross, E. (1978). *To live until we say goodbye.* Englewood Cliffs, NJ: Prentice-Hall.

Kubler-Ross, E. (1982). *Working it through.* New York: Macmillan.

Kuhn, M. E. (1983, July 31). We're old, not senile, Ronald. *New York Times.*

Kuhn, M. E., & Bader, J. E. (1991). Old and young are alike in many ways. *Gerontologist, 31,* 273–274.

Labouvie, E. V., Bartsch, T., Nesselroade, J., & Baltes, P. (1974). On the internal and external validity of simple longitudinal designs: Dropout and retest effects. *Child Development, 45,* 282–290.

Labouvie-Vief, G. (1985). Intelligence and cognition. In J. E. Birren & K. W. Schaie (Eds.), *Handbook of the psychology of aging* (2nd ed., pp. 500–530). New York: Van Nostrand Reinhold.

Labouvie-Vief, G., & Gonda, J. (1976). Cognitive strategy training and intellectual performance in the elderly. *Journal of Gerontology, 31,* 327–336; 372–382.

Labouvie-Vief, G., & Shell, D. (1982). Learning and memory in later life. In B. Wolman (Ed.), *Handbook of developmental psychology* (pp. 828–846). Englewood Cliffs, NJ: Prentice-Hall.

Lachman, J. L., & Lachman, R. (1980). Age and the actualization of world knowledge. In L. Poon, J. Fozard, L. Cermak, D. Arenberg, and L. Thompson (Eds.), *New directions in memory and aging* (pp. 285–311). Hillsdale, NJ: Erlbaum.

Lachman, J. L., Lachman, R., & Thronesbery, C. (1979). Metamemory throughout the adult life span. *Developmental Psychology, 15,* 543–551.

Lachman, M. E. (1983). Perceptions of intellectual aging: Antecedent or consequences of intellectual functioning? *Developmental Psychology, 19,* 482–498.

Lachman, M. E. (1985). Personal efficacy in middle and old age: Differential and normative patterns of change. In G. Elder, Jr. (Ed.), *Life-course dynamics: Trajectories and transitions, 1968–1980* (pp. 188–213). Ithaca, NY: Cornell University Press.

Lachman, M. E. (1986). Locus of control in aging research: A case for multidimensional and domain-specific assessment. *Psychology and Aging, 1,* 34–40.

Lachman, M. E. (1986b). The role of personality and social factors in intellectual aging. *Educational Gerontology, 12,* 399–444.

Lachman, M. E., & Jelalian, E. (1984). Self-efficacy and attributions for intellectual performance in young and elderly adults. *Journal of Gerontology, 39,* 577–582.

Lachman, M. E., & Leff, L. (1989). Perceived control and intellectual functioning: A five-year longitudinal study. *Developmental Psychology, 25,* 722–728.

Lachman, M. E., Baltes, P. B., Nesselroade, J. R., & Willis, S. L. (1982). Examination of personality-ability relationships in the elderly: The role of contextual (interface) assessment mode. *Journal of Research in Personality, 16,* 485–501.

Lachman, M. E., & McArthur, L. Z. (1986). Adult age differences in causal attributions for cognitive, physical, and social performance. *Psychology and Aging, 1,* 127–132.

Lajer, M. (1982). Unemployment and hospitalization among bricklayers. *Scandinavian Journal of Social Medicine, 10,* 3–10.

Lakatta, E. G. (1990). Heart and circulation. In E. Schneider & J. Rowe (Eds.), *Handbook of the biology of aging* (pp. 181–218). New York: Academic Press.

Langer, E. (1982). Old age: An artifact? In S. Kiesler & J. McGaugh (Eds.), *Biology, behavior, and aging* (pp. 255–281). New York: National Research Council.

Langer, E. (1983). *The psychology of control.* Palo Alto, CA: Sage.

Langer, E., & Rodin, J. (1976). The effects of choice and enhanced personal responsibility: A field experiment in institutionalized setting. *Journal of Personality and Social Psychology, 34,* 191–198.

Langer, E., Rodin, J., Beck, P., Weinman, C., & Spitzer, L. (1979). Environmental determinants of memory improvement in late adulthood. *Journal of Personality and Social Psychology, 37,* 2003–2013.

Larson, R. (1978). Thirty years of research on the subjective well-being of older Americans. *Journal of Gerontology, 33,* 109–125.

Larson, R., Mannell, R., & Zuzanek, J. (1986). Daily well-being of older adults with friends and family. *Psychology and Aging, 1,* 117–126.

LaRue, A., Bank, L., Jarvik, L. F., & Hetland, M. (1979). Health in old age: How do physicians' ratings and self-ratings compare? *Journal of Gerontology, 34,* 687–691.

LaRue, A., Dessonville, C., & Jarvik, L. F. (1985). Aging and mental disorders. In J. E. Birren & K. W. Schaie (Eds.), *Handbook of the psychology of aging* (pp. 664–702). New York: Van Nostrand Reinhold.

Lauer, J., & Lauer, R. (1985, June). Marriages made to last. *Psychology Today.*

Lauriant, P., & Rabin, W. (1976). Characteristics of

new beneficiaries by age at entitlement. In *Reaching retirement age: Findings from a survey of newly entitled workers 1968–1970* (pp. 11–29). Washington, DC: US Department of Health, Education and Welfare, Social Security Administration.

Laws, J. L. (1980). Female sexuality through the lifespan. In P. B. Baltes & O. G. Brim, Jr. (Eds.), *Life-span development and behavior* (Vol. 3, pp. 208–252). New York: Academic Press.

Lawton, M. P. (1975). The Philadelphia Geriatric Morale Scale: A revision. *Journal of Gerontology, 30,* 85–89.

Lawton, M. P. (1978). Clinical geropsychology: Problems and prospects [lecture]. Washington, DC: American Psychological Association.

Lawton, M. P. (1980a, November). Do elderly research subjects need special protection? Psychological vulnerability. Washington, D.C.: Department of Health, Education and Welfare, Institutional Review Board.

Lawton, M. P. (1983). Environment and other determinants of well-being in older people. *Gerontologist, 23,* 349–357.

Lawton, M. P. (1985). Housing and living environments of older people. In R. Binstock & E. Shanas (Eds.), *Handbook of aging and the social sciences* (pp. 450–478). New York: Van Nostrand Reinhold.

Lawton, M. P. (1991, Winter). Functional status and aging well: The usual definitions are limited. *Generations,* 31–35.

Lawton, M. P., & Gottesman, L. E. (1974). Psychological services to the elderly. *American Psychologist, 29,* 689–693.

Lawton, M. P., & Nahemow, L. (1973). Ecology and the aging process. In C. Eisdorfer & M. P. Lawton (Eds.), *The psychology of adult development and aging* (pp. 619–674). Washington, DC: American Psychological Association.

Lawton, M. P., Moss, M., & Moles, E. (1984). Pet ownership: A research note. *Gerontologist, 24,* 208–210.

Lawton, M. P., Whelihan, W., & Belsky, J. K. (1980). Personality tests and their uses with older adults. In J. E. Birren & R. B. Sloane (Eds.), *Handbook of mental health and aging* (pp. 537–553). Englewood Cliffs, NJ: Prentice-Hall.

Layton, J., & Siegler, I. (1978, November). Mid-life: Must it be a crisis? [paper]. Annual convention of the Gerontological Society, Dallas.

Lazarus, L. W., Groves, L., Guttmann, D., Ripekyjin, A., Frankel, R., Newton, N., Gruner, J., & Havasy-Galloway, S. (1987). Brief psychotherapy with the elderly: A study of process and outcome. In J. Sadavoy & M. Leszcz (Eds.), *Treating the elderly with psychotherapy* (pp. 5–22). Madison, CT: International University Press.

Lazarus, L. W., Stafford, B., Cooper, K., Cohler, B., & Dysken, M. (1981). A pilot study of an Alzheimer patients' relatives discussion group. *Gerontologist, 22,* 353–358.

Lazarus, R. S., & Delongis, A. (1983). Psychological stress and coping in aging. *American Psychologist, 38,* 245–254.

Lazarus, R. S., DeLonges, A., Folkman, S., & Gruen, R. (1985). Stress and adaptational outcomes: The problem of confounded measures. *American Psychologist, 40,* 770-779.

Lebowitz, B. (1988). Mental health services. In G. Maddox (Ed.), *Encyclopedia of aging* (pp. 440–442). New York: Springer.

Lee, D. T., & Markides, K. S. (1990). Activity and mortality among aged persons over an eight-year period. *Journal of Gerontology: Social Sciences, 45,* S39–42.

Lee, G. L., & Shehan, C. L. (1989). Retirement and marital satisfaction. *Journal of Gerontology, 44,* S226–230.

Lee, J. A. (1991). Through the looking glass: Life after Isherwood—A conversation with Don Bachardy. *Journal of Homosexuality, 20,* 33–64.

Leech, S., & Witte, K. L. (1971). Paired-associate learning in elderly adults as related to pacing and incentive conditions. *Developmental Psychology, 5,* 180.

Lefcourt, H. M. (1981). *Research with the locus-of-control construct: Assessment methods* (Vol. 1). New York: Academic Press.

Lehman, H. C. (1953). *Age and achievement.* Princeton, NJ: Princeton University Press.

Leifer, M. (1977). Psychological changes accompanying pregnancy and motherhood. *Genetic Psychology Monographs, 95,* 55–96.

Lemon, B., Bengtson, V., & Peterson, J. (1972). An explanation of the activity theory of aging: Activity tapes and life satisfaction among in-movers to a retirement community. *Journal of Gerontology, 27,* 511–523.

Lerner, R. M. (1986). *Concepts and theories of human development.* Reading, MA: Addison-Wesley.

Lerner, R. M., & Spanier, G. (1978). A dynamic, interactional view of child and family development. In R. M. Lerner & G. Spanier (Eds.), *Child influences on marital and family interaction* (pp. 1–22). New York: Academic Press.

Lerner, R. M., & Ryff, C. D. (1978). Implementation of the life-span view of development: The sample case of attachment. In P. B. Baltes & O. G. Brim, Jr. (Eds.), *Life-span development and behavior* (Vol. 1, pp. 2–44). New York: Academic Press.

Lesser, J., Lazarus, L. W., Frankel, R., & Havasy, S.

(1981). Reminiscence group therapy with psychotic geriatric inpatients. *Gerontologist, 21,* 291–296.

Levav, I. (1989–1990). Second thoughts on the lethal aftermath of a loss. *Omega, 20,* 81–90.

Levenson, H. (1972). Distinctions within the concept of internal-external control: Development of a new scale. *Proceedings of the 80th Annual Convention of the American Psychological Association,* 261–262.

Levinson, B. M. (1972). *Pets and human development.* Springfield, IL: Thomas.

Levinson, D. J. (1978). *The seasons of a man's life.* New York: Knopf.

Levinson, D. J. (1986). A conception of adult development. *American Psychologist, 41,* 3–13.

Levy, S. M. (1990). Humanizing death. In G. Herek, S. Levy, S. Maddi, S. Taylor, & D. Wertleib (Eds.), *Psychological aspects of serious illness* (pp. 189–213). Washington, DC: American Psychological Association.

Levy, S. M., Derogatis, L. R., Gallagher, D., & Gatz, M. (1980). Intervention with older adults and the evaluation of outcome. In L. Poon (Ed.), *Aging in the 1980s: Psychological issues* (pp. 41–64). Washington, DC: American Psychological Association.

Lewinsohn, P. M., & Teri, L. (Eds.) (1983). *Clinical geropsychology: New directions in assessment and treatment.* Elmsford, NY: Pergamon Press.

Lewinsohn, P. M., Rohde, P., Seeley, J. R., & Fischer, S. A. (1991). Age and depression: Unique and shared effects. *Psychology and Aging, 6,* 247–260.

Lewis, E. (1979). Mourning by the family after a stillbirth or neonatal death. *Archives of Disease in Childhood, 54,* 303–306.

Lewis, R. A., & Spanier, G. B. (1979). Theorizing about the quality and stability of marriage. In W. Burr, R. Hill, F. Nye, & I. Reiss (Eds.). *Contemporary theories about the family, Vol. 1* (pp. 268–294). New York: Free Press.

Lichtenberg, P. (1990). Remembering Becky. *Omega, 21,* 83–89.

Lieberman, M. A. (1965). Psychological correlates of impending death: Some preliminary observations. *Journal of Gerontology, 20,* 181–190.

Lieberman, M. A. (1975). Adaptive processes in later life. In N. Datan & L. Ginsburg (Eds.), *Life-span developmental psychology: Normative life events* (pp. 135–159). New York: Academic Press.

Lieberman, M. A. (1978, November). Methodological issues in the evaluation of psychotherapy with older adults [paper]. Annual meeting of the Gerontological Society, Dallas.

Lieberman, M. A., & Peskin, H. (1992). Adult life crises. In J. E. Birren, R. B. Sloane, & G. D. Cohen (Eds.), *Handbook of mental health and aging* (pp. 120–146). New York: Academic Press.

Liebowitz, B., & Niederehe, G. (1992). Concepts and issues in mental health and aging. In J. E. Birren, R. B. Sloane, and G. D. Cohen (Eds.), *Handbook of mental health and aging* (pp. 3–25). New York: Academic Press.

Lindemann, E. (1944). The symptomatology and management of acute grief. *American Journal of Psychiatry, 101,* 141–148.

Lindley, C. J. (1989). Assessment of older persons in the workplace. In T. Hunt & C. J. Lindley (Eds.), *Testing older adults: A reference guide for geropsychological assessments* (pp. 232–257). Austin, TX: Pro-Ed.

Liss, L., & Gomez, F. (1958). The nature of senile changes of the human olfactory bulb and tract. *Archives of Otolaryngology, 67,* 167–171.

Liu, W. T., & Yu, E. (1985). Asian/Pacific American Elderly: Mortality differentials, health status, and use of health services. *Journal of Applied Gerontology, 4,* 35–64.

Livson, F. B. (1981). Paths to psychological health in the middle years: Sex differences. In D. Eichorn, N. Haan, J. Clausen, M. Honzik, & P. Mussen (Eds.), *Present and past in middle life* (pp. 195–221). New York: Academic Press.

Livson, N. (1973). Developmental dimensions of personality: A lifespan formulation. In P. B. Baltes & K. W. Schaie (Eds.), *Life-span developmental psychology: Personality and socialization* (pp. 98–122). New York: Academic Press.

Livson, N., & Peskin, H. (1981). Psychological health at age 40: Prediction from adolescent personality. In D. Eichorn, N. Haan, J. Clausen, M. Honzik, & P. Mussen (Eds.), *Present and past in middle life* (pp. 183–194). New York: Academic Press.

Long, G. M., & Crambert, R. F. (1990). The nature and basis of age-related changes in dynamic visual activity. *Psychology and Aging, 5,* 138–143.

Long, H. B. (1990). Educational gerontology: Trends and developments in 2000–2010. *Educational Gerontology, 16,* 317–326.

Lopata, H. Z. (1973). *Widowhood in an American city.* Cambridge: Schenkman.

Lopata, H. Z. (1975). Widowhood: Societal factors in life-span disruptions and alternatives. In N. Datan & L. Ginsburg (Eds.), *Life-span developmental psychology: Normative life crises* (pp. 217–234). New York: Academic Press.

Lopez, F. G. (1983). A paradoxical approach to vocational indecision. *Personal and Guidance Journal, 59,* 433–439.

Lorr, M. (1978). The structure of the California Q-set. *Multivariate Behavioral Research, 13,* 387–393.

Lorsbach, T. C., & Simpson, G. B. (1988). Dual-task

performance as a function of adult age and task complexity. *Psychology and Aging, 3,* 210–212.
Love, D. O., & Torrence, W. D. (1989). The impact of worker age on unemployment and earnings after plant closings. *Journal of Gerontology: Social Sciences, 44,* S190–195.
Lowenthal, M. F., & Chiriboga, D. (1973). Social stress and adaptation: Toward a life-course perspective. In C. Eisdorfer & M. P. Lawton (Eds.), *The psychology of adult development and aging* (pp. 281–310). Washington, DC: American Psychological Association.
Lowy, L. (1980). Mental health services in the community. In J. E. Birren & R. B. Sloane (Eds.), *Handbook of mental health and aging* (pp. 827–853). Englewood Cliffs, NJ: Prentice-Hall.
Ludeman, K. (1981). The sexuality of the older person: Review of the literature. *Gerontologist, 21,* 203–208.
Lumsden, D. B. (Ed.). (1985). *The older adult as learner.* Washington, DC: Hemisphere.
Lund, D., Caserta, M. S., & Dimond, M. F. (1986). Gender differences through two years of bereavement among the elderly. *Gerontologist, 26,* 314–320.
Lund, D., Dimond, M., Caserta, M., Johnson, R., Poulton, J., & Connelly, J. (1986–1987). Identifying elderly with coping patterns two years after bereavement. *Omega, 16,* 213–224.
Lupri, E., & Frideres, J. (1981). The quality of marriage and the passage of time: Marital satisfaction over the family life cycle. *Canadian Journal of Sociology, 6,* 283–305.
Lutsky, N. S. (1980). Attitudes toward old age and elderly persons. *Annual Review of Gerontology and Geriatrics, 1,* 287–336.
Lynn, J. (1990, Winter). Dying well: What becomes, or continues to be, important? *Generations,* 69–73.
Maas, H., & Kuypers, J. (1974). *From thirty to seventy.* San Francisco: Jossey-Bass.
Mace, N. L., & Robbins, P. V. (1991). *The 36-hour day.* Baltimore: Johns Hopkins University Press.
Macklin, E. (1987). Nontraditional family forms. In M. Sussman & S. Sternmetz (Eds.), *Handbook of marriage and the family* (pp. 320–354). New York: Plenum.
Madden, J. D. (1982). Age differences and similarities in the improvement of controlled search. *Experimental Aging Research, 8,* 91–98.
Madden, J. D. (1984). Date-driven and memory-driven selective attention in visual search. *Journal of Gerontology, 39,* 72–78.
Madden, J. D. (1990). Adult age differences in the time course of visual attention. *Journal of Gerontology: Psychological Sciences, 45,* P9–16.
Maddi, S. (1990). *Personality theories: A comparative analysis.* Homewood, IL: Dorsey Press.
Maddox, G. L. (1964). Disengagement theory: A critical evaluation. *Gerontologist, 4,* 80–83.
Maddox, G. L. (1965). Fact and artifact: Evidence bearing on disengagement theory from the Duke Longitudinal Study. *Human Development, 8,* 117–130.
Maddox, G. L. (1991, Winter). Aging with a difference: Heterogeneity, intervention, and the future. *Generations,* 7–11.
Maddox, G. L., & Douglass, E. B. (1974). Aging individual differences: A longitudinal analysis of social, psychological, and physiological indicators. *Journal of Gerontology, 29,* 555–563.
Maddox, G. L., & Eisdorfer, C. (1962). Some correlates of activity and morale among the elderly. *Social Forces, 40,* 254–260.
Maeda, D. (1980). Japan. In E. Palmore (Ed.), *The international handbook on aging* (pp. 253–270). Westport, CT: Greenwood.
Maeda, D. (1983). Family care in Japan. *Gerontologist, 23,* 579–583.
Mages, N. L., & Mendolsohn, G. A. (1979). Effects on patients' lives: A personalized approach. In G. Stone et al. (Eds.), *Health psychology: A handbook* (pp. 255–284). San Francisco: Jossey-Bass.
Maiden, R. J. (1987). Learned helplessness and depression: A test of the reformulation model. *Journal of Gerontology, 42,* 60–64.
Maldonado, D., Jr. (1975). The Chicano aged. *Social Work, 20,* 213–216.
Maldonado, D., Jr., & Applewhite-Lozano, S. (1986). *The Hispanic elderly: Empowerment through training.* Arlington, TX: Center for Chicano Aged.
Mallinckrodt, B., & Fretz, B. R. (1988). Social support and the impact of job loss on older professionals. *Journal of Counseling Psychology, 35,* 281–286.
Marcia, J. E. (1966). Development and validation of ego-identity status. *Journal of Personality and Social Psychology, 3,* 551–558.
Marcus, S., & Hayslip, B. (1987, April). Effects of maternal employment and family life-cycle stage on the psychological well-being of women [paper]. Annual convention of the Society for Research in Child Development, Baltimore.
Markides, K. S. (1983b). Minority aging. In M. W. Wiley, B. B. Hess, & K. Bond (Eds.), *Aging in society: Selected reviews of recent research* (pp. 115–137). Hillsdale, NJ: Erlbaum.
Markides, K. S., & Mindel, C. H. (1987). *Aging and ethnicity.* Newbury Park, CA: Sage.
Markus, H. R., & Herzog, A. R. (1992). The role of self-concept in aging. In K. W. Schaie & M. P.

Lawton (Eds.), *Annual Review of Gerontology and Geriatrics* (pp. 110–143). New York: Springer.

Markus, H. R., & Warf, E. (1989). The dynamic self-concept: A social psychological perspective. *Annual Review of Psychology, 38,* 299–337.

Marsden, C. D. (1978). The diagnosis of dementia. In A. D. Isaacs & F. Post (Eds.), *Studies in geriatric psychiatry* (pp. 99–118). New York: Wiley.

Marshall, J. (1983). Reducing the effects of work-oriented values on the lives of male American workers. *Vocational Guidance Quarterly, 32,* 109–115.

Marshall, L. (1981). Auditory problems in aging listeners. *Journal of Speech and Hearing Disorders, 46,* 226–240.

Marshall, M. (1989). Assessment of persons with hearing disabilities. In T. Hunt & C. J. Lindley (Eds.), *Testing older adults: A reference guide for gerontological assessment* (pp. 150–162). Austin, TX: Pro-Ed.

Marshall, V. (1980). *Last chapters: A sociology of aging and dying.* Belmont, CA: Brooks/Cole.

Marshall, V. W., & Levy, J. A. (1990). Aging and dying. In R. Binstock & L. George (Eds.), *Handbook of aging and the social sciences* (pp. 245–267). New York: Academic Press.

Martin, C. E. (1981). Factors affecting sexual functioning in 60–79-year-old married males. *Archives of Sexual Behavior, 10,* 399–420.

Mass, H., & Kruypers, J. (1974). *From thirty to seventy.* San Francisco: Jossey-Bass.

Masters, W. H., & Johnson, V. E. (1966). *Human sexual response.* Boston: Little, Brown.

Masters, W. H., & Johnson, V. E. (1970). *Human sexual response* (2nd ed.). Boston: Little, Brown.

Masters, W. H., & Johnson, V. E. (1981). Sex and the aging process. *Journal of the American Geriatrics Society, 9,* 385–390.

Masters, W. H., Johnson, V. E., & Kolodny, R. C. (1982). *Human sexuality.* Boston: Little, Brown.

Masters, W. H., Johnson, V. E., & Kolodny, R. C. (1992). *Human sexuality.* New York: HarperCollins.

Matarazzo, J. D. (1972). *Wechsler's measurement and appraisal of adult intelligence.* Baltimore: Williams & Wilkins.

Mathieu, J., & Peterson, J. (1970, October). Some social psychological dimensions of aging. Paper presented at the Annual Scientific Meeting of the Gerontological Society. Ontario, Canada.

Matthews, K. A., & Rodin, J. (1989). Women's changing work rules: Impact on health, family, and public policy. *American Psychologist, 44,* 1389–1393.

Matthews, R., & Matthews, A. (1986). Infertility and involuntary childlessness: The transition to nonparenthood. *Journal of Marriage and the Family, 48,* 166–178.

Matthews, S. H. (1987). Perceptions of fairness in the division of responsibility for old parents. *Social Justice, 1,* 4.

Matthews, S. H., & Sprey, J. (1984). The impact of divorce on parenthood: An exploratory study. *Gerontologist, 24,* 41–47.

Matthews, S. H., Werkner, J. E., & Delaney, P. J. (1990). Relative contributions of help by employed and nonemployed sisters to their elderly parents. *Journal of Gerontology: Social Sciences, 49,* S36–44.

McCary, J. L., & McCary, S. P. (1982). *McCary's human sexuality* (4th ed.). Belmont, CA: Wadsworth.

McClelland, P. C. (1973). Testing for competence rather than intelligence. *American Psychologist, 28,* 1–14.

McContha, D., McContha, J. T., & Cinelli, B. (1991). Japan's coming crisis: Problems for the honorable elders. *Journal of Applied Gerontology, 2,* 224–235.

McCrae, R. R. (1982). Age differences in the use of coping mechanisms. *Journal of Gerontology, 37,* 454–460.

McCrae, R. R. (1989). Age differences and changes in the use of coping mechanisms. *Journal of Gerontology: Psychological Sciences, 44,* P161–169.

McCrae, R. R. (1991). The five-factor model and its assessment in clinical settings. *Journal of Personality Assessment, 57,* 399–414.

McCrae, R. R., & Costa, P. T. (1984). *Emerging lives, enduring dispositions: Personality in adulthood.* Boston: Little, Brown.

McCrae, R. R., & Costa, P. T. (1986). Personality, coping, and coping effectiveness in an adult sample. *Journal of Personality, 54,* 385–405.

McCrae, R. R., & Costa, P. T. (1990). *Personality in adulthood.* New York: Guilford Press.

McCullock, B. J. (1990). The relationship of intergenerational reciprocity of and to the morale of older parents: Equity and exchange-theory comparisons. *Journal of Gerontology: Social Sciences, 44,* S150–155.

McDowd, J. E., & Craig, F. (1988). Effects of aging and task difficulty on divided attention performance. *Journal of Experimental Psychology: Human Perception and Performance, 14,* 267–280.

McDowd, J. M. (1986). Effects of age and extended practice on divided attention performance. *Journal of Gerontology, 41,* 764–769.

McDowd, J. M., & Birren, J. E. (1990). Aging and attentional processes. In J. E. Birren & K. W. Schaie (Eds.), *Handbook of the psychology of aging* (pp. 222–233). New York: Academic Press.

McEvoy, G. M., & Cascio, W. F. (1989). Beliefs about the relationship between productiveness and age. *Journal of Applied Psychology, 74,* 11–17.

McFarland, R. A. (1968). The sensory and perceptual processes in aging. In K. W. Schaie (Ed.),

Theory and methods of research on aging (pp. 3–52). New York: Springer.

McFarland, R. A. (1973). The need for functional age measurements in industrial gerontology. *Industrial Gerontology, 1,* 1–19.

McFarland, R. A., Tune, C. S., & Welford, A. T. (1964). On the driving of automobiles by older people. *Journal of Gerontology, 19,* 190–197.

McGee, M. G., III, Hall, J., & Lutes-Dunckley, J. L. (1979). Factors influencing attitude towards retirement. *Journal of Psychology, 101,* 15–18.

McGuigan, F. J. (1983). *Experimental psychology: Methods of research.* Englewood Cliffs, NJ: Prentice-Hall.

McGuire, F. A., Dottavio, D., & O'Leary, J. T. (1986). Constraints to participation in outdoor recreation across the life-span: A nationwide study of limitors and prohibitors. *Gerontologist, 26,* 538–544.

McIlroy, J. H. (1984). Mid-life in the 1980s: Philosophy, economy, and psychology. *Personnel and Guidance Journal, 62,* 623–628.

McLloyd, V. C. (1989). Socialization and development in a changing economy: The effects of paternal job and income loss on children. *American Psychologist, 44,* 293–302.

McNeil, J. K., LeBlanc, E. M., & Joyner, M. (1991). The effect of exercise on depressive symptoms in moderately depressed elderly. *Psychology and Aging, 6,* 487–488.

McPherson, B., & Guppy, N. (1979). Preretirement life-style and the degree of planning for retirement. *Journal of Gerontology, 34,* 254–263.

Meehan, P. J., Saltzman, L. E., & Sattin, R. W. (1991). Suicides among older United States residents: Epidemiologic characteristics and trends. *American Journal of Public Health, 81,* 1198–1200.

Meichenbaum, D. (1977). *Cognitive behavior modification.* New York: Plenum.

Meichenbaum, D. (1989). *Cognitive behavior modification: An integrative approach.* New York: Plenum.

Meier, E. L., & Kerr, E. A. (1976). Capabilities of middle-aged and older workers: A survey of the literature. *Industrial Gerontology, 3,* 147–156.

Memmink, E., & Heikkila, J. (1975). Elderly people's compliance with prescriptions and quality of medication. *Journal of Social Medicine, 3,* 87–92.

Meredith, D. (1985, June). Mom, dad, and the kids. *Psychology Today,* 62–67.

Merriam, S. B. (1987). Young, middle, and preretirement adults' experiences with retraining after job loss. *Educational Gerontology, 13,* 249–262.

Meyer, B. J., & Rice, G. E. (1989). Prose-processing in adulthood: The text, the reader, and the task. In L. W. Poon, D. C. Rubin, & B. A. Wilson (Eds.), *Everyday cognition and adulthood and late life* (pp. 157–194). Cambridge: Cambridge University Press.

Mihal, W. L., & Barrett, G. V. (1976). Individual differences in perceptual-information-processing and their relation to automobile accident involvement. *Journal of Applied Psychology, 61,* 229–233.

Miles, M. S. (1984). Helping adults mourn the death of a child. In H. Wass & C. Corr (Eds.), *Childhood and death* (pp. 219–240). Washington, DC: Hemisphere/McGraw-Hill.

Miller, D., & Lieberman, M. A. (1965). The relationship of affect state and adaptive capacity to reactions to stress. *Journal of Gerontology, 20,* 492–497.

Miller, D. C., & Form, W. H. (1951). *Industrial Sociology.* New York: Harper & Row.

Miller, E. (1980). Cognitive assessment of the older adult. In J. E. Birren & R. B. Sloane (Eds.), *Handbook of mental health and aging* (pp. 520–536). Englewood Cliffs, NJ: Prentice-Hall.

Miller, M. (1978). Geriatric suicide: The Arizona study. *Gerontologist, 18,* 488–495.

Miller, M. (1979). *Suicide after sixty: The final alternative.* New York: Springer.

Miller, R. A. (1990). Aging and the immune response. In E. Schneider & J. Rowe (Eds.), *Handbook of the biology of aging* (pp. 157–180). New York: Academic Press.

Miller, S. S., & Cavanaugh, J. C. (1990). The meaning of grandparenthood and its relationship to demographic relationship, and social participation variables. *Journal of Gerontology: Psychological Sciences, 45,* P244–246.

Mischel, W. (1981). *Introduction to personality.* New York: Holt, Rinehart, and Winston.

Mobily, K. E., Leslie, D. K., Lemke, J. H., Wallace, R. B., & Kohout, F. J. (1986). Leisure patterns and attitudes of the rural elderly. *Journal of Applied Gerontology, 5,* 201–214.

Monge, R. H. (1975). Structure of the self-concept from adolescence through old age. *Experimental Aging Research, 1,* 281–291.

Monge, R. H., & Hultsch, D. (1971). Paired-associate learning as a function of adult age and the length of the anticipation and inspection intervals. *Journal of Gerontology, 26,* 157–162.

Montalvo, B. (1991). The patient chose to die. Why? *Gerontologist, 31,* 700–703.

Montpare, J., & Lackman, M. (1989). You're only as young as you feel: Self-perceptions of age, fears of aging, and life satisfaction from adolescence to old age. *Psychology and Aging, 4,* 73–78.

Moore, J. E. (1984). Impact of family attitudes towards blindness/visual impairment on the rehabilitation process. *Journal of Visual Impairment and Blindness, 78,* 100–106.

Moos, R. H., & Tsu, V. D. (1977). The crisis of physical illness: An overview. In R. H. Moos (Ed.),

Coping with physical illness (pp. 3–21). New York: Plenum.

Moran, J. M. (1979). *Leisure activities for the mature adult.* Minneapolis: MN: Burgess.

Morgan, D. L. (1989). Adjusting to widowhood: Do social networks really make it easier? *Gerontologist, 29,* 101–107.

Mortimer, J. T., Finch, M. D., & Kumka, D. (1982). Persistence and change in development: The multidimensional self-concept. In P. B. Baltes & O. G. Brim (Eds.), *Life-span development and behavior* (pp. 264–313). New York: Academic Press.

Mosatche, H. S., Brady, E. M., & Noberini, M. R. (1983). A retrospective life-span study of the closest sibling relationship. *Journal of Psychology, 113,* 237–243.

Moss, H., & Sussman, E. (1980). Longitudinal study of personality development. In O. Brim & J. Kagan (Eds.), *Constancy and change in human development* (pp. 530–595). Cambridge, MA: Harvard University Press.

Moss, M., & Moss, D. (1980). The image of the dead spouse in remarriage of elderly widow(er)s [paper]. Annual meeting of the Gerontological Society, Washington, DC.

Moss, M. S., & Moss, S. Z. (1983). The impact of parental death on middle-aged children. *Omega, 14,* 65–75.

Moss, M. S., Lesher, E. L., & Moss, S. Z. (1986–1987). Impact of the death of an adult child on elderly parents: Some observations. *Omega, 17,* 209–218.

Murphy, J. M., Olivier, D. C., Monson, R. P., Sobol, A. M., & Leighton, A. H. (1988). Incidence of depression and anxiety: The Stirling County study. *American Journal of Public Health, 78,* 534–540.

Murphy, M., Sanders, R. E., Gariesheski, A., & Schmitt, F. (1981). Metamemory in the aged. *Journal of Gerontology, 36,* 185–193.

Murphy, P., & Burck, H. (1976). Career development of men and mid-life. *Journal of Vocational Behavior, 9,* 337–343.

Murphy, P. A. (1991). Parental death in childhood and loneliness in young adults. *Omega, 23,* 25–36.

Murrell, F. H. (1970). The effect of extensive practice on age differences in reaction time. *Journal of Gerontology, 25,* 268–274.

Murrell, F. H., & Griew, S. (1965). Age, experience, and response speed. In A. T. Welford & J. E. Birren (Eds.). *Behavior, aging, and the nervous system* (pp. 60–66). Springfield, IL: Thomas.

Murstein, B. I. (1982). Marital choice. In J. Wolman (Ed.), *Handbook of developmental psychology* (pp. 652–666). Englewood Cliffs, NJ: Prentice-Hall.

Mussen, P., Honzik, M. P., & Eichorn, D. H. (1982). Early-adult antecedents of life satisfaction at age 70. *Journal of Gerontology, 37,* 316–322.

Myer, D. A. (1991). Work after cessation of career job. *Journal of Gerontology, 46,* S93–102.

Myers, G. C. (1985). Aging and worldwide population change. In R. Binstock & E. Shanas (Eds.), *Handbook of aging and the social sciences* (pp. 173–198). New York: Van Nostrand Reinhold.

Myers, J. E., & Salmon, H. E. (1984). Counseling programs for older persons: Status, shortcomings, and potentialities. *Counseling Psychologist, 12,* 39–54.

Myers, J. E., & Shelton, B. (1987). Abuse and older persons: Issues and implications for counselors. *Journal of Counseling and Development, 65,* 376–380.

Myers, J. K., Weissman, M. M., Tischler, G. L., Holzer, C. E., III, Leaf, P. J., Orvaschel, H., Anthony, J. C., Boyd, J. H., Burke, J. D., Kramer, M., & Stoltzmann, R. (1984). Six-month prevalence of psychiatric disorders in three communities. *Archives of General Psychiatry, 41,* 959–967.

Myers, W. A. (1991). *New techniques in the psychotherapy of older patients.* Washington, DC: American Psychiatric Press.

Nardi, A. H. (1973). Person-perception research and the perception of life-span development. In P. B. Baltes & K. W. Schaie (Eds.), *Life-span developmental psychology: Personality and socialization* (pp. 285–301). New York: Academic Press.

National Cancer Institute. (1991). What you need to know about cancer. Washington, DC: DHEW.

National Council on Aging. (1981). *Aging in the eighties: America in transition.* Washington, DC: Author.

National Institute on Aging. (1989). Alzheimer's disease. Washington, DC: DHEW.

Nebes, R. D., & Madden, D. J. (1988). Different patterns of cognitive slowing produced by Alzheimer's disease and normal aging. *Psychology and Aging, 3,* 102–104.

Nehrke, M. (1974, November). Actual and perceived attitudes towards death and self-concept in three-generational families [paper]. Annual meeting of the Gerontological Society, Washington, DC.

Nehrke, M., Hulicka, I., & Morganti, J. (1980). Age differences in life satisfaction, locus of control and self-concept. *International Journal of Aging and Human Development, 11,* 25–33.

Neimeyer, R. A. (1989). Death anxiety. In H. Wass, F. M. Berardo, & R. A. Neimeyer (Eds.), *Dying: Facing the facts* (2nd ed., pp. 97–136). Washington, DC: Hemisphere.

Nelson, E.A., & Daneffer, D. (1992). Aged heterogeneity: Fact or fiction? The fate of diversity in gerontological research. *Gerontologist, 32,* 17–23.

Nelson, F., & Faberow, N. (1980). Indirect self-destructive behavior in the nursing-home patient. *Journal of Gerontology, 35,* 949–957.

Nelson, K. A. (1987). Visual impairment among elderly Americans: Statistics in transition. *Journal of Visual Impairment and Blindness, 81,* 331-334.

Nesselroade, J. R. (1988). Some implications of the state-trait distinction for the study of development over the life-span: The case of personality. In P. Baltes & O. Brim (Eds.), *Life-span development and behavior* (Vol. 8, pp. 163–191). Hillsdale, NJ: Erlbaum.

Nesselroade, J. R., Siegler, I., & Baltes, P. B. (1974). Adolescent personality development and historical change: 1970–72. *Monographs of the Society for Research in Child Development, 39.*

Nesselroade, J. R., Stigler, S. M., & Baltes, P. B. (1980). Regression toward the mean and the study of change. *Psychological Bulletin, 88,* 622–637.

Neugarten, B. L. (1968). The awareness of middle age. In B. L. Neugarten (Ed.), *Middle-age and aging: A reader in social psychology* (pp. 93–98). Chicago: University of Chicago Press.

Neugarten, B. L. (1973). Personality change in late life: A developmental perspective. In C. Eisdorfer & M. P. Lawton (Eds.), *The Psychology of adult development and aging.* Washington, DC: American Psychological Association.

Neugarten, B. L. (1976). Adaptation and the life cycle. *Counseling Psychologist, 6,* 16–20.

Neugarten, B. L. (1977). Personality and aging. In J. E. Birren & K. W. Schaie (Eds.), *Handbook of the psychology of aging* (pp. 626–649). New York: Van Nostrand Reinhold.

Neugarten, B. L. (1982). *Age or need?* Belmont, CA: Sage.

Neugarten, B. L., & Datan, N. (1973). Sociological perspectives on the life cycle. In P. B. Baltes & K. W. Schaie (Eds.), *Life-span developmental psychology: Personality and socialization* (pp. 53–69). New York: Academic Press.

Neugarten, B. L., & Hagestad, G. (1976). Aging and the life course. In R. H. Binstock & E. Shanas (Eds.), *Handbook of aging and the social sciences* (pp. 35–57). New York: Van Nostrand Reinhold.

Neugarten, B. L., & Weinsten, K. K. (1964). The changing American grandparent. *Journal of Marriage and the Family, 26,* 199–204.

Newman, B., & Newman, P. (1986). *Development through life* (3rd ed.). Homewood, IL: Dorsey Press.

Newman, B., & Newman, P. (1990). *Development through life: A psychosocial approach* (4th ed.). Homewood, IL: Dorsey Press.

Newman, B. M. (1982). Mid-life development. In B. Wolman (Ed.), *Handbook of developmental psychology* (pp. 617–635). Englewood Cliffs, NJ: Prentice-Hall.

Newman, J. P., Engle, R. J., & Jensen, J. E. (1991). Changes in depression-symptoms experiences among older women. *Psychology and Aging, 6,* 212–222.

Newsweek. (1990). The search for the fountain of youth. March 5, pp. 44–47.

Newton, N. A., Brauer, D., Gutman, D., & Grunes, J. (1986). Psychodynamic therapy with the aged: A review. In T. L. Brink (Ed.), *Clinical gerontology* (pp. 205–230). New York: Haworth Press.

Nirenberg, T. D. (1983). Relocation of institutionalized elderly. *Journal of Counsulting and Clinical Psychology, 51,* 693–701.

Nock, S. L. (1982). The life-cycle approach to family analysis. In B. Wolman (Ed.), *Handbook of developmental psychology* (pp. 636–651). Englewood Cliffs, NJ: Prentice-Hall.

Noelker, L., & Harel, Z. (1978). Predictors of well-being and survival among institutionalized aged. *Gerontologist, 18,* 562–567.

Norton, A. J., & Glick, P. C. (1986). One-parent families: A social and economic profile. *Family Relations, 35,* 9–17.

Novatney, J. P. (1990, November). Grandparents' ties to step- and biological grandchildren. Paper presented at the Annual Scientific Meeting of the Gerontological Society. Boston, MA.

Obler, L. K., & Albert, M. L. (1985). Language skills across adulthood. In J. E. Birren & K. W. Schaie (Eds.), *Handbook of the psychology of aging* (pp. 463–473). New York: Van Nostrand Reinhold.

O'Brien, J. E., & Lind, D. (1976). Review of *The Honorable Elders* [by E. Palmore]. *Gerontologist, 19,* 560–561.

O'Bryant, S. L. (1990–1991). Forewarning of a husband's death: Does it make a difference for older widows? *Omega, 22,* 227–239.

Ochs, A. L., Newberry, J., Lenhardt, M. L., & Harkins, S. W. (1985). Neural and vestibular aging associated with falls. In J. E. Birren & K. W. Schaie (Eds.), *Handbook of the psychology of aging* (pp. 378–399). New York: Van Nostrand Reinhold.

O'Connor, D. W., Franz, C. P., Pollit, P. A., Roth, M., Brook, P., & Reiss, B. B. (1990). Memory complaints and impairment in normal depressed and demented persons identified in a community survey. *Archives of General Psychiatry, 47,* 224–227.

O'Donohue, W. T. (1987). The sexual behavior and problems of the elderly. In L. Carstensen & B.

Edelstein (Eds.), *Handbook of clinical gerontology* (pp. 66–75). New York: Pergamon.

Oerter, R. (1986). Developmental task through the life-span: A new approach to an old concept. In P. Baltes, D. Featherman, & R. Lerner (Eds.), *Life-span development and behavior* (Vol. 7, pp. 233–269). Hillsdale, NJ: Erlbaum.

O'Hara, M. W., Hinnicks, J. V., Kohout, F. J., Wallace, R. B., & Lemke, J. H. (1986). Memory complaint and memory performance in depressed elderly. *Psychology and Aging, 1,* 208–214.

Ohio Crime Prevention Association. (1989). *A Crime Prevention Guide for Senior Citizens for Their Safety and Peace of Mind.* Columbus, OH.

Ohta, R. J. (1981). Spatial problem-solving: The response selection tendencies of young and elderly adults. *Experimental Aging Research, 1,* 81–84.

Ohta, R. J., Carlin, M. F., & Harmon, B. M. (1981). Auditory acuity and performance on the Mental Status Questionnaire in the elderly. *Journal of the American Geriatrics Society, 29,* 476–478.

Okun, M. A. (1976). Adult age and cautiousness in decision-making: A review of the literature. *Human Development, 19,* 222–233.

Olsen-Noll, G. G., & Bosworth, M. F. (1989). Alcohol abuse in the elderly. *American Family Physician, 39,* 173–179.

Olsho, L. W., Harkins, S. W., & Lenhardt, M. L. (1985). Aging and the auditory system. In J. E. Birren & K. W. Schaie (Eds.), *Handbook of the psychology of aging* (2nd ed., pp. 332–377). New York: Van Nostrand Reinhold.

Olson, P. (1990). The elderly in the People's Republic of China. In J. Sokolovsky (Ed.), *The cultural context of aging: Worldwide perspectives* (pp. 141–161). New York: Bergin & Garvey.

Ornstein, S., & Isabella, L. (1990). Age versus stage models of career attitudes of women: A partial replication and extension. *Journal of Vocational Behavior, 36,* 1–19.

Osgood, C. E., Suci, G. J., & Tannenbaum, P. H. (1957). *The measurement of meaning.* Chicago: University of Illinois Press.

Osgood, N. J. (1983). Patterns of aging in retirement communities: Typology of residents. *Journal of Applied Gerontology, 2,* 28–43.

Osgood, N. J. (1990). Prevention of suicide in the elderly [unpublished manuscript]. Virginia Commonwealth University: Richmond, VA.

Osgood, N. J., & Brant, B. A. (1990). Suicidal behavior in long-term care facilities. *Suicide and Life-Threatening Behavior, 20,* 113–122.

Osipow, S. H. (1983). *Theories of career development.* Englewood Cliffs, NJ: Prentice-Hall.

Osipow, S. H. (1987). Counseling psychology: Theory, research, and practice in career counseling. *Annual Review of Psychology, 38,* 257–278.

Osipow, S. H., Doty, R. E., & Spokane, A. R. (1985). Occupational stress, strain, and coping across the life-span. *Journal of Vocational Behavior, 27,* 98–108.

Osterweis, M., Solomon, F., & Green, M. (1984). *Bereavement: Reactions, consequences, and care.* Washington, DC: National Academy Press.

Ostrom, J., Hammarlund, E., Christensen, D., Plein, J., & Kethley, A. (1985). Medication usage in an elderly population. *Medical Care, 23,* 157–164.

Palmore, E. (1969). Physical, mental, and social factors in predicting longevity. *Gerontologist, 9,* 103–108.

Palmore, E. (1975). *The honorable elders: A cross-cultural analysis of aging in Japan.* Durham, NC: Duke University Press.

Palmore, E. (1979). Predictors of successful aging. *Gerontologist, 16,* 441–446.

Palmore, E. (1982). Preparation for retirement: The impact of preretirement programs on retirement and leisure. In N. J. Osgood (Ed.), *Life after work: Retirement leisure, recreation, and the elderly* (pp. 330–341). New York: Praeger.

Palmore, E. (Ed.). (1980). *International handbook on aging.* Westport, CT: Greenwood Press.

Palmore, E., & Cleveland, W. (1976). Aging, terminal decline, and terminal drop. *Journal of Gerontology, 31,* 76–81.

Palmore, E., George, L. K., & Fillenbaum, G. G. (1982). Predictors of retirement. *Journal of Gerontology, 37,* 733–742.

Panek, P. E. (1982, November). Cautiousness and auditory selective-attention performance of older adults [paper]. Annual meeting of the Gerontological Society of America, Boston.

Panek, P. E. (1984, February). Stimulating classroom discussion regarding negative attitudes toward aging [paper]. Annual meeting of the Association for Gerontology in Higher Education, Indianapolis, IN.

Panek, P. E., & Reardon, J. (1987). Age and gender effects on accident types for rural drivers. *Journal of Applied Gerontology, 6,* 332–346.

Panek, P. E., & Rush, M. C. (1981). Simultaneous examination of age-related differences in the ability to maintain and reorient auditory selective attention. *Experimental Aging Research, 7,* 405–416.

Panek, P. E., & Sterns, H. L. (1985). Self-evaluation, actual performance, and preference across the life-span. *Experimental Aging Research, 11,* 221–223.

Panek, P. E., Rush, M. C., & Slade, L. A. (1984). An exploratory examination on the locus of the age-Stroop interference relationship. *Journal of Geriatric Psychology, 145,* 209–216.

Panek, P. E., Barrett, G. V., Alexander, R. A., & Sterns, H. L. (1979). Age and self-selected performance pace on a visual monitoring inspection task. *Aging and Work: A Journal on Age, Work, and Retirement, 2,* 183–191.

Panek, P. E., Barrett, G. V., Sterns, H. L., & Alexander, R. A. (1977). A review of age changes in perceptual information-processing ability with regard to driving. *Experimental Aging Research, 3,* 387–449.

Panek, P. E., Barrett, G. V., Sterns, H. L., & Alexander, R. A. (1978). Age differences in perceptual style, selective attention, and perceptual-motor reaction time. *Experimental Aging Research, 4,* 377–387.

Papalia, D., & Bielby, D. D. (1974). Cognitive functioning in middle-aged and elderly adults: A review of research based on Piaget's theory. *Human Development, 17,* 424–443.

Parham, I. A., Priddy, J. M., McGovern, T. V., & Richman, C. M. (1982). Group psychotherapy with the elderly: Problems and prospects. *Psychotherapy: Theory, Research, and Practice, 19,* 437–443.

Parke, R. D. (1988). Families in life-span perspective: A multilevel developmental approach. In E. M. Hetherington, R. M. Lerner, & P. B. Baltes (Eds.), *Child development in life-span perspective* (pp. 159–190). Hillsdale, NJ: Erlbaum.

Parkes, C. M., & Weiss, R. S. (1983). *Recovery from bereavement.* New York: Basic Books.

Parkes, G. W. (1987–1988). Research: Bereavement. *Omega, 18,* 365–378.

Parmalee, P. A., Kleban, M. H., Lawton, M. P., & Katz, I. R. (1991). Depression and cognitive change among institutionalized aged. *Psychology and Aging, 6,* 504–511.

Parnes, H. S., & Meyer, J. A. (1972). Withdrawal from the labor force by middle-aged men. In G. M. Shatto (Ed.). *Employment of the middle-aged* (pp. 63–86). Springfield, IL: Thomas.

Parnes, H. S., Crowley, J. E., Haurin, R. J., Less, L. J., Morgan, W. R., Mott, F. L., & Nestel, G. (1985). *Retirement among American men.* Lexington, MA: Lexington Books.

Patterson, R. (1987). Family management of the elderly. In L. Carstensen & B. Edelstein (Eds.). *Handbook of clinical gerontology* (pp. 267–276). New York: Pergamon.

Pattison, E. M. (1977). *The experience of dying.* Englewood Cliffs, NJ: Prentice-Hall.

Peacock, E. W., & Talley, W. M. (1985). Developing leisure competence: A goal for late adulthood. *Educational Gerontology, 11,* 261–276.

Pearce, S. D. (1991). Toward understanding the participation of older adults in continuing education. *Educational Gerontology, 17,* 451–464.

Pearlin, L. I., & Lieberman, M. A. (1979). Social sources of emotional distress. *Research in Community and Mental Health, 1,* 217–248.

Pearlman, R., & Uhlmann, R. (1988). Quality of life in chronic disease: Perceptions of elderly patients. *Journal of Gerontology: Medical Sciences, 42,* M25–30.

Peck, M. (1984). Youth suicide. In H. Wass & C. Corr (Eds.), *Childhood and death* (pp. 279–290). Washington, DC: Hemisphere/McGraw-Hill.

Peck, R. C. (1968). Psychological developments in the second half of life. In B. L. Neugarten (Ed.), *Middle age and aging* (pp. 44–49). Chicago: University of Chicago Press.

Pederson, N., Plomin, R., McClearn, G., & Firberg, L. (1988). Neuroticism, extraversion, and related traits in adult twins reared apart and reared together. *Journal of Personality and Social Psychology, 55,* 950–957.

Pelham, A. O., & Clark, W. F. (1987). Widowhood among low-income and racial groups in California. In H. Lopata (Ed.), *Widows* (pp. 191–222). Durham, NC: Duke University Press.

Pellegrino, J., & Glaser, R. (1979). Cognitive correlates and components in the analysis of individual differences. In R. Sternberg & D. Detterman (Eds.), *Human Intelligence: Perspectives on its theory and measurement* (pp. 61–88). Norwood, NJ: Ablex.

Peppers, L. (1987). Grief and elective abortion: Breaking the emotional bond. *Omega, 18,* 1–12.

Perlick, D., & Atkins, A. (1984). Variations in reported age of a patient: A source of bias in the diagnosis of depression and dementia. *Journal of Consulting and Clinical Psychology, 52,* 812–820.

Perlmutter, M. (1983). Learning and memory through adulthood. In M. W. Riley, B. B. Hess, & K. Bond (Eds.), *Aging in society* (pp. 219–242). Hillsdale, NJ: Erlbaum.

Perlmutter, M., & Mitchell, D. (1982). The appearance and disappearance of age difference in adult memory. In F. I. M. Cariak & S. Trehub (Eds.), *Aging and cognitive processes* (pp. 127–144). New York: Plenum.

Perlmutter, M., & Nyquist, L. (1990). Relationships between self-reported physical and mental health and intelligence performance across adulthood. *Journal of Gerontology: Psychological Sciences, 45,* P145–155.

Perlmutter, M., Metzger, R., Miller, K., & Nezevorski, T. (1980). Memory of historical events. *Experimental Aging Research, 6,* 47–60.

Pervin, L. A. (1968). Performance and satisfaction as a function of individual-environment fit. *Psychological Bulletin, 69,* 56–68.

Peskin, H., & Livson, F. (1981). Uses of the past in psychological health. In D. Eichorn, N. Haan, J.

Clausen, M. Honzik, & P. Mussen (Eds.), *Present and past in middle life* (pp. 153–181). New York: Academic Press.

Peterson, D. (1985). A history of education for older learners. In D. B. Lumsdem (Ed.), *The older adult as learner* (pp. 1–24). Washington, DC: Hemisphere.

Peterson, D., & Eden, D. (1981). Cognitive style and the older learner. *Educational Gerontology, 7,* 57–66.

Peterson, J. A. (1980). Social-psychological aspects of death and dying and mental health. In J. E. Birren and R. B. Sloane (Eds.), *Handbook of mental health and aging* (pp. 922–942). Englewood Cliffs, NJ: Prentice-Hall.

Pfeffer, C. R. (1984). Death preoccupations and suicidal behavior in children. In H. Wass & C. Corr (Eds.), *Childhood and death* (pp. 261–290). Washington, DC: Hemisphere/McGraw-Hill.

Pfeiffer, E. (1970). Survival in old age: Physical, psychological, and social correlates of longevity. *Journal of the American Geriatrics Society, 18,* 273–285.

Pfeiffer, E. (1976). *Multidimensional functional assessment: The OARS methodology.* Durham, NC: Center for Study of Aging and Human Development.

Pfeiffer, E. (1977). Psychopathology and social pathology. In J. E. Birren & K. W. Schaie (Eds.), *Handbook of the psychology of aging* (pp. 650–671). New York: Van Nostrand Reinhold.

Pfeiffer, E., Verwoerdt, A., & Wang, H. S. (1968). Sexual behavior in aged men and women. *Archives of Genetic Psychiatry, 19,* 753–758.

Piaget, J., & Inhelder, B. (1969). *The psychology of the child.* New York: Basic Books.

Pierce, B., & Chiriboga, D. (1979). Dimensions of adult self-concept. *Journal of Gerontology, 34,* 80–85.

Pillemer, K., & Finlelhor, D. (1988). The prevalence of elder abuse: A random-sample survey. *Gerontologist, 28,* 51–57.

Planek, T. W., & Fowler, R. C. (1971). Traffic-accident problems and exposure characteristic of the aging driver. *Journal of Gerontology, 26,* 224–230.

Plath, D. W. (1973). Ecstasy years—Old age in Japan. *Pacific Years, 46,* 421–428.

Plemons, J. K., Willis, S. L., & Baltes, P. B. (1978). Modifiability of fluid intelligence in aging: A short-term training approach. *Journal of Gerontology, 33,* 2.

Plude, D. J., & Doussard-Roosevelt, J. A. (1989). Aging, selective attention, and feature integration. *Psychology and Aging, 4,* 98–105.

Plude, D. J., & Hoyer, W. J. (1986). Age and the selectivity of visual information-processing. *Psychology and Aging, 1,* 4–10.

Plude, D. J., & Hoyer, W. J. (1981, November). Adult age differences in visual search as a function of stimulus-mapping and processing load. *Journal of Gerontology, 36,* 596–604.

Plude, D. J., Kaye, D. B., Hoyer, W. J., Post, T. A., Saynisch, M. J., & Hahn, M. V. (1983). Aging and visual search under consistent and varied mapping. *Developmental Psychology, 19,* 508–512.

Pollitt, P. A., O'Connor, D. W., & Anderson, I. (1989). Mild dementia: Perceptions and problems. *Aging and Society, 9,* 261–275.

Pomin, K., Pederson, N., McClearn, G., Nesselroade, J., & Bergman, C. (1988). EAS temperaments during the last half of the life-span: Twins reared apart and twins reared together. *Psychology and Aging, 3,* 43–50.

Ponds, R. W., Brouwer, W. H., & Van Wolffelaar, P. C. (1988). Age differences in divided attention in a simulated driving task. *Journal of Gerontology: Psychological Sciences, 43,* P151–156.

Poon, L. (1985). Differences in human memory with aging. In J. E. Birren & K. W. Schaie (Eds.), *Handbook of the psychology of aging* (pp. 427–462). New York: Van Nostrand Reinhold.

Poon, L., & Shaffer, G. (1982, August). Prospective memory in young and elderly adults [paper]. Annual convention of the American Psychological Association, Washington, DC.

Poon, L. W., Clayton, G. M., & Martin, P. (1991, Winter). Cecilia Payne Grove: In her own words. *Generations,* 67–69.

Pope, M., & Schulz, R. (1991). Sexual attitudes and behavior in mid-life and aging homosexual males. *Journal of Homosexuality, 20,* 169–178.

Popkin, S., Schaie, K. W., & Krauss, I. (1983). Age-fair assessment of psychometric intelligence. *Educational Gerontology, 9,* 47–55.

Post, F. (1980). Paranoid schizophrenialike, and schizophrenic states in the aged. In J. E. Birren & R. B. Sloane (Eds.), *Handbook of mental health and aging.* Englewood Cliffs, NJ: Prentice-Hall.

Post, F. (1987). Paranoid and schizophrenic disorders among the aging. In L. Carstensen & B. Edelstein (Eds.), *Handbook of clinical gerontology* (pp. 96–111). New York: Praeger.

Poth, M. (1989). *Is mid-life easier in a mink coat?* Buffalo, NY: Prometheus.

President's Commission on Mental Health. (1978). *Mental health in America: 1978. Findings and assessment.* Washington, DC: US Government Printing Office.

Price, R. E., Omizo, M. M., & Hammert, V. L. (1986). Counseling clients with AIDS. *Journal of Counseling and Development, 65,* 96–97.

Puder, R. S. (1988). Age analysis of cognitive-behavioral group therapy for chronic pain patients. *Psychology and Aging, 3,* 204–207.

Qassis, S., & Hayden, D. C. (1990). Effects of environment on psychological well-being of elderly persons. *Psychological Reports, 66,* 147–150.

Quilter, R. E., Giambra, L. M., & Benson, P. E. (1983). Longitudinal age changes in vigilance over an 18-year interval. *Journal of Gerontology, 38,* 51–54.

Quinn, J. F. (1977). Microeconomic determinants of early retirement: A cross-sectional view of white married men. *Journal of Human Resources, 12,* 329–346.

Quinn, J. F., & Burkhauser, R. B. (1990). Work and retirement. In R. Binstock & L. George (Eds.), *Handbook of aging and the social sciences* (3rd ed., pp. 304–327). New York: Academic Press.

Quinn, J. F., Burkhauser, R. V., & Myers, D. C. (1990). *Passing the torch: The influence of economic incentives on work and retirement.* Kalamazoo, MI: Upjohn Institute for Employment Research.

Rabbitt, P. M. A. (1965). Age and discrimination between complex stimuli. In A. T. Welford & J. E. Birren (Eds.), *Behavior, aging, and the nervous system* (pp. 35–53). Springfield, IL: Thomas.

Rabinowitz, J. C., & Craik, F. (1986). Prior retrieval effect in young and elderly adults. *Journal of Gerontology, 41,* 368–375.

Rabinowitz, J. C., Ackerman, B. P., Craik, F. I. M., & Hinchley, J. (1982). Aging and metamemory: The roles of relatedness and imagery. *Journal of Gerontology, 37,* 688–695.

Rabins, P. V. (1992). Schizophrenia and psychotic states. In J. E. Birren, R. B. Sloane, & G. D. Cohen (Eds.), *Handbook of mental health and aging* (pp. 464–477). New York: Academic Press.

Rabins, P. V., & Mace, N. L. (1986). Some ethical issues in dementia care. In T. L. Brink (Ed.). *Clinical gerontology* (pp. 503–512). New York: Haworth Press.

Rachal, J. R. (1989). The social context of adult and continuing education. In S. B. Merriam & P. M. Cunningham (Eds.), *Handbook of adult and continuing education* (pp. 3–14). San Francisco: Jossey-Bass.

Rando, T. A. (1984). Grief, dying, and death: Clinical interventions for caregivers. Champaign, IL: Research Press.

Raphael, B. (1983). *The anatomy of bereavement.* New York: Basic Books.

Raskin, A. (1979). Signs and symptoms of psychopathology in the elderly. In A. Raskin & L. Jarvik (Eds.), *Psychiatric symptoms and cognitive loss in the elderly: Evaluation and assessment techniques* (pp. 3–18). New York: Halsted.

Raskind, M. A., & Peskind, E. R. (1992). Alzheimer's disease and other dementing disorders. In J. E. Birren, R. B. Sloane, & G. D. Cohen (Eds.), *Handbook of mental health and aging* (pp. 478–516). New York: Academic Press.

Rawlins, M. E., Rawlins, L. D., & Rearden, J. (1985). Stresses and coping strategies of dual-career couples affiliated with a university. *Education Journal, 18,* 26–30.

Rebok, G. (1987). *Life-span cognitive development.* New York: Holt, Rinehart, and Winston.

Rebok, G., Offermann, L. R., Wirtz, G., & Montaglione, C. J. (1986). Work and intellectual aging: The psychological concomitants of social-organizational conditions. *Educational Gerontology, 12,* 359–374.

Reedy, M. N., Birren, J. E., & Schaie, K. W. (1982). Age and sex differences in satisfying love relationships across the life-span. *Human Development, 24,* 52–66.

Reese, H. W., & Overton, W. F. (1970). Models of development and theories of development. In L. R. Goulet & P. B. Baltes (Eds.), *Life-span developmental psychology: Research and theory* (pp. 116–145). New York: Academic Press.

Regier, D. A., Myers, J. K., Robins, L. N., Blazer, D. G., Hough, R. L., Easton, W. W., & Locke, B. Z. (1988). The NIMH catchment area program: Historical context major objectives, and study-population characteristics. *Archives of General Psychiatry, 41,* 934–941.

Reichard, S., Livson, P., & Peterson, P. (1962). *Aging and personality.* New York: Wiley.

Reidl, R. (1981). Behavioral therapies. In C. Eisdorfer (Ed.), *Annual review of gerontology and geriatrics* (pp. 148–180).

Reifler, B., Cox, G., & Hanley, R. (1981). Problems of mentally ill elderly as perceived by patients, families, and clinicians. *Gerontologist, 21,* 165–170.

Reinberg, J., & Hayslip, B. (1991, November). The effect of elder-abuse education on persons with experienced childhood violence [paper]. Annual Convention of the Gerontological Society, San Francisco.

Reinke, B. J., Holmes, D. S., & Harris, R. L. (1985). The timing of psychosocial changes in women's lives: The years 25 to 45. *Journal of Personality and Social Psychology, 48,* 1353–1364.

Reker, G. T., Peacock, E. J., & Wong, T. P. (1987). Meaning and purpose in life: A life-span investigation. *Journal of Gerontology, 42,* 44–49.

Reno, V. (1976). Why men stop working before age 65: An information paper prepared for the House Select Committee on Aging. Washington, DC: US Government Printing Office.

Repetti, R. L., Matthews, K. A., & Waldron, I. (1989). Employment and women's health: Effects of paid employment on women's mental and physical health. *American Psychologist, 44,* 1394–1401.

Report of the Secretary of Labor. (1989, January). Older-worker task force: Key policy issues for the future. Washington, DC: United States Department of Labor.

Research and Forecasts, Inc. (1980). Retirement preparation: Growing corporate involvement. *Aging and Work, 3,* 1–13.

Resnick, L. B. (1976). Introduction: Changing conceptions of intelligence: In L. Resnick (Ed.), *The nature of intelligence* (pp. 1–10). Hillsdale, NJ: Erlbaum.

Reynolds, D., & Kalish, R. (1976). Death rates, ethnicity, and the ethnic press. *Ethnicity, 3,* 305–316.

Reynolds, L. F., Masters, S. H., & Moser, C. H. (1987). *Economics of labor.* Englewood Cliffs, NJ: Prentice-Hall.

Rhodes, S. R. (1983). Age-related differences in work attitudes and behavior: A review and conceptual analysis. *Psychological Bulletin, 93,* 328–367.

Rhyne, D. (1981). Bases of marital satisfaction among men and women. *Journal of Marriage and the Family, 43,* 941–954.

Rich, B. M., & Baum, M. (1984). *The aging: A guide to public policy.* Pittsburgh, PA: University of Pittsburgh Press.

Richards, W. S., & Thorpe, G. L. (1978). Behavioral approaches to the problems of later life. In M. Storandt, I. Siegler, & M. F. Elias (Eds.), *The clinical psychology of aging* (pp. 253–276). New York: Plenum.

Riegel, K. F. (1973). Developmental psychology and society: Some historical and ethical considerations. In J. R. Nesselroade & P. B. Baltes (Eds.), *Life-span developmental psychology: Methodological issues* (pp. 1–24). New York: Academic Press.

Riegel, K. F. (1975). Adult life crises: A dialectical interpretation of development. In N. Datan & L. Ginsburg (Eds.), *Life-span development psychology: Normative life crises* (pp. 99–128). New York: Academic Press.

Riegel, K. F. (1976). The dialectics of human development. *American Psychologist, 31,* 689–700.

Riegel, K. F. (1977a). History of psychological gerontology. In J. E. Birren & K. W. Schaie (Eds.), *Handbook of the psychology of aging* (pp. 70–102). New York: Van Nostrand Reinhold.

Riegel, K. F. (1977b). The dialectics of time. In N. Datan & H. Reese (Eds.), *Life-span developmental psychology: Dialectical perspectives on experimental research* (pp. 3–45). New York: Academic Press.

Riegel, K. F., & Riegel, R. M. (1972). Development and death. *Developmental Psychology, 6,* 306–319.

Riegel, K. F., Riegel, R. M., & Meyer, G. (1967). Sociopsychological factors of aging: A cohort sequential analysis. *Human Development, 10,* 27–56.

Rife, J., & Kilty, K. (1989–1990). Job-search discouragement and the older worker: Implications for social work practice. *Journal of Applied Social Sciences, 14,* 71–94.

Riley, M. (1983). The family in an aging society: A matrix of latent relationships. *Journal of Family Issues, 4,* 439–454.

Riley, M., Foner, A., & Associates. (1968). *Aging and society: An inventory of research findings* (Vol. 1). New York: Russell Sage Foundation.

Rinaldi, A., & Kearl, M. C. (1990). The hospice farewell: Ideological perspectives of its professional practitioners. *Omega, 21,* 283–300.

Risman, B. J. (1986). Can men "mother"? Life as a single father. *Family Relations, 35,* 95–102.

Robbins, R. A. (1990–1991). Bugen's Coping-with-Death Scale: Reliability and further validation. *Omega, 22,* 287–300.

Roberto, K. A., & Scott, J. P. (1986). Friendships of older men and women: Exchange patterns and satisfaction. *Psychology and Aging, 1,* 103–109.

Roberts, P., & Newton, P. M. (1987). Levinsonian studies of women's adult development. *Psychology and Aging, 2,* 154–163.

Robertson, J. F. (1977). Grandmotherhood: A study of role conceptions. *Journal of Marriage and the Family, 39,* 165–174.

Robertson-Tchabo, E. A. (1980). Cognitive skill and training for the elderly: Why should "old dogs" require new tricks? In L. W. Poon, J. Fozard, L. Cermak, D. Arenberg, & L. Thompson (Eds.), *New directions in memory and aging* (pp. 511–518). Hillsdale, NJ: Erlbaum.

Robertson-Tchabo, E. A., Hausman, C., & Arenberg, D. (1976). A classical mnemonic for older learners: A trip that works! *Educational Gerontology, 1,* 215–226.

Robey, B. (1984, February). Entering middle-age. *American Demographics,* 4.

Robins, L. N., Helzer, J. E., Weissmann, M. M., Orvaschel, H., Gruenbert, E., Burke, J. D., & Regier, D. A. (1984). Lifetime prevalence of specific psychiatric disorders in three sites. *Archives of General Psychiatry, 41,* 959–967.

Robins, L. N., West, P. A., & Murphy, G. E. (1977). The high rate of suicide among older white men: A study testing ten hypotheses. *Social Psychiatry, 12,* 1–20.

Robinson, P. K., Coberly, S., & Paul, C. E. (1985). Work and retirement. In R. Binstock & E. Shanas (Eds.), *Handbook of aging and the social sciences* (pp. 503–527). New York: Van Nostrand Reinhold.

Robison, R. (1991, Winter). Rose Feinstein: Yoga and no chocolate. *Generations,* 29–31.

Rockstein, M., & Sussman, M. (1979). *Biology of aging*. Belmont, CA: Wadsworth.

Rodabough, T. (1980). Alternatives to the stages model of the dying process. *Death Education, 4*, 1–19.

Rodenheaver, D., & Datan, N. (1988). The challenge of double jeopardy: Toward a mental health agenda for aging women. *American Psychologist, 43*, 648–654.

Rodin, J., & Langer, E. (1977). Long-term effects of a control-relevant intervention with the institutionalized aged. *Journal of Personality and Social Psychology, 34*, 314–350.

Rogers, C. (1961). On becoming a person: A therapist's view of psychotherapy. Boston: Houghton Mifflin.

Rogers, C. (1972). *Becoming partners: Marriage and its alternatives*. New York: Delacorte Press.

Rollins, B. C., & Cannon, K. L. (1974). Marital satisfaction over the life cycle: A reevaluation. *Journal of Marriage and the Family, 36*, 271–282.

Romaniuk, J., & Romaniuk, M. (1982). Participation motives of older adults in higher education: The Elderhostel experience. *Gerontologist, 22*, 364–368.

Romaniuk, M. (1981). Reminiscence and the second half of life. *Experimental Aging Research, 7*, 315–336.

Romaniuk, M., & Romaniuk, J. (1981). Looking back: An analysis of reminiscence functions and triggers. *Experimental Aging Research, 7*, 477–490.

Rook, K. S. (1987). Reciprocity of social exchange and social satisfaction among older women. *Journal of Personality and Social Psychology, 52*, 145–154.

Roose, S. P. (1991). Diagnosis and pharmacological treatment of depression in older patients. In W. Myers (Ed.), *New techniques in the psychotherapy of older clients* (pp. 111–124). Washington, DC: American Psychiatric Press.

Root, W. (1981). Injuries at work are fewer among older employees. *Monthly Labor Review, 104*, 30–34.

Rose, C. L. (1964). Social factors in longevity. *Gerontologist, 4*, 27–37.

Rosen, B., & Jerdee, T. H. (1976). The nature of job-related stereotypes. *Journal of Applied Psychology, 61*, 180–183.

Rosenbaum, E. H. (1980). The doctor and the cancer patient. In M. Hamilton & H. Reid (Eds.), *A hospice handbook: A new way to care for the dying*. Grand Rapids, MI: Eerdmans.

Rosenstein, J., & Swenson, E. (1980). Behavioral approaches to therapy with the elderly. In S. S. Sargent (Ed.), *Nontraditional therapy and counseling with the aging* (pp. 178–198). New York: Springer.

Rosenthal, L. (1985). Kin-keeping in the familial division of labor. *Journal of Marriage and the Family, 45*, 509–521.

Rosenthal, R., & Rosnow, R. (1984). *Essentials of behavioral research: Methods and data analysis*. New York: McGraw-Hill.

Rosewater, L. B. (1985). On MMPI profiles of battered women. *Journal of Counseling and Development, 63*, 387.

Rosow, I. (1978). What is a cohort and why? *Human Development, 21*, 65–75.

Rosow, I. (1985). Status and role change through the life cycle. In R. Binstock & E. Shanas (Eds.), *Handbook of aging and the social sciences* (pp. 693). New York: Academic Press.

Ross, E. (1968). Effects of challenging and supportive instructions on verbal learning in older persons. *Journal of Educational Psychology, 59*, 261–266.

Rossi, A. F., & Rossi, P. H. (1990). *Of human bonding: Parent-child relationships across the life course*. New York: Aldine.

Roth, S., & Cohen, J. L. (1986). Approach-avoidance and coping with stress. *American Psychologist, 41*, 813–819.

Rowe, E. J., & Schnore, M. M. (1971). Item concreteness and reported strategies in paired-associate learning as a function of old age. *Journal of Gerontology, 26*, 470–475.

Rowe, G. P. (1990, November). Retirement transition of state employees: A ten year follow-up [paper]. Annual Meeting of the Gerontological Society, Boston.

Rowe, J. W. (1991, Winter). Reducing the risk of usual aging: A substantial departure from the traditional approaches in geriatric medicine. *Generations*, 25–29.

Rowe, J. W., & Kahn, R. L. (1987). Human aging: Usual and successful. *Science, 237*, 143–149.

Rowe, J. W., & Minaker, K. L. (1985). Geriatric medicine. In C. E. Finch & E. L. Schneider (Eds.), *Handbook of the biology of aging* (2nd ed. pp. 932–960). New York: Van Nostrand Reinhold.

Rowland, K. (1977). Environmental events predicting death for the elderly. *Psychological Bulletin, 84*, 349–372.

Roybal, E. R. (1988). Mental health and aging: The need for an expanded federal response. *American Psychologist, 43*, 189–194.

Rubin, L. B. (1982). Sex and sexuality: Women at mid-life. In M. Kirkpatrick (Ed.), *Women's sexual experience: Exploration of the dark continent* (pp. 61–82). New York: Plenum.

Rush, M. C., Panek, P. E., & Russell, J. (1990). Analysis of individual variability among older adults on the Stroop Color Word Interference Test. *International Journal of Aging and Human Development, 30*, 225–236.

Rybash, J. M., Hoyer, W. J., & Roodin, P. A. (1986). *Adult cognition and aging*. Elmsford, NY: Pergamon Press.

Ryff, C. D. (1984). Personality development from the inside: The subjective experience of change in adulthood and aging. In P. B. Baltes & O. G. Brim (Eds.), *Life-span development and behavior* (pp. 244–279). New York: Academic Press.

Ryff, C. D. (1989). In the eye of the beholder: Views of psychological well-being among middle-aged and older adults. *Psychology and Aging, 4*, 195–210.

Sable, P. (1991). Attachment, loss of spouse, and grief in elderly adults. *Omega, 23*, 129–142.

Sadavoy, J., & Fogel, B. (1992). Personality disorders in old age. In J. E. Birren, R. B. Sloane, & G. D. Cohen (Eds.), *Handbook of mental health and aging* (pp. 433–463). New York: Academic Press.

Salamon, M. J. (1985). Medication use and illness: The relationship between self and provider report. *Clinical Gerontologist, 3*, 17–22.

Salthouse, T. A. (1980). Age and memory: Strategies for localizing the loss. In L. Poon, J. Fozard, L. Cermak, D. Arenberg, & L. Thompson (Eds.), *New directions in memory and aging* (pp. 47–65). Hillsdale, NJ: Erlbaum.

Salthouse, T. A. (1982). *Adult cognition*. New York: Springer-Verlag.

Salthouse, T. A. (1984). The skill of typing. *Scientific American, 250*, 128–136.

Salthouse, T. A. (1985). Speed of behavior and its implications for cognition. In J. E. Birren & K. W. Schaie (Eds.), *Handbook of the psychology of aging* (2nd ed., pp. 400–426). New York: Van Nostrand Reinhold.

Salthouse, T. A. (1991, Winter). Cognitive facets of aging well: The focus on decline is controversial. *Generations*, 35–39.

Salthouse, T. A. (1991). *Theoretical perspectives on cognitive aging*. Hillsdale, NJ: Erlbaum.

Salvendy, G. (1974). Discrimination in performance assessments against the aged. *Perceptual and Motor Skills, 39*, 1087–1099.

Salzman, C., & Nenis-Olsen, J. (1992). Psychopharmacologic treatment. In J. E. Birren, R. B. Sloane, & G. D. Cohen (Eds.), *Handbook of mental health and aging* (pp. 722–763). New York: Academic Press.

Salzman, C., & Shader, R. (1979). Clinical evaluation of depression in the elderly. In A. Raskin & L. Jarvik (Eds.), *Psychiatric symptoms and cognitive loss in the elderly: Evaluation and assessment techniques* (pp. 39–74). Washington, DC: Hemisphere.

Sammartino, F. J. (1987). The effect of health on retirement. *Social Security Bulletin, 50*, 31–47.

Sanders, G. F., & Pittman, J. F. (1987). Attitudes of youth toward known and general target elderly. *Journal of Applied Gerontology, 6*, 464–475.

Sanders, K. (1979–1980). A comparison of older and younger spouses in bereavement outcome. *Omega, 11*, 217–232.

Sands, L. P., Meredith, W. (1989). Effects of sensory and motor functioning on adult intellectual performance. *Journal of Gerontology: Psychological Sciences, 44*, P56–58.

Santos, J., Hubbard, R. W., McIntosh, J. L., & Eisner, H. R. (1984). Community mental health and the elderly: Training approaches. *Journal of Community Psychology, 12*, 359–368.

Sarafino, E. P., & Armstrong, J. W. (1986). *Child and adolescent development*. St. Paul, MN: West.

Sarason, S. B. (1977). *Work, aging, and social change*. New York: Free Press.

Sarason, S. B., Sarason, E. K., & Cowden, P. (1975). Aging and the nature of work. *American psychologist, 30*, 584–592.

Sargent, S. S. (1980). Why nontraditional therapy and counseling with the aged? In S. Sargent (Ed.), *Nontraditional therapy and counseling with the aging* (pp. 1–11). New York: Academic Press.

Sargent, S. S. (1982). Therapy and self-actualization in the later years via nontraditional approaches. *Psychotherapy: Theory, Research, and Practice, 19*, 522–531.

Schaffer, G., & Poon, L. W. (1982). Individual variability in memory training with the elderly. *Educational Gerontology, 8*, 217–229.

Schaie, K. W. (1965). A general model for the study of developmental problems. *Psychological Bulletin, 64*, 92–107.

Schaie, K. W. (1967). Age changes and age differences. *Gerontologist, 7*, 128–132.

Schaie, K. W. (1970). A reinterpretation of age-related changes in cognitive structure and functioning. In L. Goulet & P. Baltes (Eds.), *Life-span developmental psychology: Research and theory* (pp. 486–508). New York: Academic Press.

Schaie, K. W. (1973). Methodological problems in descriptive developmental research on adulthood and aging. In J. R. Nesselroade & H. W. Reese (Eds.), *Life-span developmental psychology: Methodological issues* (pp. 253–280).

Schaie, K. W. (1977). Quasiexperimental designs in the psychology of aging. In J. E. Birren & K. W. Schaie (Eds.), *Handbook of the psychology of aging* (pp. 39–69). New York: Van Nostrand Reinhold.

Schaie, K. W. (1977–1978). Toward a stage theory of adult cognitive development. *Aging and Human Development, 8*, 129–138.

Schaie, K. W. (1978). External validity in the assessment of intellectual development in adulthood. *Journal of Gerontology, 33*, 696–701.

Schaie, K. W. (1979). The primary mental abilities in adulthood: An exploration in the development of psychometric intelligence. In P. Baltes & O. Brim

(Eds.), *Life-span development and behavior* (Vol. 2, pp. 68–115). New York: Academic Press.

Schaie, K. W. (1983). Age changes in intelligence. In D. S. Woodruff & J. E. Birren (Eds.), *Aging: Scientific perspectives and social issues* (2nd ed., pp. 150–163). New York: Van Nostrand Reinhold.

Schaie, K. W. (1990). Intellectual development in adulthood. In J. E. Birren & K. W. Schaie (Eds.), *Handbook of the psychology of aging* (pp. 291–310). New York: Academic Press.

Schaie, K. W., & Baltes, P. B. (1977). Some faith helps to see the forest: A final comment on the Horn and Donaldson myth of the Baltes-Schaie position on adult intelligence. *American Psychologist, 32,* 1118–1120.

Schaie, K. W., & Geiwitz, J. (1982). *Adult development and aging.* Boston: Little, Brown.

Schaie, K. W., & Gribbin, K. (1975). Adult development and aging. *Annual Review of Psychology, 26,* 65–96.

Schaie, K. W., & Hertzog, C. (1983). Fourteen-year cohort sequential analyses of adult intellectual development. *Developmental Psychology, 19,* 531–543.

Schaie, K. W., & Labouvie-Vief, G. (1974). Generational versus ontogenetic components of change in adult cognitive behavior: A 14-year cross-sequential study. *Developmental Psychology, 10,* 305–320.

Schaie, K. W., & Parham, I. (1976). Stability of adult personality traits: Fact or fable? *Journal of Personality and Social Psychology, 34,* 146–158.

Schaie, K. W., & Schaie, J. P. (1977). Clinical assessment and aging. In J. E. Birren & K. W. Schaie (Eds.), *Handbook of the psychology of aging* (pp. 692–723). New York: Van Nostrand Reinhold.

Schaie, K. W., & Willis, S. L. (1986). Can decline in adult intellectual functioning be reversed? *Developmental Psychology, 22,* 223–232.

Schaie, K. W., & Willis, S. L. (1991). Adult personality and psychomotor performance: Cross-sectional and longitudinal analyses. *Journal of Gerontology: Psychological Sciences, 46,* P275–284.

Schaie, K. W., Labouvie, G., & Barrett, T. (1973). Selective attrition effects in a 14-year study of adult intelligence. *Journal of Gerontology, 28,* 328–334.

Schaie, K. W., Rosenthal, F., & Pearlman, R. M. (1953). Differential mental deterioration of factorially "pure" functions in later maturity. *Journal of Gerontology, 8,* 191–196.

Scheibel, A. (1992). Structural changes in the aging brain. In J. Birren, R. Sloane, & G. Cohen (Eds.), *Handbook of mental health and aging* (pp. 147–174). New York: Academic Press.

Scheidt, R. (1980). Ecologically valid inquiry: Fait accompli? *Human Development, 23,* 225–228.

Scheidt, R., & Schaie, K. W. (1978). A taxonomy of situations for an elderly population: Generating situational criteria. *Journal of Gerontology, 33,* 838–857.

Schiffman, S. (1983). Taste and smell in disease. *New England Journal of Medicine, 308,* 1275–1279.

Schlossberg, N. (1989) *Overwhelmed: Coping with life's ups and downs* (pp. 28–29). Lexington, MA: Lexington Books.

Schludermann, E., & Zubek, J. P. (1962). Effect of age on pain sensitivity. *Perceptual and Motor Skills, 14,* 295–301.

Schmeck, R. R. (1983). Learning styles of college students. In R. F. Dillon & R. R. Schmeck (Eds.), *Individual differences in cognition* (Vol. 1, pp. 233–380). New York: Academic Press.

Schmidt, D. F., & Boland, S. M. (1986). Structure of perceptions of older adults: Evidence for multiple stereotypes. *Psychology and Aging, 1,* 255–260.

Schmidt, F., Murphy, M., & Sanders, R. E. (1981). Training older adults free-recall rehearsal strategies. *Journal of Gerontology, 36,* 329–337.

Schneider, D. M., & Smith, R. T. (1973). *Class differences and sex roles in American kinship and family structure.* Englewood Cliffs, NJ: Prentice-Hall.

Schonfield, D. (1982). Who is stereotyping whom and why? *Gerontologist, 22,* 267–272.

Schooler, C. (1984). Psychological effects of complex environments during the life-span. *Intelligence, 8,* 259–281.

Schooler, C. (1987). Effects of complex environments during the life-span: A review and theory. In C. Schooler & K. W. Schaie (Eds.), *Cognitive functioning and social structure over the life course* (pp. 24–29). Norwood, NJ: Ablex.

Schover, L. R. (1986). Sexual problems. In L. Teri & P. M. Lewinsohn (Eds.), *Geropsychological assessment and treatment: Selected topics* (pp. 145–187). New York: Springer.

Schuknecht, H. F., & Igarashi, M. (1964). Pathology of slowly progressive sensorineural deafness. *Transaction of the American Academy of Ophthalmology and Otolaryngology, 68,* 222–242.

Schultz, N. R., Elias, M. F., Robbins, M. A., Streeton, D. H., & Blakeman, N. (1989). A longitudinal study of the performance of hypertensive and hypotensive subjects on the WAIS. *Psychology and Aging, 4,* 496–503.

Schultz, N. R., Elias, M. F., Robbins, M. A., Streeton, D. H., & Blakeman, N. (1986). A longitudinal comparison of hypertensives and normotensives on the WAIS: Initial findings. *Journal of Gerontology, 41,* 169–175.

Schulz, R. (1978). *The psychology of death, dying, and bereavement.* Reading, MA: Addison-Wesley.

Schulz, R., & Brenner, G. (1977). Relocation of the aged: A review and theoretical analysis. *Journal of Gerontology, 32,* 323–333.

Schulz, R., & Hanusa, B. H. (1978). Long-term effects of control and predictability enhancing interventions: Findings and ethical issues. *Journal of Personality and Social Psychology, 35,* 1194–1201.

Schulz, R., & Hanusa, B. H. (1979). Environmental influences on the effectiveness of control and competence-enhancing interventions. In L. C. Perlmutter & R. Monty (Eds.), *Choice and perceived control* (pp. 315–337). Hillsdale, NJ: Erlbaum.

Schwab, D. P., & Heneman, H. G. (1977). Effects of age and experience on productivity. *Industrial Gerontology, 4,* 113–117.

Schwartz, A. N., & Peterson, J. A. (1979). *Introduction to gerontology.* New York: Holt, Rinehart, and Winston.

Schwartz, B., & Reisberg, D. (1991). *Learning and memory.* New York: Norton.

Scott, J. P. (1962). Critical periods in behavioral development. *Science, 138,* 949–958.

Sears, D., Freeman, J., & Peplau, L. (1986). *Social psychology.* Englewood Cliffs, NJ: Prentice-Hall.

Seefeldt, C., Jontz, R. K., Galper, A., & Serock, K. (1977). Children's attitudes toward the elderly: Educational implications. *Educational Gerontology, 2,* 301–310.

Seiden, R. H. (1985–1986). Mellowing with age: Factors influencing the nonwhite suicide rate. *Omega, 16,* 14–19.

Select Committee on Aging, US House of Representatives. (1981). Elder abuse (Comm. Pub. No. 97-289). Washington, DC: U.S. Government Printing Office.

Seligman, M. E. P. (1975). *Helplessness: On depression, development, and death.* San Francisco: Freeman.

Seligman, M. E. P. (1991). *Learned optimism.* New York: Knopf.

Selkoe, D. J. (1991, November). Amyloid protein and Alzheimer's disease. *Scientific American,* 68–78.

Selye, H. (1976). *The stress of life* (rev. ed.). New York: McGraw-Hill.

Sex Equity in Education Bulletin. (1983). Title IX Makes Progress. Illinois State Board of Education. Title IV Sex Desegregation Project, June.

Sexton, C. S., & Perlman, D. S. (1989). Couples' career orientation, gender-role orientation and perceived equity as determinants of mental power. *Journal of Marriage and the Family, 51,* 933–941.

Shanas, E. (1962). *The health of older people: A social survey.* Cambridge: Cambridge University Press.

Shanas, E., & Maddox, G. (1985). Health, health resources, and the utilization of care. In R. Binstock & E. Shanas (Eds.), *Handbook of aging and the social sciences* (pp. 697–726). New York: Van Nostrand Reinhold.

Share, L. (1978). Family communication in the crisis of a child's fatal illness: A literature review and analysis. In R. Kalish (Ed.), *Caring for the dying and the bereaved.* Farmingdale, NY: Baywood.

Sheehy, G. (1976). *Passages: Predictable crises of adult life.* New York: Dutton.

Sheikh, J. I. (1992). Anxiety and its disorders in old age. In J. E. Birren, R. B. Sloane, & G. D. Cohen (Eds.), *Handbook of mental health and aging* (pp. 410–432). New York: Academic Press.

Sheikh, J. I., & Yesavage, J. H. (1986). Geriatric depression scale (GDS): Recent evidence and development of a shorter version. In T. L. Brink (Ed.), *Clinical gerontology* (pp. 165–174). New York: Haworth Press.

Sheppard, H. L. (1976). Work and retirement. In R. Binstock & E. Shanas (Eds.), *Handbook of aging and the social sciences* (pp. 286–309). New York: Van Nostrand Reinhold.

Sheppard, H. L., & Rix, S. E. (1977). *The graying of working America: The coming crisis in retirement-age policy.* New York: Free Press.

Sherwood, S., & Mor, V. (1980). Mental health institutions and the elderly. In J. E. Birren & R. B. Sloane (Eds.), *Handbook of mental health and aging* (pp. 854–884). Englewood Cliffs, NJ: Prentice-Hall.

Shindell, S. (1989). Assessing the visually impaired older adult. In T. Hunt & C. J. Lindley (Eds.), *Testing older adults: A reference guide for gerontological assessment* (pp. 135–149). Austin, TX: Pro-ed.

Shock, N. W. (1977). Biological theories of aging. In J. E. Birren & K. W. Schaie (Eds.), *Handbook of psychology and aging* (pp. 103–115). New York: Van Nostrand Reinhold.

Shore, H. (1976). Designing a training program for understanding sensory losses in aging. *Gerontologist, 16,* 157–165.

Shore, R. J., & Hayslip, B. (1990, August). Predictors of well-being in custodial and noncustodial grandparents [paper]. Annual Meeting of the American Psychological Association, Boston.

Shore, R. J., & Hayslip, B. (1992). Custodial grandparenting: Implications for children's development. In A. Gottfried & A. Gottfried (Eds.), *Redefining families: Implications for children's development* (pp. 120–141). New York: Plenum.

Shulderman, E., & Zubek, P. (1962). Effects of age on pain sensitivity. *Perceptual and Motor Skills, 14,* 295–301.

Siegler, I. (1975). The terminal-drop hypotheses: Fact or artifact? *Experimental Aging Research, 1,* 169–185.

Siegler, I. (1980). Psychological aspects of the Duke longitudinal studies. In K. W. Schaie (Ed.), *Longitudinal studies of adult psychological development* (pp. 136–190). New York: Guilford Press.

Siegler, I. (1989). Developmental health psychology. In P. Costa, M. Gatz, B. Neugarten, T. Salthouse, & I. Siegler (Eds.), *The adult years: Continuity and*

Change. Washington, DC: American Psychological Association.

Siegler, I., & Botwinick, J. (1979). A long-term longitudinal study of intellectual ability of older adults: The matter of selective subject attrition. *Journal of Gerontology, 34*, 242–245.

Siegler, I., & Costa, P. T., Jr. (1985). Health-behavior relationships. In J. E. Birren & K. W. Schaie (Eds.), *Handbook of the psychology of aging* (2nd ed., pp. 144–166). New York: Van Nostrand Reinhold.

Siegler, I., George, L., & Okum, M. (1979). Cross-sequential analysis of adult personality. *Developmental Psychology, 15*, 350–351.

Siegler, I., McCarty, S., & Logue, P. (1982). Wechsler Memory Scale scores, selective attrition, and distance from death. *Journal of Gerontology, 37*, 176–181.

Sigall, H. D., & Landy, D. (1973). Radiating beauty: The effects of having a physically attractive partner on person perception. *Journal of Personality and Social Psychology, 28*, 218–224.

Silberschatz, G., & Curtis, J. T. (1991). Time-limited psychodynamic therapy with older adults. In W. Myers (Ed.), *New techniques in the psychotherapy of older clients* (pp. 95–110). Washington, DC: American Psychiatric Press.

Sill, J. (1980). Disengagement reconsidered: Awareness of finitude. *Gerontologist, 20*, 457–462.

Silverman, P. R. (1986). *Widow to widow*. New York: Springer.

Silverman, P. R., & Cooperband, A. (1984). *Widow to widow: The elderly widow and mutual help*. In G. Lesnoff-Caravaglia (Ed.). The world of the older woman: Conflicts and resolutions (pp. 40–52). New York: Human Sciences Press.

Simon, A. (1980). The neuroses, personality disorders, alcoholism, drug use and misuse, and crime in the aged. In J. E. Birren & R. B. Sloane (Eds.), *Handbook of mental health and aging* (pp. 653–670). Englewood Cliffs, NJ: Prentice-Hall.

Simonton, D. K. (1990a). Creativity and wisdom in aging. In J. E. Birren & K. W. Schaie (Eds.), *Handbook of the psychology of aging* (pp. 320–329). New York: Academic Press.

Simonton, D. K. (1990b). Does creativity decline in the later years? Definition, data, and theory. In M. Perlmutter (Ed.), *Late-life potential* (pp. 83–112). Washington, DC: Gerontological Society.

Sinclair, D. (1969). *Human growth after birth*. London: Oxford University Press.

Sinnott, J. (1989a). General systems theory: A rationale for the study of everyday memory. In L. W. Poon, D. C. Rubin, & B. A. Wilson (Eds.), *Everyday cognition in adulthood and late life* (pp. 59–72). Cambridge: Cambridge University Press.

Sinnott, J. (1989b). Prospective/intentional memory and aging. In L. W. Poon, D. C. Rubin, & B. A. Wilson (Eds.), *Everyday cognition in adulthood and late life* (pp. 352–372).

Sinnott, J., Harris, C., Block, M., Collesano, S., & Jacobson, S. (1983). *Applied research in aging*. Boston: Little, Brown.

Skolnick, B. D., Eddy, J. M., & St. Pierre, R. W. (1984). Medication compliance and the aged: An educational challenge. *Educational Gerontology, 10*, 307–315.

Sloane, R. B. (1980). Organic brain syndrome. In J. E. Birren & R. B. Sloane (Eds.), *Handbook of mental health and aging* (pp. 554–590). Englewood Cliffs, NJ: Prentice-Hall.

Slocum, J. W., & Cron, W. L. (1985). Job attitudes and performance during three career stages. *Journal of Vocational Behavior, 26*, 126–145.

Smith, G. C., Smith, M. F., & Toseland, R. W. (1991). Problems identified by family caregivers in counseling. *Gerontologist, 31*, 15–23.

Smith, M. B. (1979). Perspectives on selfhood. *American Psychologist, 33*, 1053–1063.

Smith, R. E., Sarason, I. G., & Sarason, B. R. (1982). *Psychology: The frontiers of behavior* (2nd ed.). New York: Harper & Row.

Smith, R. M., & Smith, C. W. (1981). Child-rearing and single-parent fathers. *Family Relations, 30*, 411–417.

Smyer, M. (1984). Life transitions and aging: Implications for counseling older adults. *Counseling Psychologist, 12*, 17–28.

Smyer, M., & Gatz, M. (1979). Aging and mental health: Business as usual? *American Psychologist, 34*, 240–246.

Smyer, M. A., Zarit, S. H., & Qualls, S. H. (1990). Psychological intervention with the aged individual. In J. E. Birren & K. W. Schaie (Eds.), *Handbook of the psychology of aging* (pp. 375–404). New York: Academic Press.

Snow, R., & Crapo, L. (1982). Emotional bondedness, subjective well-being, and health in elderly medical patients. *Journal of Gerontology, 37*, 609–615.

Sokolovsky, J. (1985). Ethnicity, culture, and aging: Do differences really make a difference? *Journal of Applied Gerontology, 4*, 6–17.

Sokolovksy, J., & Vesperi, M. D. (1991, Winter). The cultural context of well-being in old age: Differing notions of "success." *Generations*, 21–25.

Solomon, K. (1982). Social antecedents of learned helplessness in the health care setting. *Gerontologist, 22*, 282–287.

Solomon, K. (1984). Psychosocial crises of older men. *Hillside Journal of Clinical Psychiatry, 6*, 123–134.

Solomone, P. R. (1982). Difficult cases in career counseling II: The indecisive client. *Personnel and Guidance Journal, 60*, 496–500.

Somers, A. R. (1987). Insurance for long-term care. *New England Journal of Medicine, 317,* 23–29.

Sontag, S. (1977). The double standard of aging. In L. R. Allman & D. T. Jaffee (Eds.), *Readings in adult psychology: Contemporary perspectives* (pp. 324–333). New York: Harper & Row.

Sparrow, P. R., & Davies, D. R. (1988). Effects of age, tenure, training, and job complexity on technical performance. *Psychology and Aging, 3,* 307–314.

Spencer, G. (1984, May). Projection of the population of the United States by age, sex, and race: 1983 to 2080. *Current Population Report* (Series P-25, No. 952). Washington, DC: U.S. Bureau of Census.

Spitzer, M. E. (1988). Taste acuity in institutionalized and noninstitutionalized elderly men. *Journal of Gerontology: Psychological Sciences, 43,* P71–74.

Spitzer, R. L., Endicott, J., & Robins, E. (1978). Research diagnostic criteria: Rationale and reliability. *Archives of General Psychiatry, 35,* 773–782.

Spokane, A. R. (1985). A review of research in person-environment congruence in Holland's theory of careers. *Journal of Vocational Behavior, 26,* 306–343.

Stagner, R. (1985). Aging in industry. In J. E. Birren & K. W. Schaie (Eds.), *Handbook of the psychology of aging* (2nd ed., pp. 789–817). New York: Van Nostrand Reinhold.

Stankov, L. (1988). Aging, attention, and intelligence. *Psychology and Aging, 3,* 59–74.

Steenbarger, B. N. (1991). All the world is not a stage: Emerging contextualist themes in counseling and development. *Journal of Counseling and Development, 70,* 288–296.

Steffy, B. D., & Jones, J. W. (1988). The impact of family and career-planning variables on the organizational, career, and community commitment of professional women. *Journal of Vocational Behavior, 32,* 196–212.

Stein, J. A., Newcomb, M. D., Bentler, P. M. (1990). The relative influence of vocational behavior and family involvement on self-esteem: Longitudinal analyses of young adult women and men. *Journal of Vocational Behavior, 36,* 320–328.

Steinmetz, S., Clavan, S., & Stein, K. F. (1990). *Marriage and family realities: Historical and contemporary perspectives.* New York: Harper & Row.

Stelmach, G. E., Goggin, G. L., & Garcia-Colera, A. (1987). Movement specification time with age. *Experimental Aging Research, 13,* 39–46.

Stenback, A. (1980). Depression and suicidal behavior in old age. In J. E. Birren & R. B. Sloane (Eds.), *Handbook of aging and mental health* (pp. 616–652). Englewood Cliffs, NJ: Prentice-Hall.

Sternberg, R. J. (1979). Intelligence research at the interface between differential and cognitive psychology: Prospects and proposals. In R. Sternberg & D. Detterman (Eds.), *Human intelligence: Perspectives on its theory and measurement* (pp. 33–60). Norwood, NJ: Ablex.

Sternberg, R. J. (1985). Cognitive approaches to intelligence. In B. B. Wolman (Ed.), *Handbook of human intelligence: Theories, measurements, and applications* (pp. 59–118). New York: Wiley Interscience.

Sternberg, R. J. (1988). *The triarchic mind.* New York: Viking.

Sternberg, R. J. (1991). Theory-based testing of intellectual abilities: Rationale for the triarchic abilities test. In H. Rowe (Ed.), *Intelligence: Reconceptualization and measurement* (pp. 183–202). Hillsdale, NJ: Erlbaum.

Sternberg, R. J., & Detterman, D. (1979). *Human intelligence: Perspectives on its theory and measurement.* Norwood, NJ: Ablex.

Sternberg, R. J., Conway, B., Keton, J., & Bernstein, M. (1981). People's conceptions of intelligence. *Journal of Personality and Social Psychology, 41,* 37–55.

Sterns, H. L., & Hayslip, B. (1990, June). Retirement and reentry: What should psychologists be doing? [paper]. Annual meeting of the American Psychological Society, Dallas.

Sterns, H. L., & Mitchell, S. (1979). Personal and cognitive development across the life-span. In H. Sterns, E. Ansello, B., Sprouse, & R. Layfield-Faux (Eds), *Gerontology in higher education* (pp. 250–261). Belmont, CA: Wadsworth.

Sterns, H. L., Barrett, G. V., & Alexander, R. A. (1985). Accidents and the aging individual. In J. E. Birren & K. W. Schaie (Eds.), *Handbook of the psychology of aging* (2nd ed., pp. 703–721). New York: Van Nostrand Reinhold.

Sterns, H. L., Weis, D. M,. & Perkins, S. E. (1984). A conceptual approach to counseling older adults and their families. *Counseling Psychologist, 12,* 55–62.

Stevens-Long, J. (1984). *Adult life: Developmental processes* (2nd ed.). Palo Alto, CA: Mayfield.

Stevenson, J. (1985). *Death, grief, and mourning.* New York: Free Press.

Stewart, A. J., & Healy, J. M. (1989). Linking individual development and social changes. *American Psychologist, 44,* 30–42.

Still, J. (1980). Disengagement reconsidered: Awareness of finitude. *Gerontologist, 20,* 457–462.

Stine, E. L., Wingfield, A., & Poon, L. W. (1989). Speech comprehension and memory through adulthood: The roles of time and strategy. In L. W. Poon & Associates (Eds.), *Everyday cognition in adulthood and late life* (pp. 195–221). Cambridge: Cambridge University Press.

Stinnett, N., Walters, J., & Kaye, E. (1984). *Relationships in marriage and the family* (2nd ed.). New York: Macmillan.

Stoddard, S. (1980). Lillian Preston dies of cancer. In M. Hamilton & H. Reid (Eds.). *A hospice handbook* (pp. 3–6). Grand Rapids: MI: Eardsmans.

Stonewater, J. K., & Daniels, M. H. (1983). Psychosocial and cognitive development in a career decision-making course. *Journal of College Student Personnel, 24,* 403–410.

Storandt, M. (1983). *Counseling and therapy with older adults.* Boston: Little, Brown.

Storandt, M. (1978). Other approaches to therapy. In M. Storandt, I. Siegler, & M. Elias (Eds.), *Clinical psychology of aging* (pp. 277–293). New York: Plenum.

Storandt, M., Grant, E. A., & Gordon, B. C. (1978). Remote memory as a function of age and sex. *Experimental Aging Research, 4,* 365–375.

Stout, S. K., Slocum, J. W., & Cron, W. L. (1988). Dynamics of the career-plateauing process. *Journal of Vocational Behavior, 32,* 74–91.

Strain, L., & Chappell, N. (1982). Problems and strategies: Ethical concerns in survey research with the elderly. *Gerontologist, 22,* 526–531.

Strehler, B. (1975). Implications of aging research for society. *Federation Proceedings of American Societies for Experimental Biology, 34,* 5–8.

Streib, G. F., & Schneider, C. J. (1971). *Retirement in American Society.* Ithaca, NY: Cornell University Press.

Stroebe, W., & Stroebe, M. S. (1989–1990). Who participates in bereavement research? *Omega, 21,* 1–30.

Strom, R., & Strom, S. (1987). Preparing grandparents for a new role. *Journal of Applied Gerontology, 6,* 476–486.

Stroop, J. R., (1935). Studies of interference in serial verbal reaction. *Journal of Experimental Psychology, 18,* 643–662.

Strub, R. L., & Black, F. W. (1981). *The mental status exam in neurology.* Philadelphia, PA: Davis.

Subich, L., Cooper, E. A., Barrett, G. V., & Arthur, W. (1986). Occupational preferences of males and females as a function of sex ratios, salary, and availability. *Journal of Vocational Behavior, 28,* 123–134.

Sullivan, F. J. (1987, May 19). Testimony before the U.S. House of Representatives Committee on Government Operations, Subcommittee on Human Resources and Intergovernmental Relations, 100th Congress, 1st Session. Washington, DC: U.S. Government Printing Office.

Suls, J. (1982). *Psychological perspectives on the self.* Hillsdale, NJ: Erlbaum.

Sunderland, A., Watts, K., Baddeley, A. D., & Harris, J. E. (1986). Subjective memory assessment and test performance in elderly adults. *Journal of Gerontology, 41,* 376–384.

Sundow, D. (1967). *Passing on: The social organization of the dying.* Englewood Cliffs, NJ: Prentice-Hall.

Sung, K. (1990). A new look at filial piety: Ideals and practices of family-centered parent care in Korea. *Gerontologist, 30,* 610–617.

Super, D. E. (1953). A theory of vocational development. *American Psychologist, 8,* 178–190.

Super, D. E. (1957). *The psychology of careers.* New York: Harper & Row.

Super, D. E. (1969). Vocational development theory: Persons, positions, and processes. *Counseling Psychologist, 1,* 2–8.

Super, D. E. (1990). A life-span, life space approach to career development. In D. Brown, L. Brooks, & Associates (Eds.), *Career choice and development* (2nd ed., pp. 197–261). San Francisco: Jossey-Bass.

Surwillo, W. W. (1964). The relation of decision time to brain-wave frequency and to age. *Electroencephalography and Clinical Neuropsychology, 16,* 510–514.

Sussman, M. B. (1985). The family of old people. In R. Binstock & E. Shanas (Eds.), *Handbook of aging and the social sciences* (pp. 415–449). New York: Van Nostrand Reinhold.

Swan, G. E., Dame, A., & Carmelli, D. (1991). Involuntary retirement, Type A behavior, and current functioning in elderly men: 27-year follow-up of the Western Collaborative Group study. *Psychology and Aging, 6,* 384–391.

Taneber, C. M. (1983, September). America in transit: An aging society. *Current Population Reports* (Series P. 23, No. 128). Washington, DC: U.S. Bureau of the Census.

Tangri, S., & Jenkins, S. (1992). The women's life-paths study: The Michigan Graduates of 1967. In D. Shuster & K. Hulbert (Eds.), *Women's lives through time: Educated American women of the 20th century* (pp. 20–35). San Francisco: Jossey-Bass.

Taub, H. (1975). Mode of presentation, age, and short-term memory. *Journal of Gerontology, 30,* 56–59.

Taylor, K. M., & Popma, J. (1990). An examination of the relationships among career decision-making, self-efficacy, career-salience, locus of control, and vocational indecision. *Journal of Vocational Behavior, 37,* 17–31.

Taylor, R. H. (1972). Risk-taking, dogmatism, and demographic characteristics of managers as correlates of information-processing and decision-making behavior. *Proceedings of the 80th Annual Convention of the American Psychological Association, 7,* 443–444.

Teri, L., & Reifer, B. (1987). Depression and dementia. In L. Carstensen & B. Edelstein (Eds.), *Handbook of clinical gerontology* (pp. 112–122). Elmsford, NY: Pergamon.

Thackray, R. I., & Touchstone, R. M. (1981). Age-related differences in complex monitoring performance. (Technical Report FAA-AM-81-12). Washington, DC: Federal Aviation Administration.

Thomae, H. (1980). Personality and adjustment to aging. In J. E. Birren & K. W. Schaie (Eds.), *Handbook of mental health and aging* (pp. 285–309). Englewood Cliffs, NJ: Prentice-Hall.

Thomas, J. L. (1986). Gender differences in satisfaction with grandparenting. *Psychology and Aging, 1,* 215–219.

Thomas, J. L. (1989). Gender and perceptions of grandparenthood. *International Journal of Aging and Human Development, 29,* 269–282.

Thomas, J. L. (1990). The grandparent role: A double-bind. *International Journal of Aging and Human Development, 31,* 169–177.

Thomas, J. L., & King, C. M. (1990, August). Adult grandchildren's views of grandparents: Racial and gender effects [paper]. Annual meeting of the American Psychological Association, Boston.

Thomas, L. E. (1982). Sexuality and aging: Essential vitamin or popcorn? *Gerontologist, 22,* 240–243.

Thomas, P. D., Hunt, W. C., Garry, P. J., Hood, R. B., Goodwin, J. M., & Goodwin, J. S. (1983). Hearing acuity in a healthy population: Effects on emotional, cognitive, and social status. *Journal of Gerontology, 38,* 321–325.

Thomas, W. I., & Thomas, D. S. (1937). *The child in America.* New York: McGraw-Hill.

Thompson, K. E., & Range, L. M. (1990–1991). Recent bereavement from suicide and other deaths: Can people really imagine it as it is? *Omega, 22,* 249–260.

Thompson, L. W., & Gallagher, D. (1983). A psychoeducational approach for treatment of depression in elders. *Psychotherapy in Private Practice, 1,* 25–28.

Thompson, L. W., & Walker, A. J. (1989). Gender in families: Men and women in marriage, work, and parenthood. *Journal of Marriage and the Family, 51,* 845–871.

Thompson, L. W., Breckenridge, J. N., Gallagher, D., & Peterson, J. (1984). Effects of bereavement on self-perceptions of physical health in elderly widows and widowers. *Journal of Gerontology, 39,* 309–314.

Thompson, L. W., Davies, R., & Gallagher, D. (1986). Cognitive therapy with older adults. *Clinical Gerontologist, 5,* 245–279.

Thompson, L. W., Gallagher, D., & Breckenridge, J. S. (1987). Comparative effectiveness of psychotherapies for depressed elders. *Journal of Consulting and Clinical Psychology, 55,* 385–390.

Thompson, L. W., Gallagher, D., Cover, M., Gilewski, M., & Peterson, J. (1989). Effects of bereavement on symptoms of psychopathology in older men and women. In D. Lund (Ed.), *Older bereaved spouses* (pp. 110–131). New York: Hemisphere.

Thompson, L. W., Gantz, F., Florsheim, M., DelMaestro, S., Rodman, J., Gallagher-Thompson, D., & Bryan, S. (1991). Cognitive-behavioral therapy for affective disorders in the elderly. In W. Myers (Ed.), *New techniques in the psychotherapy of older clients* (pp. 3–20). Washington, DC: American Psychiatric Press.

Thompson, L. W., Opton, E., Jr., & Cohen, K. D. (1963). Effects of age, presentation speed, and sensory modality performance of a vigilance task. *Journal of Gerontology, 18,* 366–369.

Thompson, R. A., Tinsley, B. R., Scalora, M. J., & Parke, R. D. (1989). Grandparents' visitation rights. *American Psychologist, 44,* 1217–1222.

Thompson, R. F. (1975). *Introduction to physiological psychology.* New York: Harper & Row.

Thorson, J., Whatley, L., & Hancock, K. (1974). Attitudes toward the aged as a function of age and education. *Gerontologist, 14,* 316–318.

Thurstone, L. L., & Thurstone, T. G. (1948). *SRA Primary Mental Abilities Ages 11–17 Form.* Chicago: Science Research Associates, Inc.

Tiggemann, M., & Winefield, A. H. (1989). Predictors of employment, unemployment, & further study among school-leavers. *Journal of Occupational Psychology, 62,* 213–221.

Till, R. E. (1978). Age-related differences in binocular backward masking with visual noise. *Journal of Gerontology, 33,* 702–710.

Time (1988, February 22). Older—but coming on strong, 76–77, 79.

Timiras, P. S. (1972). *Developmental physiology and aging.* New York: Macmillan.

Timiras, P. S. (1978). Biological perspectives on aging. *American Scientist, 66,* 605–613.

Timiras, P. S. (1988). *Physiological basis of geriatrics.* New York: Macmillan.

Tittle, C. K. (1988). Validity, gender research, and studies of the effects of career development interventions. *Applied Psychology: An International Review, 37,* 121–131.

Tolbert, E. L. (1974). *Counseling for career development.* Boston: Houghton Mifflin.

Tomlin, A. M., & Passman, R. H. (1991). Grandmothers' advice about disciplining grandchildren: Is it accepted by mothers, and does its rejection influence grandmothers' subsequent guidance? *Psychology and Aging, 6,* 182–189.

Toseland, R. W., & Smith, G. C. (1990). Effectiveness of individual counseling by professional and peer helpers for family caregivers of the elderly. *Psychology and Aging, 5,* 256–263.

Treat, N., Poon, L., & Fozard, J. (1981). Age, imagery, and practice in paired-associate learning. *Experimental Aging Research, 7,* 337–342.

Treat, N., & Reese, H. W. (1976). Age, imagery, and

pacing in paired-associate learning. *Experimental Aging Research, 7,* 337–342.

Troll, L. (1980). Grandparenting. In L. Poon (Ed.), *Aging in the 1980s: Psychological issues* (pp. 475–481). Washington, DC: American Psychological Association.

Troll, L., & Bengtson, V. (1982). Intergenerational relations throughout the life-span. In J. Wolman (Ed.), *Handbook of developmental psychology.* Englewood Cliffs, NJ: Prentice-Hall.

Troll, L. E., Miller, S. J., & Atchley, R. C. (1979). *Families in later life.* Belmont, CA: Wadsworth.

Trotter, R. J. (1986). Three heads are better than one. *Psychology Today,* 56–62.

Tulving, E. (1991). Memory research is not a zero-sum game. *American Psychologist, 46,* 41–42.

Turner, M. J., Scott, J. P., & Bailey, W. C. (1990, November). Factors impacting attitude toward retirement and retirement-planning behavior among mid-life university employees [paper]. Annual Scientific Meeting of the Gerontological Society, Boston.

U.S. Bureau of the Census. (1986). *Statistical abstract of the United States.* Washington, DC: U.S. Government Printing Office.

U.S. Bureau of the Census. (1990). *Current Population Reports* (Series P-60, No. 166).

U.S. Bureau of the Census. (1990). *Statistical abstract of the United States.* Washington, DC: Department of Health, Education, and Welfare.

U.S. Bureau of the Census. (1991). *Statistical Abstract of the United States* (111th ed.). Washington, DC: U.S. Government Printing Office.

U.S. Senate Special Committee on Aging. (1985, October). *How older Americans live: An analysis of census data* (Serial No. 99-D). Washington, DC: U.S. Government Printing Office.

U.S. Senate Special Committee on Aging. (1987–1988). *Aging America: Trends and perspectives.* Washington, DC: Department of Health and Human Services.

U.S. Senate Special Committee on Aging. (1987–1988). *Aging America: Trends and Projections.* Washington, DC: U.S. Department of Health and Human Services.

Udry, J. R. (1974). *The social context of marriage.* New York: Lippincott.

Uhlenberg, P., Cooney, T., & Boyd, R. (1990). Divorce for women after mid-life. *Journal of Gerontology: Social Sciences, 45,* S3–11.

Ullman, L. P., & Krasner, L. (1975). *A psychological approach to abnormal behavior.* Englewood Cliffs, NJ: Prentice-Hall.

Underwood, D. (1984). Toward self-reliance in retirement planning. *Harvard Business Review, 62,* 18–20.

Usui, W. N. (1984). Homogeneity of friendship networks of elderly blacks and whites. *Journal of Gerontology, 39,* 350–356.

Vaitenas, R., & Weiner, Y. (1977). Developmental, emotional, and interest factors in mid-career change. *Journal of Vocational Behavior, 11,* 291–304.

Valliant, G. E. (1977). *Adaptation to life.* Boston: Little, Brown.

Valliant, G. E., & Valliant, C. O. (1990). Natural history of male psychosocial health, XII: A 45-year study of predictors of successful aging at age 65. *American Journal of Psychiatry, 147,* 31–37.

Veatch, R. (1979). Defining death anew. In H. Wass (Ed.), *Dying: Facing the facts* (pp. 320–359). Washington, DC: Hemisphere.

Verdi, J. W., & Hayslip, B. (1991, August). Occupational level and retirement satisfaction: A path-analytic solution [paper]. Annual Convention of the American Psychological Association, San Francisco.

Vernon, M. (1984). Psychological stress of hearing loss. *Shiloh,* 5(4), 3–6.

Veroff, J., Douvon, E., & Kulka, R. A. (1981a). *The inner American: A self-portrait from 1957 to 1976.* New York: Basic Books.

Veroff, J., Douvon, E., & Kulka, R. A. (1981b). *Mental health in America: Patterns of help-seeking from 1957 to 1976.* New York: Basic Books.

Verrillo, R. T., & Verrillo, V. (1985). Sensory and perceptual performance. In N. Charness (Ed.), *Aging and human performance* (pp. 1–46). New York: Wiley.

Vickio, C. J., & Cavanaugh, J. C. (1985). Relationships among death anxiety, attitudes toward aging, and experience with death in nursing home employees. *Journal of Gerontology, 40,* 347–349.

Vogel, F. S. (1977). The brain and time. In E. W. Busse & E. Pfeiffer (Eds.), *Behavior and adaptation in later life* (2nd ed., pp. 228–239). Boston: Little, Brown.

Vondracek, F. W., Lerner, R. M., & Schulenberg, J. (1986). *Career development: A life-span developmental approach.* Hillsdale, NJ: Erlbaum.

Vuchinich, S., Hetherington, E. M., Vuchinich, R. A., & Clingempeel, W. G. (1991). Parent-child interaction and gender differences in early adolescents' adaptation to stepfamilies. *Developmental Psychology, 27,* 618–626.

Wachtel, H. (1966). Hard-core unemployment in Detroit: Causes and remedies. In *Proceedings of the Industrial Relations Research Association* (pp. 233–241). Madison, WI: Author.

Walaskay, M., Whitbourne, S. K., & Nehrke, M. (1983–1984). Construction and validation of an ego-integrity status interview. *International Journal of Aging and Human Development,* 18, 61–72.

Waldman, D. A., & Avolio, B. J. (1986). A metaanalysis of age differences in job performance. *Journal of Applied Psychology, 71,* 33–38.

Wall, S., & Kaltreider, N. (1977). Changing social-sexual patterns in gynecological practice. *Journal of the American Medical Association, 347,* 565–568.

Wallerstein, A. (1989). *Second chances.* New York: Ticknor & Fields.

Wallerstein, J. (1985). Children of divorce: Preliminary report of 10-year follow-up up older children in adolescence. *Journal of American Academy of Child Psychiatry, 24,* 545–553.

Wallston, B., & Wallston, K. (1978). Locus of control and health: A review of the literature. *Health Education Monographs, 6,* 107–117.

Wantz, M. S., & Gay, J. E. (1981). *The aging process: A health perspective.* Cambridge, MA: Winthrop.

Ward, R. A. (1977). The impact of subjective age and stigma on older persons. *Journal of Gerontology, 32,* 227–232.

Ward, R. A. (1984). *The aging experience: An introduction to social gerontology* (2nd ed.). New York: Harper & Row.

Ward, R. H. (1980). Age and acceptance of euthanasia. *Journal of Gerontology, 35,* 421–431.

Ware, L. A., & Carper, M. (1982). Living with Alzheimer's disease patients: Family stresses and coping mechanisms. *Psychotherapy: Theory, Research, and Practice, 19,* 472–481.

Warshak, R. A., & Santrock, J. W. (1983). Children of divorce: Impact of custody disposition on social development. In E. J. Callahan & K. A. McCluskey (Eds.), *Life-span developmental psychology: Nonnormative life events* (pp. 241–263). New York: Academic Press.

Wass, H. (1989). An overview of the facts. In H. Wass, F. M. Berardo, & R. A. Neimeyer (Eds.). *Dying: Facing the facts* (pp. 3–12). Washington, DC: Hemisphere.

Wass, H., & Corr, C. (1981). *Helping children cope with death: Guidelines and resources.* Washington, DC: Hemisphere.

Wass, H., & Corr, C. (1984). *Childhood and death.* Washington, DC: Hemisphere/McGraw-Hill.

Wass, H., Berardo, F., & Neimeyer, R. (1988). *Dying: Facing the facts* (2nd ed.). Washington, DC: Hemisphere.

Waters, E. B. (1984). Building on what you know: Techniques for individual and group counseling with older people. *Counseling Psychologist, 12,* 81–96.

Watkins, S. C., Manken, J. A., & Bongaarts, J. (1987). Demographic foundations of family change. *American Sociological Review, 52,* 346–358.

Watson, W. H. (1990). Family care, economics, and health. In Z. Harel, E. A. McKinney, & M. Williams (Eds.), *Black aged: Understanding diversity and service needs* (pp. 50–68). Newbury Park, CA: Sage.

Wechsler, D. (1981). *WAIS-R Administration and Scoring Manual.* New York: Psychological Corporation.

Weeks, G. R., & Wright, L. (1985). Dialectics of the family life cycle. *American Journal of Family Therapy, 27,* 85–91.

Weiffenback, J. M., Tylenda, C., & Braum, B. (1990). Oral sensory changes in aging. *Journal of Gerontology, 45,* M121–125.

Weinberger, L. E., & Millham, J. (1975). A multidimensional multiple-method analysis of attitudes toward the elderly. *Journal of Gerontology, 30,* 343–348.

Weisman, A. (1990–1991). Bereavement and companion animals. *Omega, 22,* 241–248.

Weiss, A. D. (1965). The locus of reaction-time change with set, motivation, and age. *Journal of Gerontology, 20,* 60–64.

Weisz, J. R. (1978). Transcontextual validity in developmental research. *Child Development, 49,* 1–12.

Weisz, J. R. (1983). Can I control it? The pursuit of veridical answers across the life-span. In P. Baltes & O. Brim (Eds.), *Life-span development and behavior* (pp. 234–300). New York: Academic Press.

Weldon, S., & Yesavage, J. (1982). Behavioral improvement with relaxation-training in senile dementia. *Clinical Gerontologist, 1,* 45–49.

Welford, A. T. (1977). Motor performance. In J. E. Birren & K. W. Schaie (Eds.), *Handbook of the psychology of aging* (pp. 450–496). New York: Van Nostrand Reinhold.

Wellman, F. E., & McCormack, J. (1984). Counseling with older persons: A review of outcome research. *Counseling Psychologist, 12,* 81–96.

Wells, C. (1979). Pseudodementia. *American Journal of Psychiatry, 136,* 895–900.

Wells, L. E., & Stryker, S. (1988). Stability and change in self over the life course. In P. Baltes & O. Brim (Eds.), *Life-span development and behavior* (Vol. 8, pp. 191–229). Hillsdale, NJ: Erlbaum.

West, R. L. (1989). Planning practical memory training for the aged. In L. W. Poon, D. C. Rubin, & B. A. Wilson (Eds.), *Everyday cognition in adulthood and later life* (pp. 573–597). Cambridge: Cambridge University Press.

West, R. L., & Crook, T. H. (1990). Age differences in everyday memory: Laboratory analogues of telephone number recall. *Psychology and Aging, 5,* 520–529.

West, R. L., Boatwright, L. K., & Schleser, R. (1984). The link between memory performance, self-assessment, and affective status. *Experimental Aging Research, 10,* 197–200.

Wetzel, L., & Ross, M. A. (1983). Psychological and social ramifications of battering: Observations leading to counseling methodology of victims of domestic violence. *Personnel and Guidance Journal, 61,* 423–427.

Whanger, A. D. (1984). Summary of psychoactive drugs for geriatric patients. In A. D. Whanger & A. C. Myers (Eds.), *Mental health assessment and therapeutic interventions with older adults.* Germantown, MD: Aspen.

Wheeler, E., & Knight, B. (1981). Morrie: A case study. *Gerontologist, 21,* 323–328.

Wheeler, L., Reis, H., & Nezlek, J. (1983). Loneliness, social interaction, and sex roles. *Journal of Personality and Social Psychology, 45,* 943–953.

Whitbourne, S. K. (1985). *The aging body: Physiological changes and psychological consequences.* New York: Springer-Verlag.

Whitbourne, S. K. (1986). *The me I know: A study of adult identity.* New York: Springer-Verlag.

Whitbourne, S. K. (1987). Personality development in adulthood and old age: Relationships among identity style, health, and well-being. In K. W. Schaie & C. Eisdorfer (Eds.), *Annual Review of Gerontology and Geriatrics* (pp. 189–216). New York: Springer.

Whitbourne, S. K., & Weinstock, L. S. (1979). *Adult development: The differentiation of experience.* New York: Holt, Rinehart, and Winston.

Whitkin, H. A., Lewis, H. B., Hertzman, M., Machover, K., Meissner, P. B., & Wapner, S. (1954). *Personality through perception.* New York: Harper.

Whitlatch, C. J., & Zarit, S. H. (1989). Sexual dysfunction in aged married couples: A case study of behavioral intervention. *Clinical Gerontologist, 6,* 14–21.

Whitlatch, C. J., Zarit, S., & VonEye, A. (1991). Efficacy of interventions with caregivers: A reanalysis. *Gerontologist, 31,* 9–14.

Wickramaratne, P. J., Weissman, M. M., Leaf, P. J., & Holford, T. R. (1989). Age, period, and cohort effects on the risk of major depression: Results from five United States communities. *Journal of Clinical Epidemiology, 42,* 333–343.

Wilcoxon, S. A. (1987). Grandparents and grandchildren: An often-neglected relationship between significant others. *Journal of Counseling and Development, 65,* 289–290.

Wilensky, J., & Weiner, M. (1977). Facing reality in psychotherapy with the aging. *Psychotherapy: Theory, Research, & Practice, 14,* 373–377.

Wilkinson, R. T., & Allison, S. (1989). Age and simple reaction time: Decade differences for 5325 subjects. *Journal of Gerontology: Psychological Sciences, 44,* P29–35.

Williams, J. G., & Solano, C. H. (1983). The social reality of feeling lonely: Friendship and reciprocation. *Personality and Social Psychology Bulletin, 9,* 237–242.

Williams-Conway, S., Hayslip, B., & Tandy, R. (1991). Similarity of perceptions of bereavement experiences between widows and professionals. *Omega, 23,* 37–52.

Willis, S. L. (1985). Towards an educational psychology of the older adult learner: Intellectual and cognitive bases. In J. E. Birren & K. W. Schaie (Eds.), *Handbook of the psychology of aging* (2nd ed., pp. 818–847). New York: Van Nostrand Reinhold.

Willis, S. L. (1991). Current issues in cognitive training research. In E. Lovelace (Ed.), *Cognition and aging: Mental processes, self-awareness, and interventions* (pp. 263–280). Amsterdam: North Holland.

Willis, S. L. (1992). Cognitive and everyday competence. In K. W. Schaie & P. M. Lawton (Eds.), *Annual review of gerontology and geriatrics* (pp. 80–109). New York: Springer.

Willis, S. L., & Nesselroade, L. S. (1990). Long-term effects of fluid-ability training in old-old age. *Developmental Psychology, 26,* 905–910.

Willis, S. L., & Schaie, K. W. (1986). Practical intelligence in later adulthood. In R. J. Sternberg & R. K. Wagner (Eds.), *Practical intelligence: origins of competence in the everyday world* (pp. 236–268). New York: Cambridge University Press.

Willis, S. L., & Schaie, K. W. (1988). Gender differences in spatial ability in old age: Longitudinal and intervention findings. *Sex Roles, 18,* 189–203.

Wilson, A. J. E. (1984). *Social services for older persons.* Boston: Little, Brown.

Wilson, K. B., & DeShane, M. R. (1982). The legal rights of grandparents: A preliminary discussion. *Gerontologist, 22,* 67–71.

Wilson, M. N. (1986). The black extended family: An analytical consideration. *Developmental Psychology, 22,* 246–256.

Wilson, M. N. (1989). Child development in the context of the black extended family. *American Psychologist, 44,* 380–385.

Wilson, R. (1963). *Feminine forever.* New York: Bantam.

Wine, J. (1971). Test anxiety and direction of attention. *Psychological Bulletin, 76,* 92–104.

Winn, R. L., & Newton, N. (1982). Sexuality in aging: A study of 106 cultures. *Archives of Sexual Behavior, 11,* 283–298.

Witkin, H. A., Lewis, H. B., Hertzman, M., Machover, K., Meissner, P. B., & Wapner, S. (1954). *Personality through perception.* New York: Harper.

Wohlwill, J. R. (1970a). The age variable in psychological research. *Psychological Review, 77,* 49–64.

Wohlwill, J. R. (1970b). Methodology and research strategy in the study of developmental change. In L. R. Goulet and P. B. Baltes (Eds.), *Life-span developmental psychology: Research and theory* (pp. 150–193). New York: Academic Press.

Wolfson, K. P. (1976). Career development patterns of college women. *Journal of Counseling Psychology, 23,* 119–125.

Wood, V., & Robertson, J. F. (1976). The significance

of grandparenthood. In J. F. Gubrium (Ed.), *Time, roles, and self in old age* (pp. 278–304). New York: Human Sciences Press.

Wood, W. G. (1978). The elderly alcoholic: Some diagnostic problems and considerations. In M. Storandt, I. Siegler, & M. Elias (Eds.), *The clinical psychology of aging* (pp. 97–113). New York: Plenum.

Woodruff, D., & Birren, J. E. (1972). Age changes and cohort differences in personality. *Developmental Psychology, 6,* 252–259.

Woodruff, D. S. (1977). *Can you live to be 100?* Boston: Catham Square Press.

Woodruff, D. S., & Walsh, D. A. (1975). Research in adult learning: The individual. *Gerontologist, 15,* 424–430.

Worden, J. W. (1982). *Grief counseling and grief therapy.* New York: Springer.

Work in America Institute. (1980). *The future of older workers in America: New options for an extended working life.* Scarsdale, NY: Author.

Works of Aristotle Translated into English (Vol. 3). London: Oxford University Press.

Wright, J. D., & Hamilton, R. S. (1978). Work satisfaction and age: Some evidence for the job-change hypothesis. *Social Forces, 56,* 1140–1158.

Wright, L. K. (1991). The impact of Alzheimer's disease on the marital relationship. *Gerontologist, 31,* 224–237.

Wright, R. E. (1981). Aging, divided attention, and processing capacity. *Journal of Gerontology, 36,* 605–614.

Wrightsman, L. S. (1988). *Personality development in adulthood.* Newbury Park, CA: Sage.

Wu, K. (1990–1991). Family support, age, and emotional states of terminally ill cancer patients. *Omega, 22,* 139–152.

Yordi, C., Chu, A., Ross, K., & Wong, S. (1982). Research and the frail elderly: Ethical and methodological issues in controlled social experiments. *Gerontologist, 22,* 72–77.

Zajonc, R. B. (1968). Attitudinal effects of mere exposure. *Journal of Personality and Social Psychology Monograph Supplement, 9,* 1–27.

Zarit, S. (1980). *Aging and mental disorders.* New York: Free Press.

Zarit, S., & Anthony, C. (1986). Interventions with dementia patients and their families. In M. Gilhooly, S. Zarit, & J. E. Birren (Eds.), *The dementias: Policy and management* (pp. 104–121). Englewood Cliffs, NJ: Prentice-Hall.

Zarit, S., Cole, K. D., & Guider, R. L. (1981). Memory-training strategies and subjective complaints of memory in the aged. *Gerontologist, 21,* 158–164.

Zarit, S., Eiler, J., & Hassinger, M. (1985). Clinical assessment. In J. E. Birren & K. W. Schaie (Eds.), *Handbook of the psychology of aging* (pp. 725–754).

Zarit, S., Reever, K., & Bach-Peterson, J. (1980). Relatives of the impaired elderly: Correlates of feelings of burden. *Gerontologist, 20,* 649–655.

Zarit, S., Todd, P., & Zarit, J. (1986). Subjective burden of husbands and wives as caregivers: A longitudinal study. *Gerontologist, 26,* 260–266.

Zarit, S. H., Anthony, C. R., & Boutselis, M. (1987). Interventions with caregivers of dementia patients: Comparison of two approaches. *Psychology and Aging, 2,* 225–232.

Zarit, S., & Zarit, J. (1983). Cognitive impairment. In P. Lewisohn & L. Teri (Eds.), *Clinical geropsychology: New directions in assessment and treatment* (pp. 38–80). Elmsford, NY: Pergamon.

Zarit, S., Zarit, J., & Reever, K. (1982). Memory training for severe memory loss: Effects on senile dementia. *Gerontologist, 22,* 373–377.

Zautra, A., Guarnaccia, C., & Dohrenwend, B. (1986). Measuring small life events. *American Journal of Community Psychology, 14,* 629–655.

Zautra, A., Guarnaccia, C., Reich, J., & Dohrenwend, B. (1988). The contribution of small events to stress and distress. In L. Cohen (Ed.), *Life events and psychological functioning* (pp. 123–148). Newbury Park, CA: Sage.

Zeits, C. R., & Prince, R. M. (1982). Child effects on parents. In B. Wolman (Ed.), *Handbook of developmental psychology* (pp. 751–770). Englewood Cliffs, NJ: Prentice-Hall.

Zelinski, E. M., Gilewski, M., & Thompson, L. (1980). Do laboratory tests relate to everyday remembering and forgetting? In L. Poon, J. Fozard, L. Cermack, D. Arenberg, & L. Thompson (Eds.), *New directions in memory and aging* (pp. 519–544). Hillsdale, NJ: Erlbaum.

Zelinski, E. M., Gilewski, M. J., & Anthony-Bergstone, C. R. (1990). The Memory Functioning Questionnaire: Concurred validity with memory performance and self-reported memory failures. *Psychology and Aging, 5,* 388–399.

Zeplin, H., Wolfe, C., & Kleinplatz, F. (1981). Evaluation of a year-long reality-orientation program. *Journal of Gerontology, 36,* 70–77.

Zimbardo, P. G., & Anderson, S. M. (1981). Conduct hearing deficit generates experimental paranoia. *Science, 212,* 1529–1531.

Zimberg, S. (1987). Alcohol abuse among the elderly. In L. Carstensen & B. Edelstein (Eds.), *Handbook of clinical gerontology* (pp. 57–65). New York: Praeger.

NAME INDEX

Name Index

Name Index

SUBJECT INDEX

Subject Index

Subject Index

Subject Index

Subject Index

Subject Index

C R E D I T S

Photographs (listed by page numbers)

Unless otherwise acknowledged, all photographs are the property of Scott, Foresman and Company. Page abbreviations are as follows: (T) top, (B) bottom, (L) left, (R) right.

1 Jean-Claude LeJeune. **7** Stacy Pick / Stock Boston. **10** Joel Gordon Photography. **23** Elizabeth Crews / Stock Boston. **25L,R** AP / Wide World Photos. **42** David R. Frazier Photolibrary. **54** Dean Abramson / Stock Boston. **55** Dion Ogust / The Image Works. **69** Suzanne Murphy / Tony Stone Worldwide. **72** Jean-Claude LeJeune. **76** Abraham Menashe. **83** Jim Whitmer. **97** Tom McCarthy / Custom Medical Stock Photo. **114** David R. Frazier Photolibrary. **122** Michael Newman / Photo Edit. **125** Kesh Sorenson Moore / Custom Medical Stock Photo. **132L** Owen Franken / Stock Boston. **132R** Susie Fitzhugh / Stock Boston. **141** Taurus Photos. **152** The Picture Cube. **155** McKinney/FPG. **171** Bob Daemmrich / The Image Works. **176** The Picture Cube. **182** Jim Harrison / Stock Boston. **189** Jean-Claude LeJeune. **195** Robert Brenner / Photo Edit. **198** Mike Douglas / The Image Works. **205** David R. Frazier Photolibrary. **221** Janice Travia / Tony Stone Worldwide. **232** Hazel Hankin / Stock Boston. **236** Ronnie Kaufman / The Stock Market. **239** Rapho / Photo Researchers. **247** Joel Gordon Photography. **264** Mark Antman / The Image Works. **271** Jean-Claude LeJeune. **290** Joel Gordon Photography. **298** Elizabeth Crews / Stock Boston. **321** Photo Researchers. **331** Michael Keller / FPG. **336** Gary Walts / The Image Works. **349** Jim Unger / UNIVERSAL PRESS SYNDICATE. Reprinted with permission. All Rights Reserved. **353** The Picture Cube. **358** Joel Gordon Photography. **368** Joel Gordon Photography. **382** Jim Harrison / Stock Boston. **391** Jean-Claude LeJeune. **394** Jim Harrison / Stock Boston. **407L, R** Strub & Black (1982), p. 149. Organic brain syndromes: An introduction to neurobehavioral disorders. Reprinted by permission of F.A. Davis Publishers. **412** David Young-Wolff / Photo Edit. **425** The Picture Cube. **448** Susan Lapides / Design Conceptions. **453** Mark Antman / The Image Works. **464** Alan Carey / The Image Works. **466** Bob Daemmrich / Stock Boston. **477** Photo Researchers. **485** Mike Douglas / The Image Works. **506** Joel Gordon Photography. **507** Bob Daemmrich / Stock Boston. **523** Glassman / The Image Works.

Text and tables

Chapter 1

Baltes, P. B., Reese, H. W., & Lipsitt, L. P. (1980). Life-span developmental psychology. *Annual Review of Psychology, 31.* / Cowley, M. (1982). *The view from 80,* 3–6. Copyright © 1976, 1978, 1980 by Malcolm Cowley. Used by permission of Viking Penguin, a division of Penguin Books USA, Inc. / Hudson, F. (1991). *The adult years: Mastering the art of self-renewal,* 46–47 and table. Reprinted by permission of the publisher, Jossey-Bass, Inc. / Ryff, C. D. (1989). Figures from In the eye of the beholder: Views of psychological well-being among middle-aged and older adults. *Psychology and Aging, 4.* Copyright © 1989 by the American Psychological Association. Reprinted by permission. / Schlossberg, N. K. (1989). *Overwhelmed: Coping with life's ups and downs,* 28–29. Copyright © 1989 by Lexington Books. Reprinted by permission of Lexington Books, an imprint of Macmillan, Inc.

Chapter 2

Baltes, P. B. (1968). Figure and table from Longitudinal sequences in the study of age and generation effects. *Human Development, 11*: 145–171. Published by S. Karger A. G., Basel. Reprinted by permission of Ablex Publishing Company.

Chapter 3

Masters, W. H., Johnson, V. E., & Kolodny, R. C. (1992). Sex after sixty. *Human sexuality,* 262. Copyright © 1992 by HarperCollins Publishers. Reprinted by permission. / New York Times (1985). Figure from Brain growth in rich environment. *New York Times,* July 30, 1985. Copyright © 1985 by The New York Times Company. Reprinted by permission. / Shock, N. W. (1977). Biological theories of aging. In Birren, J. E. & Schaie, K. W. (Eds.), *Handbook of the psychology of aging,* 103–115. Reprinted by permission of Van Nostrand Reinhold, New York. / Siegler, I. C. (1989). Table from Developmental health psychology. In Costa, P., Gatz, M., Neugarten, B., et al. (Eds.), *The adult years: Continuity and change.* Copyright © 1989 by the American Psychological Association. Reprinted by permission of the American Psychological Association and Ilene C. Siegler. / Thompson, R. F. (1975). Figure from introduction to *Physiological psychology.* Copyright © 1975 by Richard F. Thompson. Reprinted by permission of HarperCollins Publishers. / USA Weekend (1989). The ache age. *USA Weekend* (December), 4–5. Copyright © 1989, *USA Today.* Reprinted with permission.

Chapter 4

American Association of Retired Persons (1984). Have you heard? Hearing loss and aging, 7–9. Copyright © 1984, American Association of Retired Persons. Reprinted with permission. / Panek, P. E., Barrett, H. L., Sterns, H. L., & Alexander, R. A. (1977). Figure from A review of age changes in perceptual information processing ability with regard to driving. *Experimental aging research, 3*: 338. Copyright © 1977, Beech Hill Enterprises, Inc. Reprinted by permission. / Smith, R. E., Sarason, I. G., & Sarason, B. R. (1982). Tables and figures from *Psychology: The frontiers of behavior,* 2/e, 132. Copyright © 1982 by Ronald E. Smith, Irwin G. Sarason and Barbara R. Sarason. Reprinted by permission of HarperCollins Publishers.

Chapter 5
Baskevill, B. (1991). Getting old isn't the same as aging. *Dallas Times Herald,* 1991. Reprinted by permission of Associated Press / Craik, F. (1977). Figure modified from Age differences in human memory. In Birren, J. E. & Schaie, K. W. (Eds.), *Handbook of the psychology of aging,* 386. Reprinted by permission of Van Nostrand Reinhold, New York. / Elderhostel Catalog (1988). Elderhostel: Continued opportunities for growth in late adulthood, *19* (2). Reprinted by permission of Elderhostel, Inc. / Fozard, J. (1980). A time for remembering. In L. Poon (Ed.), *Aging in the 1980's: Psychological issues,* 273–290. Copyright © 1980 by the American Psychological Association. Reprinted by permission of the American Psychological Association and the author. / Gilewski, M. J. & Zelinski, E. M. (1986). Table originally published in Zelinski, E. M., Gilewski, M. J., & Thompson, L. W. (1980), q.v. / Hayslip, B. & Kennely, K. (1985). Cognitive and non-cognitive factors affecting learning among older adults. In B. Lumsden (Ed.), *The older adult as learner,* 73–98. Reprinted by permission of Hemisphere Publishing Corp. / Kausler, D. (1991). Figure from *Experimental psychology, cognition, and human aging,* 2/e, 194. Reprinted by permission of Springer-Verlag, New York, and the author. / Rubin, L. (1991). Cartoon: Rubes published in *Dallas Times Herald,* January, 1991. Reprinted by permission of Leigh Rubin and Creators Syndicate. / Willis, S. (1985). Excerpts from Toward an educational psychology of the older adult learner: Intellectual and cognitive bases. In J. E. Birren & K. W. Schaie (Eds.), *Handbook of the psychology of aging,* 2/e, 818–847. Reprinted by permission of Van Nostrand Reinhold. / Zelinski, E. M., Gilewski, M. J., & Thompson, L. W. (1980). Table from Do laboratory tests relate to self-assessment of memory ability in the young and old? In L. W. Poon, J. L. Fozard, et al. (Eds.), *New directions in memory and aging: Proceedings of the George A. Talland Memorial Conference,* 529. Adapted by permission of Lawrence Erlbaum Associates. Reprinted in Gilewski, M. J. & Zelinski, E. M. (1986).

Chapter 6
Horn, J. L. (1970). Figure from Organization of data on life-span development of human abilities. In L. Goulet & P. Baltes (Eds.), *Life-span developmental psychology: Research and theory,* 463. Reprinted by permission of Academic Press. / Horn, J. L. (1975). Figure adapted from Gf-Gc Sampler, University of Denver mimeo. Reprinted by permission of J. L. Horn. / Horn, J. L. (1978). Excerpts from Human ability systems. In P. Baltes (Ed.), *Life-span development and behavior, 1*: 211–256. Reprinted by permission of Academic Press and the author. / The Psychological Corporation (1981). Table adapted from Wechsler Adult Intelligence Scale–Revised. Copyright © 1981, 1955 by The Psychological Corporation. All rights reserved. Reproduced by permission. / Schaie, K. W. (1977–1978). Figure from *International Journal of Aging and Human Development, 8*: 133. Copyright © 1977, Baywood Publishing Co., Inc. Reprinted by permission of Baywood Publishing Co., Inc. / Schaie, K. W. (1979). Excerpts from The primary mental abilities in adulthood: An exploration in the development of psychometric intelligence. In P. Baltes & O. Brim (Eds.), *Life-span development and behavior, 2*: 68–115. Reprinted by permission of Academic Press and the author. / Schaie, K. W. (1990). Figure from Late life potential and cohort differences in mental abilities. In M. Perlmutter (Ed.), *Late life potential,* 48. Copyright © the Gerontological Society of America. Reprinted by permission. / Schaie, K. W., Rosenthal, F., & Pearlman, R. M. (1953). Figure adapted from Differential mental deterioration of factorially "pure" functions in later maturity. *Journal of Gerontology, 8*: 191–196. Copyright © 1953 The Gerontological Society of America. Reprinted by permission. / Trotter, R. J. (1986). Three heads are better than one. *Psychology Today,* 56–62. Copyright © 1986, Sussex Publishers, Inc. Reprinted by permission of Psychology Today Magazine.

Chapter 7
Akron Beacon Journal (1991). Excerpts from *Akron Beacon Journal,* 1991. Reprinted by permission of Knight-Ridder/Tribune News Service. / Carter, B. & McGoldrick, M. (1988). Tables from *The changing family life cycle: A framework for family therapy,* 15, 22. Copyright 1988. Reprinted by permissin of Allyn and Bacon. / Gilbert, L. A. (1987). What makes dual career marriages tick? Copyright © 1987 Hogg Foundation for Mental Health. Reprinted by permission of Hogg Foundation for Mental Health and the author. / Kahn, R. & Antonucci, T. (1980). Figure from P. B. Baltes & O. G. Brim (Eds.), *Life-span development and behavior, 3*: 273. Reprinted by permission of Academic Press and the author. / Lauer, J. & Lauer, R. (1985). Marriage made to last. *Psychology Today* (June), 26. Copyright © 1985 Sussex Publishers, Inc. Reprinted by permission from Psychology Today Magazine. / Masters, W. H., Johnson, V. E., & Kolodny, R. C. (1992). Table from *Human sexuality,* 322–326. Copyright © 1992 by HarperCollins Publishers. Reprinted by permission. / Sturdivant, S. (1988). Excerpt from Divorce. *Update on Human Behavior, 8* (2). Reprinted by permission of Human Services Inc., Dallas, TX (800) 873-2834. / Trotter, R. J. (1986). The three faces of love. *Psychology Today* (September), 50. Copyright © 1986 Sussex Publishers, Inc. Reprinted by permission from Psychology Today Magazine.

Chapter 8
Costa, P. T., Jr., & McCrae, R. R. (1986b). Table adapted from Personality stability and its implications for clinical psychology. *Clinical Psychology Review, 6*: 407–423. Copyright © 1986 Pergamon Press Ltd. Reprinted by permission. / Levinson, D. J., et al. (1978). Excerpts from *The seasons of a man's life.* Copyright © 1978 by Daniel J. Levinson. Reprinted by permission of Alfred A. Knopf, Inc. / Maas, H. & Kuypers, J. (1974). Table from *From thirty to seventy,* 198. Copyright © 1974 by Jossey-Bass, Inc., Publishers. Reprinted by permission. / Ryff, C. (1989). Figure from In the eye of the beholder: Views of psychological well-being among middle-aged and older adults. *Psychol-*

ogy and Aging, *4*. Copyright © 1989 by The American Psychological Association. Reprinted by permission. / Whitbourne, S. K. (1986). Figure from *The me I know: A study of adult identity.* Copyright © 1986 Springer-Verlag. Reprinted by permission.

Chapter 9
American Association of Retired Persons (1988). How to train older workers, 13. Reprinted by permission of Business Partnership Program, AARP. / Associated Press (1991). Study challenges firm's policies on older workers. *The Advocate*, Newark, Ohio, (June 4): 11. Reprinted by permission of Associated Press. / Baskevill, B. (1992). Do we work too hard? *Dallas Times Herald*, February, 24, 1992. Reprinted by permission of Associated Press. / Crane, D. P. (1986). *Personnel: The management of human resources*, 350. Reprinted by permission of Donald Crane. / Dallas Times Herald (1991). Attitude toward older workers. *Dallas Times Herald* (May 3). Reprinted by permission of the Dallas Morning News. / Hunger, J. (1983). "Herman" cartoon, Charleston *Times-Courier* (August 20). Universal Press Syndicate. Reprinted with permission. All rights reserved. / Matthews, K. A. & Rodin, J. (1989). Women's changing work roles: Impact on health, family and public policy. *American Psychologist*, *44*: 1389–1393. Reprinted by permission of the American Psychological Association. / Osgood, N. J. (1983). Table from Patterns of aging in retirement communities: Typology of residents. *Journal of Applied Gerontology*, *2*: 28–43. Copyright © 1983. Reprinted by permission of Sage Publications, Inc. / Tangri, S. & Jenkins, S. (1992). Excerpts from The Women's Life Paths Study: The Michigan graduates of 1967. In D. Shuster & K. Hulbert (Eds.), *Women's lives through time: Educated American women of the 20th century*, (San Francisco: Jossey-Bass, 1992) 20–35.

Chapter 10
Blazer, D. (1990). Excerpts from *Emotional problems in late life.* Used by permission of Springer Publishing Company, Inc., New York, NY 10012. / Carson, R. C. & Butcher, J. N. (1991). Excerpts from A lethality scale for the assessment of suicide potential. *Abnormal psychology and modern life*, 9/e, 416. Copyright © 1992 by HarperCollins Publishers. Reprinted by permission. / Crook, T. (1987). Table from Dementia. In L. Carstensen & B. Edelstein (Eds.), *Handbook of clinical gerontology*, 100. Copyright © 1987. Reprinted by permission of Allyn and Bacon. / Foley ElderHealth Center. *Caregivers education*, Program AWARE (outline of weeks 1–8). Reprinted by permission of the Joseph M. Foley ElderHealth Center, University Hospitals of Cleveland. / Gallagher, D. and Thompson, L. (1983). Excerpt from Depression. In P. Lewisohn & L. Teri (Eds.), *Clinical geropsychology: New directions in assessment and treatment*, 7–37. Reprinted by permission of Pergamon Press, Inc. / The Gerontologist (1991). Table from Problems identified by family caregivers in counseling. *The Gerontologist*, *31*: 15–23. Copyright © 1991 The Gerontological Society of America. Reprinted by permission. / Miller, M. (1978). Excerpt from Geriatric suicide: The Arizona study. *The Gerontologist*, *18*: 488–495. Copyright © 1978 The Gerontological Society of America. Reprinted by permission. / Miller, M. (1979). Excerpts from *Suicide after sixty: The final alternative.* Used by permission of Springer Publishing Co., Inc., New York, NY 10012. / Ohio Department of Liquor Control. Directives from the Ohio Department of Liquor Control in Cooperation with the Governor's Office of Advocacy for Recovery Services and Ohio Department of Aging. Reprinted by permission. / Teri, L. & Reifler, B. (1987). Figures from Depression and dementia. In L. Carstensen & B. Edelstein (Eds.), *Handbook of clinical gerontology*, 112–122. Copyright 1987. Reprinted by permission of Allyn and Bacon. / Ware, L. A. & Carper M., (1982). Tables from *Psychotherapy: Theory, research and practice*, *19*: 472–481 (*Psychotherapy* since 1984). Reprinted by permission of the editor, *Psychotherapy.* / Wells, C. (1979). Table adapted from Pseudodementia. In P. Lewisohn & L. Teri (Eds.), *Clinical geropsychology: New directions in assessment and treatment*, 12. Copyright © 1979 The American Psychiatric Association. Reprinted by permission. Reprinted in D. Gallagher & L. Thompson (1983).

Chapter 11
Burns, D. D. (1980). Data from *Feeling good: The new mood therapy.* New York, Signet, 1980. Used in table from Thompson et al. (1991), q.v. / Gottesman, L., Quarterman, C., & Cohn, G. (1973). Table from Psychosocial treatment of the aged. In C. Eisdorfer & M. P. Lawton (Eds.), *The psychology of adult development and aging*, 378–427. Copyright © 1973 by the American Psychological Association. Reprinted by permission of the American Psychological Association and Leonard Gottesman. / Keller, J. & Hughston, G. (1981). Table from *Counseling the elderly: A systems approach.* Copyright © 1981 by James F. Keller and George A. Hughston. Reprinted by permission of HarperCollins Publishers. / Thompson, L. J., Gantz, F., Florsheim, M., et al. (1991). Table from Cognitive behavioral therapy for affective disorders in the elderly. In Myers, W. (Ed.), *New techniques in the psychotherapy of older clients*, 10–12, 14. Copyright © 1991 American Psychiatric Press, Inc., Washington, DC. Reprinted by permission.

Chapter 12
Austen, M. (1958). Paiute Indian Song from *The American Rhythm.* Copyright (renewed) 1958 by Kenneth M. Chapman and Mary C. Wheelwright. Used by permission of Houghton Mifflin Company. Reprinted in Moffat, M. J. (1982), q.v. / Barbus, A. (1975). Excerpt from The Dying Person's Bill of Rights, *American Journal of Nursing*, *1*: 99. Reprinted by permission of American Journal of Nursing Company. / Caine, L. (1974). Excerpt from *Widow.* Copyright © 1974 by Lynn Caine. Reprinted by permission of William Morrow & Company, Inc. / Cook, A. S. & Oltjenbruns, K. A. (1989). Table from *Dying and grieving: Lifespan and family perspectives*, 338. Copyright © by Holt, Rinehart and Winston, Inc. Reprinted by permission of the publisher. / Irion, P. E. (1990–1991). Changing patterns of ritual response to death. *Omega*, *22*: 159–172. Copyright © 1990, 1991 Pergamon Press, Ltd. Reprinted by permission. / Kenney, P. D. (1991). Remembrance. *Compassionate Friends.* Reprinted by permission of Priscilla D. Kenney, member, Compassionate Friends. / Lichtenberg, P. (1990). Remembering Becky. *Omega*, *21*: 83–89. Copyright © 1990 Pergamon Press, Ltd. Reprinted by permission. / Moffat, M. J. (1982). Excerpt from Paiute Indian Song from Austen, M. (1958), q.v.